FUNDAMENTALS OF COMPUTING II

Abstraction, Data Structures, and Large Software Systems

C++ EDITION

FUNDAMENTALS OF COMPUTING II

Abstraction, Data Structures, and Large Software Systems

Allen B. Tucker

Bowdoin College

Robert D. Cupper

Allegheny College

W. James Bradley

Calvin College

Richard G. Epstein

West Chester University

Charles F. Kelemen

Swarthmore College

McGRAW-HILL, INC.

New York St. Louis San Francisco Auckland Bogotá Caracas
Lisbon London Madrid Mexico City Milan Montreal New Delhi
San Juan Singapore Sydney Tokyo Toronto

FUNDAMENTALS OF COMPUTING II
Abstraction, Data Structures, and Large Software Systems,
C++ Edition

Copyright © 1995 by McGraw-Hill, Inc. All rights reserved.
Printed in the United States of America. Except as permitted
under the United States Copyright Act of 1976, no part of this
publication may be reproduced or distributed in any form or by
any means, or stored in a data base or retrieval system, without
the prior written permission of the publisher.

This book is printed on recycled, acid-free
paper containing 10% postconsumer waste .

1 2 3 4 5 6 7 8 9 0 FGR FGR 9 0 9 8 7 6 5 4

ISBN 0-07-065502-2

The editor was Eric M. Munson;
the production supervisor was Paula Flores.
Quebecor Printing/Fairfield was printer and binder.

Library of Congress Catalog Card Number: 94-79884

ABOUT THE AUTHORS

Allen B. Tucker is Professor of Computer Science at Bowdoin College; he has held similar positions at Colgate and Georgetown Universities. He earned a BA in mathematics from Wesleyan University and an MS and PhD in computer science from Northwestern University. Professor Tucker is the author or coauthor of several books and articles in the areas of programming languages, natural language processing, and computer science education. He recently served on the ACM Task Force on the Core of Computing and as cochair of the ACM/IEEE–CS Joint Curriculum Task Force that developed the report *Computing Curricula 1991*. He is a member of ACM, IEEE–CS, CPSR, and the Liberal Arts Computer Science Consortium (LACS).

Robert D. Cupper is Professor and Chair of the Department of Computer Science at Allegheny College. He received a BS from Juniata College and a PhD from the University of Pittsburgh. At Allegheny, Professor Cupper developed one of the first computer science major programs for a liberal arts college, a program that helped motivate the design of the liberal arts model curriculum. He has been an active member of ACM for several years, having served as chair of the Student Chapters Committee and as secretary-treasurer of the Special Interest Group on Computer Science Education (SIGCSE). Professor Cupper has written and spoken on the economics of computing, curriculum development, and accreditation. He is a member of ACM and a cofounder of LACS.

W. James Bradley is Professor of Mathematics and Computer Science at Calvin College. He graduated from MIT with a major in mathematics and completed a PhD in mathematics from the University of Rochester. Professor Bradley also earned an MS in computer science from the Rochester Institute of Technology. He has authored papers in game theory and computer science curriculum, as well as an introductory text in discrete mathematics. His current scholarly interests are in formal methods in decision making, database systems, ethical and social issues in computing, and computer science education. Professor Bradley is a member of MAA, ACM, CPSR, and LACS.

Richard G. Epstein is Professor of Computer Science at West Chester University. He earned a BA in physics at George Washington University and a PhD in computer science at Temple University. He has research interests in the areas of programming languages, object-oriented databases, and curriculum design. He recently served on the ACM/IEEE–CS Joint Curriculum Task Force that developed the report *Computing Curricula 1991*. Professor Epstein is a member of ACM and IEEE–CS.

Charles F. Kelemen is Professor of Computer Science and Mathematics and Director of the Computer Science Program at Swarthmore College. He earned a BA from Valparaiso University and a PhD in Mathematics from the Pennsylvania State University. He has held faculty positions at Ithaca College and LeMoyne College and was Visiting Associate Professor of Computer Science at Cornell. He has published research and educational articles in both mathematics and computer science. His research interests are algorithms and the theory of computation. He holds the Certificate in Computer Programming (Systems Programming) from the Institute for Certification of Computer Professionals. He is a member of ACM, IEEE–CS, CPSR, MAA, and LACS.

Dedicated

Allen B. Tucker: To my wife Meg

Robert D. Cupper: To my wife, Sandy

W. James Bradley: To my wife, Hope

Richard G. Epstein: To my father, David

Charles F. Kelemen: To my wife Sylvia

CONTENTS

CHAPTER 2   INHERITANCE, POLYMORPHISM AND GENERIC CLASSES

85

PREFACE

The discipline of computer science and engineering, or computing, is an extraordinary one. More than any other field of study or professional engagement, the process of solving computational problems and designing computational devices continues to evolve with relentless speed. And so must the curriculum that prepares students to confront the challenges of this unusual discipline.

This text, together with its accompanying laboratory manual and software, is designed for the second course in computing (CS2), which has traditionally confined itself to the study of data structures. Here, we broaden the study of data structures by adding the relevant theory (computational complexity and correctness), modernizing the software design process (using C++ and object-oriented methods), and focusing on the functional elements of operating systems as a compelling application for the study of data structures. The social issue of software reliability is also examined to complete this text. Thus, students who use this text and its laboratory materials will come away not only with an appreciation for the fundamental data structures of computer science but also some strong ideas about their underlying theory, their applications, and the impact of their use on the software systems that they effectively serve.

Overview of This Text

This text has ten chapters and is organized for use in a one-semester course with an accompanying laboratory component. The accompanying *Laboratory Manual* and software are designed to complement the text, so that they should be used in tandem with it. The coordination of laboratory exercises will enrich the textual material that is covered in the lectures.

Chapter 0 reviews important fundamental concepts of programming from the first course. The accompanying Chapter 0 in the laboratory manual contains a C++ tutorial and elementary exercises which can be used by students who are familiar with another language (e.g., Pascal) to gain equivalent familiarity with the elements of C++ that they would encounter in a first course. Students who have already studied C++ in their first course may skip this chapter altogether. That choice will give students more time to work with other aspects of the course.

Chapter 1 provides a detailed introduction to object-oriented software design. It illustrates the basic ideas of class and method by solving a simple programming problem using the object-oriented paradigm. The object-oriented design features of C++ that appear in this chapter are introduced in the accompanying Chapter 1 of the *Laboratory Manual*.

Chapter 2 continues this train of discussion, introducing the use of dynamic objects, virtual methods, inheritance, polymorphism, and a basic class called Element that will be used throughout the remainder of the text. Chapter 2 in the *Laboratory Manual* introduces these features as they appear in the C++ language. Because Chapter 2 is a rather long chapter, instructors are encouraged to be selective in its coverage. Sections that are more or less optional are flagged in the table of contents with an asterisk (*). (In fact, optional sections in all chapters are flagged in this way, so that students can remain focussed on the more central issues in the course.)

Chapter 3 focuses on the problem of measuring and classifying the efficiency of algorithms by introducing the notion of computational complexity. It treats the correctness and complexity of various classical sorting and searching algorithms. We recommend that, among these algorithms, students cover at least one $O(n \log n)$ sorting algorithm alongside a conventional $O(n^2)$ algorithm in order to gain an appreciation of the importance of efficiency when making choices among alternatives in algorithm design. Chapter 3 is independent from Chapter 2. It can be covered immediately after Chapter 1 or topics from Chapter 3 can be intermixed with topics from Chapter 2.

Chapters 4 and 5 develop six fundamental data structures in computer science—stacks, queues, lists, binary trees, trees, and graphs—and their applications. Each of these is characterized as a class, and its fundamental operators are identified as the methods of that class. In Chapter 4, applications of stacks are illustrated through the classical problem of evaluating Polish expressions, while applications of queues are explored through the simulation of a waiting line in a bank. There, too, the notion of pseudorandom number generation, so fundamental in the design of computer simulations, is introduced and discussed.

Binary trees, general trees, and graphs are introduced in Chapter 5. The BinaryTree class is considered as a restriction of the general Tree class, thus giving an important application of the idea of inheritance. The discussion of trees ends with an overview of compilers and the use of the tree class in the design of an expression parser.

Chapter 6 concentrates on the implementation issues that surround these six classes, including tradeoffs in time and space (computational complexity again) between linked and array representations. Chapter 6 in the *Laboratory Manual* contains additional tutorial material on the use of pointers to build linked structures that implement the various classes discussed in Chapters 4 and 5. This organization allows instructors to treat the six classes developed in Chapters 4 and 5 as abstract data types, putting off all implementation details until Chapter 6. Alternatively, it is possible to introduce a class from Chapter 4 or 5 and immediately consider its implementation details from Chapter 6 before going on to another abstract data type.

Chapter 7 draws together the study of object-oriented design and data structures into a single important computer science application—the design of an operating system. Operating systems is a fundamental subject area of computer science, but it is not normally studied until much later in a more traditional curriculum. However, this chapter combines an overview of operating systems with a detailed discussion of key operating system components, providing students with a capstone object-oriented design experience. The tree structure of a UNIX or PC/DOS directory system can be modeled and explored easily using the `Tree` class. The scheduling of memory and processes is also studied in detail. Students can exercise these operating system applications by running the simulations provided in the software and completing the work in Chapter 7 of the *Laboratory Manual*.

Chapter 8 broadens the study of software design by providing a complete overview of the process of software engineering. It contrasts the principles of object-oriented design, used in this text, with the traditional process of function-oriented design. It also introduces software management, testing methods, and the user interface. Thus, it provides a valuable prelude to an intermediate or advanced software engineering course that may appear later in the curriculum.

Chapter 9 discusses three different social dimensions of software design— the dynamics of software teams, the idea of software as property, and the reliability of large software systems. Students have an opportunity here to grapple with important issues that uniquely confront computer scientists and engineers. For instance, how is a large software project organized and managed? What are the risks and liabilities when a complex software system fails? Who owns a software product, and what are the rights and responsibilities of such ownership?

Unless students have had a thorough introduction to C++ in advance, this text provides more material than can be covered in a single semester. Below, we outline different alternative "routes" through this text and lab manual, depending on different student backgrounds and course goals.

Student Audience, Goals, and Alternative Course Organizations

This text assumes that students have already had a first course in computer science, using either Volume I in this series or another introductory text. In either case, we expect that students have had a one–semester introduction to programming and problem solving, in either C++ or another contemporary language (Pascal or Scheme, for instance). We also expect that students will have taken a college level course in discrete mathematics or calculus (or both), either in advance or in parallel with this course. The mathematical discussions are interwoven into this text so that students can see the interplay of mathematics with the study of complexity, correctness, data structures, simulation, and operating systems.

Depending on whether students have had a first course in C++ or a first course in another language, we recommend that one of two alternative "routes" through this text be followed in a one–semester (14–week) course. Route 1 is designed for students who have already had an introduction to C++ programming, while Route 2 is design for students who have not used C++ but have had an introduction to programming in another language.

Text/Lab Chapter	Topics	Route 1 Weeks	Route 2 Weeks
0	C++ tutorial; programs, functions, input/ output, arithmetic, specifications (pre– and postconditions)	1–2	
1	Software design; classes, objects, and methods	3–4	1–2
2	Generics, inheritance, polymorphism; class libraries and software reuse	5–6	3–4
3	Complexity, search, and sort; empirical evaluation of sorting	7–8	5–6
4	Stack and queue classes and their methods; the list class and its basic methods; random number generation, simulation, Polish expressions	9	7
5	Trees, binary trees, and graphs; properties and applications	10	8–9
6	Implementation of data structures; linked vs array strategies, complexity issues; C++ pointers and dynamic storage management	11–12	10–11
7	Operating systems and software design; process management, queueing, tree structured directories	13	12–13
8	Overview of software engineering	14	
9	Social issues; software reliability		14

As indicated, Route 1 requires two weeks at the beginning of the semester to bring students up to speed with C++ (Chapter 0 in the *Laboratory Manual* should be particularly helpful in this regard). This time therefore compromises both the breadth and the depth with which data structures and their applications can be covered later in the semester. A more ideal schedule is reflected in

Route 2, which assumes that students are familiar with the rudiments of C++ and can move directly into the object-oriented design aspects of the language. Route 2 provides the luxury of two full weeks' study of trees and graphs and two full weeks' study of operating system applications of data structures.

Other routes through this text are certainly feasible, depending on the instructor's preferences and the course's goals. For instance, our rather brief suggested treatment of stacks and queues (1 week) realistically allows only stacks or queues to be studied in reasonable depth; some may prefer to allocate two weeks for these topics. Courses that wish to emphasize techniques for analysis of algorithms and verification could do all of Chapter 3 immediately after Chapter 1. Different analysis techniques are illustrated in the analyses of the various algorithms presented in Chapter 3. After Chapter 3, the unstarred sections of Chapter 2 could be presented followed by all the material in Chapters 4, 5, and 6. Courses that wish to emphasize object-oriented programming should do all of Chapter 2 and could skip Chapter 3 or just cover a favorite sort. However, to incorporate a reasonable level of breadth into this course, we recommend that at least two weeks be spent working with the material in Chapters 7–9 of the text.

Coordination of Laboratory Work

Whether Route 1 or Route 2 is taken through the text, the laboratory material should be coordinated with the text on a week-by-week basis. Each chapter in the *Laboratory Manual* contains detailed descriptions (including program listings in the chapter appendices) of the C++ classes and programs discussed in the corresponding chapter of text; students should frequently reference these details as they read each chapter in the text.

The next page shows a typical laboratory schedule that can be followed for either Route 1 or Route 2. Each lab listed on the right can be done in a week's time, except for the team projects which may require more time.

The laboratory exercises are accompanied by a complete set of software—programs, classes, and data files—to facilitate student laboratory work. This software is on a diskette distributed with the *Instructors Manual*. It may also be obtained directly by sending e–mail to `allen@polar.bowdoin.edu`.

The Breadth–First Approach: The Fundamentals of Computing Series

Readers may know that the course for which this text has been developed is the second in a collection of courses proposed in *Computing Curricula 1991* [2] and labeled as the "breadth-first" curriculum. The general goal of these courses is to provide a broad view of the wide range of subjects in the discipline of computing, an integration of theory with the practice of computing, and a rigorously defined laboratory component. We hope to achieve a curriculum that has much the same goals and style as a two- or three-semester introduction to another science, such as chemistry or biology.

Text/Lab Chapter	Topic	Lab assignment(s)
0	C++ tutorial	Congressional PAC money The gradebook problem
1	Classes and objects	Using the `WeatherObs` class Implementing a class
2	Inheritance and polymorphism	`Element` classes Dynamic objects
3	Searching and sorting	Serial vs binary search Team project—empirical evaluation of sorting algorithms
4	Stacks, queues, and lists	Development of a linked queue application Comparison of random number generators
5	Trees and binary trees	Team project—linked binary tree implementation Binary search trees
6	Implementation issues	Comparison of linked and array implementations of lists
7	Operating systems	Team project—operating system simulation or job scheduler
8	Software engineering	Short (3–5 page) paper on software teams
9	Software reliability	Short (3–5 page) paper on software reliability

This text is therefore the second in a series of texts that are being developed to support the breadth-first approach for the first four courses in the introductory curriculum. At this writing, the first text in this series is also available (in both Pascal and C++ editions) and a Pascal edition of this text is also available. The third and fourth texts are planned for development over the next two or three years. The titles of these texts, which are collectively called the *Fundamentals of Computing Series*, are as follows:

Volume I: Logic, Problem Solving, Programs, and Computers
Volume II: Abstraction, Data Structures, and Large Software Systems

Volume III: Levels of Architecture, Languages, and Applications
Volume IV: Algorithms, Concurrency, and the Limits of Computation

The prerequisite structure assumed here is similar to that which is followed by these courses' counterparts in a traditional curriculum. That is, the course using *Volume I* is a prerequisite for all others, and the course using *Volume II* is a prerequisite for the course using *Volume IV*.

Any of these texts can be used interchangeably with any alternative text for any of the first four courses in the curriculum. For instance, this text can be used in the second course and some alternative for *Volume III* can be used in a more traditionally oriented computer organization course, or vice versa. We have already given some advice on how this text can be used by students whose first course used Pascal or whose first course used a different approach than the breadth-first approach in *Volume I*. In short, the *Fundamentals of Computing Series* is a "loosely coupled" collection of teaching materials designed to cover one or more of the first four courses in the computer science curriculum, and in a wide range of institutional settings.

Acknowledgments

This work results from the toil, suggestions, and support of many people—too numerous to mention individually. Since this text represents a fundamentally new approach to teaching a second course in computer science, we cannot overstate the importance of the feedback we have received from our students and colleagues who have worked through the class testing with us.

In particular, we acknowledge the work of the following reviewers for their contributions to this development and revision process: Art Farley (University of Oregon), Ralph Morelli (Trinity College), Patricia Pineo (Allegheny College), William Punch (Michigan State University), Stephen E. Reichenbach (University of Nebraska), and Antonio Siochi (Christopher Newport University). They have provided immeasurable help in what has been a significant task, and we thank them sincerely.

Allen B. Tucker, Robert D. Cupper, W. James Bradley,
Richard G. Epstein, Charles F. Kelemen

References

[1] P. Denning, D. Comer, D. Gries, M. Mulder, A. Tucker, A. Turner, and P. Young, "Computing as a Discipline," *Report of the ACM Task Force on the Core of Computer Science*, ACM, New York, 1988. Reprinted in *Communications of the ACM* (January 1989) and *Computer* (March 1989).

[2] A. Tucker (ed), B. Barnes, R. Aiken, K. Barker, K. Bruce, J. Cain, S. Conry, G. Engel, R. Epstein, D. Lidtke, M. Mulder, J. Rogers, E. Spaf-

ford, and A. Turner, *Computing Curricula 1991*, ACM/IEEE–CS Joint Curriculum Task Force, ACM and IEEE–CS Press, New York, 1991.

[3] A. Tucker and D. Garnick, "A Breadth-First Introductory Curriculum in Computing," *Computer Science Education 3* (1991), 271-295.

[4] A. Tucker, A. Bernat, J. Bradley, R. Cupper, and G. Scragg, *Fundamentals of Computing I: Logic, Problem Solving, Programs, and Computers*; Pascal and C++ editions, McGraw-Hill (1994 and 1995).

THE CRAFT
OF PROGRAMMING

This text assumes that you have already acquired some C++ programming skills. We also assume that you have some ideas about procedural abstraction (the use of functions), arguments, one-dimensional arrays, the concept of type, the distinction between variables and constants, and basic approaches to solving problems and translating solutions into programs.

This chapter reviews these basic programming concepts. We do this by presenting an example program and studying its design and implementation in detail. This example is intended to illustrate one particular set of principles for program construction. These principles, collectively called *function-oriented design*, have evolved over the last several decades. In function-oriented design, the designer focuses upon identifying the basic functions or processes that are required to solve a problem. Function-oriented design is usually performed in a top-down fashion. That is, the original problem is broken up into subproblems, and this decomposition process continues until each of the subproblems is simple enough to be solved by means of a single function.

Following this review chapter, we will develop an alternative design methodology, called *object-oriented design*. Since you may not be familiar with object-oriented design, the example program given in this chapter will be developed again in the next chapter using an object-oriented style. This will allow you to identify the differences that exist between these two design techniques, and will form a basis for further development of object-oriented design ideas throughout the remainder of the text.

SIX PRINCIPLES FOR PROGRAM DESIGN

In order to motivate a discussion of design principles, we first need to understand the context in which programs are generally developed. Most programs originate out of the needs of some *sponsor*, an individual or an organization that needs to solve a particular computational problem or to perform a particular computational task. While the sponsor initiates the project, other groups—the *developers*, the *maintainers*, and the *users*—are also involved.

For example, a corporate manager may want to develop a software product that will be used by employees, such as an automated payroll system. In this case, the corporate manager is the sponsor and the employees are the eventual users of the software. The developers are those who design and implement the software. The maintainers are those who modify the software after it has been put into productive use (for example, maintainers generally fix bugs, or errors, in the software as they are discovered and add new or changed features to the program as the need arises).

We use a simple example problem in order to introduce the principles presented in this chapter. A professor wants to sponsor a program that will automate grading procedures for his current classes. The professor hires a computer science student to develop the program. This student may also be called upon later to maintain the program as the professor discovers new tasks or functions that need to be added. In this case, the professor is the sponsor and the user of the proposed program, and the student is the developer and maintainer.

Our student programmer soon learned that the professor was somewhat uncertain about exactly what the program was supposed to do. Consequently, the programmer adopted a style of programming that made it easier to modify the program when a change was proposed. Therefore, when the professor requested that the grading program be changed, our student programmer could satisfy the new requirements by modifying several existing functions in the program. Our programmer did not need to rewrite the program from scratch. The need to respond to change also mandated careful documentation of the program. Thus, the program contained clearly stated specifications for each procedure and function.

In reflecting upon what had been learned in coursework and other practical experience, our student programmer recalled a relatively short list of principles for program design. These principles are briefly summarized below.

PROBLEM DECOMPOSITION: *Find some basis for decomposing a problem into smaller and smaller subproblems.* Every design methodology begins with some criterion for problem decomposition. In a function-oriented design, as mentioned previously, the decomposition is based upon the component parts inherent in a solution to a problem. In object-oriented design, this decomposition is based upon the data that is required to solve a problem. In either case, functions are important elements in the eventual solution.

FORMAL SPECIFICATIONS: *Provide each function with a clearly stated precondition and a clearly stated postcondition.* There really can be no formal notion of program *correctness* without the use of *formal specifications*. Each function should be clearly documented with a precondition and a postcondition. These take the form of logical assertions in a precise style, often using the notation of predicate logic.[1] The precondition specifies what must be true when the function is called. The postcondition asserts what will be true, assuming the precondition, when the function is finished executing.

FUNCTIONAL COHESION: *Each function should have a single purpose that can be explained with a simple sentence.* A function is functionally cohesive if it is dedicated to one purpose. This is an important principle for designing functions that are easy to debug, modify, and reuse in new contexts. For example, suppose a function f performs tasks A, B and C. Then, it is unlikely that we could reuse function f in a new program that just requires that we perform task A. However, if a function performs just task A, then it could be used wherever task A needs to be performed.

EXPLICIT INTERFACES: *All data being passed into and out of a function must appear explicitly in the argument list of that function.* If all of the data flowing into or out of a function is clearly reflected in that function's list of arguments, then that function is said to have an *explicit interface*. When functions have explicit interfaces, they tend to be loosely coupled (see below). Again, explicit interfaces are desirable because they make it easier to understand what a function is doing and how it interacts with its environment (i.e., with the functions that call it).

LOOSE COUPLING: *Avoid the use of global variables.* Functions are coupled to the extent that they interact. A basic consideration in writing a good program is that the couplings between functions should be explicit (through the use of explicit interfaces) and not implicit (through the use of shared *global variables*). The notions of local and global variables should be familiar ones. They are defined below for the purpose of review.

Definition   A *local variable* is a variable that is declared explicitly inside a function. Local variables can be referenced only by statements within that function.

Definition   A *global variable* is one that is declared outside of a function and may be referenced explicitly by that function and other functions within the scope of that variable's declaration.

Normally, each function in a program should be designed so that its statements reference *only* its own formal arguments and local variables. That is, references to global variables should be avoided. For example, someone who is trying to track down a bug in a program should not have to deal with obscure,

---

1.   For an introduction to the use of predicate logic in the formation of pre- and postcondition specifications, see *Fundamentals of Computing*, Volume I.

undocumented interactions between function f and function g that result from the use of some global variable—no such interaction should be permitted by the design. The most important principle for making couplings explicit, then, is to avoid the use of global variables.

Formal arguments are considered local to a function, but they are usually not considered local variables as such.

INFORMATION HIDING: *The internal details of a function (e.g., local variables and the algorithm employed) should be hidden from the rest of the program.* Information hiding is an important concept for software design. Information hiding is related to the use of formal specifications and to the principles of loose coupling and explicit interfaces. The idea of information hiding is that when a programmer wants to use a function, then that programmer should only need to know:

1. The function's interface (i.e., its argument list)
2. The function's formal specifications, i.e., its preconditions and postconditions

In particular, the programmer should not need to know anything about the algorithm that the function uses in order to satisfy its specifications, nor should the programmer need to know about any other internal detail. The use of global variables, therefore, is inconsistent with the idea of information hiding.

Our student programmer discovered that adhering to these principles allowed the program to be modified in a fairly straightforward manner in response to changing requirements. In addition, following these principles made it easier to track down bugs that were discovered during the development process and to fix the few remaining bugs that were discovered when the program was run. Our student programmer discovered that although bugs were a fact of life for a software developer, the number of bugs in the delivered program could be minimized by careful program design and development.

USING THESE PRINCIPLES IN PROGRAM DESIGN

Let us now explore the use of these six principles in designing a particular program. Recall that a function is said to be *functionally cohesive* if it has a single purpose. Functions that are not functionally cohesive are more difficult to debug, modify and reuse in new contexts.

Recall the grading program that our student programmer was asked to write. An early version of that program included a function get_and_compute that read in a student's data and then computed that student's final average. According to the professor's grading scheme, each student takes three exams (two hourly exams and a final) and receives a final average that is a weighted average of these three exam scores. The function get_and_compute passes back all of a student's data (the student's name, three exam scores, and final average) to the appropriate calling function. These considerations led to the design of the get_and_compute function sketched below:

```
//
// Get all data for an individual student and
// compute student's final average.
//
void get_and_compute(string student_name,
                     float& first_hourly,
                     float& second_hourly,
                     float& final_exam,
                     float& average)
{
    // LOCAL DATA ...
    [declare exam weights as constants]

    // STATEMENTS ...
    [ prompt user for and get student's name ]
    [ prompt user for and get exam scores:
          first_hourly, second_hourly, final_exam ]
    [ compute weighted average ]
}   // end get_and_compute
```

This function is not functionally cohesive because it combines two purposes: getting a student's data and computing that student's average. One negative consequence of a lack of functional cohesion is that this function is less reusable than it might otherwise be. For example, suppose another program requires that we input the same data, but not for the purpose of computing a final average. Then `get_and_compute` is not reusable in that other program because it has the "side effect" of computing a student average. The only way the new program could use `get_and_compute` is if the new program introduces a dummy argument to match the function formal argument, `average`. This sort of "patch" is certainly not a sound way to build software! This helps to illustrate how functional cohesiveness improves the clarity and reusability of a function.

A functionally cohesive solution might decompose `get_and_compute` into a `void` function `get_student_data` and a `float` function `compute_average`. The function `get_student_data` would read a student's data and the function `compute_average` would compute the final average, using the exam scores. With this design, any program that needs to read in the student data (student name and exam scores) could reuse the function `get_student_data` without having to work around the need for a superfluous argument. This is the design that our student programmer finally settled upon, a design that is presented in detail at the end of this chapter.

Functions should be *loosely coupled* and should have *explicit interfaces*. Functions are coupled to the extent that they interact. Thus, in any program, the couplings between functions should be obvious. The reader of a program should not have to pore over it for a long time in order to deduce the couplings between functions. A basic technique for achieving these ends is to avoid the use of global variables. Global variables can be avoided by the judicious use of arguments. If all of the data flowing into or out of a function is clearly reflected in that function's list of arguments, then that function is said to have an *explicit interface*. None of the data flowing into or out of the function is hidden away in global variables. This is very desirable because it improves the clarity of the program code.

A variable in a function is global if its declaration is not found in that function either as a local variable or as an argument. For example, if a function uses a variable x, and if that variable is neither declared as a local variable nor as an argument within that function, then the variable x must be a global variable in that function.[2] If a function f contains a global variable x, and if we try to move that function to a new program, the new program had better provide a suitable declaration for x and that new program would have to use that variable x in a manner that is consistent with its use in the function f.

Note that while the use of global variables should be avoided, the C++ language forces the programmer to use global types. For example, a certain user-defined type might be declared externally (i.e., outside any function). This constitutes a form of coupling between all functions that define variables or arguments to be of that type. However, this form of coupling is not as bad as coupling by means of global variables. Global named constants also introduce a form of coupling between functions. Global named constants are acceptable when they can be defended on the grounds of maintaining consistency. That is, if two functions use the same named constant, declaring that constant globally is preferable to the possibility of the two functions giving the constant different values.

While all of the above principles are important for writing functions that are easy to debug, modify and reuse, none of them is more important than the principle of *information hiding*. In part, this is because the concept of information hiding integrates many of the previous concepts (especially, problem decomposition, formal specifications, loose coupling and explicit interfaces).

When we decompose a problem according to some criterion (whether it is a functional decomposition into processes or an object-oriented decomposition into objects), a fundamental issue is how the various components in our solution will communicate and interact and how much one component can know about another component. For example, if part of our problem decomposition involves a main function that will call an array sorting function, how much should the main function know about the sorting function and how much should the sorting function know about the main function?

Information hiding (in this array sorting example) implies that the main function should only need to know the sorting function's formal specifications and argument list. The formal specifications would state the fact that the function sorts an array and the argument list (or explicit interface) would document the input and output arguments expected by the function. In particular, the main function would not know, or need to know, anything about local variables within the sorting function nor about the algorithm the sorting function utilizes in order to satisfy the formal specifications. Furthermore, the sorting function

---

2. This characterization will need to change when we learn about classes and objects. In that case, the data contained within an object is global (in a sense) to all functions that belong to that object's class. From a software engineering perspective, this form of data sharing is considered good.

should only have access to the main function data that it actually needs to use in order to accomplish its task.

This is a very important principle for the design of software systems that are easy to debug, modify, and reuse. For example, suppose that the array sorting function alluded to in the previous paragraph needs to be replaced by a more efficient sorting function. As long as the principle of information hiding is adhered to, this will just involve replacing the original function with a new and more efficient function that has *exactly the same formal specifications and exactly the same argument list*. The principle of information hiding implies that there will be no hidden dependencies in the software system, that is, no interactions among software components that depend upon the internal details of the function being replaced. This also suggests why it is so important to avoid global variables and how the issues of global variables, explicit interfaces and information hiding are all related.

EXERCISES

0–1 Find a program that you developed in your first computer science course and analyze it from the point of view of functional cohesion, coupling, and information hiding. Is your design consistent with these principles? Are your functions functionally cohesive? Do you use global variables? If your program violates these principles, consider the implications of these violations in terms of debugging your program, modifying it, and reusing functions in new programs.

0–2 Consider the following function. Is it cohesive? If not, how would you improve upon its design? (Note that the argument a is an array whose component type is int.)

```
//
// Reads in an array of positive integers, computes their
// sum and displays the result.
//
int sum_it_all(int a[], int& n)
{
    // LOCAL DATA ...
    const int SENTINEL = -1;
    int an_integer, sum;

    // STATEMENTS ...
    cout << "Enter a positive integer or -1 to halt: ";
    cin  >>  an_integer;
    sum = 0;
    n = 0;
    while (an_integer != SENTINEL)
    {
        a[n] = an_integer;
        n++;
        sum += an_integer;
        cout << "Enter a positive integer or -1 to halt: ";
```

```
            cin  >> an_integer;
        }
        cout << endl;
        cout << "The sum is " << sum << endl;
        return sum;
}   // end sum_it_all
```

0–3 The function `count_them` utilizes the global variables

```
int a[100];
int cut_off;
int n;
```

Here n specifies the number of elements in the array a. This function counts the number of elements in the array a whose values are at least as large as cut_off. Explore the implications of a, cut_off, and n being treated as global variables rather than as formal arguments in this function. In particular, how do the global variables impact upon the possibility of reusing this function in a new program?

```
//
// Counts the number of elements in the array a that
// exceed cut_off.  n is the number of array elements.
//
int count_them()
{
    // LOCAL DATA ...
    int count = 0;

    // STATEMENTS ...
    for (int i = 0; i < n; i++)
        if (a[i] >= cut_off) count++;
    return count;
}   // end count_them
```

0–4 Imagine a program that involves quite a few initialization steps. For example, the program might require initializing some counters, initializing some files, initializing some arrays to 0, and so forth. All of these things need to be done before the program can do anything useful. Is it a good idea to write a function that takes care of all of the initialization steps all at once? Consider the implications for debugging, modifying, and reusing different functions within the program.

APPLICATION—THE SEARCHER PROBLEM

We shall now embark upon a complete description of the program which the professor (as sponsor) has asked the student programmer (as developer) to develop and implement. We begin with a discussion of the problem statement that the professor and the programmer eventually agree upon. We say "eventually" because it took a fairly long period of negotiation between these two individuals before the exact nature of the program became clear. It is often the case that sponsors and developers must engage in a long period of negotiation before a problem description is agreed upon.

As mentioned previously, the professor hired the student programmer in order to automate his grade keeping procedures. This particular professor is quite set in his ways insofar as grading is concerned. Regardless of the course, three exams are administered: a first hourly, a second hourly, and a final exam. These are weighted 25%, 25% and 50% respectively. A student's final average is the weighted average of the three exam scores.

It took some time for the professor and the programmer to agree upon the exact nature of the grading program. At first the professor thought the programmer was not bright enough to understand exactly what was needed. The programmer had similar negative thoughts about the professor, but after a while, they learned how to communicate their ideas to one another. After all, the programmer was not familiar with being a professor and the professor knew little about programming and computers. Over time, the programmer learned to think more like a professor and the professor learned to think more like an analyst and software designer. After considerable discussion, the final problem statement was agreed upon:

The SEARCHER program will allow the professor (the user) to enter the names and exam scores for all students in a particular class. The maximum class size is to be 100. Once a student's exam scores have been entered, the program will compute that student's final average. This is the weighted average of the three exam scores. The three exam scores for a given student will be entered as float *values. The three exam scores will be assigned the following weights:*

first hourly	*25%*
second hourly	*25%*
final exam	*50%*

The names and final averages for the entire class will be stored in two parallel arrays: an array of names and an array of final averages. These arrays will be rearranged so that the names are stored alphabetically.

Finally, the program will enter a "process requests" phase during which the professor will be able to access the final average of any student simply by entering that student's name. He will be able to enter these names in a loop. The loop will terminate when the professor enters the value "*" in lieu of a student's name.

Using A Design Methodology: MAPS

In negotiating with the professor in order to arrive at this particular problem description, the programmer was actually employing the first step in a problem-solving methodology that was taught in the first computer science course. That methodology was called *MAPS*: A *M*ethodology for *A*lgorithmic *P*roblem *S*olving.[3] MAPS requires that a problem be clearly stated before any formal specifications, design or coding of the program can be attempted. The process of problem-solving is viewed in MAPS as consisting of a series of steps.

Step 1: The dialogue   Understand the problem. Read the problem statement. Ask questions about input and output expectations and limitations until the problem statement is completely clear.

Step 2: The specifications   Develop specifications from an understanding of the problem statement. Write pre- and postconditions for the whole problem that are complete and consistent. That is, be sure that the preconditions cover all (and only) the input possibilities, that the postconditions define the output for every possible input, and that the preconditions and postconditions are both internally and mutually consistent.

Step 3: The breakdown   Systematically subdivide the process into a small collection of major steps. Repeat this decomposition for each step until it makes no sense to go further. Identify the control relationships among these steps. That is, what steps must precede other steps, what steps are constituents of larger steps, what steps must be repeated within a loop, and so on? Document each step by writing a brief description of its own (local) expectations. Assign an appropriate name and a clear purpose to each variable that you discover for each new step.

Step 4: Defining abstractions Determine which of these steps you have seen before in other algorithmic problem-solving situations, recall the appropriate functions that were used in those situations, and adapt those functions for reuse in this new problem's solution. Often this activity will require combining two or more functions to form a new one, or else tailoring a function to fit a specialized new use.

Step 5: Coding   Translate each of the individual steps in the solution into C++, identifying new functions and reusing old functions as appropriate to accomplish each individual step. Connect the steps with appropriate control structures (loops, function calls, statement sequences, conditionals, etc.) in a way that agrees with your discoveries in Stage 3. Retain as C++ comments all descriptive information noted during Step 3 for each of the individual steps and corresponding variables.

---

3.   See Volume I of this series, *Fundamentals of Computing*.

Step 6: Testing and verification   Systematically test, or validate, the C++ program by running it once for each set of input values in a suite of alternatives designed to exploit the full range of inputs allowed by the problem's preconditions. For each run, check that the program's output satisfies the problem's postconditions. Alternatively, verify some or all of the program's constituent steps, using proof techniques, when appropriate.

Step 7: Presentation   Add commentary at the beginning (the "top") of the program to clarify the purpose of the program, note its authorship and date, and identify the use of functions that were developed for other purposes (and often by other programmers). Prepare a printed listing of the program, along with a printed copy of one or more sample outputs.

Bear in mind that the MAPS methodology often requires going back to an earlier step. For example, errors found during testing might require changes in coding or even in the specifications. While the MAPS methodology is useful for conceptualizing and solving modest algorithmic problems in a first course, it needs to be made more robust for use in more advanced software design situations. However, MAPS is intentionally designed as a scaled-down version of the *software lifecycle model*, a classic software design methodology introduced in the next chapter.

MAPS represents a *top-down* program design methodology using *stepwise refinement*. Stepwise refinement involves taking a problem and breaking it down into smaller and smaller subproblems. Eventually, one arrives at a set of subproblems that can be solved in a straightforward manner using C++ functions. Deciding when to stop this decomposition process is something of an art. However, recall that each function should have a single, well-defined purpose (the principle of functional cohesion). Thus, each function should encode a fundamental procedural abstraction, that is, some computational process that can often be reused in other programs. For example, our student programmer wrote a search function that was used in six different programs.

Top-down program design by step-wise refinement is an example of the function-oriented design methodology. In function-oriented design, the designer focuses his or her initial attention on identifying the basic tasks (i.e., functions in a generic sense) that need to occur in a program in order for that program to solve the given problem. Programs that are designed using this methodology tend to have a hierarchical structure that can be captured by means of diagrams.

Using Diagrams in Designing Solutions

In program design, the adage "a picture is worth a thousand words" is especially useful. From the earliest days of programming, diagrams of various sorts have been utilized to help in the design and documentation of programs. There are literally dozens of conventions for diagramming various aspects of computer systems – both hardware and software. One type of diagram, the *structure chart*, is especially useful for representing and documenting program development using a function-oriented design methodology.

A *structure chart* shows how a problem has been decomposed in terms of functions. It accomplishes this by representing functions as boxes and using lines between boxes to indicate the relationship of one function calling another. There are several ways to draw a structure chart. In this text, we use the convention that structure charts are drawn sideways, with the "top" of the chart to the left and the "bottom" of the chart to the right. This style was chosen because it simplifies the drawing of charts for large programs. In this kind of structure chart, if function f calls another function, g, then the box representing f is drawn to the left of the box representing g and a line is drawn between them. If data flows from f to g, that data is shown above the connecting line; and if data flows from g back to f, then that data is shown below the connecting line. When a function f calls a function g, we call g a *descendant* of f (don't forget that our structure charts are drawn sideways!), and f a parent (or ancestor) of g. A function may have many descendants and many parents.

Structure charts only detail the calling relationship between functions, i.e., which functions call which other functions, and the data flow between the functions. Structure charts do not show control structures such as decisions or loops, nor do they show the order in which functions are called by a given function.

Figure 0–1 shows a simple structure chart that corresponds to a program in which the main function, denoted by m in the figure, calls a function f and a function g. The functions f and g are descendants of the main function in the structure chart. The function main passes variables a, b and c to the function f. The function f modifies c and passes it back to the function main. The variables a and b are input arguments for f and c is an input-output argument. The main function passes c to the function g. The function g uses c to compute a float value, which it returns. We represent the result passed back by a non-void function by displaying the return type of the function (e.g., float or int) as an output data flow. Note that different kinds of boxes are used to distinguish between void functions (such as f) and functions that return a value (such as g).

Figure 0–2 shows the structure chart that our student programmer developed for the SEARCHER program. The structure chart reflects how the original problem was decomposed into subproblems. It also shows the data flows among the functions in the program. Figure 0–2 shows that the original problem was first decomposed into four important steps:

1. Give the professor instructions on how to use the program.
2. Get the class data from the professor, storing that class data in the arrays stu_names (sn in the chart) and stu_averages (sa in the chart). The class data includes class_size (cs in the chart), the number of students in the class.
3. Sort the class data alphabetically by name, keeping the student averages in the correct correspondence.

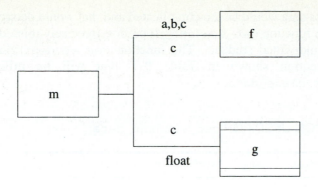

FIGURE 0–1 A simple structure chart.

4. Process requests from the professor that will enable acquisition of the final average for a particular student or termination of the program.

These four steps correspond to the four functions that constitute the second level in the structure chart.

Figure 0–2 shows that a single void function (`give_instructions`) will be used to accomplish the goal of presenting the professor with instructions. In other words, this function does not require further refinement in terms of defining additional functions. Also note that a single void function (`sort_by_name`) will be used to accomplish the task of sorting the data by student name. Thus, the functions `give_instructions` and `sort_by_name` do not have any descendants in Figure 0–2.

However, the void function `get_class_data` does have descendants, the void function `get_student_data` and the float function `compute_average`. Our student programmer decided that the process of getting the data for an entire class (consisting of many students) required a special function to get the data for an individual student. Otherwise, the procedure for reading in the

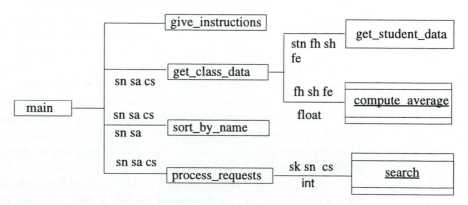

FIGURE 0–2 Structure chart for the `Searcher` program.

class data would be too complicated and that would detract from its readability. The function `get_student_data` does precisely this: it reads in the data for an individual student. The function `get_student_data` produces the information shown in Table 0–1 that will be utilized by its parent, `get_class_data`.

TABLE 0–1   NOTATION USED FOR `get_student_data`

variable name:	symbol in structure chart:
student_name	stn
first_hourly	fh
second_hourly	sh
final_exam	fe

This is shown by means of the data flow emanating from `get_student_data` in the structure chart of Figure 0–2.

The function `get_class_data` does two things with the individual student data passed back by `get_student_data` :

1. It calls the function `compute_average` in order to get a final average for a particular student, based upon that student's exam scores.
2. It places a student's name and final average in the `stu_names` and `stu_averages` arrays, respectively.

Figure 0–2 shows that the function `compute_average` utilizes the exam scores (`first_hourly`, `second_hourly`, `final_exam`) of a particular student in order to compute and pass back a float value as that student's final average.

Figure 0–2 also shows that the function `get_class_data` produces the array of names (`stu_names`), the array of averages (`stu_averages`) and the class size (`class_size`) as output for the main function. The main function passes this information (`stu_names`, `stu_averages` and `class_size`) to the function `sort_by_name`. The function `sort_by_name` modifies the values contained within the `stu_names` and `stu_averages` arrays and thus are shown as input-output arguments. The value of `class_size` is not modified by `sort_by_name` and thus appears as an input argument.

Figure 0–2 finally shows that the function `process_requests` uses the array of names, the array of averages, and the class size in order to accomplish its task of allowing the professor to access the final average for any student. Thus, the variables `stu_names`, `stu_averages` and `class_size` are shown as input arguments for the function `process_requests`. The function `process_requests` calls the function `search`. This function takes the name of a student (`search_key`), the array of student names (`stu_names`), and the class size (`class_size`) and returns a value of type `int`. The value returned by search is either the index of the location where search_key was found in the array stu_names or −1 if search_key does not occur in the array stu_names.

EXERCISE

0–5 Draw a structure chart for the following situation: The main function calls void functions q, r, and s and a float function f. The function q calls the void function t and the float function v. The function q has no input arguments, but produces the float values x, y, and z. The function r uses the values x, y and z to compute a new value for z (a float) and another new value called w (a float). The function s uses z and w, but produces no new data. The function f computes the sum of x, y and z (these are float values). The function t has no input arguments, but produces the values x and y. The float function v takes the values of x and y and produces a value for z.

A FORMAL SPECIFICATION LANGUAGE

Our second program design principle mandates the use of formal specifications for each function. These take the form of preconditions and postconditions that are included in the comments at the beginning of each function. These preconditions and postconditions are given in a formal notation called a *specification language*. In this section, we discuss the specification language that our student programmer used to document the Searcher program. This specification language is based upon mathematical logic. Preconditions and postconditions serve two fundamental purposes:

1.   They serve as program specifications.
2.   They serve as program documentation.

As program specifications. Preconditions and postconditions specify the behavior of each function in a program. Thus, they are written *before* the functions are actually coded. The code is written to satisfy the specifications and not the other way around. The precondition states what the programmer can assume is true when the function is called. The postcondition states what will be true (assuming the precondition) when the function has finished executing. A function that satisfies its postconditions for all possible values of arguments that satisfy its preconditions is said to be *correct*. One cannot formally discuss the correctness of a function except in relation to its satisfaction of these specifications.

As program documentation. In the real world of computing, many people will read a function during its lifetime. Thus, every function must contain a section of comments (at the beginning of the function) that clearly explain the purpose of that function and its specification. The purpose is given in English, but the specification is given in a more stylized language that includes formal logic. The specification is intended to make the behavior of the function both precise and clear to the reader.

Preconditions and postconditions represent special cases of the more general concept of an *assertion*. Assertions are expressed using the same notation that is used to express formal specifications. Assertions can occur at any point in a program and they are sometimes used as documentation to help clarify a program's logic. An important kind of assertion is the *loop invariant*. Loop invariants are assertions associated with program loops. A loop invariant is true just before the execution of a loop begins and remains true after each execution of the loop body. Loop invariants are important for formulating loops that are logically correct. Loop invariants are also important for program verification and for proving that a program terminates.

The rest of this section gives a brief accounting of the specification language that is used in our example program (called `Searcher`).

Specifying the State of the Computation

At any point in time, a program is operating on a set of variables and their values. These variables might be simple variables, arrays, or other kinds of structures that we shall learn about in this course. An important kind of assertion is one that makes a statement about the state of the computation. The relational operators of C++ (>, >=, <, <=) are used in the specification language. In lieu of the C++ equality operator (==) we use the usual mathematical symbol, =. We use the C++ operator != to connote inequality. The logical connectives are denoted by *and* (sometimes presented as ^) and *or*. Here are some examples of assertions.

Example 0.1   `num_students` is defined

This asserts that the variable `num_students` has some value appropriate for its type.

Example 0.2   `num_students >= 0 ^ num_students <= 100`

This assertion states that the variable `num_students` has a value of at least 0 and at most 100. This assertion also implies that `num_students` is defined.

Example 0.3   `(let_grade='A' or let_grade='B'   or`
                   `    let_grade='C') ^ average >= 70.0`

This assertion states that the variable `let_grade` has the value `'A'` or `'B'` or `'C'` and that the variable `average` is at least 70.0.

Note the use of parentheses to specify the order in which the logical connectives are evaluated. That is, the conjunction operator ^ has higher precedence than the disjunction operator `or`, and thus we need to use parentheses here. An alternative form is shown in Example 0.4.

Example 0.4   `let_grade in {'A' .. 'C'} ^ average >= 70.0`

This assertion is equivalent to the previous one. The notation first .. last will be used to define a range of ordinal (e.g., `int`, `char` or enumerated) values. Thus, 'A' .. 'C' denotes the sequence of characters 'A', 'B', 'C'. The curly braces are used to define a set. Thus {'A' .. 'C'} denotes the set that consists of the values 'A', 'B', and 'C'. We use the symbol "in" to denote the set membership test. Thus, `let_grade in {'A' .. 'C'}` will be true if the value of `let_grade` is in the indicated set. Otherwise, `let_grade in {'A' .. 'C'}` will be false.

Example 0.5   `grade_sum = sum i in {0 .. N-1} : grade[i]`

This assertion states that the variable `grade_sum` is equal to the sum of the array elements `grade[i]` for i going from 0 to N–1. The following variations are also useful:

```
max i in {0..N-1}: grade[i]
min i in {0..N-1}: grade[i]
```

These compute the maximum and minimum of `grade[0]` through `grade[N-1]`, respectively. Note that the specification given in this example is equivalent to:

```
grade_sum = sum i in {1 .. N} : grade[i-1]
```

Example 0.6   `post: num_students = old(num_students) + 1`

This postcondition states that the value of `num_students` upon leaving the function will be one more than the value `num_students` had when the function was entered.

It is sometimes important in a postcondition to state that the new value of a variable is related in some way to the value that the variable had when the function began its execution (and when the precondition was true). This example illustrates how the original value of a variable can be referenced in a postcondition by using the notation:

```
old(aVariable)
```

Specifying the Processing of Input

External sources of data (such as the keyboard and external files) are viewed as *streams*. A stream is a sequence of characters. We use the notation \n to denote the new line character that is important for keyboard input (where it corresponds to the return or enter key) and for input from text files that are organized as a sequence of lines. In general, if a function processes input from the keyboard or an external file, then the precondition and postcondition for that function must describe the processing of that input and its effect on the state of the computer's memory. The symbol input is used to refer to keyboard input.

The examples that follow show preconditions and postconditions for functions that process inputs of various kinds from various sources.

Example 0.7 pre: input = aFloat
post: input = empty ^ stu_grade = aFloat

These specifications indicate how input processing is reflected in the form of a precondition and a postcondition. The precondition simply states that the input stream contains a float value, denoted by aFloat. The postcondition states that the input stream is empty (since aFloat has been "consumed" by the function) and that the variable stu_grade now contains the value (aFloat) that was previously in the input stream.

Note that we use symbols such as aFloat, aString, anInt and so forth to indicate the type of data that is contained in the input stream.

The semantics of a precondition on an input stream needs further elaboration. The specification language that we are using intentionally avoids the difficult problem of describing the detailed interaction between the program and the user. In general, a function that is going to get input data from the user will also be prompting the user for that input data. The prompts to the screen will often alternate with the input operations at the keyboard. The specification language that we are employing ignores the prompts for input and tries to handle input processing *by describing the expected form that the input data will take*. This will enable the person who codes the function to have a fairly clear understanding of what the function does and what form the input data will take.

Another way of explaining the semantics of a precondition

    pre: input = aFloat

for a function f is that a sufficient condition for the function f to work properly is that the user will provide a float value for the function to process and not some other type of value and not no value at all.

Example 0.8 pre: input = aString \n aFloat \n
post: input = empty ^ stu_name = aString ^
stu_grade = aFloat

The precondition states that the input stream will provide a string on one line followed by a float value on the next line. The float value is followed by a new line character. The postcondition states that the input stream is empty (since both aString and aFloat have been "consumed" by the function) and that the variable stu_name now contains the value aString and the variable `stu_grade` now contains the value `aFloat`.

Of course, `aString` and `aFloat` are the values that were previously contained in the input stream. The new line characters in the precondition indicate that this function assumes that the user will press the enter (or return) key after entering the string `aString` and after entering the float `aFloat`. This information is important because it will help the implementor to decide the correct way to handle this input situation.

Example 0.9   pre: `input = N aFloat1 aFloat2 ... aFloatN`
                   post: `input = empty ^ num_grades = N ^`
                             `for all i in {1 .. num_grades}:`
                             `      grade[i-1]=aFloati`

The precondition states that the input stream contains an integer `N` followed by `N float` values. The i-th `float` value is denoted by `aFloati`. The postcondition states that the input stream has been totally consumed (`input = empty`) and that the variable `num_grades` has the value `N` (the first value in the input stream). In addition, the universal quantifier, `for all`, is used to explain the correspondence between the `N` float values in the input stream and the final values in the array `grade`. In fact, the postcondition states that the `N float` values in the input stream were read in sequence into the components of the array `grade`, so that `grade[i-1]` now contains `aFloati`. The precondition does not require new line characters in the input stream. The implication here is that any new line characters will be ignored.

Example 0.10   pre: `aTextFile =  N aFloat1 aFloat2 ...`
                            `                aFloatN restOfFile`
                    post: `aTextFile =restOfFile^num_grades = N ^`
                            `for all i in {1 .. num_grades}:`
                            `      grade[i-1]=aFloati`

This example is similar to Example 0.9 except that the input is coming from a text file. The identifier `aTextFile` represents the input file stream (`ifstream`) object used in the function to effect file input operations. When this function begins executing, the text file is positioned so that the next input value is the integer `N`. Following this integer, the file contains `N` float values, followed by some unspecified data that the symbol `restOfFile` refers to. The postcondition states that the integer and `N` float values have been consumed and that the file has been repositioned so that the next data in the file is `restOfFile`. Furthermore, `grade[i-1]` equals the i-th float value that was provided in the input file stream.

Specifying the Generation of Output

The specifications for generation of output are handled very much like those for the processing of input. Output is viewed as a stream of characters. These characters may either be sent to the computer screen or to an external file. The special symbol `output` is used to refer to the computer screen. The symbol `\n` is used to specify the new line character. Here are some examples of preconditions and postconditions for functions that generate output.

Example 0.11

```
pre:   output = empty ^ num_grades >= 0 ^
          for all i in {1..num_grades}:
              grade[i-1] is defined
post:  output = grade[0] \n... \n
          grade[num_grades - 1]
```

The precondition states that the output stream (the computer display) is empty, that the array components `grade[i-1]` are defined for `i` in `{1.. num_grades}` and that `num_grades` is at least 0. If `num_grades` is 0, then the set `{1..num_grades}` is interpreted as the empty set. If `{1..num_grades}` is the empty set then the assertion

```
for all i in {1..num_grades} : grade[i-1] is defined
```

is vacuously true. The postcondition states that the output consists of all of the values `grade[i-1]` for `i` in the set `{1..num_grades}`. Furthermore, each grade is followed by a new line character. If num_grades is 0 then no new data will be sent to the output stream.

Example 0.12

```
pre:   aTextFile = oldStuff ^ num_grades >= 0 ^
          for all i in {1..num_grades}:
              grade[i-1] is defined
post:  aTextFile = oldStuff
          grade[0] \n ...\n grade[num_grades - 1]
```

These specifications are for a function that is writing to a file that (perhaps) has already been written to. Files are referenced by using the names of output file stream (ofstream) objects. In this case, the external file (associated with the ofstream object `aTextFile`) already contains some unspecified stuff, called `oldStuff`. This function *appends* the student grades `grade[0]`, `grade[1]`, ..., `grade[num_grades-1]` to the already existing stuff in the file.

Notice how precise this notation is. The `oldStuff` is followed immediately by the grades in the file without any new line character intervening between the oldStuff and the grades.

More Examples Using Quantifiers and Informal Assertions

The universal quantifier `for all` and the existential quantifier `there exists` are used frequently in specifying functions. Let's show how these quantifiers are used in specifying functions that perform (1) sorting and (2) searching with respect to arrays.   Furthermore, we shall illustrate that, when the meaning is clear, we can substitute simple English phrases for more complicated logical expressions in our preconditions and postconditions:

Example 0.13
```
           pre:    num_grades >= 0 ^
                     for all i in {1..num_grades}:
                        grade[i-1] is defined
          post:   for all i in {1 .. num_grades - 1}:
                        grade[i-1] <= grade[i] ^
                        grade is a permutation of old(grade)
```

These specifications describe a function that will sort an array `grade` that contains `num_grades` values. The precondition states that `num_grades` is at least 0 and that all of the array components from `grade[0]` through `grade[num_grades - 1]` are defined. (If `num_grades` is 0, this is an empty set of array components, so the precondition is again vacuously true.) The postcondition states two facts: (1) that the array is now sorted, with each component less than or equal to the succeeding component, and (2) that the new array values are a permutation of the old array values, and thus contains the same values as the old array.

We used the informal assertion

```
grade is a permutation of old(grade)
```

to communicate a concept that should be familiar to the reader. To express this idea more formally would require a more complicated expression that might actually detract from the readability of the specification.

Example 0.14
```
           pre:    num_grades >= 0 ^
                     search_key is defined ^
                     grade is sorted.
          post ((there exists i in {0..num_grades - 1}:
                        search_key = grade[i]  ^  search = i)
                     or
                     (for all i in {0..num_grades - 1}:
                        search_key != grade[i]) ^ search = -1))
```

The specifications in this example describe a function `search` that searches through the array `grade` for the value `search_key`. The precondition states that `num_grades` is at least 0, that `search_key` is defined, and that the array is sorted.   The postcondition is interesting because it states two possible outcomes for the function. If there is a match for `search_key` in the array, then `search` will return the value of an index `i` that satisfies `grade[i]` = `search_key`. If there is no match for `search_key`, then `search` will return the value -1.

Note that we chose to use the informal statement "grade is sorted" rather than the formal description of what it means for an array to be sorted (as given in

Example 0.13). Note also the use of the function name in specifying the result returned by the function. Also note the way the disjunctive operator `or` is used to stipulate the two possible outcomes for the function.

Repeating Groups of Data Items within Streams

Some functions process large amounts of input data and others generate large quantities of output data. Typically, these complex streams contain repeating patterns. For example, an input stream might consist of an integer N followed by N repetitions of the following pattern: a student name, and three exam scores. We need to develop a notation for describing these complex input and output streams. Since the same principles apply to both types of streams, we shall focus our attention upon input streams only.

Example 0.15

```
pre:    input = N
        (N repetitions of aName
        FHScore SHScore FScore)
post:   input = empty ^ class_size = N ^
        for all i in {1..class_size}:
            stu_names[i-1] = i-th aName ^
            stu_averages[i-1] = weighted average of
            i-th FHScore, i-th SHScore,
            and i-th FScore
```

The precondition states that the input stream contains an integer value (N) followed by N repetitions of the pattern: a name, a first hourly score, a second hourly score and a final exam score. The postcondition states that the entire input stream has been consumed and that the variable `class_size` is N. Furthermore, `stu_names[i-1]` has the value of the i-th instance of aName and `stu_averages[i-1]` contains the weighted average of the i-th set of exam scores.

These specifications describe a function (similar to one that we shall actually need for our `Searcher` example program) that calls several additional functions in order to perform its task. (This explains why at first glance, this function might seem to violate functional cohesiveness. At its level in a program hierarchy, it performs a single task: filling in the arrays `stu_names` and `stu_averages`.)

We decided to be a bit informal in giving the postcondition. We might have been more precise by asserting the following concerning `stu_averages[i-1]`:

```
stu_averages[i-1] =
    0.25 * i-th FHScore + 0.25 * i-th SHScore + 0.5 * i-th FScore
```

However, our strategy is to leave the details as to how a weighted average is computed to the formal specifications for the function that actually computes this average. This is consistent with our program design strategy, where details are left to functions that actually must deal with those details.

It should be noted that this example describes a function that is using one of two basic strategies for processing data in an input stream. This strategy (sometimes called the *header value strategy*) involves providing a data item at the beginning of a stream (in this case N) that indicates how much data follows in the stream (in this case, N repetitions of the described pattern).

We could have used the N repetitions of notation to give the specifications presented earlier in Example 0.9. Here is a restatement of that example using this new notation:

```
pre:    input = N (N repetitions of : aFloat)
post:   input = empty ^ num_grades = N  ^
        for all i in {1..num_grades} : grade[i-1] = i-th aFloat
```

Example 0.16
```
        pre:    input =
                (repetitions of:
                   aName FHScore SHScore FScore)
                SENTINEL
        post:   input = empty ^
                class_size = number of repetitions ^
                for all i in {1..class_size} :
                   stu_names[i-1] = i-th aName ^
                   stu_averages[i-1] = weighted average
                      of i-th FHScore i-th SHScore
                      and i-th FScore
```

These specifications describe a procedure that is similar to the one given in the previous example except that it uses a *sentinel loop strategy* for processing the input data. This is the second basic strategy for organizing data in an input stream. The notation

```
(repetitions of: aName FHScore SHScore FScore)
```

indicates that the input stream consists of an indefinite number of repetitions (0 or more) of the pattern being described. A special sentinel value (SENTI-NEL in this example) marks the end of the data to be processed. When the program encounters this value in lieu of an expected student name, the input processing loop will terminate.

EXERCISES

0–6 This problem presents function prototypes (with argument names) along with the preconditions and postconditions for these functions. In each case, give an English language description of what the function does.

a. `int add_em();`
   ```
   pre:  input = N (N repetitions of : aFloat)
   post: input = empty ^
         add_em = sum i in {1..N}: i-th aFloat
   ```
b. `void compute_stats(int a[], int n, int& min_val, int& max_val, int& sum_val);`
   ```
   pre:  n > 0 ^ for all i in {1..n} : a[i-1] is defined
   post: min_val = min i in {1..n} : a[i-1]
       ^ max_val = max i in {1..n} : a[i-1]
       ^ sum_val = sum i in {1..n} : a[i-1]
   ```
c. `void zero_it(int a[], int n);`
   ```
   pre:  N > 0 ^ for all i in {1..n} : a[i-1] is defined
   post: for all i in {1..n}:
             (old(a[i-1]) < 0 ^ a[i-1] = -1)
         or (old(a[i-1]) > 0 ^ a[i-1] = 1)
   ```

0–7 Give preconditions and postconditions for each of the following functions:

a. This `void` function takes an array a with n elements and sorts that array in descending order. Give the complete specification for describing a as sorted.
b. This `float` function (`ave_elem`) returns the average of the elements in an array a that contains n elements, where n is at least 1.
c. This `int` function (`lin_search`) performs a linear search on an array that may not be sorted. The array is a and it contains n elements, where n is at least 0. The search key is called `key`. The function returns the index of `key` in the array a, if `key` is found, and −1 otherwise.
d. This `void` function merges two arrays, a with n elements and b with m elements into a third array, c with p = m + n elements. It accomplishes this by placing the elements of a at the beginning of the array c and then copying the elements of b into c. The relative order of elements in a and b is preserved in c.
e. This void function is similar to the one described in part *d* except that the arrays a and b are sorted and the elements are merged so that the array c will also be sorted.

THE `Searcher` PROGRAM WITH COMMENTARY

This section presents the `Searcher` program function by function. Each function, including the main function, is presented along with accompanying commentary that helps to clarify the design principles and decisions that the program reflects.

External definitions and declarations

The program file begins with a series of comments that give the programmer's name, the date that the program was completed, the overall behavior of the program, the input data that is expected, and the results that will be produced. These are followed by external definitions and declarations. These definitions and declarations are global throughout the rest of the program. Note that no *variables* are defined globally. The global definitions are for named constants and a `string` type; the global declarations are for functions (i.e., one global function prototype is presented).

```
/* -- Program name: Searcher



   -- Programmer:    Student programmer
   -- Date:          June 1, 1993



   -- ** Overview
   -- This program allows the user to enter student data for
   -- all students in a class.  It then allows the user to
   -- access each student's final average.



   -- The program begins by presenting the user with
   -- instructions.



   -- It then asks the user to enter the number of students in
   -- the class (an integer).



   -- It then asks the user to enter the grade data for that
   -- many students.  For each student, the following data is
   -- entered:



   --   STUDENT NAME          (a string)
   --     FIRST HOURLY SCORE  (a float)
   --     SECOND HOURLY SCORE (a float)
   --     FINAL EXAM SCORE    (a float)



   -- The program uses this information to compute a final
   -- average for each student.  The student's name and final
   -- average are then stored in parallel arrays.



   -- Once all of the student data for the class has been
   -- entered, the data in the parallel arrays is sorted
   -- alphabetically by student name.
```

```
--  Finally, the program enters a "process requests" phase
--  that allows the user to enter student names in a loop.
--  For each student name entered, the program will either
--  display that student's final average or, if no such
--  student is contained in the name array, the program
--  will display an appropriate error message.


--  The user can terminate this process by entering an
--  asterisk (*) in lieu of a student name.


--  ** Warnings
--  This program does virtually no integrity checks on the
--  input data.  The program will not check that an on
--  nerves factor is actually Y or N.  Any character other
--  than Y will be treated as an N.  Exam scores are not
--  checked for being in range (say 0 to 100).          */


#include <iostream.h>
#include <string.h>


// GLOBAL CONSTANTS AND TYPEDEF'S ...
const int MAXCLASS = 50;   // maximum number of students in class
const int MAXSTRING = 20;   // maximum student name length
const int LINESIZE  = 80;   // maximum length of input line
typedef char string[MAXSTRING];


// GLOBAL FUNCTION PROTOTYPE ...
void read_string(char*, int);
```

Almost every C++ program begins with the use of the #include preprocessor directive that pulls in header files that contain function prototypes and other information that the compiler will need in order to compile a program successfully. This program includes the `iostream.h` header file (which provides input and output operations using `cin` and `cout`) and the `string.h` header file (which provides the functions `strcmp` and `strcpy` that are needed by this program).

The global (or external) constants are `MAXCLASS`, which gives the maximum number of students in the class, `MAXSTRING`, which gives the maximum number of characters in a student name string (including one character for the string terminator character '\0') and `LINESIZE`, which gives the maximum input line length.

The `typedef` statement declares a global type: `string` The global function prototype declares a function `read_string` that has two arguments: a string that is passed by reference (by virtue of the fact that `string` is an array type) and an `int` that is passed by value. The second argument specifies the maximum number of characters that can be stored in the string that is being read. This function is used to read in the value for a string variable from the keyboard.

The function `main`

The main function consists of three parts:
1.   A part that declares function prototypes.
2.   A part that defines local variables.
3.   A statement part that contains executable code.

```
void main()
{
    // FUNCTION PROTOTYPES ...
    void give_instructions();
    void get_class_data(string[], float[], int&);
    void sort_by_name(string[], float[], int);
    void process_requests(string[], float[], int);


    // LOCAL DATA ...
    string stu_names[MAXCLASS];      // list of student names
    float stu_averages[MAXCLASS];    // list of student averages
    int class_size;


    // STATEMENTS ...
    give_instructions();
    get_class_data(stu_names, stu_averages, class_size);
    sort_by_name(stu_names, stu_averages, class_size);
    process_requests(stu_names, stu_averages, class_size);
}
```

The local data consists of an array `stu_names`, an array `stu_averages` and an `int` variable, `class_size`. Each component of `stu_names` is a string that gives the name of a student and the corresponding component of `stu_averages` gives the final average for that student.   The `int` variable `class_size` specifies how many students are in the class.

The function prototypes declare the functions called by the function `main`. These are (1) `give_instructions`, a function that explains the program to the user, (2) `get_class_data`, a function that reads in data for the arrays `stu_names` and `stu_averages`, (3) `sort_by_name`, a function that sorts the data alphabetically by student name and (4) `process_requests`, a function that allows the user to get averages for specified students.

Note that none of the main function variables represents individual student data values. This is a manifestation of information hiding. The main function does not need to know these individual student details and thus these variables are not declared at the top level in the program. Note also that the main function does not perform any input or output operations. This is a manifestation of another software design principle, mainly that the operations of getting data from the user and of displaying results to the user should be performed by functions at a lower level.

The statements in the main function simply call the functions that perform the four major steps in the problem decomposition: giving the user instructions, getting the data, sorting the data, and processing requests for individual averages.

The function `give_instructions`

This function presents the user with a brief explanation of what the program does. The `cin.get()` statement will cause the program to "hang–up" until the user presses the return key. This will assure that the user can finish reading the instructions before being asked for program data.

```
// Function: give_instructions
// Purpose:  Gives the user instructions
// Pre:      output = empty
// Post:     output contains instructions for program use
void give_instructions()
{
    cout << "This program will ask you to enter student data\n";
    cout << "It will then sort the student names and final\n";
    cout << "averages alphabetically by name.  Then, it will\n";
    cout << "allow you to request computed averages for \4
    particular\n";
    cout << "students." << endl << endl << endl;
    cout << "Press any key, then enter to continue: ";
    cin.get();
    cin.ignore(LINESIZE, '\n');
    cout << endl;
} // end give_instructions()
```

The function `get_class_data`

This function "produces" the data that the main function needs: namely, the arrays `stu_names` and `stu_averages` and the variable `class_size`. The variable `class_size` gives the actual number of students in the class. Note that this function's arguments are all output arguments and thus need to be declared as pass by reference arguments. The array arguments declared as

```
string stu_names[]
float stu_averages[]
```

are pass by reference arguments since what is actually being passed to the function are the base addresses of the two arrays. When an array argument is declared in the following manner:

```
type arr-name[]
```

then it is passed by reference and there is no need to make this explicit by means of an ampersand. The argument `class_size` is declared pass by reference, using the `&`.

```
// Function: get_class_data
// Purpose:  Gets the student names and averages for
//           students in a class.
```

---

4.   This backslash is used to allow a string constant to continue to a new line in such a manner that the string does not contain the new line character.

```
// Pre:        input = N (N repetitions of:
//                aName FHScore SHScore FScore)
// Post:       class_size = N
//                and for all i in [1..class_size] :
//                           stu_names[i-1] = i-th aName
//                and for all i in [1..class_size] :
//                       stu_averages[i-1] =
//                       weighted average determined by
//                       (i-th FHScore i-th SHScore i-th FScore)
void get_class_data(string stu_names[], float stu_averages[],
int& class_size)
{
    // FUNCTION PROTOTYPES ...
    void get_student_data(char*, float&, float&, float&);
    float compute_average(float, float, float);


    // LOCAL DATA ...
    string   student_name;
    float    first_hourly, second_hourly, final_exam;


    // STATEMENTS ...
    cout << "How many students are in the class? ";
    cin  >> class_size;
    cin.ignore(LINESIZE, '\n');    // go to beginning of next line


    for (int i = 0; i < class_size; i++)
    {
        get_student_data(student_name, first_hourly,
          second_hourly, final_exam);
        stu_averages[i] = compute_average(first_hourly,
             second_hourly, final_exam);
        strcpy(stu_names[i], student_name);
    }
} // end get_class_data
```

This function asks the user to enter a value for `class_size`. A loop is then used to do the following for each student in the class:

1. Get that student's individual data,
2. Compute that student's final average,
3. Place that student's final average in the appropriate position in the array `stu_averages`, and
4. Place that student's name in the appropriate position in the array, `stu_names`.

Step 1 is accomplished by means of a call to the function `get_student_data`. This function passes back all data for an individual student (that student's name and exam scores). Step 2 is accomplished by means of a call to the function, `compute_average`. This function takes the exam scores and returns a `float` value. Step 3 is accomplished by means of the assignment of the value returned by `compute_average` to the array component stu_averages[i]. Here, i is the loop index (note that it is defined within the for statement). The loop index is being used to keep track of where each name and average should go in the arrays stu_averages and stu_names. Step 4 is accomplished by means of a call to the strcpy function.

The function get_student_data

This function produces all of the data for an individual student. It is called within the for loop in the function get_class_data. The arguments first_hourly, second_hourly and final_exam are all output arguments and thus they are all declared as pass by reference arguments (using the &). The argument student_name is also an output argument, but it is pass by reference by virtue of the fact that string is an array type. This function simply prompts the user for the data and passes the data back to the calling function, get_class_data.

```
// Function: get_student_data
// Purpose:   Prompts the user for and gets all data
//            for one student.
// Pre:       input = aName FHScore SHScore restOfData
// Post:      input = restOfData and student_name = aName
//                and first_hourly = FHScore
//                and second_hourly = SHScore
//                and final_exam = FScore


void get_student_data(char* student_name, float& first_hourly,
    float& second_hourly, float& final_exam)
{
    // STATEMENTS ...
    cout << "Please enter the student's name: ";
    read_string(student_name, MAXSTRING);
    cout << "Please enter an exam score when prompted:\n";
    cout << "First hourly score: ";
    cin  >> first_hourly;
    cout << "Second hourly score: ";
    cin  >> second_hourly;
    cout << "Final exam score: ";
    cin  >> final_exam;
    cin.ignore(LINESIZE, '\n');    // next input on new line
    cout << endl << endl;
} // end get_student_data
```

Note that this function knows nothing about the arrays stu_names and stu_averages. This is another example of information hiding. The function get_student_data does not know about these arrays because it does not need to know about them. Nor does it need to know about class_size. The application of information hiding in this context allows the procedure get_student_data to be reusable. The function get_student_data can be moved to any other program that might need to read in data for an individual student regardless of how that other program proposes to utilize the data.

The function   `get_student_data` calls the function `read_string`, which is used to read in the value of a `string` variable. The function prototype for `read_string` was declared globally before the main function. The function definition for `read_string` will be presented and discussed later.

The function `compute_average`

The function `compute_average` takes an individual student's three exam scores and returns a `float` value that represents that student's final average. The arguments are all input arguments and are thus passed by value.

```
// Function: compute_average
// Purpose:  Returns a student's final average
// Pre:      first_hourly, seond_hourly and final_exam
//           are defined
// Post:     compute_average = maximum of ((0.25 * (first_hourly
//                             + second_hourly)
//                             + 0.50 * final_exam), 0)
float compute_average(float first_hourly, float second_hourly,
          float final_exam)
{
   // LOCAL DATA ...
   const float WEIGHT1 = 0.25,
             WEIGHT2 = 0.25,
             WEIGHTF = 0.50;
   float tent_average;    // tentative average


   // statements
   tent_average = WEIGHT1 * first_hourly
     + WEIGHT2 * second_hourly
     + WEIGHTF * final_exam;
   if (tent_average < 0.0) tent_average = 0.0;
   return (tent_average);
} // end compute_average
```

The exam weights are defined locally as named constants. This is another example of information hiding. The calling function, `get_class_data`, does not need to know about the particular details as to how a student's final average is computed. In addition, no other function in the program needs to know the three exam weights. These considerations dictated that the three exam scores should be defined locally within this function.

The function `sort_by_name`

This function uses the bubblesort algorithm to sort the array of student names (`stu_names`) alphabetically by name. As it does so, it keeps the averages in the parallel array, `stu_averages`, in the proper correspondence with the names being sorted. The arrays `stu_names` and `stu_averages` are input-output arguments which is consistent with the fact that all array arguments (declared in the manner in which these array arguments are declared) are treated as pass by reference arguments..The function `sort_by_name` declares the variable `class_size` as a pass by value argument, since the function does not update the value of this argument.

```
// Function: sort_by_name
// Purpose:  Bubblesorts the array stu_names alphabetically,
//           keeping the array stu_averages in the proper
//           correspondence
// Notation: old(a) --> b will mean that the memory cell a was
//           mapped to the memory cell b in a permutation.
// Pre:      class_size >= 0 and
//              for all i in [1..class_size] :
//                 stu_names[i-1], stu_averages[i-1] are defined
// Post:     stu_names is a permutation of old(stu_names) and
//              stu_averages is a permutation of
//              old(stu_averages) and
//              for all i, j in [1..class_size-1] :
//                 (if old(stu_names[i-1]) --> stu_names[j-1]
//                   then
//                   old(stu_averages[i-1]) --> stu_averages[j-1])
//                 and
//                 for all i in [1..class_size - 1] :
//                   stunames[i-1] < stunames[i]
void sort_by_name(string stu_names[], float stu_averages[],
                  int class_size)
{
    // LOCAL DATA ...
    enum {false, true} done = false;
    string tname;
    float tfloat;
    int limit = class_size - 1;



    // STATEMENTS ...
    // outer loop
    for (int pass = 1; !done && (pass <= limit); pass++)
    {
       done = true;
       // inner loop
       for (int i = 0; i < (class_size - pass); i++)
       {
       if (strcmp(stu_names[i], stu_names[i+1]) > 0)
       {
          strcpy(tname, stu_names[i]);
          strcpy(stu_names[i], stu_names[i+1]);
          strcpy(stu_names[i+1], tname);
          tfloat = stu_averages[i];
          stu_averages[i]   = stu_averages[i+1];
          stu_averages[i+1] = tfloat;
          done = false;
       }
       } // inner loop
    } // outer loop
} // end sort_by_name
```

Bubblesort is not a particularly efficient sorting algorithm. Later in this text, you will learn about sorting algorithms that are significantly better than bubble-sort, but bubblesort is used here because it is easy to understand. Bubblesort works by repeatedly traversing the array to be sorted (`stu_names` in this case). One traversal involves comparing each successive pair of adjacent array components and swapping those components if they are out of order. Note that the `strcmp` function must be used to compare the student names in the `stu_names` array. After one traversal, the name that belongs at the end of the array will wind up at the last position. After k traversals, the k names that belong in the last k positions will be in their proper locations. Thus, after $n - 1$ traversals, where n is the array size, the last $n - 1$ names will be in their proper locations, which implies that the entire array will be sorted. Thus, at most $n - 1$ traversals of an array that contains n elements is required to bubblesort that array. In the function `sort_by_name`, n equals `class_size`.

The inner loop in `sort_by_name` (the `for` loop) implements an array traversal. Note that the loop test value is `class_size - pass`, where `pass` is the number of passes (i.e., traversals) that have been performed so far. If `pass` traversals have been performed, there is no need for the next traversal to examine the last `pass` components in the array, since (by the logic given in the previous paragraph) they are guaranteed to be in the correct order.

Only in the worst case will all `class_size - 1` traversals be required, for if a traversal that requires no swapping occurs, then we know that the array is already sorted. The `int` variable `done` is used to detect such a situation. At the beginning of every traversal, `done` is set to 1 (true). If `done` remains `true`, that is if no swaps occur during a traversal, the outer loop will be able to determine that this was the case and the `while` loop will terminate the next time `done` is tested. If two names need to be swapped during a traversal, `done` will be reset to 0 (false). `Done` will remain `false` for the remainder of the traversal. When `done` is `false`, another traversal of the array will be performed unless `class_size - 1` traversals have already been completed.

The function `process_requests`

This function allows the professor to enter student names repeatedly. If an asterisk is entered in lieu of a student name, then the loop terminates and control returns to the main function (and the program terminates). Otherwise, a search is performed for the given value of `search_key`. The function `search` performs a linear search.

```
// Function: process_requests
// Purpose:  Processes user requests for student final averages.
// Pre:      input = (repetitions of aName) '*'
//              and output = oldStuff
// Post:     searchkey = '*' and input = empty
//              oldstuff = oldstuff \n
//                  (repetitions of : student grade report
//                      for i-th aName)
void process_requests(string stu_names[], float stu_averages[],
```

```
                int class_size)
{
    // FUNCTION PROTOTYPE ...
    int search(string, string[], int);


    // LOCAL DATA ...
    const int SENTINEL = '*';
    string search_key;
    int location;



    // STATEMENTS ...
    cout << endl << "Begin searching phase ... " << endl;
    cout << "Please enter a student's name or *: ";
    read_string(search_key, MAXSTRING);
    while (search_key[0] != SENTINEL)
    {
        location = search(search_key, stu_names, class_size);
        if (location != -1)
        cout << "This student's average is "
            << stu_averages[location] << endl;
        else
        cout << "No student in this class has that name.\n";
        cout << "Please enter a student's name or *: ";
        read_string(search_key, MAXSTRING);
    }
    // hang up program
    cout << "Press any key to exit: ";
    cin.get();
} // end process_requests
```

In order to perform its assigned task, this function needs to know the student names and averages and the class size. This procedure is a consumer of this information but it does not modify this information in any way. Note that the argument `class_size` is passed by value, but the arguments `stu_names` and `stu_averages` are passed by reference, since this is the usual manner in which arrays are passed.

The function `process_requests` uses a sentinel loop schema. This means that the loop continues executing until the user enters a special value (called a sentinel) that serves as a signal that the loop is to terminate. In this case, the sentinel value is represented by the named constant SENTINEL, whose value is '*'. So long as the value of search_key[0] (that is, the first character in search_key) is not an asterisk, the loop body will execute and another search for a student name will be conducted.

Note that the implementation of a sentinel loop requires an input variable (in this case, search_key) that needs to be compared against the sentinel (SENTINEL). Note that search_key is read in before the loop and at the end of the loop body.

If an asterisk has not been entered as the value for search_key, then the loop body executes. This begins with a call to the function search. This function either returns a −1 (if the search fails) or an array index (if the search succeeds). This array index is the location of `search_key` in the array `stu_names`. The function `process_requests` stores this index in the local variable, `location`. The value of `location` is then tested to determine whether to display an error message (if `location` is −1) or to display the average of the student that was located in the array `stu_names`.

The function `search`

This function performs a linear search upon the array of student names, `stu_names`, using the search key, `search_key`. A linear search through an array involves examining the array elements one by one, from the beginning of the array until the end. A precondition for this implementation of linear search is that the array is sorted. We take advantage of this precondition by terminating the search as soon as we determine that the `search_key` is less than the array component currently being examined (i.e., `stu_names[index]`).

```
// Function: search()
// Purpose:  Performs a linear search on the array stu_names
//           using the key search_key.  Returns location of
//           found element in the array stu_names or -1 if
//           the search fails.
// Pre:      class_size >= 0 and search_key is defined and
//            stu_names is sorted in ascending order
// Post:     ((there exists i in [1..class_size) :
//                 search_key = stu_names[i-1] ^ search_key = i)
//           or
//           ((for all i in [1..class_size) :
//                 search_key != stu_names[i-1] ^ search_key = -1)
int search(string search_key, string stu_names[], int
class_size)
{
   // LOCAL DATA ...
   int index = 0;
   enum {found, not_found_yet} status = not_found_yet;


   // statements
   while ((status == not_found_yet) && (index < class_size))
   {
       if (!strcmp(stu_names[index], search_key))
       {
      status = found;
       }
       else
       {
      index++;
       }
   } // while


   if (status == found)
      return(index);
   else
```

```
                  return(-1);
      } // end search
```

The logic of this implementation of linear search is quite simple. We iterate upon the following idea: either `search_key` is not in the array `stu_names` or `search_key` is one of a specific, ordered collection of array components. That specific collection of array components is represented symbolically by the range of indices:

```
      index .. class_size - 1
```

This idea is the key to the logic behind linear search and is called a *loop invariant*. A loop invariant is a condition which is true when we first enter a loop and which remains true after each execution of the loop body. With each iteration, we reduce by one the number of elements in this ordered collection by increasing the value of `index`. If this collection of components ever becomes empty (`index >= class_size`), then we will know that the search has failed. Another indication that the search has failed will be if `search_key < stu_names[index]`. Since the array elements are sorted, this would imply that `search_key`, if it is in the array, must have some index less than `index`. However, the logic of the loop has already eliminated all such array elements from contention.

The function `read_string`

The function `read_string` is used to read in a string value from the keyboard. This function is written so that it will work correctly even if the number of characters entered by the user is greater than `MAXSTRING - 1`, the maximum number of characters that can be stored in a variable of type `string`. Remember that the string termination character, \0, occupies one position in a string.

```
// Function:    read_string
// Purpose:     To read an input string from the keyboard.  This
//              function will truncate excess characters so that
//              the input stream position will be at the
//              beginning of the next line
// Define:      M = MAXSTRING
// Pre:         input = c1 c2 .... cN \n restOfInput, where each
//              cj is a character and N >= 0
// Post:        input = restOfInput and
//                  ((N > M ^ str = c1 c2 .... cM) or
//                   (N < M ^ str = c1 c2 .... cN))


void read_string(char* str, int len)
{
   cin.getline(str, len);
   if (cin.gcount() ==  len - 1)
   {
      cin.ignore(LINESIZE, '\n');
```

```
        }
    }  // end read_string
```

This function uses the `getline` function to read in up to `len` characters from the input stream (denoted by the object `cin`). The `gcount` function is then used to determine the actual number of characters that was read. If this is equal to the maximum allowable by the call to `getline` (i.e., `len - 1`), then the `ignore` function is called so that the rest of the input line will be ignored. This will allow the next input from the user to be accepted from the beginning of the next line.

A REVIEW OF RECURSION

Many of the algorithms presented in this text are recursive in form. Recursion is a fundamental problem-solving tool, and you may have encountered it in the first course. The nature of recursion is reviewed here so that later we can gain deeper insight into why recursion is so useful.

Consider the following recurrence relation that defines a function Max that returns the index of the largest element in a nonempty list $L = (e_0\ e_1\ ...\ e_m)$:

$$
\begin{aligned}
\text{Max}(L, m) &= 0 & &\text{if } m = 0 \\
&= m & &\text{if } m > 0 \text{ and } e_m > e_{\text{Max}(L, m-1)} \\
&= \text{Max}(L, m-1) & &\text{if } m > 0 \text{ and } e_m <= e_{\text{Max}(L, m-1)}
\end{aligned}
$$

Note that *m is the largest index in the list* and not the number of elements in the list. The number of elements in the list is m + 1 because the first index is 0. Thus, max(L,m) returns the index of the largest value among the m + 1 elements: $e_0\ e_1\ ...\ e_m$. This recurrence relation is recursive, in both its second and third lines.

A recursive function, `max`, in C++, that implements this recurrence relation for an array of integers is given below:

```
1    int max(int list[], int m)
2    {
3        if (!m)          // i.e., m == 0
4            return 0;
5        else if (list[m] > list[max(list, m-1)])
6            return m;
7        else
8            return max(list, m-1);
9    }  // end max
```

The function `max` makes two simplifying assumptions: namely, that `m >= 0` and that the actual number of elements in `list` is at least `m + 1`. We have marked this function with line numbers so that we can reference specific lines of the function in the discussion that follows. We have underlined the two places where the function calls itself recursively, that is, at lines 5 and 8.

Suppose we call the function max with list = (2 5 4 3) and m = 3. Every call of max is called an *activation* of max (some authors use the term *incarnation* instead). Each activation of max can cause up to two additional activations of max. Thus, the natural way to represent the relationship among activations is by means of a tree, called a *recursion tree*. Each node in a recursion tree represents one activation of a recursive function or procedure. We shall call these nodes *activation nodes*.

An activation node is depicted in Figure 0–3. An activation node is represented as an oval that contains a number that indicates which activation of a recursive function this is (first, second, third and so forth). Since max is an int function, an activation node for max will show the value returned by that particular activation (once it has been determined). These return values are shown alongside the up arrows in the recursion tree. The activation node will also show the values of the input arguments list and m when the function is called. These input argument values are shown alongside the down arrows in the recursion tree. When an activation creates a new activation at line 5 in max, the new activation node is shown below and to the left of the original. When an activation creates a new activation at line 8 in max, the new activation node is shown below and to the right of the original. When a particular activation is completed, an arrow will be drawn from that activation node back to the node that caused that activation and the return value will be inserted alongside that arrow.

For example, suppose we call max(list, m) with list = (2 5 4 3) and m = 3. Then, we are at activation #1. Since m is 3, the test at line 3 is false and this will cause the recursive call at line 5 to occur. This causes the creation of a new activation node in our recursion tree, as shown in Figure 0–4. This second activation node is at level 2 in the recursion (or, in the recursion tree). Note that list remains the same, but m is 2 at this level.

In activation #2, the test at line 3 is false, since m is 2. This causes max to call itself again at line 5, leading to activation #3. Activation #3 is at the third level in the tree. The argument list remains the same, but m is now 1. In activation #3, the test at line 3 is false once again, so this causes a recursive call at line 5, leading to activation #4. Activation #4 is at level 4 in the recursion tree. Since m is 0 for this activation, the test at line 3 is true. Hence, this activation does not cause any additional recursive calls. Instead, activation #4 returns a value of 0 since line 4 executes. In returning from activation #4, we reacti-

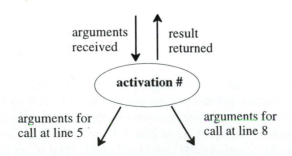

FIGURE 0–3   An activation node for recursion.

vate activation #3, which was suspended. The return value for max, 0, is inserted into the boolean expression at line 5. Since m is 1 for this activation
(activation #3), the test

```
list[m   {= 1}]   > list[max {= 0}]
```

is true, and activation #3 can return a value of 1 (i.e., the value of m). This is
due to the execution of line 6 in activation #3. This causes us to return from
activation #3 and to reactivate activation #2, which was suspended.

   At this point, the return value for max, 1, is plugged into the test at line 5.
Since m = 2 in activation #2, that expression is:

```
list[m {=2}] > list[max {=1}]
```

This evaluates to false and causes activation #2 to call max recursively at line 8.
This results in the fifth activation of max. The recursion tree at this point is
shown in Figure 0–5. Note that since we recursed at line 8, activation #5 ema-
nates from the right of activation #2.

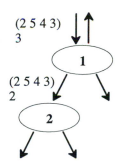

FIGURE 0–4   Recursion tree after max calls itself at line 5 for the first time.

   Figure 0–6 shows the complete recursion tree for this example. Study this
figure carefully. Note that this is not a very efficient method for computing the
index of the maximum element in a list. The function max, however, was intended to introduce a literal implementation of the given recurrence relation
and it is a good example of a double recursion. Recursive algorithms can be
reasonably efficient and very elegant when appropriately used.

   Another reason why recursion is important to the discipline is that many of
the data structures studied in computing are recursive in nature. That is, we can
give natural recursive rules for building such structures. For example, a list can
be constructed by combining a list element with an already existing list. Many
recursive algorithms are based upon the idea of decomposing a structure.

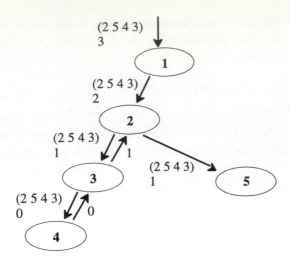

FIGURE 0–5   Recursion tree after the fifth activation of max. This occurs when the second activation of max recurses at line 8.

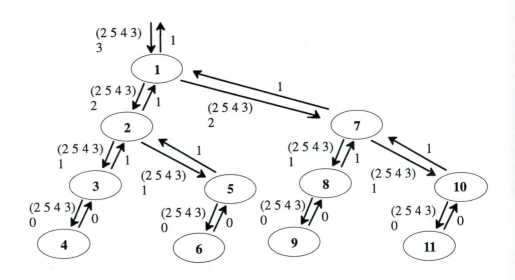

FIGURE 0–6   The complete recursion tree, showing all activations.

These algorithms work by breaking up a structure into smaller parts, and then applying themselves recursively to those smaller parts. Eventually, we obtain pieces of the original structure that are so small that the solution can be presented in straightforward terms. In the formal study of algorithms, this strategy for solving a problem by decomposing a structure is called "divide and conquer."

EXERCISES

0–8 Draw the recursion tree for max when `list` = (4 3 5 6) and m = 3.

0–9 Write a recursive function factorial(n) that will return the factorial of n. Draw the recursion tree for `factorial(n)` when n = 3 and when n = 4.

0–10 Write a recursive function `power(n, p)` that will return the value of n^p. Draw the recursion tree for `power(n, p)` when n = 2 and p = 4.

SUMMARY

Developing reliable programs for others to use is not a trivial process. It is important to design programs whose components are easy to debug, modify, and reuse. Toward this end, six fundamental program design principles are evident.

1. Problem decomposition
2. Formal specifications
3. Functional cohesion
4. Explicit interfaces
5. Loose coupling
6. Information hiding

The `Searcher` program represents most of the prerequisite programming concepts that are assumed by this text. If you understand these six principles, you are well prepared for the learning adventure that lies ahead.

SOFTWARE DEVELOPMENT
WITH OBJECTS

This book is about three major topics:

* The role of abstraction in computing

* Fundamental principles of data structures and their applications

* The design and implementation of large software systems

In this chapter, we introduce a powerful methodology, called *object-oriented design and programming*, that relates to all three of these topics. We motivate this presentation by discussing the problems that confront sponsors, developers, adaptors, and users of large software systems. Then we introduce object-oriented design and programming by again solving the `Searcher` program that was presented in Chapter 0, but this time using object-oriented design and programming techniques. This example therefore provides a useful link to the introductory course, as well as a prelude to the major topics of study in the remainder of this text.

WHAT IS SOFTWARE METHODOLOGY?

After having completed a first course in computing, you probably find algorithmic problem solving to be intellectually challenging and personally satisfying. It is important to remember, however, that the problems you tackled in the first course are qualitatively different from those that occur in actual practice. Not only are "real world" applications larger (in terms of lines of program code and related measures of complexity), they have greater impact on the quality of day-to-day life, and thus carry greater potential rewards and risks for the software designer.

Imagine the satisfaction that one would derive from helping to develop a software product that is used by thousands of others and makes a significant contribution to the quality of professional work as we know it—a word processor, for instance, or a natural language translation system. At the same time, imagine the suffering a software designer would experience if his or her design error caused a catastrophic computer system failure—for instance, an x-ray machine out of control that injures or kills a patient.

One can identify the purpose of software methodology and engineering, therefore, as the process of maximizing the quality and minimizing the risks for all people associated with a software system. These include the *sponsors* (who request the development of the system), the *developers* and *adaptors* (who are involved in its design and evolution), and the eventual *users* (who are the ultimate beneficiaries of the system). Software methodology and engineering has, as its primary goal, the development of quality software, where "quality" implies a high level of satisfaction among sponsors, developers, adaptors and users.

It will be helpful at the outset of this study for readers to appreciate the importance of the difference between "real world" applications and the sorts of programs you have developed in an introductory course. The difference is not just a matter of devoting more effort to the same sorts of problem-solving activities that were introduced in the first course. If one compares a modest problem that requires a 100-line program and one that requires several hundred thousand lines of code, it is clear that there is a fundamental difference in the way the solution is developed. A simple program development methodology (such as the MAPS methodology reviewed in Chapter 0) is not robust enough to solve truly complex problems, although its basic features provide a useful starting point. This chapter presents two alternative software methodologies (or, *software models*) that provide more robust approaches to real world software projects.

An obvious difference is that large programs are usually *group efforts* rather than the work of one individual. The kind of individuality and creativity that is rewarded in a first course may actually be frowned upon in a commercial setting where large software systems are developed.. In group efforts, individuals have a greater need to conform to group standards (for example, uniform standards for programming style, interface design, and documentation). In addition, individuals need to work within a social setting that involves interaction with many different types of personalities.

Software sponsors, developers, adaptors and users sometimes have conflicting goals and interests. Sponsors may want to increase productivity at the expense of end user satisfaction. Developers may want to deliver a system as quickly as possible, at the expense of adaptors who are vitally interested in documentation that is complete and easy to use and in program designs that are clear and easy to modify. Sponsors want to keep costs low, while developers may want to "strut their stuff," meaning, they would like to utilize the full power of their software tools and of the underlying hardware. To make matters worse (or, to make life more interesting, depending upon your point of view), sponsors, developers, adaptors and users often disagree among themselves. Consequently, one cannot overemphasize the importance of communications skills and social skills for the success of a large software project. Students of computing are well-advised to pay close attention in their English courses and also to welcome opportunities to work on team projects, to write documentation, and to present oral reports.

Communication problems among sponsors, developers, adaptors, and users are often complex and subtle. Developers need to understand the specialized language of the sponsors (e.g., the language of the stockbroker or of the furniture retail business). Sponsors need to learn some technical computer terms in order to make competent decisions for their organizations. Developers and sponsors need to understand user perspectives on the proposed system. There are also communications problems within groups. In a programming team with n members, the number of lines of communication is proportional to n^2. This means that doubling the number of programmers on the team quadruples the number of possible lines of communication. This implies that a large team needs well-defined channels of communication. Moreover, as programming teams get larger, written and formal (as opposed to oral and informal) forms of communication become increasingly important.

The proliferation of channels of communication is one factor behind Brooks' well-known principle of software design, the so-called mythical man-month[1]. As manager of a large software project involving the development of an operating system during the 1960s, Fred Brooks learned that adding new people to a late project will normally delay, rather than speed up, its completion. In order for a large software design project to succeed, communication and social skills among participants in the project must be well-developed and disciplined. The larger the programming team, the more important it is to follow rigorous standards for specifying, designing, documenting, coding, and testing systems.

EXERCISES

1–1 Make a list of conflicts that might arise between sponsors, developers, adaptors and users. Make your list as exhaustive as possible.

1–2 Why might adaptors be more interested than developers in high quality documentation?

1–3 Suppose you are working with a teammate on a program that is due the day after tomorrow. Suddenly, your professor adds two new members to your team. Discuss the problems inherent in incorporating these two new people into your project. Think about different situations in which the new team members might either help or hinder your chances of meeting the deadline.

The Ideal of "Goodness"

There is no standard definition of "goodness" with respect to software systems. There is a growing consensus that *reliability* (correctness and robustness) are foremost concerns, but reliability alone does not assure "goodness." For instance, a perfectly reliable system that has a horrendous user interface is not likely to be considered "good." Therefore, in considering the goodness of a software system, it is wise to look at all of the nine qualities listed in Figure 1–1 together.

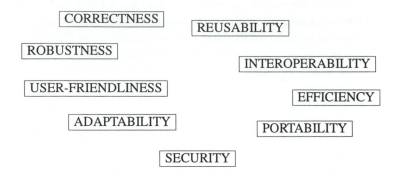

FIGURE 1–1   Nine qualities of a good software system.

Correctness   A software system is *correct* if it satisfies its specifications. The specifications describe the expected system behavior in complete detail and are the result of a negotiating process between sponsors and developers in consultation with users. The specification is usually a part of a formal, legal agreement (a business contract) between sponsors and developers. Failure to deliver a correct system can have many legal and ethical implications.

Correctness implies, at least in principle, the property of verifiability. That is, one would expect that a software system is correct only if the developers have been able to establish its correctness in some convincing manner.

Robustness   A software system is *robust* if it has the ability to function even under abnormal conditions. A specification will normally cover a list of error situations, such as illegal input values. A good specification will describe these error situations in considerable detail. Hence, a correct implementation of such a specification will be robust according to our definition.

A system which is both correct and robust is said to be *reliable*. Sponsors and users are unlikely to accept an unreliable system. The production of an unreliable system can have major, negative repercussions for a software firm. In the extreme, an unreliable system can cause enormous financial losses, bodily harm and even death.

User-friendliness   A software system is *user-friendly* if it is reliable and if the rewards of using the system are commensurate with the effort required both to learn the system and to use the system in practice. In order to be considered user-friendly, a software system must provide benefits commensurate with the investment of time users make in order to learn and to use the system. For example, the desktop publishing system which was used in the production of this book is user-friendly (according to this definition and according to the judgement of the authors) because the effort required in mastering the system (which is considerable) is well worth the benefits provided (the efficient production of this book). Some authors have characterized user-friendliness in terms of the time it takes to accomplish basic tasks upon first acquaintance with a system. This was the philosophy behind the MacIntosh interface when it was introduced in 1983. This point of view also has validity.

Adaptability   A software system is *adaptable* if it can evolve "gracefully." Like biological systems, large software systems often experience environmental stress. That stress may come from changing requirements (the desire to add new features or modify existing features in some way) or even the discovery of an error in the system. Large software systems that cannot evolve to meet changing requirements are not likely to remain useful for very long. One of the great challenges of software methodology, therefore, is to design systems in such a way that they can evolve gracefully. This can be difficult, since a fundamental law of software evolution is that systems become more complex as they evolve.

The cost of fixing bugs and adapting systems to new requirements, a process known as *software maintenance*, is high. Empirical studies have shown the cost of maintenance to be 50 to 70 percent of the cost of a software project over its lifetime [4]. Thus, another way of characterizing the quality of adaptability is that a software system should have an acceptably low maintenance cost.

Reusability   A software system is *reusable* if its components can be reused in other systems. Reusability is important because the cost of software development is becoming ever more expensive relative to the cost of hardware— software development has historically been a labor-intensive process. Sponsors and developers are always looking for ways to minimize development costs. Many important developments in programming language technology during the 1980s reflect a growing concern with the issue of software reuse. Object-oriented languages (e.g., C++, Eiffel, and Smalltalk) are likely to become dominant programming languages during the 1990s, in part because they offer features that facilitate software reuse.

Interoperability   A software system has the quality of *interoperability* if it can be easily combined with other software systems. Interoperability will be a major concern for software systems development during the 1990s and beyond. Two trends are forcing software developers to be more concerned about this issue. The first is the trend toward distributed systems, in which applications software and data files can be distributed over a computer network. In a distributed system, it is important for the individual elements to fit together nicely.[1] The second factor is the development of graphical user interface (GUI) standards (so-called *windowing environments*) for operating systems. Issues of interoperability relate to both the internal details of system communication and the user interface issues which make the combining of software components "seamless" from the user's point of view.

Efficiency   A software system is *efficient* if various costs are acceptably low. Cost can be measured using various benchmarks, or *cost metrics*. One such cost metric is the cost in dollars of developing, delivering, operating, and adapting the system. Another metric is the cost of training people to use the system. Still other cost metrics include the efficiency with which the system utilizes computer resources, such as the amount of memory space an algorithm requires (its *space complexity*), and the amount of time an algorithm takes to accomplish its task (its *time complexity*). Chapter 3 presents the principles that allow us to analyze the space and time complexity of algorithms.

Portability   A software system is *portable* if it can be moved to a new hardware or software environment with acceptably low cost. Portability is essential due to the rapid pace with which computer technology is changing. During its lifetime, a software system is likely to be ported to a new compiler, a new operating system, or a new hardware platform. The costs of this kind of refitting can sometimes exceed the original development cost of the software product itself!

Security   A software system is *secure* if it cannot be accessed, modified or damaged by unauthorized users. This includes the security of data files produced by the system. Security issues are becoming more important as software becomes more pervasive and as computer systems are interconnected in increasingly complex ways.

EXERCISES

1–4 Can you think of qualities a software system should have that are not included in Figure 1.1? List and explain briefly the additional qualities which you added.

1–5 Suppose your professor decides to allow students to use any computer and any C++ compiler in completing their assignments for this course. What kinds of interoperability and portability problems might arise as a consequence of this decision?

1–6 Retrieve one of the programs that you wrote in your introductory course and evaluate it from the perspective of portability to a new C++ compil-

---

1.   See Chapter 7 for a more complete discussion of distributed systems.

er. Which features of your program are portable? Which are not? How might you make your program more portable if it is not perfectly portable?

The Software Crisis

The view of many software engineers is implicit in the title of Fred Brooks' essay on software engineering, titled "No Silver Bullet" [2]. Software systems can be ugly beasts, indeed. The ideal of software "goodness" that was presented in an earlier section is just that—an ideal. Software methodology and engineering can be viewed as an effort to approximate that ideal as closely as possible.

The good news is that this effort for software quality will provide many opportunities for computer scientists and engineers, both in industry and in academia, to improve the process of software design as well as the software products themselves. It would not be an exaggeration to suggest that the quest for methods that assure software quality is an incredibly complex problem. In fact, some software systems are arguably the most complex artifacts ever created.

The bad news is that the field of software engineering and methodology is viewed by many as being in a state of crisis. The existence of this "software crisis" was first identified and announced in 1968 at an international conference, which in retrospect is seen as the seminal conference for the emerging field of software engineering. The notion of a software crisis recognizes that the computing industry has consistently failed to produce quality software, and further that the world's present and future needs for quality software far exceed the industry's capacity to produce it.

The symptoms of the software crisis include late completion of projects; cost overruns; systems that do not evolve gracefully; systems that are not reliable, user-friendly, or portable; and so forth. A 1979 study by the Comptroller General of the United States found that among all government-contracted software projects studied, only 2% delivered products that worked on delivery! Of the remaining 98%, 3% worked after some minor corrections, 45% were delivered but never successfully used, 20% were used, but only after extensive reworking (and eventually had to be abandoned), and 30% were paid for by the government but were never even delivered [5]. There is no evidence that this situation has improved markedly since 1979.

General factors that contribute to the emergence and persistence of the software crisis include the following:

1. Dramatic advances in hardware and operating systems
2. Dramatic decreases in hardware costs
3. Increasing demand for new software systems, with a resulting "applications backlog"
4. Haphazard approaches to software development

Ironically, the recent success and rapid evolution of computer hardware has worsened the software crisis. Not only do sponsors and end-users want more software, they also want better software.

The prospects for future progress are not altogether bleak, however. The 1980s saw important developments in the area of software methodology and engineering. The new emphasis on rigorous specifications, in the form of pre- and postconditions for software components, reflects a recent industry trend toward a more disciplined and rigorous approach to the software development process. This text reflects another important recent trend, one that the software engineer Bertrand Meyer has called "the road to object-orientedness" [3]. The object-oriented design paradigm reflects the industry's progress toward genuinely better ways of designing software components and ensuring software quality. While there is still no "silver bullet," many experts believe that the object-oriented paradigm represents a fundamental advance in addressing the software crisis.

SOFTWARE MODELS

The idea of a "software model" is a significant one for software methodology and engineering. Terms that are used synonymously with software model in the literature are "software process model" and "software engineering paradigm." There are two uses for a software model. First, a software model can be interpreted as an abstract *description* of how people actually build software systems. That is, based upon their observation and experience with software development projects, computer scientists abstract common patterns from these projects and then present this abstract description as a software model. Second, a software model can be interpreted as a *prescription* of how software should be constructed.

The *software lifecycle* and *prototyping* models are the two most significant models for the commercial world. The following section presents these models more fully. We shall focus most of our attention on the software lifecycle model.

The Software Lifecycle Model

The software lifecycle (or waterfall) model envisions software development as an essentially sequential process in which distinct stages lead one to another. This is illustrated in Figure 1–2, which resembles a waterfall (if you use your imagination).

The lifecyle model of software construction views software as being developed in six distinct stages. These are:

1.   Requirements analysis

2. Specification
3. Design
4. Implementation
5. Testing
6. Adaptation

Requirements analysis and *specification* involve interactions among sponsors, users, and developers of the software product. The purpose of requirements analysis and specification is to produce a requirements document which clearly specifies the agreed upon goals and the functionality of the proposed product, as well as the constraints under which it will be operating. "Functionality" refers to the behavior of the system, which is documented within the requirements document in complete detail.

Design involves the generation of a design document which serves as a blueprint for the proposed system. Developers and adaptors are usually involved in this process. Adaptors are involved in order to help assure that the design is consistent with a graceful evolution of the system. The design document often includes graphical depictions of system structure as well as textual material which documents the pre- and postconditions for all functions.

Implementation involves building the system described in the design document. This includes making important decisions about data structures and algorithms, as well as writing the program code itself. These decisions can have significant impact upon the efficiency of the system.

Testing involves detecting as many defects in the software system as possible. *Unit testing* seeks to find defects in individual software components (such as functions), while *integration testing* seeks to find defects that might arise when assembled components fail to work correctly in concert with one another.

Adaptation (or *maintenance*) refers to the evolution of the "completed" system.

The software lifecycle model, in practice, is not perfectly sequential. There are loops which feed back from later stages to earlier ones in the cycle. For

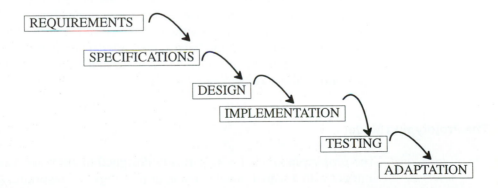

FIGURE 1–2   The software lifecycle (waterfall) model.

example, the discovery of an error during integration testing could force the developers to backtrack to the implementation or design stage. Empirical studies have clearly established that the earlier an error is found in the lifecycle, the less costly it is to correct. Thus, it is less expensive to correct an error discovered during the design stage than it is fix an error discovered during the testing or adaptation stages. It is important, moreover, in managing a project using the software model, to minimize these sorts of feedback loops as much as possible.

Over the life of a typical system, the adaptation stage is by far the most expensive. Barry Boehm, a well-known software economist and expert on software metrics (measures of software costs), identifies one typical large software project whose cost of development was $30.00 per instruction and whose cost of adaptation was $4,000.00 per instruction [6]. Figure 1.3 shows a typical percentage breakdown for the cost of a software product among the analysis, specification, design, implementation, testing, and adaptation stages of a software project. Note that analysis and specification are lumped together in this breakdown (based on data given in [4]).

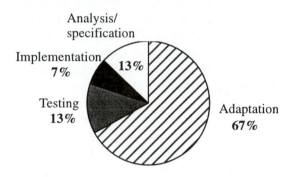

FIGURE 1–3   Typical allocation of costs among stages in the software lifecycle.

A major disadvantage of the software lifecyle model is that the sponsors and users of the system do not get to see a working model of the system until near the end of the development process. Yet it is common for sponsors and users to discover new requirements once they get a chance to interact with an operational system. Because sponsors have signed a legal contract for the product (embodied in the requirements document), it is usually too late to incorporate new suggestions into a system at such a late stage.

The Prototyping Model

The *prototyping model* is specifically designed to allow sponsors and users to interact with a scaled-down version, or prototype, of a working system before a final specification is agreed upon. Prototyping is an increasingly popular model, although it is often not considered appropriate for very large systems. The basic idea behind prototyping (and its variants) is iterative design. Early during the development cycle (and before any requirements document has been agreed upon), a prototype version of the system is delivered to the sponsors and users. Let's call this prototype #1. Prototype #1 gives sponsors and users an opportunity to clarify their needs and to express these needs to the system developers. On this basis, the developers produce a second prototype, prototype #2. This iterative design process continues until a prototype is produced which makes sponsors and users reasonably happy. In effect, this final prototype, prototype #n, becomes the system specification.

The key to successful prototyping is to assure that prototype #n is viewed as a prototype and not as a production quality system. This is crucial because prototype #n was literally thrown together without much concern for "goodness" of design and without anticipating evolving needs. Also, prototype #n may have been implemented in a special prototyping language that is unsuitable for implementing the final system.

EXERCISES

1–7 List and explain briefly factors that might make it difficult for developers to discard prototype #n.

1–8 Based upon your own programming and problem solving experience, which of the two software models—the software lifecycle model or the prototyping model—seems to be more relevant to your own programming assignments and projects? Explain.

OBJECT-ORIENTED DESIGN

In Chapter 0 we presented a program (`Searcher`) that was developed using a function-oriented design methodology. That methodology involved identifying the basic processes (i.e., functions) that were inherent in the problem solution. The result was a program whose basic building blocks were functions.

This section introduces an alternative design methodology: *object-oriented design*. Object-oriented design focuses on the concepts inherent in the problem domain rather than the processes inherent in the problem solution. When a program is designed in this manner, its basic building blocks will be objects rather than functions. (We shall soon learn the technical meaning for the term "object"). For example, if one is writing a grade-keeping program, one is able to think in terms of individual students and the sections of a course instead of about arrays of student names and averages. Object-oriented methodology is increasingly important in the practical world of software development. Many software vendors have made a firm commitment to object-oriented design and object-oriented programming languages.

There is a lot to learn about object-oriented design and programming. In this section we shall present basic guidelines for doing an object-oriented design and the rudiments of object-oriented programming. In Chapter 2 we shall discuss more advanced topics in object-oriented programming in some depth.

Object-Oriented Programming Languages

If you were to attend a research meeting of software engineers, you might very well hear a lot of talk about object-oriented this and object-oriented that. In particular, you might hear people talking about object-oriented analysis, object-oriented design, object-oriented programming, object-oriented languages, the object-oriented language paradigm, object-oriented databases and so forth. In addition, you would probably hear some of the strange terms that object-oriented advocates like to use in their conversations, terms like "encapsulation," "inheritance," "class protocols," "polymorphism," "messages," "constructors," and "destructors."

It is important to note that object-oriented design is not necessarily synonymous with programming in an object-oriented language. Object-oriented design is a design methodology that may or may not lead to an implementation in an object-oriented language. An object-oriented language is a specific kind of language that has new and powerful abstractions, including support for many of the constructs named at the end of the previous paragraph.

It is possible to do an object-oriented design and then to implement that design in a language that is not object-oriented. Conversely, using an object-oriented language does not necessarily ensure that OOD techniques have been used. If one wants to design software using object-oriented techniques, it is certainly advisable to use an object-oriented language, especially since object-oriented languages are now widely available. At the present time, the most significant object-oriented languages for commercial applications are C++, Smalltalk, and Eiffel.

Before going on to present a simple characterization of "object-oriented design," we need give some informal definitions that identify the nature of objects themselves.

Definition An *object* is a bundle of variables and behaviors. An object has a type, which is called its *class*. An object's class defines the particular variables that it contains and the behaviors that it can exhibit. The variables associated with a class are called *data members* and the behaviors are called *member functions*. Member functions are sometimes called *methods* and data members are sometimes called *instance variables*. Methods are the processes that can be activated within an object-oriented design. Thus, methods correspond to the functions of a function-oriented design.

An Object-Oriented Design Methodology

In this section we shall present a simple object-oriented design methodology. This methodology is largely based upon the early work of Abbott [1] and Booch [2], who were pioneers in the application of object-oriented thinking to software engineering. An object-oriented design methodology can be defined as follows.

Definition An *object-oriented design methodology* has four major steps.

1. Identify the classes and objects that are part of the solution.
2. Identify and describe the data members that are contained within each type of object.
3. Identify each of the member functions that can act upon each type of object.
4. For each member function, describe its purpose, arguments, preconditions, and postconditions.

This methodology can be applied to the `Searcher` problem that was introduced and solved in Chapter 0. As we develop an object-oriented solution for this problem, we will elaborate upon the four steps in our simple design methodology. Here is a brief restatement of that problem:

A professor needs a program that will allow him to compute student averages and to retrieve averages for particular students. Each student in the professor's class is represented by the following information: a name, three exam scores, and a final average.

The first step in the object-oriented design is to identify the basic classes that are inherent in the problem. A *class* is a type and *objects* are variables whose type is a class. We also say that an object is *an instance of a class*. In the case of the grade-keeping program, there are two classes inherent in the problem:

1. The class `Student`, whose instances represent individual students.
2. The class `Section`, whose instances represent individual sections of a course. A `Section` object contains a collection of `Student` objects.

The classes `Student` and `Section` identify the two basic kinds of objects that are inherent in the grade-keeping problem. We have `Student` objects (with their names, exam scores, and final averages) and we have a single `Section` object, which represents all the students in one section of a course.

The second step in an object-oriented design is to list all of the data members for each class developed in step one. The data members represent the data contained within an object. All objects in a class have the same data members, although with different values. The values of an object's data members define the *state* of that object. Here are the data members for the classes Student and Section:

1. For the class `Student`:
   a. `student_name:`   a string
   b. `first_hourly:`   a float
   c. `second_hourly:`   a float
   d. `final_exam:`   a float
   e. `average`   a float

2. For the class `Section`:
   a. `c`   an array of `Student` objects
   b. `class_size`   an integer

A particular `Student` object therefore contains five data members. A particular `Section` object contains two data members, and the first of these (c) is an array of `Student` objects.

For the third step in an object-oriented design, we need to list the *member functions* for each class. The member functions for a class define the behaviors that objects of that class can exhibit. What exactly do we mean by a "behavior"? An object's behavior might include things like:

- Providing access to that object's data members

- Allowing updates of that object's data members

- Allowing that object's data members to be tested in various ways

- Displaying that object's data on the computer screen

In practice, *classes are designed with the intention of making them generally useful*. In other words, classes are not normally designed with the idea that they will be used in one and only one program. The goal is to make them useful for many different applications that deal with the same kinds of data. Very often, the designer of a class does not even know the specific applications that are intended for that class. This principle is very much related to the issue of software *reuse* that we discussed earlier.

It needs to be stressed that we are not adhering to this principle in the grade-keeping example. We are designing the classes `Student` and `Section` specifically for one application. We defend this strategy only on pedagogical grounds: our first example of an object-oriented design should be as simple as possible and related as closely as possible to a familiar example (the earlier `Searcher` program). In fact, realistic designs for the classes `Student` and `Section` would contain many more member functions than we are providing here.

C++ classes are usually presented in two separate files: a *header file* that contains the declaration for the class plus perhaps some auxiliary declarations and definitions and a second file that gives the implementations (i.e., the definitions, using the standard C++ terminology) for all functions declared in the header file, including all member functions. We shall call the second kind of file an *implementation file*. It is universally agreed that header files should have a name that ends with `.h`. Implementation files will have a name that ends in .cxx or `.cpp` or `.c`, depending upon the compiler that you are using.

It is important to understand the relationship between the person who designs and implements a class (the class developer) and the persons who use a class (the client programmers). The class developer tries to anticipate all of the needs of client programmers. This developer-client relationship often leads to classes that contain a large number of member functions. A particular client only uses those member functions that are relevant to his or her application.

For the purposes of our example, we shall introduce only member functions that are actually needed for the application that we have in mind. Here is a list and a brief explanation of those member functions:

1. For the class `Student`:
    a. a constructor, `Student`
    b. a destructor, `~Student`
    c. a `char*` function, `get_name`, that will return a student's name
    d. a `void` function, `set_name`, that will set a student's name
    e. a `void` function, `read_in`, that will get all of a student's data from the user
    f. a `void` function, `compute_average`, that will set a student's final average based upon that student's exam scores
    g. a `void` function, `display_average`, that will display a student's final average at the computer display.
2. For the class `Section`:
    a. a constructor, `Section`
    b. a destructor, `~Section`
    c. a `Student` function, `search`, that will search a `Section` for a student with a specific name
    d. a `void` function, `read_in`, that will get all of a section's data from the user
    e. a `void` function, `compute_averages`, that will compute the final averages for each student in a section
    f. a `void` function, `add_student`, that will add a new student to a section
    g. a `void` function, `sort_by_name`, that will sort the students in a section alphabetically by name.

Constructors and destructors are special member functions that are automatically applied at the appropriate time. Constructors are applied when an object is defined and destructors are applied when the program leaves the scope of an object's definition. A class can have more than one constructor, but they must be distinguishable in terms of the number and types of their arguments. A class can only have one destructor and a destructor is not permitted to have any arguments. The name of a destructor is the name of its class preceded by a tilde (~).

The final step in an object-oriented design is to provide a specification for each of the methods in the design. We shall not present all of those specifications at this point. They are included in the program code that appears beginning in the next section.

Classes, Objects, and Methods in C++

Classes are usually presented in two files (as mentioned previously): a header file that presents the class declaration and an implementation file that presents the implementations (i.e., the definitions) of member functions. The header file will normally begin with a section of comments that summarizes the properties of the class (or classes) that it declares. This is followed by definitions of auxiliary constants and declarations for auxiliary types and functions. Finally, the header file contains the actual class declaration. The implementation file contains the implementations of member functions, as well as their specifications. In addition, the implementation file will contain definitions for non-member functions whose prototypes were given in the associated header file.

Below is the syntax for declaring the `Student` class. This declaration is contained in the `student.h` header file. That file also declares the `string` type that the `Student` class declaration assumes.

```
class Student
{
    private:
        // data members
        string student_name;
        float  first_hourly, second_hourly,
         final_exam, average;


    public:
        // member functions
        // constructor - destructor
        Student();
        ~Student();


        // access
        char* get_name();


        // modify
        void set_name(string);
        void read_in();
        void compute_average();


        // display
        void display_average();
}; // Student class
```

This declaration indicates that `Student` is the name of a class and that objects of this class have five `private` data members (`student_name`, `first_hourly`, `second_hourly`, `final_exam` and `average`). (We shall discuss the issue of privacy later.) Furthermore, this class contains seven member functions (including the constructor and destructor) and these are called `Student`, `~Student`, `get_name`, `set_name`, `read_in`, `compute_average` and `display_average`. These member functions are all declared `public`, although `private` member functions are also permitted. Their being `public` means that they are part of the *public interface* of this class and, thus, that client programmers can apply these functions to `Student` objects. The functions declared within a class declaration are presented as function prototypes. Comments are used in the class declaration to group member functions into "method categories" (e.g., constructor – destructor, access, modify and display).

We need to elaborate upon the assertion that the class `Student` "contains" seven member functions. The idea that a class contains member functions is called *encapsulation*. Another way of understanding encapsulation is to state that classes bundle data and functions together as an indivisible unit. Encapsulation is one of the fundamental abstractions supported in all object-oriented languages. It helps to force designers and programmers to couple functions more closely with the entities that they naturally associate with, and this yields a more natural description of those entities. By "more natural" we mean that people intuitively associate behaviors with objects, and encapsulation allows the software designer to do the same.

Another way of understanding encapsulation is to view member functions as messages that we send to objects. The objects "understand" the messages by executing the relevant member function definition. We send a message to an object by means of the following notation:

```
object.message()
```

This is called an *object-message pair*. In this context *object* is called the *receiver* of the message. The message part of the object-message pair takes the form of a function call. The type of the expression `object.message()` is the return type of the function `message`.

The terminology of the previous paragraph (receiver objects, messages, object-message pairs) was made popular by the Smalltalk language. The more common C++ terminology is that the function `message` *is being applied to* `object`, in the expression `object.message()`.

Suppose a function contains the following object definition:

```
Student stu;
```

It is important to remember that this definition causes the automatic application of the constructor `Student` to the object `stu`. Once `stu` has been defined, then we can manipulate it by sending it messages in accordance with the public interface of the `Student` class. For example, the following object-message pairs could be evaluated:

```
stu.get_name()
    // returns the name of the receiver, stu
stu.set_name("Allen")
    // sets the receiver's name to "Allen"
stu.read_in()
    // prompts user for and gets all input data
    // for the receiver, stu
stu.compute_average()
    // computes the receiver's final average based upon
    // the exam scores
stu.display_average()
    // displays the receiver's final average
```

When the program leaves the scope of the definition for the object `stu`, the `Student` class destructor is automatically applied to that object. In this case, the destructor will do nothing that is obviously useful, except that it will render the object `stu` unusable.

The data members of the `Student` class are all declared as `private`. This means that the only functions that have access to these data members are the member functions of the `Student` class. One could also extend the visibility of data members by declaring them `public`, but this is considered a poor practice, because it also tends to defeat some of the primary objectives of object-orientation. By declaring the data members as being private, we force client programmers to access the data members only by means of legal member functions. One consequence of this is that we might be able to modify the internal representations of data members without needing to modify the public interface of a class. In general, client programs will not require modification unless some aspect of the public interface of a class has changed. If we make a data member part of the public interface of a class and then decide to change the internal representation of that data member, then significant changes may be required in the client programs. This will increase the cost of program maintenance.

In a well-designed class, one can access and modify data members only via functions in the public interface of that class. For example, one can access a student's name by applying the `get_name` function:

```
stu.get_name()
```

and one can set a student's name by applying the `set_name` function:

```
stu.set_name(aName)
```

Here `aName` is assumed to be a variable of type `string`.

In defining a function for the class `CL` one can refer to all of the data members for that class. Suppose `func` is a member function for the class `CL` and that `dm` is a data member for that class. Then, in defining the function `func` for the `CL` class one can refer to `dm` without defining it locally. Two alternate ways of stating this are that `dm` is defined within the scope of `func` or that `dm` is visible within that function.

For example, the `set_name` member function of the `Student` class can refer to the `Student` class data member `student_name` without defining it. In the implementation of that function, the following statement sets the value of `student_name` to the value of `aName` using the `strcpy` function:

```
strcpy(student_name, aName)
```

Perhaps the most difficult point to understand (when one is first learning how to program in an object-oriented language) is that when a member function refers to a data member, *that data member is stored within the object to which the function is being applied.*

For example, the statement

```
stu.set_name(aName);
```

causes the application of the `set_name` function to the `Student` object called `stu`. The definition of this function contains the `strcpy` statement mentioned above, namely:

```
strcpy(student_name, aName)
```

In this context, the variable `student_name` is understood to be the `student_name` data member of the object that the function is being applied to, that is, the object `stu`.

A `Section` object represents a section of a course taught by the professor. The `Section` class declaration occurs in the file `section.h`. That file also presents the definition for the named constant, `MAXCLASS`. Below is the declaration for the class `Section`:

```
const int MAXCLASS = 50;

class Section
{
    private:
        // data members
        Student c[MAXCLASS];
        int class_size;


    public:
        // member functions
        // constructor - destructor
        Section();
        ~Section();


        // access
        Student search(string);


        // modify
        void read_in();
        void add_student(Student);
        void compute_averages();
        void sort_by_name();
};  // Section class
```

This declaration indicates that objects of the type `Section` contain two data members: an array, `c`, of `Student` objects and an integer, `class_size`.

Suppose a function contains the following variable definitions:

```
Section a_section;
Student stu;
string  s_name;
```

The definition for the object `a_section` causes the constructor `Section` to be applied to that object. Since a `Section` object contains a collection of

Student objects, the constructor Student will automatically be applied to each of those Student objects. Thus, the constructor Student will be called MAXCLASS times. Hence, what appears as a simple variable definition in C++ can actually cause quite a considerable amount of computing to take place.

Once the objects a_section and stu have been defined, they can be manipulated using the member functions contained in the public interfaces of the Section and Student classes. For example, the object a_section might be manipulated as follows:

```
stu = a_section.search(s_name);
        // if s_name is the name of a student in
        // a_section, stu will be that student
        // object; otherwise, stu will contain
        // a student_name that indicates an error
a_section.read_in()
        // get all data for a_section, including
        // class_size, from the user
a_section.compute_averages()
        // computes the student final averages,
        // updating each Student object in a_section
a_section.add_student(stu)
        // add stu to a_section
a_section.sort_by_name()
        // arrange Student objects in a_section
        // alphabetically by name
```

When we leave the scope of the definition of a_section, the Section class destructor (~Section) is automatically applied. In addition, the destructor ~Student is automatically applied to all of the Student objects contained within the a_section object. This amounts to fifty (MAXCLASS) calls to the Student class destructor.

Now, let us turn our attention to the implementation of member functions. Member function implementations (i.e., the function definitions) are provided in a separate file. We shall give four examples of Student and Section class member functions here, leaving a full accounting of the Student and Section member functions for later.

Here is the definition of the Section class constructor:

```
Section::Section()
{
    class_size = 0;
}   // end Section::Section()
```

The constructor header uses the *scope resolution operator* (::) to indicate that the function Section belongs to the Section class. This enables the compiler to recognize this function as a constructor for the Section class. The variable class_size in the function body is the class_size data member for the Section object to which the constructor is being applied.

Here is the implementation for the Section class destructor:

```
Section::~Section()
{
    ;
}  // end Section::~Section()
```

The use of the scope resolution operator in the destructor header and the use of the tilde in the function name tells the compiler that this function is the destructor for the `Section` class. Note that the destructor does not appear to be doing anything. This will often be the case for simple examples. Destructors will become more interesting once we learn about dynamic memory allocation and virtual functions in Chapter 2.

Here is how the `Student` class member function `get_name()` is implemented:

```
char* Student::get_name()
{
    return (student_name);
} // end Student::get_name()
```

The member function header (also called a *declarator*) uses the scope resolution operator to indicate that this function is a member of (belongs to) the `Student` class. The return type of this function is `char*`, which represents the address of a character.   It may not be obvious that this function return type is compatible with the value returned in the return statement. Seeing this requires that you understand the issues discussed in Chapter 2 that relate to address, pointers and arrays. For now, let us just state that the data member `student_name` is declared as a `string`, that is, as an array of characters. As you will learn in Chapter 2, when the name of an array is used in an expression, it represents the base address of an array. The base address of an array of characters is the address of a character.   In other words, the compiler views the expression `student_name` in the above function as being of type `char*`.

A client program that has declared `stu` as a `Student` object might use the function `get_name` as follows:

```
if (strcmp(stu.get_name(), "Aaron"))
    cout << stu.get_name();
```

In other words, if `stu`'s name is not `Aaron`, `stu`'s name will be displayed.

The implementation of the `Section` member function `add_student` is not difficult to understand:

```
void Section::add_student(Student astudent)
{
    c[class_size++] = astudent;
}  // end Section::add_student
```

The function `add_student()` is implemented as a void function with the single argument `astudent`, which is declared to be a `Student` object. Since this method belongs to the class `Section`, it has access to the data members `class_size` and `c` that belong to the receiver object. Note how an object can be copied using an assignment statement:

```
c[class_size++] = astudent;
```

This copies all of `astudent`'s data members into the array entry `c[class_size]` and then increments `class_size`.

You should now have enough information to understand the `ObjSearcher` program. This is a C++ program that is based upon the object-oriented design that we developed in this section. This program solves the same problem that was solved by the `Searcher` program that was described in the previous chapter.

EXERCISES

1–9 Develop an object-oriented design for the following situation: A service station operator wants to use a computer program to keep track of the cars being serviced on any particular day. On any day he can handle at most 25 cars. For each car, he needs to keep track of the following information:

> *a.* the owner
> *b.* the car make
> *c.* the car model
> *d.* the car year
> *e.* the type of work that needs to be done on the car (such as "oil change" or "brake relining")

Your design should provide a listing of classes, a listing of data members for the various classes, a listing of member functions for the various classes, and specifications for each member function.

1–10 Reconsider the object-oriented design presented in this section for the grade-keeping program from the perspective of making the classes Section and Student more generally useful. In other words, reconsider the design from the perspective that we might want to reuse Section and Student in a variety of programs. Essentially, this involves defining new member functions for both classes. Define and implement those new member functions and write a program that takes advantage of the new, more general, design for Section and Student.

1–11 Take one of the programs that you developed during your first course in computing (assuming that this was not done in an object-oriented style) and do an object-oriented design for the problem that your program solved. Once you have completed the design, implement the design as an actual program. Compare the original function-oriented design and your new object-oriented design from the perspective of the design principles given in Chapter 0. In particular, which program has better properties in terms of reusable software components, debugging, and maintenance?

THE `ObjSearcher` PROGRAM WITH COMMENTARY

We shall now present the complete object-oriented implementation of the `Searcher` program, which we are calling `ObjSearcher`. `ObjSearcher` is a multi-file project (`objsearc.prj` in the Turbo C++ environment) that is equivalent in behavior to the `Searcher` program that was presented earlier (except that the instructions presented to the user have been modified slightly). This means that if you run these two programs, their external behavior is identical in every regard (except for the user instructions). It is interesting that these behaviorally equivalent programs are completely different in their internal organization.

The `ObjSearcher` program is organized as a multi-file project that consists of three implementation files. Here we shall use the GNU C++ names for those files[2]:

- The file `student.cxx`, which implements the `Student` class

- The file `section.cxx`, which implements the `Section` class

- The main program file, `objsearc.cxx`.

The `student.cxx` and `section.cxx` files include the corresponding header files, `student.h` and `section.h`, respectively. The main program file, `objsearc.cxx`, includes the `section.h` header file which, in turn, includes the `student.h` header file. The `objsearc.cxx` file is a "client" of the services provided collectively by the `student.h`, `student.cxx`, `section.h` and `section.cxx` files. Thus, the `objsearc.cxx` file can declare both `Student` and `Section` objects and can manipulate those objects using the functions that are contained in the public interfaces of the `Student` and `Section` classes.

We shall first present the main program file, `objsearc.cxx`, and then we shall present the files that declare and implement the `Student` and `Section` classes, respectively. These are the `student.h` and `student.cxx` files and the `section.h` and `section.cxx` files. In doing this, we emphasize that the classes `Student` and `Section` are autonomous program components that can be reused in other client programs. They can be understood independently of their use in this particular program.

The Functions `main` and `give_instructions`

The main program file, `objsearc.cxx`, presents three functions:
- the function `main`, which defines and manipulates a `Section` object,
- the function `give_instructions`, which presents the user with instructions,
- the function `process_requests`, which allows the user to request final averages for particular students.

---

2.   Again, Turbo and Symantec C++ use .cpp in lieu of .cxx for implementation files.

In this section, we present most of the main program file. We have omitted the introductory comments, which essentially reproduce what was given earlier for the `Searcher` program, and the function `process_requests`, which we shall discuss separately in the next subsection. Here is the beginning of the main program file, including the functions `main` and `give_instructions`:

```
#include <iostream.h>
#include <string.h>
#include "section.h"


void main()
{
    // LOCAL DATA ...
    Section asection;


    // FUNCTION PROTOTYPES ...
    void give_instructions();
    void process_requests(Section&);


    // STATEMENTS ...
    give_instructions();
    asection.read_in();
    asection.compute_averages();
    asection.sort_by_name();
    process_requests(asection);
}


// Function:   give_instructions
// Purpose:    Gives the user instructions
// Pre:        output = empty
// Post:       output contains instructions for program use
void give_instructions()
{
    cout << "This program will ask you to enter student data\n";
    cout << "It will then sort the student names and final\n";
    cout << "averages alphabetically by name.  Then, it will\n";
    cout << "allow you to request computed averages for \
            particular\n";
    cout << "students." << endl << endl << endl;
    cout << "Press enter to continue: ";
    cin.get();
    cin.ignore(LINESIZE, '\n');
    cout << endl;
} // end give_instructions()


#include <iostream.h>
#include <string.h>
#include "section.h"
```

This main program file includes the `section.h` header file, which provides the declaration for the `Section` class. This file, in turn, includes the `student.h` header file, which provides the declaration for the `Student` class. This enables the main program file to define and manipulate `Section` and `Student` objects as required. (A `Student` object is required in the `process_requests` function discussed in the next section.)

The function `main` declares only one variable: `asection`. This is an object of the class `Section`. Note how the use of this one variable greatly simplifies the logic of the program and makes it much easier to understand than the earlier program (`Searcher`). If the reader understands what the `Section` class is all about, then the reader should find the main function easy to understand.

The definition of `asection`:

```
Section asection;
```

causes the constructor `Section` to be applied to the object `asection`. This initializes `class_size` to 0 and also applies the constructor `Student` to each of the `Student` objects contained within `asection`. The number of such `Student` objects is `MAXCLASS`. The constant `MAXCLASS` is defined in the `section.h` header file.

Essentially all of the internal details of what a `Section` object contains is hidden away within a `Section` object. The main function "knows" nothing of the internal structure of the object `asection`. The main function has no direct access to individual `Student` objects nor to their internal details (e.g., individual names and exam scores). This illustrates how object-oriented programming strengthens information hiding. Compare this situation against the `Searcher` program in the previous chapter which had to know about class sizes, student names and student averages.

Consider the task of writing this program (which we are calling `ObjSearcher` for ease of reference) as opposed to the earlier `Searcher` program that used a function-oriented approach. The use of the classes `Student` and `Section` allows the implementor of `ObjSearcher` to think in terms of the problem domain (i.e., in terms of students and sections) as opposed to the programming domain (the domain of arrays and array sizes). In fact, it is appropriate to decide the data that the objects in a class contain and the behaviors that those objects will exhibit before any decisions are made concerning how the data is to be stored or how the operations are to be performed. This is considered one of the major advantages of object-oriented design and programming: the client programmers can think in terms of the concepts inherent in the problem domain instead of lower level programming details.

After presenting instructions to the user, the main function sends three messages to the object, `asection`:

```
asection.read_in();
asection.compute_averages();
asection.sort_by_name();
```

The application of the function `read_in` to `asection` causes all of the data for a section of a course to be read in from the user. The application of `com-`

pute_averages to asection causes the computation of the final averages for each of the students in asection.

The application of sort_by_name to asection reorganizes the Student objects within asection so that they are arranged alphabetically by name. This is required so that the function search, which assumes a sorted array, can work properly. The function search is called within process_requests.

The function main then calls the function process_requests, passing asection as an argument. This illustrates that objects can be used both as formal and actual arguments. When objects are used as arguments, they can be declared either as pass by value or as pass by reference arguments. The function process_requests in this program is similar to process_requests in the original Searcher program. We shall discuss the new process_requests function in detail in the next subsection.

You might be wondering whether process_requests could have been implemented as a member function for the Section class. The answer is yes. However, we chose not to do so. One motivation for not implementing process_requests as a member function was to illustrate how objects can be used with nonmember functions.

When the program exits the main function, the destructor ~Section is applied to asection. This causes the Student destructor to be applied to all of the Student objects contained within asection.

The Function process_requests

This function bears a strong resemblance to the process_requests function in the original Searcher program.

```
// Function: Process_requests()
// Purpose:  Processes user requests for student final averages.
// Pre:      input = (repetitions of aName) '*' and
//           output = oldStuff
// Post:     input = empty
//           output = oldstuff \n
//              (repetitions of : student grade report
//               for i-th aName)
void process_requests(Section& asection)
{
    // LOCAL DATA ...
    const int SENTINEL = '*';
    string   search_key;
    Student astudent;


    // statements
    cin.ignore(LINESIZE, '\n');
    cout << endl << "Begin searching phase ... " << endl;
    cout << "Please enter a student's name or *: ";
    read_string(search_key, MAXSTRING);
    while (search_key[0] != SENTINEL)
    {
```

```
      astudent = asection.search(search_key);
      if (!strcmp(astudent.get_name(), "not found"))
      cout << "No student in this class has that name." << endl;
      else
      astudent.display_average();
        cout << "Please enter a student's name or *: ";
        read_string(search_key, MAXSTRING);
   }
   // hang up program
   cout << "Press enter to exit: ";
   cin.get();
} // end process_requests
```

The formal argument `asection` is declared as a pass by reference argument, although it is only used as an input argument. This was done to save
space, since a pass by reference argument is implemented as an address (i.e., as
a pointer to the original data) as opposed to a duplicate of the original data.
One `Section` object requires a considerable amount of memory, since it contains fifty (`MAXCLASS`) `Student` objects. The function `process_requests`
defines `astudent` as a local `Student` object. Note that the object `astudent`
is both created (with the constructor `Student`) and destroyed (with the destructor `~Student`) within this function.

The function `process_requests` reads in a student's name
(`search_key`) and then asks `asection` to perform a search upon itself (this is
how object-oriented people think!):

```
astudent = asection.search(search_key);
```

The result passed back by the function `search` is a `Student` object. This
result is stored in the variable `astudent`. The function `search` works as follows: If a student with the name `search_key` is found in the receiver collection of `Student` objects (i.e., `asection`), then that `Student` object is
returned as the value of the function. If no student with that name exists in the
receiver collection of `Student` objects, then the function returns a `Student`
object with a name of "not found." This serves as an error flag. If the search
succeeds, then we can display the relevant student's final average using the object-message pair:

```
astudent.display_average();
```

If the search fails, an appropriate error message is displayed at the computer
screen.

The `student.h` header file

The `student.h` header file presents the declaration for the `Student` class. In
addition, it defines the constants `MAXSTRING` and `LINESIZE` and presents a
`typedef` for the type `string`. Finally, it presents the function prototype for
the function `read_string` that we use to read in strings from the keyboard.
Here is the `student.h` header file excluding the introductory comments:

```
// GLOBAL CONSTANTS AND TYPEDEF'S ...
const int MAXSTRING = 20;   // maximum student name length
const int LINESIZE  = 80;   // maximum length of input line
typedef char string[MAXSTRING];


// GLOBAL FUNCTION PROTOTYPE ...
void read_string(char*, int);


class Student
{
    private:
        // data members
        string student_name;
        float  first_hourly, second_hourly,
         final_exam, average;


    public:
        // member functions
        // constructor - destructor
        Student();
        ~Student();


        // access
        char* get_name();


        // modify
        void set_name(string);
        void read_in();
        void compute_average();


        // display
        void display_average();
}; // Student class
```

Note that `read_string` is not a member function, but its prototype is provided here and its implementation is presented in the `student.cxx` file. One might argue that all definitions and declarations relating to the `string` type should be provided in a separate header and implementation file (say, `strg.h` and `strg.cxx`). This would certainly be the preferred strategy if many programs are going to use the `string` type, but not the `Student` type. Our design is intended to make our introduction to object-orientedness as simple as possible, so we decided not to use separate files for declaring and implementing the `string` type.

The `student.cxx` Implementation File

In this section, we present the implementations of the `Student` class member functions that are contained in the `student.cxx` file. The `student.cxx` file begins by including the `student.h` file that provides the requisite `Student` class declaration. The `student.cxx` file also provides the definition for `read_string`. That definition is identical to the one used in the `Searcher` program and is not reproduced here.

The constructor `Student` This constructor is automatically applied whenever a `Student` object is defined. This constructor initializes the data member `student_name` to the empty string.

```
// Constructor:  Student()
// Purpose:      To initialize the receiver object
// Pre:          None
// Post:         Initializes the receiver object with
//               student_name = ""
Student::Student()
{
    strcpy(student_name, "");
} // end Student::Student()
```

It is natural to express the specifications in terms of the "receiver" because the executable part of a member function describes something that is happening to a particular receiver object. Of course, this receiver will be different (in general) for various evocations of the function.

The destructor `~Student` This destructor is automatically applied to a `Student` object whenever a program leaves the scope of the definition of that particular `Student` object.

```
// Destructor:  ~Student()
// Purpose:     Destroys the receiver object
// Pre:         The receiver object is initialized
// Post:        The receiver object is destroyed
Student::~Student()
{
    ;   // no dynamic storage to be deallocated
} // end Student::~Student()
```

The function `Student::get_name` This function simply returns the value of the data member `student_name`.

```
// Function:  Student::get_name()
// Purpose:   To return the name of the receiver object
// Pre:       student_name = aName
// Post:      get_name = aName
//
char* Student::get_name()
{
    return (student_name);
} // end Student::get_name()
```

The function `Student::set_name`   This function sets the value of the data member `student_name` to the value of the string argument, aName, using the `strcpy` function.

```
// Function:  Student::set_name()
// Purpose:   Sets the receiver object's name to aName
// Pre:       The receiver is intialized and aName = aString
// Post:      student_name = aString
void Student::set_name(string aName)
{
    strcpy(student_name, aName);
} // end Student::set_name()
```

The function `Student::read_in`   The function body of this function is identical to that of the function `get_student_data` in the original `Searcher` program.   In `Student::read_in`, the identifiers `student_name`, `first_hourly`, `second_hourly`, and `final_exam` refer to the data members of the receiver object.

```
// Function:  Student::read_in()
// Purpose:   To prompt the user for and get the name and exam
//            scores for the receiver object.
// Pre:       The receiver object is initialized and
//            input = aName \n aScore1  \n aScore2  \n aScore3
//            \n restOfInput
// Post:      input = restOfInput and student_name = aName and
//            first_hourly = aScore1 and second_hourly = aScore2
//            and final_exam = aScore3
void Student::read_in()
{
    cout << "Please enter the student's name: ";
    read_string(student_name, MAXSTRING);
    cout << "Please enter an exam score when prompted:\n";
    cout << "First hourly score: ";
    cin  >> first_hourly;
    cout << "Second hourly score: ";
    cin  >> second_hourly;
    cout << "Final exam score: ";
    cin  >> final_exam;
} // end Student::read_in()
```

Note that the major difference between the function `Student::read_in` and the function `get_student_data` from the original `Searcher` program is that `Student::read_in` has no arguments, whereas `get_student_data` has to pass back all of the input data to the calling function (which was `get_class_data`). In the case of `Student::read_in`, the receiver object contains all of the data that had to be passed back by the original `get_student_data` function.   The function `Student::read_in` can access these data members directly, without the need for argument passing. This is an important advantage of object-oriented programming. Clearly, not having an argument list makes the member function easier to read and understand. It also eliminates errors associated with the passing of arguments. *Student::read_in accomplishes the elimination of arguments without introducing global variables.*

The function `Student::compute_average`   The body of this member function is similar to that of the function `compute_average` in the original `Searcher` program. This function simply computes the value of the receiver's instance variable `average`, using the data already existing within the receiver. Again note the absence of an argument list, because all of the needed data is contained within the receiver.

```
// Function:  Student::compute_average()
// Purpose:   To compute the receiver's average based
//            based upon the exam scores and exam weights
// Pre:       first_hourly, seond_hourly, and final_exam
//            are defined
// Post:      average  = WEIGHT1 * first_hourly
//                     + WEIGHT2 * second_hourly
//                     + WEIGHTF * final_exam
void Student::compute_average()
{
    // LOCAL DATA ...
    const float WEIGHT1 = 0.25,
            WEIGHT2 = 0.25,
            WEIGHTF = 0.50;


    // STATEMENTS ...
    average = WEIGHT1 * first_hourly
      + WEIGHT2 * second_hourly
      + WEIGHTF * final_exam;
} // Student::compute_average()
```

The function `Student::display_average`   This function displays the receiver's average on the screen.

```
// Function:  Student::display_average()
// Purpose:   To display the receiver's average on the
//               computer display
// Pre:       average = aFloat and output = oldStuff
// Post:      output = oldStuff This student's average
//               is aFloat \n
void Student::display_average()
{
    cout << "This student's average is " << setprecision(1)
      << average << endl;
}
```

The `section.h` Header File

The `section.h` header file contains the declaration for the `Section` class. In addition, it defines the constant `MAXCLASS`. The `section.h` header file, excluding the introductory comments, follows:

```
#include "student.h"
// GLOBAL CONSTANT DEFINITION ...
const int MAXCLASS = 50;


class Section
{
    private:
        // data members
        Student c[MAXCLASS];
        int class_size;


    public:
        // member functions
        // constructor - destructor
        Section();
        ~Section();


        // access
        Student search(string);


        // modify
        void read_in();
        void add_student(Student);
        void compute_averages();
        void sort_by_name();
};   // Section class
```

Note that the section.h header file begins by including the student.h header file. This is required so that the compiler will recognize the identifier Student as the name of a class.

The section.cxx implementation file

The constructor Section   This constructor initializes the class_size data member to 0. Also recall that the constructor Student will automatically be applied to the Student objects contained within the receiver Section after the constructor Section is called.

```
// Constructor:   Section()
// Purpose:       To initialize the receiver.  This will
//                apply the Student() constructor to all
//                Student objects in the receiver.
// Pre:           None
// Post:          The receiver is initialized and
//                for all i in [1..MAXCLASS]
//                  : c[i-1] is initialized
//                  and class_size = 0.
```

```
Section::Section()
{
    class_size = 0;
} // end Section::Section()
```

The destructor ~Section   This destructor is called after the destructor ~Student has been applied to all Student objects in the receiver collection.

```
// Destructor: ~Section()
// Purpose:    To destroy the receiver.  This will apply
//             the ~Student() destructor to all Student
//             objects in the receiver.
// Pre:        The receiver is initialized.
// Post:       The receiver is destroyed and
//                 for all i in [1..MAXCLASS]
//                    : c[i-1] is destroyed.
Section::~Section()
{
    ; // no dynamic objects to deallocate
} // end Section::~Section()
```

The function Section::search   This function performs a linear search on the array c of Student objects. This function assumes that the array is sorted alphabetically by name and it takes advantage of this fact by terminating as soon as the search_key value is smaller than the value of c[index].get_name(). The notation c[index].get_name() can be read as "the value that is returned when the function Student::get_name is applied to the object c[index], which is one of the Student objects in the array c." The variable cur_name is introduced to make the program more readable. The variable comparison is used to record the value returned by a call to strcmp so that strcmp does not need to be called unnecessarily. When search_key matches cur_name, we return from the function with the value c[index]. If the search fails, the value returned by the function will be a Student object whose name is "not found."

```
// Function: search(string)
// Used:      To search through the receiver for a Student
//            whose name is search_key.  Either returns that
//            Student object or returns a Student object whose
//            name is "not_found".  Uses a linear search.
// Pre:       class_size >= 0 and search_key is defined and
//            c is sorted in ascending order by name
// Post:      (there exists i in [0..class_size-1] :
//            c[i].get_name() = search_key
//            and search = c[i]) or
//            (for all i in [0..class_size-1] :
//            c[i].get_name() != search_key
//            and search.get_name = "not_found")
Student Section::search(string search_key)
{
```

```
// LOCAL VARIABLES ...
int index = 0;
Student astudent;
int comparison;
string cur_name;   // speeds things up a little
enum {found, not_found_yet} status = not_found_yet;


// STATEMENTS ...
while ((status == not_found_yet) && (index < class_size))
{
    strcpy(cur_name, c[index].get_name());
    comparison = strcmp(search_key, cur_name);
    if (!comparison)
    {
    // match
    status = found;
    }
    else if (comparison < 0)
    {
    // search fails
    index = class_size;
    }
    else
    {
    // try another (unless at end)
    index++;
    }
} // end while


if (status == not_found_yet)
{
    // search failed
    astudent.set_name("not found");
    }
else
{
    // search succeeded
    astudent = c[index];
}
return astudent;
} // end Section::search()
```

Note that this function needs to apply the function `Student::get_name` to a `Student` object in order to get access to the value of the `student_name` data member of that `Student` object. That is because `student_name` is private to the `Student` class and is not part of the public interface of that class. Thus, `student_name` cannot be referenced by any function that is not a member of the `Student` class (assuming what we have learned thus far).

The function `Section::read_in` This function is closely related to the function `get_class_data` in the original `Searcher` program. This function asks the user to enter the number of students in the class. Then, a `for` loop is used to read in data for that many students.

```
// Function:  Section::read_in()
// Purpose:   To read in all of the data for the
//            receiver section.
// Define:    inputPattern = aName FHScore SHScore FScore
// Define:    the notation c[i].Student::read_in()
//            means that the function read_in()
//               has been applied to the Student c[i].
//               This implies that the post condition for
//               Student::read_in() applies.
// Pre:       The receiver is initialized class_size = 0 and
//            input = N (N repetitions of: inputPattern)
//            and N <= MAXCLASS
// Post:      class_size = N and N <= MAXCLASS and
//            for all i in [1..class_size] :
//               c[i-1].Student::read_in()
void Section::read_in()
{
    // LOCAL DATA ...
    Student astudent;
    int num;


    // STATEMENTS ...
    cout << "How many students are in the class? ";
    cin  >> num;
    for (int i = 0; i < num; i++)
    {
        cin.ignore(LINESIZE, '\n');// go to beginning of next line
        astudent.read_in();
        this -> add_student(astudent);  // increments class_size
    }
} // Section::read_in()
```

All of this data is read into the local `Student` object called `astudent` before being inserted into the receiver `Section` object. Individual student data is obtained by applying `Student::read_in` to `astudent`. Once `astudent` contains a new set of student data, this latest data is added to the receiver `Section` object by applying the `Section::add_student` function to the receiver. This is accomplished by means of the special variable called **this**, as follows:

```
this -> add_student(astudent);
```

This statement says "Apply the function `Section::add_student` with the argument `astudent` to the receiver object." This causes the data contained within `astudent` to be assigned to appropriate components in the array `c`.

The keyword `this` is used in C++ whenever a member function must refer to the receiver object. Again, *the receiver object is the object to which the function is being applied in a particular evocation of that function.* In fact, **this** is a variable that contains the *address* of the receiver object. (In Chapter 2 we shall learn that `this` is thus a pointer to the receiver object.) The arrow notation is used to cause the function `Section::add_student` to be applied to the object that `this` points to, that is, to the receiver object. Once you learn more about pointers, the use of `this` will become more clear. For now, let us just say that whenever you see the pattern

```
this -> func()
```

within a member function, where `func` is the name of some function, then you should interpret this as meaning "apply `func` to the receiver object". Indeed, this construct is *usually* equivalent to calling `func` without the use of `this`:

```
func()
```

That is, the use of `this ->` is usually not required, but in our opinion, even when it is not required, it makes the logic more transparent. It stresses (for the human reader) that the function `func` is being applied to the receiver object.

Note that the `Student` and `Section` classes both have member functions called `read_in`. This is an example of *function overloading*. The type of the object to which `read_in` is being applied tells the compiler which version of `read_in` is being called. The compiler can also use distinct argument type lists to distinguish between overloaded functions. For example, the following function prototypes are for distinct, overloaded functions:

```
void add_em(int, int, int);
void add_em(float, float, float);
```

The function `Section::compute_averages`   The `Section` class function `read_in` was implemented by repeated calls to `Student::read_in`. The function `Section::compute_averages` is implemented by repeatedly calling `Student::compute_average`. One might say that `Section::compute_averages` "broadcasts" the `Student::compute_average` message to each of the `Student` objects contained within the receiver `Section` object. This "broadcasting" pattern is very common in object-oriented programming.

```
// function:  Section::compute_averages()
// Purpose:   To update each Student object in the
//            receiver by computing its final average
// Define:    the notation c[i].Student::compute_average()
//            means that the function compute_average()
//            has been applied to the Student c[i].
//            This implies that the post condition for
//            Student::compute_average() applies.
// Pre:       for i in [0..class_size-1] :
//            (c[i].first_hourly, c[i].second_hourly,
//            c[i].final_exam, c[i].on_nerves are defined)
// Post       for i in [0..class_size-1] :
//               c[i].Student::compute_average()
void Section::compute_averages()
{
    for (int i = 0; i < class_size; i++)
    {
        c[i].compute_average();
```

```
        }
    }  // end Section::compute_averages()
```

FIGURE 1–4   C++ code for `Section::compute_averages`.

The function `Section::add_student`   This function was discussed earlier. It increments `class_size` and stores `astudent` in the next available position in the array `c`.

```
// Function: Section::add_student(Student)
// Purpose:  To add astudent to the receiver section.
// Pre:      class_size = n and N < MAXCLASS
// Post:     c[N] = astudent and class_size = old(class_size) + 1
void Section::add_student(Student astudent)
{
    c[class_size++] = astudent;
}  // end Section::add_student
```

FIGURE 1–5   C++ code for `Section::add_student`.

The function `Section::sort_by_name`   This function is similar to the `sort_by_name` function that was given in the original `Searcher` program. However, this implementation is simpler than the original nonmember function version in two regards: First, the member function contains no formal argument list because all of the relevant data is contained within the receiver object; and second, the swapping process is simplified by the use of a single `Student` object, `tstudent`.

```
// Function:  Section::sort_by_name()
// Purpose:   To sort the receiver collection of Student objects
//               in ascending order by name.  Uses bubblesort.
// Pre:     class_size >= 0 and for all i in [0..class_size-1] :
//               c[i].student_name is defined
// Post:     c is a permutation of old(c) and
//               for all i in [0..class_size-2] :
//               c[i].student_name <= c[i+1].student_name
void Section::sort_by_name()
{
    // LOCAL DATA ...
    enum {false, true} done = false;
    Student tstudent;
    int limit = class_size - 1;


    // STATEMENTS ...
    // outer loop:
    for (int pass = 1; !done && (pass <= limit); pass++)
    {
        done = true;
        // inner loop:
```

```
        for (int i = 0; i < (class_size - pass); i++)
        {
        if (strcmp( c[i].get_name(), c[i+1].get_name()) > 0)
        {
            tstudent = c[i];
            c[i]    = c[i+1];
            c[i+1] = tstudent;
            done = false;
        }
        } // end inner loop
    } // end outer loop
} // end sort_by_name()
```

FIGURE 1–6   C++ code for `Section::sort_by_name`.

Note that the `Student::get_name` function must be used to access the student names that are stored in individual `Student` objects.

OBJECT-ORIENTED PROGRAMMING AND THE SIX DESIGN PRINCIPLES

Chapter 0 introduced six program design principles. These principles were developed in the 1970s in the context of function-oriented design and programming in a procedural language (e.g., Cobol, FORTRAN, PL/I, Pascal and C). However, the process of object-oriented design and programming, which has evolved more recently (i.e., the latter part of the 1980s and in the 1990s), strongly supports these very same design principles. One might say that a primary achievement of the object-oriented revolution in software development is to facilitate the creation of programs whose development and structure are consistent with these principles. Here is a brief discussion of how object-oriented techniques support these six principles.

Problem decomposition   Object-oriented design gives us a natural device for decomposing problems into subproblems. We decompose a problem by identifying the classes inherent in the problem domain. In practice, the designer tries to create classes that can be reused in many applications. The basic building blocks of an object-oriented design (classes) are explicitly designed for reuse. The basic building blocks of a function-oriented design (functions) can be reusable if we adhere to good design principles, but they can only be reused by incorporating them into a library or copying them into a new program. The very mode of problem decomposition in an object-oriented system is centered around the creation of reusable software components.   In fact, in the next and subsequent chapters we shall introduce some very powerful techniques for making our classes more general and more reusable.

Formal specifications   Formal specifications in an object-oriented design have special coherence because we are not just specifying functions in isolation, but we are specifying the behavior of objects themselves. The formal specifications in an object-oriented design consist of preconditions and postconditions for each member function contained within a class (as was shown in the `ObjSearcher` program). Since many member functions in an object-oriented design tend to be small, many of the preconditions and postconditions in an object-oriented design are consequently quite simple.

Functional cohesion   In object-oriented programming, *it is difficult*, once one has had just a little practice, *to write methods that are not functionally cohesive*. The very concept of a method suggests functional cohesion. As mentioned above, the member functions of an object-oriented design tend to be smaller than the functions of a function-oriented design. In part this is because member functions are intended to convey one particular kind of object behavior. It should be noted (by means of a contrast) that it is sometimes very difficult (in a function-oriented design) to achieve functional cohesion.

The general concept of cohesion has to do with the "glue" which holds a software component together. This concept arose in the context of function-oriented design in procedural languages, where the issue was whether a function had a strong enough conceptual glue or whether a function was just an arbitrary collection of statements. Functional cohesion was considered the best form of cohesion for a function. By definition, all the parts of a functionally cohesive function focus on a single, easily identified purpose.

However, software engineers identified additional levels of cohesion that were also considered useful. *Communicational cohesion* was viewed as the second best form of cohesion for a function (right behind functional cohesion). *A function was viewed as being communicationally cohesive if all of its parts were related to a common collection of data.* For example, a function that performed various tasks relative to a given file would be considered communicationally cohesive. Software engineers found that communicationally cohesive functions, like functionally cohesive functions, had good properties in terms of debugging, modifying, and reusing that function.

A class represents a higher level of organization than a function. Indeed, a class normally contains an entire collection of functions (the member functions). However, *as a group, all of the member functions in a class are communicationally cohesive*, in the same sense that each member function by itself might be functionally cohesive. The member functions of a class are communicationally cohesive, as defined in the previous paragraph, because they all have access to the data members of the objects in that class.

Loose coupling and explicit interfaces   The fact that the member functions within a class are communicationally cohesive (as a group) facilitates clean and clear interactions among those functions. This is reflected in the fact that the member function interfaces (argument lists) are generally much simpler than the corresponding interfaces in a function-oriented design. Much of the data that is normally passed back and forth among functions is contained within the receiver objects and does not need to appear in member function argument lists. The `ObjSearcher` program clearly showed that this led to programs that were easier to read, understand and debug.

In the context of function-oriented design we stated that interfaces should be explicit. However, an even greater goal is that interfaces should be as simple as possible, so long as one does not introduce bad forms of coupling (e.g., global variables). In an object-oriented design one can achieve the simplification of member function interfaces without introducing global variables. This makes programs easier to read and understand.

Object-oriented programming represents a major shift in the way we think about processes and data. In a function-oriented design, we think of data as being passed back and forth among functions. The functions are static (in the sense of being motionless) and the data is dynamic. In an object-oriented design, we think of the data as being static and the functions as being dynamic. The functions are passed back and forth (as messages) among objects.

Note that the member function interfaces are simplified, but not at the expense of introducing global variables. The use of global variables in an object-oriented design would seem to be either impossible, or at the very least, awkward and unnatural. The member functions naturally share the data members (an acceptable form of coupling) and this seems to supplant any need for thinking in terms of global variables.

Information hiding   Object-oriented languages automate information hiding, a goal that is sometimes difficult to achieve in a function-oriented design. This was clearly reflected in the `ObjSearcher` program, in which the main function only "knew" about a single object belonging to the `Section` class, and did not need to know any of the internal details (specifically, the `Student` object details like representation of individual student names and exam scores) contained within that `Section` object.

There are two aspects to information hiding in an object-oriented context. First, an object's data members (which should be declared private) are hidden away in that object. The only way we can get access to those data members is by sending that object appropriate messages. Furthermore, when we send an object a message, we only need to understand the precondition and postcondition associated with that message. We do not need to know how the member function is implemented.

SPECIFICATIONS AND CORRECTNESS OF PROGRAMS

Specifications are generated as part of the software design process. This implies that specifications are written as guidance for programmers. Programmers are given this charge: write functions that satisfy the formal specifications given in the software design. The question naturally arises as to how these specifications are used after the code is written. In other words, how do programmers check to see if their functions satisfy the given specifications? The process of demonstrating that a function satisfies its specifications is called *verification*.

There are at least three approaches to demonstrating that a given function satisfies its specifications:

- Software testing

- Informal verification

- Formal verification

Moreover, there are two forms of software testing: *static testing* and *dynamic testing*. In static testing, the function being tested is treated as input for a program called a static program analyzer. The analyzer checks the function for certain patterns that are considered probable sources of error. In dynamic testing, the function is run using test data. The preconditions and postconditions are used to generate test cases and expected test case results. The function is then run to see if the expected results are achieved.

Informal verification involves the use of mathematical argumentation techniques, though in a discursive style, to argue that a function satisfies its preconditions and postconditions. These informal arguments resemble the arguments mathematicians use to prove theorems in English. In fact, most mathematical proofs are done in this way. You will see examples of informal verification in this text.

Formal verification is a process by which a function, or a collection of functions that constitute a subsystem, is analyzed statically, alongside its pre- and postconditions, by someone who has the goal of rigorously and exhaustively proving that that routine or subsystem is correct. Persons who engage in formal verification of software systems adhere strictly to axioms and rules of inference about the behavior of different kinds of program constructs. Consequently, formal verification is related more closely to the methods of formal logic.

There are many situations in which mathematical verification techniques (whether formal or informal) can be used to provide assurance that the program satisfies its postconditions under all circumstances. In some of these situations, verification is in fact preferable to testing, since testing does not provide such assurance. It is also important to emphasize that the process of formal verification is not yet well enough developed to be widely used in the software industry at this time. Formal verification is still considered a research problem, and therefore, it is not used in this text.

SUMMARY

This chapter introduced software methodology in an object-oriented context. We discussed the parties that are normally involved in the development of a software project (sponsors, developers, maintainers and users) and the lifecycle that software typically undergoes. We illustrated this methodology by presenting an object-oriented design for the `Searcher` program that was originally presented in Chapter 0, along with a new program, `ObjSearcher`, that recasts `Searcher` in accordance with this design. We also showed how object-oriented design and programming facilitates the six design goals presented in Chapter 0. Finally, we presented a brief discussion of verification techniques.

References

[1] Abbott, Russell J.,"Program Design by Informal English Descriptions," *Communications of the ACM*, 26, 11 (November 1983), 882-894.

[2] Booch, Grady, *Software Engineering with Ada*, Benjamin/Cummings Publishing Company, Inc, Menlo Park, California, 1986.

[3] Brooks, Frederick P., *The Mythical Man–Month: Essays on Software Engineering*, Addison–Wesley, 1975.

[4] Brooks, Frederick P., "No Silver Bullet: Essence and Accidents of Software Engineering," *IEEE Computer*, April 1987, pp. 10–19.

[5] Meyer, Bertrand, *Object-Oriented Software Construction*, Prentice-Hall, 1988.

[6] Pressman, Roger S., *Software Engineering: A Practitioner's Approach*, 2nd ed., McGraw–Hill, 1987.

[7] Mynatt, Barbee, *Software Engineering: A Project-Oriented Approach*, Prentice-Hall, 1988.

[8] Sommerville, Ian, , 2nd Edition, Addison-Wesley, 1988.

CHAPTER 2

INHERITANCE, POLYMORPHISM AND GENERIC CLASSES

This chapter continues the introduction to object-oriented programming. It provides programming tools that will facilitate the creation of data structures with powerful characteristics. Once you master these tools, you will utilize them throughout the remainder of this text.

Data structures are a major theme in this book. Moreover, the historical trend in the treatment of data structures has been to capture the essence of these structures independent of their implementation details. Object-oriented languages represent the most recent development in this historical trend. Object-oriented languages make it easier to implement data structures that are *generic* and *heterogeneous*.

GENERIC AND HETEROGENEOUS DATA STRUCTURES

A somewhat anachronistic characterization of "data structure" follows: a data structure is a collection of elements that are related in some way. For example, the elements in a list are related by a sequential ordering. A list has a first element, a second element and so on. The elements in a tree exist in a hierarchical relationship to one another. There is a special element, called the root, that has no parent (or ancestor) in the tree. All other elements in the tree have a unique parent. This characterization is "anachronistic" in that a more modern view would include the *operations* that act upon a data structure as being an *intrinsic aspect* of that data structure. Thus, a list is not only a sequential arrangement of elements, but also the list concept includes all operations that are permitted with respect to those elements. Clearly, this more modern characterization of data structures is related to the class concept introduced in Chapter 1. In fact, we shall implement data structures as classes.

Let's consider an important data structure, the queue, and look at different ways in which a queue can be implemented. A queue is a data structure which captures the first in - first out (fifo) behavior of queues in the real world; for example, a line in front of a teller's window at a bank. Customers enter the queue at its rear and leave the queue at its front. The first person who enters the queue is the first person who leaves the queue. A queue is a sequential arrangement of elements that exhibit this first in - first out behavior.

There are many ways in which a data structure, such as a queue, can be implemented in C++. Some combinations of properties one might want to have for a data structure include:

1. nongeneric and homogeneous
2. generic and homogeneous
3. nongeneric and heterogeneous
4. generic and heterogeneous

The flexibility to obtain these properties is not available in most programming languages. By the end of this chapter you should be able to implement data structures of these four kinds. In the following paragraphs, we shall clarify the distinction between these four kinds of data structures.

If a queue implementation permits only one element type, then the queue is said to be *homogeneous*; otherwise the queue is *heterogeneous*. Figure 2–1 shows a heterogeneous queue that contains four different types of elements: a floating point number, two strings, a character, and an integer. A homogeneous queue would only permit one type of element, so we would have a queue of integers or a queue of floating point numbers, but not a queue of integers and floating point numbers together. Heterogeneity is achievable because of a powerful property of object-oriented languages called *polymorphism*. Much of this chapter is devoted to a careful presentation of this fundamental concept.

Front				Rear
3.5	"Hello"	"Goodbye!"	'Z'	17

FIGURE 2–1   A heterogeneous queue with five elements of various kinds.

In C++ the permissible element types for a queue implementation can either be given as an actual type or as a parameterized type. In the former case, the queue is said to be nongeneric and in the latter case, generic. We can build generic data structures in C++ because of the powerful template facility, which allows classes to be defined in terms of one or more type parameters. Templates will be introduced later in the text.

The choice of a programming language is very important, because not all languages support heterogeneous and generic data structures. The fact that C++ supports both heterogeneous data structures and generic data structures is partly responsible for the growing popularity of C++.

THE `Element` CLASS

We shall now begin our presentation of the concepts and tools that will be needed to create heterogeneous data structures, whether generic or nongeneric. In particular, we shall introduce the concepts of *inheritance* and *polymorphism*. These concepts have a fundamental utility in object-oriented programming beyond the implementation of heterogeneous data structures.

In the previous section, we mentioned that a data structure consists of elements. In order to achieve heterogeneity, those elements must be implemented as objects. Suppose we want to create a queue such as the one shown in Figure 2–1. This requires that we implement each data item in the queue as a kind of object. This suggests the need for four classes:

- `StringObj`   an object in this class will contain one string

- `FloatObj`   an object in this class will contain one floating point number

- `IntObj`   an object in this class will contain one integer

- `CharObj`   an object in this class will contain one character

If we consider the desired behavior of these classes, we find many similarities. In object-oriented programming, if a collection of classes share a set of common behaviors, then it is often advisable to introduce a more general class that captures the common behaviors. The more general class is implemented as a *superclass* of the original classes, which are then called *subclasses* of this more general class. Consequently, we shall introduce a superclass, `Element`, that captures the common behavior of the `StringObj`, `FloatObj`, `IntObj` and `CharObj` subclasses. The hierarchy is shown in Figure 2–2.

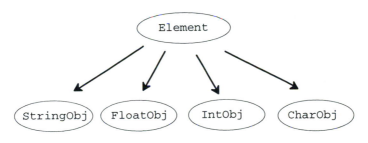

FIGURE 2–2   Creating a hierarchy of Elementary Classes.

The class `Element` will capture most, but not all, of the common behavior of the `StringObj`, `FloatObj`, `IntObj` and `CharObj` classes because we intend the class `Element` to represent *the most general kind of object* that can be used with our heterogeneous data structures. Suppose we wish to place objects that belong to the class `CL` in one of our heterogeneous data structures. Then, we must declare the class `CL` as a subclass of `Element`. The class `Element` will capture the common behaviors of all such potential subclasses and thus must exclude any behaviors peculiar to any of the `StringObj`, `FloatObj`, `IntObj`, `CharObj`, or any other, yet to be defined, classes. We shall refer to the class `Element` and all of its subclasses collectively as the "element classes." We shall refer to an instance of any element class as an "element."

Every element will contain the data member `my_class`. This data member will be inherited from the `Element` class by means of the inheritance mechanism that we shall soon describe. The purpose of the `my_class` data member is to store a string that specifies the class to which an element belongs. For example, the value of `my_class` for a `FloatObj` will be the string `FloatObj` and the value of `my_class` for a `Student` object will be the string `"Student"`.

The class `Element` will establish a *common class protocol* for all of its subclasses. The common class protocol consists of those functions that can be applied to any element (i.e., any instance of the class `Element` or any of its subclasses). The concept of a common class protocol is a design concept and not a language concept. That is, C++ has no intrinsic notion of a common class protocol, but C++ programmers need to understand this concept. The prototypes for the functions in the common class protocol for the element classes are given in Figure 2–3.

```
inline char* get_class();
     // note that this is a static
     //function
virtual  void   display();
virtual int operator ==(Element&);
virtual int operator !=(Element&);
virtual int operator >(Element&);
virtual int operator <(Element&);
virtual int operator <=(Element&);
virtual int operator >=(Element&);
virtual  void   read_in();
virtual  void   file_in(ifstream&);
virtual  void   file_out(ofstream&);
```

FIGURE 2–3   The common class protocol for "elements."

The instance variable, `class_name`, contains one of the element class names. We shall discuss the significance of the `inline` key word shortly.

Note that there are 11 functions in the common class protocol. Ten of these (`display`, the 6 comparison operators, `read_in`, `file_in` and `file_out`) are declared `virtual` and one (`get_class`) is not declared `virtual`, and is thus `static` by default. The fact that these functions are in the common class protocol means that we intend these functions to be applicable to any element. The distinction between the `static` and `virtual` functions is as follows: the `static` function, `get_class`, is implemented once and for all at the `Element` level in the hierarchy. The subclasses of `Element` inherit the function `get_class` as it is, that is without changing its implementation in any way. Said another way, `get_class` will do the same thing, that is, return the string value of the instance variable `my_class` regardless of class of the element which calls it. The `virtual` functions, on the other hand, are given only a skeletal implementation at the `Element` level. Virtual functions must be given new implementations in each subclass of `Element`.

We use the term *ubiquitous* to refer to those, necessarily `virtual`, functions in a class hierarchy that need to be implemented in nearly all (if not all) of the subclasses in a class hierarchy. Thus, the functions `display`, the comparison operators, `read_in`, `file_in` and `file_out` are ubiquitous. Each of the subclasses of `Element` that we shall discuss will have its own implementation for each of these functions.

The class `Element` is called an *abstract class* because we have no intention of ever creating an `Element` object *per se*. The purpose of the `Element` class is to allow us to implement heterogeneous data structures (using pointers to elements, as we shall see) and to introduce the common class protocol for all of the element classes. On the other hand, a class that is permitted to have instances is called a *concrete class*. For example, the classes `StringObj` and `FloatObj` are concrete classes.

The `elements.h` header file declares the type `class_name` and the class `Element`. The details are shown in Figure 2–4.

```
// This is the header file for the Element class
// that is an abstract class that serves as the
// root class for the hierarchy of element classes.


#ifndef ELEMENTS_H
#define ELEMENTS_H


#include <string.h>
#include <iostream.h>
#include <fstream.h>


// GLOBAL DECLARATION, DEFINITION ...
typedef char class_name[21];


enum boolean {FALSE,TRUE};


class Element {
    protected:
        // DATA MEMBER ...
        class_name my_class;


    public:
        // MEMBER FUNCTIONS ...
        // constructor - destructor
        inline Element();
        inline virtual ~Element();
```

```
                    // access
                    virtual char* get_class();


                // display
                virtual void display() { };
                 // not implemented at this level


                // comparison operators
                virtual int operator ==(Element&);
                virtual int operator !=(Element&);
                virtual int operator >(Element&);
                virtual int operator <(Element&);
                virtual int operator <=(Element&);
                virtual int operator >=(Element&);


                // read in
                virtual void read_in() { };
                 // not implemented at this level


                // file in - file out
                virtual void file_in(ifstream&) { };
                 // not implemented at this level
                virtual void file_out(ofstream&) { };
                 // not implemented at this level
};   // end class Element


// POINTER TYPE ...
typedef Element* ElementPtr;


#endif
```

FIGURE 2–4   The elements.h header file declaring type class_name and the class Element.

The key word *protected* in the declaration of the my_class data member means that my_class will be inherited by subclasses of Element that are declared using the public qualifier. Note that the destructor ~Element and all of the ubiquitous functions are declared virtual. This is important for the implementation of heterogeneous data structures. The full significance of the key word virtual will become apparent only when we discuss heterogeneous data structures in the next section. Ubiquitous functions in a hierarchy should certainly be declared virtual. If a function is going to be redefined in a subclass, it should be declared virtual. Destructors should be declared virtual for those classes that are going to be used in a heterogeneous data structure. Constructors are never declared virtual.

Three of the Element class member functions (the constructor, the destructor and get_class) are declared with the key word inline. An object-oriented design typically involves many small functions; functions that contain just one or two statements. Since every actual function call during a program's execution requires some run-time overhead, the large number of calls to small functions will slow down the execution of a program. Consequently, C++ allows the programmer to declare functions `inline`. This amounts to a request to the compiler that calls to such a function not be treated as ordinary function calls, but instead that the compiler substitute appropriate code for the function call *in line* in the program. For example, suppose a function `sum2ints` has the following prototype and definition:

```
prototype:      inline int sum2ints(int, int);

definition:     int sum2ints(int a, int b)
                {
                        return a + b;
                }
```

If the function `sum2ints` were to be called as follows:

```
k = sum2ints(int1, int2);
```

then the `inline` key word is a request to the compiler to attempt an in line substitution of code for the function instead generating object code that actually causes a transfer of control to the function. In this case, the in line code becomes

```
k = int1 + int2;
```

In fact, the `Element` class functions `display`, `read_in`, `file_in` and `file_out` are also inline functions. If a function prototype does not include the key word `inline` but provides a function body, then that function prototype is actually an inline function definition. The function body is the function definition. The functions `display`, `read_in`, `file_in` and `file_out` are defined so that they do nothing and documentation is provided that explains that these functions are not being implemented at this level in the hierarchy. In other words, the subclasses of `Element` are responsible for implementing these functions.

The function `get_class` is also part of the common class protocol for the element classes. Since `get_class` will not be redefined lower in the hierarchy, it is not declared `virtual` and is, therefore, `static` by default.

The comparison operator `Element` member functions contain the additional keyword `operator` which is used to "overload" built-in C++ operators. This allows an operator, such as <, to have a variety of meanings depending upon the type of its arguments. In this case, these operators will be used to make comparisons, such as == or <, between *the* `value` *data members* of objects of a given class, e.g., we can use == to determine whether two `IntObj` (described in the section below) elements are *value equal* (or, more precisely, have equal contents in their respective `value` data members.) Recall that the parameter notation (`Element&`) allows the comparison operators to have call-by-reference arguments directly. Again, the details will be found in the implementations of the particular element classes such as `IntObj`.

The definitions of the `Element` class member functions declared in the `Elements.h` header file of Figure 2–4 are given in Figure 2–5.

```
// Constructor:    Element::Element()
// Purpose:        To initialize the receiver.
// Pre:            None
// Post:           my_class = "Element"
Element::Element()
{
    strcpy(my_class, "Element");
}   // end Element::Element()



// Destructor:     Element::~Element()
// Purpose:        To destroy the receiver
// Pre:            The receiver is initialized
// Post:           The receiver is destroyed
Element::~Element()
{
    ;
}   // end Element::~Element()



// Function:       Element::get_class()
// Purpose:        Returns the class of the receiver
//                 This function is inherited by all
//                 derived classes.
// Pre:            my_class = aClassName
// Post:           get_class = aClassName
char* Element::get_class()
{
    return my_class;
}   // end Element::get_class()



// Operator:       Element::==(e)
// Purpose:        This operator introduces the notion of
//                 value identity into our class hierarchy.
//                 At this level, the function always returns 1,
//                 since any two Element objects are equal.
// Pre:            *eptr belongs to the class Element.
// Post:           ==() = 1
int Element::operator ==(Element& e)
{
    return 1;
}   // end operator Element::==



// Operator:       Element::!=(e)
// Purpose:        This operator introduces the notion of
//                 value inequality into our class hierarchy.
//                 At this level, the function always returns 0,
//                 since any two Element objects are equal.
```

```
// Pre:             *eptr belongs to the class Element.
// Post:            !=() = 0
int Element::operator !=(Element& e)
{
    return 0;
}  // end operator Element::!=



// Operator:        Element::<(e)
// Purpose:         This operator introduces the notion of a
//                  linear ordering into our class hierarchy.
//                  At this level, this operator always
//                  returns 0 since any two Element objects are
//                  equal.
// Pre:             *eptr belongs to the class Element.
// Post:            <() = 0
int Element::operator <(Element& e)
{
    return 0;
}  // end operator Element::<



// Operator:        Element::>(e)
// Purpose:         This operator introduces the notion of a
//                  linear ordering into our class hierarchy.
//                  At this level, this operator always
//                  returns 0 since any two Element objects are
//                  equal.
// Pre:             *eptr belongs to the class Element.
// Post:            >() = 0
int Element::operator >(Element& e)
{
    return 0;
}  // end operator Element::>



// Operator:        Element::<=(e)
// Purpose:         This operator introduces the notion of
//                  less than or equal to based upon value
//                  identity into our class hierarchy.
//                  At this level, the function always returns 1,
//                  since any two Element objects are equal.
// Pre:             *eptr belongs to the class Element.
// Post:            <=() = 1
int Element::operator <=(Element& e)
{
    return 1;
}  // end operator Element::<=



// Operator:        Element::>=(e)
// Purpose:         This operator introduces the notion of
//                  greater than or equal to based upon value
//                  identity into our class hierarchy.
//                  At this level, the function always returns 1,
//                  since any two Element objects are equal.
```

```
// Pre:              *eptr belongs to the class Element.
// Post:             >=() = 1
int Element::operator >=(Element& e)
{
    return 1;
}  // end operator Element::>=
```

FIGURE 2–5   Definitions of `Element` class member functions.

STANDARD CLASSES AND OBJECTS

If we want to store integers, floating point numbers, strings and characters in our heterogeneous data structures, we must introduce our own representations of these types as classes. We have already alluded to the classes `StringObj`, `FloatObj`, `IntObj`, and `CharObj` which will serve this purpose. We shall call these classes the "standard classes" because the types `int`, `char` and `float` are standard C++ classes and the `string` type is fundamental. The term "standard classes" is not standard, but it gives us a means of referring to these classes as a group. (Since we shall implement the standard classes as subclasses of `Element`, the standard classes are also element classes, according to our terminology.) We have two motivations for introducing the standard classes at this time. First, they provide a context for a discussion of inheritance and virtual functions. Second, they provide a framework for a discussion of dynamic objects in the next section.

We are not suggesting that programming with objects in C++ requires that you dispense with the standard types (e.g., `float`, `int`, and `char`). The standard classes are, however, especially relevant in the present discussion, which is leading towards the implementation of heterogeneous data structures. For example, if you want to store an integer in such a data structure, you must first convert that integer into an `IntObj`.

Inheritance and Virtual Functions

The relationship between the `Element` class and the standard classes is shown graphically in Figure 2–2 above. These classes constitute what is called a *class hierarchy*. `Element` is the root class and the standard classes are descendants of the root class in this hierarchy. Recall that `Element` is called the *superclass*, and its descendants in the diagram are called its *subclasses*.

Because of this organization, the standard classes can provide objects that can be incorporated into heterogeneous data structures, such as a heterogeneous list, queue, or tree. Since each standard class is a subclass of `Element`, each standard class *inherits* the `my_class` data member and all of the functions in the public interface of the class `Element` as shown in Figure 2–4. In particular, the standard classes inherit the common class protocol that was introduced by the class `Element`.

Definition   A subclass is said to *inherit* members (instance variables and member functions) from its superclass if it has access to those members without needing to redeclare them.

The term *base class* is used in C++ to describe a class from which another class inherits. The class doing the inheriting is called a *derived class* (in C++ parlance). A derived class does not inherit all of the members (i.e., data members and member functions collectively) of its base class. The members that are inherited depend upon the way in which a derived class is declared. We shall always declare a derived class using the following inheritance pattern:

```
class DerivedClass : public BaseClass
{
      ..... etc.
};  // end class DerivedClass
```

The key word `public` indicates the way in which `DerivedClass` will inherit from `BaseClass`. In this type of inheritance, `DerivedClass` will inherit all `protected` and `public` members of `BaseClass`. `DerivedClass` will not inherit the `private` members of `BaseClass`. Many experts consider this the only acceptable form of inheritance, although C++ provides for other inheritance mechanisms. What is significant about this acceptable form of inheritance is that the derived class inherits the *entire* public interface of the base class.

The power that follows from inheriting member functions from a superclass is that all objects in the subclass will understand all of the messages that are already understood by objects in its superclass. Moreover, *any subclass can redefine any inherited member functions as appropriate to its particular needs.* However, whenever a subclass redefines a superclass member function, the superclass function must be declared `virtual`. Once declared `virtual`, a function remains `virtual` throughout the hierarchy. For the sake of clarity, we prefer to redeclare a function as `virtual` throughout a hierarchy, but this is not necessary.

Great care must be taken to consider the implications of function redefinition within the hierarchy, a process called *overloading*. Two functions `Class1::func` and `Class2::func` where `Class2` inherits from `Class1` are the same function if they have the same prototype. Then, declaring `Class1::func` virtual will mean that `Class2::func` will also be virtual. However, if `Class1::func` and `Class2::func` have different prototypes (e.g., they might have different argument types or different return types), then they are not the same function, and declaring `Class1::func` virtual will have no implications for `Class2::func`.

The ability to redefine member functions in a class hierarchy gives us our first notion of polymorphism, the idea of *polymorphic redefinition*:

Definition   When a subclass redefines a member function that is contained in its superclass, that function is said to be *polymorphically redefined.*

We can only have polymorphic redefinition if the function in the subclass has the same prototype (i.e., the same return type and the same list of argument types) as the function in the superclass. Otherwise, we are actually introducing a new function (by means of function overloading).

The concepts of inheritance and polymorphic redefinition can be illustrated by considering the declaration and implementation of one of the standard classes. All four standard classes are implemented in an almost identical manner, so we shall only present and discuss the implementation of the `IntObj` class. The class declaration for the `IntObj` class is shown in Figure 2–6.

```
class IntObj : public Element
{
    protected:
        // DATA MEMBER ...
        int value;


    public:
        // MEMBER FUNCTIONS ...
        // constructors - destructor
        inline IntObj(int);
        inline IntObj();            // default constructor
        inline virtual ~IntObj();


        // display
        virtual void display();


        // convert to and from standard int
        inline virtual int get_val();
        inline virtual void set_val(int);


        // comparison operators
        virtual int operator ==(Element&);
        virtual int operator !=(Element&);
        virtual int operator >(Element&);
        virtual int operator <(Element&);
        virtual int operator <=(Element&);
        virtual int operator >=(Element&);


        // file in / file out
        virtual void file_in(ifstream&);
        virtual void file_out(ofstream&);
};   // end class IntObj
```

FIGURE 2–6 The class declaration for `IntObj`.

The declaration on line 1 indicates that `IntObj` is a subclass of the class `Element`. Thus, objects in the class `IntObj` contain two data members: the variable `my_class` that is inherited from the class `Element` and the new data member value.   If `my_class` had been declared `private` in `Element`, it would not be inherited by the `IntObj` class. The variable `value` is of type `int`. Figure 2–7 shows an `IntObj` object called `IObj` whose value is 3.

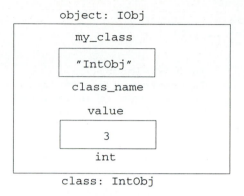

object: IObj

class: IntObj

FIGURE 2–7   An object in the class IntObj whose value is 3.

The class `IntObj` inherits the functions in the common class protocol established by the class `Element`. With the exception of `get_class`, these could not be implemented properly for each of the different types of element at the `Element` class level. Thus, the inherited functions `display`, the comparison operators, `read_in`, `file_in` and `file_out` must be redefined in the class `IntObj`.

We now examine the `IntObj` member functions, starting with the constructors and the destructor. The class `IntObj` has two constructors: `IntObj(int)` and `IntObj()`. The former initializes an `IntObj` object with an integer value passed as an argument (e.g., `IntObj i(3)` sets up an `IntObj` named `i` and initializes its `value` instance variable to 3) whereas the latter does not initialize the value of the `IntObj` object to which it is being applied. The C++ language mandates that the second constructor must be provided if we intend to store `IntObj` objects in an array (since a constructor must be applied to the objects in such an array when the array is defined). The code for the `IntObj` constructors and destructor follows in Figure 2–8.

```
// Constructor:     IntObj::IntObj(an_int)
// Purpose:         Initializes the receiver and sets its
//                  value to an_int.
// Pre:             an_int = anInt
// Post:            my_class = "IntObj" and value = anInt
IntObj::IntObj(int an_int)
{
    strcpy(my_class, "IntObj");
    value = an_int;
}   // end IntObj::IntObj(int)


// Constructor:     IntObj::IntObj()
// Purpose:         Initializes the receiver without
```

```
//                     initializing its value.
// Pre:               None
// Post:              my_class = "IntObj"
IntObj::IntObj()
{
    strcpy(my_class, "IntObj");
}   // end IntObj::IntObj()


// Destructor:        IntObj::~IntObj()
// Purpose:           To destroy the receiver
// Pre:               The receiver is initialized
// Post:              The receiver is destroyed
IntObj::~IntObj()
{
    ;
}   // end IntObj::~IntObj()
```

FIGURE 2–8   Implementation of `IntObj` constructors and destructor.

It is important to realize that a subclass constructor implicitly calls the *argumentless* constructor for its superclass. If there is no such constructor, the default constructor is applied. This implicit constructor call can be overridden by an explicit call to a particular superclass constructor.[1] A subclass destructor implicitly calls the destructor for its superclass. For example, suppose we have classes A, B and C where C is a subclass of B and B is a subclass of A. Then, the definition:

```
C cobj;
```

will cause the application of the constructors A(), B() and C() to cobj *in that order*. When we leave the scope of the definition of cobj, the destructors ~C(), ~B(), ~A() will be applied to cobj *in that order*. Be aware of the fact that these guidelines were not part of earlier C++ language standards and may not be implemented correctly on all compilers.

Let us now turn our attention to the remaining `IntObj` class member functions. The implementations are shown in Figure 2–9. Note that all the "ubiquitous functions," `display`, the comparison operators, `read_in`, `file_in`, and `file_out`, introduced by the class `Element` are polymorphically redefined here. On the other hand, the function `Element::get_class` is not polymorphically redefined here. This is because the correct implementation of `get_class` for class `IntObj` is identical to its implementation in the class `Element`. Finally, note that two new `virtual` functions, `get_val` and `set_val`, have been added:. These have been declared `virtual` to allow for the possibility that we might want to implement subclasses of `IntObj`. For, example, we might want to implement a class `VeryLongIntObj` that will support extra long integer values.

---

1. One of the Professor class constructors discussed later in the chapter will illustrate how one can override this default.

```
//
// display
//


// Function:      IntObj::display()
// Purpose:       To display a representation of the receiver
//                at the computer screen
// Pre:           value = anInt and output = oldStuff
// Post:          output = oldStuff anInt \n
void IntObj::display()
{
   cout << value << endl;
}  // end IntObj::display()



//
// convert to and from standard int
//


// Function:      IntObj::get_val()
// Purpose:       To return the value of the receiver as an
//                integer
// Pre:           value = anInt
// Post:          get_val = anInt
int IntObj::get_val()
{
   return value;
}  // end IntObj::get_val()



// Function:      IntObj::set_val(an_int)
// Purpose:       To set the receiver's value to an_int
// Pre:           an_int = anInt
// Post:          value = anInt
void IntObj::set_val(int an_int)
{
   value = an_int;
}  // end IntObj::set_val()



//
// comparison operators
//


// Operator:      IntObj::==(e)
// Purpose:       Returns true if receiver and *eptr are
//                value equal. ASSUMES *eptr IS AN IntObj.
// Pre:           e.get_class() = "IntObj" and
//                e.get_val() = firstInt
//                and value = secondInt
// Post:          ==() = (firstInt = secondInt)
int IntObj::operator ==(Element& e)
{
```

```
        return (value == ((IntObj&) e).get_val( ));
}   // end IntObj::operator ==



//
// file in / file out
//


// Function:        IntObj::file_in(in_file)
// Purpose:         To read in a value for the receiver from a
//                  text file, in_file.  This function assumes
//                  that the line containing the class string has
//                  already been read in.
// Pre:             in_file = anInt restOfFile
// Post:            in_file = restOfFile and value = anInt
void IntObj::file_in(ifstream& in_file)
{
    in_file >> value;
    in_file.ignore(LINESIZE, '\n');
}   // end IntObj::file_in()


// Function:        IntObj::file_out(out_file)
// Purpose:         To write out a representation of the receiver
//                  to a text file, out_file.
// Pre:             out_file = oldStuff and my_class = "IntObj"
//                     and value = anInt
// Post:            (oldStuff != "" and out_file = oldStuff
//                     \n "IntObj" \n anInt) or
//                  (oldStuff = "" and out_file = oldStuff
//                     "IntObj" \n anInt)
void IntObj::file_out(ofstream& out_file)
{
    if (out_file.tellp())
    {
    // this is not first object in file
    // need to advance to new line
    out_file << endl;
    }
    out_file << my_class << endl;
    out_file << value;
}   // end IntObj::file_out()
```

FIGURE 2–9 Implementation of `IntObj` ubiquitous member functions.

As you can see, these functions are very simple and many of them, e.g., get_val and set_val, could have been declared `inline`. This is not unusual in an object-oriented design. Note that when we display an `IntObj`, we do not display the value of `my_class`, but just the value of the data member, `value`. In Figure 2–9, we have shown the implementation for the == comparison operator only. The other comparison operators are implemented similarly. The function `file_in` reads in an integer value from a text file and uses that to set the `value` data member of the receiver object. The function `file_out` writes out a representation of the receiver (including a string that identifies its class) to a file. The detailed reasoning behind the design of `file_in` and `file_out` will be clarified in a later section.

EXERCISES

2–1 Provide implementations for one or more of the other standard classes: `StringObj`, `CharObj`, and `FloatObj`.

2–2 Consider the enumerated type `veggie`:

```
enum veggie {carrot, onion, broccoli, spinach, kale};
```

Implement a class `VeggieObj` that will allow users to store values of type `veggie` as objects. The class declaration for `VeggieObj` is given below.

```
class VeggieObj : public Element
{
    protected:
        // DATA MEMBER ...
        veggie value;

    public:
        // MEMBER FUNCTIONS ...
        // constructors / destructor
        inline VeggieObj(veggie);
        inline VeggieObj();
        inline virtual ~VeggieObj();

        // display
        virtual void display();

        // read in
        virtual void read_in();

        // convert to and from a veggie
        inline virtual veggie get_val();
        inline virtual void set_val(veggie);

        // file in - file out
        virtual void file_in(ifstream&);
        virtual void file_out(ofstream&);
};    // end class VeggieObj
```

2–3 This exercise extends the original declaration for the class `VeggieObj` introduced in exercise 2–2 to include a new member function whose prototype is:

```
int is_green_veggie();
```

This function returns 1 if the receiver veggie is green and 0 if the receiver veggie is not green.

(For readers who do not eat their veggies, carrots are orange, onions are yellow, broccoli, spinach, and kale are green.)

POINTERS AND DYNAMIC OBJECTS

In most applications, objects are declared as *dynamic objects*. This was not the case in our first object-oriented program, `ObjSearcher`. Heterogeneous data structures depend heavily upon the properties of dynamic objects.

Recall that `FloatObj` (as well as `CharObj` and `StringObj`) has declarations analogous to those of `IntObj` discussed just above. Consider the following sketch of a function definition:

```
void do_whatever()
{
    // LOCAL DATA ...
    FloatObj   r(3.5);

    // STATEMENTS ...
    .....   // whatever
}   // end do_whatever
```

Consider the following question: When is memory allocated for the object `r` that is defined in this function?

The answer is that the memory for the object `r` is allocated at program execution (run) time, when the function `do_whatever` is *called*. This is also the point in time at which the constructor `FloatObj(float)` is applied to `r`. The memory allocated for `r` is deallocated when the function `do_whatever` is finished executing. Before the memory is deallocated, the destructor `~FloatObj` is applied to `r`. This memory allocation strategy is called *automatic* storage allocation and the variable `r` is called an *automatic variable*. The memory for all local variables defined within a function is allocated in this manner (unless that variable is specifically declared `static`, in which case memory is allocated at compile time). The C++ run time system handles the allocation and deallocation of automatic variables.

It is often desirable for the programmer to have control of memory allocation. This is the key concept behind *dynamic objects* and *dynamic storage allocation*. Dynamic objects are allocated and deallocated at run-time by means of programmed, explicit calls to the operators `new` and `delete`.

In order to create a dynamic object, one must define a pointer variable that can be used to point to that dynamic object. For example, in order to create a dynamic `FloatObj` object, one must declare a pointer variable whose base class is `FloatObj`; that is, one must declare a `FloatObj` pointer. The following statement defines a `FloatObj` pointer called `foptr`:

```
FloatObj *foptr;
```

This definition establishes the variable `foptr` as a pointer variable, whose base class is `FloatObj`. The value of `foptr` can be *the address* of any object that belongs to the class `FloatObj`. When `foptr` contains the address of a `FloatObj` object, we conceptualize it as pointing to that object. The variable `foptr` does not necessarily contain a valid address. For example, the above definition leaves `foptr` undefined. Another problem situation is one in which `foptr` contains the address of an object that has been deallocated. Care must be taken to assure that we use the value of `foptr` only when `foptr` is pointing to a valid object.

Consider the following definitions for the variables `foptr`, `flobj1` and `flobj2`:

```
FloatObj *foptr, flobj1, flobj2(3.5);
```

These variables are quite different. The variable `foptr` is a `FloatObj` pointer. The system will allocate enough space to store just one address (i.e., a pointer) and the value of `foptr` is left undefined. The variables `flobj1` and `flobj2`, on the other hand, are `FloatObj` objects. The system allocates enough space for one `FloatObj` object for each of these variables. The system applies the `FloatObj()` constructor to `flobj1` and the `FloatObj(float)` constructor to `flobj2`. This leaves the value of `flobj1` undefined and the value of `flobj2` is set to 3.5.

Pointer variables such as `foptr` can be used to create, manipulate and (ultimately) destroy dynamic objects. The creation, manipulation and destruction of a dynamic `FloatObj` object is illustrated in the following function:

```
void dynaexample()
{
    // LOCAL DATA ...
    FloatObj *foptr;

    // STATEMENTS ...
    foptr = new FloatObj(3.5);
    ....  // foptr now points to a dynamic FloatObj
    ....  // object whose value is 3.5
    cout << foptr -> get_val() << endl;
         // value contained within *foptr is displayed
    delete foptr;
         // dynamic object is destroyed
}
```

FIGURE 2–10   A function that creates, displays, and destroys a dynamic object.

The definition

```
FloatObj *foptr;
```

establishes `foptr` as a `FloatObj` pointer whose value is undefined. The assignment

```
    foptr = new FloatObj(3.5);
```

establishes `foptr` as a pointer to a dynamic `FloatObj` object. The new operator in this statement does the following:

- It allocates space for one `FloatObj` object in dynamic memory.

- It applies the constructor `FloatObj(float)` to that dynamic `FloatObj` object.

- It returns the address of that dynamic `FloatObj` object as its result.

The address that the `new` operator returns is stored in the variable `foptr`. The net result is that `foptr` is a pointer to a dynamic `FloatObj` object, as shown in Figure 2–11. Note that the value of the dynamic `FloatObj` object is 3.5 because of the application of the constructor `FloatObj(float)`.

The dynamic object that `foptr` points to (in Figure 2–11) has no name. For this reason, dynamic variables are sometimes called *anonymous variables*. A special area of memory, called the *heap*, is dedicated to dynamic storage allocation. At any point in time, a portion of the heap, called *free storage*, is available for the allocation of new dynamic objects. Whenever the `new` operator is applied, memory is taken from free storage and is allocated for the creation of one or more dynamic objects.[2]   This decreases the amount of free storage that is available. It is possible for insufficient free storage to remain to allow the `new` operator to create a dynamic object. If this is the case, the `new` operator returns the special pointer value `NULL`.   `NULL` is defined in the `stdlib.h` header file. `NULL` represents an address that could not possibly be the legal address of any variable, dynamic or otherwise.

One sends messages to a dynamic object *by indirection*. This is illustrated by the following statement from the function `dynaexample` of Figure 2–10.

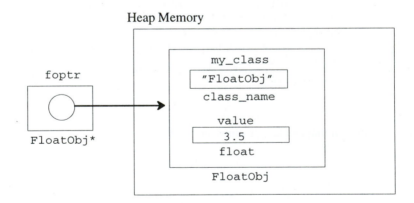

Heap Memory

FIGURE 2–11   The pointer variable `foptr` points to a dynamic object whose class is `FloatObj`.

---

2.   The `new` operator can be used to allocate arrays of objects. For example, a dynamically allocated array of 10 FloatObj objects can be created using:

```
foptr = new FloatObj[10];
```

The type of a dynamic variable need not be a class. For example, if str is declared as a `char*` variable, then one can dynamically allocate an array of 21 chars (i.e., a string) by means of

```
str = new char[21];
```

```
cout << foptr -> get_val() << endl;
```

This statement contains the expression `foptr -> get_val()`. This is a float valued expression that is computed by applying the function `get_val` to the object to which `foptr` points. In other words, we are sending the message `get_val` to an object indirectly by means of a pointer to that object. The indirection is encoded in the arrow (–>) operator. In general, if `ptr` is a pointer to an object that belongs to class `CL` and if `func` is a member function of `CL`, then the notation

```
ptr -> func()
```

always means "apply the function `CL::func` to the object that `ptr` points to."
The following notations are always equivalent:

```
ptr -> func()
*ptr.func()
```

The latter notation will help us to gain greater insight into the meaning of the arrow operator. The operator (*) is used to access the variable that a pointer variable points to. This is called dereferencing the pointer and * used in an expression preceding an identifier is the dereferencing operator. Thus, `*ptr` means the variable that `ptr` points to. Since we are assuming that `ptr` points to a `CL` object, the type of `*ptr` is `CL`. Thus, we can apply a member function, such as `CL::func`, to `*ptr` using the dot operator:

```
*ptr.func()
```

This pattern of dereferencing a pointer and then applying the dot operator to the dereferenced pointer is so common, that the arrow operator was introduced to allow this sequence to be captured by means of a single operator.
The `delete` operator returns memory to free storage that was allocated for a dynamic object. In the function `dynaexample` of Figure 2–10, the statement

```
delete foptr;
```

does the following:

- It applies the destructor `~FloatObj` to the object that `foptr` points to.

- It returns the memory occupied by the object `*foptr` to free storage.

After the application of the `delete` operator,[3] the `foptr` should not be used without assigning it a new valid value (perhaps by use of the `new` operator). This is because `foptr` is now pointing to an area of heap memory that has been returned to free storage. That area of memory can be utilized by some other function for the creation of new dynamic objects and variables.

---

3. If `new` were to be used to allocate an array, as in:
```
foptr = new FloatObj[10];
```
then the call to `delete` should have the form:
```
delete []foptr;
```

On the other hand, it is important to apply the `delete` operator before we leave the function `dynaexample`, because otherwise the memory for `foptr` will be deallocated (in the run-time stack memory because, as a local variable in a function, it is an automatic variable) without the memory for the object that it points to being deallocated (in heap memory). Assuming no other variable is pointing to that particular object, the result is wasted storage, since an object that is no longer needed takes up space that should have been returned to free storage.

Suppose `ptr1` and `ptr2` are declared as pointer variables (e.g., of type `FloatObj *`). Then, the assignment statement:

```
ptr1 = ptr2;
```

copies the address stored in `ptr2` into `ptr1`. It is important to realize that this assignment statement does not cause `ptr1` to point to a *copy* of the object that `ptr2` points to. Rather, *it causes ptr1 and ptr2 to point to the same object*.

Care must be taken, when using the `delete` operator with respect to one pointer variable, not to delete a dynamic object referenced by another pointer variable. For example, consider the following C++ statements:

```
FloatObj *ptr1, *ptr2;
ptr1 = new FloatObj(3.5);
ptr2 = ptr1;
      // ptr2 and ptr1 now both point to the same object
delete ptr2;
      // the object ptr1 points to is also being deleted
```

After the application of the `delete` operator to `ptr2`, the programmer must realize that `ptr1` is no longer pointing to a valid `FloatObj` object. The object that `ptr1` points to is the same object that `ptr2` was pointing to, and that object has been deallocated. If an attempt is made to dereference `ptr1` in any way, an error results. This kind of error is known as a *dangling reference*.

In summary, there are four basic things you need to know about programming with dynamic objects:

1. One creates a dynamic object with the `new` operator.
    e.g., `foptr = new FloatObj(3.5);`
2. One destroys a dynamic object with the delete operator.
    e.g., `delete foptr;`
3. One sends dynamic objects messages by indirection.
    e.g., `foptr -> set_val(3.56);`
4. The assignment statement, when used with pointer variables, copies pointers and not the objects that the pointers point to.

EXERCISES

2–4 Convert the following program, which uses standard float variables, into one that uses dynamic `FloatObj` objects exclusively:

```
#include <iostream.h>
```

```
void main()
{
    // LOCAL DATA ...
    float r1, r2, r3, sum;

    // STATEMENTS ...
    cout << "Please enter first value: ";
    cin  >> r1
    cout << "Please enter second value: ";
    cin  >> r2;
    cout << "Please enter third value: ";
    cin  >> r3;
    sum = r1 + r2 + r3;
    cout << endl
         << "Their sum is " << sum << endl;
}   // end main
```

2–5 Write a program that will read in the names and grades for students in a class in a sentinel loop. The program will display the name and grade for the student with the highest grade. Your program must represent all data in terms of dynamic objects (e.g., dynamic `StringObj` objects and dynamic `FloatObj` objects) instead of the standard types (`string` and `float`).

POINTERS AND ARRAYS

The preferred way to manipulate an array in C++ is by using pointers in lieu of indices. This is because every time the compiler encounters an expression such as `c[i]`, where `c` is an array and where `i` is an index, the compiler will generate code which will cause the system to compute the address of `c[i]` when the program executes. For example, consider the expression

```
c[i] > c[i+1]
```

that might occur in an implementation of a sorting algorithm. The compiler translates this into code which (among other things) computes the addresses of both `c[i]` and `c[i+1]`.

Let's examine this issue a bit further. Assume that the components of the array `c` are declared to be of type `T` (e.g., `T` might be `FloatObj` or just `float`). An array is stored in memory as a sequence of bytes. The name of the array, the symbol `c`, denotes the address of the first byte in the array. This address is called the base address of the array `c`. This notation has been chosen because *C++ views the name of an array, when used in an expression, as the base address of the array.* All of the components in an array require the same amount of storage. The C++ expression for the number of bytes occupied by one component of an array of type `T` is `sizeof(T)`. The `stdlib.h` header file provides the prototype for the `sizeof` function. The address of `c[i]` is given in Figure 2–12.

```
c + i * sizeof(T),   i = 0, 1, 2, ....
```

FIGURE 2–12   Expression used to compute address of ith element of an array of type T.

The compiler expands every reference to `c[i]` to machine code to perform that computation. Note that this computation involves one addition and one multiplication. A multiplication operation is more expensive (in terms of time) than an addition operation.

Consider the following loop for displaying n elements stored in the array `c` as shown in Figure 2–13.

```
for (int i = 0; i < n;
i++)
    cout << c[i] <<
endl;
```

FIGURE 2–13   C++ code for displaying the elements on an array using subscript notation.

The compiler might translate the above `for` loop into object code with logic corresponding to the following pseudo-code:

```
// PSEUDO-CODE !!!
for (int i = 0; i < n; i++)
{
    register = c + i * sizeof(T);
    cout << *register << endl;
}
```

This logic implies that each time through the loop, the compiler will compute the address of `c[i]` using the expression of Figure 2–12 given earlier.   This requires n multiplication operations.

A more efficient approach would be to initialize a pointer variable to the base address of the array and then to add `sizeof(T)` to that pointer variable each time through the loop. This would obviate the need for the n relatively expensive multiplication operations.   The pseudo-code might look like this:

```
// PSEUDO-CODE !!!
T *ptr = c;   // initialize ptr to base address of c
for (; ptr < last address in array c; ptr = ptr + sizeof(T))
    cout << *ptr << endl;
```

In fact, C++ allows us to accomplish this, but in a straightforward and elegant manner. C++ supports pointer comparisons and pointer arithmetic. Suppose `ptr1` and `ptr2` are pointer variables. Then, `ptr1 == ptr2` is 1 (or, true) if and only if `ptr1` and `ptr2` contain the same address. Similarly, `ptr1 < ptr2` is 1 (or, true) if and only if the address of `ptr1` is less than the address of `ptr2`. In particular, if `ptr1` points to `c[i]` and `ptr2` points to `c[j]` then `ptr1 < ptr2` if and only if `i < j`.

Pointer arithmetic in C++ is very powerful. Suppose `ptr` is a pointer variable whose type is `T*`. Then, the compiler views the expression

```
ptr + i
```

as actually meaning

```
ptr + i * sizeof(T)
```

Does this look familiar? The beauty of pointer arithmetic in C++ is that the programmer need not explicitly specify the `sizeof` function. This interpretation of the plus (+) operator for pointers is extended in a consistent manner for the operators –, — and ++. Thus, suppose `ptr` points to an array component, `c[i]`. Then,

```
ptr++
```

is interpreted as meaning "add `sizeof(T)` to `ptr`." Consequently, `ptr` will be changed to point to `c[i+1]`. *Incrementing a pointer variable that points into an array is the same as advancing one position forward in that array.*

Recall that whenever the name of an array is used in an expression, the array name is interpreted as the base address of the array. Suppose the array c contains n components. Then, the address of the last component is given by the expression `c + n - 1`. In particular, if `ptr` is a pointer into the array c that contains n components, then `ptr` is pointing to a valid component of c so long as `ptr >= c` and `ptr < c + n`. In other words, if we are advancing through the array c and `ptr` equals `c + n`, then `ptr` is no longer pointing to a valid data component.

Consequently, the following C++ code will allow us to display the n elements in the array c whose component type is T in a manner which will allow the compiler to generate very efficient object code:

```
T *ptr = c;  // initialize ptr to base address of c
for (; ptr < c + n; ptr++)
   cout << *ptr << endl;
```

This code works as follows: We initialize the pointer variable `ptr` to the base address of c. So long as `ptr < c + n`, the value of `*ptr` is displayed (assuming that the `<<` operator will accept an argument of type T). `ptr` is then incremented using `ptr++`. Recall that this expands to:

```
ptr = ptr + sizeof(T)
```

which does not require the expensive multiplication operation. In other words, this code requires n fewer multiplication operations than a straightforward compilation of the code with upon array indexing given in Figure 2–13.

You might be wondering whether it was worth it to devote so much effort to getting rid of those n multiplication operations. There are situations in which it is very important to improve the efficiency of a program. This is especially true when a particular section of code (e.g., a particular function) is consuming an inordinate amount of time or space (relative to other functions). Later in this text you will study the *complexity of algorithms*, which includes the formal study of such problems.   For the time being, let us just say that professional C++ programmers almost always use pointers in lieu of indices in manipulating arrays. It is considered the efficient and professional way of handling arrays in C++.

The Section Class Revisited

In Chapter 1 we presented the ObjSearcher program that included a class, Section. A Section object represented a section of a class taught by a particular professor. A Section object contains an array of Student objects. We shall now present alternative implementations for the Section class member functions add_student, compute_averages and sort_by_name. These new implementations use pointers instead of indices. You should compare them with the versions given in the corresponding sections, Figures 1–5, 1–4, and 1–6, respectively, of Chapter 1.

The function Section::add_student   The C++ code of Figure 2–14 that follows implements the Section::add_student function using pointers. The expressions involving pointers are shown in **boldface** for emphasis.

```
// Function:Section::add_student(astudent)
// Purpose: To add astudent to the receiver section.
// Pre:     class_size = n and N < MAXCLASS
// Post:    c[N] = astudent and class_size = old(class_size) + 1

void Section::add_student(Student astudent)
{
    // LOCAL DATA ...
    Student *stuptr = c + class_size;


    // STATEMENTS ...
    *stuptr = astudent;
    class_size++;
}   // end Section::add_student
```

FIGURE 2–14   C++ implementation of Section::add_student using pointers.

The pointer variable, stuptr, is initialized to c + class_size. This sets stuptr so that it points to the location in the array c where the next Student object belongs. The assignment

```
    *stuptr = astudent;
```

can be read as "assign the values stored in the data members of astudent to the data members of the object that stuptr points to."

The function Section::compute_averages   The function Section::compute_averages in Figure 2–15 shows the most typical for loop pattern for traversing an array using pointers. Again, expressions using pointers are in **boldface** to draw them to your attention.

```
// function:  Section::compute_averages()
// Purpose:   To update each Student object in the
//            receiver by computing its final average
// Define:    the notation c[i].Student::compute_average()
//            means that the function compute_average()
//            has been applied to the Student c[i].
//            This implies that the post condition for
//            Student::compute_average() applies.
// Pre:       for i in [0..class_size-1] :
//                (c[i].first_hourly, c[i].second_hourly,
//                 c[i].final_exam are defined)
// Post       for i in [0..class_size-1] :
//                c[i].Student::compute_average()

void Section::compute_averages()
{
    // LOCAL DATA ...
    Student *stuptr = c;


    // STATEMENTS ...
    for (; stuptr < c + class_size; stuptr++)
    {
        stuptr -> compute_average();
    }
}   // end Section::compute_averages()
```

FIGURE 2–15   C++ implementation of Section::compute_averages using pointers.

The pointer stuptr is initialized to the base address of c. The program loops as long as stuptr < c + class_size, and stuptr is incremented using stuptr++. Within the loop, the Student::compute_average function is applied to the object that stuptr points to.

The function Section:sort_by_name   The function Section::sort_by_name, shown in Figure 2–16, performs a bubblesort of the array c that is contained within a Section object. Again, the expressions with pointers are shown in **boldface** for emphasis.

```
// Function:  Section::sort_by_name()
// Purpose:   To sort the receiver collection of Student objects
//            in ascending order by name.  Uses bubblesort.
// Pre:     class_size >= 0 and for all i in [0..class_size-1] :
//              c[i].student_name is defined
// Post:    c is a permutation of old(c) and
//              for all i in [0..class_size-2] :
//                  c[i].student_name <= c[i+1].student_name

void Section::sort_by_name()
```

```
{
    // LOCAL DATA ...
    Student *stuptr;
    enum {false, true} done = false;
    Student tstudent;
    int limit = class_size - 1;



    // STATEMENTS ...
    // outer loop:
    for (int pass = 1; !done && (pass <= limit); pass++)
    {
        done = true;
        stuptr = c;
        // inner loop:
        for (; stuptr < (c + class_size - pass); stuptr++)
        {
            if (strcmp(stuptr -> get_name(),
                (stuptr + 1) -> get_name()) > 0)
            {
                tstudent  = *stuptr;
                *stuptr   = *(stuptr + 1);
                *(stuptr + 1) = tstudent;
                done = false;
            }
        } // end inner loop
    } // end outer loop
} // end sort_by_name()
```

FIGURE 2–16 C++ implementation of `Section::sort_by_name` using pointers.

The pointer variable `stuptr` is not initialized where it is defined. Instead, it is reset to the base address of the array in the inner loop, since the inner loop involves performing a traversal of part of the array. We continue a traversal so long as `stuptr < (c + class_size - pass)`, the variable `pass` being a factor since with each successive pass we need to look at one fewer array components. We advance through the array by incrementing `stuptr`. The variable `stuptr` points to the first of the two `Student` objects involved in the bubblesort comparison. The expression `stuptr + 1` is the address of the next `Student` object. Consequently, the call to `strcmp` involves the comparison of `stuptr -> get_name()` against `(stuptr + 1) -> get_name()`. The swapping process involves swapping the `Student` object that `stuptr` points to and the `Student` object that `(stuptr + 1)` points to.

HETEROGENEOUS DATA STRUCTURES AND TRUE POLYMORPHISM

We can now explore the full power of object-oriented programming by developing a truly heterogeneous data structure: a set of elements. Recall from mathematics the following definition:

Definition   A *set* is a collection of elements in which no two elements are identical. The elements in a set are not generally presumed to be ordered or indexed in any way.

Computer scientists usually characterize a set as a data structure with certain associated operations. In order to keep the discussion as simple as possible, we ignore many of the familiar set operations (unions, intersections, set differences and so forth) and focus on a rather simple-minded characterization. We could, of course, implement those operations to obtain a more complete representation of sets.

The class declaration for a simple-minded set data structure is given in Figure 2–17.

```
const int CAPACITY = 100;


class ElementSet
{
    protected:
        // DATA MEMBERS ...
        ElementPtr s[CAPACITY];
        int current;  // index of current ElementPtr
        int size;


    public:
        // MEMBER FUNCTIONS ...
        // constructor - destructor
        inline ElementSet();
        inline virtual ~ElementSet();


        // test
        int is_member_of(ElementPtr);
        int cardinality();
        inline int is_full();
        inline int is_empty();


        // access
        ElementPtr get_any();


        // modify
        virtual int add(ElementPtr);
        void clear();


        // display
        virtual void display();
};   // end class ElementSet
```

FIGURE 2–17   Class declaration for a simple set data structure.

The data member s represents a set using an array of `Element` pointers. The type `ElementPtr` was declared using the following `typedef` statement in the `elements.h` file:

```
typedef Element* ElementPtr;
```

The declaration of s in Figure 2–17 restricts our sets to CAPACITY (100) elements. The data member `size` stores the number of elements in the set at any time. The data member `current` is an index that indicates the current element in the set. This value is manipulated by the function `get_any` to return a pointer to the current object in the set. At any given time, the objects in a set are the objects that the pointers `s[0]`, `s[1]`, ... , and `s[size - 1]` reference.

The constructor, `ElementSet()`, sets up an empty set (`size = 0`). The `is_member_of` member function is used to test whether a given object (whose *address* is passed as an argument) is a member of the receiver set. Here we are using the set-theoretical notion of "membership." The `cardinality` member function is used to return the cardinality of the receiver set (i.e., the number of elements it contains). The `is_full` member function is used to test whether the receiver set is full (i.e., contains CAPACITY elements). The `is_empty` member function is used to test whether the receiver set is empty. The `get_any` member function returns a pointer to the current object in the set and updates the value of `current`. This function is our only means of retrieving individual objects once they have been added to an `ElementSet`. The `add` member function is used to add a new element to an `ElementSet`. The `add` function returns 1 if the attempt to add a new element succeeds and 0 otherwise. The attempt to add a new element will fail if the receiver set is full or if the proposed new element is already in the set. The `clear` member function resets the receiver set to an empty set, deallocating all the objects that were added to the set.

The ElementSet class implements a heterogeneous set. What enables heterogeneity is the use of the type `ElementPtr`. The array s is an array of `Element` *pointers* and many of the functions have `Element` pointers as parameters. This is significant because `Element` pointers are intrinsically polymorphic. This means that an `Element` pointer can point to any kind of element.

Since the component type of the array s is `ElementPtr`, the array components, `s[i]`, are *polymorphic*. This means that type of the object `*s[i]` (for a particular i) cannot be determined without additional information. The type of `*s[i]` might be `IntObj` or `FloatObj` or some other type in the hierarchy of `Element` classes given in Figure 2–2. Furthermore, the type of `*s[i]` can change from moment to moment. The compiler views `s[i]` as being of type `ElementPtr` for the purposes of compile-time type checking, but it is possible to dynamically force `s[i]` to point to a `FloatObj` or an `IntObj` or a `Student` (we shall introduce the element class `Student` later in this chapter), as will be the case if the following statements were to be executed at various points in time:

```
s[i] = new FloatObj;
s[i] = new IntObj;
s[i] = new Student;
```

Again, s[i] is permitted to point to any kind of object in the hierarchy of element classes. This is related to the root meaning of "polymorphism": polymorphic objects are permitted to take a variety of forms.

You might be wondering why the functions add and display in Figure 2–17 are declared virtual while most of the other functions are not. This is because it is our intention to define subclasses that are specialized versions of ElementSet. These subclasses might need to redefine the functions add and display, but it is very unlikely that they will need to redefine any of the other functions. We should also mention that, insofar as declaring functions virtual is concerned, collection classes (classes that consist of collections of objects, such as ElementSet) are treated differently from element classes (classes that provide individual objects for heterogeneous data structures). Almost all functions in an element class should be declared virtual. This is important for enabling *true polymorphism*, a concept to be discussed below. Unfortunately, "polymorphism" has several distinct meanings in object-oriented programming. We use the term *true polymorphism* to refer to the polymorphism of function calls, that is , calls to a single function name can refer to different function implementations depending upon the class of the receiver. This is distinct from the polymorphism of objects, as described in the previous paragraph.

We shall now discuss the implementations of the ElementSet member functions.

The constructor ElementSet   What is noteworthy here is that the ElementSet constructor, in contrast to the Section constructor (Figure 1.d) discussed in Chapter 1, does not cause the automatic application of any constructor to the individual array components, s[i]. This is because s, unlike the array c of the Section class example, is not an array of objects; it is an array of pointers. The implementation is shown in Figure 2–18.

```
// Constructor: ElementSet::ElementSet()
// Purpose:     To initialize the receiver set
// Pre:         None
// Post:        size = 0 and current = -1
ElementSet::ElementSet()
{
   size = 0;
   current = -1;
}  // end ElementSet::ElementSet()
```

FIGURE 2–18   C++ implementation of the constructor ElementSet.

The destructor ~ElementSet   This destructor applies the delete operator to each pointer in the array s that points to a dynamic object. The implementation is given in Figure 2–19. *Note that the pointer variable,* ptr, *that is used to traverse the array,* s, *is a pointer to an Element pointer!* Pointers to Element pointers are required in several of the ElementSet member functions because the array s is an array of pointers and to manipulate that array using pointers requires pointers to those pointers. Thus, ptr is defined as follows:

```
ElementPtr *ptr = s;
```

Thus, ptr is a pointer to an ElementPtr and it is appropriately initialized to the base address of s, *which is the address of an Element pointer.* The application of delete in this function is to *ptr and not to ptr because delete ptr would mean delete the thing that ptr points to, but ptr points to one of the array elements, s[i], and these cannot be deleted because they were not dynamically allocated.

```
// Destructor:  ElementSet::~ElementSet()
// Purpose:     To destroy the receiver set, deallocating
//              memory for all of its elements
// Pre:         size = N
// Post:        for all i in [0..N-1] : *s[i] has
//              been deallocated
ElementSet::~ElementSet()
{
    // LOCAL DATA ...
    ElementPtr *ptr = s;


    // STATEMENTS ...
    for (; ptr < s + size; ptr++)
    {
        delete *ptr;
    }
}   // end ElementSet::~ElementSet()
```

FIGURE 2–19   C++ implementation of the destructor, ~ElementSet.

The function ElementSet::is_member_of   The function is_member_of returns 1 if its argument (eptr) points to a member of the receiver set and 0 otherwise. The implementation is given in Figure 2–20.

```
// Function:  ElementSet::is_member_of(eptr)
// Purpose:   To test whether *eptr is already in the
//            receiver set. Returns 1 if *eptr is
//            in set and 0 otherwise.  Uses value
//            identity to determine set membership.
// Pre:       size = N and *eptr is initialized.
// Post:      (for all i in [1..N] : *s[i-1] != *eptr
//            and is_member_of = 0) or
//            (there exists i in [1..N] : *s[i-1] = *eptr
```

```
//            and is_member_of = 1)
int ElementSet::is_member_of(ElementPtr eptr)
{
    // LOCAL DATA ...
    ElementPtr *ptr = s;
    class_name eptr_class;    // class *eptr belongs to
    class_name set_class;     // class current set element
                // belongs to


    // STATEMENTS ...
    // Get class of *eptr
    strcpy(eptr_class, eptr -> get_class());


    // search for element equal to *eptr
    for (; ptr < s + size; ptr++)
    {
        // Get class of current set element
        strcpy(set_class, (*ptr) -> get_class());
        if (!strcmp(eptr_class, set_class))
        {
        // belong to same class; can compare using ==
        if ( **ptr == *eptr) // == requires object arg
        {
            return 1;
        }
        }
    }  // end for


    // match not found
    return 0;
}  // end ElementSet::is_member_of()
```

FIGURE 2–20   C++ implementation of `ElementSet::is_member_of`.

The argument `eptr` in this function is polymorphic.   That is, `eptr` may point to any kind of element. Thus, this function can be called with actual arguments of a variety of pointer types, including `FloatObj*`, `IntObj*` and `StringObj*`.   This function, of course, requires some notion of equality of objects.   That is, in order to determine whether e is a member of a set of objects $\{e_1, e_2, ..., e_n\}$ we need some concept of equality so that we can decide whether an object, e, is equal to another object, e_i, for each i.   The concept used here is called *value identity* because we check whether the contents of the `value` data members of the two objects are equal.   This is facilitated by the use of the overloaded operator, `==`, as shown in the comparison statement

```
        if ( **ptr == *eptr)
```

of Figure 2–20.   An example implementation of the overloaded operator, `==`, was shown earlier in Figure 2–9 for `IntObj` objects. Similar implementations apply in the member functions associated with the other `Element` classes. (Remember, the variable `ptr` is a pointer to an `ElementPtr` and thus needs to be dereferenced twice before being compared to the value of `eptr`.)

The `ElementSet` functions `cardinality`, `is_full` and `is_empty` These functions, given in Figures 2–21, 2–22, and 2–23, are straightforward and require no explanation.

```
// Function:  ElementSet::cardinality()
// Purpose:   Returns the number of elements in the
//            receiver set.
// Pre:       size = N
// Post:      cardinality = N
int ElementSet::cardinality()
{
    return size;
}   // end ElementSet::cardinality()
```

FIGURE 2–21 C++ implementation of `ElementSet::cardinality`.

```
// Function:  ElementSet::is_full()
// Purpose:   Returns 1 if the receiver set is full
//            and 0 otherwise.
// Pre:       size is defined
// Post:      (size = CAPACITY and is_full = 1)
//            or (size < CAPACITY and is_full = 0)
int ElementSet::is_full()
{
    return (size == CAPACITY);
}   // end ElementSet::is_full()
```

FIGURE 2–22 C++ implementation of `ElementSet::is_full`.

```
// Function:  ElementSet::is_empty()
// Purpose:   Returns 1 if the receiver set is empty
//            and 0 otherwise.
// Pre:       size is defined
// Post       (size = 0 and is_empty = 1)
//            or (size > 0 and is_empty = 0)
int ElementSet::is_empty()
{
    return (!size);
}   // end ElementSet::is_empty()
```

FIGURE 2–23 C++ implementation of `ElementSet::is_empty`.

The function ElementSet::get_any   This function returns a pointer to the current element in the receiver set. It also manipulates the data member current. The implementation appears in Figure 2–24. If the receiver set is empty, then current will be 0, and get_any will return the value NULL (the pointer value that cannot point to anything). If the receiver set is nonempty, then the pointer stored in s[current] is returned and then the value of current updated. The data member current cycles if current is already at the "end" of the set.

```
// Function:  ElementSet::get_any()
// Purpose:   Returns a pointer to the current element
//            in the receiver set and advances current
//            to next element.
// Pre:       size = N and current = P
// Post:      (P = -1 and get_any = NULL)
//            or
//            (P >= 0 and P < size - 1
//            and get_any = s[P] and current = old(P) + 1)
//            or
//            (P >= 0 and P = size - 1
//            and get_any = s[P] and current = 0)
ElementPtr ElementSet::get_any()
{
    // LOCAL DATA ...
    ElementPtr ptr;


    // return NULL if current was never set
    if (current == -1)
    {
        return NULL;
    }


    // current was previously set
    ptr = s[current];
    if (current == size - 1)
    {
        // at end; reset to beginning
        current = 0;
    }
    else
    {
        // not at end; advance to next
        current++;
    }
    return ptr;
}   // end ElementSet::get_any()
```

FIGURE 2–24   C++ implementation of ElementSet::get_any.

The function ElementSet::clear   Like the destructor, ~ElementSet, this function returns all of the objects included in the receiver ElementSet to

free storage. In addition, the function `clear` resets `size` to 0 and `current` to
−1. The details are in Figure 2–25.

```
// Function:  ElementSet::clear()
// Purpose:   To reset the receiver set to the empty set,
//            deallocating all objects the set contains.
// Pre:       size = N
// Post:      for all in in [1..N] : s[i-1] is deleted
//            and size = 0 and current = -1
void ElementSet::clear()
{
    // LOCAL DATA ...
    ElementPtr *ptr = s;


    // STATEMENTS ...
    for (; ptr < s + size; ptr++)
    {
        delete *ptr;
    }
    size = 0;
    current = -1;
}   // end ElementSet::clear()
```

FIGURE 2–25   C++ implementation of `ElementSet::clear`.

The function `ElementSet::add`   The C++ implementation of the member function, add, is shown in Figure 2–26. The argument `eptr` is polymorphic. This has the consequence that *this function can add any kind of dynamic
object to the receiver set so long as that dynamic object is a member of the
class `Element` or any of its subclasses.*   In some sense, the add function is
what makes the class `ElementSet` able to represent a heterogeneous data
structure.

The function add returns 1 if it succeeds and 0 if it fails. The function fails
if either the set is full to `capacity` or if the object that `eptr` points to is already in the set (based upon the object identity test).

```
// Function:  ElementSet::add(eptr)
// Purpose:   To add the element eptr points to to the receiver
//            set.  This function returns 1 if add succeeds
//            and 0 if add fails.  Add will fail if receiver
//            set is already full or if *eptr is a duplicate
//            element.  This function will set current to 0
//            if current was never set.
// Pre:       size = N and *eptr is intialized
// Post:      (N = 0 and size = 1 and s[0] = eptr and
//            current = 0 and add = 1)
//            or
//            (N = CAPACITY and size = old(size) and add = 0)
//            or
//            (N > 0 and there exists i in [1..N] :
```

```
//              *s[i-1] = *eptr and size = old(size) and add = 0)
//              or
//              (N > 0 and for all i in [1..N] : *s[i-1] != *eptr
//              and size = old(size) + 1 and s[size] = eptr
//              and add = 1)
int ElementSet::add(ElementPtr eptr)
{
    // LOCAL DATA ...
    ElementPtr *ptr = s;


    // STATEMENTS ...
    // check if receiver is already full
    if (this -> is_full())
    {
        return 0;    // set already full
    }


    // not full; check if *eptr is already in set
    if (this -> is_member_of(eptr))
    {
        return 0;       // duplicate; already in set
    }


    // not full; not duplicate.
    // insert
    ptr = s + size;   // set pointer to end
    *ptr = eptr;
    size++;
    // set current if this is first element
    if (size == 1) current = 0;
    return 1;   // success flag
}   // end ElementSet::add()
```

FIGURE 2–26   C++ implementation of `ElementSet::add`.

The first thing that this function does is to check whether the receiver set is full (`this -> is_full()`). If this is true, the function exits with the value 0 without adding `*eptr` (i.e., the object that `eptr` points to) to the receiver set. If the receiver is not full, a search is performed in order to determine whether `*eptr` is already in the set. If `*eptr` is already in the set, we exit the function with the value 0 without adding `*eptr` to the set. Otherwise, we add `*eptr` to the receiver (by storing the value of `eptr` in the array `s`). Note that we need to set `current` to 0 if `*eptr` is the first element in the receiver set.

True Polymorphism: The function `ElementSet::display()` The simplicity of this function is striking. As shown in Figure 2–27, an Element-Set object displays itself by broadcasting the `display()` message to each of its constituent objects (i.e., all of the dynamic objects in the set). In broadcasting the `display()` message to each constituent object in the receiver set, this function is demonstrating what is called *true polymorphism*.

```
// Function:  ElementSet::display()
// Purpose:   To display each of the elements in the
//            receiver set.
// Pre:       size = N
// Post:      for all in in [1..N] : s[i-1] -> display()
void ElementSet::display()
{
    // LOCAL DATA ...
    ElementPtr *ptr = s;


    // STATEMENTS ...
    for (; ptr < s + size; ptr++)
    {
        (*ptr) -> display();
    }
}   // end ElementSet::display()
```

FIGURE 2–27   C++ implementation of `ElementSet::display`.

True polymorphism occurs when a polymorphic object[4] possesses (or, behaves as if it possesses) the power to select the appropriate implementation for a message that it receives.   Stated differently, true polymorphism means that when we apply a function to a polymorphic object, that object can dynamically select the appropriate definition for that function.   This is a subtle concept that is related to the need for `virtual` functions in our class declarations.

Suppose `sptr` is a polymorphic object and that `sptr` could point to any object that belongs to a set of classes {`C1`, `C2`, ... , `CN`} where `C1` is the root class of a hierarchy in which the other classes participate. Suppose further that *each* of the classes has a `virtual void` member function declared:

```
virtual void display();
```

The fact that these functions are declared `virtual` is highly significant. Consider the following code:

```
sptr -> display()
```

Since `sptr` is polymorphic, which function is being called? Are we calling `C1::display`, `C2::display`, ..., or `CN::display`?

Obviously, if `sptr` points to an object of the class `Cj`, we would like to call `Cj::display`. However, since `sptr` is polymorphic, the type of object that `sptr` points to is determined dynamically (i.e., during the execution of the program) and can change dynamically! In other words, *it should now be clear that the compiler, which processes the program before execution time, cannot possi-*

---

4.   Recall that the array components, s[i], are polymorphic.

bly know which of the N display functions is the correct function because the compiler cannot possibly know what kind of object sptr *will point to at any given point during the program's execution!* Consequently, C++ must provide some kind of run-time (i.e., dynamic) binding of function calls to function implementations. Virtual functions allow for this kind of *deferred binding*.

Deferred binding is an important concept in object-oriented languages and it is a fundamental key to the power of the object-oriented paradigm. Deferred binding means that function calls are bound to object code (i.e., compiled function implementations) dynamically, at execution time. Deferred binding is accomplished by means of virtual functions and a construct called a *virtual functions table (VFT)*. The VFT is a system internal table that is not visible to the programmer. However, understanding that the VFT exists can help in understanding true polymorphism.

Each class has a virtual functions table which contains the name of each virtual function for that class as well as a pointer to the compiled code for that function. Thus, each of the N classes above has a virtual functions table that includes an entry for the function display and a pointer to the compiled code for the display function for that class. Every object is tied in to the VFT for its class. When the compiler encounters the statement:

```
sptr -> display();
```

it checks to see if display is a function for the class C1 (the root class). This is because the compiler sees sptr (our polymorphic object) as a C1 pointer. So long as display is a function at that level in the hierarchy, the compiler is satisfied. Next, the compiler checks to see whether display is declared virtual or static (the latter being the default). If display is static, then the compiler views this as a call to C1::display. There is no opportunity for true polymorphism since the decision as to which version of display is intended was determined statically (i.e., at compile-time). If display is declared virtual at the C1 level (in the hierarchy), then the compiler takes a different approach. The compiler generates code that will enable the dynamic (run-time) determination of which function is intended. Instead of generating object code for a particular implementation of display, the compiler generates object code that will cause a run-time search of the appropriate VFT for the implementation of display corresponding to the class of the receiver object. In other words, the generated object code will say: *Determine the class that* *sptr *belongs to and retrieve the virtual functions table for that class. Search the VFT for the function* display. *If found, follow the pointer in the virtual functions table to the object code that will get executed.* The compiler sets up the code searching the VFT and transferring control to the appropriate function at compile-time, but the determination of the particular object code (i.e., that which corresponds to the proper implementation of the named function) to execute occurs dynamically, at run-time. Note that this setup (by the compiler) allows the object *sptr to behave as if it can *select* its own implementation for the message that it has received (i.e., display()). In short, this setup enables true polymorphism.

We have seen three distinct uses for the term polymorphism in this chapter. In summary these are:

- The polymorphic redefinition of a function in a class hierarchy.

- The polymorphism of objects, which enables a given pointer variable to point to objects of a variety of types.

- True polymorphism, in which a polymorphic object can dynamically select the interpretation for a message that it receives.

EXERCISES

2–6 Extend the declaration of `ElementSet` to include a new member function, `is_subset_of`, whose prototype is:

```
int is_subset_of(ElementSet&);
```

This function will return 1 (true) if every object in the receiver is also contained in the argument `ElementSet`, and 0 (false) otherwise.

2–7 Assume a type `ElementSetPtr` declared as follows:

```
typedef ElementSet* ElementSetPtr;
```

Implement the function `is_subset_of` described in the previous exercise using the following prototype in lieu of the original one:

```
int is_subset_of(ElementSetPtr);
```

2–8 Extend the `ElementSet` class declaration to include a function, `union_with`, whose prototype is:

```
int union_with(ElementSet& first, ElementSet& second);
```

This function should compute the union of the receiver `ElementSet` with the first argument, the `ElementSet` `first`, returning this result via the second argument, the `ElementSet` `second`. The function `union_with` returns 1 if the union was computed successfully and 0 if the union "overflows" because the value of:

```
this -> cardinality()  +  first.cardinality()
```

exceeds `CAPACITY`. Note that the union of the two sets should not contain any duplicate objects.

2–9 Implement the function `union_with` as a stand-alone function whose prototype is:

```
int union_with(ElementSet& first, ElementSet& second, Element-
Set& result);
```

This function computes `result` as the union of the sets `first` and `second`. The function returns 1 if the union is computed successfully and 0 otherwise (due to the "overflow" error situation described in the previous exercise).

2–10 Implement a stand-alone function `intersection_with` whose prototype is:

```
void intersection_with(ElementSet& first, ElementSet& second,
ElementSet& result);
```

This function will compute the intersection of the sets `first` and `second`, returning the result by means of the argument, `result`.

2–11 Implement the class `Point`, which is declared at the end of this exercise. A `Point` object contains two data members: x and y. These represent the x and y coordinates of a point in the Cartesian plane. Each is a dynamic `FloatObj` object. The functions `xval` and `yval` return (as float values) the values of the x and y coordinates stored within a `Point` object. The display function displays the x and y coordinate values with appropriate labels. The setx and sety functions are used to set the values of the x and y coordinates. The move function adds the x coordinate of the argument to the x coordinate of the receiver and does the same for the y coordinates. The functions file_in and file_out have their usual meanings.

```
class Point : public Element
{
    private:
        // DATA MEMBERS ...
        FloatObj* x, y;

    public:
        // MEMBER FUNCTIONS ...
        // constructor - destructor
        Point(float, float);
        Point();
        inline virtual ~Point();

        // access
        inline float xval();
        inline float yval();

        // display
        virtual void display();

        // modify
        inline void setx(float);
        inline void sety(float);
```

```
inline void move(Point);

    // file in - file out
    virtual void file_in(ifstream&);
    virtual void file_out(ofstream&);
};   // end class Point
```

2–12 Design and implement a class `Complex` that is a subclass of `Element` and allows programmers to manipulate complex numbers. An object of this class will have two float-valued instance variables: `RealPart` and `ImaginaryPart`. A complex number will be initialized by the following definition:

```
Complex z(3.4, -1.2);
```

This implies the availability of a constructor whose prototype is:

```
Complex(float rpart, float ipart);
```

Design the class `Complex` to include member functions that will provide the ability to:
  a.   access each of the real and imaginary parts of a complex number
  b.   modify the real and imaginary parts of a complex number individually
  c.   display a complex number at the screen
  d.   add and multiply two complex numbers
  e.   retrieve and save a complex number in a file

Suppose *Z1* and *Z2* are objects that belong to the class `Complex`. Then, we can add *Z2* into *Z1* by executing the following statement:

```
Z1.add_in(Z2);
```

Similarly, we can multiply *Z2* into *Z1* (so that the new value of *Z1* will be *Z1* * *Z2*) by executing the following statement:

```
Z1.multiply_by(Z2);
```

Recall that the sum and product of two complex numbers

$$Z_1 = R_1 + I_1i \qquad \text{and}$$
$$Z_2 = R_2 + I_2i$$

are defined respectively as

$$R_1 + R_2 + (I_1 + I_2)i \qquad \text{and}$$
$$R_1R_2 - I_1I_2 + (R_2I_1 + R_1I_2)i.$$

USING THE ElementSet CLASS: TYPE CASTING

In this section, we present the Setter program which utilizes the services provided by the ElementSet class. These services include the ability to define and manipulate ElementSet objects. The Setter program introduces the use of *type casting*. We need to use type casting in order to accomplish certain tasks when we are working with a heterogeneous data structure.

The main program file, setter.cxx The Setter program consists of the following implementation files:

- elements.cxx,[5] which implements the Element class,

- standobj.cxx, which implements all of the standard classes (IntObj, FloatObj, CharObj and StringObj)

- eleset.cxx, which implements the ElementSet class

- setter.cxx, which is the main program file.

In order to understand the Setter program, we need only discuss the setter.cxx file, since we have already discussed the contents of the other implementation files.

The idea behind the Setter program is quite simple. The main function defines an ElementSet object named the_set, which is then manipulated by calls to the stand-alone functions get_set, display_one, display_two and display_three. The function get_set adds various kinds of objects to the_set. The display functions then illustrate three different ways in which objects in the_set can be accessed and displayed. The code for the beginning of the setter.cxx file, including the functions main and prompt_user, is shown in Figure 2–28. The get_set function and the three display functions will be discussed separately.

```
// Program: setter.cxx
//
// This program illustrates the use of the ElementSet class.
// It creates a set that contains floats, integers, strings
// and characters.  It then shows three distinct ways to
// display the elements in the set.
//
#include <ctype.h>      // for toupper()
#include <string.h>
#include <iomanip.h>
#include "elements.h"
#include "eleset.h"
#include "standobj.h"


void main()
{
```

---

5.   The .cxx suffix is used in GNU C++; it is .cpp in Turbo and Symantec C++.

```
// DATA MEMBER ...
ElementSet the_set;


// FUNCTION PROTOTYPES ...
void get_set(ElementSet&);
void display_one(ElementSet&);
void display_two(ElementSet&);
void display_three(ElementSet&);


// STATEMENTS ...
get_set(the_set);
display_one(the_set);
display_two(the_set);
display_three(the_set);
}   // end main()


// Function:  prompt_user()
// Purpose:   To prompt user with menu of choices.
// Pre:       output = oldStuff
// Post:      output = oldStuff <presentation of menu>
void prompt_user()
{
    cout << "Enter F if you want to enter a float, " << endl;
    cout << ".....  S if you want to enter a string," << endl;
    cout << ".....  C if you want to enter a character, " << endl;
    cout << ".....  I if you want to enter an integer, " << endl;
    cout << ".....  Q if you want to quit." << endl;
}
```

FIGURE 2–28 C++ code for the `Setter` program `main` and `prompt_user` functions.

The function `get_set` This function, as shown in Figure 2–29, uses a sentinel loop to get new set elements from the user. If the user enters an `'F'`, the user is prompted to enter a float value. Then, the system creates a dynamic `FloatObj` object which is then added to `the_set` (the pass by reference argument that corresponds to the `the_set` variable in the main function). Similarly, if the user enters an `'S'`, a `'C'` or an `'I'`, a dynamic object of type `string`, `character`, or `integer`, respectively, is created and added to the set. Note that the variable `dynaobj` is polymorphic because its type is `ElementPtr`.

```
// Function:  get_set(the_set)
// Purpose:   To get values of various types from the user and
//            place them in the_set.
// Pre:       the_set is initialized and input =
//            (N repetitions of : aChar aValue)
// Post:      the_set contains the N values that were in the
//            input stream, unless there were duplicates and
//            input = empty.
```

```cpp
void get_set(ElementSet& the_set)
{
    // DATA MEMBERS ...
    char menu_choice;
    ElementPtr dynaobj;
    float      rvalue;
    string     svalue;
    char       cvalue;
    int        ivalue;


    // FUNCTION PROTOTYPE ...
    void prompt_user();


    // STATEMENTS ...
    prompt_user();
    cin >> menu_choice;
    menu_choice = toupper(menu_choice);
    while ( menu_choice != 'Q' && !the_set.is_full())
    {
        cin.ignore(LINESIZE, '\n');
        switch (menu_choice)
        {
        case 'F':
            cout << "Enter a float value: ";
            cin  >> rvalue;
            dynaobj = new FloatObj(rvalue);
            break;  // create a FloatObj
        case 'S':
            cout << "Enter a string value: ";
            read_string(svalue, MAXSTRING);
            dynaobj = new StringObj(svalue);
            break;  // create a StringObj
        case 'C':
            cout << "Enter a character value: ";
            cin  >> cvalue;
            dynaobj = new CharObj(cvalue);
            break;  // create a CharObj
        case 'I':
            cout << "Enter an integer value: ";
            cin  >> ivalue;
            dynaobj = new IntObj(ivalue);
            break;  // create an IntObj
        }  // end switch
        if(the_set.add(dynaobj))
        {
         // successful add
         cout << "New object added to set.\n";
        }
        else
        {
         // could not add; delete dynamic object
         cout << "Duplicate object. Did not add.\a\n";
         delete dynaobj;
        }
        prompt_user();
```

```
            cin >> menu_choice;
            menu_choice = toupper(menu_choice);
        }   // end while
    }   // end get_set()
```

FIGURE 2–29   C++ code for the `get_set` function used in the `Setter` program.

This function uses the `toupper` function whose prototype is provided in the `ctype.h` header file. This function takes a character argument and returns the upper case version of the argument if that argument was a lowercase letter. Otherwise, the function returns the same value as the argument. The use of `toupper` allowed us to simplify the `while` loop condition and the `case` labels within the `switch` statement.

The function `display_one`   This function displays the contents of `the_set` using the function `ElementSet::display`. Recall from the `display` function of Figure 2–27, this function takes advantage of true polymorphism and "broadcasts" the `display` message to each object in the receiver set. The details are shown in Figure 2–30.

```
// Function:  display_one(the_set)
// Purpose:   To display the elements in the_set using the
//            function ElementSet::display()
// Pre:       the_set is initialized
// Post:      All elements in the_set are displayed at the screen
void display_one(ElementSet& the_set)
{
    cout << endl
        << "Here are the set elements shown using " << endl
        << "ElementSet::display(): " << endl;
    the_set.display();
    cout << endl;
    cin.get();
}   // end display_one()
```

FIGURE 2–30   C++ code for the function `display_one`.

The function `display_two`   This function displays `the_set` by sending the `display` message to each of the individual elements in `the_set`. As shown in Figure 2–31, it accomplishes this by use of the function `ElementSet::get_any`, which returns a pointer to an element in `the_set`. Every time `get_any` is called again, it returns a pointer to another element in `the_set`.

```
// Function:  display_two(the_set)
// Purpose:   To display the elements in the_set using the
//            functions get_any and display() (polymorphically)
```

```
// Pre:       the_set is initialized
// Post:      All elements in the_set are displayed at the screen
void display_two(ElementSet& the_set)
{
    // DATA MEMBER ...
    int set_size = the_set.cardinality();


    // STATEMENTS ...
    cout << endl
      << "Here are the set elements shown using " << endl
      << "get_any() and Element::display(): " << endl;
    for (int i = 0; i < set_size; i++)
    {
        the_set.get_any() -> display();
    }
    cout << "STRIKE ANY KEY" << endl;
    cin.get();
}   // end display_two()
```

FIGURE 2–31   C++ code for the function `display_two`.

If we call `get_any` as many times as there are objects in `the_set`, then all of the objects in `the_set` are retrieved. The expression

`the_set.get_any()`

evaluates to an `Element` pointer. Thus, we can send the message `display` to the object that `the_set.get_any()` points to using the arrow operator. *This is possible because display is implemented as a virtual function in the* `Element` *class itself.* Thus, true polymorphism applies, and the various objects referenced by the_set.get_any() can select the proper implementation for the display message that they receive.

The function `display_three`: Type Casting   This function, shown in Figure 2–32, displays `the_set` by applying the function `get_val` to each of the objects in `the_set` and then using `cout` to display the values of the individual objects. The code is reproduced as Figure 2–32. This is possible because each of the objects in `the_set` belongs to a standard class and `get_val` is implemented in each standard class.

```
// Function:  display_three(the_set)
// Purpose:   To display the elements in the_set using the
//            functions get_any and get_val().  This requires
//            type casting.
// Pre:       the_set is initialized
// Post:      All elements in the_set are displayed at the screen


void display_three(ElementSet& the_set)
{
    // DATA MEMBERS ...
    int set_size = the_set.cardinality();
    ElementPtr eptr;
```

```
    // STATEMENTS ...
    cout << endl
      << "Here are the set elements shown using " << endl
      << "get_any() and the appropriate version " << endl
      << "of the get_val() function: " << endl;
    for (int i = 0; i < set_size; i++)
    {
        // capture pointer, since every use of get_any()
        // will change current object in set
        eptr = the_set.get_any();
        if (!strcmp(eptr -> get_class(), "FloatObj"))
        {
        cout << ((FloatObj*) eptr) -> get_val() << endl;
        }
        else if (!strcmp(eptr -> get_class(), "StringObj"))
        {
        cout << ((StringObj*) eptr) -> get_val() << endl;
        }
        else if (!strcmp(eptr -> get_class(), "CharObj"))
        {
        cout << ((CharObj*) eptr) -> get_val() << endl;
        }
        else // must be IntObj
        {
        cout << ((IntObj*) eptr) -> get_val() << endl;
        }
    }  // end for
    cout << "STRIKE ANY KEY" << endl;
    cin.get();
}  // end display_three()
```

FIGURE 2–32   C++ code for the function `display_three`.

You might be wondering why the following code was *not* used to apply the `get_val` function to the various objects in the set:

```
for (int i = 0; i < set_size; i++)
{
        eptr = the_set.get_any();
        cout << eptr -> get_val() << endl;
}
```

In fact, this code yields a fatal compiler error. In particular, *the compiler views the "cout statement" as being in error because the function `get_val` is not implemented at the `Element` level in the class hierarchy.* In other words, when the compiler encounters the expression

```
eptr -> get_val()
```

it sees that `eptr` is an `Element` pointer and thus it checks to see if the function `get_val` is declared for the `Element` class. Since it is not, it then checks to see if `get_val` might be declared in a superclass of `Element`, but `Element` has no superclasses. This is a situation in which a message is not understood by the receiver of that message. In order to apply `get_val` to `*eptr`, we must type cast `eptr` to a new pointer type, a type that corresponds to a class (in this case, one of the standard classes) that understands the `get_val` message. In order to accomplish this we must be able to determine the class of `*eptr` dynamically (i.e., during the execution of the program).

In order to determine the class of `*eptr` dynamically, we need only apply the function `get_class`, which is declared at the `Element` level. This returns the name of the class of `*eptr` as a string, and this can then be compared against the strings `"FloatObj"`, `"IntObj"`, `"StringObj"`, and `"CharObj"`. Using this information, we type cast `eptr` to be an appropriate pointer type.

> **Example 2.1**   Suppose we determine that `eptr` is pointing to a `FloatObj` object. Then we type cast `eptr` as a `FloatObj*` using the expression `(FloatObj*) eptr`.

The example, `setter.cxx`, includes the following expressions and their corresponding types as shown in Table 2–1.

TABLE 2–1 TYPE CAST EXPRESSION TYPES FROM `Setter.cxx`

expression:	type:
eptr	Element*
(FloatObj*) eptr	FloatObj*
(char *) eptr	char*

Basically, type casting is used to convert a pointer of one type into a pointer of another type, when necessary, so that the compile will not fail due to violation of the type rules of the language. Since `eptr` is of type `Element*`, the expression

```
eptr -> get_val()
```

is illegal (as we have seen). But, since the expression `(FloatObj*) eptr` is of type `FloatObj*`, the expression

```
((FloatObj*) eptr) -> get_val()
```

is legal. The compiler says, in effect: "The expression `(FloatObj*) eptr` is of type `FloatObj*`, so the function `get_val` had better be declared for the `FloatObj` class, and, of course, type casting assures that this is so."

Type casting is an important technique for dealing with heterogeneous data structures whenever it is necessary to "broadcast" a message that is not implemented in the root class of the relevant class hierarchy.

*RESTRICTING HETEROGENEITY

Although heterogeneous data structures (such as `ElementSet`) are very powerful, we sometimes need to implement a data structure whose elements are limited to one or more specified classes. In this section, we shall implement such a restricted data structure as a class called `PersonSet`. We shall assume that a `PersonSet` is a set of objects that belong to one of the following classes: `Person`, `Professor`, or `Student`. These are three new element classes that we shall introduce in this section.

There are two important reasons for implementing restricted data structures:

1. For safety; we can check to make sure that only objects that belong to a specified class or classes are being incorporated into the heterogeneous data structure that we are using.

2. For persistence;[6] we sometimes need to write data structures to a file and then retrieve those data structures from that file using a different (or, even the same) client program. When the items to be written are objects, this requires that they be restricted in certain ways.

For example, consider the function `PersonSet::file_in` that we shall soon introduce. This function allows a `PersonSet` to be constructed using data stored in a text file. That text file contains string representations of `Person`, `Professor`, and `Student` objects. This construction is possible because the `PersonSet::file_in` function "knows" how `Person`, `Professor`, and `Student` objects are stored in a file. It would be impossible to implement this function at the `ElementSet` level, *since the class `ElementSet` is unrestricted.* Any object in any element class can be added to an `ElementSet`, and the set of element classes can grow over time (i.e., we can always add new element classes to the hierarchy). For example, the element class hierarchy is augmented by addition of Persons, Professors, and Students as shown in Figure 2–33.

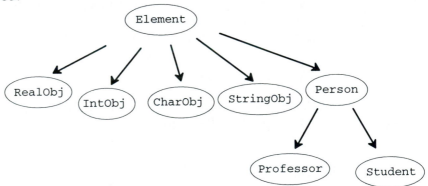

FIGURE 2–33   The subclasses of `Element` including the `Person`, `Professor`, and `Student` classes.

---

6. Many articles and even entire books have been written about the issue of "persistence" in object-oriented systems and we do not wish to trivialize the subject here. Basically, we are using this term to refer to the ability to store objects in a file and to retrieve them from that file.

Consequently, the class `ElementSet` cannot predict in advance the names and structures of all possible element classes. If this is not clear at this point, it should become clear when you see how the `PersonSet::file_in` function is actually implemented.

The functions `file_in` and `file_out` were part of the common protocol introduced by the `Element` class. Indeed, they are ubiquitous functions. Thus, subclasses of `Element` are expected to provide their own definitions for the `file_in` and `file_out` functions. In order for our design to be successful, it is important that `file_in` and `file_out` be given consistent interpretations throughout the class hierarchy. Our intention is that when `file_out` is applied to an object, it will write out a representation of that object, including the name of its class, to a text file. The function `file_in`, when applied to an object, will set the data member values for that object equal to values found in a text file. These values will normally be the "file out" of an object that belongs to the same class as the object that is being "filed in." Thus, the `file_in` and `file_out` functions can be used to give objects some kind of *persistence* beyond the life of a program.

Before we can discuss the `PersonSet` class in detail, we need to discuss the `Person`, `Student` and `Professor` classes.

Persons, Students, and Professors

The `Person` class is a subclass of `Element`. This will allow us to store `Person` objects in any of the data structures, such as `ElementSet`, that are implemented using `Element` pointers. As a subclass of `Element`, the `Person` class inherits the `my_class` data member and the (static) member function `get_class` from the class `Element`. The four ubiquitous functions: `display`, `read_in`, `file_in` and `file_out` are polymorphically redefined in the `Person` class. In addition, two new data members, `name` and `phone`, of type `string` are introduced. These new data members are declared "protected" so that they will be inherited by the subclasses of `Person`, that is, the classes `Professor` and `Student`. Further, the `Person` class declares and defines the following new public member functions that are used to access and modify individual data members: `get_name`, `get_phone`, `set_name`, and `set_phone`. These functions are declared `static` because they will be implemented in the same way and inherited directly by all classes that are derived from the `Person` class.

The declaration for the `Person` class that is provided in the `persons.h` header file is shown in Figure 2–34.

```
class Person : public Element
{
    protected:
        // DATA MEMBERS ...
        string name, phone;

    public:
        // MEMBER FUNCTIONS ...
```

```
// constructor - destructor
Person(string, string);
inline Person();
inline virtual ~Person();


// display
virtual void display();


// access
inline char* get_name();
inline char* get_phone();


// comparison operators
virtual int operator ==(Element&);
virtual int operator <(Element&);
// inherited by all Person subclasses


// modify
virtual void read_in();
inline void set_name(string);
inline void set_phone(string);


// file in - file out
virtual void file_in(ifstream&);
virtual void file_out(ofstream&);
};    // end class Person
```

FIGURE 2–34 Declaration for the `Person` class from `persons.h` header file.

Note that two `Person` class constructors are provided. The constructor `Person(string, string)` will initialize the `name` and `phone` data members using the strings that are passed as arguments. The constructor `Person()` will initialize `name` and `phone` each to the empty string. Both constructors initialize `my_class` to `"Person"`.

The `Professor` class is declared as a subclass of `Person`. The `Professor` class inherits the `my_class`, `name` and `phone` data members. In addition, the `Professor` class introduces a new `float` data member called `salary`. The `Professor` class inherits all of the static functions that the `Person` class either inherited or introduced (i.e., `get_class`, `get_name`, `get_phone`, `set_name` and `set_phone`) and it polymorphically redefines the four ubiquitous functions: `display`, `read_in`, `file_in` and `file_out`. In addition, the `Professor` class introduces the following new public member functions: `display_as_advisor` (displays `Professor` data in the context of being a student's advisor), `get_salary` and `set_salary` (access and modify functions for the new `salary` data member), `is_paid_well` (checks to see if a `Professor` is getting what he or she deserves), and `change_salary` (adds an amount to a `Professor`'s salary).

The declaration for the `Professor` class that is provided in the `persons.h` header file is given below in Figure 2–35.

```
class Professor : public Person
{
    protected:
        // DATA MEMBERS ...
        float salary;


    public:
        // MEMBER FUNCTIONS ...
        // constructor - destructor
        Professor(string, string, float);
        inline Professor();
        inline virtual ~Professor();


        // display
        virtual void display();
        virtual void display_as_advisor();


        // access - test
        float get_salary();
        int is_paid_well();


        // modify
        virtual void read_in();
        void set_salary(float);
        void change_salary(float);


        // comparison operators
        virtual int operator ==(Element&);


        // file in - file out
        virtual void file_in(ifstream&);
        virtual void file_out(ofstream&);
};   // end class Professor
```

FIGURE 2–35   Declaration for the `Professor` class from `persons.h`.

Again, two constructors are provided for the `Professor` class. The constructor `Professor(string, string, float)` will initialize the name, phone and salary of a `Professor` object to the values passed as arguments. The constructor `Professor()` will initialize the name and phone data members to the empty string and the salary to 0.0. Both constructors initialize the `my_class` data member to "Professor".

The `Student` class is also a subclass of `Person`. Consequently, the `Student` class inherits the `my_class`, name and phone data members. The `Stu-`

dent class introduces the following new, protected data members: `major` (a string), `gpa` (a `float`) and `advisor` (a pointer to a `Professor` object). The `Student` class inherits all static `Element` and `Person` class member functions; namely, `get_class`, `get_name`, `get_phone`, `set_name` and `set_phone`.   The `Student` class polymorphically redefines the four ubiquitous element class functions: `display`, `read_in`, `file_in` and `file_out`. The `Student` class introduces the following access and modify functions for the data members `major`, `gpa` and `advisor`: `get_major`, `get_gpa`, `get_advisor`, `name_of_advisor`, `set_major`, `set_gpa` and `set_advisor`.

The declaration for the `Student` class that is provided in the `persons.h` header file appears in Figure 2–36.

```
class Student : public Person
{
    protected:
        // DATA MEMBERS ...
        string major;
        float  gpa;
        Professor* advisor;


    public:
        // MEMBER FUNCTIONS ...
        // constructor - destructor
        Student(string, string);
        inline Student();
        inline virtual ~Student();


        // display
        virtual void display();


        // access
        inline string& get_major();
        inline float get_gpa();
        inline char* name_of_advisor();
        inline Professor* get_advisor();


        // comparison operators
        virtual int operator ==(Element&);


        // modify
        virtual void read_in();
        inline void set_major(string);
        inline void set_gpa(float);
        inline void set_advisor(Professor*);


        // file in - file out
        virtual void file_in(ifstream&);
```

```
        virtual void file_out(ofstream&);
};   // end class Student
```

FIGURE 2–36   Declaration for the Student class from persons.h.

Again note the existence of two Student constructors: Student(string,string) and Student(). The former initializes name and phone to the strings that are passed as arguments, while the latter initializes name and phone to the empty string. Both constructors initialize my_class to "Student", major to the empty string and gpa to 0.0. Finally, both constructors initialize advisor so that it points to a new Professor object. All Student objects contain a pointer to a Professor object and thus, in some sense, every Student object contains a Professor object. This represents a new kind of relationship between classes (in addition to the more obvious base class — derived class relationship).

The Person, Professor and Student classes extend the possible kinds of objects that can be included in heterogeneous data structures such as ElementSet. This hierarchy is pictured in Figure 2–33.

The Person class constructors and destructor   This subsection and subsequent subsections present the implementations of the Person, Professor, and Student class member functions. The Person class constructors and destructor are shown in Figure 2–37.

```
// Constructor:    Person::Person(nm, ph)
// Purpose:        Initializes a Person object with name = nm
//                 and phone = ph
// Pre:            nm is defined and ph is defined
// Post:           my_class = "Person" and name = nm and
//                 phone = ph
Person::Person(string nm, string ph)
{
    strcpy(my_class, "Person");
    strcpy(name, nm);
    strcpy(phone, ph);
}   // end Person::Person(string, string)


// Constructor:    Person::Person()
// Purpose:        Initializes a Person object.
// Pre:            None
// Post:           my_class = "Person" and name = "" and
//                 phone = ""
Person::Person()
{
    strcpy(my_class, "Person");
    strcpy(name, "");
    strcpy(phone, "");
}   // end Person::Person()


// Destructor:     Person::~Person()
// Purpose:        Destroys a Person object.
```

```
// Pre:              Receiver is initialized.
// Post:             Receiver is destroyed.
Person::~Person()
{
}  // end Person::~Person()
```

FIGURE 2–37   C++ implementations for `Person` class constructors and destructor from `persons.cxx`.

We have already discussed these functions. For example, the following definition creates two `Person` objects: a `Person` object `per1` whose name is `"Doe, John"` and whose phone is `"555-1212"` and a `Person` object `per2` whose `name` and `phone` are initialized to empty strings:

```
Person per1("Doe, John", "555-1212"), per2;
```

In other words, the definition for `per1` calls the constructor `Person(string, string)` whereas the definition for `per2` calls the constructor `Person()`.

The `Person` class access and display functions   These functions, with implementations shown in Figure 2–38, do not require additional commentary.

```
// Function:       Person::display()
// Purpose:        To display receiver's data at computer screen.
// Pre:            output = oldStuff and name is defined and
//                 phone is defined
// Post:           output = oldStuff
//                 "Person's name and phone:" \n
//                 name \n phone \n \n
void Person::display()
{
    cout << "Person's name and phone: " << endl;
    cout << name << endl;
    cout << phone << endl;
    cout << endl;
}   // end Person::display()


// Function:       Person::get_name()
// Purpose:        To return the name of the receiver.
// Pre:            name is defined
// Post:           get_name = name
char* Person::get_name()
{
    return name;
}   // end Person::get_name()


// Function:       Person::get_phone()
// Purpose:        To return the phone number of the receiver.
// Pre:            phone is defined
```

```
// Post:          get_phone = phone
char* Person::get_phone()
{
    return phone;
}   // end Person::get_phone()
```

FIGURE 2–38   C++ implementations for the `Person` class access and display
functions from `persons.cxx`.

The `Person` class comparison operators The comparison operators for
equality and less than are implemented as shown in Figure 2–39.

```
//
// comparison operators
//


// Operator:      Person::==(p)
// Purpose:       To determine whether the receiver and p
//                are value equal.  This operator assumes that
//                p is a Person object.
// Pre:           p is a Person object and
//                    name = nmString1 and phone = phString1 and
//                    p.get_name() = nmString2 and
//                    p.get_phone() = phString2
// Post:          ==() = (nmString1 = nmString2) and
//                          phString1 = phString2)
int Person::operator ==(Element& p)
{
    // LOCAL DATA ...
    Person* perptr = (Person*) &p;    // type cast


    // STATEMENTS ...
    if (!strcmp(name, perptr -> get_name())
      && !strcmp(phone, perptr -> get_phone()))
        return 1;
    else
        return 0;
}   // end Person::operator ==


// Operator:      Person::<(p)
// Purpose:       Returns true if the receiver's name comes
//                earlier, lexicographically, than the name of
//                p. This operator is inherited by all
//                Person subclasses.  ASSUMES p is a kind of
//                person.
// Pre:           name = nmString1 and
//                    p.get_name() = nmString2
// Post:          <() = (nmString1 < nmString2)
int Person::operator <(Element& p)
```

```
    {
        if (strcmp(name, ((Person*) &p) -> get_name()) < 0)
            return 1;
        else
            return 0;
    }   // end Person::operator <
```

FIGURE 2–39   C++ implementations for `Person` class comparison operators from `persons.cxx`.

The implementations of the equality operator, `== (p)`, is indicative of the style. The input argument, `p`, a pass-by-reference argument referring to an element, is type cast into a pointer to a `Person` in the local data definition. Then, if the name and phone number of the object `p` match those of the receiver, the equality operator returns 1, otherwise, it returns 0.[7] The implementation for `< (p)` is similar.

The `Person` class modify functions   Note that the `Person::read_in` function shown in Figure 2–40 requires the `read_string` function that was first introduced in Chapter 0.

```
// Function:        Person::read_in()
// Purpose:         To prompt user for and get the name and
//                  phone number of the receiver.
// Pre:             input = aName \n aPhone restOfStuff
// Post:            input = restOfStuff and name = aName and
//                  phone = aPhone
void Person::read_in()
{
    cout << endl;
    cout << "Enter person's name: ";
    read_string(name, MAXSTRING);
    cout << "Enter person's phone: ";
    read_string(phone, MAXSTRING);
}   // end Person::read_in()


// Function:        Person::set_name(aname)
// Purpose:         To set the receiver's name to aname.
// Pre:             aname is defined
// Post:            name = aname
void Person::set_name(string aname)
{
    strcpy(name, aname);
}   // end Person::set_name()


// Function:        Person::set_phone(aphone)
// Purpose:         To set the receiver's phone to aphone.
// Pre:             aphone is defined
// Post:            phone = aphone
```

---

7.   Recall that `strcmp` returns zero when the strings being compared are the same.

```
void Person::set_phone(string aphone)
{
    strcpy(phone, aphone);
}    // end Person::set_val()
```

FIGURE 2–40   C++ implementations for the `Person` class modify functions from `persons.cxx`.

The `Person` class `file_in` and `file_out` functions   We assume that all `file_in` functions are called after the class name string has already been read in. Thus, the code for a `file_in` function is not the perfect inverse of the code for a `file_out` function in its class, since the latter writes out all data members, including the class name. This lack of symmetry in the code is required in order for us to be able to file in ad hoc and heterogeneous collections of `Person` objects. Note, however, that the program can read files that it has output, thus achieving data persistence. The details are given in Figure 2–41.

```
// Function:      Person::file_in(in_file)
// Purpose:       To read in the name and phone number of the
//                receiver from in_file
// Pre:           in_file is a text file open for input and
//                in_file = aName \n aPhone \n restOfStuff
// Post:          in_file = restOfStuff and name = aName
//                and phone = aPhone
void Person::file_in(ifstream& in_file)
{
    in_file.getline(name, MAXSTRING);
    in_file.getline(phone, MAXSTRING);
}    // end Person::file_in()


// Function:      Person::file_out(out_file)
// Purpose:       To write out a representation of the receiver,
//                including the receiver's class, to out_file.
// Pre:           out_file is a text file open for output and
//                out_file = oldStuff and name is defined and
//                phone is defined.
// Post:          (oldStuff = "" and
//                    out_file = "Person" \n name \n phone)
//                  or
//                (oldStuff != "" and
//                    out_file = \n "Person" \n name \n phone)
void Person::file_out(ofstream& out_file)
{
    if (out_file.tellp())
    {
    // this is not first person in file
    // need to advance to new line
    out_file << endl;
    }
    out_file << my_class << endl;
    out_file << name << endl;
```

```
        out_file << phone;
}       // end Person::file_out()
```

FIGURE 2–41   C++ implementations for the `Person` class file_in and file_out functions from `persons.cxx`.

The function `Person::file_in` assumes that the ifstream object `in_file` is a text file that is positioned so that the next character to be read in from the file represents the beginning of a new `Person` name.   The `Person::file_out` function writes out the values of the receiver's `my_class`, name and `phone` data members to an ofstream object, `out_file`. The function `tellp` returns an integer value that represents the position of `out_file` for output.   If this is not 0, then this is not the first data being written out to the file and a new line character must be written in order to separate the new data from the previous.   If `tellp` returns 0, then this is the first data being written out to the file, and a new line character is not written.   Note that we do not write out a new line character after writing out the value of `phone`.   These considerations are required so that the end of file function (`eof`) will work properly when a heterogeneous sequence of elements is filed in.   This pattern has been applied consistently in all of the `file_out` functions in all of the element classes (although we deferred discussion of these details until now).

The `Professor` class constructors and destructor   The `Professor` class constructors and destructor are presented in Figure 2–42.

```
// Constructor:   Professor::Professor(nm, ph, sal)
// Purpose:       Initializes a Professor object with name
//                = nm, phone = ph and salary = sal
// Pre:           nm is defined and ph is defined and sal is
//                defined
// Post:          my_class = "Professor" and name = nm and
//                phone = ph and salary = sal
Professor::Professor(string nm, string ph, float sal)
    : Person(nm, ph)
{
    strcpy(my_class, "Professor");
    salary = sal;
}     // end Professor::Professor(string, string, float)


// Constructor:   Professor::Professor()
// Purpose:       Initializes a Professor object.
// Pre:           None
// Post:          my_class = "Professor" and name = "" and
//                phone = "" and salary = 0.0
Professor::Professor()
{
    strcpy(my_class, "Professor");
    salary = 0.0;
}     // end Professor::Professor()
```

```
// Destructor:      Professor::~Professor()
// Purpose:         Destroys a Professor object.
// Pre:             Receiver is initialized.
// Post:            Receiver is destroyed.
Professor::~Professor()
{
}    // end Professor::~Professor()
```

FIGURE 2–42   C++ implementation for the `Professor` class constructors and destructor from `persons.cxx`.

The function header for the constructor `Professor(string, string, float)` indicates that this constructor is implemented by first calling the `Person(string, string)` constructor as opposed to the `Person()` constructor which would be called by default. In addition, the arguments `nm` and `ph` that are passed in the call to `Professor(string, string, float)` are passed on as arguments to `Person(string, string)`. Consequently, the definition

```
Professor prof("Jones, Sally", "555-1212", 40000.0);
```

will:
1. create a `Professor` object called `prof`,
2. apply the `Person(string, string)` constructor to `prof`, passing `"Jones, Sally"` for initializing `name` and `"555-1212"` for initializing `phone`,
3. execute the body of the constructor `Professor(string, string, float)`, which initializes `my_class` to `"Professor"` and `salary` to `40000.0`.

Note that the `my_ class` data member is set twice: first to `"Person"` by the `Person` constructor and then to `"Professor"` by the `Professor` constructor. Obviously, the order in which these events occur is critical.

All other `Professor` class member functions   The remaining `Professor` class member functions in Figure 2–43 are followed by a brief commentary.

```
//
// display
//
```

```
// Function:     Professor::display()
// Purpose:      To display receiver's data at computer screen.
// Pre:          output = oldStuff and name is defined and
//               phone is defined salary is defined
// Post:         output = oldStuff "Professor's name, phone
//               and salary:" \n name \n phone \n salary \n \n
void Professor::display()
```

```
{
    cout << "Professor's name, phone and salary: " << endl;
    cout << name << endl;
    cout << phone << endl;
    cout << salary << endl;
    cout << endl;
}    // end Professor::display()



// Function:      Professor::display_as_advisor()
// Purpose:       To display receiver's data at computer screen
//                labelled as a student advisor.
// Pre:           output = oldStuff and name is defined and
//                phone is defined and salary is defined
// Post:          output = oldStuff "Advisor's name, phone
//                and salary:" \n name \n phone \n salary \n \n
void Professor::display_as_advisor()
{
    cout << "Advisor's name, phone and salary: " << endl;
    cout << name << endl;
    cout << phone << endl;
    cout << salary << endl;
    cout << endl;
}    // end Professor::display_as_advisor()



//
// access - test
//



// Function:      Professor::get_salary()
// Purpose:       To return the salary of the receiver.
// Pre:           salary is defined
// Post:          get_salary = salary
float Professor::get_salary()
{
    return salary;
}



// Function:      Professor::is_paid_well()
// Purpose:       Returns 1 if receiver's salary is greater than
//                CUT_OFF ($50,000.00) and 0 otherwise.
// Pre:           salary is defined
// Post:          is_paid_well = (salary > CUT_OFF)
int Professor::is_paid_well()
{
    // LOCAL DATA ...
    const float CUT_OFF = 50000.0;


    // STATEMENTS ...
    return (salary > CUT_OFF);
}    // end Professor::is_paid_well()
```

```
// Operator:    Professor::==(pr)
// Purpose:        To determine whether the receiver and pr
//                 are value equal.  This operator assumes that
//                 pr is a Professor object.
// Pre:           pr is a Professor object and
//                    name = nmString1 and phone = phString1 and
//                    salary = salary1 and
//                    pr.get_name() = nmString2 and
//                    pr.get_phone() = phString2 and
//                    pr.get_salary() = salary2
// Post:          ==() = (nmString1 = nmString2) and
//                         phString1 = phString2 and
//                         salary1 = salary2)
int Professor::operator ==(Element& pr)
{
    // LOCAL DATA ...
    Professor* profptr = (Professor*) &pr;


    // STATEMENTS ...
    if (!strcmp(name, profptr -> get_name())
      && !strcmp(phone, profptr -> get_phone())
      && salary == profptr -> get_salary())
        return 1;
    else
        return 0;
}   // end Professor::operator ==


//
// modify
//


// Function:      Professor::read_in()
// Purpose:       To prompt user for and get the name,
//                phone number and salary of the receiver.
// Pre:           input = aName \n aPhone \n aFloat restOfStuff
// Post:          input = restOfStuff and name = aName and
//                phone = aPhone salary = aFloat
void Professor::read_in()
{
    cout << endl;
    cout << "Enter professor's name: ";
    read_string(name, MAXSTRING);
    cout << "Enter professor's phone: ";
    read_string(phone, MAXSTRING);
    cout << "Enter professor's salary: ";
    cin  >> salary;
    cin.ignore(LINESIZE, '\n');
        // new line
}   // end Professor::read_in()


// Function:      Professor::set_salary(asalary)
// Purpose:       To set the receiver's salary to asalary.
```

```
// Pre:            asalary is defined
// Post:           salary = asalary
void Professor::set_salary(float asalary)
{
    salary = asalary;
}    // end Professor::set_salary()



// Function:       Professor::change_salary(asalary)
// Purpose:        To add asalary to the receiver's salary.
// Pre:            asalary is defined
// Post:           salary = old(salary) + asalary
void Professor::change_salary(float achange)
{
    salary +=achange;
}    // end Professor::change_salary()



//
// file in - file out
//



// Function:       Professor::file_in(in_file)
// Purpose:        To read in the name, phone number and salary
//                 of the receiver from in_file
// Pre:            in_file is a text file open for input and
//                 in_file = aName \n aPhone \n aFloat \n restOf-
Stuff
// Post:           in_file = restOfStuff and name = aName
//                 and phone = aPhone and salary = aFloat
void Professor::file_in(ifstream& in_file)
{
    Person::file_in(in_file);
    in_file >> salary;
    in_file.ignore(LINESIZE, '\n');
        // new line
}    // end class Professor::file_in()



// Function:       Professor::file_out(out_file)
// Purpose:        To write out a representation of the receiver,
//                 including the receiver's class, to out_file.
// Pre:            out_file is a text file open for output and
//                 out_file = oldStuff and name is defined and
//                 phone is defined and salary is defined.
// Post:           (oldStuff = "" and
//                     out_file = "Professor" \n name \n phone
//                     \n salary) or
//                 (oldStuff != "" and
//                     out_file = \n "Professor" \n name \n phone
//                     \n salary)
void Professor::file_out(ofstream& out_file)
{
    Person::file_out(out_file);
```

```
        out_file << endl << salary;
}   // end Professor::file_out()
```

FIGURE 2–43   C++ implementations of `Professor` class member functions from `persons.cxx`.

The only new element here is that the functions `Professor::file_in` and `Professor::file_out` explicitly call the functions that they are polymorph-ically redefining. This requires the use of the scope resolution operator (::). Thus, note that the function body for `Professor::file_out` reads:

```
Person::file_out(out_file);
out_file << endl << salary;
```

This causes the function `Person::file_out` to be applied to the receiver `Professor` object, and that, in turn, will cause the `name` and `phone` data members of the receiver `Professor` object to be written out to `out_file`. This is a common pattern of code reuse in object-oriented programming.

The `Student` class constructors and destructor   The `Student` class constructors and destructor are designed analogously to those of the `Profes-sor` class. The code is given below in Figure 2–44. The constructor `Stu-dent(string, string)` follows the pattern established by the constructor `Professor(string, string, float)` in the manner in which it calls the superclass constructor `Person(string, string)`. Both `Student` class constructors use the `new` operator to allocate space for a `Professor` object that represents a student's advisor. The `Student` class destructor applies the `delete` operator to the `Professor` pointer, `advisor`, in order to deallocate the `Professor` object that `advisor` references.

```
// Constructor:    Student::Student(nm, ph)
// Purpose:        Initializes a Student object with name = nm,
//                 phone = ph
// Pre:            nm is defined and ph is defined
// Post:           my_class = "Student" and name = nm and
//                 phone = ph and major = "" and gpa = 0.0
//                 and *advisor = a new Professor
Student::Student(string nm, string ph)
    : Person(nm, ph)
{
    strcpy(my_class, "Student");
    strcpy(major, "");
    gpa = 0.0;
    advisor = new Professor;
}   // end Student::Student(string, string)


// Constructor:    Student::Student()
// Purpose:        Initializes a Student object.
// Pre:            None
// Post:           my_class = "Student" and name = "" and
```

```
//                      phone = "" and major = "" and gpa = 0.0
//                      and *advisor = a new Professor.
Student::Student()
{
    strcpy(my_class, "Student");
    strcpy(major, "");
    gpa = 0.0;
    advisor = new Professor;
}   // end Student::Student()



// Destructor:     Student::~Student()
// Purpose:        Destroys a Student object and that Student's
//                 advisor.
// Pre:            Receiver is initialized.
// Post:           *advisor is deallocated and the receiver
//                 is destroyed.
Student::~Student()
{
    delete advisor;
}   // end Student::~Student()
```

FIGURE 2–44 C++ implementation of Student class constructors and destructor from persons.cxx.

The Student class display, access and modify member functions The Student class display, access and modify member functions are given in Figure 2–45. These are followed by a brief observation.

```
//
// display
//



// Function:       Student::display()
// Purpose:        To display receiver's data at computer screen.
// Pre:            output = oldStuff and name is defined and
//                 phone is defined and major is defined and
//                 gpa = aFloat and *advisor = aProfessor
// Post:           output = oldStuff "Student's personal info: "
//                 \n name \n phone \n major \n gpa \n
//                 aProfessor.display_as_advisor()
void Student::display()
{
    cout << "Student's personal info: " << endl;
    cout << name << endl;
    cout << phone << endl;
    cout << major << endl;
    cout << gpa << endl;
    advisor -> display_as_advisor();
}   // end Student::display()
```

```
//
// access
//


// Function:       Student::get_major()
// Purpose:        To return the major of the receiver.
// Pre:            major = is defined
// Post:           get_major = major
string& Student::get_major()
{
   return major;
}  // end Student::get_major()


// Function:       Student::get_gpa()
// Purpose:        To return the gpa of the receiver.
// Pre:            gpa is defined
// Post:           get_gpa = gpa
float Student::get_gpa()
{
   return gpa;
}  // end Student::get_gpa()


// Function:       Student::name_of_advisor()
// Purpose:        To return the name of the receiver's advisor.
// Pre:            advisor -> get_name() = aName
// Post:           name_of_advisor = aName
char* Student::name_of_advisor()
{
   return advisor -> get_name();
}  // end Student::name_of_advisor()


// Function:       Student::get_advisor()
// Purpose:        To return a pointer to the receiver's advisor.
// Pre:            advisor = aProfessorPointer
// Post:           get_advisor = aProfessorPointer
Professor* Student::get_advisor()
{
   return advisor;
}


// Operator:     Student::==(st)
// Purpose:        To determine whether the receiver and st
//                 are value equal.  This operator assumes that
//                 st is a Student object.
// Pre:            st is a Student object
// Post:           ==() = true if all of the data members of
//                 the receiver equal all of the data members
//                 of st and false otherwise.
int Student::operator ==(Element& st)
{
    // LOCAL DATA ...
    Student* stuptr = (Student*) &st;      // type cast
```

```
    // STATEMENTS ...
    if (!strcmp(name, stuptr -> get_name())
      && !strcmp(phone, stuptr -> get_phone())
      && !strcmp(major, stuptr -> get_major())
      && gpa == stuptr -> get_gpa()
      && *advisor == *(stuptr -> get_advisor())))
        return 1;
    else
        return 0;
}    // end Student::operator ==




//
// modify
//




// Function:        Student::read_in()
// Purpose:         To prompt user for and get all of the
//                  receiver's data, including all data for
//                  the receiver's advisor.
// Pre:             input = aName \n aPhone \n aMajor \n
//                  aFloat \n aProfName \n aProfPhone \n
//                  aProfSalary \n restOfStuff
// Post:            input = restOfStuff and name = aName and
//                  phone = aPhone and major = aMajor and gpa =
//                  aFloat and advisor -> get_name() = aProfName
//                  and advisor -> get_phone() = aProfPhone and
//                  advisor -> get_salary() = aProfSalary
void Student::read_in()
{
    cout << endl;
    cout << "Enter student's name: ";
    read_string(name, MAXSTRING);
    cout << "Enter student's phone: ";
    read_string(phone, MAXSTRING);
    cout << "Enter student's major: ";
    read_string(major, MAXSTRING);
    cout << "Enter student's gpa: ";
    cin  >> gpa;
    cin.ignore(LINESIZE, '\n');
     // new line
    cout << "Enter advisor data when prompted: " << endl;
    advisor -> read_in();
}    // end Student::read_in()




// Function:        Student::set_major(amajor)
// Purpose:         To set the receiver's major to amajor.
// Pre:             amajor is defined
// Post:            major = amajor
void Student::set_major(string amajor)
{
    strcpy(major, amajor);
}    // end Student::set_major()
```

```
// Function:        Student::set_gpa(gp)
// Purpose:         To set the receiver's gpa to gp.
// Pre:             gp is defined
// Post:            gpa = gp
void Student::set_gpa(float gp)
{
    gpa = gp;
}    // end Student::set_gpa


// Function:        Student::set_advisor(profpt)
// Purpose:         To set the receiver's advisor equal (in value)
//                  to *profpt
// Pre:             *profpt is initialized
// Post:            all *profpt data members are equal to
//                  corresponding *advisor data members.
void Student::set_advisor(Professor* profpt)
{
    *advisor = *profpt;
}    // end Student::set_advisor()
```

FIGURE 2–45   C++ implementations of the Student class display, access, and
modify member functions from persons.cxx.

These functions are fairly straightforward. Perhaps of greatest interest is the manner in which Professor class methods are called when the advisor data member is involved.   In some sense, the Student class is reusing code that is already provided by the Professor class. This pattern is seen, for example, in the Student::read_in member function which calls Professor::read_in as follows:

```
advisor -> read_in();
```

The Student class file_in and file_out functions   The Student::file_in function shown in Figure 2–46   calls the Person::file_in function to read in a student's name and phone number. It then reads in a student's major and gpa. Finally, it reads in the data for a student's advisor by applying Professor::file_in to the Professor object that the data member advisor points to.

```
// Function:        Student::file_in(in_file)
// Purpose:         To read in the receiver's name, phone number,
//                  major, gpa and advisor data from in_file
// Pre:             in_file is a text file open for input and
//                  in_file = aName \n aPhone \n aMajor \n aGpa \n
//                  aProfName \n aProfPhone \n aSalary restOfStuff
// Post:            in_file = restOfStuff and name = aName
//                  and phone = aPhone and major = aMajor and
//                  gpa = aGpa and advisor -> get_name() =
//                  aProfName and advisor -> get_phone() =
```

```
//                    aProfPhone and advisor -> get_salary() = aSa-
lary
void Student::file_in(ifstream& in_file)
{
    // STATEMENTS ...
    Person::file_in(in_file);
    in_file.getline(major, MAXSTRING);
    in_file >> gpa;
    in_file.ignore(LINESIZE, '\n');
        // new line
    advisor -> file_in(in_file);
}   // end Student::file_in()
```

FIGURE 2–46 C++ implementation of `Student::file_in` member function from `persons.cxx`.

The function `Student::file_out`, shown in Figure 2–47, calls `Person::file_out` in order to file out a student's class, name and phone. It then writes out the student's major and gpa. Finally, it writes out the name, phone and salary of a student's advisor by applying the `get_name`, `get_phone` and `get_salary` functions to the `Professor` object that the data member `advisor` references. We did not use the statement

```
advisor -> file_out(out_file);
```

to file out a student's advisor because that would write out a superfluous class name string (with the value "`Professor`") to the external file.

```
// Function:       Student::file_out(out_file)
// Purpose:        To write out a representation of the receiver,
//                 including the receiver's class, to out_file.
// Pre:            out_file is a text file open for output and
//                 out_file = oldStuff and name is defined and
//                 phone is defined and major is defined and
//                 gpa is defined and advisor -> get_name() =
//                 prName and advisor -> get_phone() = prPhone
//                 and advisor -> get_salary() = prSalary
// Post:           (oldStuff = "" and
//                     out_file = "Student" \n name \n phone \n
//                     major \n gpa \n prName \n prPhone \n
//                     prSalary)   or
//                 (oldStuff != "" and
//                     out_file = \n "Student" \n name \n phone \n
//                     major \n gpa \n prName \n prPhone \n
//                     prSalary)
void Student::file_out(ofstream& out_file)
{
    Person::file_out(out_file);
    out_file << endl;
    out_file << major << endl;
    out_file << gpa << endl;
    out_file << advisor -> get_name() << endl;
    out_file << advisor -> get_phone() << endl;
```

```
        out_file << advisor -> get_salary();
}   // end Student::file_out()
```

FIGURE 2–47   C++ implementation of `Student::file_out` member function from `persons.cxx`.

EXERCISE

2–13 Design and implement the following classes: `Politician`, `Senator` and `CongressPerson`. `Senator` and `CongressPerson` are subclasses of `Politician` and `Politician` is a subclass of `Person` (as described in the text). A `Politician`, in addition to having a `name` and a `phone`, has a `party` and a `state`.[8] A `Senator` has a `rank` (junior or senior) and a `CongressPerson` has a `district` (given as an integer: 1, 2, ...). Your design should include methods for initializing, accessing, modifying, displaying, filing in and filing out.

*BUILDING A RESTRICTED DATA STRUCTURE

We now turn our attention to the design and implementation of a restricted data structure, `PersonSet`. A `PersonSet` is a specialized `ElementSet` that can only contain person objects (i.e., objects that belong to the classes `Person`, and the derived classes `Professor`, and `Student`). The main objectives of our `PersonSet` design are the following:

1. To restrict membership in a set to `Person`, `Professor`, and `Student` objects.
2. To allow a set to be written out to a file.
3. To allow a set to be reconstructed from data contained in a file.

Our discussion of the design and implementation of the `PersonSet` class will stress the ways in which we can reuse the code that is already available in the `ElementSet` class.

Designing the `PersonSet` class

A `PersonSet` is an `ElementSet` whose membership is restricted to `Person`, `Professor` and `Student` objects. Intuitively, a `PersonSet` would seem to be a special kind of `ElementSet` and, thus, it seems appropriate to implement the `PersonSet` class as a subclass of `ElementSet`. In so doing, we hope to

---

8.   ...and a price, according to many political observers, but you can ignore this "real world" consideration for the purposes of this exercise.

reuse as many of the `ElementSet` member functions as possible. Indeed, the `PersonSet` implementation presented in the next section will reuse the following `ElementSet` functions without modification:

```
is_member_of    cardinality    is_full      is_empty
get_any         clear          display
```

`PersonSet` will reuse these functions simply by inheriting them. These functions represent seven out of the eight member functions in the `ElementSet` class (not counting the constructor and the destructor). The reader should again study the implementation of these member functions to see why they can be reused by `PersonSet` without modification. For example, it is clear that there is nothing about the inherited function `ElementSet::display` (which is reproduced here as Figure 2–48) that in any way is affected by the fact that the `PersonSet` subclass will have restricted membership:

```
void ElementSet::display()
{
    // LOCAL DATA ...
    ElementPtr *ptr = s;


    // STATEMENTS ...
    for (; ptr < s + size; ptr++)
    {
        (*ptr) -> display();
    }
}   // end ElementSet::display()
```

FIGURE 2–48   C++ implementation of `ElementSet::display`.

We can *reuse* the `ElementSet::display` function by inheriting it because `*ptr` is polymorphic (i.e., `*ptr` can point to any kind of element, including, now, a `Person`, a `Student` or a `Professor`).

The `PersonSet` class will need a constructor and a destructor. The only `ElementSet` function that needs to be polymorphically redefined is the virtual function, `add`. In addition, `PersonSet` will include a `file_in` function for filing in person objects from a file and a `file_out` function for writing out person objects to a file. The declarations are found in the header file of Figure 2–49.

```
class PersonSet : public ElementSet
{
    public:
        // MEMBER FUNCTIONS ...
        // constructor - destructor
        PersonSet();
        virtual ~PersonSet();
```

```
                    // modify
                    virtual int add(ElementPtr);


                    // file in - file out
                    virtual int file_in(string);
                    virtual void file_out(string);
          };   // end class PersonSet
```

FIGURE 2–49   Declarations for the `PersonSet` class from `perset.h`.

Implementing the `PersonSet` Class

In this section, we present the definitions of the `PersonSet` member functions.

The `PersonSet` constructor and destructor   We prefer to provide an explicit constructor and destructor for every class. If a constructor or a destructor were not provided, the defaults would come into effect. In this case, our explicit constructor does exactly what the default constructor would do: it applies the `ElementSet` constructor to the `PersonSet` object being defined. This has the effect of establishing an empty `PersonSet`. Similarly, our explicit destructor does what the default destructor would do: it applies the `ElementSet` destructor to the relevant `PersonSet` object. This will deallocate all memory that was allocated for the various kinds of person objects stored in the `PersonSet`. The details are shown in Figure 2–50.

```
// Constructor:     PersonSet::PersonSet()
// Purpose:         Creates a new PersonSet object.
// Pre:             None
// Post:            current = -1 and size = 0    (i.e.,
//                  post for constructor ElementSet())
PersonSet::PersonSet()
{
    ; // Constructor ElementSet() called automatically
}   // end PersonSet::PersonSet()


// Destructor:      PersonSet::~PersonSet()
// Purpose:         Destroys the receiver PersonSet.
// Pre:             size = N
// Post:            for all i in {1..N} : *s[i-1] is
//                  deallocated (i.e., post for destructor
//                  ~ElementSet())
PersonSet::~PersonSet()
{
    ; // Destructor ~ElementSet() called automatically
}   // end PersonSet::~PersonSet()
```

FIGURE 2–50   C++ implementation of the constructor and destructor for the `PersonSet` class from `perset.cxx`.

The `PersonSet::add` function   You might be surprised that this function is so simple. Nonetheless, it contains the key idea that needed to understand implementation of restricted data structures. We first check to see if the argument `eptr` is pointing to an object that belongs to one of the valid classes (`Person`, `Professor`, or `Student`). If `eptr` points to any other kind of object, `PersonSet::add` returns 0, and `*eptr` (the object `eptr` points to) is not added to the receiver `PersonSet`. Otherwise (if `eptr` does point to some kind of person object), we simply invoke the `ElementSet::add` function to perform the actual addition. This is, again, an example of the reuse of previously developed code facilitated by the object-oriented approach to program development. The details are shown in Figure 2–51.

```
// Function:   PersonSet::add(eptr)
// Purpose:    To add the person that eptr points to
//             to the receiver PersonSet.
// Pre:        eptr is initialized and size is defined
// Post:       (eptr -> get_class in {"Person", "Student",
//             "Professor"} and post for ElementSet::add(eptr)
//             holds) or
//             (eptr -> get_class not in {"Person", "Student",
//             "Professor"} and add = 0 and size = old(size))
int PersonSet::add(ElementPtr eptr)
{
    // LOCAL DATA ...
    string recvr_class;


    // STATEMENTS ...
    strcpy(recvr_class, eptr -> get_class());
    if (!strcmp(recvr_class, "Person")
      || !strcmp(recvr_class, "Professor")
      || !strcmp(recvr_class, "Student"))
      return ElementSet::add(eptr);
    else
      return 0;
}   // end PersonSet::add()
```

FIGURE 2–51   C++ implementation of `PersonSet::add` from `perset.cxx`.

Note that if `*eptr` belongs to one of the legal classes, then the value returned by `PersonSet::add` is the value returned by `ElementSet::add`. That is, if the receiver set is full or if `*eptr` represents a duplicate object, then `PersonSet::add` will return 0; otherwise `ElementSet::add`, and thus, `PersonSet::add` will return 1.

Recall that the postcondition for the `ElementSet::add` is quite complicated. Rather than repeating it in the post-condition here, we refer to it as:

```
Post for ElementSet::add(eptr)
```

In other words, we are stating that if `eptr` points to a person object of some kind, then the postcondition for the `ElementSet::add` function will hold. This notation simplifies the statement of the post-condition.

The `PersonSet::file_out` function   The postcondition states in informal terms the idea that the `PersonSet::file_out` function achieves the filing out of each person in the receiver set.   The implementation of `PersonSet::file_out` is very simple.   We broadcast the message "`file_out(outfile)`" to each person object in the receiver set.   All of the element classes (including the three person classes) are expected to implement the `file_out(ofstream&)` functions in a consistent manner.   These functions always write out the name of the receiver's class and the value of all of the receiver's data members to the output file stream referenced in the argument. The complete implementation of `PersonSet::file_out` is given in Figure 2–52.

```
// Function:    PersonSet::file_out(file_name)
// Purpose:     To write out the contents of the receiver
//              set to the file whose name is file_name
// Pre:         size = N
// Post:        for i in {1..N} : s[i-1] has been filed out
//              to file whose name is file_name
void PersonSet::file_out(string file_name)
{
    // LOCAL DATA ...
    ofstream outfile;
    ElementPtr *ptr = s;

    // STATEMENTS ...
    outfile.open(file_name, ios::out);
    for (; ptr < s + size; ptr++)
    {
        (*ptr) -> file_out(outfile);
    }
    outfile.close();
}  // end PersonSet::file_out()
```

FIGURE 2–52   C++ implementation of `PersonSet::file_out` from `perset.cxx`.

Note that `PersonSet::file_out` is not one of the ubiquitous `file_out` functions; it is simply a function that overloads the `file_out` name.   The "ubiquitous" `file_out` functions are those that are implemented in the hierarchy of element classes and `PersonSet` is not part of that hierarchy.   Note also that `PersonSet::file_out` expects the name of a file and not a file object as an argument.

The `PersonSet::file_in` function   It is interesting to note that `PersonSet::file_in` and `PersonSet::file_out` for collection classes are so asymmetrical in their design.   This is related to the issue of persistence and the fact that there is no standard method for writing objects out to disk and then rebuilding them based upon the information stored on the disk.   Regrettably, we have to hand code functions to perform these tasks.   The code appears in Figure 2–53.

```
// Function:    PersonSet::file_in(file_name)
// Purpose:     To build the receiver PersonSet using the
```

```
//              data stored in a file whose name is file_name.
// Pre:         (file with name file_name does not exist) or
//              (file with name file_name does exist and is
//              a sequence of M Person file outs) and size = N
// Post:        (file with name file_name does not exist
//              and size = old(size) and file_in = 0) or
//              (file with name file_name does exist and
//              M+N <= CAPACITY and size = M+N and M Person
//              objects have been added to the receiver) or
//              (file with name file_name does exist and
//              M+N = CAPACITY+k and k > 0 and size = CAPACITY
//              and M - k Person objects have been added to
//              the receiver and all M Person objects have been
//              processed)
//
int PersonSet::file_in(string file_name)
{
    // LOCAL DATA ...
    ifstream infile;
    string class_id;
    Person  *perptr;


    // STATEMENTS ...
    infile.open(file_name, ios::in | ios::nocreate);
    if (infile.fail())
    {
        cout << "Could not open file.  It may not exist." << endl;
        return 0;  // failure
    }
    else
    {
        while (!infile.eof())
        {
        infile.getline(class_id, MAXSTRING);
        if (!strcmp(class_id, "Person"))
        {
            // create new dynamic Person object
            perptr = new Person;
        }
        else if (!strcmp(class_id, "Professor"))
        {
            // create new dynamic Professor object
            perptr = new Professor;
        }
        else // must be a Student
        {
            // create new dynamic Student object
            perptr = new Student;
        }


        // get rest of data; add new object to receiver
        perptr -> file_in(infile);
        add(perptr);
        } // while
        infile.close();
```

```
        return 1;   // success
    }  // else
}  // end PersonSet::file_in()
```

FIGURE 2–53   C++ implementation for `PersonSet::file_in` from `perset.cxx`.

The precondition presents several important simplifying assumptions that we have made. First, we are assuming that the file being read in is well-formed, that is, that it consists of "file outs" of `Person`, `Professor`, and `Student` objects only. We make no commitment to handling an ill-formed file correctly.   This function will work correctly even if the receiver `PersonSet` already contains some objects.   However, as the postcondition states, if the number of objects provided in the external file exceeds the number that can be accommodated, then any extra objects will simply be ignored.

This function reads in the first line of the file, which is assumed to be a class string. If this string is not in the set `{"Person"`, `"Professor"`, `"Student"}`, then the file is not a well-formed file and this function is not guaranteed to work properly. If this string is `"Person"`, the function creates a new dynamic `Person` object. If this string is `"Professor"`, the function creates a new dynamic `Professor` object and if this string is `"Student"`, then a new dynamic `Student` object is created.   Regardless of the type of person object that is created, `perptr` points to that object.   We then take advantage of polymorphism and the ubiquitousness of ubiquitous `file_in` functions to read in the data for the object that `perptr` points to, using:

```
perptr -> file_in(infile);
```

Finally, we add the object that `perptr` references to the receiver `PersonSet` using:

```
add(perptr);
```

This function is quite significant because it goes to the heart of the persistence issue and the need for restricted data structures if we are going to construct data structures from data in a file. This function requires a knowledge of the kinds of class strings that might be contained in a well-formed file. This function could not be implemented properly at the `ElementSet` level because there is no way to anticipate all possible element classes that might be implemented.

EXERCISES

2–14 Following the pattern established by `PersonSet`, design and implement a restricted set data structure called `PoliticianSet`. This will be an `ElementSet` whose membership is restricted to `Politicians` (see Exercise 2–13).

2–15   Following the pattern established by `PersonSet`, design and implement a restricted set data structure called `PointSet`. This will be an `ElementSet` whose membership is restricted to `Point` objects (see Exercise 2–11).

2–16   Extend your implementation of `PointSet` to include the following member functions:
   a.   `leftmost_point`
   b.   `rightmost_point`
   c.   `topmost_point`
   d.   `bottommost_point`

Each of these new functions will return a value of type `Point*`. The function `leftmost_point` returns a pointer to the `Point` in the receiver set that has the least X coordinate value. The function `rightmost_point` returns a pointer to the `Point` in the receiver set that has the greatest X coordinate. The function `topmost_point` returns a pointer to the `Point` in the receiver set that has the greatest Y coordinate and the function `bottommost_point` returns a pointer to the `Point` in the receiver set that has the least Y coordinate.

*A `PersonSet` CLIENT PROGRAM

In this section, we present the program `PSetter`, which acts as a client with respect to the `PersonSet` class. This program will create a `PersonSet` object called `perset`. The program will then file in data for `perset` from an external file called `"perdat.txt"`. The program will then allow the user to add new `Person`, `Professor` and `Student` objects to the `PersonSet`, using a loop similar to the one used in the earlier `Setter` program of Figure 2–28. The `PSetter` program will then use two functions to display the contents of the `perset`. Finally, the program will overwrite the text file `"perdat.txt"` with the latest contents of the `perset`.

We present only the new code in the subsections that follow. In particular, the functions `display_one` and `display_two` are not presented because they are identical to the `display_one` and `display_two` functions of the `Setter` program in Figures 2–30 and 2–31.

The main program file, `psetter.cxx`   The `PSetter` program consists of the following implementation files:

- `elements.cxx`, which implements the `Element` class,

- `strg.cxx`, which implements the `read_string` function,

- `persons.cxx`, which implements the `Person`, `Professor` and `Student` classes,

- `eleset.cxx`, which implements the `ElementSet` class,

- perset.cxx, which implements the PersonSet class,

- psetter.cxx, the main program file, which includes the main function and the following additional functions: prompt_and_get, get_per_set, display_one, and display_two.

The only new material that we need to present here are the functions main, prompt_and_get and get_per_set that are contained in the psetter.cxx file.   The beginning of the psetter.cxx file, including the function main is shown in Figure 2–54[9]

```
// This program illustrates the use of the PersonSet class.
// It initializes a PersonSet using data stored in a text
// file (perdat.txt). It then allows the user to add new
// Persons, Professors and Students to the PersonSet.
// It then uses two different functions to display the
// updated PersonSet before it writes the updated PersonSet
// out to a file.


#include <ctype.h>
#include <iostream.h>
#include <string.h>   // for strcpy
#include "strg.h"     // for LINESIZE
#include "perset.h"


void main()
{
    // LOCAL DATA ...
    PersonSet perset;


    // FUNCTION PROTOTYPES ...
    void get_per_set(PersonSet&);
    void display_one(PersonSet&);
    void display_two(PersonSet&);


    // STATEMENTS ...
    // load data from external file, if it exists
    //
    if (!perset.file_in("perdat.txt"))
    //
    // The Microsoft C/C++ compiler 7.00
    // fails to promote the char[] automatically
    // so you must resort to a string copy
    // string tmp;
    // strcpy(tmp,"perdat.txt");
    // if (!perset.file_in(tmp))
    {
```

---

9.   In Turbo C++, the #include "strg.h" must be #include "a:strg.h" to indicate that the strg.h file will be found on a disk in drive a.

```
          cout << "Starting with empty set. " << endl;
      }
      else
      {
          cout << "Starting with non-empty set." << endl;
      }


      // get new data from user and display updated set
      get_per_set(perset);
      display_one(perset);
      display_two(perset);


      // write out updated set to file
      perset.file_out("perdat.txt");
      //
      // The Microsoft C/C++ compiler 7.00 complication
      //perset.file_out(tmp);
}    // end main
```

FIGURE 2–54   The main function of the Psetter program.

Recall that the PersonSet::file_in function returns 0 if the file whose name was passed as an argument could not be opened successfully. Thus, the expression

```
!perset.file_in("perdat.txt")
```

is true if file_in returns 0 and there is no data to be read in. In this case, perset is an empty PersonSet. The function get_per_set (which is discussed in the next subsection) allows the user to add new person objects to perset. The perset is then displayed twice (first using display_one and then using display_two). Finally, the statement

```
    perset.file_out("perdat.txt");
```

either creates a new file called "perdat.txt"[10] or overwrites the file with that name. The objects in perset are "filed out" to the file "perdat.txt".

The functions get_per_set and prompt_and_get   The function get_per_set prompts the user for and gets data to be added to the PersonSet argument, perset, which is a pointer to a PersonSet. The function prompt_and_get is used to prompt the user with a menu of choices and to return an uppercase character that represents the user's choice. The logic of get_per_set is similar to the logic of get_set in the Setter program. For example, the statements:

---

10. In the Turbo C++ version of the software the a: indicates the disk drive that will contain the per-dat.txt file.

```
perptr = new Person;
perptr -> read_in();
perset.add(perptr);
```

executed in sequence (they are not contiguous in the code) will set `perptr` to a pointer to a new, dynamically allocated, `Person` object. The constructor `Person()` will be called in this case. Polymorphism will cause the function `Person::read_in` to be applied to the object that `perptr` points to, and finally, the object that `perptr` points to will be added to the `PersonSet`, that `perset` points to. The remaining details are in Figure 2–55.

```
// Function:        get_per_set()
// Purpose:         To get Person, Professor and Student data from
//                  the user and to add new objects to perset.
// Pre:             size = N and input = (M repetitions of :
//                      aMenuChoice PersonData)
// Post:            size = M + N and M new Persons have been added
//                  to perset.
void get_per_set(PersonSet& perset)
{
    // LOCAL DATA ...
    char menu_choice;
    Person *perptr;


    // FUNCTION PROTOTYPE ...
    char prompt_and_get();


    // STATEMENTS ...
    menu_choice = prompt_and_get();
    while (!perset.is_full() && menu_choice != 'Q')
    {
        switch(menu_choice)
        {
        case 'P':
            perptr = new Person;
            break;
        case 'F':
            perptr = new Professor;
            break;
        case 'S':
            perptr = new Student;
            break;
        }   // end switch
        perptr -> read_in();
        if (perset.add(perptr))
        {
        // add successful
        cout << "Person added to set.\n";
        }
        else
        {
        // duplicate person. could not add.
        cout << "Duplicate.  Could not add person to set.\a\n";
```

```
            delete perptr;
        }


        // get next menu choice
        menu_choice = prompt_and_get();
    } // end while
} // end get_per_set()
```

FIGURE 2–55 C++ implementation of get_per_set from psetter.cxx.

The prompt_and_get function is, similarly, analogous to prompt_user in the setter program. As shown in Figure 2–56, it basically prompts the user and gets a character code distinguishing Person, Professor, and Student objects, and a special quit code, Q. The character code is returned to the caller by prompt_and_get.

```
// Function:    prompt_and_get()
// Purpose:     Returns a menu choice from user
// Pre:         input = a legal menu choice restOfStuff
// Post:        prompt_and_get = a legal menu choice and
//              input = restOfStuff
char prompt_and_get()
{
    // LOCAL DATA ...
    char ch;


    // STATEMENTS ...
    cout << endl;
    cout << "Enter P if you want to create a Person, " << endl
      << "..... F if you want to create a Professor, " << endl
      << "..... S if you want to create a Student," << endl
      << "..... Q if you want to quit." << endl;
    cin >> ch;
    ch = toupper(ch);
    cin.ignore(LINESIZE, '\n');
    return ch;
} // end prompt_and_get()
```

FIGURE 2–56 C++ implementation of prompt_and_get from psetter.cxx.

EXERCISES

2–17 Following the model provided by the PSetter program, write a program that will read in politician information from a file, creating a PoliticianSet from this information (see Exercise 2–14). The program will then allow users to enter new politician data. The program will display the updated `PoliticianSet` and will write the updated `PoliticianSet` out to the original file.

2–18 Following the model provided by the `PSetter` program, write a program that will read in a set of `Point` objects from a file, creating a `PointSet` from this information (see Exercise 2–15). The program will then allow users to enter new point data. The program will display the updated `PointSet` and will write the updated `PointSet` out to the original file.

OBJECT-ORIENTED DESIGN AND SOFTWARE REUSE

A primary justification for the migration to object-oriented software development is that object-oriented languages support powerful forms of software reuse. A software component (such as a function or a class definition) is reusable to the extent that it can be employed in a variety of programs without modification. We now know enough about object-orientation to discuss the relationship between object-oriented languages and software reuse. In this chapter, we have illustrated four important forms of reuse: reusing object definitions, heterogeneity, reusing individual functions in a hierarchy, and reusing methods by "tweaking" a general structure.

Reusing object definitions   When we implement classes in which the classes are declared in header files and implemented in implementation files, we can reuse those classes in many different client programs. For example, there is no limit (in principle) to the number of programs that could use the `Person`, `Professor`, and `Student` classes as presented in this chapter. This frees the client programmers from having to reimplement these classes. This form of reuse is not peculiar to object-oriented languages. Indeed, it is not unlike the old idea of a software "library." Historically, a software library consisted of a collection of routines (procedures and functions) that were generally useful, especially routines that related to numerical and statistical computations.

Heterogeneous data structures   This represents a powerful form of reuse that is almost exclusively associated with object-oriented languages. Clearly, a heterogeneous queue (for example) is more reusable than a queue of integers or a queue of strings, or even a generic, but homogeneous, queue in some applications. Object-oriented languages facilitate the creation of heterogeneous data structures.

Reusing functions in an object-oriented design   A common pattern of reuse in object-oriented programming is when a ubiquitous function in one class calls the related ubiquitous functions in one or more related classes. This pattern was evident in several of the Student functions. For example, the function Student::file_in (reproduced here with the ubiquitous file_ins in bold for emphasis as Figure 2–57) calls both Person::file_in and Professor::file_in (since advisor is a Professor pointer):

```
void Student::file_in(ifstream& in_file)
{
    // STATEMENTS ...
    Person::file_in(in_file);
    in_file.getline(major, MAXSTRING);
    in_file >> gpa;
    in_file.ignore(LINESIZE, '\n');
        // new line
    advisor -> file_in(in_file);
}   // end Student::file_in()
```

FIGURE 2–57   C++ implementation of Student::file_in.

The fact that Student::file_in can be implemented in this way not only means that code from other classes can be reused, it also means that the resultant code is easier to understand than it might otherwise have been. The clarity stems from the fact that the ubiquitous file_in functions all have the same semantics throughout the hierarchy of element classes.

Reusing methods by "tweaking" a general structure   The PersonSet class illustrated this form of reuse. The general pattern there was to create a specialized structure from a more general structure. That is, the PersonSet class is a specialized version of the more general ElementSet class. The specialized structure was created by "tweaking" the more general structure. As we shall see, this represents a powerful form of reuse because the specialized structure is often able to use most of the functions of the more general structure without modification.

Another way of seeing that "tweaking" is a powerful form of reuse is to consider a context in which a software vendor has provided a collection of heterogeneous data structures (queues, stacks, lists, trees, graphs, and so forth). It is a simple matter for client programmers to create restricted structures from these heterogeneous structures. This does not involve modifying the given structures in any way. It involves implementing subclasses of the original classes, subclasses that inherit without modification many of the functions in the superclass. We shall see examples of this in later chapters, specifically in Chapter 7, when these classes are used in a program that simulates a simple operating system.

SUMMARY

This chapter has presented a number of important concepts and techniques for programming in an object-oriented language. Our primary goal has been to demonstrate how to implement heterogeneous and / or generic data structures, such as those that will be used in many of the subsequent chapters in this book. A number of important related concepts, including inheritance, virtual methods, polymorphic redefinition, deferred binding, true polymorphism, polymorphic objects, and persistence, have been discussed. The important class `Element`, along with some of its subclasses, `IntObj`, `FloatObj`, `CharObj`, `StringObj`, `Person`, `Professor`, and `Student`, were introduced. We showed the important role played by dynamic objects and implemented a class, `ElementSet`, that captures the intuitive notion of a set. A heterogeneous data structure was altered to create a restricted data structure. Finally, we looked at the important role played by ubiquitous functions and the interesting patterns of reuse that they enable.

CHAPTER 3

COMPLEXITY, SEARCHING, AND SORTING

In Chapter 1, we looked at several qualities of good software—correctness, robustness, user–friendliness, adaptability, reusability, interoperability, efficiency, portability, and security. In this chapter, we focus our attention on one quality of good software—*efficiency*. Efficiency in programs is desirable for a number of reasons, including its relation to the real cost of computers and computation. As a vehicle for studying efficiency, we introduce two general applications of considerable importance—sorting and searching. By searching, we mean the process of determining if an element is in a list. By sorting, we mean the process of rearranging the elements in a list so that they are in increasing (or decreasing) order. In this chapter, our lists will be arrays of integers. In Chapter 4, we will introduce the class `List` and discuss how the algorithms developed here can be applied to the heterogeneous data structures developed in Chapter 2.

INTRODUCTION TO COMPLEXITY

To begin, let us consider two alternative algorithms for sorting an array of integers from smallest to largest. Throughout this chapter, we will assume the following declarations.

```
const MAXARRSIZE=1000;
typedef int IntArr[MAXARRSIZE];
```

We assume that a is an array of type `IntArr`.

Definition We use the notation `a[0..n]` to denote the elements of an array with indices from 0 to n inclusive. `a[0..n]` *is sorted* means that for all j in {1..n}   `a[j-1]` ≤ `a[j]`.

Example 3.1 For example, `a[0..n]` = (3, 17, 4, 6, 15, 2) means that n = 5 and `a[0]` =3, `a[1]` = 17, ... , `a[5]` = 2, and `a[0..n]` *is sorted* means that `a[0]` = 2, `a[1]` = 3, `a[2]` = 4, `a[3]` = 6, `a[4]` = 15, and `a[5]` = 17.

When we make the assertion that a[0..n] is sorted, we assume implicitly that the final array, a, contains the same elements that the original array contained. That is, no elements have been created or destroyed. This prevents such 'trick' sorts as:

```
for (int i=0; i<=n; i++) a[i]=0;
```

which do, in fact, leave the array, a, in nondecreasing order; but do so by 'cheating'. We shall, from time to time, abuse the term *ascending* and use it to mean what is more properly called *nondecreasing*. Further, we assume the existence of the four additional functions, sortedp, maxloc, swap and permute, given in Figure 3–1.

```
//Function:sortedp (a, n)
//Purpose: To return 1 if a[0..n] is sorted; return 0 otherwise
//Pre:      0 <= n < MAXARRSIZE
//Post:     Let r be the value returned.  Then
//          a[0 .. n] is unchanged ^
//          ((r = 1)   ^   (a[0..n] is sorted) )  or
//          ((r = 0)   ^   (a[0..n] is not sorted) )

//Function:maxloc(a, n)
//Purpose: To return the index of the element of maximum value
//         in a[0..n]
//Pre:      0 <= n < MAXARRSIZE
//Post:     Let r be the value returned.  Then
//          ((0 <= r <= n)   ^   (for all j in {0..n}
//          a[j] <= a[r] ))

//Function:swap(a, i, j)
//Purpose: To interchange the elements at locations i and j in
//         array a
//Pre:      0 <= i,j < MAXARRSIZE
//Post:     The elements of a are unchanged except for  those at
//          indices i and j and
//          (a[i] = old a[j])  and  (a[j] = old a[i])

//Function:permute(a, n)
//Purpose: To permute the elements of a[0..n]
//Pre:      (0 <= n < MAXARRSIZE)   ^
//          (elements of a[0..n] are distinct)
//Post:     a[0..n] = the next permutation of
//          old (a[0], a[1], ..., a[n]) in lexicographic order
//          unless old (a[0], a[1], ..., a[n]) are in decreasing
//          order.  In that case, a[0..n] = a rearrangement of
//          (a[0], a[1], ..., a[n]) in increasing order. }
```

FIGURE 3–1   Specifications for the functions sortedp, maxloc, swap, and permute.

For instance, the next permutation of (1 2 3 4) is (1 2 4 3); the next permutation of (1 2 4 3) is (1 3 2 4); and the next permutation of (4 3 2 1) is (1 2 3 4). Our first sorting algorithm is given as Example 3.2.

Example 3.2 The following sorting function finds permutations of `a[0..n]` until `a[0..n]` is sorted.

```
void Sort_by_Perm(IntArr a, int n)
{
  while ( !sortedp(a,n) ) permute(a, n);
}
```

FIGURE 3-2 C++ code for a Sort by Permutation Algorithm.

Suppose we regard a deck of cards as sorted if all the clubs are first, then the diamonds, then the hearts, and lastly the spades and if the cards in each suit are arranged with the two first, the three second, up to the ace. `Sort_by_Perm` sorts the deck by rearranging it, determining if it is sorted, and if even one card is out of order, rearranging again. Thus, it could take an *extremely long time* to sort the deck (unless we happen to be very lucky). However, since the process of generating the permutations is done in a systematic way so that all possible permutations are cycled through, eventually the correct one will be found. If the permutations were generated randomly (for instance, by shuffling), the procedure conceivably could continue forever.[1] Certainly, no reasonable person would sort this way! However, it will illustrate some valuable points as we continue.

Our second algorithm (Example 3.3) searches through the deck card by card until the highest ranking card is found, puts it on the right, then searches for the next highest, puts it to the left of the first, etc. Continuing in this way, finally, the deck becomes sorted.

Example 3.3 This sorting algorithm rearranges the array element by element. It first finds the location of the largest number of the original array and swaps that element with the rightmost element. That element is then removed from consideration by reducing the right index, `topuns`. The variable `topuns` is used to hold the top (rightmost) index of unsorted left part of the array. Repeating the same sequence of operations on the shorter array finds the next-largest element and swaps it with the next-to-rightmost location of the original array, and so on until the array is sorted. A detailed discussion of the operation of `SelectionSort` is presented at the beginning of the next section.

```
//Function:selectionsort(a, n)
//Purpose: To sort the array  a[0..n]  into ascending order
//Pre:     0 <= n < MAXARRSIZE
//Post:    a[0..n] is in ascending order
void selectionsort(IntArr a, int n)
```

---

1.   We tried this process 5 times on a deck of just 3 cards. It took successively 3, 5, 4, 5, and 3 shuffles. We were not patient enough to try it on 4 cards!

```
  {
    int maxl;


    for (int topuns=n; topuns >= 1; topuns--)
    {
      maxl = maxloc(a,topuns);
      swap(a, topuns, maxl );
      //inv: (a[topuns .. n] is sorted) ^
      // (for all i in {0..topuns} a[i] <= a[topuns])
    }
  }  // end selectionsort
```

FIGURE 3–3   C++ code for a Selection Sort Algorithm.

These two examples illustrate some basic ideas about efficiency of algorithms.

1. Efficiency can refer to two factors—how the algorithm uses *space* and how it uses *time*. In most cases, it is quite easy to see how much space an algorithm consumes, but it is not so easy to estimate its time requirements; thus we will focus most of our efforts on considerations of time. In fact, if we speak about the "efficiency of an algorithm" we will mean time efficiency unless we explicitly refer to space. For instance, the algorithm Sort_by_Perm will normally take considerable time, whereas SelectionSort will take less time.

2. The time and space each sorting algorithm uses depends on the size of the array.

3. The time spent sorting an array may or may not depend on the initial arrangement of its items. For instance, if an array is already sorted, Sort_by_Perm only has to read through the array once, whereas SelectionSort requires approximately the same number of steps no matter what the initial arrangement is. The worst case (i.e., the case requiring the longest possible time) for Sort_by_Perm occurs when the sorted order is the last permutation to be examined—i.e., n! permutations have to be examined before the ordered one is found. For instance, if the array is initially (1 3 2), Sort_by_Perm has to successively test (1 3 2), (2 1 3), (2 3 1), (3 1 2), (3 2 1), and finally (1 2 3). SelectionSort, on the other hand, would go through the array and pick the 3, swap it with something, then go through and pick the 2, swap it with something, and lastly pick the 1, independently of what the initial arrangement was.

Many implementation factors influence the time a computer takes to execute an algorithm, including the following:

• The programming language in which it is written

• The machine code that a particular compiler generates for the program, and

- The time each of the machine instructions takes to execute.

We would like to find a way to determine the efficiency of an algorithm that is independent of these implementation factors. To do this, we look at the algorithm itself (expressed in C++ or pseudocode) and count the number of *steps* the algorithm takes. There are several alternative ways we can do this:

1. We can simply count the number of steps the algorithm requires, taking into account that this depends on the size of the input data. The disadvantage of this is that steps vary greatly in how long they take—for instance, generating a permutation in `Sort_by_Perm` will take considerably longer than swapping elements in `SelectionSort`.
2. We can look more closely at each step and count the number of *operations* (additions, multiplications, assignments, comparisons, etc.) the algorithm uses. This is better, but it still suffers from the same problem as counting steps—for instance, a multiplication may take fifty times as long to execute as an addition.
3. We can count the most costly operations. Unfortunately, this is unreliable because the most costly operations may occur very infrequently.
4. We can attempt to identify the *critical steps* in an algorithm and count the number of times these are executed. The critical steps are those that consume the most time; typically these are the steps that are contained in an innermost nested loop.

The fourth approach is the one we will take. It may happen that there are several steps in the innermost nested loop. These particular steps will be called the *dominant segment* of the program.

Definition   The *dominant segment* of a program is that collection of steps that consume the most time, which is usually measured by the number of times they are executed. The dominant segment often occurs within the innermost loop and/or the most deeply nested calling level for a method.

We are interested in the number of times the dominant segment in a program is executed.

Within the dominant segment, there is often one *dominant operation*, such as a multiplication. In this case, we ignore the other steps and look at the complexity of the algorithm in terms of the number of multiplications it requires. Alternatively, if there is no single dominant operation, we can identify one operation (often a comparison) in the dominant segment as the "essence" of the algorithm and regard it as the dominant operation.

Definition   The *complexity* of an algorithm is the number of times the dominant operation in the dominant segment is performed.

For instance, the dominant segment of `Sort_by_Perm` is the statement

```
permute(a, n);
```

Thus, we can identify the complexity of `Sort_by_Perm` as the number of permutations generated.

Alternatively, we can look at the implementation of an algorithm and express the complexity in terms of the types of operations done in it. For instance, the dominant segment of `SelectionSort` is

```
for (int topuns=n; topuns >= 1; topuns--)
{
    maxl = maxloc(a,topuns);
    swap(a, topuns, maxl );
}
```

We can state the complexity in terms of whichever one of these steps is likely to be the most time-consuming. The time each will take depends on its implementation. However, `maxloc(a,topuns)` requires examination of each element of `a[0..topuns]`, which the other operations may or may not require. Thus it is reasonable to regard the call to `maxloc` as the dominant operation. Since `maxloc` involves another loop, namely one that compares values of `a[0..topuns]` to decide which is largest, we can state the complexity of `SelectionSort` as the number of comparisons involved. We prefer to state it this way and not as the number of calls to `maxloc` since a comparison is a primitive operation and thus its time requirements are known for any given CPU.

Thus, to determine the complexity of an algorithm, we need to identify its dominant segment and then determine how many times the dominant operation in the dominant segment is performed. Since this often depends on the size, n, of the input data, an algorithm's complexity is usually stated as a function of n. Recall, however, that complexity also depends on the initial arrangement of the input data. Thus we can often distinguish a worst-case complexity, an average-case complexity, and a best-case complexity.

> **Definition**   The *worst-case complexity* of an algorithm is the maximum number of times the dominant operation in the dominant segment can be performed. The *average-case complexity* is the average number of times the dominant operation in the dominant segment will be performed taken over all possible arrangements of the input data. The *best-case complexity* is the minimum number of times the dominant operation in the dominant segment can be performed.

For instance, if we take n to be the number of items in the array, the worst-case complexity of `Sort_by_Perm` is $n!$ permutations. The average case is $\frac{1}{2}n!$ and the best case is 1. The worst case, average case, and best case for `SelectionSort` are all the same, namely:

$$n + (n - 1) + (n - 2) + \ldots + 1$$

comparisons, since the number of elements to check in each call to `maxloc` decreases by one at each iteration of the inner loop. This sums to $\dfrac{n(n + 1)}{2}$. Finding the average case complexity of an algorithm is often difficult, however.

One of the main benefits of this kind of complexity analysis is that it gives us a metric for comparing *algorithms* with respect to efficiency. However, we need to be careful that we are comparing "apples to apples." For instance, `Sort_by_Perm` requires n! permutations in the worst case and `Selection-Sort` requires $\dfrac{n(n + 1)}{2}$ comparisons. Thus we cannot say that `Sort_by_Perm` is less efficient unless we add the fact that it takes longer to generate a permutation than to do a comparison. We also need to know that for all positive integers n, $n! > \dfrac{n(n + 1)}{2}$. Thus to compare the complexity of algorithms, we need some mathematical tools that will allow us to compare functions. It is common practice to use the letter n to indicate the number of objects under consideration. It is also common to use n as the top index in an array, e.g. `a[0..n]`. In C and C++, all arrays have a lower index of 0, so that the number of elements in the array `a[0..n]` is really $n+1$. For now, we will try to be precise about whether the n we are talking about is the number of elements in an array or the top index of the array. Later, we will expect the reader to decide based on context.

> **Definition** A function g *dominates* another function f if either $g(x)$ or some constant multiple of $g(x)$ exceeds $f(x)$ for all values of x (except possibly for small values). We use the notation $O(g(n))$ [read "big-oh" of $g(n)$] for the set of functions dominated by $g(n)$.

Thus, for instance, $n!$ dominates n^2 (see Figure 3–4). Note that for $n = 2$ and $n = 3$, $n^2 > n!$. But for $n > 4$, $n! > n^2$. Thus n^2 belongs to $O(n!)$ but $n!$ does not belong to $O(n^2)$. We can establish the following hierarchy of relationships where each set on the left is a *proper* subset of the set on its right:

$$O(1) \subset O(\log_2 n) \subset O(n) \subset O(n \log_2 n) \subset O(n2) \subset O(n^3) \subset ... \subset O(n^k) \subset O(2^n) \subset O(n!)$$

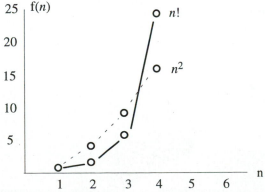

FIGURE 3–4 Comparison of $n!$ and n^2.

For a further illustration of the concept of domination, see Figure 3–5. Note that n dominates $\log_2 n$ which in turn dominates 1.

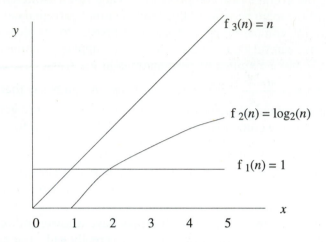

FIGURE 3–5   Asymptotic domination of several functions.

One important feature of the concept of domination is that functions which differ by a constant multiple dominate each other and hence can be regarded as *equivalent*. For instance, $O(3n) = O(n)$. Even though $3n$ clearly grows faster than n, we regard them as equivalent because they both increase linearly. That is, they grow "in the same way" (see Figure 3–6). Thus, when using big-oh notation as a complexity measure, we can ignore leading constants.

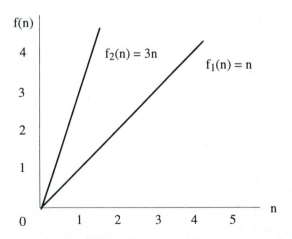

FIGURE 3–6   Comparison of two "equivalent" functions which differ by a constant multiple.

A second feature of this notation is that adding dominated functions to an expression can be ignored. For instance $n^2 + n$ is equivalent to n^2 since n is dominated by n^2. Combining these two observations, we see, for instance, that $n^2 + 3n + 2$ is in $O(n^2)$.

There are two additional notations you will see from time to time, $\Theta(\mathbf{f})$ and $o(f)$. $\Theta(\mathbf{f})$ denotes the set of functions equivalent to f and $o(f)$ denotes all functions that are *strictly dominated* by f—functions dominated by f which are not equivalent to it. Thus, $o(f) \equiv O(\mathbf{f}) - \Theta(\mathbf{f})$.

If the number of steps in the dominant segment of an algorithm is equivalent to (for instance) n^2 we say that *the algorithm is* $O(n^2)$. An $O(n^2)$ algorithm is more efficient than an $O(n^3)$ algorithm since n^3 dominates n^2. The number of steps required by a more efficient algorithm is always dominated by the number of steps required by a less efficient algorithm. Another way of looking at this concept is to think of n^3 as "growing faster" than n^2. This difference in growth rate can be quite substantial. See Table 3–1 for a comparison of the growth rates of some common functions.

TABLE 3–1   GROWTH OF FIVE COMMON FUNCTIONS

n	$\log_2 n$	n	n^2	n^3	2^n
1	0	1	1	1	1
10	3.3	10	100	1000	1024
100	6.6	100	10^4	10^6	$>10^{30}$
1000	10.0	1000	10^6	10^9	$>10^{300}$
10000	13.3	10000	10^8	10^{12}	$>10^{3000}$

EXERCISES

3–1 Sketch the functions $f(n) = 2n + 5$ and $g(n) = n^2$. Show graphically that g dominates f.

3–2 Sketch the functions $f(n) = n^2 + 2$ and $g(n) = 2^n$. Show graphically that g dominates f.

3–3 Let $f(n) = 18n - 1$ and $g(n) = 0.01n^2 + n + 1$. For what positive values of n is $g(n) > f(n)$? Which function is dominant?

3–4 Separate the following list of expressions into collections that are equivalent to each other:

$\log n$ $\qquad\qquad$ $n + \log n$ $\qquad\qquad$ 37

$2^{\log_2 n}$ $\qquad\qquad$ $n^2 + 16n + 1$ $\qquad\qquad$ $n + \dfrac{18}{n}$

$$3n + 2 \qquad\qquad 5n^2 + 2\log n \qquad\qquad 10^{-5}n^2$$
$$13n + \log n + 6 \qquad (3n + 1)(2 + \log n) \qquad 16n + 5n\log n$$

3–5 Find an example of a function in $O(1)$ that is not a constant function.

SEARCHING

One of the most frequent applications of computers is searching quantities of data for a particular item. Computer scientists have devised several data structures that allow rapid access to data and easy updates as well. Our focus in this section is on the design and complexity of algorithms that are used to search ordered and unordered arrays. We will examine the problem of searching more complex structures in subsequent chapters.

Linear Search

We begin with the most basic structure, an unsorted array, and the simplest search algorithm. Suppose `a[0..n]` denotes an unsorted array of `n+1` integers and `x` is a particular integer. Our objective is to search `a[0..n]` to determine whether or not `x` occurs there and, if so, to determine its index in `a[0..n]`.

```
//Function: linSearch(a, n, x)
//Purpose: To return the index of the first occurence of x in
//          a[0..n] or to return -1 if x is not in a[0..n]
//Pre:      0 <= n < MAXARRSIZE
//Post:     Let r be the value returned.  Then
//          ( (r = -1)   ^   (x is not in a[0..n]) )      or
//          ( (x=a[r])   ^   (0 <= r <= n)   ^
//          (x is not in a[0..r-1]) )
int linSearch(IntArr a, int n, int x)
{
  if (n >= MAXARRSIZE)
  {
    cout << endl << "You asked for a linear search through \
    more elements than allowed." << endl;
    cout << "I will give you a search through MAXARRSIZE \
    elements." << endl;
    n = MAXARRSIZE;
  }


  for (int i=0; i <= n; i++)
    {
      if (x == a[i]) break;
      //inv: x is not in a[0..i]
    }  //end for
  if (i <= n)
    return i;  // found at location i
  else
```

```
        return (-1);   // x is not in a[0..n]
}   //end linSearch
```

FIGURE 3–7   C++ code for a Linear Search Algorithm.

> **Example 3.4**   Consider the array a[0..11] = (4 9 7 11 3 8 13 6 8 19 3 5).
>
> *a.*   LinSearch(a, 11, 8) searches a for the number 8. Since a[5] == 8, the if statement causes a break from the for loop with i == 5. Because this value of i is less than or equal to n (11), LinSearch returns a result of 5. Note that the first 8 is the only one found by this version of LinSearch.
>
> *b.*   LinSearch(a, 11, 21) searches a for 21. In this case, 21 is not in the array. Thus the loop terminates with i == 12, one more than the top index, n, of the range to be searched. Hence, the if (i <= n) statement causes –1 to be returned.

Note that if there is more than one occurrence of x in a, LinSearch always finds the first one.

Verification of Linear Search   Now we verify the correctness of this algorithm. Most of the algorithms you will see in this chapter will be verified in the text—some verifications will be left to the exercises. Our purpose in verifying these algorithms is to help you begin to develop techniques for establishing the correctness of the algorithms. Acquiring these tools, however, is not easy! The following is a brief introduction to verification.

To verify an algorithm, we need to show that its code is consistent with its pre- and postconditions. This can be done in the following steps.

1.   Assume that the precondition is valid; i.e., that we have some particular input for which the precondition is true.
2.   Move through the algorithm step by step, noting relationships that follow from the precondition and transforming these relationships at each step in accordance with the particular statements encountered.
3.   Determine that the postcondition is satisfied at the end of this process.

Step 2 involves using mathematical induction on each loop in the algorithm. This assures that the loop's invariant is satisfied.[2]

The verification of LinSearch is relatively short and straightforward. The verifications we do later will be longer and more detailed. Carrying out the

---

2.   Some texts prefer to start with the postcondition and work backward. They look at the states that satisfy the postcondition and calculate the inverse image of that set under the last step of the algorithm. The inverse image of this set is then calculated for the second to the last step. This process continues all the way back to the beginning of the algorithm. If the resulting preimage contains the set of states satisfying the precondition, the algorithm is verified. For an introduction to verification, we find that working forward is easier to understand, since it mirrors the step-by-step execution of the algorithm itself.

steps of a verification can often seem tedious and frustrating because there are so many details. However, it is precisely this attention to detail that provides the greatest value in verification! Subtle (or even egregious) errors frequently occur in seemingly innocent code. When we attempt to verify this code, the necessity of evaluating what happens in each case uncovers situations in which the algorithm might fail. Furthermore, we have found that carefully verifying an algorithm often leads us to a depth of understanding that we have been unable to acquire in any other way.

We suggest, however, that you do not simply read through a verification. Instead, try keeping one finger on the algorithm, another on the verification, and pencil and paper on the side. Then walk through the verification step by step, checking each of its assertions as you go. At the end, go back and read through the algorithm again, to "nail it down" in your memory, and to see how much more clearly you understand it. Now let us begin the verification of LinSearch (don't forget the pencil and paper):

1. The precondition guarantees that the for-loop will be entered. If x == a[0], then the first if-statement will break out of the for-loop and the second if-statement will cause the correct index of 0 to be returned. To check the loop invariant, proceed inductively. For the initialization step, note that when i == 0, the failure to break out of the for-loop means that x is not equal to a[0] so x is not in a[0..0]. For the induction step, we suppose i is such that x is not a member of a[0..i] at the foot of the for-loop. The for-loop causes i to be incremented and if i is still in the range of interest (i <= n), the statement if (x == a[i]) break; is executed. If the break is not executed then x != a[i] and the invariant is true for the new value of i.

2. Now we consider two cases separately, depending on whether or not the loop finds x. First, suppose it does find x at index r. The if-statement after the loop returns the value r. Since the invariant held on the previous pass through the loop, x is not in a[0..(r-1)] giving the correct postcondition in this case. Second, suppose x is not in a[0..n]. Then at the conclusion of the for-loop, i = n + 1 so that the final if-statement will cause the value -1 to be returned.

This completes the verification of LinSearch.

Complexity of Linear Search   The dominant segment of this program is the loop:

```
for (int i=0; i <= n; i++)
    {
      if (x == a[i]) break;
      //inv: x is not in a[0..i]
    }  //end for
```

The operation that most characterizes this loop is the comparison of x to a[i]; thus we think of the complexity of this algorithm in terms of number of occurrences of this comparison.

The worst case complexity occurs when x is not in the array; in this case n+1 comparisons are required. Thus the worst case complexity of LinSearch is $O(n)$. The average case takes into account two possibilities—x is in a[0..n] and x is not. Suppose the probability that x is in a[0..n] is p. Suppose also that each of the locations a[0] ... a[n] is equally likely to be the location of x. Then the probability that a[i] == x is $\frac{p}{n+1}$. Thus the average number of comparisons is given by the expression:

$$1\frac{p}{n+1} + 2\frac{p}{n+1} + \ldots + (n+1)\frac{p}{n+1} + (1-p)(n+1)$$

$$= \frac{(n+2)}{2}p + (1-p)(n+1)$$

This is also in $O(n)$. Note that if $p = 0$, this becomes $n + 1$, which is the value we obtained for the worst case complexity. If $p = 1$ (wherein x is certain to be in a[0..n]), this becomes $\frac{(n+2)}{2}$, indicating that we would expect to search roughly half the array.

If we have no information about how the data in a list is arranged, a worst case complexity of $O(n)$ is the best we can expect to achieve. Since the list is unordered, *any* algorithm must examine every member before we can say that an element is not in the list; thus any algorithm for searching the list must have a worst case complexity of at least $O(n)$. But linear search is in $O(n)$; thus no algorithm can do better than linear search in terms of big-O. Similarly, it is impossible to find an algorithm that improves on the average case complexity of linear search for the same reason—every item in the list has to be examined and each is equally likely to be the desired element. Thus, in terms of big–O, linear search is an optimal algorithm for the problem of searching an unordered list. But the fact that linear search is asymptotically optimal for unordered lists does not mean that there are not better searches. Big–O notation hides constant factors. A careful look at the linear search algorithm shows that there are really 2 comparisons done each time through the for-loop.

```
for (int i=0; i <= n; i++)
   {
      if (x == a[i]) break;
   }  //end for
```

One is the element comparison, x == a[i], which we have counted. But each time through the loop, the comparison, i <= n, is also made to prevent the index i from going out of the range of interest. This latter comparison is likely to be performed very quickly because most machine languages have special looping instructions to facilitate just this kind of comparison. On the other hand, there is an elegant way to do away with this second comparison altogether. The idea is to guarantee that x will always be found so that there is no need to check in the loop if the index has gone too far. This search is called a sentinel search and the details are given in Figure 3–8.

```
//Function:sentinelSearch(a, n, x)
//Purpose: To return the index of the first occurence of x in
//          a[0..n] or to return -1 if x is not in a[0..n]
//Pre:      0 <= n < MAXARRSIZE - 1
//Post:     Let r be the value returned.   Then
//                ( (r = -1)   ^   (x is not in a[0..n]) )      or
//                ( (x=a[r])   ^   (0 <= r <= n)   ^
//                (x is not in a[0..r-1]) )
int sentinelSearch(IntArr a, int n, int x)
{
   if (n >= MAXARRSIZE - 1)
   {
      cout << endl << "You asked for a sentinel search through
more elements than allowed." << endl;
      cout << "I will give you a search through MAXARRSIZE - 1
elements." << endl;
       n = MAXARRSIZE - 1;
   }


   a[n+1] = x;  //set the sentinel to guarantee termination of
for loop
      for (int i=0; ; i++)
      {
         if (x == a[i]) break;
         //inv: x is not in a[0..i]
      }   //end for

      if (i <= n)
         return i;   // found at location i
      else
         return (-1);   // found sentinel so x is not in a[0..n]
}   //end sentinelSearch
```

FIGURE 3–8   C++ code for a Sentinel Search Algorithm.

The for-loop no longer contains a termination test because the if–statement inside the loop is guaranteed to find a match, either in the range 0..n or at n+1 because we put a copy of x into a[n+1]. There are two things to keep in mind about the sentinel search.

1.   One extra element of the array is needed for the sentinel. Thus, one cannot do a sentinel search if the array is filled to its maximum capacity.
2.   Although both linear search and sentinel search are O(n), in every realistic situation, if a search of an unordered array is called for, sentinel search is to be preferred.

You might note that the for-loop could be replaced by code such as:

```
int i = -1;
while (x != a[++i]);
```

This empty while-loop is elegant in some ways and many C programmers like its brevity. For the purpose of this text, however, we prefer code that makes the functioning of the algorithm clear even if it is a bit more wordy.

As stated above, algorithms that have a running time of $O(n)$ are the best one can hope for in searching an unordered array. However, if we can assume that the data are arranged *a priori* in some kind of order, substantial improvements are possible.

Binary Search

Suppose we have an array, a[0..n], whose elements are arranged in order from smallest to largest, such as the names in a telephone directory. The elements can be of type int, float, or string—in general, any type for which there is a natural ordering. Suppose also we have an element x and we would like to determine if x is in a[0..n] and, if it is, locate it.

For instance, looking up someone's name in a telephone directory is an example of this sort of problem. A common strategy for looking up a telephone number is to make an arbitrary guess at its location by opening up the directory somewhere near the middle, try this guess, check whether the phone number precedes or follows that guess, and then make another try. In the next try, however, we only look at the remaining half of the directory that was not eliminated by the first try.

Binary search is an algorithm very much like this. We always start at the middle of the array and decide which half our desired element is in. Once that is decided, we ignore the "wrong" half and repeat the process until we either find the element or conclude that it is not in the array. The code is presented in Figure 3–9.

```
//Function:binarySearch(a, n, x)
//Purpose: To return the index of an occurence of x in a[0..n]
//          or to return -1 if x is not in a[0..n]
//Pre:      (0 <= n < MAXARRSIZE - 1)  ^  (a[0..n] is sorted
//          in ascending order)
//Post:     Let r be the value returned.  Then
//          ( (r = -1)  ^  (x is not in a[0..n]) )      or
//          ( (x=a[r])  ^  (0 <= r <= n) )
int binarySearch(IntArr a, int n, int x)
{
  int lo=0, hi=n, mid;


  if (n >= MAXARRSIZE)
  {
    cout << endl << "You asked for a binary search through \
        more elements than allowed." << endl;
    cout << "I will give you a search through MAXARRSIZE \
        elements." << endl;
    n = MAXARRSIZE;
  }
```

```
      while (hi>lo)
      {
        mid = (lo + hi) / 2;
        if (x <= a[mid])     //then x is in lower half so
          hi = mid;        //lower hi
        else      //otherwise x is in upper half so
          lo = mid+1;    //raise lo
        //inv:   ( a[lo] <= x <= a[hi] )   or ( x is not in a[0..n] )
      }  //end while

      if (x == a[lo])
        return lo;  // found at location lo
      else
        return (-1);  //  x is not in a[0..n]
    }  //end binarySearch
```

FIGURE 3–9   C++ code for a Binary Search Algorithm.

Example 3.5   Consider a[0..12] = (1 3 3 4 6 8 9 10 13 14 17 17 18). We can apply `BinarySearch` to look up (*a*) 8, (*b*) 0, (*c*) 3, (*d*) 21, and (*e*) 12.

a.   Since n = 12, the values of lo, hi, mid, and a[mid] on each pass through the loop are shown in Table 3–2.

TABLE 3–2   VALUES OF KEY VARIABLES FOR n = 12

loop pass	lo	hi	mid	a[mid]
1	0	12	6	9
2	0	6	3	4
3	4	6	5	8
4	4	5	4	6
5	5	5		

Note that a[mid] = 8 on the third pass through the loop. Alternate versions of binary search test if x == a[mid] and, if so, drop out of the loop rather than just testing if x ≤ a[mid]. One of the exercises will ask you to explore whether or not this change actually makes binary search more efficient.

b.   If x = 0, the intermediate values become those given in Table 3–3.

TABLE 3–3 VALUES OF KEY VARIABLES FOR x = 0

loop pass	lo	hi	mid	a[mid]
1	0	12	6	9
2	0	6	3	4
3	0	3	1	3
4	0	1	0	1
5	0	0		

c. If x == 3, we get the sequence of values in Table 3–4.

TABLE 3–4 VALUES OF KEY VARIABLES FOR x = 3

loop pass	lo	hi	mid	a[mid]
1	0	12	6	9
2	0	6	3	4
3	0	3	1	3
4	0	1	0	1
5	1	1		

d. When x == 21, the result is Table 3–5.

TABLE 3–5 VALUES OF KEY VARIABLES FOR x = 21

loop pass	lo	hi	mid	a[mid]
1	0	12	6	9
2	7	12	9	14
3	10	12	11	17
4	12	12		

e. Finally, if we set x = 12, Table 3–6 captures the result.

TABLE 3–6 VALUES OF KEY VARIABLES FOR x = 12

loop pass	lo	hi	mid	a[mid]
1	0	12	6	9
2	7	12	9	14
3	7	9	8	13
4	7	8	7	10
5	8	8		

The final value of lo is 8. Note that if we wanted to insert the element of value 12 into a[0..n], it should go 'between' index 7 and index 8. In some situations, this knowledge is of interest.

Verification of BinarySearch   The verification of the binary search algorithm is more complicated than that for linear search. But this will illustrate another value of verification—besides demonstrating that the algorithm is correct, the verification provides a careful explanation of exactly what the algorithm is doing and why it works. We shall see this below.

To verify BinarySearch, we first check that the loop terminates. Suppose hi - lo > 1 at the beginning of some iteration of the while loop. Then, that iteration of the loop will give a value of mid between lo and hi which differs from both of them. Thus, letting hi = mid or lo = mid+1 will bring hi and lo closer together, so that each pass through the loop makes progress toward termination. Now suppose hi - lo = 1. In this case, mid becomes lo. This is why the else clause in the loop assigns lo the value mid+1 rather than mid—the latter alternative would cause an infinite loop. As written, however, either hi becomes mid (which equals lo) or lo becomes mid+1 (which equals hi), but either alternative causes the loop to terminate since mid is guaranteed to be assigned a new value during each iteration of the loop.

We also need to check the loop invariant, using induction. Before the loop begins, we can make the following assertion:

```
(a[lo] <= x <= a[hi])   or   ( x is not in a[0..n])
```

because lo was set to 0, hi was set to n, and the array a is sorted in ascending order. Thus the invariant holds initially, and we have established the basis step for the induction. Now suppose the invariant holds after some number i of passes through the loop. We have three cases:

1. If x is not in a[0..n], the invariant still holds after completion of the i+1st pass.
2. Suppose x is in a[0..n], then the invariant at the end of the ith pass guarantees that a[lo] <= x <= a[hi] immediately before the i+1st

pass. If $x < $ a[mid], then the new hi = mid, lo stays the same, so, after the completion of the i+1st pass, it is still true that a[lo] <= x <= a[hi] in terms of the new values of lo and hi. On the other hand if x >= a[mid], it must be that $x > $ a[mid+1], since x is in a[0..n] and a[0..n] is sorted in ascending order. Then assigning lo = mid + 1 maintains the invariant a[lo] <= x <= a[hi] after completion of the pass.

We can now check whether the postcondition holds. If n = 0, the loop is never entered because lo = hi = 0. The if-statement after the loop guarantees the postcondition.

If n > 0, the loop will be entered so we can apply the loop invariant to conclude that when we fall out of the loop, a[lo] <= x <= a[hi] or x is not in a[0..n]. Since lo = hi on loop termination, this means that either x = a[lo] or x is not in a[0..n]. The if-statement after the loop ensures that the correct value will be returned to obtain the postcondition.

Complexity of BinarySearch   Now we need to analyze the complexity of BinarySearch. The dominant segment is the while loop and the dominant operation is comparison which occurs twice in each iteration of the loop. Thus, we can compute the time complexity of BinarySearch by counting the iterations. At any given step, we take the set of elements of a[lo..hi] and cut it roughly in half; this is why algorithms like binary search are called *divide and conquer* algorithms. If we let *m* be the size of the subarray a[lo..hi], then $m = $ (hi - lo + 1) and we can tabulate the size of the resulting subarrays as shown in Table 3–7.

TABLE 3–7   SIZE OF THE DIVIDED ARRAY

If m is:	subarray	size
odd	a[lo..mid]	(m+1)/2
odd	a[(mid+1) .. hi]	(m−1)/2
even	a[lo..mid]	m/2
even	a[(mid+1) .. hi]	m/2

Evidently, the size of the resulting subarray never exceeds $\frac{m+1}{2}$. In general, then, for an array of size *n*, we can tabulate the progress each iteration makes in reducing the size of the subarray being examined as shown in Table 3–8.

TABLE 3–8   SUCCESSIVE REDUCTIONS IN THE SIZE OF THE ARRAY

Iteration	Upper Bound for Size of Subarray
0	n
1	$(n+1)/2$
2	$(n+3)/4$
3	$(n+7)/8$
...	
k	$(n-1+2^k)/2^k$

Thus after k iterations, an upper bound for the size of the remaining subarray is $(n-1)/2^k + 1$. Hence if k is large enough that

$$\frac{n-1}{2^k} + 1 < 2$$

we are certain that the size of the remaining subarray is 1—i.e., the size is an integer and is less than or equal to $(n-1)/2^k + 1$. Hence, if $(n-1)/2^k + 1 < 2$, the size must be 1. Thus `lo == hi` and the loop is done. The previous expression is equivalent to $n-1 < 2^k$ and thus the number of iterations required cannot exceed $\lceil \log_2(n-1) \rceil$. Since this is an awkward expression to work with, we can use the following relation to simplify it.

$$\lceil \log_2(n-1) \rceil < 1 + \log_2(n-1) < 1 + \log_2(n)$$

That is, the worst case complexity of binary search is in $O(\log_2 n)$. A lower bound for the best case can be found by taking the size of the subarray after splitting to be $(n-1)/2$. A similar analysis to what was done above shows that the best case complexity is also in $O(\log_2 n)$. (See the exercises.) Hence the average case is in $O(\log_2 n)$ also.

This does not mean that the best, worst, and average case searches for any specified value of n are always the same, however. For instance, in Example 3.5, each case except case d required five iterations, whereas case d required four. Rather, it is the *growth* of time that is common across all cases. An algorithm with a complexity of $O(\log_2 n)$ is very efficient (see Table 3–1). Binary search enables extremely large tables to be searched very quickly.

Hashing

Linear and binary search are two of the most commonly used searching algorithms. But there is one more frequently used searching technique that we need to examine in order to complete our study of searching, and that is hashing.

A typical and very important application of hashing is in building the symbol table used by a compiler. For instance, consider a C++ program which includes the following variable declarations:

```
int i, j, k;
char username[20];
float amount1, amount2;
int flag, xflag;
char response;
```

FIGURE 3–10   Declarations for a C++ Program Fragment.

and which begins with the executable code shown in Figure 3–11.

```
i = 0; j = 0; k = 0;
cout << "Enter first amount: ";
cin >> amount1;
...
```

FIGURE 3–11   Beginning Executable Statements of a C++ Program Fragment.

One of the first steps a compiler takes when it processes a program such as this is to use the variable declarations to build a table of the names of the variables which have been declared and two pieces of information about each—its type and the memory location has been assigned to it. The place where this information is stored is called the *symbol table*. Memory locations are specified relative to the start of the activation record for the function. For this example, we will assume that local variables occur first in the activation record. The symbol table entries for the first four variables in the above program fragment are shown in Table 3–9.

TABLE 3–9   PART OF A COMPILER SYMBOL TABLE FOR THE PROGRAM FRAGMENT OF FIGURES 3–10 AND 3–11

Symbol	Type	Location
i	int	0
j	int	4
k	int	8
username	char	12
amount1	float	32

When the compiler scans the executable part of the program (Figure 3–11), it checks the symbol table for each variable name as it is encountered and generates an error message if it is not found. It then uses the type information to do further error checking and to select the appropriate machine language instructions to generate; it also replaces the reference to the variable name with the unsigned binary representation of its memory address. In the process of building and referencing a symbol table, compilers usually use hashing. We illustrate the concept of hashing by constructing the beginning of a symbol table for this simple program fragment.

To keep the explanation focussed on the main issues, we make a few simplifying assumptions. First, we assume the hash table is an array of length 17 indexed from 0 to 16. The fixed length of the array is an essential feature of hashing. The restriction to a length of 17 is quite unrealistic, however; the actual length would normally be a prime number larger than the largest number of variables we would expect a program to contain. We will explain why it needs to be prime below; our choice of 17 for now is simply to keep the example to a manageable size. Also, for now, we ignore the type and memory location fields and only store and retrieve the variable names. A full symbol table might use an array of `structs` rather than a simple array of keys (the variable names).

Our strategy for placing a variable name in the array is this: we will look only at the first character in the name and calculate its position in the alphabet i.e., `'a'` $= 1$, `'b'` $= 2, \ldots,$ `'z'` $= 26$. The position in the table to be used will be the remainder after that number is divided by 17. In essence, our computation is based on the formula:

```
position =( ( (int) buffer[0]) - ((int) 'a') + 1 ) % htablength;
```

where `buffer[0]` denotes the first character in the variable name and `htablength` is 17 for this example. Such a formula is called a *hash function*. See Figure 3–12 for the result of placing the first five symbols in the table using this hash function. Note, for example that `j` goes to position 10, i.e., `10 % 17 = 10` and `username` would go to position 4, i.e., `21 % 17`. This formula is very naive and is being used here to illustrate the ideas of hashing.

Our first problem occurs when it is time to enter the variable `amount2`. See Figure 3–13 for the symbol table at that point. Application of the hash func-

0			0			0			0			0	
1			1			1			1			1	amount1
2			2			2			2			2	
3			3			3			3			3	
4			4			4			4	username		4	username
5			5			5			5			5	
6			6			6			6			6	
7			7			7			7			7	
8			8			8			8			8	
9	i		9	i		9	i		9	i		9	i
10			10	j		10	j		10	j		10	j
11			11			11	k		11	k		11	k
⋮	⋮		⋮	⋮		⋮	⋮		⋮	⋮		⋮	⋮
15			15			15			15			15	
16			16			16			16			16	

FIGURE 3–12 Symbol table for the first five entries from the Program Fragment of Figure 3–10.

tion suggests that the symbol `amount2` should be entered in position 1; however, that location is already occupied by `amount1`. This situation is an example of a "collision," which is defined as follows:

> **Definition** When inserting values into a hash table, a *collision* is said to occur whenever the calculated position for a new entry is already occupied by an earlier entry.

There are two popular methods for dealing with collisions, called *separate chaining* and *linear probing*. In separate chaining, each cell in the hash table is a pointer to a linked list, one list element for each value that maps to that location. Linked lists will be discussed in detail in Chapter 6. Figure 3–14 shows the completed hash table for the example of Figure 3–10 using separate chaining. Note that `response` also has a hash value of 1 and thus is added to the linked list beginning at 1. In linear probing, the values are entered directly into the table, at the first available position after the calculated position. Figure 3–15 shows the completed hash table using linear probing. Note that `response` ends up in position 3, since it encounters a second collision in position 2.

Linear probing and separate chaining each have advantages and disadvantages. Linear probing has the advantage of being very simple to implement both for insertions and for searches. It has the disadvantage that as the hash table becomes full, both insertions and searches degenerate toward linear search. Furthermore, as the table fills up, additional entries can cause a table overflow. The number of possible entries is not limited in separate chaining since the linked list can be extended dynamically. However, it is more compli-

0	
1	amount1
2	
3	
4	username
5	
6	
7	
8	
9	i
10	j
11	k
⋮	⋮
15	
16	

FIGURE 3–13 Symbol table after seven entries.

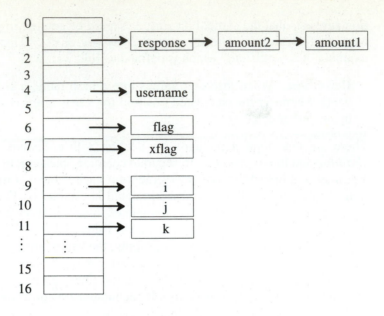

FIGURE 3–14 Completed hash table using separate chaining.

cated (and thus is more error-prone) because of the overhead involved in maintaining the linked lists. Thus, if the maximum number of entries to a hash table is known, normally a table about half again as large as that maximum is allocated and linear probing is used. If the maximum is unknown or frequently

0	
1	amount1
2	amount2
3	response
4	username
5	
6	flag
7	xflag
8	
9	i
10	j
11	k
⋮	⋮
15	
16	

FIGURE 3–15 Completed hash table using linear probing.

approached, separate chaining is used. Note also, that the operation of deletion can be implemented with separate chaining fairly easily, but it cannot be easily implemented with linear probing. (See Exercise 3–17.)

Let us now return to the example program of Figures 3–10 and 3–11 for a moment and consider the process of searching. When a C++ compiler begins to process the executable code, it first encounters the line

```
i = 0; j = 0; k = 0;
```

These assignment statements each require an access of the symbol table. First the position of i is calculated using the same hash formula as was used for insertion, namely:

```
position =( ((int) buffer[0]) - ((int) 'a') + 1 ) % htablength
```

giving a value of 9. The ninth position in the table is checked. Suppose linear probing is being used; if i is in position nine, its type and location are read and the compiler proceeds. If i is not there, the table is searched sequentially until either i is found or an empty cell is encountered. If separate chaining is being used, the linked list which originates at position 9 is searched until i is found or the list is exhausted. In either case, if i is not found, an error message is generated. Once i has been processed, the same pattern repeats for j, k, amount1, and the other variables.

Possible improvements   Now that we have seen the basic idea of how hashing works, we can examine a number of possible improvements and generalizations. These are:

1. better selection of a hash function
2. optimal selection of the table size
3. better schemes to handle collisions

We start with the hash function. An ideal hash function would have two properties: *uniformity* and *randomness*. By uniformity, we mean that the set of possible table entry keys are distributed equally to each cell in the hash table. By randomness, we mean that *in practice*, each cell will actually receive about the same number of keys. Consider the example of Figures 3–10 and 3–11 above and suppose variable names are restricted to being strings of six lowercase characters. Then the hash function

```
position =( ((int) buffer[0]) - ((int) 'a') + 1 ) % htablength
```

is not uniform since cells 1 through 9 are assigned twice as many variable names as cells 0 and 10 through 16—i.e., names beginning with 'a' or 'r' are assigned to cell 1, 'b' or 's' are assigned to cell 2, etc., while only keys beginning with 'q' are assigned to cell 0, only keys beginning with 'j' are assigned to cell 10, etc. Moreover, this function is not random either, since the distribution of first letters of variable names is far from even. Thus cell 0, for instance, is far less likely to be used than, say, cell 1.

It is possible to tell whether a proposed hash function is uniform for a specified set of possible keys; however, checking for randomness depends on knowing the actual set of keys that will be used. Many schemes for improving the uniformity and randomness of hash functions have been studied. One improvement is to use more than the first letter of a name to compute the position. For instance, suppose that keys are character strings, at least eight characters in length. (Shorter keys can be padded with blanks if necessary.) Then one common way to compute the position of a key in a hash table is to use an algorithm such as that shown in Figure 3–16.

```
//alternate hash computation  for identifiers up to 8 chars long
        {unsigned long temp=0;
        int mask4 = 0x0f;
        int shiftamt = 4;
        for (int i=0; i<strlen(buffer); i++)
        {
        temp = (temp << shiftamt) |
                ((unsigned long) (buffer[i] & mask4));
        }  // end for

        position = temp % htablength;
```

FIGURE 3–16   A Hashing Function Using Bits from Characters in a Table Key.

With the mask shown (1111 in binary), the & calculation selects the rightmost four bits of the ASCII code for a character. The shift (<<) shifts the previous bits 4 to the left. Thus, the algorithm assembles the rightmost four bits of the ASCII code for each of the first eight characters in the key into a 32-bit word. For instance, if we consider the key amount1, we have the following ASCII values and rightmost four bits:

character	ASCII	valuebits
a	61	0001
m	6D	1101
o	4F	1111
u	75	0101
n	66	1110
t	74	0100
1	31	0001
space	20	0000

Thus, immediately before position is calculated, we have

```
h = 00011101111101011110010000010000
```

which is 502,653,968 in decimal. Hence if htablength is 919, for instance, position becomes 485.

If further efforts to improve the probability of uniformity and randomness are desired, additional steps can be taken before moding by htablength. For instance, in the *middle square method*, h is squared (in our case producing a

64-bit number) and some collection of bits out of the middle of the resul are selected.

Another technique, known as *random hashing*, uses a random number generating technique to distribute the values of h. A typical formula is:

```
h = ((a * h + b) % M;
```

where M is $2^{\frac{L}{2}}$ and L is the length, in bits, of an integer on the machine being used. Thus, on a machine with 32-bit integers, $\frac{L}{2} = 16$ and M $= 65536$. In this case, we would want h to be 16 bits in length rather than 32, so that the product a*h does not overflow. This can be accomplished by masking and shifting by 2 bits and selecting a and b as prime numbers smaller than M. For example, a could be 16411 and b could be 11471.

Let us now turn our attention to the issue of table size. We have indicated earlier that htablength should be a prime number. The previous calculation of h shows us why. For instance, suppose htablength is a power of 2, say 256. When the calculation

```
position := h % htablength;
```

is made, only the last two characters of the key will be significant since all others have been multiplied by a multiple of 256 (because we shifted them by at least 8 bits). Since the last two characters are very likely to be blanks, our distribution is far from random. The easiest way to avoid this kind of problem is to simply make the table length a prime.

Suppose we are using linear probing and suppose we let α denote the proportion of the table which is full; i.e., $\alpha = \dfrac{N}{\text{TableLength}}$ where N denotes the number of entries. α is usually called the *load factor*. It has been proven that the average number of probes required is $\frac{1}{\alpha}\ln\dfrac{1}{1-\alpha} + \frac{1}{\alpha}$ for a successful search; and $\dfrac{1}{1-\alpha}$ for an unsuccessful search. Thus, suppose a table is $\frac{2}{3}$ full. The average number of probes required for a successful search is about 3 and for an unsuccessful search is about 3. This is quite reasonable. This explains why we said earlier that the hash table should be about half again as long as the largest number of keys to be entered.

Additional improvements can be made by finding better ways to handle collisions. The most common way to improve collision handling is called *double hashing* and is used just with linear probing. In double hashing, instead of resolving a collision by using the next available space, a second hash function is calculated to decide on a step size to the next location to be used. Since these step sizes vary for every location in the table, this improves randomness. We will leave further examination of double hashing for the exercises.

Comparison of searching methods Linear search is the simplest of the four methods but it is very slow; its complexity is O(n). Sentinel search is always better but still O(n). The only time we would use either is when we are given a collection of unordered data and all of it must be searched. Binary search has a complexity of $O(\log_2 n)$, which is quite fast; it has the disadvantage of requiring that a list be sorted before binary search can be used and sorting is quite slow relative to searching as we shall see in the next few sections.

As long as a hash table can be kept from becoming too full, hashing is the most efficient of the three search methods. As indicated above, if a table is less than $\frac{2}{3}$ full and linear probing is used, the average unsuccessful search takes only 3 comparisons; i.e., the complexity is $O(1)$—independent of the size of the table! A binary search would require five comparisons with a table as small as 32 members. Thus, hashing is a valuable searching tool and is, consequently, widely used. It has only one major limitation, but in many applications (such as most databases), that limitation is critical. The problem is that searching via hashing requires an exact match of the table entry and the key being searched for since the value of `position` is determined by a formula whose input is the key.

However, many database applications require searches like this:

Find all records such that $K_1 < key < K_2$

To carry out such a search via hashing would require a means to list all possible key values between K_1 and K_2, and then look them up one at a time. If the type of `key` is `float` or `string`, this could be so time consuming that any advantage gained from the efficiency of hashing is lost. For such searches, maintaining a sorted table and using binary search is the most viable approach. A technique called indexing is an alternative approach which is faster than binary search; however, we save examination of indexing for a later volume in this series.

EXERCISES

3–6 Suppose a[0..4] = (0 6 15 51 95) and x = 95. Trace both `Sentinel-Search` and `BinarySearch` for these values by giving the values of the variables after each iteration of the loop.

3–7 Suppose [0..4] = (0 6 15 51 95) and x = 94. Trace both `Sentinel-Search` and `BinarySearch` for these values.

3–8 Modify `LinSearch` so that it counts the number of occurrences of x.

3–9 Write pre- and postconditions and a loop invariant for your answer to the previous exercise. Then verify it.

3–10 Modify `BinarySearch` so that it counts the number of occurrences of the item being searched for.

3–11 The game "Guess my number" is played like this. The first player selects a number between 1 and 100. The second player makes a guess.

The first player responds by telling whether the guess was too high, too low, or correct. The second player then makes another guess. The object of the game is to find the correct number in as few guesses as possible. Write a function for the second player based on the concept of a binary search.

3–12 Verify the function you wrote in the previous exercise.

3–13 An important variant of `BinarySearch` can be used to find the roots of equations by the "midpoint method." For instance, suppose $f(x) = x^2 + 16x + 1$. If $x = 1$, the right hand side of this equation will be 18, which is positive. If $x = -1$, the right hand side will be -14, which is negative. By the intermediate value property for continuous functions, f must have a root between 1 and -1. Choose the number midway between 1 and -1, namely 0, and recalculate $f(x)$, getting 1, again positive. Hence there is a root between 0 and -1. Now take a number midway between 0 and -1. Continue in this fashion until the difference between the numbers is arbitrarily small (for instance, less than 10^{-3}.) Write a function to find the roots of any continuous function $g(x)$ using this method. You may pass initial values x_1 and x_2 to it where $g(x_1) < 0$ and $g(x_2) > 0$.

3–14 Verify the function you wrote in Exercise 3–13 above.

3–15 Note that in `BinarySearch` `hi` = `mid` but `lo` = `mid` + 1. One might expect the operations to be symmetrical—e.g., `hi` = `mid` and `lo` = `mid`. Construct an example to show that if `lo` = `mid` + 1 is replaced by `lo` = `mid`, `BinarySearch` is in error and explain why the error occurs. (Hint: start by determining where the verification of `BinarySearch` would fail if this change were made. For simplicity assume the array is of length 2^n and its length is cut exactly in half at each iteration.)

3–16 Modify `BinarySearch` so that it tests if `x` == `a[mid]` and if so, drops out of the loop. Estimate the average case complexity of this revised `BinarySearch`. Is it a significant improvement? (Hint: calculate the probability that `x` == `a[mid]` on the first pass through the loop, then on the second pass, etc.)

3–17 Explain why the deletion operation would be easy to implement with separate chaining but difficult with linear probing.

3–18 A hash table of length 23 will be used to store names. Enter the following list into such a table:

```
joseph, thomas, alice, frederick, elizabeth, george,
gracie, kenneth, sanjay, zelda, oscar, rita, tanya, walter,
edward, fauntleroy
```

Do this twice—once using linear probing, and once using separate chaining. Use the hash function based on the alphabetic position of the first letter. For this size table, explain why this hash function is neither uniform nor random.

3–19 Repeat Exercise 3–18 above using linear probing, but this time resolve collisions by double hashing. As a second hash function, use:

```
position = 1 + (((int)buffer[0]) - ((int)'a') + 1 )) % 8.
```

3–20 Write a C++ program in which you implement hashing via linear probing. Use eight characters from each variable name, a table of length 23, and mask and shift by one. Enter the list of names from Exercise 3–18; your program should then print out the table showing what is entered in each location or that the location is empty.

3–21 Suppose a list of n keys were to be entered to an empty hash table implemented with linear probing. What are the best and worst cases for the number of table accesses required? Repeat with separate chaining. Count reads and writes as separate accesses.

SORTING

As the binary search example has shown, the need to create an ordered linear list out of an unordered one is fundamental to the efficient operation of searching algorithms. Many computer applications require sorted data.

Because of its central role in various applications—data processing, artificial intelligence, mathematics, science—the development of efficient sorting algorithms has been studied widely by computer scientists. Although it is not possible to derive a general *Sort* algorithm with complexity $O(n)$—that is, one with efficiency is directly proportional to the size, n, of the list being sorted—we shall see that some clever and intricate approaches to sorting algorithm design have made significant improvements upon the more straightforward approaches, such as selection sort, which have complexity $O(n^2)$.

We begin by discussing two algorithms known as "Selection Sort" and "Insertion Sort." These algorithms are conceptually straightforward, although they are inefficient for arrays that are large. Following this, we study four additional sorting algorithms which are conceptually more intricate than the first two, but which yield significant gains in efficiency. These are known as "Shell Sort," "MergeSort," "QuickSort," and "HeapSort." Each method is illustrated with an example and evaluated for complexity in terms of its *average case* performance. That is, we assume that the array to be sorted initially appears in random order, so that an average number of comparisons (a[i] vs a[j]) will occur.

In practice, this "average case" assumption is often not valid. That is, many applications encounter lists that are partially ordered, and thus the performance of the sorting algorithm can be (adversely or favorably) affected by such additional preconditions. To help clarify these effects, we will draw distinctions between worst case, best case, and average case assumptions, and their effects upon the performance of the various sorting algorithms.

We conclude this development by exercising the different sorting methods using an array of random numbers.

This chapter covers some popular sorting algorithms. Many others are also in use. For a more complete treatment of the field of sorting, the reader is referred to Knuth's classic work, *The Art of Computer Programming*, *Volume 3*: *Sorting and Searching* [2]. This chapter will, however, leave the reader with an appreciation of several important sorting algorithms and serve as a basis for studying additional sorting strategies and implementations in the future.
We will use the following array to illustrate the different sorting algorithms.

Example 3.6   Let

```
a[0..9] = (49 42 23 80 25 46 39 96 73 74).
```

Of course, after sorting we should obtain

```
a[0..9] = (23 25 39 42 46 49 73 74 80 96).
```

Sometimes we will depict an array left to right as above. Smaller indices are assumed to be to the left. Other times (in figures) we will illustrate an array as a column as in Figure 3–17 with smaller indices above larger indices. Nonetheless, when we talk about a lower index, we mean a smaller index and a higher index refers to a bigger index. In Chapter 4, we will show how to extend these sorting algorithms to more complicated objects. For now, this particular example will be used throughout this chapter, so that we may focus our attention on the details of the different algorithms themselves.

Selection Sort

Selection Sort (sometimes called *Interchange Sort* or *Exchange Sort*) was introduced earlier in this chapter. We will discuss it more thoroughly here. It begins with an array `a[0..n]`, of n+1 elements, selects the largest element, and then exchanges that element with the last element, `a[n]`. Thereby, two goals are satisfied; the largest element is in its final position and the remainder of the array to be sorted is of length *n* (rather than *n+1*). At this point, the same procedure is repeated with the subarray `a[0..(n-1)]`. The next-largest element is interchanged with `a[n-1]` and the problem is thus reduced to an (n–1)-element sort. Repeating this procedure exactly n times therefore leaves the array sorted.

Example 3.7   As an example, conside, again, the array:

```
a[0..9] = (49 42 23 80 25 46 39 96 73 74).
```

We use the variable `topuns` to indicate the top index of the unsorted part of the array. In the first stage of the algorithm described above, we fix our attention on the position of the last element, 74, and mark that index with the variable `topuns` = n, i.e. the whole array is unsorted. We then search `a[0..n]` to select the index `maxl` of the largest element; in this example, `maxl` = 7, the index of the element containing 96. Thus, we exchange `a[7]` with `a[9]`, leaving

```
a[0..9] = (49 42 23 80 25 46 39 74 73 96)
```

We now select the shorter array `a[0..8]` by decrementing `topuns` and searching that subarray to find the index `maxl` of the largest remaining element. The entire sequence of stages for this sort is summarized in Figure 3–17, for this particular array. The diagrams show the state of `a[0..9]` immediately before execution of `Swap(a, topuns, maxl)`. (See the function `SelectionSort` in Figure 3–3.)

Selection Sort is implemented in three parts; the function `SelectionSort` and the auxiliary functions `maxloc` and `swap`. The function `maxloc` finds the index `maxl` of the largest element `a[maxl]` in the subarray `a[0..topuns]`.

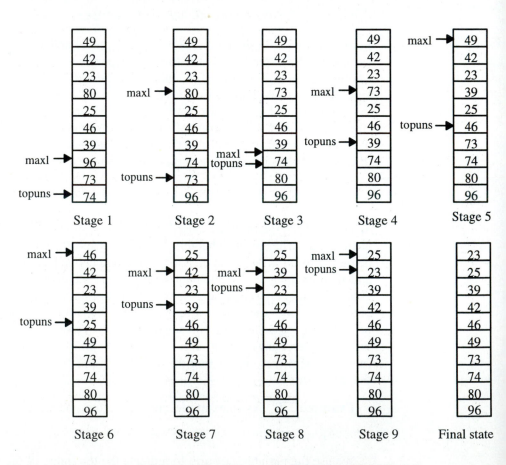

FIGURE 3–17   Stages in the execution of SelectionSort with L=(49 42 23 80 46 39 96 73 74).

Swap performs a single exchange of element a[topuns] with element
a[maxl].

SelectionSort controls the index topuns as described above, invokes
the function maxloc to set the index maxl of the largest element in the subarray a[0..topuns], and invokes Swap to exchange a[topuns] and
a[maxl]. The implementation of maxloc is simple, and appears, along with
SelectionSort in Figure 3–18.

```
//Function:selectionsort(a, n)
//Purpose: To sort the array  a[0..n]  into ascending order
//Pre:      0 <= n < MAXARRSIZE
//Post:     a[0..n] is in ascending order
void selectionsort(IntArr a, int n)
{
  int maxl;


  for (int topuns=n; topuns >= 1; topuns--)
  {
    maxl = maxloc(a,topuns);
    swap(a, topuns, maxl );
    //inv: (a[topuns+1 .. n] is sorted) ^
    //  (for all i in {0..topuns} a[i] <= a[topuns+1])
  }
}  // end selectionsort


//Function:maxloc(a, n)
//Purpose: To return the index of the element of maximum value
//          in a[0..n]
//Pre:      0 <= n <= MAXARRSIZE
//Post:     Let r be the value returned.   Then
//          ( (0 <= r <= n)  ^
//          (for all j in {0..n} a[j] <= a[r] )  )
int maxloc(IntArr a, int n)
{
  int maxsofar = a[0];
  int maxsofarloc = 0;


  for (int imax=1; imax<=n; imax++)
  {
    if (maxsofar < a[imax])
    {
      maxsofar=a[imax];
      maxsofarloc=imax;
    }
  }
  return maxsofarloc;
}  //end max
```

FIGURE 3–18   C++ code for the functions SelectionSort and maxloc.

For documentation, the bodies of these functions include precise comments
about their respective purposes.

Verification of Selection Sort Verifying `SelectionSort` is similar to other verifications we have done; we assume the preconditions and use mathematical induction to show that the invariant holds. We then use the invariant to show that the postcondition must hold also. We will assume `maxloc` is correct, leaving its verification for the exercises. Thus, we only need to verify the function `SelectionSort`.

First, we assume the preconditions, `0<= n < MAXARRSIZE,` and without stating it explicitly, we always assume that `a[0..n]` exists. We now check the invariant inductively, starting with `topuns = n`. After the first step in the `for` loop, `maxl` is the index of the greatest element in `a[0..n]`. After the second step, that greatest element is placed at the end of the array. Thus `a[topuns..topuns]` is sorted and `a[k] < a[topuns]` for all `k` less than `topuns`. So the invariant holds in this case.

Now assume the invariant holds after the `i`-th iteration of the loop, for some particular value of `i`. I.e.,

```
(a[topuns..n] is sorted)    ^
(for all i in {0.. topuns-1} a[i] <= a[topuns])
```

`topuns` is decremented by 1 and if `topuns` is still ≥ 1 the `for`-loop is entered again. Now, at the top of the `for`-loop, the invariant reads:

```
(a[topuns+1..n] is sorted)    ^
(for all i in {0.. topuns} a[i] <= a[topuns+1])
```

in terms of the new value of `topuns`. In the first step, `maxl` becomes the index of the greatest element in `a[0..topuns]` (for the new value of `topuns`). In the second step, that element is swapped to position `topuns`. Since `a[topuns+1..n]` is sorted by the induction step and the new `a[topuns]` is less than or equal to the elements of that subarray, we can conclude that `a[topuns..n]` is now ordered. Also we can conclude that all elements `a[k]` (`k < topuns`) are less than or equal to `a[topuns]` since `a[maxl]` was selected to be the maximum of `a[0..topuns]`. Hence, we have established that the invariant holds.

To complete the proof that `SelectionSort` is correct, we have to consider the two cases, `n=0` and `n>0`. If `n=0`, then there is only one element in the array, the `for`-loop is never entered so `SelectionSort` does nothing, leaving the one element array sorted. Now consider the case where `n>0`. In this case, the `for`-loop is entered and terminates when `topuns` gets decremented to `0`. Just before `topuns` is decremented that last time, `topuns` is equal to `1`, and the loop invariant at the foot of the loop guarantees: `a[1..n]` is sorted and `a[0] <= a[1]`. This conjunction implies that the postcondition `a[0..n]` is sorted is true.

Complexity of Selection Sort: Best, Average, and Worst Case Assumptions As we saw earlier, `SelectionSort` is $O(n^2)$ in complexity for best, average, and the worst case. For increasing values of n, the value of n^2 grows rapidly, as shown in Table 3–10.

TABLE 3–10   GROWTH OF THE FUNCTION $f(n) = n^2$

n value	n^2 value
1	1
10	100
100	10,000
1,000	1,000,000
10,000	100,000,000
100,000	10,000,000,000

We should also note that the comparison count for SelectionSort does not vary with respect to different assumptions about the degree to which the initial array is already in order. Other sort strategies, as we shall see, do have varying step counts as we make different assumptions about the initial ordering of the array.

Insertion Sort: An Improvement under Best Case Assumptions

In the case of a selection sort, the total number of steps does not vary from the average case to either the best case or the worst case. Its step count is always the same, as we have seen earlier. *Insertion Sort* is another simple sorting algorithm which, although $O(n^2)$ in complexity in the average and worst cases, approaches $O(n)$ complexity under best case assumptions. Readers may have already seen this sort in a previous course.

Insertion Sort searches a[0..n] serially from the beginning until an element, a[firstuns], is found which is out of order with respect to its predecessor, a[firstuns - 1]. When such an element is found, it is saved in a temporary location and the preceding element is shifted into location firstuns, creating a potential hole at location firstuns-1. By shifting preceeding array values towards the end of the array, we move the potential hole forward until the appropriate place for the value saved in temp is found. As the potential hole is moved towards the beginning of the array, the place to insert the value in temp is the first potential hole (from the rear) such that a[pothole-1] ≤ temp. All of this is embodied in the function in Figure 3–19.

```
//Function: insertionsort(a, n)
//Purpose: To sort the array  a[0..n]   into ascending order
//Pre:      0 <= n < MAXARRSIZE
//Post:     a[0..n] is in ascending order
void insertionsort(IntArr a, int n)
{
    int pothole, temp;
```

```
for (int firstuns=1; firstuns <= n; firstuns++)
{
   //inv: a[0.. firstuns-1] is sorted

   if (a[firstuns - 1] > a[firstuns])
   { // shift some of a [0.. firstuns-1] back to
     // make place for a[firstuns]
     temp=a[firstuns];
     pothole=firstuns;
      //saved value in temp,potential hole at firstuns
     do
     {
   //inv: temp < a[pothole-1]
   pothole--;
   a[pothole+1] = a[pothole];
     } //inv: temp < a[pothole+1] = a[pothole]
     while ((pothole>0) && (temp < a[pothole-1]));

     a[pothole] = temp; //found the right spot so put temp into
it
   } //end if
 } //end for
}   // end insertionsort
```

FIGURE 3–19   Function InsertionSort.

Verification and Complexity of Insertion Sort   We will leave verification of InsertionSort for the exercises. In the average case, it is not difficult to show that this function is $O(n^2)$ in complexity. In the best case, however, the initial ordering of a[0..n] allows all n steps of the for loop to be executed without a single execution of the embedded do-while loop. That is, the fact that the a[0..n] is sorted guarantees that a[firstuns - 1] ≤ a[firstuns] for every value of firstuns from 1 to n. Thus, the shift toward the end of elements within a[0..n], to allow extraction of element a[topuns] and reinsertion into its proper position, never needs to take place. Therefore, the complexity of InsertionSort is $O(n)$ in this best case.

Shell Sort

Returning to the average case, we note a serious deficiency in the performance of the selection and insertion sorts. Because the size of the array changes by 1 at each step, and each change requires performance of an algorithm with complexity $O(n)$, the complexity of these algorithms is $O(n^2)$.

Shell Sort was invented by Donald Shell in 1959 [4]. It attempts to reduce the number of passes required during the sorting of an array. To accomplish this, we initially define a minimum distance, or *gap*, arbitrarily as $\left\lfloor \frac{n}{3} \right\rfloor + 1$, where *n* is the number of elements in the array (not the top index). We imagine our array being broken into subarrays consisting of those elements which are

$\left\lfloor \frac{n}{3} \right\rfloor$ + 1 apart. We then use a specialized sort function (e.g., an insertion sort) that will sort each subarray separately. The effect of this initial step, using our example 10-element array and a gap size of 4, is shown in Figure 3–20. Here, the index k is used to identify the starting index for each such group, and the elements of the group that are to be sorted are indicated. We are assuming again that our initial a[0..9] = (49 42 23 80 25 46 39 96 73 74). As the reader can see, a swap of the numbers 25 and 49 places them both nearer to their final destination.

Next, the gap size is recomputed using the expression $\left\lfloor \frac{n}{3} \right\rfloor$ + 1 again where n is now the previous gap size. This is done as many times as necessary until the gap size becomes 1. Thus, for an array of size 10, the initial four sorts of groups separated by 4 is followed by two sorts of groups separated by 2, and finally one sort of the group of elements separated by 1 (which is the entire array). The subarrays separated by 2 are shown in Figure 3–21. Since the size of the subarrays grows exponentially rather than linearly, fewer passes through the array are required than with the selection or insertion sort.

Implementation of Shell sort is done in two parts. The first part, called gap-sort, is a variation of an insertion sort, except that it sorts only that sublist of a[0..n] that begins with index k and whose elements are separated by gap g. It is given in Figure 3–22.

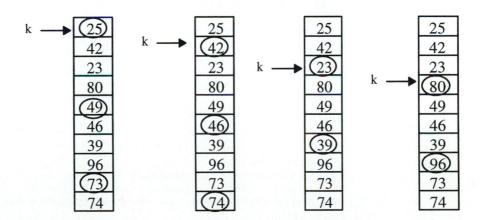

FIGURE 3–20   Initial subarrays for Shell Sort after each is sorted.

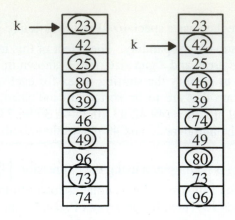

FIGURE 3–21 The second set of subarrays for Shell Sort after each is sorted.

```
//Function:gapsort(a, k, g, n)
//Purpose: To sort the elements  (a[k], a[k+g], a[k+2g],
//            .., a[k+((n/g)g)]into ascending order
//Pre:      0 <= n < MAXARRSIZE  ^  (0 <= k, g <= n)
//Post:     (a[k], a[k+g], a[k+2g], .., a[k+((n/g)g])
//          is in ascending order


void gapsort(IntArr a, int k, int g, int n)
{
  int pothole, temp;



  for (int firstuns=k+g; firstuns <= n; firstuns += g)
  {
    //inv: (a[k], a[k+g], a[k+2g], .., a[firstuns-g]) is sorted
    if (a[firstuns - g] > a[firstuns])
    {
      //shift some of (a[k], a[k+g], a[k+2g], .., a[firstuns-g])
back
      temp=a[firstuns]; //to make a place for a[firstuns]
      pothole=firstuns;
         //saved value in temp,potential hole at firstuns



      do
      { //inv: temp < a[pothole-g]
    pothole-=g;
    a[pothole+g] = a[pothole];
      }//inv: temp < a[pothole+g] = a[pothole]
      while ((pothole>k) && (temp < a[pothole-g]));

      a[pothole] = temp;
    } //end if
```

```
    } //end for
  }  // end gapsort
```

FIGURE 3–22   C++ code for the `gapsort` function.

The second part of the Shell sort controls the overall process, recomputing the gap size at each pass. This is given in Figure 3–23.

```
//Function:shellsort(a, n)
//Purpose: To sort the array  a[0..n]  into ascending order
//Pre:      0 <= n < MAXARRSIZE
//Post:     a[0..n] is in ascending order
void shellsort(IntArr a, int n)
{
   int gap= ((n+1)/3) + 1;


   while (gap > 1 )
   {
      for (int k=0; k < gap; k++)
        gapsort(a, k, gap, n);
      gap = (gap/3) + 1;
   }

   // gapsort last time with gap of 1
   gapsort(a, 0, 1, n);
 }  // end shellsort
```

FIGURE 3–23   C++ code for the ShellSort function.

Complexity of Shell Sort   Analysis of the Shell sort is a very difficult matter. In fact, the average number of comparisons for the Shell sort has never been algebraically derived. Bold readers may wish to scan pages 85–95 of Knuth's *Sorting and Searching* [2] to gain a feeling for the complications that surround the analysis of Shell sort.

However, empirical studies show that it is in the vicinity of $O(n^{1.25})$ whenever the array size n is in the range between 100 and 60,000. For large values of *n*, this is a significant improvement over the selection and insertion sorts. Thus, for an array of size 1000, we would expect Shell sort to take roughly one–half of 1% of the time required by a selection or insertion sort. Later in the chapter, we shall return to the question of empirical evaluation of sorting efficiency with some comparative data for different sorts.

Verification of Shell Sort   The verification of Shell sort is simple—the last step in Shell sort is `gapsort(a, 0, 1, n)` which is an invocation of `InsertionSort`. `InsertionSort`, however, was verified as an exercise in the previous subsection.

MergeSort

The divide and conquer strategy is useful in sorting algorithms as well as in searching. A "MergeSort," for example, splits the original array into two subarrays, say L1 and L2, which are individually sorted and then merged together to yield the result. Because sorting the two shorter subarrays and merging them can be performed faster than directly sorting the original array by any of the methods above, a merge sort leads to an attractive algorithm. For example, consider the 10-element array of Example 3.6.

```
a[0..9] = (49 42 23 80 25 46 39 96 73 74)
```

We first split it into two subarrays, say L1 and L2:

```
L1 = a[0..4] = (49 42 23 80 25)  and
L2 = a[5..9] = (46 39 96 73 74)
```

Next, we sort L1 and L2 individually, so they they become:

```
L1 = (23 25 42 49 80)  and  L2 = (39 46 73 74 96)
```

Finally, the two subarrays are recombined, or merged, into a single sorted array L as follows:

```
L = a[0..9] = (23 25 39 42 46 49 73 74 80 96)
```

These steps form, as the reader can see, a naturally recursive algorithm since the sorting of the smaller lists L1 and L2 can be handled by invoking the same function twice more. The stopping point for recursive invocation occurs when the size of L1 or the size of L2 is reduced to 1 in the course of a split. An outline of a merge sort illustrating the subdivision of the array and then the merging back together is shown in Figure 3–24 for the example array. The top half of the figure shows the subdividing and the bottom half of the figure shows the results of the merging calls. In both parts, array elements with lower indices are above those with higher indices.

The code for the function MergeSort appears below in Figure 3–25. It is the task of MergeSort to divide the incoming array range in half, recursively call itself to sort the two halves, then to call the function, merge, to merge together the two sorted halves.

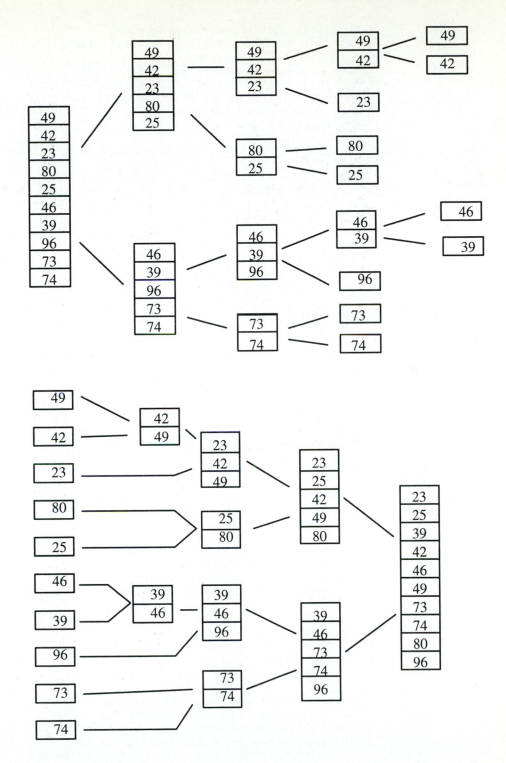

FIGURE 3–24   Outline of the MergeSort.

```
//Function:mergesort(a, first, last)
//Purpose: To sort the array  a[first..last] into ascending or-
der
//Pre:      0 <= first <= last < MAXARRSIZE
//Post:     a[first..last] is in ascending order
void mergesort(IntArr a, int first, int last)
{
  int lf,ll, rf, rl;

  if ((last - first) > 0)  //there is something here to sort
  {
    lf = first;      //first index of left half
    ll = (first+last)/2; //last index of left half
    rf = ll + 1;     //first index of right half
    rl = last;       //last index of right half
    mergesort(a, lf, ll); //sort left half
    mergesort(a, rf, rl); //sort right half
    merge(a, lf, ll, rf, rl);  //merge the 2 sorted halves
  }  // end if
}  // end mergesort
```

FIGURE 3–25   C++ code for MergeSort.

The comments adjacent to the first use of each identifier describe its purpose.

The function merge, shown in Figure 3–26, merges the two subarrays a[lfirst..llast] and a[rfirst..rlast] into a temporary array, temp, assuming that each of the subarrays is sorted. After the merging is complete, the sorted array temp is copied back into a[lfirst..rlast]. It is assumed that rfirst = llast + 1.

```
//Function:merge(a, lfirst, llast, rfirst, rlast)
//Purpose: To merge 2 sorted sublists of the array a
//         into 1 sorted list
//Pre:       (a[lfisrt..llast] is sorted)   ^
//           (a[rfirst..rlast] is sorted)   ^
//           (rfirst = llast + 1)
//Post:     a[lfirst..rlast] is sorted
void merge(IntArr a, int lfirst, int llast, int rfirst, int
rlast)
{
  IntArr temp;
  int tempind=0;
  int lfirstsav=lfirst;


  while ((lfirst <= llast)  && (rfirst <= rlast))
      //both sublists have elements
    if (a[lfirst] <= a[rfirst])
      temp[tempind++] = a[lfirst++];
      //move element from left sublist to temp
    else
      temp[tempind++] = a[rfirst++];
      //move element from right sublist to temp
```

```
// now one of the sublists is empty so find out which


if (rfirst > rlast)
        // then right sublist is empty so move rest of
        // left sublist
    while (lfirst <= llast)
      temp[tempind++] = a[lfirst++];
else
        // left sublist is empty so move rest of right sublist in
    while (rfirst <= rlast)
      temp[tempind++] = a[rfirst++];

//  now temp has the merged sublist, so copy back to a
lfirst = lfirstsav;
tempind = 0;


  while (tempind <= (rlast – lfirstsav) )
    a[lfirst++] = temp[tempind++];
}  // end merge
```

FIGURE 3–26   C++ code for the function merge.

It is important to understand the behavior of merge. Suppose L1 = a[0..4] and L2 = a[5..9] are the ordered subarrays of length 5 shown in Figure 3–27. Initially, lfirst and rfirst index the first elements in these two subarrays, respectively. The index tempind indexes the position of the next empty location in array temp. Thus, the initial iteration of the first while-loop leaves lfirst, rfirst, and tempind as shown in Figure 3–27 and the second iteration leaves lfirst, rfirst, and tempind as shown in Figure 3–28.

Subsequent steps in the loop add one element at a time (from either one or the other of the subarrays L1 or L2) to the merged array temp, until one of the two subarrays becomes exhausted. Since we cannot predict which one that will be, the final two while loops cover both cases. In our example, L1 becomes exhausted first, leaving rfirst indexing the tail end of L2 (the element 96). Thus, the second of these two while loops completes the merge process by simply copying the remainder of L2 over to the merged array temp. You may wonder whether the extra space used by the array temp is necessary. We leave it as an exercise to discover that one cannot naively merge in place. However, it is possible to reduce the amount of extra space used by designing a more complicated (and time–consuming) algorithm. As a practical matter, most merge sorting programs do use extra space.

Complexity of MergeSort   Let n be the number of elements in the array to be sorted (not the top index). Before we analyze MergeSort, let us analyze

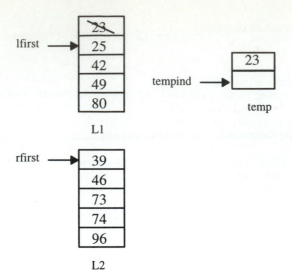

FIGURE 3–27   Initial step in the merge of L1 and L2.

the function merge. At first, it is not clear what should be selected as the dominant operation. After some reflection, it turns out that choosing tempindex++ is right. There are a number of different comparisons one might choose, but the number of occurrences of any one of them is bounded above by the the number of occurrences of tempind++. Thus, getting an upper bound on the number of times tempind++ is executed provides an upper bound for any other dominant operation we might have chosen. For convenience, we assume that the initial

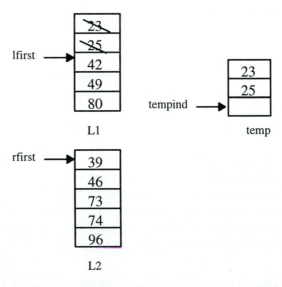

FIGURE 3–28   Second step in the merge of L1 and L2.

number of items to be sorted is $n = 2^k$ for some integer k.

Let T(n) be the number of times `tempind++` is executed when `MergeSort` is called to sort an array with n elements. Note that T(1) = 0. In general, T(n) is the number of times `tempind++` is executed in `MergeSort` for the left half, T($n/2$), plus the number of times `tempind++` is executed in `MergeSort` for the right half, T($n/2$), plus the number of times `tempind++` is executed in merging the two halves, n. That is, we have

$$T(n) = n + 2T(n/2) \tag{3.1}$$

But, since the list is repeatedly split in two, we plug $n/2^i$ into equation (3.1) successively and simplify to obtain:

$$
\begin{aligned}
T(n) \;&= n + 2T(n/2) \\
&= n + 2(\, n/2 \, + \, 2T(n/2^2)) = 2n + 2^2 T(n/2^2) \\
&= 2n + 2^2(\, n/2^2 \, + \, 2T(n/2^3)\,) = 3n + 2^3 T(n/2^3) \\
&\quad\cdot \\
&\quad\cdot \\
&= kn + 2^k T(n/2^k)
\end{aligned}
$$

Recalling our assumption that $n = 2^k$ implies that $k = \log_2 n$, this simplifies to :

$$
\begin{aligned}
T(n) \;&= n \log_2 n \, + \, nT(1) \\
&= n \log_2 n \, + n\,0 \\
&= n \log_2 n
\end{aligned}
$$

Relaxing this assumption, if n were not, in fact, an exact power of 2, T(n) can be bounded by:

$$T(n) \le n + 2T(\, (n+1)/2\,) \tag{3.2}$$

since the larger half at each splitting in `MergeSort` has at most $(n+1)/2$ elements in it. This recurrence is harder to solve but still has a solution that is O($n \log_2 n$). We conclude that the worst–case complexity of `MergeSort` is O($n \log_2 n$), which represents a major gain over selection and insertion sorts. Keeping in mind that the number of element comparisons were bounded above by the number of executions of `tempind++`, we can also say that the number of element comparisons used by `MergeSort` is O($n \log_2 n$). The merge sort algorithm is important in its own right. Merging, however, is also important when sorting amounts of data so large that internal sorting routines[3] are not possible. The kind of merge used above in `MergeSort` was a two–way merge.

---

3.   Internal sorting routines are those which can be used when the size of the set of data to be sorted is such that all of its elements can be stored in the computer's main memory simultaneously.

One can imagine a k–way merge that merges k sorted lists into one sorted list. Many external sorting algorithms divide the external data up into blocks small enough that each block can be sorted internally. Then, the sorted blocks are merged together using a multiway merge.

QuickSort

Another approach to sorting, called *QuickSort*, was discovered by C.A.R. Hoare in 1962. Unlike `MergeSort`, which uses a significant amount of extra storage for the `temp` array, a quick sort operates directly on a single copy of the array, and still maintains an average complexity of $O(n \log_2 n)$. Thus, in the average case, the use of extra storage can be avoided without sacrificing sorting efficiency.

Our approach to the quick sort algorithm is motivated by Jon Bentley's piece, "How to Sort," in his column "Programming Pearls" in the *Communications of the ACM* [1]. `QuickSort` uses a divide and conquer strategy in the following way. An element is chosen from the array and called the pivot element. The array is then rearranged (called partitioning) so that the pivot element is in its proper sorted location and all the elements with values less than or equal to the pivot value are moved to locations with indices less than the pivot element's index. Similarly, all the elements with values greater than the pivot value are moved to locations with indices greater than the pivot index. After partitioning, `QuickSort` is then called recursively on the two smaller parts. Suppose again that we begin with the array of Example 3.6.

```
a[0..9] = (49 42 23 80 25 46 39 96 73 74)
```

If the initial pivot element chosen were `a[4]` = 25, then after partitioning, we have

```
a[0..9] = (23 25 42 80 49 46 39 96 73 74)
```

Let `partdiv` be the new index of the pivot element, in this case `partdiv` = 1. Since `a[0..(partdiv-1)]` ≤ `a[partdiv]` < `a[(partdiv+1)..9]`, we see that `a[partdiv]` is in its final sorted position and that properly sorting the left part, `a[0..(partdiv-1)]`, and the right part, `a[(partdiv+1)..9]`, independently of each other, will leave all of `a[0..9]` sorted. In order to understand the function `QuickSort`, one must know the specifications of the function `partition`. We will examine the implementation of the function `partition` shortly. Its specifications are given in Figure 3–29.

```
//Function:partition(a, first, last, pivloc)
//Purpose: Let pivotval be the value in a[pivloc] before the
//         call.  Let r be the value returned.  Then a call to
//         partition rearranges the array a so that
//         (a[first..r-1] <= pivotval < a[r+1..last])   ^
//         (a[r] = pivotval)
//Pre:     first <= pivloc <= last
//Post:    (a[first..r-1] <= pivotval < a[r+1..last])   ^
```

```
//                  (a[r] = pivotval)
```

FIGURE 3–29   Specifications for the Function `partition`.

As mentioned at the beginning of this chapter, it is always the case that we do not throw away or invent elements. That is, the array after partitioning contains exactly the same elements as it did before, just in a different order. The function `QuickSort` itself is

```
//Function: quicksort(a, first, last)
//Purpose: To sort the array  a[first..last]   into
//          ascending order
//Pre:      0 <= first <= last < MAXARRSIZE
//Post:     a[first..last] is in ascending order
void quicksort(IntArr a, int first, int last)
{
   int pivotind; // pivot index before partitioning
   int partdiv;  //partition division point after partitioning


   if ((last - first) > 0)     //there is something here to sort
   {
     pivotind = (first+last)/2;   //pivot on middle element
     partdiv = partition(a,first, last, pivotind);

     quicksort(a, first, partdiv-1); //sort left part
     quicksort(a, partdiv+1, last);  //sort right part
   }  // end if
}   // end quicksort
```

Verification of `QuickSort`   The verifications we have done so far have all depended on the principle of mathematical induction. If $P(n)$ is some proposition, (often a loop invariant) where n is a natural number, we show that two statements are true:

(1) $P(0)$
(2)   for all n: $P(n-1) => P(n)$

From the truth of these, we conclude that $P(n)$ is true for all n (perhaps restricted by some finite maximum possible value). Intuitively, using this method of induction, we can show $P(4)$ is true as follows:

(a)   show $P(0)$ is true
(b)   using (2) above with $n = 1$ and (a), conclude $P(1)$
(c)   using (2) above with $n = 2$ and (b), conclude $P(2)$
(d)   using (2) above with $n = 3$ and (c), conclude $P(3)$
(e)   using (2) above with $n = 4$ and (d), conclude $P(4)$.

To verify QuickSort, however, we will need a slightly different form of the principle of mathematical induction. Again, we want to establish the truth of *P(n)*. This time, however, we show that the statements:

(3)   P(0)
(4)   *for all n:* (P(0) ... P(*n*–1)) => P(*n*)

are true. From these we can conclude that *P(n)* is true for all *n*. This second form of induction is sometimes called *complete induction*. The difference is that our second version of induction has the same basis step but makes a stronger assumption in the induction step than the first version, namely that *all* of P(0), ..., P(*n*–1) are true, not just P(*n*–1). Intuitively, using complete induction, we show P(4) is true as follows:

(a)   show P(0) is true
(b)   using (4) above with *n* = 1 and (f), conclude P(1)
(c)   using (4) above with *n* = 2 and (f) and (g), conclude P(2)
(d)   using (4) above with *n* = 3 and (f) and (g) and (h), conclude P(3)
(e)   using (4) above with *n* = 4 and (f) and (g) and (h) and (i), conclude P(4).

It can be shown that the two principles of induction are equivalent[3]. However, the form of the second one will be more useful to us here because we will want to split a list of size *n* into two sublists whose sizes may be anywhere between 1 and *n*–1.

For this argument we assume that partition is correct. We will verify partition in a separate argument shortly. The proof is by induction. If QuickSort is called on an empty subarray (indicated by first > last) or a single element array (indicated by first = last), the if-statement guarantees that it will do nothing, leaving the subarray sorted in either case. Thus, the base case is established. Now assume that QuickSort is called on a subarray a[first..last] with *n* elements where $n \geq 2$. The condition in the if-statement is true so the body of the if-statement is entered. The index, pivotind is calculated and satisfies the preconditions of partition, first $\leq$ pivotind $\leq$ last so that after the invocation of partition we may be sure that its postcondition holds. In this case, that means that

a[first..(partdiv-1)]$\leq$a[partdiv] < a[(partdiv+1)..last]   (3.3)

Furthermore, the number of elements in both a[first..(partdiv-1)] and a[(partdiv+1)..last] is less than *n*. Complete induction allows us to assume P(*j*) for all *j* < n. Thus, by induction, we may certainly assume that the two recursive calls to QuickSort result in both a[first..(partdiv-1)] in ascending order and a[(partdiv+1)..last] in ascending order. That combined with (3.3) guarantees that a[first..last] is sorted. So, QuickSort is correct by induction.

We now consider the implementation and correctness of the function partition which appears in Figure 3–30.

```
//Function:partition(a, first, last, pivloc)
//Purpose: Let pivotval be the value in a[pivloc] before the
//          call.  Let r be the value returned.  Then a call to
//          partition rearranges the array a so that
//          (a[first..r-1] <= pivotval < a[r+1..last])   ^
//          (a[r] = pivotval)
//Pre:      first <= pivloc <= last
//Post:     (a[first..r-1] <= pivotval < a[r+1..last])   ^
//          (a[r] = pivotval)
int partition(IntArr a, int first, int last, int pivloc)
{
   int pivotval;
   int ll;   //last index of left section;
             //ll+1 is the first index of the right section
   int rl;   //last index of right section

   pivotval = a[pivloc];  //get pivot value
   swap(a, first, pivloc); //set up invariant
   ll = first;

   for (rl = first+1; rl <= last; rl++)
      //inv: a[first..ll] <= pivotval < a[ll+1..rl-1]
      if (a[rl] <= pivotval)
          swap(a, ++ll, rl); // maintains invariant for new ll
             //otherwise we know a[first..ll] <= pivotval <
             //a[ll+1..rl]

      swap (a, first, ll);  // to guarantee pivotval at location
ll
      return ll;
}  //end partiton
```

FIGURE 3–30   C++ code for the function partition.

Before we proceed, we should clarify one point. Recall that the notation a[i..j] was a short hand for the set of values { a[i], a[i+1], ..., a[j] }. If i > j, this set is empty. Now, if the pivot element is the smallest element in the subarray then r, the value returned by partition, will equal first and the first part of the post condition reads a[first..(first-1)] <= pivotval. This is vacuously true because every element of the empty set a[first..(first-1)] is less than or equal to pivotval. Similar considerations apply to the loop invariant in partition and to the post condition if the pivot value is the largest element in the subarray.

Let n be the number of elements in the subarray a[first..last]. The precondition for partition requires that $n \geq 1$. If $n = 1$, then first = last = pivloc and a look at the first few statements show that the for-loop will not be entered and that first will be the value returned. In this case, the post-condition is clearly satisfied. If $n > 1$, then the for-loop must be entered. The statements before the for-loop guarantee that the invariant is satisfied the first time the loop is entered. Let us now assume the invariant and look at the body of the `for`-loop. The invariant says that the portion of the array that we are interested in has been divided up into three pieces.

- the left part so far, `a[first..ll]`, each of which is less than or equal to `pivotval`,

- the right part so far, `a[ll+1 .. rl-1]`, each of which is greater than `pivotval`,

- the rest, `a[rl..last]`, which we do not know about yet.

As we begin the next iteration of the `for`-loop, we must decide where to put `a[rl]`. If `a[rl] > pivotval`, then by doing nothing, we can conclude that `a[first..ll] <= pivotval < a[ll+1..rl]` at the foot of the loop. If `a[rl] ≤ pivotval` then we must make room for it in left part. This can be achieved by incrementing `ll` so that it points to the first element in the right part (`> pivotval`) and interchanging it with `a[rl]` (which was `≤ pivotval`). This effectively extends the right end of the left part to what was the left end of the right part. What used to be in left end of the right part is swapped to the right end of the right part (location `rl`). Thus, in this case, after the swap at the end of the `for`-loop, we obtain `a[first..ll] <= pivotval < a[ll+1..rl]`. When `rl` is increased by the `for`-loop, we obtain the invariant at the top of the loop on the next iteration. When the loop terminates, `rl = last + 1`, so that the invariant guarantees that `a[first..ll] <= pivotval < a[ll+1..last]`. Before the `for`-loop, we put the pivot value in `a[first]`. After the `for`-loop, swapping `a[first]` with `a[ll]` combined with the invariant guarantees the postcondition. Thus, `partition` is correct.

Best and Worst Case Analysis of `QuickSort`   The dominant operation we shall count in this analysis is the comparison, `(a[rl] <= pivotval)`, in the `if`-statement,

```
if (a[rl] <= pivotval)
        swap(a, ++ll, rl);
```

that is inside the `for`-loop of the function `partition`. The complexity of `QuickSort` depends upon the initial ordering of the array `a[first..last]`. That is, the arbitrary identification of the pivot as the value of the middle element, `pivotind = (first+last)/2`, assumes that approximately half of all the elements will be less than `a[pivotind]` and half will be greater. If that is the case, then the boundary for the partition of `a[first..last]` into subarrays `a[first..r-1]` and `a[r+1..last]` will be close to `pivotind`, and the recursive calls to `QuickSort` will be each working on subarrays of approximately half the size of the original array.

Suppose we use this particular "best case" assumption for *every* level of recursion. We could derive a recurrence equation as we did for `MergeSort` and solve it. That kind of top-down analysis is extremely useful in analyzing recursive functions. We leave that analysis for an exercise. In order to illustrate another useful technique, we choose to use a kind of bottom-up analysis here.

Assuming, for simplicity, that n is a power of 2, Table 3–11 gives the subarray size, the number of subarrays, and the maximum number of invocations of QuickSort occurring at each level of recursion:

TABLE 3–11   COUNTING THE NUMBER OF INVOCATIONS OF QuickSort

Level of recursion	Subarray size	Number of subarrays	Invocations of QuickSort
0	n	1	2
1	$\leq n/2$	2	4
2	$\leq n/4$	4	8
s	$\leq n/2^s$	2^s	2^{s+1}
$\log_2 n - 1$	≤ 2	$n/2$	n
$\log_2 n$	1	n	0

Each invocation of QuickSort (with subarray size $n/2^s$) will require at most $n/2^s - 1$ dominant comparisons in the invocation of partition at this level. Multiplying by the number of subarrays of this size and summing this over all the values of s from 0 to $\log_2 n$ we have the following complexity for Quick-Sort under these assumptions.

$$\sum_{s=0}^{\log_2 n} 2^s \left(\frac{n}{2^s} - 1 \right) \quad = \sum_{s=0}^{\log_2 n} (n - 2^s)$$

$$= n \log_2 n - \sum_{s=0}^{\log_2 n} 2^s$$

$$= n \log_2 n - 2n + 2$$

Thus, QuickSort is $O(n\log_2 n)$ in complexity. This result is subject to our best case assumption that the pivot element in each subarray will divide it into two equal halves in preparation for the next level of invocation.

However, this best case is not always guaranteed by the initial ordering of the array. For instance, the initial ordering of the 10-integer array a[0..9] of Example 3.6 caused a first partition into one-element and eight-element subarrays. In the worst possible case, one can imagine an array in which the first partitioning will yield subarrays of sizes 0 and $n - 1$, the second will yield subarrays of sizes 0 and $n - 2$, and so forth. In this case, the total number of recursive invocations of QuickSort will be $n-1$, rather than $\log_2 n$, and its complexity will become, therefore, $O(n^2)$. This performance is, therefore, no better than that of `SelectionSort` which was presented at the beginning of this section.

In between these two extremes, however, experience has shown that `Quick-Sort` performs quite well for lists of reasonably large size and randomness. Furthermore, simple refinements can be made to the pivot selection procedure so that the worst case $O(n^2)$ complexity can be eliminated. We shall now examine the average case complexity of `QuickSort` in detail. We shall consider some empirical evidence concerning the performance of `QuickSort` at the end of the chapter.

Average Case Analysis of `QuickSort`   The mathematics of this analysis is quite a bit more difficult than what we have done so far. However, it is quite accessible to a student who has completed calculus through introductory integration and has some algebra skill. We encourage you to work through it with us as it is a good example of how careful mathematical analysis can establish valuable results in computing.

Recall that the expected value of n events $E_1, E_2, ..., E_n$ with corresponding values $v_1, v_2, ..., v_n$ is given by the formula:

$$\text{ExpVal} = v_1 * P(E_1) + v_2 * P(E_2) + ... + v_n * P(E_n)$$

where $P(E_i)$ is the probability that E_i occurs. In the case of `QuickSort`, E_i will be the event that the pivot element picked is the ith element and v_i will be the number of dominant comparisons in this case. $P(E_i)$ will equal $1/n$ if we assume that it is equally likely that the pivot element belongs first, second, etc., in the final ordering.

`QuickSort` splits an array, a, into two subarrays which are recursively sorted. If the pivot element picked is the $k+1$st, then the sizes of these subarrays are k and $n - k - 1$. Suppose we let S_n denote the expected number of dominant operations (comparisons) `QuickSort` requires for an array of size n. Note, $S_0 = 0$, $S_1 = 0$. If $n > 1$, we have the following numbers of comparisons:

1. $n - 1$ comparisons in the call to `partition` at this level,
2. S_k comparisons to sort the left partition, and
3. S_{n-k-1} comparisons to sort the right partition

Summing, we have

$$S_n = n - 1 + S_k + S_{n-k-1}$$

We would like to solve for S_n. However, we do not know k. In fact, k can be any value between 0 and $n - 1$. If we assume that each of these possibilities is equally likely, i.e., each possible partitioning of a is equally likely, we get the expected number of comparisons by summing over the number of comparisons for each possible partition multiplied by the probability that that partition occurs ($1/n$). This yields

$$S_n = \sum_{k=0}^{n-1} \frac{1}{n}\left(n - 1 + S_k + S_{n-k-1}\right)$$

$$= n - 1 + \frac{1}{n}\sum_{k=0}^{n-1}\left(S_k + S_{n-k-1}\right)$$

$$= n - 1 + \frac{1}{n}\sum_{k=0}^{n-1} S_k + \frac{1}{n}\sum_{k=0}^{n-1} S_{n-k-1}$$

$$S_n = n - 1 + \frac{2}{n}\sum_{k=0}^{n-1} S_k \tag{3.4}$$

This complicated expression can be greatly simplified by the following trick. Replace n by $n - 1$ in the above expression (3.4). We get

$$S_{n-1} = n - 2 + \frac{2}{n-1}\sum_{k=0}^{n-2} S_k. \tag{3.5}$$

Multiplying (3.4) by n, we have

$$nS_n = n(n - 1) + 2\sum_{k=0}^{n-1} S_k \tag{3.6}$$

and multiplying (3.5) by $(n-1)$

$$(n - 1)S_{n-1} = (n - 2)(n - 1) + 2\sum_{k=0}^{n-2} S_k. \tag{3.7}$$

Subtracting (3.7) from (3.6), we get

$$nS_n - (n - 1)S_{n-1} = n(n - 1) - (n - 2)(n - 1) + 2S_{n-1}$$

which simplifies to

$$nS_n - (n + 1)S_{n-1} = 2(n - 1).$$

Dividing by $(n + 1)(n)$ we get

$$\frac{S_n}{n + 1} = \frac{S_{n-1}}{n} + \frac{2(n - 1)}{n(n + 1)}.$$

Now let T_n denote $\dfrac{S_n}{n+1}$. Then T_{n-1} denotes $\dfrac{S_{n-1}}{n}$ and in terms of T, the recurrence becomes:

$$T_n = T_{n-1} + \frac{2(n-1)}{n(n+1)}. \tag{3.8}$$

Recall that $S_0 = 0$, $S_1 = 0$, thus $T_0 = 0$, $T_1 = 0$. Since $n > 1$ implies

$$\frac{(n-1)}{(n+1)} < 1.$$

we can simplify (3.8) to obtain the inequality

$$
\begin{aligned}
T_n &< T_{n-1} + \frac{2}{n} \\
&< T_{n-2} + \frac{2}{n-1} + \frac{2}{n} \\
&< T_{n-3} + \frac{2}{n-2} + \frac{2}{n-1} + \frac{2}{n}
\end{aligned}
$$

so that

$$T_n < T_1 + \sum_{k=2}^{n} \frac{2}{k} = \sum_{k=2}^{n} \frac{2}{k}$$

But the latter expression can be approximated by

$$\int_{2}^{n} \frac{2}{k}\, dk = 2\ln(n) - 2\ln(2)$$

Hence

$$S_n = (n+1)T_n \approx (n+1)(2\ln(n) - 2\ln(2)).$$

Because $\log_2$ is a constant multiple of the natural log, ln, we see that the average case complexity of QuickSort is $O(n\log_2 n)$, as well as its best case. Because, in practice, QuickSort seems to outperform most other sorting algorithms, it is frequently used.

HeapSort

The final sort algorithm to be presented in this chapter is the so-called "Heap-Sort." It was discovered in 1964 by J.W.J. Williams [5], has worst case complexity of $O(n\log_2 n)$, and avoids the extra storage requirements of the merge sort. To understand the heap sort algorithm, we first define the notion of a "heap:"

> **Definition**   A *heap* is an array a[1..n] in which each element a[i] is greater than or equal to both of the elements a[2i] and a[2i+1] if they exist, for all i = 1, . . ., n/2.

In this discussion, in order to follow tradition and keep the exposition uncomplicated, we will ignore a[0] and consider only the portion of an array starting at index 1. It is possible to redefine a heap for arrays starting at index 0 in a fairly natural way; however, doing so introduces a bit more complexity into the code for very little gain. Thus, a[1..n] is a heap if a[1] ≥ a[2] and a[1] ≥ a[3], a[2] ≥ a[4] and a[2] ≥ a[5], and so forth. An attractive way to look at this is to view the array as a binary tree with a[1] as the root as shown in Figure 3–31.

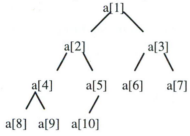

FIGURE 3–31   Graphical illustration of a heap.

We will study trees in more depth in Chapter 5. For now, the following terminology will suffice. The *left child* of a[i] is a[2i] and the *right child* of a[i] is a[2i+1]. The *parent* of a[j] is a[j/2] where the division is integer division. Then when an array is viewed as a binary tree, it has the heap property if the value of every parent is greater than or equal to the value at either of its children. Our original array from Example 3.6, reindexed to a[1..10] = (49 42 23 80 25 46 39 96 73 74) is not a heap. The following three reorderings of a[1..10] however, are all heaps:

```
a₁[1..10]  =  (96 80 74 73 46 42 49 25 39 23)
a₂[1..10]  =  (96 74 80 73 46 42 49 25 39 23)
a₃[1..10]  =  (96 80 74 73 49 46 42 39 25 23)
```

Figure 3–32 provides a graphical illustration showing that the original ordering of a[1..10] is not a heap, but the reordering a₁[1..10] is a heap—i.e., each element is greater than or equal to the two elements immediately below it. Note that if the elements of the diagram are read from top to bottom and left to right, they are arranged in the same order as the corresponding array. We see that a heap does not necessarily reflect a reverse ordering for an array, although it can. We see also that the very largest element in any heap must appear first, even though there is some flexibility in arranging the remaining elements.

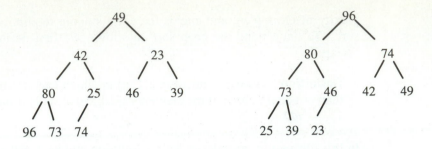

$a[1..10] = (49\ 42\ 23\ 80\ 25\ 46\ 39\ 96\ 73\ 74)$ $a[1..10] = (\ 96\ 80\ 74\ 73\ 46\ 42\ 49\ 25\ 39\ 23)$

(a) not a heap   (b) a heap

FIGURE 3–32   Graphical illustration of two lists; one (a) is not a heap and the other (b) is a heap.

The `HeapSort` algorithm uses a function `heapify` whose specification is:

```
//Function:heapify(a, left, right)
//Purpose: To make a[left..right] satisfy the heap property
//Pre:    a[(left+1) .. right] satisfies the heap property
//Post:    a[left .. right] satisfies the heap property
```

Beginning with an initial array a[1..10], the heapsort algorithm proceeds through two major loops. The first loop rearranges the elements of a[1..10] so that they form a heap. The second loop begins by exchanging a[1] and a[n] in the heap (thus placing the largest element in its final position for the sort), and then remaking a heap out of the remaining subarray a[1 .. (n–1)]. The main logic of `HeapSort` is provided in the comments of the code portrayed in Figure 3–33.

```
//Function:heapsort(a,last)
//Purpose: To sort the array  a[1..last]  into ascending order
//Pre:    1 <= last < MAXARRSIZE
//Post:    a[1..last] is in ascending order
void heapsort(IntArr a, int last)
{
  if ((last - 1) > 0)      //there is something here to sort
    {  //start at leftmost element s.t. all elements to its right

      //are guaranteed to satisfy heap property.  Then heapify
      //moving left one element at a time maintaining the
      //heapify precondition
    for (int left = last/2; left >=1; left--)
      heapify(a, left, last);  //now a[1..last] is a heap

    for (int right=last; right > 1; )
    {
      swap(a, 1, right--);    //swap biggest (1st) element to
                              //right end and then cut off right
                              //end by decrementing right
      heapify(a, 1, right);   //then heapify the remaining array
```

```
        } //end for loop
      }   //end if
    }   // end heapsort
```

FIGURE 3–33   C++ Code for the Function `HeapSort`.

Essential to both the initial loop (which builds the heap) and the final loop (which maintains the heap) is the function `heapify`. This function assumes that `a[(left+1) .. right]` satisfies the heap property and makes `a[left .. right]` into a heap. If `a[left]` is bigger than its larger child, then `a[left .. right]` is already a heap, otherwise `a[left]` is swapped with its bigger child. Now the new `a[left]` satisfies the heap property but the position that used to hold the bigger child may not. So, we make that position a parent and repeat the process, pushing the value that was originally in `a[left]` further down the tree. There is one technicality. At each iteration, we must check to see if the parent has two children in the range of interest. If so, we pick the child with a bigger value. If the parent has only one child then we select it (the left child) to use as the `bigchild`. The code follows in Figure 3–34.

```
//Function:heapify(a, left, right)
//Purpose: To make a[left..right] satisfy the heap property
//Pre:      a[(left+1) .. right] satisfies the heap property
//Post:     a[left .. right] satisfies the heap property
void heapify(IntArr a, int left, int right)
{
  int parent, lchild, bigchild;

  parent = left;   //the only element that may not
                   //satisfy heap property
  lchild = parent*2;   //its left child
    if ((lchild + 1) <= right) // then parent has two children
                               // so find index of bigger child
      bigchild = (a[lchild] >= a[lchild+1]) ? lchild : lchild+1;
    else
      bigchild = lchild; //  because lchild is the only
                         // child in tree

  while ( (bigchild <= right) && (a[bigchild] > a[parent]) )
  {
    swap(a, parent, bigchild);
      //now parent satisfies heap property but bigchild may not
    parent = bigchild;
      //so replace parent by bigchild and check its children
    lchild = parent*2;
    if ((lchild + 1) <= right)
      bigchild = (a[lchild] >= a[lchild+1]) ? lchild : lchild+1;
      //find bigger child
    else
      bigchild = lchild;
      //  because lchild is the only child in tree
```

```
    }   //end while
}   //end heapify
```

FIGURE 3–34   C++ Code for the Function `heapify`.

To illustrate this process, consider our example array once again, where `Heap-Sort` initially invokes `heapify` with the subarray `a[5..10]`, as shown in Figure 3–35. Note that `left` is initially 5 in `HeapSort` and that `a[6..10]` satisfies the heap property. The variable `last` equals 10 throughout Figure 3–35. Again we show both the actual array and a graphical illustration.

Each of the diagrams shows the array after the return from `heapify(a, left, last)` for the value of last shown. The portion of the array in the curly brackets satisfies the heap property. After the first invocation of `heapify`, the elements 25 and 74 are swapped, so that `a[5]=74` and `a[10]=25`. After the second invocation, the larger of `a[8]` and `a[9]`, or 96, is swapped with `a[4]=80`, since `a[4]` is not the largest of the three. Similarly, the third invocation leaves `a[3]=23` swapped with the larger of `a[6]` and `a[7]`. Note, in the next invocation of `heapify`, that `a[2]=42` is first swapped with the larger of 96 and 74, but then the process is not finished; that is, since placing 46 in location `a[4]` leaves it not the largest among `a[8]` and `a[9]`, it is further swapped with `a[8]`, leaving 42 finally in `a[8]` and 80 in `a[4]`. Readers should carefully review these steps, to become convinced that a heap is indeed created at the point where `left` is finally reduced to 1.

The final loop in the `HeapSort` algorithm removes element `a[1]` from the heap and swaps it with `a[last]`; since `a[1]` is the largest element in the heap, it ultimately belongs in the rightmost position. Thereafter, the array is reduced by 1 at its right end by decrementing the variable right, the function `heapify` is recalled to restructure this shorter array as a heap, and the next-largest element is thus extracted. One by one, the elements of `a[1..n]` are thus placed in their final positions. The first step is shown in Figure 3–36. Initially `a[1]` and `a[10]` are swapped; secondly the heap condition is restored but only on the subarray `a[1..9]`.

Note here that, at any stage, the only element in the subarray `a[1..right]` that is swapped out is `a[1]`, and therefore only *one* pass through the array by `heapify` (beginning at `a[1]`) is needed in order to restore the integrity of the heap.

Analysis of `HeapSort`   Let us consider the dominant operation to be the comparison `(a[bigchild] > a[parent])` in the condition part of the `while`-statement of the function `heapify`. The complexity of `HeapSort` can be determined by observing first that `heapify`, for a subarray of size k, requires at most $\log_2 k$ iterations of its `while` loop and k is always less than or equal to n. In the first loop within `HeapSort` itself, at most $\frac{n}{2} + 1$ invocations of `heapify` are executed, with subarrays of size increasing by 1 at each invocation so the total number of critical operations form this part of `HeapSort` is bounded above by $(\frac{n}{2} + 1) \log_2 n$. In its second loop, `HeapSort` invokes

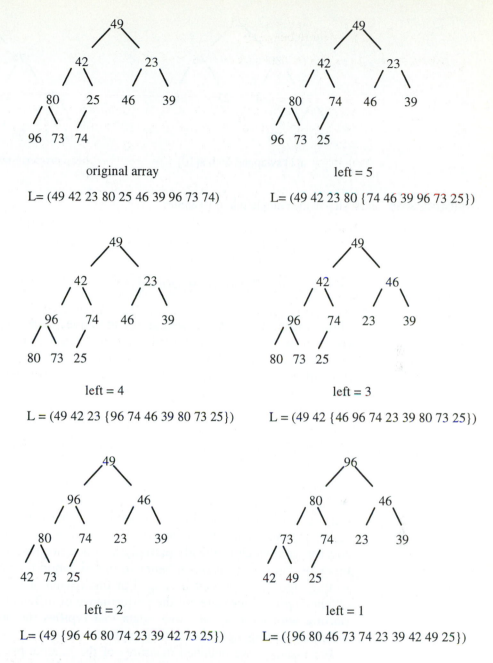

FIGURE 3–35   Initial building of the heap in HeapSort.

heapify $n-1$ times, with subarrays of size k decreasing by 1 at each invocation. Again k is always less than or equal to n, so an upper bound on the total
number of dominant operations from this second loop is $(n-1)\log_2 n$. Combining these observations, we have the following upper bound for the complexity of HeapSort:

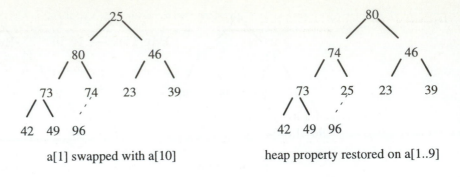

a[1] swapped with a[10]   heap property restored on a[1..9]

FIGURE 3–36   First step in the completion of HeapSort.

$$[\frac{n}{2} + 1 + (n - 1)] \log_2 n = O(n \log_2 n)$$

This estimate should be viewed as conservative, since most of the actual in-vocations of `HeapSort` are for subarrays of a size k that is far smaller than the original array size n. A more exact calculation of this complexity is difficult, and will not be developed here. We will leave the verification of `HeapSort` for the exercises.

Empirical Evaluation of Sorting Algorithms

As suggested above, the performance of most sorting algorithms depends upon the initial ordering of the array. For instance, we noted that the quick sort algorithm is particularly poor in the "worst case" that the partitioning repeatedly yields quite unequal-sized subarrays. Furthermore, some applications require a sort for data which is already partially in order. Sorting algorithms can some-times be "tuned" to perform better in this situation than any of the standard sorting algorithms presented here. For this reason, it is sometimes useful to obtain *empirical* measures of the performance of different sorting algorithms, starting with an array of "live" data that typifies the actual application to which the sorting algorithm will be applied.

For instance, we obtained measures of the relative performance of the six different sorting algorithms in this chapter. For this, we took an array of 5000 random integers, and exercised each of the sorting algorithms with those inte-gers. Furthermore, we exercised the six sorting algorithms again using a 5000-element array that was already ordered. These runs were made on a Sun Sparcstation ELC, and the results are shown in Table 3–12. In the lab manual, we will discuss how further timing information and other empirical means can be used in order to corroborate the derived complexities that were obtained by computing step counts.

TABLE 3–12 RUN TIMES (SECONDS) FOR SORTING A LIST OF 5000 INTEGERS

Sorting Algorithm	Run Time—List in Random Order	Run Time—List in Ascending Order
Selection	10.3	14.9
Insertion	9.9	0.02
Shell	0.2	0.07
Merge	0.3	0.27
Quick	0.17	0.12
Heap	0.23	0.25

These results are interesting. The insertion sort, as predicted, performs dramatically better when the list is already ordered. However, in the general case, the quick, Shell, heap, and merge sorts are substantially better. It is interesting to ponder the fact that the selection sort is much worse if the array is already sorted. Why? Remember that the empirical timing counts all the operations performed by the algorithm.

Final Remarks on Efficiency

At the beginning of this chapter, we commented that we would take it for granted that efficiency is desirable. We are now in a position where we can intelligently question that assumption.

Efficiency is not an end in itself—ultimately, we concern ourselves with efficiency of algorithms in order to enable people to use their resources of time and money more effectively. Thus whenever improving *machine* efficiency increases *human* time and cost, it is probably not worth it. For instance, you might have an inefficient algorithm to carry out a task which only needs to be done once. It is not likely to be worth the time and effort to find and master a more efficient algorithm to carry out that task. Alternatively, you might have two algorithms which could be used in a program which is to be maintained by someone else. It might be better to select the slower one if it is easier for the maintainer to understand. Finally, you might have a relatively slow but effective program for carrying out a task when a newer, faster method becomes available. It may be too expensive to purchase it and train users to justify the improvement.

All other things being equal, however, a more efficient algorithm is preferable to a less efficient one. Dramatic savings of human time and cost (and frustration) are often possible with more efficient algorithms.

SUMMARY

Our primary tool for comparing the computational complexity of algorithms is big–oh notation. In this notation, sums of functions are equivalent to that individual function in the sum which grows the fastest for large n; also functions which are constant multiples of each other are equivalent. Thus, we represent a family of equivalent functions (and all those which grow more slowly) by $O(f(n))$ where $f(n)$ is the simplest of the fastest growing functions.

We examined four important searching techniques: linear search, sentinel search, binary search, and hashing. These have complexities $O(n)$, $O(n)$, $O(\log n)$ and $O(1)$ respectively. Thus, hashing is used whenever possible; however, it is not appropriate in some situations such as searches involving inequality constraints on keys. Also searching an unordered list requires a linear or sentinel search.

We examined two sorting algorithms whose average case complexity is $O(n^2)$: the selection sort and insertion sort. These were presented primarily because of their conceptual simplicity, although the insertion sort is widely used on nearly sorted lists. We also examined three sorting algorithms with an average case complexity of $O(n\log n)$: the heap sort, merge sort, and quick sort. Empirically, the quick sort has been shown to be the fastest on randomly arranged lists; in spite of this fact, however, it has a worst case complexity of $O(n^2)$. Because the quick sort algoritnm requires recursion, it is often combined with a call to an insertion sort for small lists to produce an even faster sorting method. A sixth method, the Shell sort, was presented. Although its average case complexity is unknown, it has been empirically shown to be approximately $O(n^{1.25})$. It is often used in languages which do not support recursion.

EXERCISES

3–22 Give a loop invariant for the function `maxloc` (invoked by `SelectionSort`). Verify this function.

3–23 Alter the `SelectionSort` function so that it invokes `swap` to interchange `a[topuns]` and `a[maxl]` *only* whenever `topuns` and `maxl` point to *different* elements (it's useless to swap an element with itself). What impact, if any, does this refinement have on the complexity of this sort? Explain.

3–24 Write a function `sorted` that determines whether an array is arranged in nondecreasing order and returns `1` or `0` accordingly.

3–25 The "bubble sort" is a straightforward sorting procedure, which readers may recall from an earlier course. Here, a series of complete passes is made over the entire array until the it is ordered. For a single pass, every adjacent pair of elements `a[i]` and `a[i+1]` is examined and, if they are out of order with respect to each other, they are swapped. Otherwise, they are left alone. When an entire pass is made over the array (say, for `i=0` to `n-1`) in which *no* such swaps are needed, the array is known to be ordered. Illustrate the bubble sort for the array a[0..9] of Example 3.6. Implement a function `BubbleSort` which embodies this strategy, using the auxiliary function `swap` as well. Show that the average case complexity of `BubbleSort` is $O(n^2)$, but that its best case complexity is $O(n)$.

3–26 Exercise the `InsertionSort` function given in the text, by showing the resulting element sequence in the array after each successive iteration of the `do-while` loop. Use as an example the array a[0..9] of Example 3.6.

3–27 Show that the average case complexity of `InsertionSort` is $O(n^2)$; show that in the case of an already sorted array, it is $O(n)$.

3–28 Verify `InsertionSort`.

3–29 Show that the function `InsertionSort` is equivalent to the function `gapsort` in the special case where `k = g = 1`.

3–30 Verify `gapsort` by giving preconditions and postconditions, and arguing systematically that the postconditions for `gapsort` are satisfied for any subarray of a[0..n] defined by beginning element k and gap size g.

3–31 Would the complexity of `ShellSort` change significantly if a selection sort were used to sort the subarrays rather than an insertion sort? Why or why not?

3–32 Complete the trace of `merge` begun in Figures 3–27 and 3–28.

3–33 Write an appropriate loop invariant for the first `while`-loop in the `merge` function. Verify this function.

3–34 Verify `MergeSort` assuming the correctness of `merge`.

3–35 Trace execution of `QuickSort` for an array which is already ordered, such as a[0..4] = (1 2 3 4 5). How many assignments and comparisons are executed? Do the same for an array which is in reverse order, such as a[0..4] = (5 4 3 2 1).

3–36 Because it uses recursion, `QuickSort` is inefficient with small arrays. `InsertionSort`, on the other hand, is very efficient with small arrays. Write a function, `FastSort`, which uses `QuickSort` above a size, N, but shifts to `InsertionSort` when the recursive invocation of `QuickSort` produces a list below this size. Exercise your function on a set of 1000 random integers and empirically determine the optimal size for N.

3–37 Let a[0..3] = (4 7 8 9). Show that for the function `heapify` in `Heap-Sort`, the order in which a[0..3] is converted into a heap is crucial.

That is, if `heapify` were invoked in a loop that varied the index `left` from 1 up to $\frac{last}{2}$, rather than from $\frac{last}{2}$ down to 1, the result would not necessarily be a heap.

3–38 Write loop invariants for both loops in `HeapSort` and verify the algorithm assuming the correctness of `heapify`.

3–39 Sometimes, we want to find the element that would be in the *k*th position in an array, a[0..n], if a[0..n] were ordered (for example, finding the median or a certain percentile). We can create a method, `Kselect`, a modification of `QuickSort`, to do this without sorting a[0..n]. The idea is this: If we apply `partition` to a[0..n], the array is divided into two subarrays with the smaller elements at the beginning. Checking the position of the pivot, we can decide which subarray the *k*th element is in. `Kselect` is then recursively called for the relevant subarray. Implement `Kselect` and exercise it on the sample array of Example 3.6.

3–40 Verify your version of `Kselect` (see Exercise 3–39).

3–41 Show that `Kselect` (Exercise 3–39) has average case complexity $O(n)$ by assuming that the array is split roughly in half at each recursive call to `Kselect`. Thus, for finding the median or a percentile of a set of data, using `Kselect` is significantly faster than sorting the data.

References

[1]   Bentley, Jon L., "How to Sort," in the column "Programming Pearls," *Communications of the ACM*, 27,4 (April 1984), 287-291.

[2]   Knuth, Donald E., *The Art of Computer Programming,* Volume 3: *Sorting and Searching*, Addison-Wesley Publishing Company, Reading, Massachusetts, 1973.

[3]   Manna, Zohar and Waldinger, Richard, *The Logical Basis for Computer Programming, volume 1: Deductive Reasoning*, Addison-Wesley Publishing Company, Reading, Massachusetts, 1985.

[4]   Shell, Donald L., "A High-Speed Sorting Procedure," *Communications of the ACM*, 2 (July 1959), 30-32.

[5]   Williams, J. W. J., "Algorithm 232: Heapsort," *Communications of the ACM*, 7 (June 1964), 347-348.

CHAPTER 4

LISTS, STACKS, AND QUEUES

In this chapter, we return to our exploration of data abstractions from the point of view of their applications. We introduce the class *list* which will be used in this and subsequent chapters. Lists are one of the simplest and most natural data structures since a great deal of data that we encounter comes to us in list form. We will see that the *list* abstraction is useful for applying fundamental searching and sorting algorithms to arbitrary sequences of elements. Two other abstractions, known as *stacks* and *queues*, are introduced in this chapter. These are useful in the many applications where insertions and deletions are allowed at one end or the other of the sequence, but nowhere else.

The *stack* is a special class of sequences in which insertions and deletions are made only at one end (called the *top* of the stack). The *queue* is a special class of sequences in which all insertions are made at one end (called the *rear* of the queue) and all deletions are made at the other (called the *front* of the queue).

The `List` subclass of sequences provides a flexible device for visualizing and manipulating a sequence of elements because it allows *any* element in the list to be altered, retrieved, inserted, or deleted, regardless of its position in the list. However, such flexibility comes at a price, since the efficiency (complexity) of list insertion and deletion, in time and/or in space, is inferior to that for stacks and queues. In stack and queue applications, flexibility for insertion and deletion is not required. These applications only require that the element at one end (or the other) needs to be accessed, inserted, or deleted. The positions and values of the vast majority of the elements are therefore unaffected.

We shall see some of these special applications in this chapter. Stacks are useful when writing programs that evaluate special forms of arithmetic expressions, called "Polish expressions." Queues are useful when writing programs that simulate a waiting line—such as a line of people waiting for teller service at a bank, or checkout service at a grocery store. That is, people normally enter the line at the rear and leave from the front. When stacks and queues are used for these applications, both storage flexibility and efficiency of insertion and deletion can be gained. Efficiency of the implementations of the member functions for lists, stacks, and queues will be studied in a later chapter.

THE List CLASS

The List class bears some resemblance to the ElementSet class presented in Chapter 2. A List differs from a set in two major ways: the elements in a List have a definite order and duplication of elements is allowed. We can access the elements of a List by specifying their location in the List. For example, we can ask for the third element in a List. Similarly, we can store an element into a List by specifying the location where we want the insertion to occur. Additionally, we can delete elements from a List (again, by specifying the location from which a deletion occurs) and we can swap two elements in a List (by specifying the locations of those two elements).

Some of the programs of this chapter are, in fact, clients of the List class implementation. Thus, we are more interested in learning how to use List objects than we are in how the List class is implemented. Chapter 2 gave you some indication of how data structures can be implemented and subsequent chapters (especially, Chapter 6) will discuss the implementation details of Lists and other data structures in greater detail. At this point, we are interested only in the behavior of Lists and their member functions, so that we can use them in solving problems.

The List class is implemented as a subclass of Sequence (as shown in Figure 4–1). Note that the classes Stack and Queue are also subclasses of Sequence. This is because there are some properties that Lists, Stacks, and Queues all share, and we implemented these properties as a separate class, Sequence. This enables us to avoid reimplementing certain operations over and over again—that is, to reuse certain methods for all three classes without reimplementing them. We shall consider Stack and Queue later in this chapter.

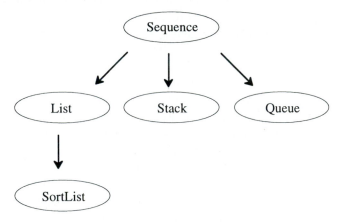

FIGURE 4–1   The Sequence class hierarchy.

We shall begin by focusing on the relationship between Sequences, Lists, and SortLists.

Definition A *Sequence* is a series of zero or more elements, written as $(e_1\ e_2\ \ldots\ e_n)$, where $n \geq 0$ is the size of the sequence.

Sequences have the associated member functions shown in Figures 4–2 and 4–3.

```
// Class description: The class Sequence provides the
//    methods that are shared by lists, stacks, and queues.
//    In our specifications a Sequence is represented as
//    Seq = (e[1] e[2] .... e[n])
//    where each e[i] denotes an object. The empty sequence
//    is denoted by Seq = ().


#ifndef SEQUENCE_H
#define SEQUENCE_H


#include <iostream.h>
#include <fstream.h>
#include "elements.h"


const int MAXELEMENTS = 500;


class Sequence
{
    protected:
        // DATA MEMBERS ...
        ElementPtr e[MAXELEMENTS];   // array of pointers to
                                     // elements
        int size;                    // number of elements


    public:
    // MEMBER FUNCTIONS ...
    // constructor - destructor
    inline Sequence();
    inline virtual ~Sequence();


    // test
    int is_full();
    int is_empty();


    // access
    int get_size();
    virtual void empty();


    // display
    virtual void display();
};   // end class Sequence
#endif
```

FIGURE 4–2 Declaration for the Class Sequence.

```
// ***Formal specifications for the Sequence class.
//


//
// constructor - destructor
//


// Sequence::Sequence();
// Used: To initialize receiver sequence.
// Pre:  None
// Post: Receiver is intialized and size = 0 and Seq = ()


// Sequence::~Sequence();
// Used: To destroy the receiver sequence.
// Pre:  Receiver has been initialized.
// Post: Receiver is destroyed.


//
// test
//


// Sequence::is_full();
// Used: To determine if the receiver sequence is full.
// Pre:  Receiver is initialized.
// Post: result = (size == MAXELEMENTS)


// Sequence::is_empty();
// Used: To determine if the receiver sequence is empty.
// Pre:  Receiver is initialized
// Post: result = (size == 0)


//
// access
//


// Sequence::get_size();
// Used: To determine the size of the receiver sequence.
// Pre:  Receiver is initialized
// Post: result = size



// Sequence::empty()
// Used: Resets the receiver to an empty sequence.
// Pre:  receiver is initialized.
// Post: size = 0, Seq = () and each object in
//    the Seq is destroyed.
```

```
//
// display
//


// Sequence::display();
// Used: Displays each object in receiver sequence.
// Pre:  Seq = (e[1] e[2] ... e[n]) and size = n
//    and display() is defined for each object in Seq.
// Post: for all I in [1..n] : the object e[i]
//    is displayed on the screen.
```

FIGURE 4–3   Formal Specifications for the Class Sequence.

A *List* is a sequence that has the following additional methods:

Retrieve   Store   Insert   Remove   Swap

The definition of the class List follows in Figures 4–4 and 4–5.

```
#ifndef LIST_H
// Class description: The class List implements a list
//    of objects. The list class allows objects to be
//    inserted into and deleted from any position.
//    In our specifications a List is represented as
//    L = (e[1] e[2] .... e[n])
//    where each e[i] denotes an object.  The empty list is
//    denoted by L = ().


#define LIST_H


#include <stddef.h>
    // required by Microsoft compiler 7.0 for NULL
#include "sequence.h"


class List : public Sequence
{
    public:
        // MEMBER FUNCTIONS ...
        // constructor - destructor
        List(){ };
            // this is an inline definition.
            // Sequence constructor is called.
        ~List() { };
            // this is an inline definition
            // Sequence destructor is called.


        // access
        ElementPtr retrieve(int);
```

```
                    // modify
                    int store(ElementPtr, int);
                    int insert(ElementPtr, int);
                    int remove(int);
                    int swap(int, int);
          };   // end class List


          #endif
```

FIGURE 4–4 Declaration for the Class `List`.

```
          // ***  Formal specifications for the List class.

          //


          //
          // constructor - destructor
          //


          // Constructor: List::List();
          // Used: To initialize a receiver list.
          // Pre:  None
          // Post: Receiver is initialized and size = 0 and L = ().


          // Destructor: List::~List();
          // Used: To destroy the receiver list
          // Pre:  Receiver has been initialized
          // Post: Receiver is destroyed


          //
          // access
          //


          // Function: List::retrieve(int i);
          // Used: To retrieve a pointer to the i-th element in list L.
          // Pre:  L = (e[1] e[2] ... e[n]) and 1<=i<=n
          // Post: (i is out of range and result = NULL) or
          //       (result = e[i])


          //
          // modify
          //


          // Function: List::store(ElementPtr eptr, int i);
          // Used: Stores eptr in place of i-th element in list L.
```

```
// Pre:   L = (e[1] e[2] ... e[n]) and size = n
// Post: (i is out of range and result = 0) or
//        (L = (e[1] ... e[i-1] Eptr e[i+1] ... e[n]) and
//        result = 1)


// Function: List::insert(ElementPtr eptr, int i);
// Used: Inserts eptr in the i-th position in list L.
// Pre:   L = (e[1] e[2] ... e[n]), size = n and 1<=i<=n+1
// Post: (i is out of range and result = 0) or
//        L = (e[1] ... e[i-1] eptr e[i+1] ... e[n]) and
//        (size = n + 1) and (result = 1)


// Function: List::remove(int i);
// Used: Deletes the i-th element in the list L.
// Pre:   L = (e[1] e[2] ... e[n]) and size = n
// Post: (i is out of range and result = 0) or
//        (L = (e[1] ... e[i-1] e[i+1] ... e[n]) and
//        size = n - 1 and result = 1)


// Function: List::swap(int i, int j);
// Used: Swaps i-th and j-th elements in a list L.
// Pre:   L = (e[1] ... e[i] ... e[j] ... e[n])
//        and 1<=i<=n and 1<=j<=n
// Post: i or j is out of range and result = 0
//        or L = (e[1] ... e[j] ... e[i] ... e[n])
```

FIGURE 4–5   Formal Specifications for the Class `List`.

A `SortList` is a `List` that has the following additional method:

`QuickSort`

We could introduce all the sorting and searching methods from the previous chapter into the class `SortList`. We choose to illustrate how this could be done by showing how `QuickSort` can be implemented using the methods of the `List` class.

To illustrate the basic features of the `Sequence` and `List` classes, we introduce some of the member functions and provide a brief example of each in the paragraphs below. (A full set of specifications for all these methods is given in Appendices A and B of the *Laboratory Manual*.) We then examine the `SortList` method in detail.

The `List` methods enable basic manipulation of the individual elements within a sequence—the `Sequence` methods by themselves provide only input and output of entire sequences. In particular, `Retrieve` and `Store` provide access to the `i`th element in the `Sequence`; `Retrieve` returns a pointer to this `i`th element, and `Store` replaces it with a different element. `Insert` adds a new element at position `i` of a `List`, and `Remove` deletes the element at position `i` (simultaneously moving the remaining elements "up" one position in the

List. Finally, Swap exchanges the two elements at positions i and j in a List. Here is an example of their use.

Example 4.1   The following is the edited output of a program to exercise the List class that is provided in Appendix C of the accompanying *Laboratory Manual*. The program provides a menu and asks the user to select a number for the List operation desired. We have omitted the menu output and replaced numbers by names of operations invoked for this example. User input is shown in boldface. A definition and formal specifications for the class Morpheme will be given below. For now, it is sufficient to think of them as short character strings that contain no blanks. Recall that List positions are indexed beginning with 1.

```
1) get       2) insert   3) retrieve   4) empty
5) display   6) remove   7) store      8) swap
9) size      10) quit

Select a function: get

How many Morphemes will be added to the list? 5
Enter a Morpheme: at
Enter a Morpheme: bat
Enter a Morpheme: 3.5
Enter a Morpheme: data
Enter a Morpheme: 50

Select a function: display

at
bat
3.5
data
50


Select a function: insert
Enter the position of the insertion: 2
Enter item to insert: ratatat

Select a function: display

at .
ratatat
bat
3.5
data
50
```

Note that insertion into position 2 moved the elements from old positions 2, 3, 4, and 5 back one place to positions 3, 4, 5, and 6, respectively, to make room for the element to be inserted. The `List` now has size 6.

```
Select a function: retrieve
Enter position of the item to be retrieved: 4
Item at position 4 is: 3.5

Select a function: remove
Enter position of item to remove: 3

Select a function: display

at
ratatat
3.5
data
50
```

Remove from position 3 deletes the item at position 3 and closes the gap. The `List` is now has size 5.

```
Select a function: store

Enter position of item to store: 4
Enter item to store: newitem


Select a function: display

at
ratatat
3.5
newitem
50


Select a function: swap
Enter 2 list positions to swap separated by a blank: 1 4


Select a function: display

newitem
ratatat
3.5
at
50
```

```
Select a function: size

List size = 5
```

Note that `Lists` inherit all the methods of `Sequences`, so that we can reuse the member function `get_size` for a `List` as well as for a `Sequence`. Second, many useful things can be done with lists without knowing the details of the implementation of a `List`. Before we go on, we will explain the idea of a `Morpheme`.

THE CLASS `Morpheme`

The `Morpheme` class is implemented as a subclass of `Element`. It is analogous to the standard classes of Chapter 2 in the following sense. A `Morpheme` is a short character string that contains no blanks, and carries some intrinsic meaning for the application program that uses it.[1] For instance, persons' surnames (`"Tucker"`, `"Cupper"`, and so forth), the arithmetic operators (`"+"`, `"-"`, and so forth), the punctuation marks (`"."`, `":"`, and so forth), are all examples of morphemes in this sense. We shall use the class `Morpheme` in many of the example applications presented in this text. A more formal definition will clarify the details:

> **Definition** A `Morpheme` is a string of 16 or fewer readable characters from the ASCII character set. It is a subclass of the `Element` class, and has the specifications given in Figures 4–6 and 4–7.

```
// FILENAME:  MORPHEME.H

// Morphemes are used in combinataion with Input_strings
// to provide generalized user input and parsing.
// A Morpheme is a string of 16 or fewer readable
// characters from the ASCII set.

#ifndef Morpheme_h
#define Morpheme_h

#include "elements.h"
#include <fstream.h>


// prototypes
boolean is_white_space (char c);
boolean is_delimiter (char c);
```

---

1. The *New Webster's Dictionary* defines a morpheme as "the smallest meaningful unit of a language that cannot be divided into smaller meaningful parts." We intend to capture this spirit when defining morphemes as a general class of elements for computational purposes. As such it provides a rich foundation, especially for applications where the standard types are inadequate.

```
const MAXMORPHEME = 16;   // Maximum characters in a Morpheme.

class Morpheme: public Element
{
    private:
      char value[MAXMORPHEME+1];

    public:


      Morpheme();
      virtual ~Morpheme();


      void virtual display();


      // access
      void get(char* prompt);
      virtual char* get_val();
      virtual void set_val(char* astring);
      Morpheme set_val(float arg);
      float to_float();
      boolean is_word();
      boolean is_float();
      virtual int operator == (Element& e);
      virtual void file_in(ifstream& afile);
      virtual void file_out(ofstream& afile);
}; //Morpheme

typedef Morpheme* MorphemePtr;


    #endif
```

FIGURE 4–6   Declaration for the Class Morpheme.

```
// ******* Formal specifications for the Morpheme class. *******

// Morpheme();
// Used: To set up receiver with its virtual methods;
// Pre:  None
// Post: Receiver is initialized and my_class = "Morpheme"

// virtual ~Morpheme();
// Used: To render receiver useless.
// Pre:  Receiver is initialized.
// Post: Receiver is no longer usable.

//access/test
// void virtual display();
```

```
// Used: To display a Morpheme.
// Pre:
// Post: Receiver.value is displayed to the screen.

// virtual char* get_val();
// Used: To retrieve the value of a morpheme
// Pre:
// Post: Returns the string value of the receiver

// virtual char* get_class();
// Used: To test class membership of the receiver.
// Pre:  Receiver is intialized.
// Post: result = receiver's class

// boolean is_float();
// Used: To determine if m takes the form of
//       a real (float) number.
// Pre:
// Post: Returns TRUE iff m takes the form of afloat number

// boolean is_word();
// Used: To distinguish punctuation from other morphemes.
// Pre:
// Post: Returns TRUE iff receiver.value has
//       no punctuation or white spaces.

// file in / file out
// virtual void file_out(ofstream& afile);
// Used: To write a representation of the receiver to afile.
// Pre:  afile is opened for text output and afile = oldStuff
// Post: afile = oldStuff Receiver.value

// virtual void file_in(ifstream& afile);
// Used: To read a representation of the receiver from a file
// Pre: afile is opened for text input and = stuff restofstuff
// Post: afile = restofstuff and receiver.value = stuff

//
// modify
//

// void get(char* prompt);
// Used: To input a Morpheme from the keyboard.
// Pre:  Prompt is a string used to prompt the user for input.
// Post: Returns a Morpheme read from the keyboard.

// virtual void set_val(char* astring);
// Used: To change the string value of a morpheme
// Pre:
// Post: Receiver's value = astring

// float to_float();
// Used: To convert a Morpheme to a float.
// Pre:
// Post: Returns the float value of m or 0 if NOT is_float(m).
//       This can can lead to an overflow error if m is too big.
//       Since different platforms have different maximum
```

```
//          floating point values, the overflow checking is left to
//          the client programmer.

// Morpheme set_val(float);
// Used: To store a float variable in a Morpheme.
// Pre:
// Post: Returns the Morpheme representation of the argument up
//          to MAXMORPHEME length.  The value will be rounded so
//          that it will fit in the Morpheme's value data member.


//
// Operator
//


// virtual int operator == (Element& e);
// Used: To test for equality of two morpheme values.
// Pre:
// Post: (result = 1 and this.value == e.value) or
//          (result = 0 and this.value != e.value)
```

FIGURE 4–7   Formal Specifications for the Class `Morpheme`.

Because the `Morpheme` class is a subclass of `Element`, the `get_class()` member function and the `my_class` instance variable are inherited. Practically speaking, a `Morpheme` is a special kind of string that provides robust input and output of strings and conversions between various data formats (e.g., from strings to numbers).

The `get_val` and `set_val` member functions are analogous to their counterparts for the standard `Element`s; one retrieves and the other stores the current 16 character `value` of the receiver object.[2] The `get` member function inputs a `Morpheme` value from the keyboard after issuing a prompt. The `display` member function displays the value of the receiver `Morpheme` on the user's computer or terminal screen. The member function `is_float` and `is_word` identify the nature of the `string` stored in the receiver `Morpheme` — a number causes `is_float` to return 1; a string of characters without punctuation marks, spaces, or control characters causes `is_word` to return 1. Finally, the member function `to_float` facilitates conversion from the receiver `Morpheme` value stored internally as a string to an internal float representation.

The specifications for the `Morpheme` class is replicated in Appendix D of the *Laboratory Manual*.

The `InputString` class provides a means to capture a line of input text as a whole and then subdivide it into its constituent `Morpheme`s. This is a powerful device for a variety of text and language processing applications as we shall see shortly. The `InputString` class is also a subclass of `Element` and is defined as follows:

---

2.   Note, there are two versions of `set_val` — one to change the `string` value of a `Morpheme`, the other to change a `float` value.

Definition An `InputString` is a string of 255 or fewer characters from the ASCII character set.

An `InputString` has several member functions:

```
InputString      ~InputString      ReFormat
MorphemeCount    Retrieve(i)
```

An `InputString` has a data member, `value`, which is a `string`. The `value` may be stored and displayed using C++ I/O objects. The `ReFormat` member function converts an `InputString` into another `string` in which individual delimiters and punctuation marks are separated from adjacent `Morphemes` by a blank space. `MorphemeCount` is a function that returns the number of `Morphemes` in a reformatted `InputString`. Precise specifications for these member functions are given in Appendix E of the *Laboratory Manual*.

Since `InputString` is a subclass of `Element`, an `InputString` inherits all of the `Element` member functions. Here is a brief example to provide an indication of the power to the classes `Morpheme` and `InputString`.

Example 4.2 Suppose that we have the following declarations;

```
    InputString in;
    int count;
Morpheme second_morpheme;
```

and the following statements in a program:

```
cin >> in;
in.ReFormat;
if in.MorphemeCount >= 2
    second_morpheme.set_val (in.Retrieve(2));
```

This code would cause the second `Morpheme` from any input string that has at least two `Morphemes`, to be retrieved and placed in the `Morpheme` second_morpheme. For instance, if the input were

```
    Hark, Hark A Lark!
```

after the call to `ReFormat`, the `value` of `in` would be

```
"Hark , Hark A Lark !"
```

(Note the spaces inserted before each of the two punctuation marks.) Thus, the second `Morpheme` is the comma (not the second word `Hark`), which is stored by the last statement as the `value` of the object `second_morpheme`.

These methods are particularly useful when we design programs that parse complex arithmetic expressions and other heavily parenthesized representations of data structures, such as trees. Many examples of the utility of these elementary classes are given throughout the text. To summarize, the `Element`, `Morpheme`, and `InputString` classes are related as shown in Figure 4-8.

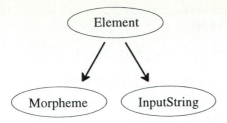

FIGURE 4–8   Another Hierarchy of Elementary Classes.

THE SortList CLASS

Two operations one might want to perform on lists are searching and sorting. Fortunately, the algorithms presented in Chapter 3 for searching and sorting arrays of integers can all be extended to lists with little difficulty. For some of these, the only operations needed are retrieve and ==. For others, more of the list operations and more relational operators are needed.   For quicksort, we need retrieve, swap, and <=. That is, if we want to quicksort a list of elements, we must be able retrieve any single element, swap any pair of elements, and compare any two element values with <=. The declaration of the SortList class as a subclass of List is:

```
class SortList : public List
{
 public:
   SortList() { };
   ~SortList() { };

   void read_in() { };
   int stream_in(char* file_name) {return 0; };
   int stream_out(char* file_name) {return 0; };
   int partition(SortList&, int, int, int);
   void sublist_quicksort (SortList&, int, int);
   void quick_sort();
}; // end class SortList
```

The input/output methods are not implemented at the SortList level. They are needed to insure that the class or classes to be operated on have the same implementation of <=. The sorting work is done by the methods partition, sublist_quicksort, and quick_sort whose definitions follow.

```
int SortList::partition(SortList& a, int first, int last,
                        int pivloc)
{
  ElementPtr pivotptr;
  int ll;
  int rl;
```

```
      pivotptr = a.retrieve(pivloc);
      a.swap(first, pivloc);
      ll = first;
      for (rl = first+1; rl <= last; rl++)
        {
        if ( *(a.retrieve(rl)) <= *pivotptr )
          a.swap(++ll, rl);
        }
    a.swap (first, ll);
    return ll;
  }   //end partiton

void SortList::sublist_quicksort (SortList& l, int first,
                                           int last)
{
  int pivotind;
  int partdiv;
   if ((last - first) > 0)
      {
      pivotind = (first+last)/2;
      partdiv = partition(l, first, last, pivotind);
    sublist_quicksort(l, first, partdiv-1);
    sublist_quicksort(l, partdiv+1, last);
      }
  }    // end sublist_quicksortvoid

SortList::quick_sort()
{
   sublist_quicksort(*this, 1, get_size());
 } //end quick_sort
```

Except for the type and name of the first parameter, `sublist_quicksort` is identical to the `quicksort` procedure of Chapter 3. Even `partition` for `lists` is almost identical to `partition` for arrays. The only difference is that `list` `element` values must be accessed indirectly. For example the if–statement in Chapter 3 was `if (a[rl] <= pivotval)` while for `lists` this must become `if ( *(a.retrieve(rl)) <= *pivotptr )` in order to access the values of the `element` pointers stored in the `list`. These are the only essential changes necessary to sort a list of objects instead of an array of integers.

Unfortunately, there is still an important detail to be considered. While our `lists` may be heterogeneous, the `<=` comparison must be between values for which it is defined. We have not defined `<=` between a `StringObj` and an `IntObj` so we should not allow such a comparison to be requested. In order to insure that this does not occur, we will invoke `quick_sort` only on a subclass of `SortList` that is guaranteed to allow this comparison. For example, here is the declaration for a class that can only contain integer objects:

```
class IntSortList : public SortList
{
   public:
      // constructor - destructor
      IntSortList() { };
```

```
        ~IntSortList() { };

        // modify
        int store(ElementPtr, int);
        int insert(ElementPtr, int);
        void read_in();

        // stream in and stream out
        int stream_in(char* file_name);
        int stream_out(char* file_name);
};   // end class IntSortList
```

This class is a `SortList` subclass whose elements are restricted to the type `IntObj`. The functions `store` and `insert` are polymorphically redefined to limit elements in an `IntSortList` to the class `IntObj`. For example, `IntSortList::store` simply determines that the element to be stored is an `IntObj` and then invokes the `List::store` method. The code for `IntSortList::store` is shown in Figure xx.

```
int IntSortList::store(ElementPtr eptr, int i)
{
  if (strcmp(eptr -> get_class(), "IntObj"))
  {
    cout << "Can only store IntObj objects in an IntSortList.";
    return 0;
  }
  else
    return List::store(eptr, i);
}   // end IntSortList::store()
```

FIGURE 4–9 C++ code for `IntSortList::store`.

The functions `read_in`, `stream_in`, and `stream_out` are implemented here for ease of reading in, filing in and filing out a stream of integer values. The identifier, `il`, can be declared to be of class `IntSortList` by the declaration: `IntSortList il`. Then data can be read in from the terminal or a file by `il.read_in` or `il.stream_in`, respectively. To sort `il`, we just invoke: `il.quicksort()`.

In a similar fashion, if we want to create and sort a list of string objects, we can define a subclass, `StrSortList`, of `SortList`, that restricts the type of its elements to `StringObj`. Details can be found by reviewing the software files, `sortlist.h` and `sortlist.cxx` which are provided in the system directory for this course or the distribution diskette.

Finally, it should be noted that any of the searching and sorting methods of Chapter 3 can be extended to the class `SortList` in a manner exactly analogous to the way we extended `quicksort`. These other methods also require that the relational operators used (e.g. `==`, `<`, etc.) be used only on operands for which they are defined. So invoking them on objects from a more restricted class such as `IntSortList` or `StrSortList` is advised.

STACKS

We now turn our attention to another abstract data type, the stack. Informally, a stack can be visualized as a kind of pile, in which elements are added by placing them on top of the pile and elements are removed by taking them off the top of the pile. A pile of trays in a cafeteria provides a good example for visualizing these stack actions. For this reason, stacks are often called *push-down* lists, or *last-in-first-out* (*LIFO*, for short) lists. A more precise definition follows.

> **Definition**   The `Stack` class is any sequence of elements, $S = (e_1\ e_2\ ...\ e_n)$ in which e_n is identified as the *top* element and insertions and deletions can only be made at the top. Insertions in a stack are called *Push*, and deletions from a stack are called *Pop*. The principal methods for the `Stack` class are:
>
> | | | | | |
> |---|---|---|---|---|
> | `is_full` | `is_empty` | `get_size` | `empty` | `display` |
> | `push` | `pop` | `top` | | |

`Stacks` also have the instance variable `size` that keeps track of the current number of elements. The constant `MAXELEMENTS` inherited from the class `Sequence` defines an upper limit for the size of a `Stack`.

Note that the first five of these methods are inherited from the class `Sequence`. The methods `is_full`, `is_empty`, `get_size`, `empty`, and `display` have the same meanings for a `Stack` as they do for a `Sequence` or `List`. That is, these methods are *reused* for `Stacks`. The methods `push`, `pop`, and `top` are unique to `Stacks`.

Stack Method Definitions

The specifications for the member functions for the class `Stack` are given in Figures 4–10 and 4–11.

```
// Class description: The class Stack is a sequence in
//     which objects can only be inserted or retrieved from
//     one end of the stack (called its top).
//     In our specifications a Stack will be denoted by
//         S = (e[1] e[2] .... e[n])
//     where each e[i] denotes an object. The empty
//     stack is denoted by S = ().


#ifndef Stack_h
#define Stack_h


#include <stddef.h>
     // required for Microsoft compiler 7.0 for NULL
#include "sequence.h"

class Stack : public Sequence
{
```

```
        public:
            //constructor / destructor
            Stack() { };
            ~Stack() { };

            // modifying
            int push(ElementPtr);
            ElementPtr pop();

            // access
            ElementPtr top();

            // display
            virtual void display();
    };   // end class Stack

    #endif
```

FIGURE 4–10   Declaration for the Class Stack.

```
// ********  Formal specifications for the Stack class  ********

//
//constructor / destructor
//

// Stack();
// Used: To initialize the receiver stack.
// Pre:  None
// Post: Receiver stack is initialized and size = 0 and S = ()

// virtual ~Stack();
// Used: To destroy the receiver stack.
// Pre:  Receiver is initialized.
// Post: Receiver stack is destroyed.


//
// accessing / modifying
//

// int push(ElementPtr eptr);
// Used: To add a new element onto the top of the stack.
// Pre:  S = (e[1] e[2] ... e[n]) and size = n
// Post: n < MAXELEMENTS and size = n+1 and
//       S = (e[1] e[2] ... e[n] eptr) and result = 1
//       or n = MAXELEMENTS and result = 0

// ElementPtr pop();
// Used: To remove the top element from the stack.
// Pre:  S = (e[1] e[2] ... e[n]) and size = n
// Post: (n = 0 and result = 0) or
//       (n > 0 and S = (e[1] e[2] ... e[n-1]) and size = n-1
//       and result = ElementPtr)
```

```
// virtual ElementPtr top();
// Used: To access the element at the top of the stack
// Pre:  S = (e[1] e[2] ... e[n]) and size = n
// Post: (n = 0 and result = NULL) or
//       (n > 0 and result = e[N])

// virtual void display();
// Used: To display the conntents of the stack object
// Pre: S = (e[1] e[2] ... e[n]) and size = n
// Post: output = S
// Note: user MUST implement display for each type
```

FIGURE 4–11   Formal Specifications for the Class `Stack`.

The stack visualized in Figure 4–12 would result from the execution of : `push(s1), push(s2), ... push(sn)` in that order.

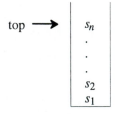

FIGURE 4–12   Visualization of Stack $S = (s_1\ s_2 \dots s_n)$.

Example 4.3   Suppose we have a `Stack` to keep track of the individual subjects that undergraduates will study in college. First, we declare the variable `subjectstack` to hold these values:

```
Stack subjectstack;
Morpheme *morph;
```

We can initialize this variable with the `value (economics history math-ematics computing)` using the following statement.

```
for (int i = 1, i ,= 4, i++)
     {
        morph -> get ("Please enter a subject name: ");
```

```
      subjectstack.push(morph);
}
```

Executing this statement will leave the variable `subjectstack` in the following state:

```
subjectstack = (economics history mathematics computing)
```

provided that the user types these four subjects, in order, in response to the prompts. If we follow these statements with

```
subjectstack.display;
```

this particular `Stack` of subjects will be displayed on the screen.

Example 4.4   Suppose we have the stack

```
subjectstack = (economics history mathematics computing)
```

and we want to push the subject `sociology` onto the top of the stack. This can be accomplished by the statements:

```
subject.set_val("sociology");
subjectstack.push(&Subject);
```

Here, we have assumed that `subject` has been declared to be of class `Morpheme`, and has been properly initialized. Note that the address of `subject` is provided as an argument, since that is the requirement of the method `push`. As a result, the value of `subjectstack` will be changed as shown below (see also Figure 4–13).

```
SubjectStack =
         (economics history mathematics computing sociology).
```

If, instead of adding a subject, we simply want to examine the top element of the original `subjectstack` to determine whether or not its value is `sociology`, we should write the following:

```
if MorphemePtr(subjectstack.Top)->get_val = "sociology"
   { ...
```

The type cast `MorphemePtr` is needed in order to interpret the top element of `subjectstack` as the address of a `Morpheme` (rather than a `Person`, or other subclass of `Element`), and the suffix `->get_val` dereferences that pointer and specifies the value of the top element, which is a `string`.

If, instead of examining the top element of the original `subjectstack`, we want to remove that element, we write the following statement:

```
subjectstack.pop
```

This leaves `subjectstack` in the following state:

```
SubjectStack = (economics history mathematics computing)
```

since `sociology` has been removed (by `pop`) from the `Stack`. The variable `size` which was inherited from `Sequence`, keeps track of the number of elements in a stack, and its value can be interrogated any time by an application program. Consider the following example.

Example 4.5 Suppose we have the `Stack` `numbers` and we enter the numbers (`42 23 80 25 46 39 96 73 74`) in response to the statement

```
for (int i = 1, i <= 9, i++)
    {
        tint ->get ("Please enter an integer: ");
        numbers.push(tint);
    }
```

As a result, `numbers.top` returns 74 (that was the last one typed), and `size` for `numbers.size` is 9. If, later in the processing of this stack, `size` for `numbers` were to become 0 and we tried to issue the instruction `numbers.pop` to remove an element from its top, `pop` would return 0. This indicates that the attempt to `pop` failed and the stack itself is left unchanged.

Run-Time Stacks and Function Activation

In any discussion of computer organization, the idea of a so-called *run-time stack* is central. The run-time stack in a computer keeps an up-to-date record of all the active function calls for a program which is running, and in the order in which they have been activated. To illustrate, consider the skeleton C++ program shown in Figure 4–14.

The program `main` calls functions P, Q, and R, and function R is the first to be activated from the program's body at the instruction just before memory loca-

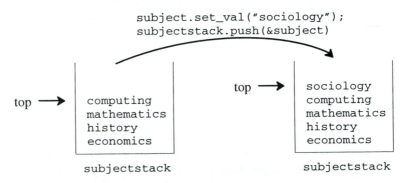

FIGURE 4–13 Execution of `subject.set_val("sociology");`
`subjectstack.push(&subject)`.

tion 0500. Later during program execution, function P or R will invoke Q, and function R will also invoke P. The numbers in the right-hand column are addresses of the memory locations that contain the machine code for the instruction immediately following the jump to the function for each of these calls at run time. Each of these numbers is, then, a return address.

When main program execution begins, an invocation of R is first activated. At that point, the system must *save* that return address (0500) of the main program, so that later, when R completes its task, control will return to the next machine instruction following that function call. In fact, considerably more information is kept in the stack including local variables, and argument information (if any). For this example, we will show only return addresses. Similarly, when R invokes procedure P, the return address 0300 must also be saved. Furthermore, it must be *pushed* on top of the prior return address on the run-time stack because of the fact that the invocation of P by R has occurred more recently than that of R by the main program. Finally, P invokes Q, causing that return address (0100) to be pushed onto the run-time stack.

Thus, at the time Q is finally activated, three different return addresses will have been saved on the run-time stack. The *order* in which they are saved is critical; that is, the *last* one saved is necessarily the *first* one to be retrieved. For instance, when Q finishes its execution, it must return control to the address

```
Statement              Address

main()
{
  ...
  R                     0500
  ...
} // end main
int P()
{
  Q();                  0100
  ...
} //end P

int Q()
{
  ...                   0200
}  //end Q

int R()
{
  ...
  P                     0300
  ...
  Q                     0400
  ...
} //end R
```

FIGURE 4–14   Skeletal C++ program with function calls.

0100 within P from where it was originally called, and neither of the other two addresses.

To emphasize this point, we can look further into the execution of this program and see that Q will eventually be invoked again, this time from address 0400 inside procedure R. At that time, this new return address must be effectively maintained so that Q can return control properly upon completion.

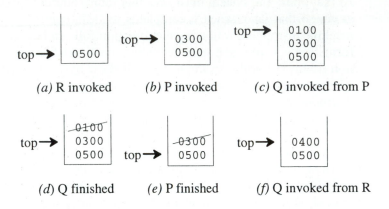

(a) R invoked   (b) P invoked   (c) Q invoked from P

(d) Q finished   (e) P finished   (f) Q invoked from R

FIGURE 4–15   Run-time stack for sample procedure invocations.

Because of this last-in-first-out structure of storing and retrieving return addresses during procedure invocation and termination, computer organizations usually include a *run-time stack* for keeping track of these return addresses. A push operation, in this setting, is synonymous with the invocation of a procedure, and a pop operation is synonymous with the return of control at the completion of a procedure invocation. The address that is retrieved in this fashion always tells the system where to resume execution inside the calling procedure. Figure 4–15 shows the contents of the run-time stack as procedures P, Q, and R are invoked. (This illustration assumes that no additional invocations of P, Q, and R appear in the program, and that none of the invocations appears inside a loop.)

Thus, the stack class, with its associated push and pop operations, plays a fundamental role in the control of program execution that includes multiple function calls. For this reason, the run-time stack and these methods are usually implemented in the machine instruction set of modern computers.

Stack Machines

A second impact that stacks have had in the area of computer organization is in the realization of so-called *stack machines*. Here, the entries in a run-time stack are arithmetic operands and the machine instruction set contains arithmetic operators (addition, subtraction, and so forth) that pop the top two operands off the stack and push the results back onto the stack. By contrast, a conventional machine instruction for adding two integers performs addition by explicitly specifying the two registers where the integers to be added currently reside and by returning its result to one of those registers.

For example, suppose we have three numbers—say 35, 17, and 40—and we want to use a stack machine to add the first to the product of the second and the third. In C++, we can specify this calculation as follows:

```
35 + 17 * 40
```

Our familiarity with expression evaluation, and especially the fact that multiplication takes precedence over addition, guarantees that this expression describes the calculation we want.

A conventional von Neumann machine language would provide the following sequence of instructions to accomplish this calculation:

```
LOAD R1,17      Load 17 into register 1
MUL  R1,40      Multiply by 40
ADD  R1,35      Add 35 to the result
```

Here, we are assuming that these instructions use "immediate" operands and that register `R1` is used as a temporary location where arithmetic operations can be performed, and the results of `MUL` and `ADD` are individually left in that same register. Thus, the final result, 715, of evaluating the expression `35+17*40` is left in register `R1` after these three machine instructions are executed.

If, instead, a stack machine were used to carry out this same calculation, the run-time stack would first need to be loaded with all three of the operands, and in the order that their respective operations (* followed by +) should be applied. That is, at the time the multiplication instruction is executed, the stack must contain all three operands, in the order shown in Figure 4–16a.

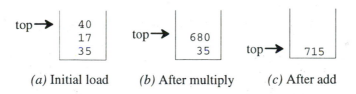

(a) Initial load   (b) After multiply   (c) After add

FIGURE 4–16   Stack machine execution of `35+17*40`.

Stack machines provide `PUSH`, `POP`, `ADD`, and `MUL` instructions, along with the run-time stack itself. Binary arithmetic instructions, like `ADD` and `MUL`, are always written without operands, since they implicitly `POP` two operands from the top of the stack and `PUSH` their result back onto the top of the stack. Thus, the following sequence of instructions to a stack machine will realize the correct calculation.

```
PUSH 35
PUSH 17
PUSH 40
MUL
ADD
```

Completion of the third PUSH instruction in this sequence leaves the stack as shown in Figure 4–16a, the MUL instruction leaves the stack as shown in Figure 4–16b, and the ADD instruction leaves the stack as shown in Figure 4–16c. That is, the single result, 715, is left at the top of the stack at the end of an expression evaluation.

Application: Evaluating Polish Expressions

Consider now the problem of designing programs that will evaluate arithmetic expressions. If the expressions are written in ordinary infix form, the development of an algorithm to evaluate them is not a simple matter. That is, the rules for handling the precedence of multiplication over addition, left-to-right scanning, and using parentheses to force a nested order of evaluation all must be designed to work together within such a program. Consider the following expression:

```
35 + 17 * (40 - 9) - 7
```

The program should interpret the evaluation rules so that the subtraction of 9 from 40 will occur first, the multiplication by 17 will occur second, the addition of 35 will occur third, and the subtraction of 7 will occur fourth.

Rather than taking on this problem all at once, we are tempted to ask whether or not there is any simpler way of writing an arithmetic expression that would allow the cumbersome rules about parentheses and precedence to be dropped without losing their inherent expressive power. Happily, the answer to this question is "yes." An alternative method of writing and interpreting expressions was invented by the Polish mathematician Lukasiewicz. Because of its origins, this different style of writing expressions is called *Reverse Polish notation* (*RPN* for short), and expressions that are written in this style are called *Polish expressions*.[3] Let us see what they look like.

Definition   A *Polish expression* is any series of arithmetic operands *x*, *y*, . . . and binary arithmetic operators *op* (typically +, −, *, and /), that can be formed using the following rules:

1.   Any operand *x* is a Polish expression.
2.   If *p1* and *p2* are Polish expressions, then *p1 p2 op* is a Polish expression.

Because this definition is recursive, it allows Polish expressions of arbitrary length to be constructed.

---

3.   In fact, there are four different variations of Polish expressions. In this discussion, we use the one where the expression is scanned from left to right and the operators are placed to the right of their respective operands. This particular variation is sometimes called *postfix notation*. The other three variations are achieved by changing the direction of the scan (right to left) and/or placing each operator before (rather than after) its respective operands. Placing the operator before its operands in a Polish expression yields the so-called *prefix notation*. Our conventional method of writing expressions with the operator between its operands is sometimes called *infix notation*.

Example 4.6 Here are three examples of Polish expressions, with their conventional infix equivalent expressions shown on the right.

```
17 40 *                      17 * 40
35 17 40 * +                 35 + 17 * 40
35 17 40 9 – * + 7 –         35 + 17 * (40 – 9) – 7
```

The evaluation of a Polish expression is governed by two simple rules. These rules are continuously applied until the expression is reduced to a single value.

1. Scan the expression from left to right until the first operator *op* is reached.
2. Apply this operator to the two operands *p1* and *p2* that appear immediately on its left, obtaining the result *p*, and then replace the triple *p1 p2 op* in the expression by *p*.

The scan begins with the leftmost token in the expression, and each repetition of the scan resumes where it left off within the expression.

To illustrate this simple algorithm, suppose we wish to evaluate the third expression in Example 4.6. Then we would apply these rules four successive times, once for each operator, to obtain the final result. The result is summarized in Figure 4–17.

Step   Expression (next operation underlined)

```
1    35 17 40 9 – * + 7 –
2    35 17 31 * + 7 –
3    35 527 + 7 –
4    562 7 –
5    555
```

FIGURE 4–17 Evaluating the Polish expression `35 17 40 9 – * + 7 –` in four steps.

In each of the first four steps, an underlined part indicates the next operation to be applied. The step below it shows the expression after that operation is complete. For example, the second step shows the result (`31`) of applying the operator – to the operands `40` and `9`. Continuing this scan forces the operator `*` to be applied to operands `17` and `31`, whose result (`527`) appears on the next line, and so on.

It is not difficult to see how Polish notation can be used to write *any* arithmetic expression, so that the use of parentheses and precedence rules can be dropped altogether. Whenever parentheses would be used to force one operator to be applied before another in an ordinary expression, the equivalent Polish expression simply places that operator on the left of the other. This forces it to be executed first in the left-to-right scan. In general, if we look at an infix expression alongside its Polish equivalent (see Example 4.6 again), we notice that the operands in the two forms always appear in the same order. We also notice that, in the Polish expression, each operator always appears in *exactly* the order in which it will be evaluated.

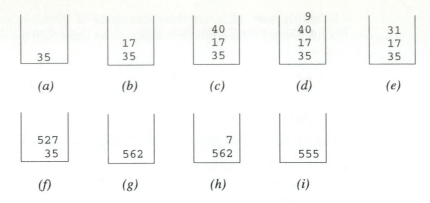

FIGURE 4–18   Operand stack contents for evaluating the expression 35 17 40 9 − * + 7 − .

The reason for using a stack in the evaluation of Polish expressions may now be evident. If we look at an arbitrary Polish expression and have a mechanism for scanning it from left to right, we see that at any point in the scan, the two most-recently-scanned operands are the ones that will be needed at the time the *first* operator is encountered. Moreover, the result of applying that operator replaces these operands in the expression just before the scan resumes. Further, the operands in the expression are treated in a last-in-first-out manner (i.e., as a *stack*) as the expression is evaluated. An informal algorithm that captures this process can be designed around an "operand stack" as follows:

1.   While there are still characters in the expression, perform step 2.
2.   Scan the expression from left to right.
     As each operand is reached, perform Step 3.
     As each operator is reached, perform Step 4.
3.   *Push* the operand onto the operand stack.
4.   *Pop* the topmost two operands from the stack,
     apply this operator to them, and
     push the result onto the stack.

This simple algorithm will, when the scan is completed, leave the final value of the Polish expression on the stack. Its action is illustrated in Figure 4–18 for the example expression 35 17 40 9 − * + 7 − . Here, we see in the first four steps (*a* through *d*) that the stack increases in size until the first operator (−) is reached. The result of applying that operator (*e*) is a stack with three operands in it, the topmost being the result of subtracting 9 from 40. The remaining stages in the evaluation are summarized in Figure 4–18 (*f* through *i*).

The C++ program named Simplerp.cxx, shown below in Figure 4–19, implements this algorithm. The program evaluates arbitrary Polish expressions typed at the keyboard and displays the stack contents as each operand or operator is entered. The final stack contents displayed by the program is the final value of the expression itself. The program also protects itself against improper input by displaying a message and skipping the invalid operand or operator. This program uses the previously described implementations of the `Stack` and `Morpheme` classes.

```cpp
//SimpleRPNcalc evaluates Polish expressions
#include "stack.h"
#include "morpheme.h"
#include <string.h>

const char prompt[] = "Enter a Polish expression (one element
per line), followed by 'quit'";

enum operator_type {no_op, plus, minus, times, divide, quit};

Stack s;
Morpheme* m;
int i;
float p1, p2;


operator_type is_operator(Morpheme* m)
{
  cout << m->get_val() << endl;
  if (!strcmp(m->get_val(), "+"))
    return plus;
  else if (!strcmp(m->get_val(), "-"))
    return minus;
  else if (!strcmp(m->get_val(), "*"))
    return times;
  else if (!strcmp(m->get_val(), "/"))
    return divide;
  else if (!strcmp(m->get_val(),"quit"))
    return quit;
  else
    return no_op;
}

void show_error (char* message)
{
  cout << "Error: " <<message << endl;
}

void main()
{
  //pre: input = a Polish expression followed by 'quit'

  cout << prompt << endl;

  do
  {
    // Show stack contents after each step.
    cout << "\n\r      Stack Contents\n\r \
          ==============\n\r";
    if (s.is_empty())
      cout << "          (empty)";
    else
      s.display();
```

```
cout << endl;
m = new Morpheme;
m->get(">");
// Push real numbers onto the stack.
if (m->is_float())
{
  m->set_val(m->to_float()); // Accomplishes right justify
  s.push(m);
}
else  // Handle operators on a FIFO basis.
{
  operator_type op = is_operator(m);
  if (op == plus || op == minus || op == times ||
    op == divide)
  {
if (s.get_size() >= 2 )
{
  m = (Morpheme*)(s.top());
  p2 = m->to_float();
  s.pop();
  delete m;
  m = (Morpheme*)(s.top());
  p1 = m->to_float();
  s.pop();
  delete m;
  m = new Morpheme;
  switch (op)
  {
    case plus:
      m->set_val(p1 + p2);
      s.push(m);
      break;
    case minus:
      m->set_val(p1 - p2);
      s.push(m);
      break;
    case times:
      m->set_val(p1 * p2);
      s.push(m);
      break;
    case divide:
      m->set_val(p1 / p2);
      s.push(m);
      break;
  } // end switch
}
else
  show_error("Stack has too few operands");
  } // end if (op == ...)
  if (op == quit)
  { }
  if (op == no_op)
  {
char tempstr[80];
strcpy(tempstr,"invalid operator or operand "),
strcat(tempstr, m->get_val());
show_error(tempstr);
```

```
        }
      } // end if (m->is_float())
    } while ( is_operator(m) != quit);

  //post: output = a series of displays of the stack as each
  //step in the evaluation of the expression is completed
  } //SimpleRPNcalc
```

FIGURE 4–19   C++ Code for the Simple Reverse Polish Notation Calculator.

Using the following input,

```
35 17 40 9 - * + 7 - quit
```

Figure 4–20 shows the program's output for the input which is processed as
shown in Figure 4–18.


```
sage% rpn
Enter a Polish expression (one element per line), followed by
'quit'
 Stack Contents
      =============
          (empty)
>35

 Stack Contents
      =============
              35

>17

 Stack Contents
      =============
              17
              35
>40

 Stack Contents
      =============
              40
              17
              35
>9

 Stack Contents
      =============
               9
              40
              17
              35
 >-

 Stack Contents
      =============
```

```
                    31
                    17
                    35
    >*

Stack Contents
        ==============
                   527
                    35
    >+

Stack Contents
        ==============
                   562
    >7

Stack Contents
        ==============
                     7
                   562
    >-

Stack Contents
        ==============
                   555
    >quit
```

FIGURE 4–20   Output of the `SimpleRPNcalc` program.

This program relies heavily on the availability of methods from the `Stack` and `Morpheme` classes. The beauty of separate compilation and data abstraction in this example is that the development of implementation details for these methods, which is not a trivial task, can be temporarily isolated from the present task of illustrating the behavior of stacks in evaluating Polish expressions. The result is a greatly simplified Polish expression evaluation program; one that mirrors directly the fundamental process that is described in the original four-step algorithm. That is, the implementation details of the methods `is_float`, `push`, `pop`, and so on, are hidden from view as we concentrate on the application at hand.

Readers should note the use of type casting and coercion, in order to accommodate the type restrictions of C++. We shall later see examples where a `Stack` is used to store nonnumeric entries, so that the more generic nature of the `Stack` becomes essential to support those examples.

Note that the program `SimpleRPNcalc` issues a gentle error message when either of two events occurs. In the first event, the element it encounters is neither a floating point number nor one of the operators +, −, *, or /, in which case it is simply skipped and processing continues with the next element. In the second event, the `Stack` has too few operands (0 or 1) to evaluate the current operator. That is, the operator has occurred too early in the Polish expression. For instance, two different error messages will be displayed during the evaluation of the following expression:

```
35 17 40 hello! 9 - * - + 7 quit
```

Readers should exercise this program with various (valid and invalid) Polish expressions that simulate these events. In doing this, you will discover that the program does *not* guard against *all* errors. That is, some sequences of operators and numbers do not form valid Polish expressions and are not detected by the program. For instance, every Polish expression must contain exactly one less operator than it does operands. In the erroneous event that the number of operands *exceeds* the number of operators by more than one, the `Stack` will contain more than one entry upon termination of the program. The task of modifying the program to accommodate this additional error situation is left as an exercise.

The development of a more extensive and robust RPN calculator program is suggested in the laboratory manual. That one actually simulates the behavior of electronic calculators, such as those manufactured by Hewlett-Packard Corporation, that are based on stacks and Polish expressions.

EXERCISES

4–1 Suppose that `Colors` is a `Stack` that contains only colors, and `m` is a pointer to a `Morpheme`. Show what that `Stack` will look like after each of the following messages is processed in turn.

    a.   `Stack Colors;`
    b.   `m = new Morpheme; m.set_val('Red'); Colors.push(m);`
    c.   `m = new Morpheme; m.set_val('Green'); Colors.push(m);`
    d.   `m = new Morpheme; m.set_val('Blue'); Colors.push(m);`
    e.   `Colors.pop;`
    f.   `m = new Morpheme; m.set_val('Violet'); Colors.push(m);`

4–2 Why are the two statements `m = new Morpheme` and `m.set_val` required every time a new value is to be pushed onto the `Stack Colors` in the previous exercise? That is, why can't we just say `Colors.push('Red')`, instead of the three statements `m = new Morpheme; m.set_val('Red');` and `Colors.push(m)`? What if, on the other hand, we just skipped the statement `m = new Morpheme` in each of parts b, c, d, and f of the previous exercise? What would be the effective contents of the stack at the end of this sequence?

4–3 Suppose we have the stack `SubjectStack` with the following contents:

```
SubjectStack = (economics history mathematics computing)
```

    a.   Write a simple C++ loop that will display a list of the elements in such a `Stack` from the top to the bottom. What will its output look like?
    b.   Write another C++ loop that will display a list of the elements in a `Stack`, but in reverse order (from the bottom to the top). What will its

output look like? (*Hint:* consider creating an auxiliary stack to store the intermediate elements.)

4–4 Referring to Figure 4–14, suppose this program were changed to contain an invocation of Q embedded within Q itself (i.e., Q is recursive) at address 0250. Show how the run-time stack now behaves by tracing its contents; use the same addresses for all other procedure calls that appear in Figure 4–14.

4–5 Considering the example in Figure 4–14 once again, discuss the effect on the stack's contents if any of the procedure invocations there were embedded inside a loop.

4–6 Convert each of the following arithmetic expressions to Polish form. In part *e*, assume that the operator ^ denotes exponentiation, and has higher precedence than * and /.
  a. 3 – 7 – 4
  b. 3 – (7 – 4)
  c. a + b / c * 3
  d. a – b + 2 * (a + b)
  e. 0 – b + (b * b – 4 * a * c) ^ 0.5 / (2 * a)

4–7 Evaluate each of the Polish expressions you obtained in Exercise 4–6, showing the stack contents at each step. In parts *c–e*, assume that a, b, and c are C++ variables with values 5, 10, and 3, respectively.

4–8 Extend the definition of Polish expressions to include unary operators, such as sqrt and chs (denoting the square root and negation, respectively). How would the rules for evaluating a Polish expression be changed to accommodate unary operators? Show how the expression in Exercise 4–6e could be rewritten and evaluated using this extended idea of Polish expressions.

4–9 Suppose we wanted to extend the program SimpleRPNcalc. In order to evaluate Polish expressions of the form

    p1 p2 ^

we would need to have access to a function Power. Define pre- and post-conditions for such a function, and then implement it as an extension of the program that appears in Figure 4–19. Implement that module and that function, so that for any arguments x and i, the invocation Power(x,i) computes the result x^i. Be sure to include accommodations for the special cases i=0 and i<0, as well as the usual case i>0. Suggest additional functions that can be utilized to extend this RPN calculator.

4–10 Refine the program SimpleRPNcalc so that it recognizes the additional error situation described in the text (i.e., not enough operators for the number of operands that are presented) and displays an appropriate error message.

QUEUES

Informally, a queue can be visualized as a kind of waiting line, in which a person may enter only at the *rear* of the line and persons may leave only from the *front* of the line. A waiting line of persons at the teller's window at the bank, or a line of airplanes at the takeoff runway at the airport, provide good examples of queues. Because of this behavior, queues are often called *first-in-first-out* (*FIFO*, for short) lists. A more precise definition of queue follows.

> **Definition**   The Queue class is any list of elements $Q = (q_1\ q_2 \ldots q_n)$, with $n \geq 0$, in which q_1 is identified as the *front* and q_n is identified as the *rear*. Insertions can be made only at the rear (after q_n) and deletions can be made only at the front (by removal of q_1). These methods are called Enter and Leave, respectively. The member functions for the Queue class include:

```
enter     remove      front      rear
empty     rotate      display    get_size
```

A Queue inherits the instance variable size from the class Sequence. The value of size indicates the current size of the queue. The constant MAX-ELEMENTS inherited from Sequence defines the limit on the size of a queue.

Queue Method Definitions

Specifications for the Queue class follow in Figures 4–21 and 4–22. Note that the Queue methods identified above overlap significantly with those for Lists and Stacks.

```
// Class description: The class Queue implements a
//     FIFO (first in - first out) sequential data
//     structure. The queue class allows objects to
//     enter at one end (the rear) and leave from the
//     other (the front). In our specifications a Queue is
//     denoted by:  Q = (e[f] e[next] .... e[r])
//     where e[f] is the object at the front of the queue,
//     e[next] is the next object and e[r] is the object at
//     the rear of the queue.  The empty queue is denoted by
//     Q = ().

#ifndef QUEUE_H
#define QUEUE_H
```

```
#include <stddef.h> // for NULL
#include "sequence.h"


class Queue : public Sequence
{
    protected:
    int f, r;

    public:
    //constructor - destructor
    Queue();
    virtual ~Queue();

    // modify
    int enter(ElementPtr);
    ElementPtr remove();
    virtual void empty();
    void rotate();

    // access
    ElementPtr front();
    ElementPtr rear();

    // display
    virtual  void display();
};   //end class Queue


#endif
```

FIGURE 4–21   Declaration for the class Queue.

```
// Formal specifications for the Queue class

//
//constructor / destructor
//

// Queue();
// Used: To initialize the receiver queue.
// Pre:  None
// Post: The receiver queue is intialized and
//       size = 0 and f = 1 and r = 0 and Q = ()

// ~Queue();
// Used: To destroy the receiver queue.
// Pre:  Receiver queue is initialized.
// Post: The receiver queue is destroyed.

//
// access / modify
```

```
//

// int enter(ElementPtr eptr);
// Used: To add a new object to the rear of the receiver queue
// Pre:  Q = (e[f] ... e[r]) and size = n
// Post: (size = MAXELEMENTS and result = 0) or
//       (size < MAXELEMENTS and Q = (e[f] ... e[r] eptr
//       and size = n + 1 and result = 1 and
//       r = (old r) + 1 % MAXELEMENTS)

// ElementPtr remove();
// Used: To remove an object from the front of the queue.
// Pre:  Q = (e[f] e[next] ... e[r]) and size = n
// Post: (size = 0 and result  = 0)
//       (or n > 0 and Q = (e[next] ... e[r]) and size = n-1 and
//       result = 1 ) and receiver = e[f] and
//       f = (old f) + 1 % MAXELENTS)


// void empty();
// Used: to empty the receiver queue
// Pre: Q = (e[f] ... e[r]) and size = n
// Post Q = () and size = 0 and each Element in Q is destroyed

// void rotate();
// Used: To move the object at the front of the queue
//       to the rear
// Pre:  Q = (e[f] e[f+1] ... e[r]) and size = n
// Post: Q = (e[f+1] ... e[r] e[f]) or n = 0

// ElementPtr front();
// Used: To access the object at the front of the queue.
// Pre:  Q = (e[f] ... e[r]) and size = n
// Post: (size = 0 and result = NULL) or
//       (or size > 0 and result = e[f])

// ElementPtr rear();
// Used: To access the object at the rear of the queue.
// Pre:  Q = (e[f] ... e[r]) and size = n
// Post: (size = 0 and result = NULL)
//       (or size > 0 and result = e[r])

// void display();
// Used: To display the conntents of the queue object
// Pre:  Q = (e[f] ... e[r]) and size = n
// Post: output = Q
// Note: user MUST implement display for each type
```

FIGURE 4–22   Formal Specifications for the Class `Queue`.

A `Queue` can be visualized as in Figure 4–23. Example 4.7 illustrates the use of several of the above methods.

Example 4.7   Suppose we declare the object `CashierQueue`, representing the names of persons waiting in line for the cashier at a grocery store, as fol-

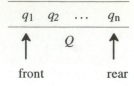

$$q_1 \quad q_2 \quad \cdots \quad q_n$$

$$\uparrow \qquad Q \qquad \uparrow$$

front   rear

FIGURE 4–23   Visualization of queue $Q = (q_1 \; q_2 \; \cdots \; q_n)$.

lows:

```
Queue CashierQueue;
```

We can initialize this object with the names

```
(Mary Stan Edward Natalie)
```

by constructing Morphemes containing the names and using the Queue en-ter method on each morpheme in order.

This will leave the object CashierQueue in the following state:

```
CashierQueue = (Mary Stan Edward Natalie)
```

In this queue, Mary is at the front of the queue and Natalie is at the rear.

If we follow these statements with

```
CashierQueue.display;
```

this particular queue of subjects will be displayed on the screen.
Like Lists and Stacks, Queues are generic and polymorphic. That is, they can contain a mixture of elements of any type—Students, Professors, Morphemes, numbers, etc. Examples 4.8 and 4.9 illustrate Queue methods for the case where the Queue contains Morphemes.

Example 4.8   Suppose we have the queue

```
CashierQueue = (Mary Stan Edward Natalie)
```

and the MorphemePtr person. Suppose further that we wish to record the arrival of another person, say Gregory, at the rear of the queue. This can be accomplished by assigning person the value "Gregory" and executing:

```
CashierQueue.enter(person)
```

As a result of this new entry, the value of CashierQueue will be changed to

```
CashierQueue = (Mary Stan Edward Natalie Gregory)
```

as illustrated in Figure 4–24. Note here that a new instance of the `MorphemePtr person` must be dynamically created, so that its entry into the `CashierQueue` will leave a unique value there.

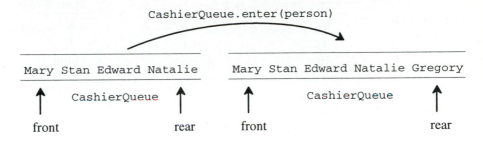

FIGURE 4–24   Execution of `enter` when person is `'Gregory'`.

Example 4.9   If, instead of adding a person to the `Queue`, we want to assign the name of the person who is at the front of `CashierQueue` to the `MorphemePtr NowBeingServed`, we would write

```
NowBeingServed = CashierQueue.front();
```

which leaves the variable `NowBeingServed` pointing to `Mary`, while `CashierQueue` remains unchanged. If, in addition, we want to *remove* this person from the queue when we assign it to this variable, we write two statements:

```
NowBeingServed = CashierQueue.remove();
```

This leaves these two variables in the following state:

```
NowBeingServed = Mary and CashierQueue = (Stan Edward Natalie)
```

This activity is pictured in Figure 4–25.

The instance variable `size` contains the current number of elements in a `Queue`, while the method `empty` empties a `Queue` of all its `Elements`. Example 4.10 illustrates the use of these member functions.

Example 4.10   Suppose we have the `Queue` Numbers = (42 23 80 25 46 39 96 73 74), so that `Numbers.size` = 9. Then, the statement
```
Numbers.empty();
```
leaves the queue in the following state,
```
Numbers = ()
```
with `Numbers.size` = 0.

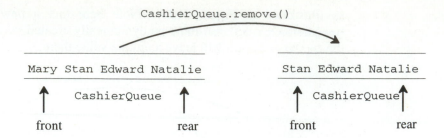

FIGURE 4–25 Execution of `CashierQueue.remove()`.

An Overview of Simulation

Computer simulation is a tool that has been used by scientists and engineers for a wide variety of system design situations—both inside and outside the computing discipline. The value of simulation as a tool is most pronounced whenever a system's behavior or cost is impossible to predict in advance of its actual design and implementation. Instead of waiting until the actual system is built to learn its cost or behavior, a simulation of the system can often be built instead. That simulation is actually an approximate model of the actual system, with many of its component characteristics and parts greatly simplified in order to make the modeling process practical.

One of the oldest simulations, and perhaps the most widely known, is that of an aircraft in flight. Flight simulation has been used for decades to train pilots for unfamiliar aircraft prior to flying the actual aircraft itself. The advantages of simulation over live flight training are several:

- Simulation is less expensive than live training.

- The cost of having a simulated "crash" is less than that of an actual crash.

- Experience gained in the simulated "flights" can often suggest design improvements for the aircraft itself.

The earlier flight simulators had the pilot sitting at the controls in a cockpit, and the controls were connected to a camera mounted on a boom over a scale model landscape and runway. Pilots had to fly dozens of these simulated take-offs and landings before they were cleared to fly an actual plane. Early versions of this simulator in fact became quite costly to maintain, since whenever a novice pilot crash-landed, the camera itself was destroyed and had to be replaced! Needless to say, flight simulators today are much more sophisticated than their ancestors were.

In general, simulation is a computing tool that is used to model a real system in advance of that system's actual design or implementation. The model helps predict the behavior and responsiveness of that system under various sets of assumptions, and thus helps refine the design of the actual system itself. Systems that have been effectively simulated prior to actual design and implementation include the following:

- Telephone networks: simulating the design of various alternative intercity connections to determine the one that minimizes both cost and customer waiting time.

- Production scheduling operations: simulating the design of various alternative production line setups to determine which one provides the best productivity and minimizes the time to process an individual order.

- Banking services: simulating the design of alternative bank floor plans and teller window configurations to minimize customer waiting time and operational cost without compromising bank security.

The list of applications for computer simulation is long and varied.

However, these different simulations have several characteristics in common. First, an effective simulation must be run *many times*—perhaps several hundred or several thousand—in order for its results to be reasonably generalizable. For instance, if we simulate the waiting line for a particular bank floor plan, we must observe changes in customer waiting time over a simulated period of hundreds of hours, and under a range of different assumptions about such factors as the number of tellers serving the line, the average time it takes a teller to serve an individual customer, and the expected arrival rate of customers at the bank.

The second common characteristic is that effective simulations must be *reasonably realistic* in the way they model a system. For instance, the number of tellers in a bank line simulation, the speed of assembly in a production line simulation, or the number of phone lines connecting cities must be specified within the realm of what is physically possible and financially feasible.

The third common characteristic of simulations is that the input "data" for a run are usually generated automatically, using so-called *random numbers* as a basis for modeling events that occur in an unpredictable manner. We used large sets of random numbers in Chapter 3 to facilitate the empirical analysis of different sorting algorithms.

In simulating the dynamics of a bank line, the simulation program should generate a new random number periodically, and then test to see whether or not that number is within the range that indicates that a customer has just entered the bank. If so, that person is added to the waiting line; otherwise, the line remains unchanged. In simulating the dynamics of a production line, a random number generated each time interval governs whether a new order enters the production line during that interval (say, an hour of the working day). In simulating the dynamics of a telephone network, a random number generated each time interval determines whether a new call will be placed during that interval.

The fourth common characteristic of simulations is that they embody many *simplifying assumptions*, assumptions that will not generally occur in the real system that the simulation is modeling. However, the assumptions are made in the interest of practicality, so that the simulation can be achieved with a reasonable amount of effort, and with the hope of not totally undermining the basic validity of the model itself. For instance, in the bank line simulation, it is simpler to assume that customers arrive at the same rate all day, even though, in practice, the lunch hour will produce a heavier flow of traffic at the bank.

The fifth common characteristic of simulations, and the reason why we introduce them in this particular chapter, is that they usually require some sort of waiting line, or *queue*, at the heart of the model. In the case of the bank line, the queue is the line of customers waiting to be served. In the production line simulation, the queue is the line of orders waiting to be manufactured. In the case of the phone network simulation, the queue is the line of phone calls waiting to be served.

Random Number Generation

As noted above, the need to generate random numbers is an important one in many computing applications. We took for granted the method for producing a large file of random numbers as we explored various sorting strategies in Chapter 3. In this section, we are faced with the need to generate random numbers for an entirely different purpose—to supply input data for a simulation. The need for a method that effectively generates large sequences of random numbers is therefore a fundamental requirement of various scientific disciplines, including the discipline of computing itself. Sequences of random numbers are, in fact, central to the activities of simulation, random sampling, numerical analysis, computer program testing and verification, executive decision making, gambling, and many others.

The problem of effectively generating random numbers is not, however, an easy one to solve. What often seems intuitively to be a good algorithm for generating random numbers often turns out to perform rather poorly.

Definition A sequence of integers $X_1X_2 \ldots X_n$ in a particular range, say $\{0, \ldots, m\}$, is said to be *random* if every possible value in that range is *equally likely* to occur *anywhere* within the sequence.

In this sense, as the number n of values in a random sequence grows large, the number of values in each of, say, k equal intervals of size m/k should become nearly equal. Many algorithms have been developed over the last several decades that use computers to aid in the task of random number generation. Some have proven to be very effective while others have turned out to be quite ineffective, when the sequences of numbers they generate are subjected to various tests for randomness.

One of the first scientists to suggest using computer arithmetic to generate random numbers was John von Neumann in 1946.[4,5] The method he suggested is called the *middle square method*. This is an iterative process in which each new random number is derived mathematically from the previous one by squaring it and extracting the middle digits from the result. This method, however, turned out to be not so effective, and was soon replaced by the *linear congruential method*, introduced by D. H. Lehmer[2] in 1948. In this method, a modulus m is chosen, together with a multiplier a, an increment c, and a starting value X_0 (called the *seed*). Each successive random number X_{i+1} is then computed from its predecessor in the sequence X_i by the following formula:

$$X_{i+1} = (aX_i + c) \% m$$

Now the problem is to find values for a, c, m, and X_0 that will result in a *good* sequence of random numbers.

What makes a random number sequence good? Given a sequence of integers $X_1 X_2 \ldots X_n$ in the range $\{0, \ldots, m\}$, various tests for randomness can be applied. Two important tests are

1. that it contain *no cycles*, or repeated occurrences of the same sequence of integers, and
2. that its integers are *evenly distributed* over the entire range of possible values, so that they are not clustered in "bunches."

The particular choices that we make for a, c, m, and X_0 in the linear congruential method can dictate whether or not a good random number sequence will emerge. For example, if we pick

$$X_0 = a = c = 7 \text{ and } m = 10$$

the following sequence of numbers will be generated.

$$7, 6, 9, 0, 7, 6, 9, \ldots$$

This sequence is a particularly poor random number sequence, since it has a cycle length of 4 and it is not evenly distributed over the range $\{0, \ldots, 9\}$.

However, other choices for these parameters in the linear congruential method will yield very good random number sequences. For example, if we choose

$$a = 25173, \quad c = 13849, \text{ and } m = 65536$$

the linear congruential method produces a sequence in which *every* integer in the range $\{0, \ldots, 65535\}$ (which is the entire range of integers that can be

---

4. See Knuth [1], page 3.

5. The general problem of random number generation has been the subject of serious study by mathematicians and computer scientists for some time. Interested readers are referred, for example, to Knuth's *Seminumerical Algorithms*[1], which contains a detailed and contemporary survey of this problem.

stored in a 16-bit word) will occur exactly once before the first duplication occurs. Furthermore, this property holds no matter what value we choose for the initial seed X_0.[5] This is an ideal situation for implementations restricted to 16–bit words. The function random, shown in Figure 4–26, computes this sequence. Here, the variable m is given as a parameter, so that alternative ranges can be specified in addition to the one used here. Popular values for 32–bit words were proposed in 1988 by Park and Miller[3]. They are $a = 16807$, $c = 0$, and $m = 2^{31} - 1$.

```
long random(long &x, long m)
// Returns a random integer between 0 and m-1.
{
  x = 25173 * x + 13849;
  return ((x % m) + m) % m;
}
```

FIGURE 4–26   A random number generator function.

To test a function and evaluate the randomness of the sequence it generates, we developed the driver program main() shown in Figure 4–27 below. It is designed to generate several sequences, choosing different values for n, m, and p for each sequence. The variable c is initialized with the seed value of 0 for each sequence, which is an arbitrary starting value.

```
void main()
{
  Morpheme input;
  int i, n, p;
  long m, c;
  List a;
  IntObj* x;
  char ch;
  char savefile[13];
  cout << "Begin random number generator driver:" << endl;
  do
    {
      do
      {
        input.get("Enter a count n (n=0 means 'quit'): ");
        n = (int)input.to_float();
        if ( n < 0 || n > MAXELEMENTS)
          cout << "Enter a number between 0 and "
                 << MAXELEMENTS << endl;
      } while ( n < 0 || n > MAXELEMENTS);
```

---

5.   Note that if we use the same seed X_0 and coefficients a, c, and m to generate two successive sequences of random numbers, we will reproduce identically the same sequence both times. The ability to reproduce the same sequence over and over again is important in testing programs that use random numbers for input. When generated in this "predictable" way, these numbers are sometimes called *pseudorandom* numbers.

```
          if (n != 0)
        {
          cout << "Enter a range m and number of intervals p: ";
          cin >> m >> p;
          a.empty();
          c = 0;
          for (i = 1; i <= n; i++)
            {
              x = new IntObj;
              x->set_val(random(c,m));
              a.insert(x, i);
            }
          do
            {
              cout << "Do you wish to save the data to a file? \
                      (Y/N)" << endl;
              cin >> ch;
              ch = toupper(ch);
            } while( (ch != 'Y') && (ch != 'N') );
          if (ch == 'Y')
            {
              cout << "Type a file name for saving: ";
              cin >> savefile;
              stream_out(savefile, a);
            }
          cin.ignore(80, '\n');
          formatted_display(a);
          test_random(a, n, m, p);
        }
      } while (n != 0);
    cout << "End random number generator driver." << endl;
  }
```

FIGURE 4–27   C++ Driver Program for Generating, Displaying, and Saving a `List`
of Random Numbers.

This program also allows the user to save a copy of the random numbers on a
separate disk file. This option is useful for creating large random input files for
applications like simulation and sorting. The simulation program that will be
discussed in the next section was exercised using the output from this program.

`main()` uses the function `test_random` shown in Figure 4–28 which
checks the n-integer list generated by the series of n calls to `Random`, finding
possible cycles in that list and counting the number of integers in the list that
fall into each of p equal intervals in the range $\{0, \ldots, m-1\}$.

```
void test_random (List& a, int n, long m, int p)
{
  // This procedure tests the randomness of the n values in
  // the list A, using the range 0..m-1.  It finds the length
  // of a possible cycle in A, as well as the number of
  // values in each of the p intervals of length m/p.
  // Ideally, the number of values in each interval should
  // be the same. The maximum number of intervals is 1000.
  int i, j, k;
```

```
IntObj xx, yy;
long cyclelength = m, cyclebegin = 0;
int counts[1000];
int cycle=0;
   // 0 if there is no cycle  becomes 1 if there is a cycle

// pre: A is a list of n integers in the range 0..m-1
//      and p>0 is the number of intervals.
for (int *iptr = counts; iptr < (counts + p); iptr++)
   *iptr = 0;
for (i = 1; i <= n; i++)
{
  xx.set_val(((IntObj*)(a.retrieve(i)))->get_val());


  if (!cycle)
  {
    for (j = i + 1; j <= n; j++)
    {
    yy.set_val(((IntObj*)(a.retrieve(j)))->get_val());
    if ((xx == yy) && (!cycle) )
    {
      cyclelength = j - i;
      cyclebegin = i;


      // we now have a possible cycle; we found a repetition
      cycle=1;


      for ( int cyci=i; cyci + cyclelength <= n; cyci++)
      {
        if ((((IntObj*)(a.retrieve(cyci)))->get_val()) !=
            ( ((IntObj*)(a.retrieve(cyci + cycle-
length)))->get_val()) )        {
          cycle = 0;
          break;
        }
      }//end for cyci
      if (cycle) break;
    }
    }// end for j

  } //if !cycle


  k = p * xx.get_val() / m;
  counts[k]++;
}// end for i
cout << "Range m and number n of values: ";
cout.width(6);
cout << m;
cout.width(6);
cout << n << endl;
if (cycle)
```

```
{
  if ( (cyclelength + cyclebegin) < n)
  {
    cout << "There is a cycle starting at: "
         << cyclebegin << endl;
    cout << "of length " << cyclelength <<endl;
  }
  else
  {
    cout << "Possible cycle start and length: ";
    cout.width(6);
    cout << cyclebegin;
    cout.width(6);
    cout << cyclelength << endl;
  }
}
cout << "Distribution of values over p equal intervals \
         in this range: " << endl;
for (iptr = counts; iptr < (counts + p); iptr++)
{
  cout.width(6);
  cout << *iptr;
  if ( ((iptr - counts) != 0) &&
     (((iptr - counts)+1) % 10 == 0 ) )
    cout << endl;
}
cout << endl;
//post: output = m, n, the starting index and length of the
//       possible cycle, and the distribution of the n values
//       from A over p equal intervals.
}
```

FIGURE 4–28   A C++ Function to Test Random Numbers.

For example, when n=10 and m=100 the following sequence of integers is generated by the program of Figure 4–27:

```
49 26 19 96 17 30 79 0 29 94
```

It should be noted that because the seed is passed by reference, its value is not decreased by the modulus m. It is possible to have some repetition of the random values generated without having true cycling of the random number generator.   Since the word length of an integer of type long is finite, the replacement statement in Figure 4–26 that computes the next seed,

```
x = 25173 * x + 13849
```

is equivalent to

```
x = (25173 * x) % L;
x = (x + 13849) % L;
```

where L is the wordlength of the type long on the machine being used. Thus, the modulus used in computing the next seed is L while the modulus used to limit the range of the random number returned is m. If m is smaller than L, it is possible for a value returned to repeat a previous one without having the seed repeat a previous seed. For another example, we used n = 100 and m = 32768, and the program gave the following sequence on one of our machines:

```
21451  20520  20067  21712  12411  30200  21011   7072   2859  11720
13251   5232   9179  14232  13171  32576  14987  21352   4387   7184
 3899  16696   3283  10976  25067  16648  26243  27568  29339   4824
24115   7808    331  30376  13283    848  19963  11384  10131  23072
 6315  29768  31043  25328   8539   3608  26867  24000  10251  14824
13987   2704  27835  14264   8787  10592  12139  18312  27651  31280
12315  10584  21427  15616  11979   7464   6499  12752  27515  25336
32019   6304   9771  15048  16067  12656   7899  25752   7795   1542
 5515   8296  23587  30992  19003  11832  14291  10208  31979  19976
29059   2224  28059  16344  18739  23424  23627  17320  32483  24656
```

In this sequence, no cycles occur and the integers are fairly well spread among the 100 intervals in the range {0, …, 32767}. This is shown in Figure 4–29, which gives the output for this particular run of the program of Figure 4–27.

```
Range m and number n of random values: 32768    100
Distribution of values over p intervals:
    0   1   1   0   0   0   1   0   2   0
    1   2   0   1   1   1   1   0   0   3
    0   2   1   2   1   1   2   0   1   1
    1   2   2   1   1   1   2   3   2   0
    3   0   1   3   0   3   0   2   0   2
    2   0   1   0   0   1   0   2   0   0
    2   1   1   0   1   3   1   0   0   0
    1   2   1   2   0   1   1   2   1   0
    1   1   0   1   3   1   0   0   1   1
    1   0   2   0   2   1   0   2   0   2
```

FIGURE 4–29   Summary output of the program of Figure 4–27 with n=100 and m=32768.

If we rerun the program with m=32768 and increase the number n of integers to, say, 1000, their distribution over these 100 intervals will become increasingly more even.

Application: Bank Line Simulation

The Queue class, along with a random number generator such as the one developed in the previous section, provide sufficient tools for developing a wide range of programs that simulate actual systems. The particular simulation we use to illustrate the value of these tools is that of a waiting line of customers at a bank. The purpose of this kind of simulation is to provide a bank manager with the means for predicting the effects of varying the number of tellers serving customers on the overall level of customer service, as the random arrival rate of customers is set at a particular level.

Statisticians have studied the distribution of arrivals in various situations and much can be learned by studying this literature. For the purposes of illustration, we will use a statistically naive simulation. The randomness of customer arrivals is captured by the user entering the probability, or chance, of a person arriving during each minute the bank is open. The number of tellers can vary from one run to the next, and is captured by the variable max_tellers. When a person arrives at the bank and all max_tellers are busy serving other customers, the new arrival enters a waiting line, which is a Queue called simply line. Thus, the bank's level of service during a particular time interval can be characterized by the average and maximum lengths of this waiting line throughout the interval of the simulation, which is typically several hours, or several hundred minutes. For our purposes, we will run the simulation for 500 minutes before reporting the resulting average and maximum line lengths.

When a person enters the Queue, that person is identified uniquely by the time (minute) when he or she arrived at the bank. (For simplicity, we assume that no more than one person can arrive, with the probability chance, at the bank during the same minute.) The basic program loop, therefore, cycles once each minute, and during that cycle, a single person may or may not arrive at the bank. A typical scenario is pictured in Figure 4–30 for a bank with four tellers, a waiting line of 7 customers, the last one arriving at minute 33.

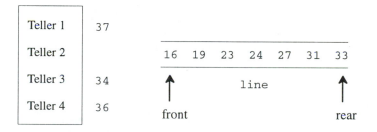

FIGURE 4–30   Bank line simulation after 33 minutes have passed.

At this particular moment, Teller 2 is the only one available to serve the Queue at this minute—all the others are busy. This scenario also shows that a customer entered the bank during each of minutes 16, 19, 23, 24, 27, 31, and 33 but no one entered during any of the intervening minutes. These arrivals are governed by the random number generator and the probability of a customer arriving at any particular minute during the simulation run.

The second element of randomness in this simulation is the amount of time it takes for a teller to serve a customer. This is modeled by the user entering the maximum and minimum number of minutes per customer, and the program then generating a random integer in that range for each customer being served by a teller. If these two limits are given by the variables max_teller_time and `min_teller_time`, then `teller[i]` will begin serving a customer at time `cur_time` and finish serving that customer at time:

```
cur_time + random(randomseed, max_teller_time - min_teller_time)
+ min_teller_time
```

This simulation runs for MAX_TIME minutes (set at 500 minutes for this illustrative run), so that it can gather enough activity to report the following results for a given number of tellers, customer arrival rate, and service rate (interval of times to serve an individual customer):

```
Number of people served
Average Waiting Time
Average Line Length
Maximum Line Length
```

We ran this simulation with a three-teller bank, varying the arrival rate and service rates. The results of one run are shown in Figure 4–31, where the arrival rate was defined by the probability 0.7 and the time for a teller to serve a customer varied between 2 and 7 minutes.

```
Sample Space:            500 minutes
Number of Tellers:         3
People Served:           333 people
Average Waiting Time:    3.8 minutes
Average line Length:     2.5 people
Maximum line Length:       8 people
```

FIGURE 4–31 Example run of the bank line simulation, with `MaxTellers` = 3 and `MaxTime` = 500 minutes.

The program itself is designed to take advantage of the `Queues` and `Element` classes, as well as the random number generator `random` of Figure 4–26. The pre- and postconditions for this program, which we call `BankLine`, are stated below in Figure 4–32.

```
// pre:   input = chance MaxTellers MaxTellerTime MinTellerTime ^
//        0 <= chance <= 1 ^ 0 < MaxTellers <= 100 ^
//        0 < MinTellerTime <= MaxTellerTime ^ MaxTime = 500 }
// post:  output = Sample Space:MaxTime
//        Number of Tellers:  MaxTellers
//        People Served:  peopleserved
//        Average Waiting Time: waittime / peopleserved
//        Average Line Length:
//        Sum i in [1...MaxTime]: QueueLength(line)[i] / MaxTime
//        Maximum Line Length:   Max i in [1...MaxTime]:
//                    QueueLength(line)[i] }
```

FIGURE 4–32 Pre- and Postconditions for the `BankLine` Program.

As the postconditions show, two additional variables are introduced: the total waiting time for all customers (`wait_time`) and the total number of customers served (`people_served`). A complete list of all the constant and variable declarations, along with a skeleton of the program itself, is given in Figure 4–33.

```
const int MAX_TIME = 500; // The number of one minute loops in
the program.

int max_tellers;          // The number of tellers available.
int min_teller_time;      // minimum minutes per teller
int max_teller_time;      // maximum minutes per teller
float chance;             // prob. of entering at each minute
int teller[100];          // Maximum of 100 tellers.
int cur_time;             // The current time [0..MAX_TIME]
Queue line;               // The line of customers.
float ave_length;         // Average waiting time per customer.
int max_length;           // Max length of waiting line.
int i;
IntObj* person;           // The person waiting in line.
long wait_time;           // Total time spent waiting by
                       // everyone.
int people_served;        // The MacDonald's Factor.
long randomseed;          // Seed for random number generation.
Morpheme inputstr;        // Input string.

// FUNCTION PROTOTYPE

long random(long &x, long m);   // prototype;


{Step 1.  Read input parameters chance, MaxTellers,
 MinTellerTime, and MaxTellerTime, initialize the waiting line,
 the tellers, and the variables waittime, peopleserved,
 avelength, and maxlength.}

{Step 2.  Cycle through the simulation MaxTime times, keeping
 track of the line, the status of each teller, and average and
 maximum queue lengths.}

{Step 3.  Compute and display the results of the run.}
```

FIGURE 4–33   Skeleton of the `BankLine` program.

The details of this program are given below in Figure 4–34. The four do–while loops in the first step initialize each of four variables, respectively. The use of do–while loops in this situation, instead of a simple read statement, allows the user to make a mistake entering a parameter and the program to gracefully respond by giving the user an opportunity to reenter it correctly. The value of each element in the `teller` array is the time when the teller can serve another customer. Setting this equal to `cur_time` means that the teller is available to serve another customer. Thus, all entries in the `teller` array are initially set to the initial `cur_time`, indicating that all tellers are available for serving customers. Finally, initializing the variable `randomseed` to 0 guarantees that the *same* set of random numbers will be used for every rerun of the simulation.

```
void main()
{
  // Get probability
  do
    {
      cout << "Enter the probability of someone entering the\
             bank each minute(0.1 - 1.00): ";
      inputstr.get("");
      chance = inputstr.to_float();
    } while (!((chance > 0) && (chance <= 1)));

  // Get the number of bank tellers
  do
    {
     inputstr.get("Enter the number of bank tellers(1 - 100):
");
     max_tellers = (int)inputstr.to_float();
    }while (!((max_tellers > 0) && (max_tellers <= 100)));

  // Get minimum teller minutes per customer
  do
    {
     inputstr.get("Enter min no of mins to serve a customer: ");
     min_teller_time = (int)inputstr.to_float();
     while (!( min_teller_time > 0));

  // Get maximum teller minutes per customer
  do
    {
     inputstr.get("Enter max no of mins to serve a customer: ");
     max_teller_time = (int)inputstr.to_float();
     }while (!(max_teller_time > min_teller_time));

  cout << endl;
  cout << "Computing..." << endl;

  // Initialize the starting time.
  cur_time = 0;

  // Initialize the teller array.  The value of each element in
  // the teller array is the time when the teller can serve the
  // next customer.  Whenever this equals the time counter, the
  // teller can help a customer at that time.
  for (int* iptr = teller; iptr < teller+max_tellers; iptr++)
    *iptr = cur_time;

  // Right now, no time has been spent waiting
  // and no one has been served.
  wait_time = 0;
  people_served = 0;
  ave_length = 0;
```

```cpp
max_length = 0;
randomseed = 0;


while (cur_time < MAX_TIME)
  {
    if (((float)(random(randomseed,32768)) / 32768) <= chance)
    // Did someone just walk in?  If so,
    // put the person in line.
    {
      person = new IntObj(cur_time);
      line.enter(person);
    }

    // Someone is waiting in line, so try to serve that person.
     if (line.get_size() > 0)
    {
      i = 0;                      // Check for an open teller.
      while ((teller[i] > cur_time) && (i < max_tellers))
        i++;
      if (i < max_tellers)  // If so, serve next person in line
        {
          // Keep track of the waiting time.
          wait_time +=  cur_time
                  - ((IntObj*)(line.front()))->get_val();
          delete (IntObj*)(line.remove());
           //Remove the person from the line
          people_served++;  // Keep track of the people served.
          // Occupy the teller for a random number of minutes.
          teller[i] = cur_time +
        random(randomseed, max_teller_time - min_teller_time)
                  + min_teller_time;
        }
    }
      // Compute the average and maximum waiting line length.
      ave_length = (cur_time * ave_length
              + line.get_size()) / (cur_time + 1);
    if (line.get_size() > max_length)
   max_length = line.get_size();
      cur_time++;                 // Keep track of the time.

  }

cout << endl;
cout << "Sample Space:           ";
cout.width(5);
cout << MAX_TIME << " minutes" << endl;
cout << "Number of Tellers:     ";
cout.width(5);
cout << max_tellers << endl;
cout << "People Served:         ";
cout.width(5);
cout << people_served << " people" << endl;
if (people_served > 0)
  {
    cout << "Average Waiting Time: ";
    cout.width(5);
```

```
            cout.precision(2);
            cout <<  (((float)wait_time) / people_served)
                 << " minutes" << endl;
        }
    cout << "Average line Length:   ";
    cout.width(5);
    cout.precision(2);
    cout <<  ave_length << " people" << endl;
    cout << "Maximum line Length:   ";
    cout.width(5);
    cout << max_length <<   " people" << endl;
}
```

FIGURE 4–34   C++ Code for the BankLine Program.

Note that the random number generator is used twice; once to decide whether or not a customer has arrived during this minute and another time to decide how many minutes to occupy teller[i] with the next person arriving at the window from the front of the Queue. The reader should study Figure 4–34 until the details are clear.

SUMMARY

The List, Stack and Queue classes have many applications in computing. We have examined some of them in this chapter. Some of the Stack and Queue methods (e.g., display) are inherited from Sequence and have the same meaning as their counterparts for Lists. Others are unique to the special nature of Stacks (push, pop, and top) and Queues (enter, remove, front, and rear).

Stacks and Queues are designed to be fully generic, so that their individual elements can be any type that is needed by the application. In the Polish expression evaluation algorithm, for example, we saw the use of the type Morpheme (short string) to store individual operators in the stack, while in the bank line simulation, we saw that individual Queue elements were treated as IntObjs. In either case, the application program has the responsibility to coerce an element to the desired type before any methods that are distinct to that type can be applied to it. For instance, one cannot do arithmetic using an integer in a Queue before coercing it from the generic class Element to the numeric type int.

EXERCISES

4–11 Using the driver, exercise the random number generator random twice, once for n=1000 and once for n=10000, in the range {0, ... , 32767}. Exercise it again, generating 1000 integers in the range {0, ... , 100}. For each of these runs, what is the shortest cycle length and how well do the numbers distribute over the given range?

4–12 Suppose that `Planes` is a `Queue` of airplanes waiting to take off at O'Hare Airport, and `aPlane` is a pointer to a `Morpheme` representing a single plane. Each element in the `Queue` is an integer that represents the flight number of a plane. An instance of `enter` thus signifies that a plane has just joined the tail end of the line from a gate at the terminal, while an instance of `remove` signifies that a plane has just taken off. Show what `Planes` will look like after each action in the following sequence:

a. `Queue Planes;`
b. `aPlane = new Morpheme;`
   `aPlane.set_val(1015);`
   `Planes.enter(aPlane);`
c. `aPlane = new Morpheme;`
   `aPlane.set_val(74);`
   `Planes.enter(aPlane);`
d. `aPlane = new Morpheme;`
   `aPlane.set_val(363);`
   `Planes.enter(aPlane);`
e. `Planes.remove;`
f. `Planes.remove;`
g. `aPlane = new Morpheme;`
   `aPlane.set_val(440);`
   `Planes.enter(aPlane);`
h. `Planes.remove;`

4–13 Suppose we have the `Queue CashierQueue` with the following elements:

`CashierQueue = (Stan Edward Natalie)`

Write C++ statements that will simulate each of the following events, and show the resulting value of `CashierQueue` after each event has completed. (Assume these three events take place one after the other.)

a. Two new persons, `Frankie` and `Johnnie`, enter the `Queue`.
b. The person at the front of the `Queue` is served, and then one new person, `Alice`, enters the `Queue`.
c. The three persons at the front of the `Queue` are served.

4–14 Below is an alternative random number generator that is also fashioned on the linear congruential method, but this one uses different values for the constants in the equation $X_{i+1} = (aX_i + c) \% m$.

```
long random (long &x, long m)
// Returns a random integer between 0 and m-1.
//This is a fairly standard
//pseudorandom number generator.
```

```
        }
      {
      // 648477559 and 216159179 are prime.
      //The first mod m puts the value
      // between -(m-1) and m-1.
      //Adding max then taking the result mod m
      //again puts the value between 0 and m-1.
        X := 648477559 * X + 216159179;
        random = ((X % m) + m) % m;
      }
```

Exercise this alternative function using the random number driver program. What is its minimum cycle length and how do its values distribute over the intervals, assuming an initial seed value $X_0=0$ and $m=32768$?

4–15 When m is much smaller than 65536, the method `random` nevertheless takes the remainder modulo m of the value computed for X_{i+1}. However, this particular situation has been shown not to generate particularly good random number sequences.

    a. Test that finding by generating sequences of $n=100$ numbers, first with $m=100$ and then with $m=10$.

    b. What is the shortest cycle length in each of these cases?

    c. Suggest other strategies of extracting two- or three-digit integers from the result returned by `random(c,m)` that might yield better sequences than this method, and then test your strategy for goodness using the driver program of Figure 4–27.

4–16 The results of running the bank line simulation program shown in Figure 4–31 are based on an arrival probability of 0.7, an availability of 3 tellers, and a range of teller service from 2 to 7 minutes. Make educated guesses for the following variations on these parameters:

    a. How would the number of people served and the average `Queue` length be affected if we increased the number of tellers from 3 to 4? If we decreased the number of tellers from 3 to 2?

    b. What would an increase in the arrival probability from 0.7 to 0.8 do to the average waiting time and the maximum `Queue` length?

    c. What would happen to these results if we changed the teller service to a range of 3 to 5 minutes? What if we changed it to 1 to 3 minutes?

Run the simulation using each of these variations to obtain exact results. Do the results of these runs agree with your intuition about (and your experience waiting in) bank lines?

References

[1]   Knuth, Donald E., *The Art of Computer Programming,* Volume 2: *Seminumerical Algorithms*, (2e), Addison-Wesley Publishing Company, Reading, Massachusetts, 1981.

[2]   Lehmer, Derrick Henry, *Proceedings of the 2nd Symposium on Large-Scale Digital Computing Machinery*, Harvard University Press, Cambridge, Massachusetts, 1951, 142-145.

[3]   Park and Miller, "Random Number Generators: Good Ones are Hard to Find," *Communications of the ACM*, 31, 10(Oct 1988) , pp. 1192–1201.

CHAPTER 5

TREES AND GRAPHS

So far in this text, we have been working with collections of data—Lists, Stacks, Queues—that are strictly linear in nature. While these data structures are suitable for a wide range of applications, they are inadequate for many others. Consider this analogy: we compared linear search and binary search earlier and found that binary search is computationally much more efficient. In some cases, then, it is clear that data can be organized in ways that provide much faster access than can be provided by a linear structure. Moreover, many problems are more naturally modeled by a nonlinear structure than a linear one. Forcing such problems into a linear structure alters the problem in significant and unproductive ways. We shall see several examples of such problems in this chapter.

Specifically, we introduce here the tree, the binary tree, and the graph. We will also introduce several common applications of these three structures—the primary application being the design of a compiler. We shall see not only that this is a complex software system, but also that it utilizes a tree structure as an intermediate representation for program text while it is being translated to machine language.

TREES

Consider, for a moment, the Library of Congress system for classifying books. Suppose you want to locate the book *The Art of Computer Programming, Volume 1*, by Donald Knuth. You would access the (electronic or physical) library catalog and learn that the call number for Knuth's book is QA76.5.K57. Then, you would go to the section of the library that contains the QA's (which designates mathematics and computing books), find 76.5 (which designates computing books) and, within that section, find K57, and find the position of the book on the shelf. Thus, a simple three level classification scheme allows you to find one book out of thousands or, if the library were very large, millions. This scheme can be diagrammed in the shape of a hierarchy, or *tree*, as shown in Figure 5–1.

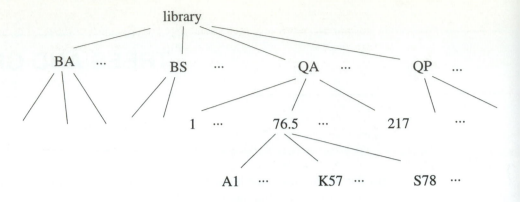

FIGURE 5–1   A portion of the Library of Congress classification tree.

Definition and Examples

Treelike structures such as the one in Figure 5–1 are very common in computing; perhaps only the linear list is more common. Trees arise frequently in computing because of the behavior we saw in the Library of Congress example—they enable us to store large volumes of information in such a way that any particular item can be reached very quickly. Typically, tree structures in computing are drawn "upside down" from their natural, biological orientation, so that the root is at the top and the branches spread out downwards. Occasionally, we represent trees in such a way that the root is at the left and the branches spread out to the right. We formalize the notion of tree as follows:

> **Definition**   A *tree* is either empty, designated by (), or a finite set of vertices, designated by $(r\ T_1\ T_2\ ...\ T_m)$, in which:
> (*i*)   The vertex r is designated as the *root* of the tree, and
> (*ii*)   The remaining vertices are divided into $m \geq 0$ disjoint sets,
> $T_1, T_2, ...,$ and T_m, each of which is itself a tree.
>   These sets are called the *subtrees* of the root r.

One reason that this definition is valuable is that it is recursive; i.e., a tree is made up of trees. The definition is not circular because as we break a tree down into subtrees, we eventually arrive at a tree which has a root but no subtrees. Later in this chapter, we shall see examples of powerful algorithms which can be written very simply by capitalizing on this recursive structure. That is, to carry out some comprehensive action on all the nodes of a tree, we first apply that action to the root and then recursively apply the same action to each of its subtrees.

There are a number of basic concepts that will help us discuss the properties of trees more effectively:

> **Definition**   An *edge* in a tree is a line joining its root to the root of any of its subtrees. If r is the root of a tree and t is the root of one of its subtrees, then r

is the *parent* of *t* and *t* is the *child* of *r*. Two or more children of the same parent are *siblings*. Moreover, the children of any parent are ordered by age from left to right, so that the oldest is on the left and the youngest is on the right. If there is any sequence of edges joining the root *r* to another vertex *v*, *r* is an *ancestor* of *v* and *v* is a *descendant* of *r*. Vertices with no children are *leaves*, and vertices with children are *internal vertices*. If a sequence of edges join vertices u and v, the set of vertices on that sequence of edges designates a *path*. The *length* of a path is its number of edges. The *depth* of any node in a tree is the length of a path from it to the root. The *height* of a tree is the maximum depth of any leaf.

Example 5.1   Consider Figure 5–2. The vertex A is the root, while the line joining A to C is an example of an edge. The root A is the parent of C and B, while C and B are siblings and C is the oldest child of A. The vertices A and C are ancestors of G, while G is a descendant of A. C, B, and A are all examples of internal vertices, whereas E, F, G, and D are leaves. The depth of B is 1, and the height of this tree is 2.

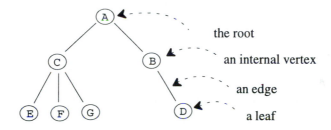

FIGURE 5–2   Parts of an unordered tree.

Besides a graphical representation as shown in Figure 5–2, we can also use a textual notation for describing a tree that is reminiscent of the notation for lists. This follows directly from the recursive nature of the definition of trees. Thus, a tree with root *r* and subtrees T_1, ..., T_m is written (r T_1 T_2 ... T_m), and the empty tree is written (). Thus the tree in Figure 5–2 is written as:

    (A (C (E) (F) (G)) (B (D)))

To simplify the representation, we generally write the leaves of the tree without their enclosing parentheses, and the first item of each sublist is understood to be the root of a subtree. Thus, the above representation can be rewritten as:

    (A (C E F G) (B D))

Example 5.2   Figure 5–3 shows an example of a *parse tree*; that is, the internal representation a typical compiler would use to represent a mathematical expression like the following:

$$\frac{3}{x^2y + 3x}(z - 1)$$

This tree has * as its root and two subtrees, with roots / and –, respectively, as shown in Figure 5–3.

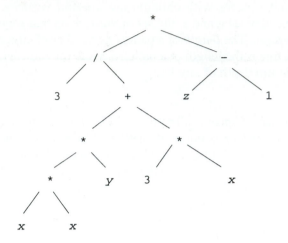

FIGURE 5–3   Example of a tree.

Our textual representation of this tree would be as follows (we have broken it into several lines to clarify the nested structure of its subtrees):

```
(*   (/   3
          (+  (*   (*  x  x )
                   y
              )
              (*  3  x )
          )
     )
     (-   z  1  )
)
```

We will say more about parse trees later in the chapter.

Trees are useful in describing a wide variety of phenomena, both within the computing discipline and outside it. The following examples illustrate some useful computing applications.

Example 5.3   A portion of the directory structure of a computer running under the UNIX operating system is shown in Figure 5–4. Here, the vertex / denotes the root directory, while each of the internal nodes is itself a subdirectory and the leaves are the names of individual files. Most contemporary operating systems organize their directories as trees; for example, both MS–DOS and the Macintosh systems are organized this way. Some systems provide graphics tools for visualizing the directory tree. Note the tree's recursive structure. An internal node has the same structure as the entire tree; it is, itself, the root of a tree containing files and other directories.

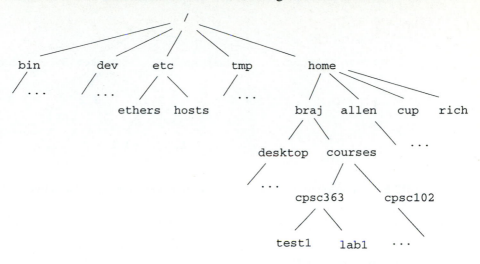

FIGURE 5–4   Portion of a UNIX directory tree structure.

Example 5.4   A `struct` in C++ defines a tree structure. For instance, suppose we define the types `point` and `triangle` as:

```
typedef struct { float x, y, z } point;
typedef struct { point v1, v2, v3 } triangle;
```

We can diagram the relationship between these structures in the form of a tree, as shown in Figure 5–5.

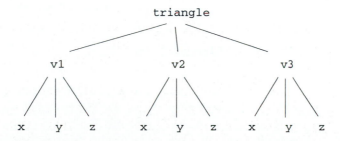

FIGURE 5–5   A structure represented as a tree.

Example 5.5   The table of contents of a book can also be represented as a tree. A portion of such a representation is drawn in Figure 5–6.

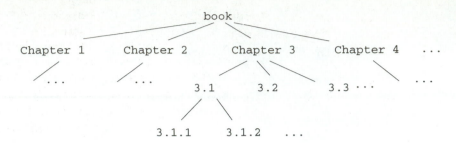

FIGURE 5–6   Portion of the table of contents of a book represented as a tree.

Specifications for the `Tree` Class

We can define the class `Tree` as follows.

Definition   The class `Tree` is the set of all objects of the form $(r\ T_1\ T_2\ ...\ T_m)$ where r is an element and each T_i is also a `Tree`. The `Tree`, itself, is represented as a `struct` of `Tree_nodes` declared as shown in Figure 5–7.

```
struct Tree_node
{
  ElementPtr e;            // value stored in the node.
  int level;              // Level of Generation.  Root = 0.
  Tree_node* parent;      // Pointer to parent (nil if Root)
  Tree_node* right_sib;    // Pointer to Right Sibling
                          // (nil if none)
  Tree_node* left_child;  // Pointer to Left Child
                          // (nil if none)
  Tree_node* right_child;  // Pointer to Right Child
                          // (nil if none)


  Tree_node(ElementPtr eptr)
  {
   e = eptr;
   parent = right_sib = left_child = right_child = NULL;
  }
```

FIGURE 5–7   Declaration for a `Tree_node`.

`Tree_nodes` are pointed to by `tree_links`.

```
typedef  Tree_node*  tree_link;
```

The associated methods for the class `Tree` are as follows:

```
file_out    search      retrieve    insert
remove      store       parse       step
graft       get         is_leaf     display
traverse    empty
```

`Trees` also have associated member variables, which hold the following information:

```
size            Number of nodes in the tree
height          Longest path from a root to the leaf
columns         0 for linear display; >0 for tabular display
width           Width of each column
current         Pointer to the current node
root            Pointer to the root node
error           Records the error state
```

These variables, though not directly accessible to application programs, can be examined by appropriate `get` and `set` functions. For example, the function `get_size` returns the current number of nodes in a `Tree`.

Finally, `Trees` have the associated types `step_type` and `traverse_type`, which facilitate moving among the nodes of a `Tree`. These types have the following values:

```
// GLOBAL DATA
enum step_type {to_root, to_parent, to_left_sib, to_right_sib,
                to_l_child, to_r_child};
enum traverse_type  {breadth_first, depth_first, pre_order,
                in_order, post_order};
```

The complete set of specifications for `Trees` and their member functions can be found in Appendix A of the accompanying *Laboratory Manual*.

To begin working with `Trees`, it is useful to separate the above methods into two groups: essential methods, which are intrinsic to working with `Trees`; and inessential methods, which are useful additions to to the repertoire but not essential. The essential methods are:

```
store       get         step        display
insert      remove      retrieve    is_leaf
```

As with other classes, the function `new` can be used to bring a `Tree` into existence, and, similarly, `delete` takes it out of existence. The method `insert` inserts an element either as the root of an empty `Tree` or as a new right (youngest) child of the current node in the `Tree`, thus increasing the `size` of the `Tree` by 1. The method `remove` removes not only the current node but also the entire subtree of which that node is the root. The specifications are given in Figure 5–8.

```
// virtual void insert(ElementPtr eptr);
// Used: To insert element elem as the new right child of the
//       current node, or as the new root of an empty tree.
// Pre:
// Post: Leaf is allocated.   Receiver is nonempty ^
//       current^.right_child^.e = elem, or receiver is empty ^
//       current = root and current^.e = elem


// virtual void remove(tree_link delete_me);
// Used: To remove all the nodes under (and including)
//       the current tree node.
// Pre:  delete_me != nil
// Post: Deletes all nodes in the subtree whose root is the
//       delete_me. The current node changes to the parent of
//       that node if it was in delete_me.
```

FIGURE 5–8   Specifications for the `Tree` member functions `insert` and `remove`.

The member functions `retrieve` and `store` are analogous to their counterparts for `Lists`—`retrieve` produces the value of the `current` node, while `store` changes it to a new value. The specifications are given in Figure 5–9.

```
// ElementPtr retrieve();
// Used: To fetch the contents of the current tree node.
// Pre:  current != nil
// Post: Result = current^.e


// ElementPtr store(ElementPtr m);
// Used: To change the value of the element in the current node.
// Pre:  current != nil
// Post: The value at the current node is replaced by m
//       and result = old current->e
```

FIGURE 5–9   Specifications for the `Tree` member functions `retrieve` and `store`.

The methods `get` and `display` are "extensions" of the `get` and `display` methods for `Elements` and perform the obvious functions. The member function `get` inputs and inserts, at the current node, a `Tree` typed at the keyboard (or in a separate file); the member function `display` shows the current value of the `Tree` on the screen. The specifications are detailed in Figure 5–10.

```
// void get (char* prompt);
// Used: To input and insert a complete tree at the current
//       node (root for new trees).
// Pre:  Prompt is the string used to prompt the user for input.
// Post: Receiver = the tree read.
```

```
// virtual void display();
// Used: To display a tree.
// Pre:  display() must be called for each Tree_mode.e
//       in receiver
// Post: columns = 0 and a linear representation is shown on
//       the screen, or columns > 0 and a tabular
//       representation is shown.
```

FIGURE 5–10   Specifications for the `Tree` member functions `get` and `display`.

The method `step` is a rather interesting and very useful `Tree` member function. It enables moving the `current` node pointer so that it is the `parent`, the `left_child`, the `right_child`, the `right_sib`, or the `root`, as specified by its parameter of type `step_type`. The `is_leaf` member function returns the value 1 if and only if the `current` node is a leaf (i.e., has no children). The details are in Figure 5–11.

```
// void step (step_type to_where);
// Used: To move the current tree node.
// Pre:  Destination node != nil
// Post: Moves current to the place designated by to_where or,
//       if undefined, leaves current where it is and
//       sets Error to true.
```

```
// int is_leaf();
// Used: To  determine whether the current node is a leaf.
// Pre:  current != nil
// Post: current^.left_child =nil and current^.right_child=nil
//       and result = true, or result = false.
```

FIGURE 5–11   Specifications for the `Tree` member functions `step` and `is_leaf`.

A brief illustration of these methods is given in Example 5.6.

Example 5.6   Reconsider the tree in Figure 5–2, whose parenthesized representation can be typed as (A (C E F G) (B D)). If we declare the object `my_tree` to be of class `Tree`, then the following methods will initialize and establish it with this value, and also display it on the screen.

```
my_tree = new Tree;
my_tree -> get("Enter a tree in parenthesized notation:");
my_tree -> display();
```

At this point, the `current` node is the `root`. Suppose that now we want to insert the `Element` H as a new `right_child` of C, insert I as the new `right_child` of A, and `remove` the `Element` D, leaving the `Tree` as shown in Figure 5–12. This can be done as follows:

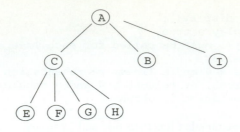

FIGURE 5–12   A new tree derived from Figure 5–2 after two insertions and a deletion.

```
my_morpheme = new Morpheme;
my_morpheme -> set_val("H");
my_tree -> step(to_l_child);
my_tree -> insert(my_morpheme);
my_tree -> step(to_right_sib);
my_tree -> remove();
my_tree -> step(to_parent);
my_morpheme = new Morpheme;
my_morpheme -> set_val("I");
my_tree -> insert(my_morpheme);
```

Note here that the new `Morpheme` `my_morpheme` has been dynamically created in two instances, once prior to each different insertion into the tree.

BINARY TREES

One structure that arises particularly often in computing is the binary tree. Figure 5–13 contains three examples of binary trees. Note in these examples that no parent has more than two children. In this section, we shall look at some important examples and properties of binary trees; subsequent sections will present the specifications for binary trees, two techniques for representing binary trees, and some important applications of binary trees.

Definition and Examples

We begin by formalizing the concept of binary tree.

Definition   A *binary tree* is a tree in which no vertex has more than two children, and the children of a parent are distinguished as the *left child* and the *right child*.

Binary trees can vary quite a bit in shape. In Figure 5–13a, every parent has exactly two children and all of the leaves are on the bottom level. This particular shape is known as a *complete* binary tree. In Figure 5–13c, the binary tree degenerates to a linked list, since every interior vertex has only a right child.

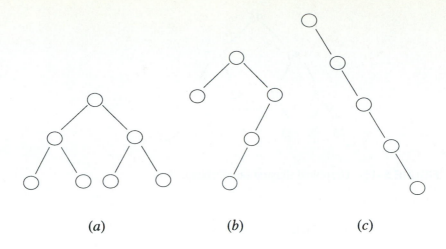

(a)　　　　　　*(b)*　　　　　　*(c)*

FIGURE 5–13   Different shapes for binary trees.

The distinction between the right and left child is always important in binary trees—for instance, the two trees illustrated in Figure 5–14 are not the same tree; the root vertex in the left-hand tree has only a right child, while the root in the right-hand tree has only a left child. If these were general trees, they would have the same shape: a root with one child.

FIGURE 5–14   Two binary trees that are not the same.

Many useful and interesting and useful examples of binary trees can be found in a variety of settings. Here are four:

Example 5.7   In Chapter 3, we introduced the notion of a *heap*. For instance, Figure 5–15 shows a heap. Note that a heap is a binary tree with the special property that every parent contains a value which is greater than the value of each of its children.

Example 5.8   Figure 5–16 illustrates the southeast pairings for the NCAA basketball tournament, 1992. Note that it is a binary tree with its root on the right. Single elimination tournaments such as this are binary trees with the winner being the root, the winner and the runner-up being its children, etc. Note that in this case, several distinct nodes may contain the same data.

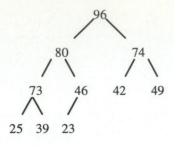

FIGURE 5–15   Graphical illustration of a heap.

FIGURE 5–16   The southeast portion of the 1992 NCAA basketball tournament.

Example 5.9   Recall the parse tree (Figure 5–3) which we examined earlier. Although we presented it there as an example of a general tree, it can be viewed as well as a binary tree since no node has more than two children.

Example 5.10   Morse code is a collection of strings of dots and dashes which denote letters of the alphabet. (See Figure 5–17.) If we let the empty string correspond to the root, we can use a binary tree such as Figure 5–18 to decode any valid sequence of Morse code symbols. As we process a string of dots and dashes, we follow the left branch if the next symbol is a dot and the right branch if it is a dash; we read the node label if the next symbol is a long pause (i.e., a blank).

A	·—	M	——	Y	—·——		
B	—···	N	—·	Z	——··		
C	—·—·	O	———	1	·————		
D	—··	P	·——·	2	··———		
E	·	Q	——·—	3	···——		
F	··—·	R	·—·	4	····—		
G	——·	S	···	5	·····		
H	····	T	—	6	—····		
I	··	U	··—	7	——···		
J	·———	V	···—	8	———··		
K	—·—	W	·——	9	————·		
L	·—··	X	—··—	0	—————		

FIGURE 5–17   Morse code.

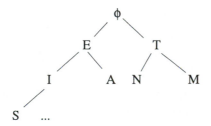

FIGURE 5–18   Part of a binary tree for interpreting Morse code.

The linear notation that we introduced earlier for trees can be extended to binary trees as well; however, it requires the use of a special symbol to denote the case where a parent has a right child but no left child. We use the symbol () to denote the empty left child, as illustrated in the binary tree

        (M (E B K) (X () Z))

which is pictured in Figure 5–19.

At this point, you have seen several interesting and useful examples of binary trees and have seen how to use a text string notation to denote binary trees. However, the real usefulness of binary trees arises from three basic char-

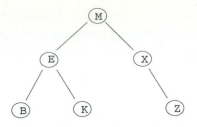

FIGURE 5–19   The binary tree (M (E B K) (X () Z)).

acteristics:

1. Binary trees are fairly simple. Unlike general trees, every parent has 0, 1, or 2 children. Like general trees, binary trees are defined using a simple recursive structure.
2. Large amounts of information can be stored in a binary tree that is not very deep.
3. Any information that can be represented by a general tree can be represented by a binary tree.

We have already discussed the first property; we will now spell out more clearly what we mean by "large amounts of data" and "not very deep." We will do this using two theorems along with the concept of "balance" for binary trees.

Theorem   A binary tree of height h has between $h+1$ and $2^{h+1}-1$ nodes.

To prove this theorem, first note that if a binary tree has height h, it must have at least one node at each of the levels $\{0, ..., h\}$. Thus, it has at least $h+1$ nodes. Also it cannot have more than $1 + 2 + 4 + 8 + ... + 2^h = 2^{h+1} - 1$ nodes, since the number of nodes cannot more than double as we move from one level in the tree to the next. A corollary of this theorem is the following:

Theorem   A binary tree with n nodes has a maximum height of $n-1$ and a minimum height of $\lfloor \log_2 n \rfloor$.

The maximum height is obvious, since $n > h+1$ and thus $h < n-1$. To see that the minimum height is $\lfloor \log_2 n \rfloor$, consider a tree T with n nodes and minimum height. That is, assume that T is complete, so that each level i, except the last, has 2^i nodes. (If not, we could move nodes from the last level to open spaces in the other levels until T is complete; this process cannot empty the last level, since we are assuming that T has minimal height.) Thus, T has between 1 and 2^h nodes at level h and has exactly 1, 2, 4, ... , 2^{h-1} nodes at the other levels. That is,

$$1 + 2 + ... + 2^{h-1} + 1 \quad \leq n \quad < 1 + 2 + ... + 2^{h-1} + 2^h$$
$$(2^h - 1) + 1 \leq n \quad < 2^{h+1} - 1$$
$$2^h \, < n \quad \leq 2^{h+1} - 1 < 2^{h+1}$$
$$h \quad \leq \log_2 n < h+1$$

Since h is an integer, $h = \lfloor \log_2 n \rfloor$.

Figure 5–20 shows a tree that is not complete and also does not have minimal height.

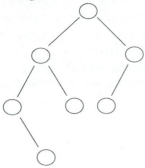

FIGURE 5–20 A binary tree that is not complete and whose height can be reduced by moving a node.

Definition A *balanced binary tree* with n nodes is a binary tree with height $\lfloor \log_2 n \rfloor$.

Thus, if a tree has n nodes and its height is $\lfloor \log_2 n \rfloor$, it is balanced. Note, however, that a balanced binary tree need not be full. The most important characteristic of balanced binary trees is that the longest path from the root to a leaf has length $\lfloor \log_2 n \rfloor$. This property gives certain binary tree searching algorithms a complexity of O(log$_2$n); i.e., they are very efficient. Also, a binary tree of height h can store O(2^h) nodes. This exponential–logarithmic relationship is what we meant earlier by "large amounts of data" and "not very deep."

Specifications for the class `BinaryTree`

Applying the general tree class to binary trees is not quite as simple as merely restricting the number of child nodes a parent can have to two. The problem is that in a binary tree, the left and right children are distinguished, whereas in a general tree they are not. For instance, the two trees in Figure 5–14 are the same if we look at them as trees, but are different if we look at them as binary trees.

Definition The class `BinaryTree` is a subclass of the class `Tree` in which no parent has more than two children and the left and right children are distinguished. In addition to the inherited `Tree` methods, the class `BinaryTree` has the following distinctive methods:

```
insert_left      insert_right
```

Because we have implemented the class `BinaryTree` as a subclass of `Tree`, they inherit all the `Tree` member functions listed in the definition of the class `Tree`. However, some of the `Tree` methods have been redefined to accommodate the special restrictions that a binary tree requires. Those methods are `insert`, `remove`, `parse`, `get`, `step`, `search`, and `graft`. A complete set of specifications for the `BinaryTree` member functions is given in Appendix B of the accompanying *Laboratory Manual*.
The specifications for the new methods are given below in Figure 5–21.

```
// void insert_left(ElementPtr elem);
// Used: To insert element elem as the new left child of the
//       current node, or as the new root of an empty
//       binary tree.
// Pre:  Receiver is empty, or current^.LeftChild is empty
// Post: Leaf is allocated.   Receiver is nonempty
//       ^ current^.LeftChild^.e = elem, or receiver is empty
//       ^ current = root and current^.e = elem

// void insert_right(ElementPtr elem);
// Used: To insert element elem as the new right child of
//       the current node, or as the new root of an empty
//       binary tree.
// Pre:  Receiver is empty, or current^.RightChild is empty
// Post: Leaf is allocated.   current is a leaf and
//       current^.LeftChild = () and current^.RightChild = elem,
//       or current^.RightChild = elem, or receiver is empty
//       ^ current = root and current^.e = elem
```

FIGURE 5–21   Specifications for `insert_left` and `insert_right`.

Implementation Considerations   A full discussion of implementation for various classes—`Lists`, `Stacks`, `Queues`, `Trees`, and `BinaryTrees`—will be given in the next chapter. However, a few key considerations are introduced here to emphasize the need for implementations to account for the subtle differences between `Trees` and `BinaryTrees`.

One way to implement `BinaryTrees` is to use an array to store the individual elements. The convention for storing vertices in an array is that the vertex in position k in the array has its left and right children stored in positions $2k+1$ and $2k+2$, or, if the index of the first element is 1, rather than 0, the convention for C++, $2k$ and $2k+1$, respectively. For example, the binary tree in Figure 5–22a can be represented in the array of Figure 5–22b. Note the use of the symbol ? to denote the missing left child of vertex X. Thus, E is in position k = 1 and its children, B and K, are in positions 3 (= 2 * 1 + 1) and 4 (= 2 * 1 + 2).

The use of an array is a simple and efficient way to implement a `Binary-Tree`. The disadvantage of an array is that it has fixed length. However, if there is a known upper bound for the number of nodes in a particular `Binary-Tree`, and if the tree is relatively balanced, then the array is the best storage method. But, restricting the size of the tree to a fixed maximum number of nodes is often undesirable. Moreover, the array option is not available for general trees, since the number of children for each node cannot be predicted.

An alternative approach for implementing `BinaryTrees` is built on the implementation of general trees. Recall, that we defined a general tree as an object of the form $(r\ T_1\ T_2\ ...\ T_m)$ where r is the root and the T_i's are also trees. Thus, we could view a `BinaryTree` as a general `Tree` in which m is restricted to never exceed 2. But, the `BinaryTree` has the additional property that the left and right child are distinguished. Thus, for instance, if a node in a general tree has no children and a child node is inserted, it automatically becomes the left child. For a binary tree, however, we may want to insert a right child even though there is no left child! Thus, the methods `insert_left` and `insert_right` are added to those for general `Trees`, and the `Tree` method `insert` is restricted so that it handles only certain kinds of insertions.

If we choose to implement the `BinaryTree` as a special case of a general `Tree`, we must adopt some sort of convention for distinguishing between a `left_child` insertion and a `right_child` insertion. This can be done by using a "dummy node" containing the `Morpheme` () to represent a missing `left_child` when a `right_child` is present. This is illustrated in Figure 5–23. Note that this is the same notation that we used earlier to represent an empty tree.

Thus, the methods for general `Trees` and `BinaryTrees` are almost the same; the only two significant differences are in the insertion methods and in the treatment of the instance variable `size`. For general `Trees`, `insert` is simple—whatever the `current` node is, `insert` adds a `right_child` and increases the `size` variable by 1. For the `BinaryTree`, we need two different insertion methods, `insert_left` and `insert_right`. The method `insert_left` checks to see if the `current` node is a leaf or has an empty `left_child`; in either of these cases, it carries out the requested insertion and adds 1 to `size`; otherwise, it sets `error` to true(1). `Insert_right` is slightly more complex; if the current node has no children, it first inserts the dummy

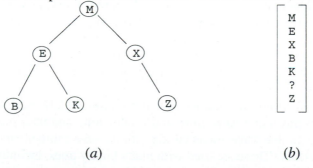

(a)   (b)

FIGURE 5–22   (a) A binary tree and (b) its array representation.

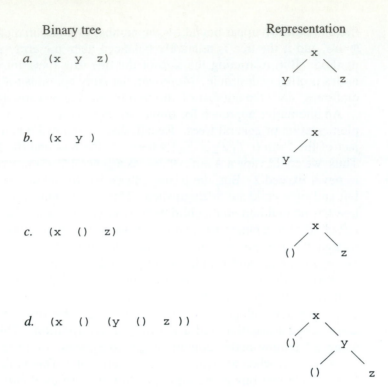

FIGURE 5-23 Examples of binary trees.

node as a `left_child`, then performs the requested insertion and adds 1 (not 2) to the `size` variable. Again, it sets error to true(1) if this insertion cannot be done. The nonspecific method `insert` is modified so that if the `current` node is a leaf, it inserts left; if the current node has only a `left_child`, it inserts right; if a node already has a `right_child`, it sets error to true(1); if the `Tree` is empty it inserts at the root.

There are a few other minor differences in the implementation of the member functions for `BinaryTrees` which will be evident if you look into the implementation of the two classes. However, we have discussed the significant ones.

Applications of Binary Trees

In this section, we discuss two of the most widely used applications of binary trees: traversing parse trees and establishing and utilizing binary search trees. We examine three traversal algorithms—the inorder, preorder, and postorder traversals. These are used with many binary trees, including parse trees. However, parse trees are very important and will serve as a nice vehicle for us to introduce the traversal algorithms.

Suppose we have a parse tree, such as the one in Figure 5-24, and that we want to "visit" every node in it. Visit could mean display the data contained in each node, look at each node in a search for a particular item, modify each node in an appropriate way, and so forth. The recursive structure of a binary tree lends itself very nicely to this type of problem. For instance, we could visit the root, recursively visit the left subtree, and then recursively visit the right subtree. If we let N denote the root node, L the left subtree, and R denote the right subtree, this sequence of visitation could be denoted NLR.

In fact, there are six possible sequences in which we can systematically visit each node, which can be, similarly, represented as:

         NLR   LNR   LRN
         NRL   RNL   RLN

The usual convention is to visit in a left-to-right fashion, which leaves us with the first three alternatives: NLR, LNR, and LRN (which are also called the "preorder," "inorder," and "postorder" traversal strategies). Using the binary tree in Figure 5–24, we get the following three expressions when visiting its nodes in these three ways:

NLR: + a * b c
LNR: a + b * c
LRN: a b c * +

These expressions are known as the prefix, infix, and postfix notations, respectively. Note that postfix is the Polish notation used for the RPN calculator that we studied in the previous chapter.

Consider now the implementation these three visitation algorithms. For the remainder of this section, we assume that the underlying `Element` type for our `BinaryTree` is `Morpheme`. Also, we interpret "visit" as simply meaning "display the data contained in a node."

The three functions `pre_order`, `in_order`, and `post_order` given in Figure 5–25 are designed to simply display the nodes in a binary tree in the sequences NLR, LNR, and LRN, respectively.

```
void  pre_order (tree_link root);
// pre: root is a pointer to the root node of a binary tree
// post: output = the pre-order (NLR) display of the binary tree
{
    if (root != NULL)
```

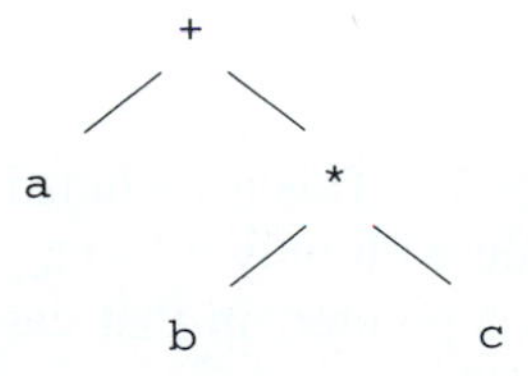

FIGURE 5–24   A simple parse tree for the expression a + b * c.

```
            {
                root->e->display;
                if left_child != NULL
                    pre_order(left_child);
                if (right_child != NULL && right_child != left_child)
                    pre_order(right_child);
            }
        }


        void  in_order (tree_link root);
        // pre: root is a pointer to the root node of a binary tree
        // post: output = the in-order (LNR) display of the binary tree

        {
            if (root != NULL)
            {
                if (left_child != NULL)
                    in_order(left_child);
                root->e->display;
                if (right_child != NULL && right_child != left_child) then
                    in_order(right_child);
            }
        }


        void  post_order (tree_link root);
        // pre: root is a pointer to the root node of a binary tree
        // post: output = the post-order (LRN) display of the binary
        tree
        {
            if (root != NULL)
            {
                if (left_child != NULL)
                    post_order(left_child);
                if (right_child != NULL && right_child != left_child)
                    post_order(right_child);
                root->e->display;
            }
        }
```

FIGURE 5–25   C++ code for the preorder, inorder, and postorder traversals of a `BinaryTree`.

Note the use of the expression:

```
right_child != left_child
```

in each of the functions of Figure 5–25. This is included because, in our implementation of `BinaryTrees`, a node with only a `left_child` will not have a NULL value for its `right_child` pointer; in that case, `right_child` will equal `left_child`.

Example 5.11   Consider Figure 5–24 again. Traversing this parse tree using each of the three functions of Figure 5–25 in turn gives the following results:

Inorder: a + b * c
Preorder: + a * b c
Postorder: a b c * +

Note that the inorder traversal gives an expression which is ambiguous in the mathematical sense; i.e., the binary tree in Figure 5–26 has the same inorder traversal as the binary tree in Figure 5–24. However, the other two travers-

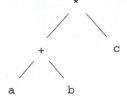

FIGURE 5–26   Another parse tree.

als of Figure 5–24 do not give the same result:

Preorder: * + a b c
Postorder: a b + c *

To avoid the ambiguity of infix notation and to provide for fast processing, a compiler normally stores an algebraic expression as a parse tree and then traverses it using a preorder or postorder traversal.

Binary Search Trees   Another major application area for binary trees is based on a binary search tree. Binary search trees (*BST*s for short) provide a valuable structure for storing data for rapid retrieval. If a BST contains n items, and if it is nearly balanced, any item can be found in roughly $\log_2 n$ lookups. The formal definition established the ground rules.

Definition   A *binary search tree* is a binary tree with the added property that for every vertex x having left and/or right children x_l and x_r, the relationships $x_l \leq x$ and $x \leq x_r$ hold.

While the definition of binary search trees does not guarantee a balanced tree, if a large amount of data is entered into a BST in a reasonably random order, the average height of the resulting BST will not vary greatly from $\log_2 n$.

Example 5.12   Figure 5–27 is a binary search tree in which the letters of the word MICROWAVE appear in alphabetical order.

A new class, `BinarySearchTree`, can be defined as a subclass of `BinaryTree`. `BinarySearchTree`, then, inherits its basic structure and methods from `BinaryTree` and `Tree`. Now, we can define two new member functions for the `BinarySearchTree` class. The first is a binary search algo-

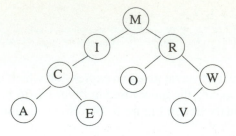

FIGURE 5–27 A binary search tree.

rithm with $O(\log_2 n)$ complexity if the `BinarySearchTree` is balanced. It assumes that a `BinaryTree`, T, has the properties of a BST and searches for an item, x. The details are in Figure 5–28.

```
int binary_search (Element* x);
// Used: To search the BST, T, for an item, x
// Pre:   current is the root of T
// Post: If x is found, current is set to that node and
//          result = true(1).  Otherwise,
//          current is set to the node
//          below which x would be inserted and result = false(0).

{
    int found = ((MorphemePtr)x->get_val() ==
                    (MorphemePtr)current.e->get_val());

    while (!found && !is_leaf)
    {
      if ((MorphemePtr)x->get_val() <
          (MorphemePtr)current.e->get_val())
            step(to_l_child);
      else if ((MorphemePtr)x->get_val() >
                  (MorphemePtr)current.e->get_val())
                step(to_r_child);
      found = ((MorphemePtr)x->get_val() ==
                  (MorphemePtr)current.e->get_val());
    }
    if ((MorphemePtr)current.e->get_val()) == "()")
      step(to_parent);
    return found;
}
```

FIGURE 5–28 C++ code for the `binary_search` function.

The second algorithm builds a binary search tree from a randomly ordered `List`. It assumes that the `List` has no duplicates. The code appears in Figure 5–29.

```
void  build (List L);
// Used: to build a BST from a List having no duplicates
```

```
// Pre:   L is a non-empty List with elements of type Morpheme.
// Post: this is a binary search tree containing the elements
//       of L. The root of this is L[1].  If L contains duplicates
//       or is empty, Error is set to TRUE(1).
{
    int leng = L.get_size;
    int n;
    Element* eptr;

    error = (leng == 0);
    if !error
    {
      empty();
      insert(L.Retrieve(1));
      n = 2;
    }
    while (n < leng && !error)
    {
      eptr = L.Retrieve(n);
      error = binary_search(eptr);
      if (!error)
        if ((MorphemePtr)eptr->get_val() <
            (MorphemePtr)current.e->get_val())
          insert_left(eptr);
        else
          insert_right(eptr);
      n = n + 1;
      step(to_root);
    }
}
```

FIGURE 5–29   C++ function to build a `BinarySearchTree` from a randomly ordered `List`.

Thus we have algorithms both for building a binary tree and for searching one. This process illustrates how objects can be used to build complex programs fairly simply. That is, we first developed specialized binary tree methods out of the tree methods. We then wrote `binary_search` using just the fundamental operators `get_val`, `is_leaf`, and `step`. Next we wrote `build` using `search`. As each procedure emerges, it becomes available for reuse as a "black box" at the next level of design.

EXERCISES

5–1 Draw the trees corresponding to the following linear representations:

a.   (A (B C D) E)

b.   (A B (C (D E) (F G)) H (I J K))

5–2 Show the linear written representation for the tree in Figure 5–30. Identify each of the following characteristics for this tree.

a.   Its root

 b.   Its height
 c.   Its size
 d.   The subtree with root B
 e.   The number of children for B
 f.   G's parent
 g.   The descendents of B
 h.   The level of node D

5–3   Sketch binary trees having the following characteristics or show why this cannot be done:
 a.   height of four, four vertices
 b.   height of three, fifteen vertices
 c.   height of four, ten vertices, balanced

5–4   Show that in a single elimination tournament the number of matches is one less than the number of players.

5–5   Implement the binary tree operator `get_size` using the operators of the `Tree` class.

5–6   Give pre- and postorder traversals of the tree in Figure 5–27.

5–7   Draw the tree, including dummy nodes, that would be built when the list L = (C O M P U T E R) is used to build a binary search tree by the method `build`.

5–8   Implement the following additional `BinaryTree` operators. With each one give appropriate pre- and postconditions. You may use any of the `Tree` or `BinaryTree` operators that are defined in this section or the Appendix to Chapter 5 of the accompanying *Laboratory Manual*.
 a.   `inorder_traverse` carries out an inorder traversal of a `Binary-Tree`—i.e., a traversal in the order LNR.

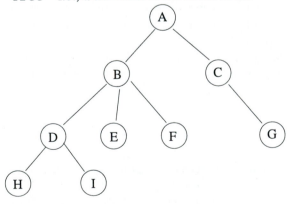

FIGURE 5–30   A tree with nine vertices.

b. `is_ordered` identifies whether the items stored in the `BinaryTree` are arranged in ascending order when the tree is visited via an inorder traversal.

COMPILING AND PARSE TREES

In this section, we illustrate how classes can be used to build very complex programs by developing part of a compiler. A *compiler* is a complex piece of software designed to accomplish the translation of programs from a "high-level language" (like C++) called the "source" language into a "machine-level language" such as the machine language introduced in Volume I of this series. A functional diagram of a compiler is shown in Figure 5–31. The compiler program, itself, is often coded (either partially or fully) in a langage such as C++.

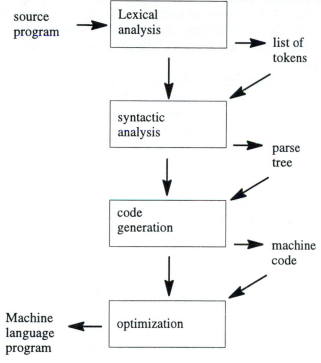

FIGURE 5–31   Overview of a compiler.

As we can see, a compiler processes the text of a source (written perhaps in C++) program in four major stages, called *lexical analysis, syntactic analysis, code generation*, and *optimization*. Many compilers have more stages, but these four are the principal ones.

The task of the lexical analysis stage is to transform the text of the source program from its form as input to the compiler, which is essentially a character string, into a list of lexical "tokens" (identifiers, constants, operators, reserved

words, delimiters, and so forth). This transformation also results in the generation of a "symbol table," which is a list of all identifiers defined in the program
along with their associated types. For example, Figure 5–32 shows a simple
C++ program and the result of lexical analysis of that program.

Syntactic analysis, sometimes called *parsing*, takes this list and transforms it
into a structural description of the program, called a "parse tree." This tree is
generated under the guidance of a formal syntactic description of C++, such as
that given in Appendix I of the *Laboratory Manual*. An abbreviated example
of the parse tree for the program in Figure 5–32 is shown in Figure 5–33.

The code generation phase of a compiler traverses the parse tree and generates a list of machine language instructions from that traversal. The traversal
method is essentially "depth–first," which allows the machine instructions to
be generated in the correct sequence. In the case of arithmetic expressions
within a program's parse tree, they generally take the form of binary trees, and
a postorder (LRN) traversal is appropriate for generating the machine instructions in the correct sequence. An illustration of code generation for the subtree
in the lower right-hand portion of the parse tree of Figure 5–33 is shown in Figure 5–34.

The optimization phase of a compiler is an optional phase, and its purpose is
to improve the run-time efficiency of the code generated by the previous phase.
For instance, most code generators have procedures for finding redundant subexpressions within an arithmetic expression, such as the following:

```
x = (a + b) * c + (a + b) * d ;
```

Once found, the generated code for this expression is replaced by code that
mirrors a more efficient equivalent program, such as the following:

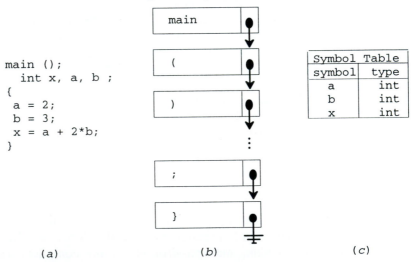

```
main ();
   int x, a, b ;
{
  a = 2;
  b = 3;
  x = a + 2*b;
}
```

| Symbol | Table |
symbol	type
a	int
b	int
x	int

(a)   (b)   (c)

FIGURE 5–32   A C++ program and the result of its lexical analysis.

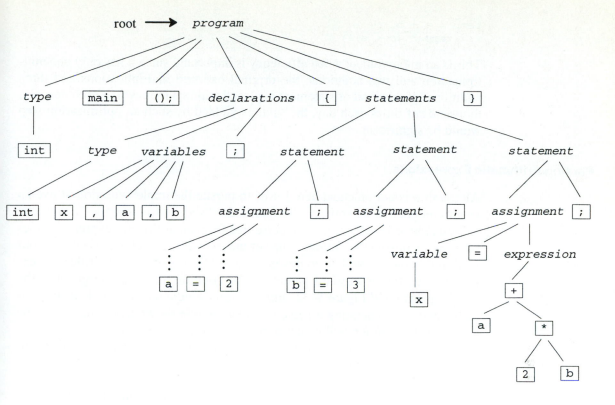

FIGURE 5–33 Partial parse tree resulting from syntactic analysis.

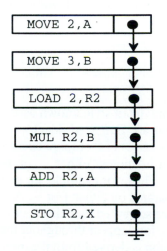

FIGURE 5–34 Sample code generated for the program of Figure 5–32(*a*).

```
temp = a + b ;
x = temp * (c + d) ;
```

This is an improvement when efficiency is important, since it has only one multiplication and two additions; the original had two multiplications and three additions. If this kind of statement is placed within a loop which executes, say, thousands of times each day, the savings yielded by such an optimization step would be significant.

Parsing Arithmetic Expressions

Although it is not practical here for us to pursue the implementation of even a small compiler in its entirety, that particular "slice" of a compiler's syntactic analysis phase which produces a parse tree from an arithmetic expression does serve as a valuable illustration of use of the `BinaryTree` class. Therefore, our goal in this section will be to develop a program that takes any arithmetic expression written in standard parenthesized notation, like the one given in the sample program of Figure 5–32, and perform the equivalent of lexical and syntactic analysis, generating a parse tree like the one shown in Figure 5–3. The output of the program will be a binary tree for the expression.

This exercise is also valuable because it combines the implementations of several different classes—`BinaryTrees`, `Strings`, `Lists`, and `Stacks`—in the development of a robust solution to a rather difficult problem.

For the purposes of this problem, we assume that an arithmetic expression is a series of `Morphemes`, each representing either a variable name (known as an *identifier*), a number, an operator (+, –, *, /, or ^), or a left or right parenthesis, which are separated from each other by one or more blanks. These `Morphemes` must occur in such a way that they satisfy the following syntax rules:

```
expression = term { + term | - term }
term = factor { * factor | / factor }
factor = identifier | number | ( expression ) |
         identifier ^ factor | number ^ factor |
         ( expression ) ^ factor
```

These rules are written in an abbreviated style known as Backus-Naur form or simply, BNF. Briefly, terms that are *italicized* denote syntactic entities, the curly braces, { and }, denote "any series of 0 or more occurrences" of whatever they enclose, and the vertical bar | denotes "either ... or, but not both" of the alternatives on its left and right. Thus, for example, an *expression* can be any sequence of terms which are separated by either + or –. A *term*, in turn, can be any sequence of factors which are separated by either * or /.

Examples of arithmetic expressions appear throughout the text. The strategy for parsing an arithmetic expression is derived from the more general technique called "precedence parsing," which was developed in the 1960's when compiler design was in its infancy. This particular method is still widely used in compiler design, and has particularly strong intuitive appeal (as we shall see).

The idea behind precedence parsing is that, when one scans an arbitrary arithmetic expression from left to right, certain relationships should be preserved in the resulting parse tree for that expression. First, the operands (identifiers and numbers) which appear in the expression form the leaves of the resulting parse tree, and their left-to-right order is preserved. This is shown, for instance, in the parse tree of Figure 5–3. Second, the operators in the expression always appear as the nonleaf nodes, and their position in the tree reflect the order in which they will be applied to their operands (using a postorder traversal for execution), rather than their textual order of appearance in the original expression. For instance, the expression

```
a + 2 * (b – c)
```

contains the operators +, *, and – in that order, yet the corresponding parse tree contains these operators in a different (postorder traversal) order, in which – appears first, followed by *, and finally followed by +.

For this reason, a left-to-right scan of the original expression can be designed in such a way that the operands are immediately added to an array of single-leaf trees as they are encountered. But when we encounter each operator during such a scan, we cannot determine its structural position in the resulting parse tree until after we have examined the next operator on its right and compared the precedences of the two. Compare, for example, the following two expressions:

```
a + 2 + b                 a + 2 * b
```

In the expression on the left, the operands a and 2 are joined directly in the tree by the operator + as their parent, because the precedence of the next operator in the expression (also +) is not greater than that of the first +. In the expression on the right, the operands a and 2 cannot be so joined, since the second operator (*) has higher precedence than +. Instead, 2 and b are joined by * as their parent, and this subtree finally becomes the right child of the parent + in the final tree for the expression a+2*b. These two situations are distinguished in Figure 5–35.

An additional consideration must be made in a left-to-right scan when we encounter a parenthesized (sub)expression as an operand. That is, the parse of the expression enclosed within the parentheses must take precedence over the just scanned operator, in the sense that all operations embedded between the left and right parentheses must be attached to the parse tree in such a way that they are executed *before* that operator.

These two considerations suggest that we need to have two supporting data structures in the formation of a parse tree for an arithmetic expression; a stack for holding operators and left parentheses, and an array for holding single-leaf trees for each of the operands as well as partially constructed subtrees as they are developed during the parse. In the following program, this stack is called `operators` and this list of trees is called `parse_trees`.

The algorithm proceeds as follows: the expression is scanned from left to right, one token (operand, operator, left parenthesis, or right parenthesis) at a time. If the token is an operand, it is immediately converted into a single–leaf tree and added to the `parse_trees` list. This is shown for the first token a in the expression a+2*b in Figure 5–36(a).

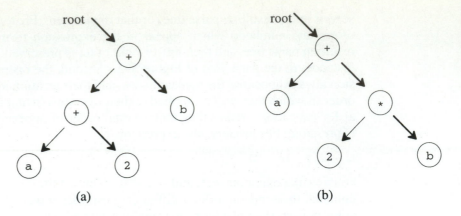

FIGURE 5–35   Parse trees for (*a*) the expression a+2+b and (*b*) the expression a+2*b.

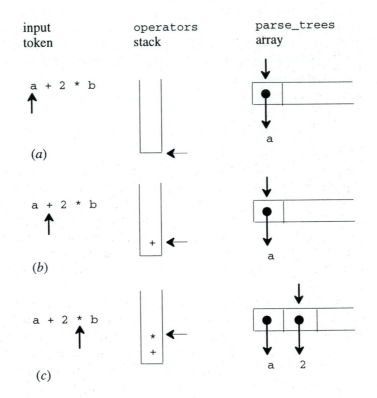

FIGURE 5–36   Initial steps in the parse of `a+2*b`; (a) scanning the first operand a, (b) scanning the first operator, +, and (c) scanning the second operator, *.

If, on the other hand, the token is an operator its priority is compared with that of the top operator on the stack (if there are any). If the topmost operator (called `toptoken` in the program below) has lower priority than the current token (or if the stack is empty or the current token is a left parenthesis), the current token is pushed onto the stack. This is the case when the token + is encountered in the expression a+2*b (Figure 5–36(*b*)), and again when the * is encountered (Figure 5–36(*c*)).

If the topmost operator in the stack has equal or higher priority, then it is popped off the stack and combined with the two most recently added trees in the array to form a new tree in this array in their place. This combining activity is accomplished by the auxiliary function combine_trees. Thus, the array parse_trees is treated as a stack of partially constructed trees, representing the different subexpressions that have been recognized and parsed at some intermediate point in the left-to-right scan. This would occur, for example, in the expression a*2+b when the token + is encountered, causing the * to be popped from the stack and combined with the two trees (a) and (2), forming the new tree (* a 2).

Finally, encountering a right parenthesis in an expression (or the end of the expression itself) causes the stack to be emptied, one operator at a time, with each operator combined with the rightmost two parse trees in the output list to form a new parse tree. This emptying process is stopped by the next occurrence of either a left parenthesis (denoting completion of the parse for some parenthesized subexpression within the larger expression) or the bottom of the stack. The main program for parsing arithmetic expressions appears below in Figure 5–37.

```
#include "elements.h"
#include "tree.h"
#include "inputstr.h"
#include "morpheme.h"
#include "sequence.h"
#include "stack.h"
#include <string.h>


const MAX_TREES = 20;

typedef TreePtr tree_list[MAX_TREES];

// global variables
Input_string inputexpression;   // a line of input to be parsed
MorphemePtr token,              // current token
        toptoken,               // token on top of
                                // operators stack
        bottommarker;           // special token "$$", to mark
                                // the bottom of the
                                // operators stack
Stack operators;                // Stack of Morphemes
tree_list parse_trees;          // list of Trees
int nparse_trees;               // and its length
int i, j, level, nmorphs;
TreePtr t;                      // Ptr to Trees of
                                // subexspressions

int syntax_error;
```

```
        void write_error ...

        int priority ...

        int is_operator ...


        void combine_trees ...

        void main()
        {
        char ch;

        //pre: input = an arithmetic expression


        // Step 1. Initialize variables and structures
        toptoken = new Morpheme;
        bottommarker = new Morpheme;
        bottommarker->set_val("$$");
        operators.push(bottommarker);
        nparse_trees = -1;
        level = 0;
        char tempstr[256];

        // Step 2. Obtain an arithmetic expression
        cout << "Enter an arithmetic expression: ";
        cin.getline(tempstr,255);
        inputexpression.set_val(tempstr);
        inputexpression.reformat(level);
        nmorphs = inputexpression.morpheme_count();
        syntax_error = FALSE;

        // Step 3. Process the expression one token
        //         at a time, and build the list of trees
        i = 1;


        while ( (i <= nmorphs) && !syntax_error)
        {
          token = inputexpression.retrieve(i);
          //cout << "token #" << i << " " << token->get_val() << endl;


          if (token->is_float() || token->is_word() )
          { // if it's a number or identifier
            t = new Tree;  // insert it at the root of a new tree
            t->insert(token);
            parse_trees[++nparse_trees] = t;
          }
          else if (is_operator(token) )// if it's an operator,
                                      // decide whether
          {          // to push it or build a subtree with it
            toptoken = (MorphemePtr)(operators.top());
            while ( strcmp(toptoken->get_val(), "$$") &&
                 strcmp(toptoken->get_val(), "(")  &&
```

```
                        (priority(toptoken) >= priority(token)) &&
                        !syntax_error
                    )
                {
                  combine_trees(toptoken, parse_trees, nparse_trees);
                  operators.pop();// don't delete because its in a tree
                  toptoken = (MorphemePtr)(operators.top());
                } // end while
                operators.push(token);
            } // end if(is_operator)
            else if ( token->get_val()[0] == '(' )
            {
                operators.push(token);
            }
            else if ( token->get_val()[0] == ')' )
            {
                while(((MorphemePtr)(operators.top()))->get_val()[0] != '('
      )
                {
                  combine_trees((MorphemePtr)(operators.pop()), parse_trees,
                              nparse_trees);
                }

                delete operators.pop();
            }
            else
                write_error(syntax_error);


            i++;
        } // while


        // Step 4. Clear the stack and combine remaining trees using its
        //         operators

            while(strcmp(((MorphemePtr)(operators.top()))->get_val(),
                    "$$") && !syntax_error)
            {
                combine_trees((MorphemePtr)(operators.pop()), parse_trees,
                            nparse_trees);
            } // end while

        // Step 5. Display the resulting parse tree(s)
            cout << "Result of the parse: \n\r";
            for (i = 0; i <= nparse_trees; i++)
            {
                parse_trees[i]->set_columns(parse_trees[i]->get_height()+1);
                parse_trees[i]->display();
            }
        //post:  output = a display of the parse tree for the
        //         input expression
        } // ExpressionParser
```

FIGURE 5–37 The ExpressionParser main program.

This program uses four auxiliary functions, called `write_error` (to display an error message), `priority` (to compute the priorities of the operators +, -, *, /, and ^ as 0, 0, 1, 1, and 2 respectively), `is_operator` (to determine whether or not the currently scanned token is an operator or not), and `combine_trees` (to combine an operator with two trees as its left and right children, forming a new tree in their place). These are shown in Figures 5–38 and 5–39, respectively.

```
void write_error(int &syntax_error)
{
    syntax_error = TRUE;
    cout << "Syntax Error:  processing stops.\n\r\n\r";
}   //write_error

int priority (Morpheme* op)
{
    switch (op->get_val()[0])
    {
       case '+':
       case '-':
       return 0;
       case '*':
       case '/':
       return 1;
       case '^':
       return 2;
       case '$':
       case '(':
       return -1;
       default :
       cout << "error in priority" << endl;
       write_error(syntax_error);
       return 9;
    }
} // Priority
```

FIGURE 5–38   Auxiliary functions `write_error` and `priority`.

```
int is_operator(Morpheme* s)
{
    char opval = s->get_val()[0];

    if ((opval == '+') ||
      (opval == '-') ||
      (opval == '*') ||
      (opval == '/') ||
      (opval == '^') )
        return TRUE;
    else
        return FALSE;
} // is_operator
```

```
void combine_trees (MorphemePtr newroot, tree_list parse_trees,
int &nparse_trees)
// Form a new tree t with the given root, and with
// parse_trees[nparse_trees-1] and parse_trees[nparse_trees]
// as its left and right subtrees, respectively  Replace
// parse_trees[nparse_trees-1] by t and decrement nparse_trees.
{
    TreePtr t;
    t = new Tree;
    t->insert(newroot);                         //create a new tree
    t->graft(parse_trees[nparse_trees - 1]);    //graft left subtree
    t->graft(parse_trees[nparse_trees]);        //and right subtree
    parse_trees[nparse_trees - 1] = t;          //insert new tree
                                                // into the list of
                                                // trees and
    nparse_trees--;                             //decrement count
} // combine_trees
```

FIGURE 5–39   Auxiliary functions `is_operator` and `combine_trees`.

To illustrate the activity of this program, a trace of the operators stack and the output list of parse trees is shown in Figure 5–40, for certain key steps in parsing the expression

$$\frac{((a + b)^2 - c^2)}{(2 * a)}.$$

A careful reading of this program reveals that the class implementations from previous chapters—`Elements`, `Stacks`, when combined with `Trees`—play an essential role in the solution of this problem. It illustrates the fundamental idea of *reuse* in software design; that is, we try not to reinvent software components—classes and methods—that are already available and known to be reliable. To solve this problem without the use of such powerful abstractions would require many times the effort that went into this program.

EXERCISES

5–9 Suggest ways in which the `ExpressionParser` program can be made more *robust*, in the sense that it will recognize the errors represented in Exercise 5–12 and report an error message.

5–10 Trace execution of the `ExpressionParser` program by showing the sequence of values in the stack and output list of trees, when it is applied to each of the following input expressions:
a. `a + b * c / d * e - f`
b. `a * ( b + c * ( d + e * f ) )`
c. `2.5 * b - 5.4 * d - 4 * f`

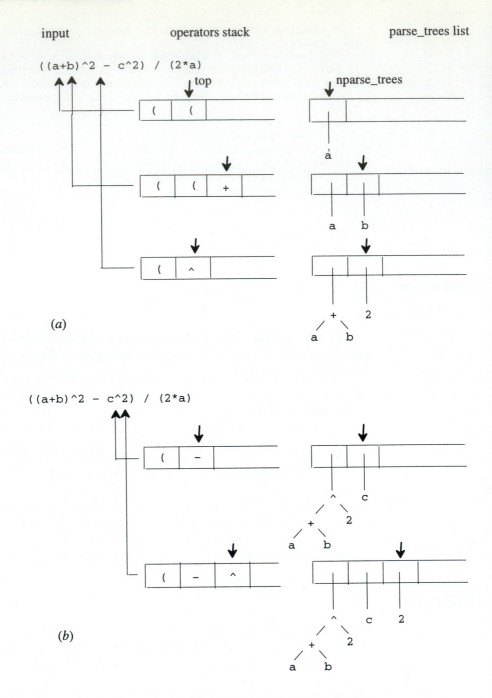

FIGURE 5–40   Trace of certain steps in the parse of the expression `((a+b)^2-c^2)/(2*a)`.

5–11 The `ExpressionParser` program stops when certain kinds of input errors occur as it builds a parse tree for an arithmetic expression. What is wrong with each of the following, and how does the program respond to such an error?

a.   +
b.   a + b ; c

5–12 The `ExpressionParser` also *fails* to recognize certain other kinds of erroneous expressions, moving right along as if nothing wrong has happened. What does it do when each of the following is presented as input?

a.   a + b *
b.   a b c
c.   + a b

INTRODUCTION TO GRAPHS

The tree is a special case of a more generalized structure, which is called the *graph*. Graphs are of considerable interest in computing. Any situation in which one wants to represent information about a finite number of elements and relationships among those elements (where "relationship" can be defined very broadly) is a candidate for modeling by means of a graph. Thus, molecular structure, electronic circuits, kinship relationships in primitive cultures, the possible routes for a new highway system, and many other situations can be represented by graphs. Graph theory as an area of study within mathematics, had its origins in the work of Leonhard Euler in 1736.[1] However, the study of graph algorithms as an area within computing is relatively new—the first textbooks on graph algorithms appeared in the late 1970s. Today, this is an active area of research in computing.

Our goals in this section are very modest. Graph theory is a large topic and there is much that can be said about it. Here, we simply introduce the basic definitions associated with graphs and show several examples. This is to enable you to recognize graphs as a common pattern useful in computing. A thorough treatment of graphs and presentation of the class *Graph* will be reserved for Volume IV of this series.

In order to manage information, we need to have ways to represent it. For instance, consider the *semantic network* representation of two species of mammals that is shown in Figure 5–41. The figure contains boxes (called *vertices* or *nodes*) which surround objects (such as `Ranger` and `Butterscotch`) and classes of objects (such as `dog`, `mammal`, etc.). It also includes arrows (called *edges* or *arcs*) labelled by properties (`is_a`, `color`, `structure`). Semantic networks such as this are used in artificial intelligence to represent the relationships between concepts; such a representation is preliminary to entering the information into a special type of database from which a machine can make

---

1.   See Knuth [1], page 373.

logical inferences (such as answering questions like "Is Ranger a vertebrate?").

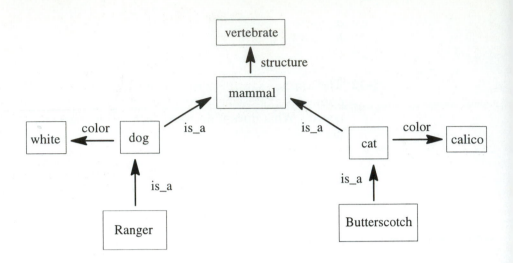

FIGURE 5–41   A semantic network.

A diagram similar to Figure 5–41 is found in Figure 5–42. This diagram represents the relationship "are_acquainted" among the players on a softball team before the first day of practice, and is formally known as a *sociogram.* Note again that the diagram consists of vertices (in this case the names of players on the team) and edges, representing the fact that some of the players were already acquainted before joining the team. This time, however, the edges do not have a direction associated with them.

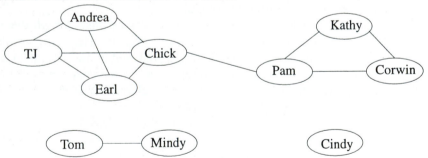

FIGURE 5–42   A sociogram.

Both of these figures are examples of graphs; this is quite a different notion of graph from what is studied in algebra or analytic geometry. This chapter is about graphs and some of the situations that can be modeled by them. We begin by carefully developing a formal definition of the notion of graph. This is necessary so that we know precisely what we are doing when we work with graphs. We will also establish some basic properties of graphs and examine two ways to represent graphs as data structures in C++.

Definitions and Examples

We begin with a collection of basic definitions. There are several important nuances to the situations we will want to model with graphs. These nuances require several variations on the basic definition. However, all of the variations share the concepts of vertices and edges as the fundamental ideas on which they are built.

> **Definition**   A graph is a nonempty set *V* of *vertices* (or *nodes*), and a set *E* of *edges* (or *arcs*) such that each edge is associated with a pair of vertices. We typically denote a graph as an ordered pair (*V*, *E*). If an edge *e* is associated with a particular vertex *v*, *e* is said to be *incident on v*.

Figure 5–42 is a representation of a graph under this definition, using lines for edges and ovals for vertices. The line joining `Andrea` and `Earl`, for instance, is an edge. This line is associated with the pair (`Andrea`, `Earl`) under the definition. It is incident on both the vertices `Andrea` and `Earl`.

In general, many different diagrams can be drawn of the same graph; for instance, consider the two diagrams in Figure 5–43. They both have five vertices and eight edges, and the connections among the vertices are the same. That is, one can be obtained from the other by moving the middle vertex horizontally so that it is outside (inside) the rectangular array of the other four vertices, while keeping the connections among the edges intact.

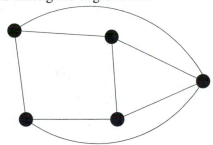

FIGURE 5–43   Two different diagrams of the same graph.

> **Definition**   A *loop* is an edge for which the associated vertices are identical. Two distinct edges are *parallel* if they are associated with the same pair of vertices. A graph with parallel edges is a *multigraph*. A graph with neither parallel edges nor loops is a *simple graph*. A graph which has a numerical value associated with each edge is a *weighted graph*.

If we just use the term "graph" with no modifiers, we usually mean a graph with no parallel edges and no weights on its edges, but possibly with loops. Figure 5–44 illustrates these concepts. Note that although we have introduced a term for graphs with weighted edges, we have not introduced a term for graphs with weighted nodes; we will deal with weighted nodes later.

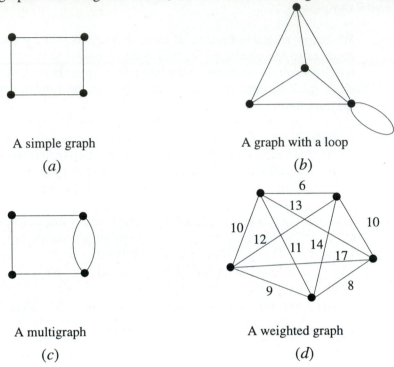

A simple graph

(a)

A graph with a loop

(b)

A multigraph

(c)

A weighted graph

(d)

FIGURE 5–44   Some different types of graphs.

The most important difference between the graphs in Figures 5–41 and 5–42 is that all of the edges in the semantic network are directional, whereas the acquaintanceships in the sociogram are mutual. This variation occurs frequently, so we need to identify it.

Definition   A *directed graph* (or *digraph*) is a nonempty set V of vertices and a set E of edges, such that each edge e is associated with *an ordered pair* of vertices. A digraph in which each edge has a numerical value associated with it is a *network*.[1]

We can also distinguish simple digraphs from multidigraphs. Note that the essential difference between graphs and digraphs is that graphs represent two-

---

1.   Unfortunately, the terminology of graph theory is not standardized. Thus "network" and other terms may have different meanings in other writings. We have tried to select the names that we see used most frequently.

way relationships while digraphs represent one-way relationships. Thus, we can regard a graph as a special kind of digraph; one in which whenever there is an edge from *A* to *B*, there is also an edge from *B* to *A*. In fact, all of our variations could be viewed as special cases of networks; networks whose edges all have weight of 1 are simply digraphs. However, we do not pursue this line of development any further, since all these variations have valuable and distinctive applications in computing.

More Examples

Let us examine several situations that arise in computing to illustrate the broad applicability of graphs and to deepen our understanding of these basic definitions. We have already seen two such illustrations—the semantic network of Figure 5–41 as a digraph and the sociogram of Figure 5–42 as a simple graph.

Example 5.13   Suppose we are assigned the task of laying out the wiring for a local area network (LAN) in a building. The points where the workstations need to be located are marked with dots on the floor plan in Figure 5–45, while the lines indicate some of the possible connections between these locations along with the length of cable needed to make those connections. Note that the dots and their connecting lines form a weighted graph. The problem is selecting those edges that connect all of the workstations in such a way that the total length of cable used is minimized.

Example 5.14   As we shall see in Chapter 8, data flow diagrams (DFD) are a popular tool for modeling the functional requirements of a system. Figure 5–46 is a typical DFD. Note that a DFD is a digraph.

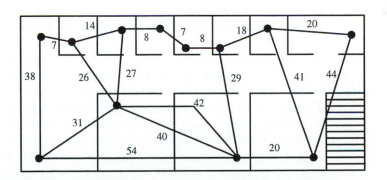

FIGURE 5–45   Connecting a LAN.

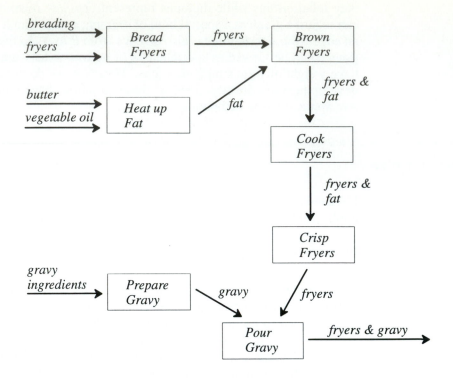

FIGURE 5–46   Data flow diagram for preparing fried chicken.

Example 5.15   Consider again the weighted graph in Figure 5–44, but this time attach the names of communities to the vertices, which gives us the graph in Figure 5–47. The edge weights now represent distances between pairs of communities. Suppose we want to find the shortest route connecting all of the cities and returning to the one at which we start. This problem is known as the travelling salesperson problem and is one of the most widely cited problems in computing; for large numbers of vertices, there are no known efficient solutions. We will discuss it more extensively when we study more complex algorithms in Volume IV of this series.

Example 5.16   Figure 5–48 contains a graph that represents the states of a "110 recognizer," which is a device which accepts binary input strings (such as 001110100101001) and identifies subsequences of the form 110. The recognizer consists of three states denoted X, Y, and Z and directed edges that indicate transitions between those states. The notation 0/1, for instance, means that the input corresponding to a particular transition is a 0 and the output is a 1. Thus, the recognizer makes the transition from state X to state Z, outputting a 1, if and only if the sequence 110 has been encountered. For the string given, the output would be 000001000000000. Digraphs based on

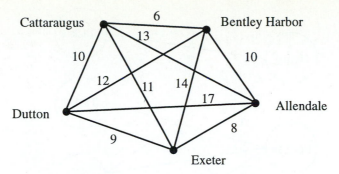

FIGURE 5–47   The travelling salesperson problem.

this principle are used in the design of compilers and hardware components.

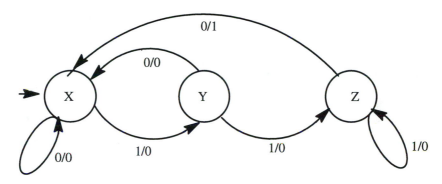

FIGURE 5–48   A 110 recognizer.

Example 5.17   There are many applications of graphs in decision-making; one of the most useful is to problems which involve matching. For instance, suppose we have three skilled workers and four tasks that need to be done. Both workers and tasks are represented by vertices in a graph. Each worker can only do some of the tasks—this capability is indicated as an edge joining that worker to that task; the time each worker will require for each job is specified as a weight on the edge. The problem is to find an optimal assignment of workers to tasks. A typical example is given in Figure 5–49.

In these examples, Figures 5–45 and 5–47 are graphs; 5–46 and 5–48 are digraphs, and 5–49 is represented as a graph, but can also be represented as a digraph. Only 5–48 has loops and only 5–45 involves a multigraph. These example graphs also include two important types of graphs that arise quite often in practice, however. The travelling salesperson problem portrayed in Figure 5–47 is an example of a *complete* graph; i.e., a graph in which every pair of vertices is joined by a single edge. The job scheduling problem of Figure 5–49 is an example of a *bipartite graph*; i.e., a graph in which the vertices can

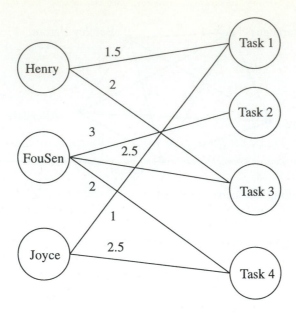

FIGURE 5–49   A job scheduling problem.

be partitioned into two subsets, *A* and *B*, in such a way that edges always join a vertex in *A* to a vertex in *B* (so there are no edges joining two vertices in *A* or two vertices in *B*).

Properties of Graphs

Graphs have many properties that are useful in classifying them, comparing them for similarities and differences, and answering questions about particular graphs. We will focus here on two elementary but useful graph properties, which rely on the following definition.

Definition   The *degree* of a vertex *v*, denoted deg(*v*), is the number of edges that are incident on it.

For instance, the graph in Figure 5–49 has one vertex with degree 3 (FouSen), five vertices with degree 2 (Henry, Joyce, Task1, Task3, and Task4), and one vertex with degree 1 (Task2). The complete graph in the travelling sales-person example has 5 vertices each of degree 4; in fact, a complete graph with *n* vertices has degree *n*–1 for all of its vertices. A loop in a graph always con-tributes a count of 2 to the degree of the vertex to which it is connected.

Checking the degrees of vertices is a quick way to show that two graphs which have different looking diagrams are in fact different. That is, if the de-grees do not correspond for any pairing of the vertices, the graphs are different. However, the converse is not true; the vertices can be matched in such a way that their respective degrees correspond even though the graphs are different. The following theorem is often useful.

Theorem   For any graph G

$$\sum_{v \in V} \deg(v) = 2|E|$$

where $|E|$ denotes the number of edges in E.

The proof of this theorem is very simple—we just note that each edge contributes two to the total degree count.

One application of this theorem is to provide a kind of "integrity check" on graphs. For instance, suppose we conjecture that a certain graph has 21 vertices and each vertex has degree 3. We can see immediately that this conjecture is impossible. This theorem can be easily extended to cover digraphs; that extension and its proof are left for the exercises.

Another set of useful concepts and properties deals with the *connectedness* of graphs. For instance, in the semantic network example of Figure 5–41, the fact that Ranger is connected by a set of directed edges to vertebrate allows us to infer that Ranger's structure is vertebrate.

Definition   A *walk* is a list $(v_1\ e_1\ v_2\ e_2\ ...\ v_n\ e_n\ v_{n+1})$ of alternating vertices and edges such that each e_i is incident on v_i and v_{i+1}. For graphs or digraphs without parallel edges, the e_i's in a walk may be omitted. That is, the list of vertices $(v_1\ v_2\ ...\ v_n\ v_{n+1})$ in a walk is sufficient to describe it. A *path* is a walk that has no repeated edge. A *simple path* is a path with no repeated vertex, with the possible exception that v_1 and v_{n+1} may be identical. The *length* of a path is the number, n, of edges it contains.

Example 5.18   In the travelling salesperson example of Figure 5–47, the list (Cattaraugus, Bentley Harbor, Dutton, Cattaraugus, Bentley Harbor, Allendale) is a walk but is not a path. (Cattaraugus, Bentley Harbor, Dutton, Cattaraugus, Exeter, Allendale) is a path, but not a simple path, whose length is 5. (Allendale, Bentley Harbor, Cattaraugus, Dutton, Exeter, Allendale) is a simple path, also of length 5.

Definition   A graph is *connected* if any two of its vertices can be joined by a path.

For instance, the travelling salesperson example (Figure 5–47) is a connected graph, while the sociogram (Figure 5–42) is not a connected graph. Note also that each of the concepts of walk, path, simple path, length, and connected can be extended to digraphs as well. Connectedness is an especially useful concept. For instance, suppose a problem is represented by a graph where one vertex denotes a starting state and another represents the solution. If the graph is connected, we are guaranteed a solution; if not, the problem may be unsolvable. The following theorem is helpful in reducing the number of steps it takes to get from one vertex to another.

Theorem   Suppose that in a graph G there is a walk beginning at a vertex u and ending at a vertex v. Then there is also a simple path beginning at u and ending at v.

The proof of this theorem can be done by induction on the length n of the walk. Suppose, first, that n = 1. Then the walk uv is already a simple path, even if u and v are identical. Now suppose that n > 1 and assume for the induction step that all walks of length n − 1 or less can be replaced by simple paths. Any walk of length n must join two vertices, say u and v. If this walk is a simple path, we are done. If it is not a simple path, there must be some vertex w along this walk that is visited twice. So, remove from this walk all vertices between the first appearance of w and the second, including one of these two appearances of w itself. The result is still a walk joining u and v and, since we have removed at least one vertex, its length must be n − 1 or less. Hence, by our assumption, this shorter walk can be replaced by a simple path.[2]   (If you haven't already done so, sketch a sample graph G, then follow the steps of the proof to convince yourself that it is effective.)

Note that the maximum length of any simple path in a connected graph with n vertices is n.

Representing Graphs

While the diagrams we have been using throughout this section to represent graphs are very helpful to people, they have some definite disadvantages—they do not represent the relationships between the vertices in a way convenient for computer manipulation, they are not unique (i.e., there can be infinitely many different diagrams for the same graph), and they become confusing and hard to draw for large graphs. Therefore, we need some different representation schemes. Two are commonly used—boolean matrices and linked lists. Let us begin with boolean matrices. First, assume the vertices have each been assigned a number from 1 to n. In a computer program, this can be accomplished by including a function that will take the names of each of the vertices and assign a numerical value to them. Subsequently, users of the program refer to the vertices by name, and the function supplies the corresponding numerical value. The representations developed here are not applicable to multigraphs.

Definition   The *adjacency matrix* of a graph (V, E) is a boolean matrix whose ijth entry is 1 if there is an edge joining nodes i and j, and 0 if there is no such edge.

---

2.   Note that this may not be the *shortest* path joining u and v, even though it is simple.

Example 5.19   The adjacency matrix for the graph of Figure 5–50*a* is:

$$\begin{bmatrix} 0 & 1 & 1 & 1 \\ 1 & 0 & 1 & 1 \\ 1 & 1 & 0 & 1 \\ 1 & 1 & 1 & 1 \end{bmatrix}$$

Note, though, that the matrix depends on the numbering of the vertices. For instance, the numbering in Figure 5–50*b* results in a different matrix:

$$\begin{bmatrix} 0 & 1 & 1 & 1 \\ 1 & 1 & 1 & 1 \\ 1 & 1 & 0 & 1 \\ 1 & 1 & 1 & 0 \end{bmatrix}$$

The C++ declaration for the data type *graph* is straightforward if we use adjacency matrices to represent graphs:

```
typedef int arr[NVERTICES] [NVERTICES] graph ;
```

The advantage of this representation is its (conceptual) simplicity; the disadvantage is its (algorithmic) complexity. That is, the space required for an adjacency matrix is $O(n^2)$, where n is the number of vertices in the graph being represented. If we are dealing with graphs of, say, 1000 or more vertices, this can become a serious limitation. Furthermore, many graphs we deal with are *sparse*; i.e., they have relatively few edges compared with their number of vertices. For a sparse graph, therefore, most of the entries in the adjacency matrix will be 0. Also, many algorithms we would like to apply to graphs are substan-

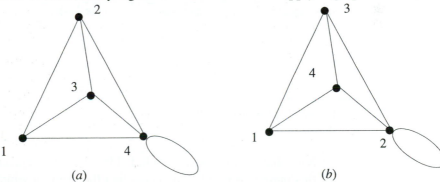

FIGURE 5–50   Two numberings for the vertices of a graph.

tially more time-complex when we use adjacency matrices to represent them than if we use linked lists.

The opposite of a sparse graph is a *dense* graph; one which has a large number of 1's in relation to its size. For dense graphs, the adjacency matrix is a computationally more efficient representation. (The concepts of dense and sparse are not precisely defined. However, one rule of thumb for distinguishing dense from sparse is that a number of edges exceeding $|V|\log_2|V|$ signifies a dense graph; otherwise, the graph is sparse.)

In order to address this efficiency problem more directly, we turn our attention to a more commonly used computer representation, known as *adjacency lists*. A C++ declaration for the type *graph* using adjacency lists is:

```
const NVERTICES = 20;
typedef vertex* vertex_ptr;
struct vertex
{
  int vertex_number;
  sometype vertex_data;
  vertex_ptr nextvert;
}
vertex_ptr [1..NVERTICES] graph;
```

Note that we have included the field `vertex_data` to provide a place to store information about each vertex. For instance, the graph of Figure 5–50a can be represented as the adjacency list shown in Figure 5–51.

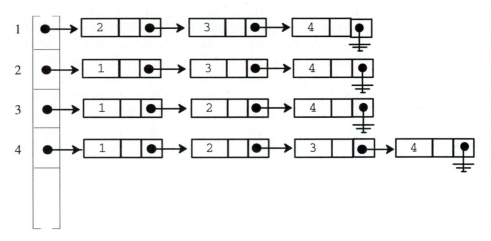

FIGURE 5–51   Adjacency list representation of a graph.

Note that every vertex is included twice in the adjacency list representation of this particular graph. Also note that the order in which vertices are inserted into each list is arbitrary. It should be clear that for dense graphs, the linked list representation is much less space efficient than the adjacency matrix representation. However, for sparse graphs the converse is true: there will be at most a few nodes in each list, so that the space consumed will be about $O(n)$. Algorithms that traverse these graphs will become fairly efficient, since they only need to examine short lists. We will return to this issue in Volume IV of this series, where an extensive study of graph algorithms will appear.

THE RELATIONSHIP BETWEEN GRAPHS AND TREES

The following definition of a tree is commonly used in mathematics.

> **Definition** A *cycle* in a graph is a path which has the same starting and ending vertices. A *tree* is a connected graph with no cycles (i.e., is *acyclic*) and one vertex is designated as the *root*.

Earlier in this chapter, we defined a tree as either empty or a set of the form $(rT_1T_2 ... T_m)$. The major advantage of the mathematical definition is that it ties trees into the study of graphs and allows us to use all of the concepts and representation tools we developed there in dealing with trees. This definition also lends itself easily to useful variations—for instance, an acyclic graph which is not necessarily connected is a *forest*. Some useful properties of trees can be easily established under this definition—for instance, any tree with n vertices must have $n-1$ edges. (See if you can convince yourself of this.) Likewise, any acyclic connected graph with $n-1$ edges must be a tree.

The two definitions are nearly equivalent, but not quite. The recursive definition has the added feature that there is an ordering associated with the subtrees. Sometimes trees defined like this are called *ordered trees* (as contrasted to *unordered trees*). If we ignore the ordering, the two definitions are equivalent. Thus, all of the properties of trees mentioned in the previous paragraph apply equally to trees defined with the recursive definition.

EXERCISES

5–13 Each of the following situations can be modeled as a graph. In each case, identify the edges and vertices, tell whether the situation would be modeled with a simple graph, a graph with loops, a multigraph, or a digraph and draw an example graph:
  a. the spread of a contagious disease
  b. a matching question in a test
  c. cities that have direct airline connections
  d. the motion of a knight on a chessboard

5–14 Draw graphs with the following characteristics if possible or explain why it is impossible. Let n represent the number of vertices.
  a. $n > 4$, no simple path has length more than 2
  b. $n > 3$, every vertex is of odd degree
  c. $n > 8$, no simple path has a length more than 4
  d. $n = 5$, each vertex has precisely three vertices incident on it

    e.   G is connected but removing any edge makes it disconnected
    f.   G is connected and removing any edge leaves G connected
    g.   G is connected and removing exactly one edge makes G disconnected

5–15 Revise the theorem containing the assertion $\displaystyle\sum_{v\in V} \deg(v) = 2|E|$ so that it applies to digraphs and show why your revision must be true.

5–16 Show that $2|E| \le |V|^2 - |V|$ for simple graphs.

5–17 Implement the function `adjacent (G, i, j)`, which returns 1 or 0 depending on whether the `i`th and `j`th vertices of `G` are adjacent, assuming the boolean matrix representation for graphs. Do the same for the function `degree (G, i)`, which returns the degree of `G`'s `i`th vertex.

5–18 How would the linked list representation of graphs be different for digraphs than for graphs? Create an example to illustrate your answer.

5–19 Show that a tree with *n* vertices must have *n*–1 edges.

5–20 For each of the following, state whether it is true or false, then prove your answer:

    a.   Every path in a tree is simple.
    b.   Adding an edge to a tree without adding vertices creates a cycle.
    c.   A graph with fewer than *n*–1 edges is a forest.

SUMMARY

This chapter has presented and introduced important applications for two fundamental nonlinear structures in computing: trees and graphs. Each one can be presented as a complete class, with methods that are useful in a wide range of applications. We have illustrated the use of trees in compiler design with an arithmetic expression parser. We have presented the binary tree as an important subclass of trees, and explored its special uses and distinguishing features. Graphs are a more general kind of data structure than trees, and their applications range widely through the discipline of computing, such as the design of computer networks and optimal transportation routes. The implementation considerations that are inherent in trees and graphs were introduced here, and will be studied in more detail in Chapter 6.

References

[1]   Knuth Donald E., *The Art of Computer Programming*, Volume 1: *Fundamental Algorithms* (2e), Addison–Wesley Publishing Company, Reading, Massachusetts, 1973.

IMPLEMENTATION OF CLASSES

This chapter addresses important considerations and options for implementing the various classes presented in earlier chapters. What considerations must be taken into account when implementing the `List`, `Stack`, `Queue`, and `Tree` objects and their member functions? What are the alternative strategies for representing these data structures in memory, and what is the impact of choosing one alternative over the other on the ultimate efficiency and versatility of the accompanying member functions? These are the questions that will be addressed in this chapter.

We shall see that in each case, the software designer must consider space-time tradeoffs in choosing an appropriate data structure. Verification also has a central role in the implementation of these classes and their member functions since, as we have seen, they are designed to be reused across a wide spectrum of applications such as those shown in the earlier chapters. We shall, therefore, informally verify several of these methods as their implementations are presented.

ARRAY VS. LINKED STORAGE

The array is a stalwart companion when we consider implementing structured data. Arrays provide a convenient means of efficiently storing, altering, and retrieving an arbitrary element in a long list of values.

However, arrays have their disadvantages as well. The major disadvantage is their inflexibility in size. That is, once the program declares an array to have a maximum of, say, 100 elements, it cannot later change the size to accommodate an unexpectedly larger input size. The programmer must intervene and alter the program text, then recompile the program to effect this sort of change. This inflexibility is not always desirable, especially in cases where the application program needs to handle widely varying input sizes.

Fortunately, there's an alternative strategy for storing lists of numbers. This alternative requires the program to build a so-called *linked structure* that will grow and shrink in size as the amount of input varies. Ideally, then, one can write a program for all feasible input sizes, not limiting the program to some arbitrary maximum limit, such as 100.

Example 6.1   Suppose we want to design a program that will read an arbitrary series of integers and display them in reverse order from that in which they appear in the input. Here are the specifications for this problem.

```
// pre:  input = e[1] e[2] ... e[n] ^ n>=0
// post: output = e[n] e[n-1] ... e[1]
```

For instance, if the input data were

```
14 29 6 48 50 73 22
```

then the output should be as follows:

```
22 73 50 48 6 29 14
```

Thus, the input is treated as a stack and the applications for this kind of program are many.

If we choose to solve this problem using an array to store the *n* input values, we must arbitrarily limit the maximum size *n* of the input. That is, the upper bound for the array must be a constant. (Readers should be convinced that this problem cannot be solved without requiring *n* auxiliary storage locations.) If we choose instead to solve the problem using a stack with no upper bound on its size, input values can be continuously pushed until there are no more, and then output values could be continuously popped until the stack is empty.

A simple array-based solution of the problem described in Example 6.1 is shown in Figure 6–1. This program requires that no more than 499 numbers be entered, since the maximum size of the array is 500, and the end of the input is flagged by the sentinel value `MyStack[n]=999`.

If we had used the `Stack` class to solve this problem, we would have gained some simplification, but no relief for the problem of limiting the input size to 499. That is because the `Stack` class is implemented using a maximum-sized array of 500 elements, so that we are up against the same constraints that the program in Figure 6–1 raises. In general, the use of a class does not necessarily alleviate all the constraints that a solution imposes.

C++ Pointers and Dynamic Data Structures

In order to implement a more flexible solution for problems like Example 6.1, we need to understand how pointers and dynamic storage allocation can be used in C++ to build dynamic data structures. The discussion below introduces the basic facilities for creating linked structures, which are intrinsically more flexible than arrays for storing data. We introduced pointers in Chapter 2 to achieve polymorphism. Here we will use pointers to build diverse data structures. To do this in a way that students are likely to encounter, especially in ordinary C programs, we will use `structs`.

```
//   Program name: ReverseNumbers
//   Pre:    (input = e[1] e[2] ... e[n])   ^ (n >= 0)
//   Post:   output = e[n] e[n-1] ... e[1]
#include <iostream.h>
const int MAXSTACK = 500;
                //maximum number of elements in array
int main()
{
  int mystack[MAXSTACK];
  int i, n;   // STATEMENTS ...
  n = 1;
  cin >> mystack[n];
  while ( (n < MAXSTACK) && (mystack[n] != 999) )
    {
      n++;
      cin >> mystack[n];
    }
  for ( i = --n; i > 0; i--)    cout << mystack[i] << endl;
}
```

FIGURE 6–1   A simple program to display numbers in reverse order.

An array is an aggregate of homogenous data. The data structure struct provides a way to define an aggregate of heterogeneous data. Of course we could do this with a class, but structs are common enough that students should see them. A C++ *structure* type is essentially a class whose members are public by default. A structure type is declared as shown in Figure 6–2.

```
struct struct-type-name
{
     data member declarations
};   // end struct-type-name
```

FIGURE 6–2   Declaration of a C++ structure type.

Data members in a C++ structure are accessed by the dot (.) operator. For example, the following declares a structure type named student with data members name and year.

```
struct student
{
  char* name;
  int year;
};
```

Once the struct is defined, to define two particular students we write:

```
student stu1, anotherstu;
```

They can be assigned values as follows.

```
stu1.name = "Jane";
stu1.year = 98;
anotherstu.name = "John";
anotherstu.year = 99;
```

Since C does not have classes, structures are essential in C for the kind of data structures we are about to introduce. In C++, classes could be used instead of structures, but many authors use structures as we shall do.

The variables, arrays, `structs`, and classes that are declared in a C++ program are activated exactly when the functions that declare them are called. It is preferable to defer the memory allocation for such data structures until after the program or function has begun its execution, so that the program can dynamically adjust the amount of storage it uses to the size of the input. Without such a facility, we are forced to overestimate the amount of storage required in order to prepare for the worst case—that is, the largest amount of input that could possibly occur.

To accommodate this need, C++ provides facilities by which a program or function may *dynamically* activate an object. These facilities are provided by two language elements: the pointer type, and the `new` and `delete` procedures. We have already seen the use of the pointer in earlier chapters, where we used it to create dynamic objects. Here, we shall use the pointer to directly reference a block of storage. There are two parts to this process.

1. A *pointer* is a variable whose value is the address of a particular kind of memory block (which contains, in turn, a scalar, array, class, or `struct` value in memory). A pointer can be declared in either of the following ways:

```
typename* ptr;   // alternative 1, * appended to typename
typename *ptr;   // alternative 2, * prepended to pointer vari-
able name
```

Here, `typename` names the type of object to which the variable `ptr` points. In reality, a pointer is nothing more than an address, in the sense described in Chapter 2, and a pointer variable is thus a variable which is used to indirectly *address* the value of another variable in memory. Alternative 1 can be a bit misleading in C++. For example,

```
int* p, q, r;
```

declares `p` to be a pointer to an integer, but `q` and `r` are just ordinary integer variables. If you want all of these variable names to be pointers to integers, you should write:

```
int *p, *q, *r;
```

2. The `new` and `delete` functions allocate and deallocate, respectively, a memory block when they are invoked in a program.

To illustrate, the following declarations identify two new types, an array and a `struct`. These are followed by declarations for the variables p, q, ap, and rp which are two pointers to `integers`, a pointer to an array, and a pointer to a `struct`, respectively.

```
typedef int intarr[9];
struct sturec
    {
        char* name;
        int score;
    };

int* p;
int *q;
intarr* ap;
sturec* rp;
```

Neither the integers, the array, nor the `struct` has any storage associated with it following these declarations. Instead, only a single word of memory is allocated for each of the associated pointers p, q, ap, and rp. When we are ready to allocate a block of storage for such an integer, array, or `struct`, we write the following statements:

```
p = new int;
ap = new intarr;
rp = new sturec;
```

Executing these statements creates new blocks of memory and assigns the *addresses* of those blocks to the associated pointer variables. This outcome is shown graphically in Figure 6–3.

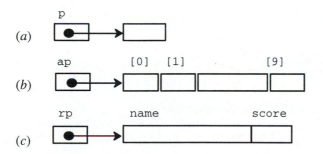

FIGURE 6–3 Dynamic allocation of storage for (a) an integer, (b) an array, and (c) a `struct`.

The arrows in this figure denote the idea that a pointer is a memory address, without needing to identify the exact binary value of that address.

To reference the value stored in each of these memory blocks, we must qualify it by identifying the pointer variable which currently contains its address.

That is, during the execution of a program, *one or more* instances of such a memory block may have been allocated. For instance, Figure 6–4 shows the effect of dynamically allocating two `integer` blocks, one referenced by p and the other reference by q. In order to distinguish the block addressed by p from

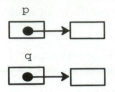

FIGURE 6–4   Two instances of a dynamically allocated memory block.

the block addressed by q, we use the reference `*p` or `*q`, respectively. Similarly, we can address the ith entry in the dynamically allocated array, using the notation `*ap[i]`. Finally, to reference an individual field within a dynamically allocated record, we use the notations `rp -> name` or `rp -> score`. In this example, since the `name` is itself a string, we may use the notation
`rp -> name[i-1]` to reference the ith character within that string referenced by `rp`.

A pointer variable may either have no value, have the value NULL (which means that it points nowhere), or have a value which references a memory block for its associated type. The distinction between the NULL value and a non-NULL reference is conventionally depicted in graphical form by a tree-shaped pointer and an arrow, as shown in Figure 6–5.

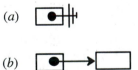

FIGURE 6–5   (*a*) NULL and (*b*) Non-NULL pointer values.

References to dynamically allocated storage blocks may occur in C++ programs in any way that a conventional variable may occur. That is, such a reference may appear within an arithmetic expression, on the left of an assignment statement, as an argument in a function call, and so on. For example, the statement *p=49 assigns the value 49 to the `integer` memory block currently addressed by p, as shown in Figure 6–6.

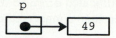

FIGURE 6–6 Result of the assignment `*p = 49`.

A pointer variable may also be assigned either the value of another pointer variable or NULL, using an assignment statement. For instance, if p is initially as shown in Figure 13–5, then the following pair of statements

```
q = p;
p = NULL;
```

leaves p and q as shown in Figure 6–7.

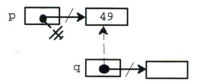

FIGURE 6–7 Result of executing `q = p; p = NULL`.

Figure 6–7 also illustrates the notational convention of showing a *change* to a pointer value by way of a *dashed* line for the new value and a diagonal line through the former pointer value.

When a dynamically allocated memory block is of no further use to the program, it may be released by the program and returned to the system by the de-lete statement. The statement delete p, for instance, releases the memory block currently addressed by p (along with any value that may be stored there) and may make undefined the value of the pointer p itself. No further access to that particular memory block or its value should be attempted after such a statement has been executed. No further use of the reference *p should be made until after p itself has been assigned a new value (either by an assignment statement or by a p = new int statement).

Linking Memory Blocks Together: the Node Additional flexibility is gained when we define blocks of memory in such a way that any number of them may be created and linked together in a chain whose size may grow and shrink as the size of the data input dictates. We wish to avoid declaring more than two or three pointer variables in order to gain this flexibility, and we wish to find a way for each such memory block to be connected, or linked, to another memory block of the same type.

Definition A *node* is a dynamically allocated `struct` which contains both a piece of information and a pointer that connects the node to another `struct` of the same type.

Schematically, we represent a node as shown in Figure 6–8, where p is a pointer to the node that is dynamically allocated and `link` is a pointer embedded within the `struct` that connects this node to another node.

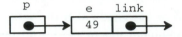

FIGURE 6–8 Structure of a node referenced by pointer p.

The declaration of this sort of node in C++ is given as follows:

```
struct Node
    {
    int   e;       // element at this node
     Node* link;   // pointer to next node
     };

Node *p, *q, *head;    // pointers to nodes
```

Here, the variables p and q are declared so that they can be used as auxiliary pointers for building a chain of these nodes in various ways. The pointer variable head is specially designated for referencing the *first* node in the chain.

To dynamically create and link a single pair of nodes to each other, the following sequence of C++ statements can be used.

```
p = new Node;
q = new Node;
p -> link = q;
```

These statements generate exactly the list fragment shown in Figure 6–9.

Note that these statements do not store any item of information in either node; they just establish a connection between them. To store information, an assignment must be made. For example, the following assignments

```
p->e = 49;
q->e = 42;
q->link = NULL;
```

leave the values 49 and 42, respectively, in the e field of the nodes referenced by p and q, and the value NULL in the link field of the node referenced by q. This is shown graphically in Figure 6–10.

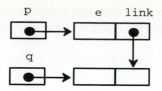

FIGURE 6–9   Linking two nodes together.

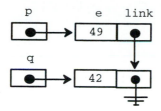

FIGURE 6–10   Assigning values to two nodes.

Dynamic Storage Management: Building a Single-Linked Chain

If we abandon the fixed-sized array for problems that require storage flexibility, the programmer must take the responsibility for building a chain of individual values one-by-one. That is, whenever a new value is read from the input, a new storage location is allocated for it and linked to the most-recently-read value using a pointer.

The simplest strategy to accomplish this is to have the program build a so-called *single-linked chain*. That is, each entry in the chain is linked via a single pointer to the one following it, as shown in Figure 6–11.

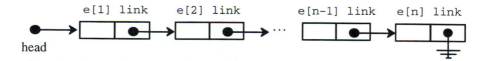

FIGURE 6–11   A single-linked chain.

However, there's a penalty attached to choosing this strategy over the array. That is, the only way to directly access an entry in this chain is through its *head* pointer, which references the first entry e[1]. If the program wants to access, say, the entry e[55], a loop must be written. If we had used an array for storing these elements, we would only need to say e[55] (or e[54] if the indexing started at 0) to retrieve the value of the fifty-fifth entry. So there's a trade-off; linked chains provide storage flexibility, but at the price of less efficient access to an individual entry.

Let's examine the programming implications of building a linked chain such as the one shown in Figure 6–11 to solve the simple problem described in Example 6.1 of displaying a series of numbers in reverse order. The program to do this is shown in Figure 6–12.

```
//    Program name:    Linked ReverseNumbers
//    Pre:    (input = e[1] e[2] ... e[n])   ^ (n >= 0)
//    Post:   output = e[n] e[n-1] ... e[1]

#include <iostream.h>

int main()
{
    struct stacknode
        { int   e;
          stacknode* link;
    }; stacknode* head;     // pointer to header node of stack
       stacknode* i;        // working pointer
       head = new stacknode;
       head -> link = NULL;
    cin >> head -> e;
     while ( head -> e != 999 )
     { i = head;
        head = new stacknode;
        head -> link = i;
        cin >> head -> e;
     }
     i = head -> link;  // skip sentinel
     while (i != NULL)
        {cout << i -> e << endl;
          i = i -> link;
        }
}
```

FIGURE 6–12   C++ code for a number reversing program that uses a linked chain.

This program requires some scrutiny. First, note that it contains no constant upper bound on the number of values that can be entered. The only practical limit is the maximum size of storage in which the program is allowed to run, which may be anywhere from, say, 256k bytes to 5 megabytes; surely enough to handle a wider range of input sizes than the array implementation.

Second, notice carefully how the program builds a linked chain and then displays its entries in reverse order. The first three statements initialize the chain with a single member, distinguished as the *head* of the chain. This is shown in Figure 6–13, where we assume that the first number read by the program is 14. Three steps are needed to accomplish this; allocating storage for the node (i.e., the element and its link to the next node — head = new stacknode;), setting its link to NULL (signifying the end of the chain — head -> link =

NULL;), and finally reading the input value 14 — cin>>head->e.

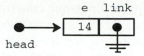

FIGURE 6–13   Initializing the single-linked chain with the value 14.

Third, notice the process that ensues each time a new node is added to the head of the chain. It is a four-step event, as illustrated in Figure 6–14 where 22 is read and added to the chain in front of 73, which had been most recently added. The pointer i is set to point to the node that contains 73 (i = head), and then head is reset to point to a new node where the 22 will be stored (head = new stacknode). Then this new node's link is set to point to the node containing 73 (head -> link = i) and finally the value 22 is read and stored in the new head node (cin >> head -> e).

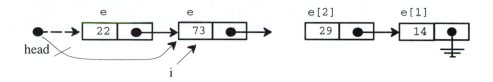

FIGURE 6–14   Adding the number 22 at the head of a single-linked chain.

Finally, the last loop in the program displays the numbers, by using the auxiliary pointer i as shown in Figure 6–15. There, we assume that 22 is the last number entered before the sentinel value 999. Thus, i is made to point to the *second* element in the list, rather than the head element. Each iteration of this loop displays the value of the element at the ith node and then moves i forward in the chain. This loop finally terminates when i = NULL, which is the convention we use to indicate the end of the chain. Thus, the last value displayed will be identical to the first value entered.

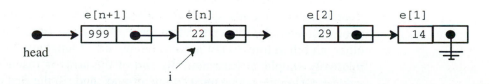

FIGURE 6–15   Displaying a single-linked chain; first step.

Evaluating Alternatives: Time, Space, and Program Simplicity

This example reveals several characteristics of the trade-offs that occur between arrays and linked strategies for manipulating data structures. Arrays are surely easier to use, as an individual entry in an array is easier to access. Arrays are therefore more efficient, since we can always access individual elements in a nonsequential, or random, manner. On the other hand, arrays are more rigid in their storage limits than linked chains, and this is a serious constraint for many types of problems.

Consider the various sorting exercises in the laboratory material for Chapter 3. We may need to alter the maximum size of the array used to store a sequence when we are sorting large lists of numbers. However, once we do this, the array implementation appears intuitively to be more efficient than the linked chain implementation, since it allows random access to all of its entries for the purposes of comparison and swapping.

Arrays also seem to be easier to work with from the programming standpoint, as this example illustrates. Working with arrays seems to be less tedious and error-prone than working with linked structures. However, since linked structures are important for a large class of problems, we need to master the program design techniques that they require. The remainder of this chapter, along with related sections of the *Laboratory Manual*, will provide many opportunities to gain insight into the manipulation of dynamically linked structures.

CIRCULAR ARRAYS, DOUBLE-LINKED CHAINS, AND OTHER STORAGE STRATEGIES

In addition to the array and the single-linked chain, many other strategies are also useful when choosing a storage scheme for a data structure. We introduce three of these alternatives here, in preparation for the discussions of particular class implementations later in this chapter.

Circular Arrays   In applications where data values are always entered and removed from an array at the same end, we can anchor the other end at a fixed location in the array, usually the first location, and let the index, or position, of the other end vary as values enter and leave. This is the action that a stack requires, as pictured in Figure 6–16.

However, if we think of the action that a queue requires, *both* ends are fluid. That is, values enter the queue at one end, while values leave at the other. Values in between the two ends retain their relative positions with respect to each other, and therefore do not need to be moved. Managing this data structure is relatively simple, at least until the end of the array is reached, when the next value entering the queue must "wrap around" and fill the first entry in the array. This wrap-around is shown in Figure 6–17. When used in this way, the array is called a *circular array*, and the index $n+1$ is always calculated modulo the

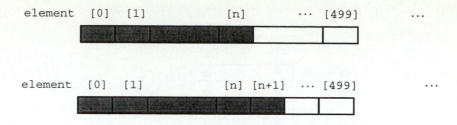

FIGURE 6–16   Adding an entry at one end of an array; the first element remains anchored.

length of the array. This calculation guarantees that the index will be reset to 0 whenever the end of the array, say the 499th entry, is reached.

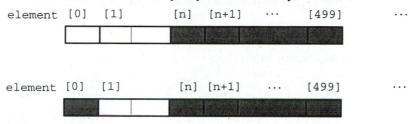

FIGURE 6–17   Adding an element to a circular array when the last entry has been filled.

Double-linked Chains   A linked chain allows us to navigate from one element to the one that immediately follows it by simply following the chain of pointers called link. This was illustrated in the previous example. However, this sort of chain becomes awkward to manage when we want to navigate through the chain backward as well as forward. For instance, suppose we are at the nth element in the chain and we want to access the $(n-1)$th element. To accomplish this using a single-linked strategy, we would have to begin all the way back at the head of the chain and then loop forward $n-1$ times, a time-consuming proposition.

Consider the alternative chaining scheme in which each node is linked both to its successor by one link, say next, and to its predecessor by another link, say previous. This node design leads to a *double-linked chain* as shown in Figure 6–18. Note there that the chain can be entered at either end, at the head or at the tail, and that navigation within the chain can proceed either forward or backward from any node.

Other Storage Strategies   Nonlinear data structures such as trees and binary trees demand different storage strategies. While studying heapsort in Chapter 3, we had a glimpse of an array storage strategy for binary trees. However, this particular strategy is not easily adapted to general trees, since the lat-

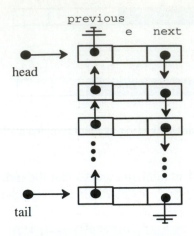

FIGURE 6–18   A double-linked chain.

ter vary more widely in shape—that is, general trees are not restricted to have exactly two children at each node. In fact, since `Trees` vary widely in size as well as in shape, a linked strategy is appropriate. This strategy is also adaptable to graphs as well as general trees, although that will not be explored in this chapter.

In the array storage strategy for binary trees, we identified the child of each interior node e_i with the array entries at locations $2i$ and $2i+1$. This strategy does not extend itself gracefully to general trees, since each interior node may have any number of children. To accommodate the storage of general trees, we will use the somewhat more complex node structure shown in Figure 6–19.

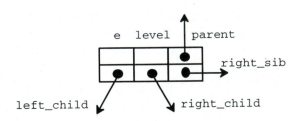

FIGURE 6–19   Node structure for a general tree.

This design allows us to move directly from a single node to either its left-most child, its rightmost child, its right sibling, or its parent, by selecting one of the pointer values `left_child`, `right_child`, `right_sib`, or `parent`, respectively. It also allows us to represent all the children of a particular node as a single-linked chain in which the head is the parent's `left_child` pointer and the children are linked to each other by a sequence of `right_sib` pointers. The last child in the chain has a `NULL` `right_sib` pointer.

> **Example 6.2** Such a structure is illustrated in Figure 6–20 for the simple tree (A B C D). Notice that the children B, C, and D of A are connected to

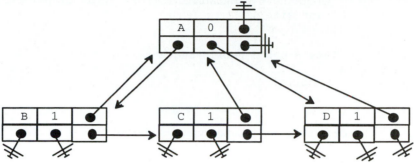

FIGURE 6–20   Linked structure representing the tree (A B C D).

each other by a linked chain; that is, they form a list, in which B (the oldest child) is at the head and D (the youngest) is at the tail.

While this structure is complex, it does facilitate movement among the various elements in a tree, and this sort of movement will be important for implementing the member functions that manipulate trees. We shall therefore use this strategy in our discussions of tree implementation in a later section. We shall also show how binary trees can be implemented as a special case of this strategy, so that we do not have to invent an entirely separate storage scheme for binary trees. This also allows many of the tree member functions to be reused for binary trees.

AN ARRAY IMPLEMENTATION FOR Sequence AND Stack

Our implementation of `Stack`s and their member functions is done using an array as the basic storage mechanism, under the assumption that the maximum `Stack` size will be relatively small. In particular, the `Stack` is implemented as a specialization of the more general class, `Sequence`, which abstracts common features of stacks and lists. With this choice, we are consciously trading off some storage flexibility in favor of programming simplicity.

The basic declarations used in the implementation of `Sequence`s and `Stack`s are shown in Figure 6–21. There, we see the the declaration of 500 (MAXELEMENTS) as the maximum `Sequence` size; the identification of `ElementPtr` as the basic class for each individual entry in a `Sequence`; and the instance variable `size` that keeps track of the current size of a `Sequence`. Since a `Stack` is a subclass of `Sequence`, any `Stack` object will inherit these

```
const int MAXELEMENTS = 500;

class Sequence
{
 protected:
  // DATA MEMBERS ...
  ElementPtr e[MAXELEMENTS]; // array of pointers to elements
   int size;
 ...

class Stack : public Sequence
{
    public:  ...
```

FIGURE 6–21   C++ declarations for the array implementation of Sequences and Stacks.

data members. The Stack is realized by the e array whose first size entries are occupied and whose remaining entries are unused.

Example 6.3   Consider Figure 6–22, where the Stack, S, (35 17 40 9) is shown both in its visual form on the left and in its actual array representation on the right.

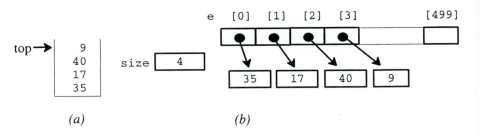

(a)   (b)

FIGURE 6–22   (a) The stack (35 17 40 9) and (b) its internal array representation.

Notice here that each entry in the array is actually a pointer to an object of class Element and hence Stacks may be heterogeneous. For example, the elements could be Morphemes, which in turn contain the text representation of the individual number in the Stack. In this case, application programs that need to manipulate individual stack entries as numbers must first coerce these values to equivalent reals before performing any arithmetic operations on them.

When we think about implementing the Stack member functions using this storage scheme, several considerations must be kept in mind. First, the size field must be initialized to 0. Since this is necessary for Lists and Queues, it is best accomplished by the constructor for Sequence. Second, the value of the size field for any Stack is the key to its status and the feasibility of certain operations to be carried out. For instance, a push can only be done effectively if size is less than MAXELEMENTS (500). Similarly, a pop can only be carried out successfully if the value of size is nonzero.

Beyond these considerations, implementation of the Stack member functions is straightforward. The operations push, pop, and top are accomplished relative to the element at location size in the array. The constructor for Sequence and the implementation of push for Stack are shown in Figures 6–23 and 13–23, respectively.

```
Sequence::Sequence()
{
    size = 0;
} // end Sequence::Sequence()
```

FIGURE 6–23   C++ code for the constructor for Sequence.

```
int Stack::push(ElementPtr eptr)
{
  if (this -> is_full())
    return 0;
  else
  {
    e[size++] = eptr;
    return 1;
  }
}   // Stack::push()
```

FIGURE 6–24   C++ code for the push member function implementation.

The method push inserts the reference eptr into the array at position size and post increments size. This can only be done if the length of the stack is less than 500, which is tested by the auxiliary method is_full.

Example 6.4   The dynamics of push are illustrated in Figure 6–25 for the Stack shown in Example 6.3 and the Morpheme pointer t, whose associated Morpheme's value is '21'.

The member functions top and pop are shown in Figure 6–26. Note that NULL is returned in the marginal event that the Stack is empty.

Operation of the member functions is illustrated in Figure 6–27 for the familiar Stack, S.

Example 6.5   Assume that x is a Morpheme whose value should be assigned a copy of the value stored at the top of Stack S. This is accomplished by the following statement:

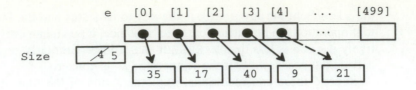

FIGURE 6–25   Execution of t -> set_val("21"); S.push(t) when S=(35 17 40 9).

```
ElementPtr Stack::pop()
{ if (this -> is_empty())
     return NULL;
  else
  {
    return e[--size];
  }
}   //Stack::pop


ElementPtr Stack::top()
{   if (this -> is_empty())
       return NULL;
    else
       return  e[size-1];
}   //Stack::top
```

FIGURE 6–26   C++ code for the Stack methods top and pop.

```
x.set_val( (MorphemePtr(S.top())) ) -> get_val() )
```

This says, literally, to assign as the value of x a copy of the value that is referenced by the pointer at the top of the Stack, S and is interpreted as a Morpheme. The effect of this statement is shown in Figure 6–27. There, we see that the value 21 at the top of the stack is assigned to x, but the length of the Stack is unaffected.

For the statement S.pop, the instance variable S.size is decreased by 1. However, note that the pointer to the morpheme value 21 is not removed physically from S.e[4]; it will simply be overwritten later, whenever a subsequent push operation causes this 5th location to be reused.

EXERCISES

6–1 Rewrite the program in Figure 6–1 so that it uses the Stack class and appropriate methods, rather than an explicit array.

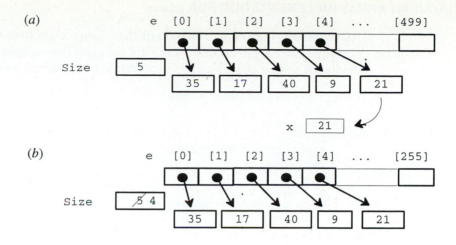

FIGURE 6–27 Execution of (a) `x.set_val( (MorphemePtr(S.top())) -> get_val() )` and (b) `S.pop()`, assuming in each case that `S = (35 17 40 9 21)`.

6–2 Assuming the array implementation of `Sequences` and `Stacks` that is discussed in this section, implement the methods `Sequence::empty()` and `Sequence::is_full()`. The complete specifications for these two methods are given in an appendix to Chapter 4 of the accompanying *Laboratory Manual*.

6–3 For each individual `Element` in a `Stack` or `Sequence`, we have already defined a member function that displays its value. For instance, if we have a `Morpheme`, `m`, the member function, `m.display()` shows its value on the screen. Taking advantage of this fact, define a member function that implements the display method for an entire `Sequence` in such a way that its individual values appear on the screen enclosed in parentheses, (and). The exact specifications for `Sequence::display()`, which are slightly more detailed, are given in an appendix to Chapter 4 of the accompanying *Laboratory Manual*.

6–4 Suppose we decide to implement `Sequences` and `Stacks` using a single-linked chain, as described in the previous section. What would be an appropriate declaration for the instance variables in this alternative implementation?

6–5 For the implementation of `Stacks` defined in Exercise 6–4, how would the constructor and the member functions `push` and `pop` be rewritten?

6–6 What are the trade-offs in efficiency, storage flexibility, and programming ease when you compare the array implementation of `Stacks` given in this section with the alternative single-linked chain implementation? Consider the constructor and the methods `push`, and `pop` specifically when answering this question.

A CIRCULAR ARRAY IMPLEMENTATION FOR Queue

As suggested, our implementation of the Queue class uses the circular array strategy. The data members f and r for the class Queue specializes the implementation so that queues can be implemented as a subclass of Sequence.

```
const int MAXELEMENTS = 500;

class Sequence
{   protected:
        ElementPtr e[MAXELEMENTS];
        int size;

.......
class Queue : public Sequence
{   protected:
        int f, r;
```

The definition of Queue as a subclass of the class Sequence enables us to retain the original usage and meaning for the Sequence data members (see Figure 6–21). The new variables f and r keep track of the positions of the front and rear of the Queue inside the array that contains its individual entries.

Example 6.6   A sample Queue Q = (Mary Stan Edward Natalie) and its circular array representation are shown in Figure 6–28. Note that the first element in the Queue is not at position 1 in the array, since several departures as well as new entries may have occurred since it was first initialized.

Initialization of a Queue by its constructor is relatively easy, since some of this member function's responsibilities are inherited from the constructor for sequences. The Queue constructor is shown in Figure 6–29. Its front and rear indices are set so that the first enter will occur at position 0 of the array and no one can leave.

Addition of a new entry into a Queue is successful only if there is space in the array for the new entry. In this case, the position of the new entry is calculated using modular arithmetic, to accommodate the case where the rear of the Queue actually wraps around to the beginning of the array. In that special case, Q.r becomes 0. Otherwise, the recalculation of Q.r is the equivalent of adding 1 to it. These steps are shown in Figure 6–30. Note also that 0 is returned in the event that the Queue is full at the time enter is called.

Example 6.7   Figure 6–31 illustrates the activity of the statements
m -> set_val('Gregory'); Q.enter(m) where m is a Morpheme pointer and Q = (Mary Stan Edward Natalie), as shown in Figure 6–28.

Here, we see that the index r is incremented, as is the size of the Queue, and Gregory enters the array as the seventh element of the array, just after

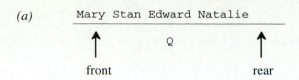

(a)

Mary Stan Edward Natalie

front   rear

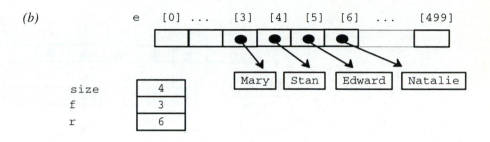

(b)

e   [0] ...   [3] [4] [5] [6] ...   [499]

Mary   Stan   Edward   Natalie

size   4
f   3
r   6

FIGURE 6–28   (a) A queue Q = (Mary Stan Edward Natalie) and (b) its circular array representation.

```
Queue::Queue()
{
    f = 0;
    r = -1;
}
```

FIGURE 6–29   C++ code for the constructor for an object of class Queue.

```
int Queue::enter(ElementPtr eptr)
{   if (this -> is_full())
        return 0;
    else
    {   r = (r + 1) % MAXELEMENTS;
        e[r] = eptr;
        size++;
        return 1;
    }
}   // end Queue::enter()
```

FIGURE 6–30   C++ code for implementation of the enter method for a circular list implementation of the Queue.

Natalie. If, on the other hand, Natalie had been in position 499 of the array, then r would have been reset to 0 and Gregory would have been placed in that entry, taking advantage of the array's circular nature. This alternative is pictured in Figure 6–31.

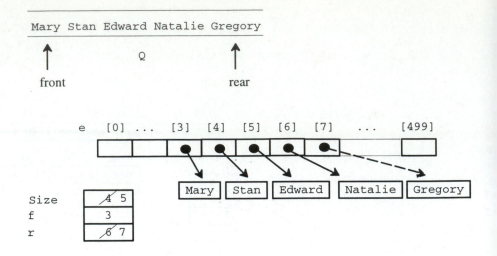

FIGURE 6–31 Result of `Q.enter(m)` when Q=`(Mary Stan Edward Natalie)` and `m -> value='Gregory'`.

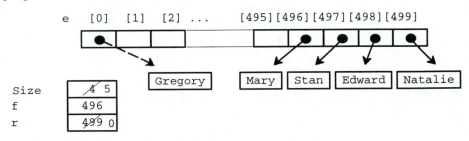

FIGURE 6–32 Result of `Q.enter(m)` when Q = `(Mary Stan Edward Natalie)`, `m->value = 'Gregory'`, and `Natalie` is in position 499.

Implementation of the `remove` method for `Queues` takes similar situations into account. That is, an empty `Queue` will cause `NULL` to be returned; otherwise the element at the front of the `Queue` is deleted by simply altering the value of `f` (see Figure 6–33). Note also that the `%` function makes allowance for the special case in which the front element moves from position 499 to position 0 after the `remove` method is invoked.

Example 6.8 Figure 6–34 shows what happens when the `remove` method is applied to the example `Queue` shown in Figure 6–28. Note that the only change is to the variables `f` and `size`. The pointer to the value `Mary` remains passively in the array, even though it is no longer accessible. That is, the indices `f` and `r` define the range of entries that remain in the queue.

```
ElementPtr Queue::remove()
{ if (this -> is_empty())
    return NULL;
  else
  { int tempint = f;
    f = (f + 1) % MAXELEMENTS;
    size--;
    return e[tempint];
  }
}  // end Queue::remove()
```

FIGURE 6–33   C++ code for implementation of the `remove` member function for the `Queue` class.

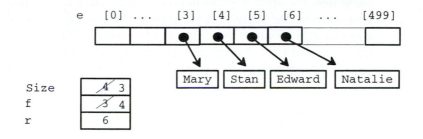

FIGURE 6–34   Effect of invoking `Q.remove()` when `Q = (Mary Stan Edward Natalie)`.

EXERCISES

6–7 Consider an alternative implementation of `Queues` as a single-linked chain. What specific pointers are needed to keep track of the status of a `Queue` in this manner? Can you think of any advantages that this alternative strategy might have over the circular array? Explain.

6–8 Re–implement a constructor and the `enter` and `remove` member functions under the alternative strategy suggested in Exercise 6–7. Compare this programming effort with the programming effort that is required in the circular array implementation.

6–9 What is the complexity of the `enter` and `remove` member function implementations for `Queues`? That is, how many steps are executed for any invocation? Is it a function of the length of the `Queue`? What would be the complexity of these methods if `Queues` had instead been implemented as a single-linked chain? Explain.

LINKED VS. ARRAY IMPLEMENTATIONS FOR `List`

Our implementation of the class `List` takes advantage of certain member functions that exist for the superclass sequence. For this reason, the array storage scheme for Sequence is shared by the class List as well as the Stack and Queue classes. Rather than dwelling solely on the details of the the array implementation for Lists, this section considers the ramifications of an alternative implementation strategy. That is, suppose we use a single-linked strategy for Sequence and List. What are its implementation characteristics, and how does that implementation contrast with the array implementation of the List class?

A Linked Implementation Strategy for Sequence and List

The linked implementation of Sequence and List is somewhat more complicated than the array implementation. One would choose this implementation strategy over the array in applications where storage flexibility is more of a concern than efficient access to the *i*th element. Nevertheless, we cannot ignore the need to access the *i*th element in a linked implementation. The data members for the class Sequence are shown in Figure 6–35.

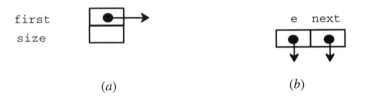

first
size

e   next

(*a*)   (*b*)

FIGURE 6–35   (*a*) Sequence data members and (*b*) general node structure for the linked implementation of the Sequence class.

Each node of the Sequence is a struct with the Element pointer e pointing to the Element at this location in the Sequence and the pointer next pointing to the next node in the Sequence. The variable first points to a "header" node whose next pointer points to the Sequence. The use of a header node allows all deletions to be treated in the same way (using a struct's next pointer), including a deletion from the beginning of the sequence. As before, the integer variable size is used to keep track of the current number of Elements in the Sequence.

The declarations for the struct seqnode and the data members of the classes Sequence and List are shown in Figure 6–36, along with some documentation about the purpose of their individual fields. Note that an individual Sequence item is of type ElementPtr, so that a Sequence or List is heterogeneous in the same sense as the array implementations of Sequence, Stack, or Queue.

The class List inherits data members from the class Sequence and has no new data members of its own. The class List does have many more member functions than the class Sequence as we shall see soon. There is no need to declare the maximum size of a Sequence using this implementation strategy

```
struct seqnode
{   ElementPtr e;     // pointer to element at this node
    seqnode* next;    // pointer to next node in sequence
};

class Sequence
{ protected:
      seqnode* first;   // pointer to header node of sequence
      int size;         // number of elements
   ....
}  // end Sequence

class List : public Sequence
{
   ...
```

FIGURE 6–36   C++ declarations of data members for the linked implementations of the
`Sequence` and `List` classes.

because of the dynamic nature of the linked structure. The only constraint on
the maximum size of a `List`, therefore, is the storage capacity of the machine
in which the application program runs.

Thus, the linked implementation of a `List L` will consist of an object of type
`Sequence` (inherited), followed by n structs of type `seqnode`, which are
themselves connected in a single-linked chain via the pointer `next`.

Example 6.9   This implementation strategy is illustrated in Figure 6–37,
where the `List L` is assumed to contain the five integers (`49 42 23 80
25`).

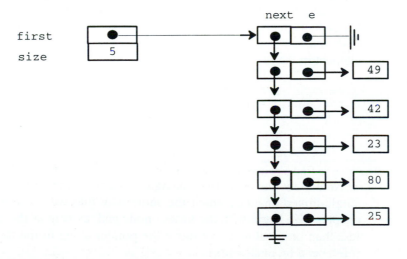

FIGURE 6–37   Linked implementation of the `List L` = (`49 42 23 80 25`).

We can now consider the implementation of individual member functions under this strategy. The constructor for an object of class `Sequence` is given in Figure 6–38. This is a straightforward procedure, in which `size` is set to 0, `first` is made to point to a new header node and the element pointer and next pointer of the header node are initialized to NULL. The constructor for an object of type `List` does nothing, relying on the execution of the inherited constructor for `Sequence` to initialize a `List` object. Thus, an empty `List`, L is signaled by the value `L.size=0`.

```
Sequence::Sequence()
{
    size = 0;
    first = new seqnode;
    first -> e = NULL;
    first -> next = NULL;
} // end Sequence::Sequence()
```

FIGURE 6–38   The constructor for the linked implementation of `Sequence`.

The remaining member functions are slightly more difficult to implement than they would be for an array implementation, due to the difference in roles between a `List` index value, say `i,` and its companion pointer value, say `p`, which references the corresponding node containing the element, e_i. Any of the `List` member functions, such as `insert` or `remove`, when given an index value `i` as an argument from an application program, must translate that value into the corresponding pointer value `p` in order to reference the node where the *i*th element e_i is stored. For an array implementation, this duality of usage is not a problem, since the index value `i` serves directly as a subscript to reference the array element `e[i]`.

In the linked implementation of `Lists`, this translation is accomplished by the code segment shown in Figure 6–39, whose task is simply to set the value of the pointer `ptr` to point to the node whose element pointer points to the `i`th element in the list.

```
// find pointer to node  position i
seqnode* ptr=first;
for (int j = 1; j <= i; j++)
    ptr = ptr->next;
```

FIGURE 6–39   The loop to find a pointer to position `i` for `Lists` under a linked implementation.

Note how the `for–loop` navigates through the individual nodes of the single-linked chain in much the same way that we illustrated earlier in this chapter. We begin with the header node and, as long as the current position is less than or equal to `i`, we move the pointer along to the next node, which is referenced by `ptr->next`.

Example 6.10   Figure 6–406 illustrates the changes in `ptr` and `j` as the loop to find a pointer to position 2 is executed. Initially `ptr` points to the header node and j = 1. Then the loop body is entered, ptr is advanced to the struct after the header node (i.e. the struct whose Element pointer points to the first element of the List) and j is increased to 2. Since 2 <= 2, the loop body is entered one more time advancing ptr to point to the struct that represents the second element of the List and then j is incremented to 3.

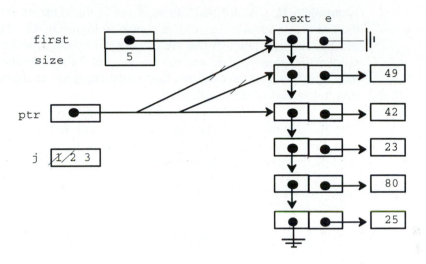

FIGURE 6–40   Finding the pointer to the second element in the linked implementation of the List L = (49 42 23 80 25).

With the ability to find a pointer to the List node that points to the ith element in hand, an implementation of the member function retrieve is relatively straightforward. This is shown in Figure 6–41. Here, the structure of the

```
ElementPtr List::retrieve(int i)
{   if ((i < 1) || (i > size))
        return NULL;
    else
      { // find pointer to node  position i
        seqnode* ptr=first;
        for (int j = 1; j <= i; j++)
          ptr = ptr->next;

        return (ptr->e);
      }
}   // end List::retrieve()
```

FIGURE 6–41   C++ code for implementation of the List.retrieve member function.

List is unaffected. This method finds the pointer to the ith List node and then returns the element pointer of that node.

The implementations of the member functions `insert` and `remove` use almost the same `for`–loop to find the `List` node that points to the `ith` `List` node. The important characteristic of an insertion into a linked chain is that it can be accomplished in a fixed number of steps once we get to the insertion point. By comparison, if we used an array representation for implementing `List` insertion, a loop would be needed in order to make space for the element to be inserted.

Example 6.11   To illustrate, an insertion of the value `80` into position 4 of the `List` L=(49 42 23 25) is shown in Figure 6–42. The dashed lines indicate the new pointers that are established by the insertion; i.e. the `next` pointer for the new node and the `next` pointer for its predecessor. Notice that `first` and all the other pointers in the chain are unaffected by an insertion, regardless of the length of the chain.

The `insert` method makes an insertion at a numerical index position `i` in the list. For instance, the insertion specified in Figure 6–42 can be accomplished by the following call, assuming that `m` is a `Morpheme` pointer:

```
m->set_val("80");
L.insert(m, 4);
```

The `insert` member function itself is shown in Figure 6–43.

Note that three different kinds of insertions are possible: at the beginning of the `List`, after the last node, and between two nodes. The use of a header node allows us to handle each of these situations with exactly the same pointer manipulation code. Without a header node, inserting a new element at the begin-

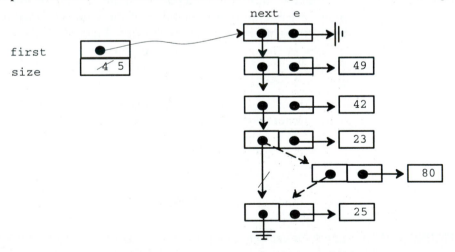

FIGURE 6–42   Pointer adjustments for inserting the `Element` 80 into position 4 of the List L=(49 42 23 25).

```
int List::insert(ElementPtr eptr, int i)
{
  if ( i < 1 || i > (size+1))
    return 0;
  else
    {
      // find pointer to node that points to position i
      seqnode* ptr=first;
       for (int j = 1; j < i; j++)
         ptr = ptr->next;

      seqnode* temp = ptr -> next; //temp points to ith node
      seqnode* newnode = new seqnode;
      ptr->next = newnode;
      newnode->next = temp;
      newnode->e = eptr;
       size++;
       return 1;
    }
}  // end List::insert()
```

FIGURE 6–43   Details of the `insert` member function for a linked implementation of the `List` class.

ning of the `List` would require manipulating the pointer `first` instead of the `next` pointer of a list node.

Deletion of a node from a `List` incorporates similar considerations. Implementation of `remove` is shown in Figure 6–44. There again, because of the use of a header node, we see that the three different cases can be handled by the same pointer manipulation code.

Example 6.12   For instance, Figure 6–45 shows how the element 42 is deleted from the `List` (49 42 23 80 25).

Figure NO TAG shows shows the status of the pointers in the member function `remove` just before the `return` statement is executed. After execution of the `return`, the pointers `ptr` and `temp` will no longer exist. The `List` is still accessible by following `next` pointers from `first`, yielding the `List` (49 23 80 25). But the element containing 42 and the `List` node pointing to it will not be accessible by this route after the `return`. If nothing points to these two structures, we will have created "garbage," storage that we dynamically obtained from the system heap that is no longer accessible. Many languages in the Lisp family provide automatic "garbage collection"; C++ does not. If we know *for sure* that nothing else will point to these locations, we should insert the following code just before the return in the member function `remove`.

```
delete (temp -> e);
delete temp;
```

```
int List::remove(int i)
{
  if ( (i < 1) || (i > size) )
    return 0;
  else
    {  // find pointer to node that points to position i
      seqnode* ptr=first;
      for (int j = 1; j < i; j++)
        ptr = ptr->next;

      seqnode* temp = ptr->next;  //temp points to ith node
      (ptr->next) = (temp->next);

      size--;
      return 1;
    }
} // end List::remove()
```

FIGURE 6–44 C++ code for linked implementation of the `remove` method for the class `List`.

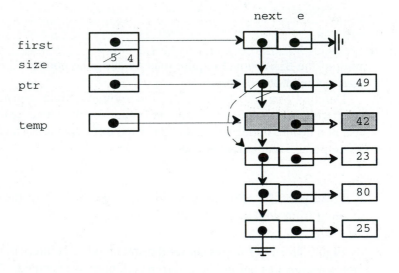

FIGURE 6–45 Pointer values just before the return after removing the element 42 from position 2 of the `List` L=(49 42 23 80 25); the shaded node has been removed from the `List` beginning at first.

The second of these is almost surely appropriate. The first is potentially dangerous. The second delete, `delete temp`, will return to the system heap the `List` node whose element pointer pointed to the element containing 42. In a well–crafted program, nothing else should be pointing to this `List` node. The first delete, `delete (temp -> e)`, would return to the heap the storage used for the element 42. If the `List` class is to be used as part of a bigger software system, it is possible that many other structures may point to the element containing 42. Thus, executing the first `delete` would make those other pointers dangling references as discussed in Chapter 2. This could be catastrophic. The first `delete` should only be used in special cases when it is known that *every* use of the class will have no other pointers pointing to a `List` element.

The complexity of the `insert` and `remove` member functions for the linked implementation of `List`s is O(1) pointer operations after the insertion point has been found. This is because in a linked structure, neither insertion nor deletion requires moving existing elements in the `List`.

However, because a linked list provides no way to directly access the ith element, each of these member functions requires a loop to find the insert or remove point. In the general case, the complexity of this loop is O(n), where n is the size of the list. Therefore, only under the most ideal circumstances is the linked `insert` or `remove` method unusually efficient. The most important advantage, therefore, for the linked implementation of `List`s is the storage size flexibility that it offers.

Array Implementation for `List`

The array implementation for the class `List` utilizes the data members and many of the member functions that were described earlier for the array implementation of the classes `Sequence` and `Stack` (see Figure 6–21). Even though accessing a particular position in an array is fast, i.e., O(1), insertion and deletion into an array implemented `List` takes O(n) steps, where n is the size of the `List`. That is evident when we examine the `insert` and `remove` member functions for `List`s that are shown in Figures 6–46 and 6–47.

```
int List::insert(ElementPtr eptr, int i)
{
   if (this -> is_full() || i < 1 || i > (size+1))
      return 0;
   else
   {
      // move elements e[i]..e[size] down one
      for (ElementPtr* j = e + size; j >= e+i; j--)
         *j = *(j - 1);

      e[i - 1] = eptr;
      size++;
      return 1;
   }
}  // end List::insert()
```

FIGURE 6–46 C++ code for the `List` `insert` member function under the array implementation.

In each of these cases, all the elements in the array that follow the index `i` (where the insertion or deletion is to be made) must be shifted upward or downward by one position. The number of iterations of the `for`–loop in each of these cases is dependent on both the `size` of the `List` and the value of `i` relative to that of `size`. For large lists, this process can be time-consuming. It

```
int List::remove(int i)
{
    if ( (i < 1) || (i > size) )
        return 0;
    else
    {
    // Move elements e[i+1] .. e[Size] up one
        delete e[i-1];
        for (ElementPtr* j = e + i ; j < (e + size); j++)
            *(j-1) = *j;

        size--;
        return 1;
    }
} // end List::remove()
```

FIGURE 6–47   C++ code for the List remove member function under an array implementation.

should be evident that the complexity of these methods is O(*n*) in general, where *n* is the size of the list. In our array implementation, each array element is a pointer to an object; thus pointers are being shifted. If the array elements are the actual objects and if the objects are large, then the time complexity for shifting the array elements can be very prohibitive.

EXERCISES

6–10 Implement the List methods swap and store using the linked implementation strategy. Refer to an appendix to Chapter 4 of the accompanying *Laboratory Manual* for their specifications.

6–11 Draw a diagram of the insertion in the List L shown in Figure 6–42, except assume that the insertion takes place at position 5 rather than position 4. Draw another diagram assuming that the insertion will be in position 1.

6–12 Give a revised declaration of the Sequence and List classes from that shown in Figure 6–36 that would allow us to re–implement Lists using a double-linked strategy. Show how the implementation of the constructor and the methods insert and remove would be altered to support this alternative implementation strategy.

A MULTILINKED IMPLEMENTATION FOR THE Tree CLASS

Because it is a two-dimensional data structure, the tree has a more complex implementation than any of the simpler linear classes that are discussed above. As suggested at the beginning of the chapter, we have adopted a multilinked implementation strategy for the class Tree. The data members for a Tree include a pointer to the root node, and each node has the structure shown in Figure 6–48. We have omitted the data member `should_delete` because it is used only in the constructor and destructor to signal permission to delete all elements in a `Tree` object when the destructor for that `Tree` object is executed.

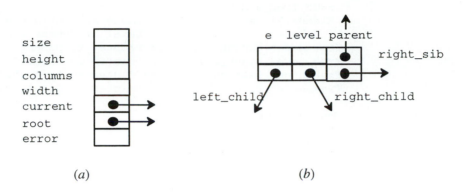

(a)   (b)

FIGURE 6–48   (a) Data members and (b) node structure for implementing the `Tree` class.

The basic declarations for implementing the `Tree` class in this way are shown in Figure 6–49. The data members also contain basic information about the status of the tree—how many nodes it has (its `size`), its `height`, the number of `columns`, and the `width` of columns when the `Tree` is displayed. Each node has four pointers: one to its parent, one to its right sibling, and two to its left and right children. Since each node in a `Tree` can have any number of children, these are connected to each other in a linked chain, as shown in Figure 6–20.

The convention for flagging the absence of a `left_child`, `right_child`, `right_sib`, or `parent` is to set the appropriate pointer to NULL. This convention helps the various member functions in their navigation among the nodes in a `Tree`. For instance, if a node's `parent` is NULL, that node must be the root, since every other node in a `Tree` has a parent. If a node's `right_sib` is NULL, it must be the youngest (most-recently-added) sibling. Furthermore, if a node's `left_child` and `right_child` are the same, the node has only one child. However, if a node's `left_child` is NULL, the node must be a leaf, since all interior vertices of trees will have non-NULL `left_child` and `right_child` pointers.

Using these conventions, an implementation of the constructor for the `Tree` class is shown in Figure 6–50. The result of declaring a `Tree` object T and thus invoking the constructor is illustrated in Figure 6–51.

The constructor `Tree_node(ElementPtr eptr)` in Figure 6–49 is used by the tree method `insert` when it executes the statement   node =

```
enum step_type {to_root, to_parent, to_left_sib, to_right_sib,
                to_l_child, to_r_child};
enum traverse_type  {breadth_first, depth_first, pre_order,
                in_order, post_order};

class Tree
{
  protected:
    struct Tree_node
     { ElementPtr e;              // value stored in the node.
       int level;                 // Level of Generation. Root = 0.
      Tree_node* parent;          // Pointer to parent (nil if Root)
      Tree_node* right_sib;       // Pointer to Right Sibling (NULL i
      Tree_node* left_child;      // Pointer to Left Child (NULL if n
      Tree_node* right_child;     // Pointer to Right Child (NULL if

       Tree_node(ElementPtr eptr)
        {e = eptr;
         parent = right_sib = left_child = right_child = NULL;
         }
       };

typedef Tree_node* tree_link;
enum tree_delete {yes_delete, no_delete};

 int size;                // Number of nodes in the tree.
 int height;              // Longest path from the root to a leaf
 int columns;             // columns for display; 0 means linear,
                          // >0 means tabular.
 int width;               // Width of each column
 Tree_node* current;      // Pointer to the current node.
 Tree_node* root;         // Pointer to the root node.
 int error;
 ....
};

typedef Tree* TreePtr;
```

FIGURE 6–49   C++ code for the node structure and data members for the `Tree` class.

new `Tree_node(elem)`. This simply allocates a new node, initializes all its tree pointers to NULL and initializes its `Element` pointer to `elem`. The effect of `node = new Tree_node(elem)` is pictured in Figure 6–52.

Once a `Tree` is created, movement from one node to another is facilitated by the `step` member function. This member function is also used by several of the other `Tree` member functions to be discussed below. It serves only to change the current node to a neighboring node or the root itself, so that some subsequent action, such as insertion or removal, can be done at that new location. This member function is shown in Figure 6–53.

Implementations of the member functions `insert` and `remove` are more involved, since the particular pointer adjustments that need to be made depend upon the location of the node to be inserted or removed (i.e., upon the value of

```
Tree::Tree() // Plant a tree.
{
     set_size(0);               // Nobody in the family.
     height = -1;
     columns = 0;               // Output has nested parentheses
     width = MAXMORPHEME;       // and MaxMorpheme chars per column
     root = NULL;
     set_current(NULL);
     set_error( FALSE );
     should_delete = yes_delete;

}
```

FIGURE 6–50   C++ code for the constructor for the Tree class.

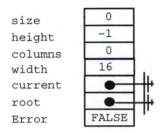

size	0
height	-1
columns	0
width	16
current	●
root	●
Error	FALSE

FIGURE 6–51   Values of T's data members after declaring T to be an object of class Tree.

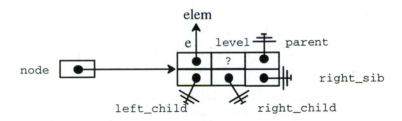

FIGURE 6–52   Effect of node = new Tree_node(elem); a new Tree node is created and initialized.

the current node pointer). The implementation details of insert are shown in Figure 6–54. Note that this method uses the statement node = new Tree_node(elem) described above. By convention, insert(elem) always inserts the new element elem as the right-hand (youngest) child of the current node. If the current node is a leaf, insert(elem) inserts elem as an only child. The remaining statements in this function establish the value of the node, compute its level in the Tree, and update the Tree's height and size.

```
void Tree::step(step_type to_where)
{
    // Move the current node pointer within the tree.
    tree_link temp;
    set_error( FALSE );
    switch (to_where)
    {
        case to_root:
            set_current( root );
            break;

        case to_parent:
            if ( (current != NULL) && (current->parent != NULL) )
            set_current( current->parent );
            else
            set_error( TRUE );
         break;

        case to_l_child:
            if (current->left_child != NULL)
            set_current ( current->left_child );
            else
            set_error( TRUE   );
         break;

        case to_r_child:
            if (current->right_child != NULL)
            set_current ( current->right_child );
            else
            set_error( TRUE );
         break;

        case to_right_sib:
            if (current->right_sib != NULL)
            set_current ( current->right_sib );
            else
            set_error( TRUE );
         break;

        case to_left_sib:
            if (current->parent != NULL)
              if (current->parent->left_child != current)
                { //search for left sibling through the parent
                temp = current->parent->left_child;
                while (temp->right_sib != current)
                  temp = temp->right_sib;
                set_current( temp );
                }
              else
              set_error( TRUE );
            else
              set_error( TRUE );
         break;
    } // switch
}
```

FIGURE 6–53   C++ code for implementation of the `step` member function for the `Tree` class.

```
void Tree::insert(ElementPtr elem)
{tree_link node;
 // Insert a new node into the tree, either as the right child}
 // of the current node or as the root of an empty tree.
 set_error( FALSE );
 if ((current != NULL) || (size == 0))
  { node = new Tree_node(elem);

    // New children are the youngest, so they may have only left
    // (older) siblings, but no right siblings or children.
    node->parent = current;
    node->level = -1;

    if ((size > 0) && (current != NULL))
     { // tree is nonempty
       node->level = current->level + 1;
       // Tell the previously youngest child about its new
       // sibling and establish the new sibling as the youngest.
       if (current->right_child != NULL)
         {
           current->right_child->right_sib = node;  // Sib -> Right
           current->right_child = node;     // parent -> right_child
         }
       else    // only child
         {
           current->left_child = node;      // parent -> left_child
           current->right_child = node;     // parent -> right_child
         }
     }
   else if (size == 0)   // insertion into an empty tree;
     {
       node->level = 0;
      set_current(node);
       root = current;
     }
     else
      set_error( TRUE );

   if (node->level > height)
     // new node is farthest from the root
     height = node->level;
      set_size(size + 1);
   }
  else
    set_error( TRUE );
 }
```

FIGURE 6–54   C++ code for implementation of the `insert` member function for the `Tree` class.

Example 6.13   Consider the insertion shown in Figure 6–55, where we want to insert a new child G into the `Tree`

```
(A (C E F) (B D))
```

assuming that C is the current node. Note that the entire insertion is made by the establishment of three pointers: two back and forth between the new node and its parent, and one between the new node and the sibling on its left (its older sibling).

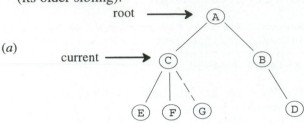

(a)

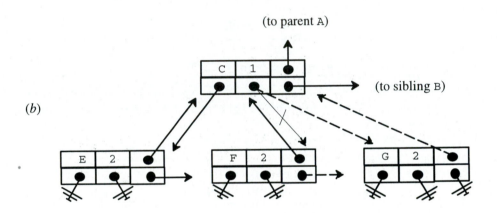

(b)

FIGURE 6–55   Insertion of G as the new child of C in the Tree (A (C E F) (B D)) *(a)* schematically, and *(b)* showing actual pointers.

The member function remove removes the current node, along with the entire subtree for which it is the root. If the current node is a leaf, remove therefore deletes only a single node. The only discriminations that need to be made are among three cases (which may overlap):

1. The node to be removed is a left child, in which case its parent's left_child pointer must be adjusted.
2. The node is a right child, in which case its parent's right_child pointer must be adjusted.
3. The node has a left sibling, in which case that sibling's right_sib pointer must be adjusted to skip over the node.

In addition to these cases, remove must systematically visit all the nodes in the subtree below the current node and remove them one by one, before finally remove the current node. Because this process requires a traversal of the subtree, we shall return to it after we have discussed the mechanics of tree traversal.

Tree Traversal and Search Since they are two-dimensional structures, trees can be searched in a variety of different ways; sometimes visiting only a few nodes, and at other times visiting some nodes over and over again. Whenever we search a tree in such a way that each node is visited exactly once, we are said to be "traversing" the tree.

Definition When we visit each node of a tree (or subtree) in such a way that every node is visited once and only once, this is called a *traversal* of the tree (subtree).

Two common strategies for traversing trees are called *breadth-first* traversal and *depth-first* traversal. (In the case of binary trees, the depth-first traversal is identical to a *postorder* traversal. However, the breadth-first traversal is not identical to the *preorder* traversal for binary trees.)

As its name suggests, the breadth-first strategy reaches broadly across a tree, visiting each node at a given level i before proceeding to the next level $i + 1$. The depth-first strategy reaches deeply as far as possible to the leftmost leaf, and then to the next-leftmost leaf, and so forth before retreating to the next higher level.

Example 6.14 The breadth-first, depth-first (postorder), and preorder traversal methods are illustrated in Figure 6–56 for the tree (A (B C D E) (F G)). The nodes are numbered in the order that they are visited.

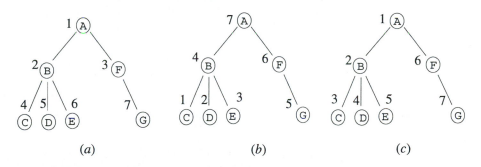

(a)   (b)   (c)

FIGURE 6–56 (a) Breadth-first, (b) depth-first (postorder), and (c) preorder traversal for the tree (A (B C D E) (F G)).

Implementation of the method search(x) requires that the Tree be traversed one node at a time, continuing until either a match for x is found or the Tree is fully traversed without a match.

To help implement a complete breadth-first or depth-first Tree traversal, the member function traverse has been designed. Its function is simply to move from the current node to the next node in the breadth-first or depth-first sequence. For instance, if the current node in the Tree, t, of Figure 6–56*b* is B, the single invocation

```
t.traverse(depth_first)
```

will change the current node to G. A complete display of the elements in a depth-first traversal of a Tree object, t, is achieved by the following loop, which begins with setting current to NULL.

```
t.set_current(NULL);
t.set_error(FALSE);
while ( !t.get_error() )
  {
    (t.current) -> e -> display();
    t.traverse(depth_first);
  }
```

A partial implementation of the traverse member function is shown in Figure 6–57. For the depth–first search, note that, after the first node has been reached, two alternative directions for moving to the next node are possible; to (the leftmost child of) a right sibling or to the parent. If neither of these moves is possible, we must be at the root, so the flag Error is set to true to indicate completion of the traversal. Implementation of the preorder traversal involves similar considerations.

Returning to the search method, its implementation is shown in Figure 6–58. Its purpose is solely to reset the current node pointer to the first node whose Element matches the value of the parameter elem, using a depth-first search strategy. It follows the specifications for search, especially in the case where the argument elem is not anywhere in the tree. Note that this case leaves the current node unchanged from its position before the search began.

This implementation is made simple by the presence of the traverse member function that was introduced above. Alternatively, the search member function could have been implemented recursively, using a strategy similar to that which was introduced for the traversal of binary trees.

Tree graft and remove Member functions   While insertion allows a single node to be added to a Tree, the graft and remove member functions allow an entire subtree to be appended to or removed from another Tree. These actions are illustrated in Figures 6–59 and 6–60. In the case of T.graft(B), notice that B is appended to T and simultaneously loses its own identity as a result. In the case of T.remove(T.get_current()), notice that the entire subtree whose root is the current node in T loses its identity.

These two methods are useful in situations where an entire subtree should be attached to, or detached from, a particular tree. We encountered one such situation in the ExpressionParser program in the previous chapter.

```
void Tree::traverse(traverse_type how)
{
    // Starting with the current node, move the current node pointer
    // to the next node in a pre-order or depth-first traversal.
    // For a complete traversal, current must be initialized to NULL.
    set_error( FALSE );
    switch (how)
    { case depth_first:
      case post_order:
        if (current == NULL)
          if (size > 0)
          { step(to_root);
            while (! is_leaf() )
                step(to_l_child);
          }
          else
            set_error( TRUE );
        else if (current == root)       // done if now at the root
          set_error( TRUE );
          else if (current->right_sib != NULL)   // look for right sibling
          { step(to_right_sib);
            while (! is_leaf() )                  // look for left child's leaf
                step(to_l_child);
          }
          else
            step(to_parent);
        break;

      // case breadth_first:  implementation is an exercise
      case pre_order:
        if (current == NULL)
          if (size == 0)
            set_error( TRUE );
          else
            step(to_root);
        else
        { if (is_leaf())               // current is a leaf
            if (current->right_sib != NULL)
              {step(to_right_sib);}
            else if (current->parent != NULL)
            {
              step(to_parent);
              if (current != root)
              { //look for a higher nonvisited rightsib
                while ((current != root) && (current->right_sib == NULL))
                  set_current ( current->parent );
                if (current->right_sib != NULL)
                  set_current( current->right_sib );
                else
                  set_error( TRUE );
              }
              else
               set_error( TRUE );
              }
            else
              set_error( TRUE );
          else                                   // current is not a leaf
              step(to_l_child);
        }
        break;
    } //case
}
```

FIGURE 6–57   C++ code for the `traverse` member function of the class `Tree`.

```
int Tree::search(Element* elem)
{
    // Search for elem.  If found, go to the node with elem and r
    // Otherwise, don't move anywhere and return FALSE.
    tree_link tempnode;
    int found = FALSE;

    // Record the current position.
    tempnode = current;

    // Start searching at the root.
    set_current( NULL );
    set_error( FALSE );
    traverse(depth_first);
    while ((! found) && (! get_error()))
    {
    if (!strcmp(current->e->get_class(),elem->get_class()))
       if ( *(current->e) == *elem )
          found = TRUE;
       else
          traverse(depth_first);
     else
       traverse(depth_first);
    }

    if (found)
     return TRUE;
    else
     {
       // Go back to where we were.
       set_current ( tempnode );
       return FALSE;
     }
} // TreeSearch
```

FIGURE 6–58 C++ code for implementation of the search member function for the class Tree, using depth-first traversal.

The implementation of graft is shown in Figure 6–61. Graft proceeds by attaching b's root as the current node's right_child. Other accommodations are made for the special case where the Tree is empty. The details of the particular graft illustrated in Figure 6–59 appear in Figure 6–62.

Implementation of remove involves a recursive series of leaf removals, beginning with the leftmost leaf below the current node. As leaves are removed, parent and sibling pointers are updated. The order in which these nodes are visited and removed is a *depth-first* traversal. Thus, for the Tree illustrated in Figure 6–60, node C is first to be removed, followed by node B. Finally, the current node is reset to become the parent of the last node removed. In our example, the new current node would be node D. Details of the remove method are shown in Figure 6–63. In this code, we chose to remove both Tree nodes and Elements pointed to by Tree nodes. As mentioned in the discus-

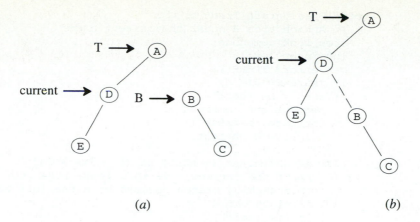

(a)   (b)

FIGURE 6–59   (b) The result of T.graft(B) with (a) the trees B = (B C) and T = (A (D E)), assuming that the current node is D.

sion of the List member function remove, the latter is dangerous if other objects could point to the same elements.

Specialization of the Tree Member Functions for the BinaryTree Class

The BinaryTree class could be built as a totally new class. Here we will consider the option of making the BinaryTree class a subclass of the Tree class, and therefore inheriting member functions from the class Tree. However, some of these member functions must be re–coded in order to make special provision for the dummy nodes that were described for binary trees in a previous section.

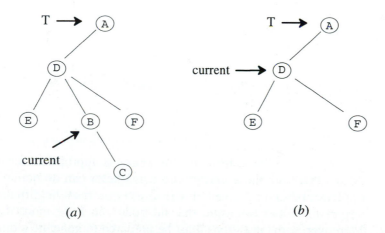

(a)   (b)

FIGURE 6–60   (b) The result of T.remove(T.get_current()), assuming (a) the Tree T = (A (D E (B C) F)) and the current node is B.

```
      void Tree::graft(Tree* b)
    { // Attach tree B under the current node.
      tree_link tempnode;
      int insertlevel;
      set_error( FALSE );
      if (size == 0)
        { root = b->root;
          set_current( b->root );
          set_size( b->size );
          height = b->height;
        }
      else if ((current != NULL) && (b->size > 0))
        {    // If the current node is a leaf,  the root of the
             // attaching branch becomes both the left and the
             // right child.
          if (is_leaf())
            current->left_child = b->root;    // parent -> left_child
        else   // Otherwise the Right Child is now second to right.
          current->right_child->right_sib = b->root;
               // Sib -> right_child
        current->right_child = b->root;
        b->root->parent = current;     // parent <- right_child
          // Traverse the grafted subtree and adjust all
          // the node levels.
        insertlevel = current->level + 1;
        b->set_current( NULL );
        do
        { b->traverse(depth_first);
          b->current->level = b->current->level + insertlevel;
        } while (!( b->current->parent == current));
          // Now B->current = B->root again
          // Recalculate the Tree's size and height.
        set_size( size + b->size );
        if (height < insertlevel + b->height )
          height = insertlevel + b->height;
      b->set_delete(no_delete); // Don't delete b's elements
        delete b;
        }
      else if (b->size > 0)
        set_error( TRUE );
    }
```

FIGURE 6–61   C++ code for implementation of the graft member
function for the class Tree.

For instance, the constructor for Trees is appropriate for BinaryTrees as
is, and therefore the BinaryTree constructor can do nothing. However, the
implementation of insert in BinaryTrees must be different from its coun-
terpart in Trees to ensure that no node can have more than two children.
Moreover, some insertions must be prepared to generate a dummy node in the
special case where the insertion of a right_child is needed for a node that
has no left_child. To distinguish these, the method insert for the class
BinaryTree will only insert a new node at the root of an empty tree, a new

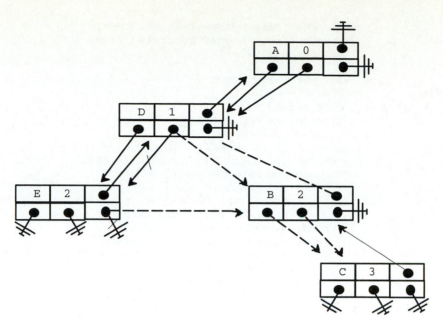

FIGURE 6–62   Details of a graft.

`left_child` for a leaf node or a node with empty `left_child`, or a new `right_child` for a node that currently has only a `left_child`. This limited re–implementation of `insert` for the `BinaryTree` class is shown in Figure 6–64.

In situations where a new `right_child` is to be inserted for a leaf node, or a new `left_child` is to be inserted for a node that has no `left_child`, the special methods `insert_left` and `insert_right` are required. In-sert_left and `insert_right` can use the method `insert` as a tool. Their implementations are left as an exercise.

Implementations of several other `Tree` member functions must also be spe-cialized for `BinaryTrees`. These include `step`, `get`, `traverse`, `search`, and `display`. Readers are encouraged to think about the special constraints that `BinaryTrees` place on the more general implementations that are dis-cussed for `Trees`.

EXERCISES

6–13 If we wanted to save a copy of the `Tree`, B, before it is grafted to the `Tree`, T, we could imagine a generally useful member function `B.Copy(C)` that would make a copy of the *entire* `Tree`, B, and identify it as the new `Tree`, C. Write specifications for the new member func-tion, `copy`, and then develop its implementation using the data members and node structure for `Trees` given in this chapter.

```
        void Tree::remove(tree_link delete_me)
        { static long unsigned recursion_level = 0;
          recursion_level++;
          if (size == 0)
              set_error( TRUE );
          else
          {set_error( FALSE );
           if (delete_me == NULL)
             delete_me = root;
               // is it a leaf?
           while (delete_me->left_child != NULL)
             remove(delete_me->left_child);
               // This node is now a leaf, so okay to remove.
               // If not the root (i.e. a parent exists) make sure
               // its left and right children pointers remain okay.
           if (delete_me->parent != NULL)
            {tree_link p = delete_me->parent;
             if (p->left_child == p->right_child) // only child
               { p->left_child = NULL;
                 p->right_child = NULL;
                }
               // not only child, see if its leftmost.
             else if (p->left_child == delete_me)
                 // is leftmost, so change parent's left_child pointer
               p->left_child = delete_me->right_sib;
               else
                 // not leftmost, locate the current node's
                 // *LEFT* sibling
                {for (tree_link left_sib = p->left_child;
                  left_sib->right_sib != delete_me;
                  left_sib = left_sib->right_sib) {  }
                    // tell left sibling to point to current's
                    // right sibling
                 left_sib->right_sib = delete_me->right_sib;

                    // if current was previous right child, make its
                    // left_sib right_child
                 if (p->right_child == delete_me)
                    p->right_child = left_sib;
                 }
             }
             if (delete_me->parent == NULL)
               current = root = NULL;  // empty tree;
             else if (current == delete_me)
               step(to_parent);
             delete delete_me->e;    // potentially dangerous
             delete delete_me;
             size --;
           }
          recursion_level--;
           if (recursion_level == 0)
             height = max_depth(this);
        } // remove
```

FIGURE 6–63 C++ code for implementation of the `remove` member function for the class `Tree`.

```
void BinaryTree::insert(ElementPtr elem)
// Insert a new node into the tree, either as the left child
// of the current node (if current is a leaf), as the right
// child of the current node (if current has a single left
// child), or as the root of an empty tree.
{ tree_link node;
  error = FALSE;
  if (size == 0)
    { // tree is empty, insert as root
      node = new Tree_node(elem);
      node->level = 0;
      current = node;
      root = current;
    }
  else if (current != NULL )
    {
    if (is_leaf() ||
        (current->left_child == current->right_child))
      {      // current has no children or has a
             // non-empty left_child
      node = new Tree_node(elem);
      node->parent = current;
      node->level = current->level + 1;
      if (is_leaf() )
           // if it has no children add to the left
        {current->left_child = node;
         current->right_child = node;
         }
        else // add to the right
          { current->right_child = node;
           current->left_child->right_sib = node;
           }
      }
     else if (empty_leaf(current->left_child))
            // if left_child is empty
      {current = current->left_child;
       delete store(elem);
       node = current;
       step(to_parent);
       }
       else
       {error = TRUE;
        cout << "attempt to add a third child \
                 to a binary tree\n";
        }
    }
    else
    {error = TRUE;
     cout << "Error: Tree size != 0 but root = NULL\n";
     }
    if (!error )
    {  if (node->level > height )
       // new node is farthest from the root
       height = node->level;
       size++;
    }
}
```

FIGURE 6–64   C++ code for limiting the options for insertion into a BinaryTree.

6–14 Illustrate the `remove` member function by:

    a. Showing all the relevant pointer adjustments that are required for removing the node D from the `Tree (A (B C D) (E F))`.

    b. Showing the effects of removing the node C from this `Tree`.

    c. Showing the effects of removing the subtree `(B C D)`.

6–15 Implement a recursive member function to perform breadth-first traversal for `Trees`, using a strategy similar to the one given earlier for binary trees.

6–16 Consider the implementation of an iterative algorithm to do a preorder traversal of binary trees. To what extent can such an algorithm be built by reusing the code for the iterative method that was presented in this chapter for `Trees`? Explain any differences that would have to be accommodated because of the need for dummy nodes in a binary tree.

6–17 What are the particular cases where `T.insert(x)` will cause `T.Error` to become true, for an arbitrary `BinaryTree`, `T`, and `Element` pointer, `x`?

6–18 Implement the member functions `insert_left` and `insert_right` for `BinaryTrees`, using the specifications given for them in an appendix to Chapter 5 of the accompanying *Laboratory Manual*.

6–19 Design and implement a function `T.IsVacant(Where)` which, for an arbitrary `BinaryTree`, `T`, would return the value `TRUE` or `FALSE` depending on whether the current node's `left_child` (`Where=to_l_child`) or `right_child` (`Where=to_r_child`) is absent or present, respectively. What sort of use would such a function have in the implementation of the other member functions for `Binary-Trees`, such as `insert`, `insert_left`, and `insert_right`?

6–20 What does the member function, `T.display`, do when `T` is a `Binary-Tree`? In particular, how does it display the dummy nodes on the screen? Suggest a modification of this member function that would skip the `display` of a node if it were a dummy node.

6–21 Consider the creation of an independent class `BinaryTree`. That is, do not make it a subclass of any other class. Design the class, give specifications for its member functions and implement the class.

VERIFICATION AND COMPLEXITY OF THE IMPLEMENTATIONS

In this section, we take an *analytical* look at these classes—`List`, `Stack`, `Queue`, and `Tree`—and their member function implementations. That is, we are interested in assuring that the member function implementations are correct, and we are interested in estimating their complexity. For the former, we shall use the informal verification methods developed in Chapter 2, and for the latter we shall examine the dominant segments of code and develop average case measures of complexity for various implementation strategies.

Verification and Complexity of the `Stack` Member Functions

Correctness of our implementations of the member functions `Stack.push` and `Stack.pop` can be established by examining the bodies of these member functions to assure that they satisfy their respective postconditions for every possible `Stack` that satisfies their preconditions. For instance, we'll look at the code for `Stack.push` that appears in Figure 6–65, where its lines are numbered on the left to make the description of the verification easier.

```
     int Stack::push(ElementPtr eptr)
       {
1      if (this -> is_full())
2         return 0;
3      else
          {
4         e[size++] = eptr;
5         return 1;
          }
       }   // Stack::push()

// Used: To add a new element onto the top of the stack.
// Pre:  S = (e[1] e[2] ... e[n]) and size = n
// Post: n < MAXELEMENTS and size = n+1 and
//         S = (e[1] e[2] ... e[n] eptr) and result = 1
//       or n = MAXELEMENTS and result = 0
```

FIGURE 6–65   Preparing to verify the `push` method for the class `Stack`.

To verify this method, we note that lines 4 and 5 are executed only if the `Stack`, S, is not full—that is, $n < MAXELEMENTS$ so that there is room to add one more element at the end of the array. In this case, execution of line 4 guarantees that the new element, `eptr`, gets assigned to the top of the `Stack` and that the `size` of the `Stack` increases by 1. Recall that in the array implementation of the class `Stack`, we have used the convention that additions and deletions always take place at the right end of the active portion of the array (recall Figure 6–16). Also recall that since C++ starts all array indexing at 0, the `ith` element in our specification, `e[i]`, is really stored in the implementation in location `e[i-1]`.

Complexity of this method is $O(1)$, since exactly three steps are executed (lines 1, 4, and 5) in the normal case where the precondition is satisfied. Complexity of the other `Stack` member functions is either $O(1)$ or $O(n)$, depending on whether they require traversal of the entire `Stack` for their completion. For instance, `top` and `pop` are both $O(1)$, since their execution always requires a constant number of steps. However, `display` is $O(n)$, since all n entries in the `Stack` are output.

Verification and Complexity of the `Queue` Member Functions

The complexities of the basic `Queue` member functions `enter` and `remove` are also O(1). A total of four steps is needed for the `enter` member function, while a total of five steps is needed for `remove` (lines 1, 3, 4, 5, and 6 in Figure 6–66), under normal circumstances where their preconditions are satisfied.

Verification of the `Queue` member function implementations can be done by making similar refinements to its pre- and postconditions as were made above for `Stacks`, and then systematically observing that the postconditions are satisfied under all cases. Suppose we wish to verify the `remove` member function, which is rewritten in Figure 6–66 with its full specifications and line numbers added for clarification.

```
    ElementPtr Queue::remove()
1   { if (this -> is_empty())
2       return NULL;
    else
3     { int tempint = f;
4       f = (f + 1) % MAXELEMENTS;
5         size--;
6       return e[tempint];
      }
    }   // end Queue::remove()

// Used: To remove an object from the front of the queue.
// Pre:   Q = (e[f] e[next] ... e[r]) and size = n
// Post: (size = 0 and result  = NULL)
//        or ( n > 0 and Q = (e[next] ... e[r]) and size = n-1
//             and result = e[f] and f = (old f + 1) % MAXELEMENTS)
```

FIGURE 6–66   C++ code for implementation of the `remove` member function of the `Queue` class.

Here, recall that the circular array implementation is used for `Queues`, so that the entry at the front of the `Queue` (the one that has been there the longest) is about to leave, and this entry is at the left-hand end of a contiguous sequence of entries in the array. Also, that sequence wraps around to the beginning of the array, as shown in Figure 6–17, whenever the right end of the array is reached by a series of new entries. Whenever the length n of the `Queue`, Q, is nonzero, therefore, the value of $Q.f$ is incremented modulo the size of the array (MAX-ELEMENTS) so that the departing entry is no longer within the range of indices $Q.f$, $Q.f+1$, ..., $Q.r$. This departure is guaranteed by line 4 in the `remove` member function. Line 5, in turn, decrements the size of the `Queue` to reflect that it now has one entry less than it had before the invocation.

Other `Queue` member functions can be verified using similar observations.

Verification and Complexity of the `List` Member Functions

To verify the `List` member functions, we need to take similar steps to refine their respective preconditions and postconditions and number their lines to facilitate the analysis. For example, consider the `insert` member function that is refined in this way in Figure 6–67.

```
     int List::insert(ElementPtr eptr, int i)
     {
1      if ( i < 1 || i > (size+1))
2        return 0;
       else
         {
         // find pointer to node that points to position i
3          seqnode* ptr=first;
4          for (int j = 1; j < i; j++)
5            ptr = ptr->next;

6          seqnode* temp = ptr -> next; //temp points to ith node
7          seqnode* newnode = new seqnode;
8          ptr->next = newnode;
9          newnode->next = temp;
10         newnode->e = eptr;
11         size++;
12         return 1;
         }
     }   // end List::insert()

// Function: List::insert(ElementPtr eptr, int i);
// Used: Inserts eptr in the i-th position in list L.
// Pre:   L = (e[1] e[2] ... e[n]), size = n and 1<=i<=n+1
// Post: (i is out of range and result = 0) or
//    L = (e[1] ... e[i-1] eptr e[i] ... e[n]) and
//    (size = n + 1) and (result = 1)
```

FIGURE 6–67   Verification setup for the List Insert member function.

Here, three different cases must be considered; an insertion at the head of a List, an insertion at the end of a nonempty List, and an insertion in between two elements of a nonempty List. In all three cases, we need to show that the integrity of the linked chain is preserved, and a new node with the item eptr is inserted into the proper location within that chain. Note first that lines 3–12 are executed for any legitimate value of i. If i is out of range, 0 is returned (lines 1 and 2) and the function terminates. However, under normal circumstances, the for–loop (lines 4,5) sets ptr to point to the i–1st node in the chain (the predecessor of the node to be inserted), the new node is allocated, and its item field is assigned the value of eptr.

Now consider the case where the insertion is made at the head of the List. This happens when i=1. Line 3 sets ptr to the header node whose next pointer points to the first element of the List. Since i=1, the for–loop is not entered and at line 6 ptr still points to the header cell so temp is made to point to the old first element in the List. Line 7 gets a new node. Line 8 makes the next pointer of the header point to the new node (effectively making the new node the first node in the List). Line 9 makes the new node's next pointer point to the former first node, and line 10 sets new node's element pointer to eptr. Finally line 11 increments size. This properly inserts the new node at the beginning of the chain.

In the case where the insertion is made at the end of a nonempty `List`, the `for`–loop guarantees that `ptr` points to the last node in the `List` at step 6. So `temp` gets `NULL`. Line 8 makes the old last node point to the `newnode` and line 9 properly makes the new node's `next` pointer `NULL`. The case where the insertion is made between two elements of a nonempty `List` is illustrated in Figure 6–42, where we see that the (`i-1`)st item's `next` pointer is redirected to the new node. The new node's `next` pointer is directed toward the old `i`th item. In each of these cases, `eptr` is inserted as the item in the new node and the size of the `List` is incremented.

Thus, each of the three cases effectively inserts a new node into the linked chain and maintains the relevant pointers and indices correctly. We have thus given an informal argument that the postcondition for `insert` is satisfied.

We have already begun to discuss the complexity of the `List` methods in a previous section, pointing out the differences that occur when comparing array and linked strategies. To reiterate, the complexity of `insert` and `remove` in the linked implementation of `Lists` is O(1), or constant, AFTER the insertion or deletion point has been obtained. Finding this point takes O(n) pointer replacements. For the array implementation, the complexity of insertion or removal is O(n) array element moves.

It is important to consider the effect of an implementation strategy on the complexity of methods that are implemented for any particular class. For instance, the linked implementation of `Lists` might have been replaced by an array implementation, with the hope of improving the efficiency of some of its member functions. For instance, the `retrieve(i)` method, upon which many list applications depend, can be implemented in O(1) complexity for the array implementation, where it is O(n) for the linked implementation.

Another significant question surrounds the impact of different linear list implementation strategies on the performance of list sorting algorithms in general. Recall from Chapter 3 that `quicksort` could sort a randomly ordered array of 5000 integers in 0.17 seconds on a Sun Sparc ELC. Using `Sortlist` from Chapter NO TAG to `quicksort` a list of 5000 randomly ordered integer objects took 0.47 seconds on the same machine with the array implementation of `Lists`. But with the linked implementation of `Lists`, sorting the same list of 5000 integer objects using the same `Sortlist` code on the same machine took 560 seconds (more than 9 minutes). These results are summarized in in Table 6–1.

TABLE 6–1   RUN TIMES (SECONDS) FOR `quicksort` FOR A LIST OF 5000 INTEGERS

Simple Array	Array Implementation of a `List` of `IntObjs`	Linked Implementation of a `List` of `IntObjs`
0.17	0.47	560.0

As the table suggests, the use of an array for implementing linear lists yields significant performance gains, even though this practice loses flexibility in storage utilization.

In general, the array implementation is ideally suited to applications in which the number of insertions and removes is relatively small, and hence the overall list size is relatively stable and predictable in advance. As insertion and deletion activity grows, it may make more sense to use the linked implementation. Even here, however, it is important to realize that *all* of these member functions have O(n) complexity in cases where the invocations are not centered on a particular location in the List.

Thus, when choosing an implementation strategy for Lists, one must examine the application with these considerations in mind. The choice of a strategy will vary with the number and locality of List insertions and removals, as well as the expected variability in the overall size of the list during a run of the program. Moreover, if the list size n is relatively small, the choice of implementation strategy is really insignificant with respect to its overall impact on the efficiency of the application. For large database applications, hash structures and balanced binary trees are appropriate.

EXERCISES

6–22 The member function, L.empty, has the role of deleting all the nodes of a List. Implement this member function, being sure your implementation frees all nodes that had been allocated for the elements of L.

6–23 Using the same techniques shown for insert, verify the member function remove. That is, show that the postconditions are satisfied by the procedure's body whenever its preconditions are met.

6–24 Can the BinarySearch member function be applied to the linked implementation for Lists? If so, how? If not, why not?

6–25 Verify the retrieve(i) member function that is defined for the linked implementation of the List class.

6–26 Show that the complexity of the retrieve(i) member function in the linked implementation of Lists has $O(n)$ complexity in the average case, by counting the number of steps executed as a function of the List size n.

6–27 Verify the implementation of the Queue member function remove.

6–28 For a binary tree, consider defining and implementing a member function IsVacant(ToWhere), which determines whether or not the current node's ToWhere element (to_l_child, etc.) is vacant. Now implement functions that determine each of the following characteristics for the current node of a BinaryTree, T:

  a. IsLeaf determines whether the current node is a leaf.
  b. IsNonLeaf determines whether the current node is a nonleaf.

   c.   `IsRoot` determines whether the current node is the root.

6–29 A binary tree is said to be *balanced* if it has a minimum height for its size. That is, it has no node that could be relocated elsewhere in the tree that would reduce the height of the tree. Define and implement an member function, `IsBalanced`, that would determine whether an arbitrary `BinaryTree` is balanced or not. What is the complexity of this member function's implementation? Explain.

6–30 Using `quicksort` to order 5000 `IntegerObjects`, the difference between the array implementation of `Lists` and the linked implementation is tremendous. By considering the two different implementations of `Lists` and the code for `Sortlist`, explain in some detail the reasons for this discrepancy. Discuss ways to design a `quicksort` member function especially for linked `Lists` that might reduce the discrepancy.

6–31 Implement and test the `quicksort` designed for linked `Lists` from Exercise 6–30 above.

SUMMARY

In this chapter, we have examined various alternative implementation strategies for some of the basic classes in computing. We have learned that different strategies are ideal under different assumptions about their use. For instance, if the maximum size of a `List`, `Stack`, or `Queue` is known and its size does not vary greatly from one application to another, then the simple array implementation strategy may be preferable on the grounds of its efficiency. On the other hand, efficiency is not lost in the linked implementation of `Stacks` and `Queues`, due to the restricted ways in which an individual element is stored and retrieved. For `BinaryTrees`, a similar tradeoff between array and linked implementations is apparent. For general `Trees`, however, a robust implementation should embrace a multilinked strategy such as the one used in this chapter.

Reuse is a strong principle reinforced in this chapter. We considered the complex task of implementing and verifying the member functions of a class as a separate exercise from its various potential and known applications. Once its member functions are defined, the class plays the role of a language extension—the overall organization of application programs that use it thus becomes less cluttered, and the solution can often be clearly laid out using only a modest number of documentary comments. When the member functions of a class are well-defined, application programs can be written more easily and clearly.

The second principle that this chapter clarified is that separating the implementation of a class from its definition allows different, competing implementations to be developed independently. It also allows an implementation to be used by different applications, thus saving significant amounts of software development effort as a result. Much of this saving comes indirectly; that is from the reliability derived from the use of rigorous standards of verification—both empirical and analytical.

History tells us that, if such principles are not systematically followed, software developers will essentially start every new application with an empty software library, thus redeveloping and reverifying common methods (such as the ones which implement the linear `List` member functions) redundantly.

CHAPTER 7

OPERATING SYSTEMS AND SOFTWARE DESIGN

After introducing the principles of software system design and computational complexity, previous chapters of this text developed the classes List, Stack, Queue, and Tree. We continued with the design of a suite of member functions for each of these classes, along with a study of their design, implementation, and verification. These classes have thereby become the building blocks for the software design methodology that was proposed in Chapter 1. The utility of these tools is, as we might sense, directly proportional to the size and complexity of the software development project where they are used.

We need to begin to experience the use of these tools in designing and implementing a large program. A fundamental and profound example of such a software development project is the design, implementation, and testing of a computer's operating system. The purpose of this chapter is to provide an introduction to what an operating system is and does; how such a system might be structured and subdivided; and finally, how one might approach the design and implementation of some components of an operating system.

The chapter begins by tracing the historical evolution of operating systems, paying special attention to how the components of today's operating system have evolved out of the practical needs of users and the physical hardware technological advances that have occurred over the years. Next, we consider how the design of an operating system might be structured, and what resulting component parts need to be designed and implemented. These principles and concepts are then illustrated with a discussion and description of the UNIX operating system, which is one of the the most important operating systems in use today.

The remainder of the chapter is devoted to a more detailed discussion of several key aspects of operating systems design and implementation. First, we look at the concept of a *process*—a program in execution—as the most basic unit of account in an operating system, and describe the components of the operating system responsible for facilitating the execution of processes. This leads to a discussion of the issues of scheduling and allocation of the computer's central processing unit. Next, memory management, the scheduling and allocation of use of the system's memory, is considered. Finally, we consider briefly some of the problems involved in facilitating and managing the use of the system's peripheral (input/output) devices.

To be sure, we are not attempting to provide a complete discussion of operating systems; that study would involve at least a whole semester course. But a limited examination of some essential features of operating systems provides an opportunity to appreciate the tools we have created and their utility in the design and implementation of a large system. Moreover, we hope to convey some of the excitement of systems programming—that branch of programming that deals with design and implementation of software which runs most directly on, and facilitates the use of, the computer itself. Finally, the techniques we present will be useful in a wide variety of important applications areas, such as database systems and simulation systems.

WHAT IS AN OPERATING SYSTEM?

So far, most of the computer programs we have encountered—in textbook examples, in laboratory projects, and in programming exercises—have been been prepared and executed in some sort of a Pascal or C++ environment. That is, we used an editor to input and modify our original program, a compiler (or interpreter) to translate the source program to an object (or binary) code, a loader to place the object code into memory for execution, and some sort of controlling program to monitor the progress of the program's execution and to help with difficult matters such as the particulars of input-output codes.

This contrasts sharply with the process of programming directly in the machine language of the computer, as readers may have experienced in other courses. In fact, if it were necessary to program in a machine language environment, the detailed knowledge of the hardware and the extreme effort that would be required to successfully complete even the simplest of programs would ensure that few programs would be written at all and consequently the computer may well have become a seldom-used artifact.

In fact, what high-level language programmers and most computer users deal with is really a *virtual computer*. The actual software bridge, which plays the role of the interlocutor between the actual hardware and the computer user's environment, is known as the *operating system*.

Functionally, the computer system we use is made up of elements that fall into three classes. First, the *computer hardware* itself includes the central processing unit, the memory, the arithmetic-logic unit, and the various bulk storage, I/O, and peripheral devices. The second component of the computing system includes the *systems programs*—the software elements which facilitate the use of the computer by programmers and problem solvers—programs like the C++ compiler, the editor, the loader, and the operating system. Finally, the computing system is rounded out by the provision of *application programs* specifically tailored for certain tasks—programs like word processors, database systems, spreadsheet programs, and so forth. Thus, a computer system can be portrayed as shown in Figure 7–1.

It is the second component—the systems programs—that interests us here. Systems programs are programs written for direct execution on the computer

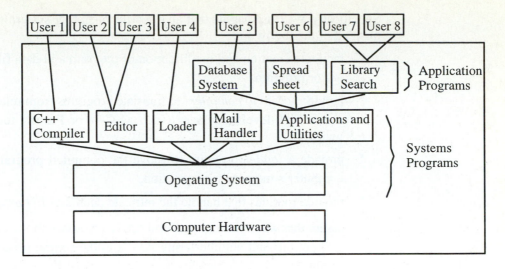

FIGURE 7–1   Conceptual view of a computing system.

hardware in order to make the power of the computer fully and efficiently accessible to applications programmers and other computer users. Systems programming is different from application programming because it requires an intimate knowledge of the computer hardware as well as of the end users' needs. Moreover, systems programs are often larger and more complex than application programs, although that is not always the case. Since systems programs provide the foundation upon which application programs are built, it is most important that systems programs be reliable, efficient, and correct. For these reasons, designing and writing systems programs is difficult and, consequently, success as a systems programmer requires knowledge of, and use of, all of the software development tools that have been introduced so far. This chapter is designed, in part, to make this assertion clear. We begin by characterizing the notion of a computer operating system and some of its component parts.

While there is no universally agreed upon definition of the concept of a computer operating system,[1] we offer the following as a reasonable starting point:

Definition   A computer's *operating system* (OS) is a group of (systems) programs designed to serve two basic purposes:

1. to control the allocation and use of the computing system's resources among the various users and tasks, and
2. to provide an interface between the computer hardware and the programmer that simplifies and makes feasible the creation, coding, debugging, and maintenance of applications programs.

---

1.   Try to find a universally agreed-upon definition of, say, "artificial intelligence" or "mathematics" or "computer science"!

Specifically, we can imagine that an effective operating system should accomplish all of the following:

- facilitate creation and modification of program and data files through an *editor* program,

- provide access to *compilers* to translate programs from relatively simple-to-use high-level languages (such as C++ or Pascal) to machine language,

- provide a *loader* program to move the compiled program code to the computer's memory for execution,

- provide routines that handle the intricate details of *I/O programming*,

- assure that when there are several active processes in the computer, each will get fair and noninterfering *access* to the central processing unit for execution,

- take care of storage and device *allocation*,

- provide for *long term storage* of user information in the form of files, and

- permit system resources to be *shared* among users when appropriate, and be *protected* from unauthorized or mischievous intervention as necessary.

Though systems programs such as editors and translators, and the various utility programs (such as sort and file transfer programs) are not usually considered part of the operating system, the operating system is responsible for providing access to these system resources. The programs that make up the operating system may be implemented in either software or "firmware" (i.e., some hardware/software combination), with some of the code permanently resident in main storage and the other code remotely accessed from on-line disk storage when needed.

Modern computer operating systems may be classified into three groups, which are distinguished by the nature of interaction that takes place between the computer user and his or her program during its processing. These classifications are called *batch*, *time-shared*, and *real time*.

In a *batch processing* operating system environment, users submit jobs to a central place where these jobs are collected into a batch and subsequently placed on an input queue at the computer where they will be run. In this case, the user has no interaction with the job during its processing, and the computer's *response time* is the *turnaround time*—the time from submission of the job until execution is complete and the results are ready for return to the person who submitted the job.

Another mode for delivering computing services is provided by the *time-sharing* operating system. In this environment, a computer provides computing services to several or many users concurrently on-line. Here, the various users are sharing the central processor, the memory, and other resources of the computer system in a manner facilitated, controlled, and monitored by the operating system. The user, in this environment, has nearly full interaction with the program during its execution, and the computer's *response time* may be expected to be no more than a few seconds.

The third class of operating system, the *real time* operating system, is designed to service those applications where response time is of the essence in order to prevent error, misrepresentation, or even disaster. Examples of real time operating systems are those which handle airlines reservations, machine tool control, and monitoring of a nuclear power station. The systems, in this case, are designed to be interrupted by external signals that require the immediate attention of the computer system.

In fact, many computer operating systems are *hybrids*, providing for more than one of these types of computing service simultaneously. It is especially common to have a background batch system running in conjunction with one of the other two on the same computer. The computing environment with which you may be most familiar—the stand-alone or networked PC or Macintosh—is the simplest form of the time-shared system; a single-user multitasking system with almost complete interaction between the programmer and the program while it is running.

A number of other definitions are important to gaining an understanding of operating systems:

> **Definition**   A *multiprogramming* operating system is an OS which allows more than one active user program (or part of user program) to be stored in main memory simultaneously.

Thus, it is evident that a time-sharing system is a multiprogramming system, but note that a multiprogramming system is not necessarily a time-sharing system. A batch or real time operating system could, and indeed usually does, have more than one active user program simultaneously in main storage. Another important, and all too similar, term is "multiprocessing."

> **Definition**   A *multiprocessing* system is a computer hardware configuration that includes more than one independent processing unit.

The term "multiprocessing" is generally used to refer to large computer hardware complexes found in major scientific or commercial applications, such as the National Weather Bureau's satellite imaging facilities.

> **Definition**   A *networked computing system* is a collection of physically interconnected computers. The operating system of each of the interconnected computers must contain, in addition to its own stand-alone functionality, provisions for handling communication and transfer of programs and data among the other computers with which it is connected.

> **Definition**   A *distributed computing system* consists of a number of computers that are connected and managed so that they *automatically* share the

job processing load among the constituent computers or separate the job load as appropriate among particularly configured processors. Such a system requires an operating system which, in addition to the typical stand-alone functionality, provides coordination of the operations and information flow among the component computers.

The networked and distributed computing environments and their respective operating systems are, in fact, realized by augmenting the basic types we have already described with more complex functional capabilities.

EXERCISES

7–1 Consider the following computing system components:

    a.   the CPU
    b.   the C++ compiler
    c.   the memory management program
    d.   a spreadsheet
    e.   the keyboard
    f.   the processor manager program
    g.   a text editor
    h.   the system accounting routines
    i.   a database system
    j.   the system scheduler

Which of these are part of an operating system?

7–2 What are the three types of operating systems? Name and list two distinguishing characteristics for each type.

7–3 Distinguish between a time-sharing and a real-time operating system.

7–4 Distinguish between a networked computing system and a distributed computing system. Which type is in the laboratory you use for this course? Which type exemplifies your campus computing system?

7–5 Distinguish between system response time and system turnaround time.

7–6 We have seen that two of the tasks of an operating system are memory allocation and device allocation. What is the fundamental difference between the allocation of memory and the allocation of a system printer among several programs that are concurrently active in the system.

HISTORY AND EVOLUTION OF OPERATING SYSTEMS

The modern computer operating system is powerful and sophisticated. This power and sophistication has evolved over the years with technological advances in computer hardware and the parallel growth of the number of computer users and their various applications. The following historical perspective will provide insight into why the various components of the modern operating system have evolved into their present form.

Because the history of computer operating systems parallels that of computer hardware, it can be generally divided into five distinct time periods, called *generations*, that are characterized by hardware component technology, software development, and mode of delivery of computer services.

The Zeroth Generation

The term zeroth generation is used to refer to the period of development of computing which predated the the commercial production and sale of computer equipment. The period might be dated as extending from the mid-1800s, and Charles Babbage's Analytical Engine, to the development of the first commercial computer in 1951.[2] In particular, this period witnessed the emergence of the first electronic digital computers—the ABC, designed by John Atanasoff in 1940; the Mark I, built by Howard Aiken and a group of IBM engineers at Harvard in 1944; and the ENIAC, designed and constructed at the University of Pennsylvania by Wallace Eckert and John Mauchly. Perhaps the most significant of these early computers was the EDVAC, developed in 1944–46 by John von Neumann, Arthur Burks, and Herman Goldstine, since it was the first to fully implement the idea of the stored program and serial execution of instructions. The development of EDVAC set the stage for the evolution of commercial computing and operating system software. The hardware component technology of this period was electronic vacuum tubes.

The actual operation of these early computers took place without the benefit of an operating system. Early programs were written in machine language and each contained code for initiating operation of the computer itself. The mode of operation was called "open-shop" and this meant that users signed up for computer time and when a user's time arrived, the entire (in those days quite large) computer system was turned over to the user. The individual user (programmer) was responsible for all machine set up and operation, and subsequent clean-up and preparation for the next user. This system was clearly inefficient and depended on the varying competencies of the individual programmers as operators.

The First Generation, 1951-1956

The first generation marked the beginning of commercial computing, including the introduction of Eckert and Mauchly's UNIVAC I in early 1951, and a bit later, the IBM 701, which was also known as the Defense Calculator. The first generation was characterized again by the vacuum tube as the active component technology.

---

2.   See Chapter 1, *Fundamentals of Computing I: Logic, Problem Solving, Programs, and Computers*, McGraw–Hill, Pascal Edition Revised, 1994, or C++ Edition, 1995.

Operation continued without the benefit of an operating system for a time. The mode was called "closed shop" and was characterized by the appearance of hired operators who would select the job to be run, initial program load (or "boot") the system, run the user's program, and then select another job, and so forth. Programs began to be written in higher level assembly and procedure oriented languages, and thus the operator's routine expanded. The operator now selected the job, ran the translation program to assemble or compile the source program, combined the translated object program along with any existing library programs that the program might need for input to the linking program, loaded and ran the composite linked program, and then handled the next job in a similar fashion. This process is pictured in Figure 7–2.

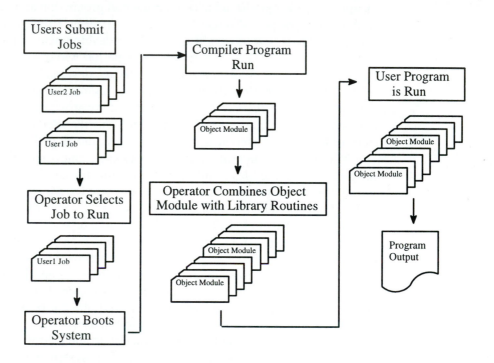

FIGURE 7–2 Computer operations in a "closed shop."

Application programs were run one at a time, and were translated with absolute computer addresses that bound them to be loaded and run from these preassigned storage addresses set by the translator, obtaining their data from specific physical I/O devices. There was no provision for moving a program to a different location in storage for any reason. Similarly, a program bound to specific devices could not be run at all if any of these devices were busy or broken.

The inefficiencies inherent in the open and closed shop methods of operation led to the development of the *monoprogrammed operating system*, which eliminated some of the human intervention in running jobs and provided programmers with a number of desirable functions. The OS consisted of a continuously resident *kernel* in main storage, and a job scheduler and a number of "utility programs" kept in secondary storage. User application programs were preceded by *control* or *specification* cards (in those days, computer programs were submitted on data cards) which informed the OS of what system resources (software resources such as compilers and loaders; and hardware resources such as tape drives and printers) were needed to run a particular application.

The system job scheduler selected jobs in first-come-first-served (FCFS) order, activated the system resources needed, and then passed control to the system (compiler or loader) and/or user program as needed. In addition to greatly streamlining the job to job transition, the monoprogrammed operating system afforded some useful features for computer users. These included: the ability to link two or more independently compiled object modules; provision for assigning actual physical I/O devices to a particular job just prior to its execution thus mitigating the need to delay or cancel a job in the case where a particular device was busy or broken; and making available basic utilities such as sorting and device-to-device data transfer, access to system libraries, and so on. These early systems, as the name "monoprogrammed" implies, processed but one task at a time, including I/O requests, and were designed to be operated as *batch processing systems*.[3]

These systems continued to operate under control of a human operator who would initiate operation by mounting a magnetic tape that contained the operating system executable code onto a "boot device," and then pushing the IPL (initial program load) or "boot" button to initiate the *bootstrap loading* of the operating system.[4] Once the system was loaded, the operator entered the date and time, and then initiated the operation of the job scheduler program which read and interpreted the control statements, secured the needed resources, executed the first user program, recorded the timing and accounting information, and then looped back to begin processing of another user program, and so on as long as there were programs waiting in the input queue to be executed.

The first generation saw the evolution from hands-on operation to closed shop operation to the development of the monoprogrammed operating system. At the same time, the development of programming languages was moving away from the basic machine languages; first to assembly languages, and later to procedure oriented languages, the most significant being the development of FORTRAN by John W. Backus in 1956. Several problems remained, however. The most obvious was the inefficient use of system resources, which was most evident when the CPU waited while the relatively slower, mechanical I/O de-

3.   Recall from the previous section that in a batch processing environment, users submit programs for execution which are collected into a "batch" which becomes an input stream to the computer. The OS job scheduler selects the next job to enter the system from this input stream.

4.   The "IPL" or "boot" button initiates a very small program in read-only memory (ROM) which causes one record to be read from the boot device and then a branch to the newly read information which consists of a program designed to read the rest of itself. In this way the system "bootstraps" itself into existence and hence the term "boot" which is still in use today.

vices were reading or writing program data. In addition, system protection was a problem because the operating system kernel was not protected from being overwritten by an erroneous application program. Moreover, other user programs in the queue were not protected from destruction by executing programs.

The Second Generation, 1956 - 1964

The second generation of computer hardware was most notably characterized by transistors replacing vacuum tubes as the hardware component technology. In addition, some very important changes in hardware and software architectures occurred during this period. For the most part, computer systems remained card- and tape-oriented systems. Significant use of random access devices, that is, disks, did not appear until towards the end of the second generation. Program processing was, for the most part, provided by large centralized computers operated under monoprogrammed batch processing operating systems.

The most significant innovations addressed the problem of excessive central processor delay due to waiting for input/output operations. Recall that programs were executed by processing the machine instructions in a strictly sequential order. As a result, the CPU, with its high speed electronic components, was often forced to wait for completion of I/O operations which involved mechanical devices (card readers and tape drives) that were orders of magnitude slower. This problem led to the introduction of the *data channel*, an integral, special purpose computer with its own instruction set, registers, and control unit, designed to process input/output operations separately and asynchronously from the operation of the computer's main CPU near the end of the first generation, and its widespread adoption in the second generation.

The data channel allowed some I/O to be *buffered*. That is, a program's input data could be read "ahead" from data cards or tape into a special block of memory called a *buffer*. Then, when the user's program came to an input statement, the data could be transferred from the buffer locations at the faster main memory access speed rather than the slower I/O device speed. Similarly, a program's output could be written to another buffer and later moved from the buffer to the printer, tape, or card punch. What made this all work was the data channel's ability to work asynchronously and concurrently with the main processor. Thus, the slower mechanical I/O could be happening concurrently with main program processing. This process was called I/O *overlap*.

The data channel was controlled by a channel program set up by the operating system I/O control routines and initiated by a special instruction executed by the CPU. Then, the channel independently processed data to or from the buffer. This provided communication from the CPU to the data channel to initiate an I/O operation. It remained for the channel to communicate to the CPU such events as data errors and the completion of a transmission. At first, this communication was handled by *polling*—the CPU stopped its work periodically and polled the channel to determine if there were any messages.

Polling was obviously inefficient (imagine stopping your work periodically to go to the post office to see if an expected letter has arrived) and led to another significant innovation of the second generation—the *interrupt*. The data channel was now able to interrupt the CPU with a message—usually "I/O complete." In fact, the interrupt idea was later extended from I/O to allow signalling of a number of exceptional conditions such as arithmetic overflow, division by zero, and time-run-out. Of course, interval clocks were added in conjunction with the latter, and thus operating systems came to have a way of regaining control from an exceptionally long or indefinitely looping program.

These hardware developments led to enhancements of the operating system. I/O and data channel communication and control became functions of the operating system, both to relieve the application programmer from the difficult details of I/O programming and to protect the integrity of the system's operation. The timing facilities mentioned above allowed the operating system to provide improved service to users by segmenting jobs and running shorter jobs first (during "prime time") and relegating longer jobs to lower priority or night time runs. System libraries became more widely available and more comprehensive as new utilities and application software components were made available to programmers.

In order to further mitigate the I/O wait problem, systems were set up to *spool* the input batch from slower I/O devices such as the card reader to the much higher speed tape drive and similarly, the output from the higher speed tape to the slower printer. Initially, this was accomplished by means of one or more physically separate small satellite computers. In this scenario, the user submitted a job at a window, a batch of jobs was accumulated and spooled from cards to tape "off line," the tape was moved to the main computer, the jobs were run, and their output was collected on another tape that later was taken to a satellite computer for off line tape-to-printer output. Users then picked up their output at the submission window.

Toward the end of this period, as random access devices became available, tape-oriented operating systems began to be replaced by disk-oriented systems. With the more sophisticated disk hardware and the operating system supporting a greater portion of the programmer's work, the computer system that users saw was more and more removed from the actual hardware—users saw a *virtual machine*.

The second generation was a period of intense operating systems development. It was the capstone period for sequential batch processing. But the sequential processing of one job at a time remained a significant limitation. Thus, there continued to be low CPU utilization for I/O bound jobs and low I/O device utilization for CPU bound jobs. This was a major concern, since computers were still very large (room size) and expensive machines. Researchers began to experiment with multiprogramming and multiprocessing in their quest for greater efficiency. They also developed a new form of delivering computing services called the *time-sharing* system. A noteworthy example is the the Compatible Time Sharing System (CTSS), developed at MIT during the early 1960s.

The Third Generation, 1964–1979

The third generation officially began in April 1964 with IBM's announcement of its System/360 family of computers. Hardware technology began to use *integrated circuits* (ICs) which yielded significant advantages in both speed and economy.

Operating systems development continued with the introduction and widespread adoption of multiprogramming. This was marked first by the appearance of more sophisticated I/O buffering in the form of spooling operating systems, such as the HASP (Houston Automatic Spooling) System that accompanied the IBM OS/360 system. These systems worked by introducing two new systems programs, a *system reader* to move input jobs from cards to disk, and a *system writer* to move job output from disk to printer, tape, or cards. Operation of the spooling system was, as before, transparent to the computer user who perceived input as coming directly from cards and output going directly to the printer.

The idea of taking fuller advantage of the computer's data channel I/O capabilities continued to develop. That is, designers recognized that I/O needed only to be initiated by a CPU instruction—the actual I/O data transmission could take place under control of a separate and asynchronously operating *channel program*. Thus, by switching control of the CPU between the currently executing user program, the system reader program, and the system writer program, it was possible to keep the slower mechanical I/O devices running and minimize the amount of time the CPU spent waiting for I/O completion. The net result was an increase in system throughput and resource utilization, to the benefit of both users and providers of computer services.

This concurrent operation of three programs (more properly, apparent concurrent operation, since systems had only one CPU, and could, therefore, execute just one instruction at a time) required that additional features and complexity be added to the operating system. First, the fact that the input queue was now on disk, a direct access device, freed the system scheduler from the first-come-first-served policy so that it could select the "best" next job to enter the system (looking for either the shortest job or the highest priority job in the queue). Second, since the CPU was to be shared by the user program, the system reader, and the system writer, some processor allocation rule or policy was needed. Since the goal of spooling was to increase resource utilization by enabling the slower I/O devices to run asynchronously with user program processing, and since I/O processing required the CPU only for short periods to initiate data channel instructions, the CPU was *dispatched* to the reader, the writer, and the user program in that order. Moreover, if the writer or the user program was executing when something became available to read, the reader program would preempt the currently executing program to regain control of the CPU for its initiation instruction, and the writer program would preempt the user program for the same purpose. This rule, called the *static priority rule with preemption*, was implemented in the operating system as a system *dispatcher* program.[5]

The spooling operating system in fact had multiprogramming since more than one program was resident in main storage at the same time. Later, this basic idea of multiprogramming was extended to include more than one active *user* program in memory at a time. To accommodate this extension, both the scheduler and the dispatcher were enhanced. The scheduler became able to manage the diverse resource needs of the several concurrently active user programs, and the dispatcher included policies for allocating processor resources among the competing user programs. In addition, memory management became more sophisticated in order to assure that the program code for each job, or at least that part of the code being executed, was resident in main storage.

The advent of large scale multiprogramming was made possible by several important hardware innovations. The first was the widespread availability of large capacity, high speed disk units to accommodate the spooled input streams and the memory overflow concomitant with the maintenance of several concurrently active programs in execution. The second was relocation hardware which facilitated the moving of blocks of code within memory without an undue overhead penalty. Third was the availability of storage protection hardware to ensure that user jobs are protected from one another and that the operating system itself is protected from user programs. Some of these hardware innovations involved extensions to the interrupt system in order to handle a variety of external conditions such as program malfunctions, storage protection violations, and machine checks in addition to I/O interrupts. In addition, the interrupt system became the technique for the user program to request services from the operating system kernel. Finally, the advent of privileged instructions allowed the operating system to maintain coordination and control over the multiple activities now going on within the system.

Successful implementation of multiprogramming opened the way for the development of a new way of delivering computing services—*time-sharing*. In this environment, several terminals, sometimes up to 200 of them, were attached (hard wired or via telephone lines) to a central computer. Users sat at their terminals, "logged in" to the central system, and worked interactively with the system. The system's apparent concurrency was enabled by the multiprogramming operating system. Users shared not only the system's hardware but also its software resources and file system disk space.

The third generation was an exciting time, indeed, for the development of both computer hardware and the accompanying operating systems. During this period, the topic of operating systems became, in reality, a major element of the discipline of computing.

---

5. The term *dispatcher* is used to distinguish this function of scheduling the processor among the active programs within the system from the function of the system scheduler program which selects the next job to enter the system and initiates setup of the resources needed to process that job.

The Fourth Generation, 1979–the Present

The fourth generation is characterized by the appearance of the personal computer and the workstation. Miniaturization of electronic circuits and components continued and *large scale integration* (LSI), the component technology of the third generation, was replaced by *very large scale integration* (VLSI), which characterizes the fourth generation. VLSI, with its capacity for containing thousands of transistors on a small chip, made possible the development of desktop computers with capabilities exceeding those that filled entire rooms and floors of buildings just twenty years earlier.

The operating systems that control these desktop machines have brought us back, in a sense full circle, to the open shop type of environment where each user occupies an entire computer for the duration of a job's execution. This works better now, not only because the desktop computer is so much more economical and ubiquitous, but also because the progress made over the years has made the virtual computer resulting from the operating system/hardware combination so much easier to use or, in the words of the popular press, "user-friendly."

However, improvements in hardware miniaturization and technology have evolved so fast that we now have inexpensive workstation class computers[6] capable of supporting multiprogramming and time-sharing. Hence the operating systems that support today's personal computers and workstations look much like those which were available for the minicomputers of the third generation—examples are Microsoft's DOS for IBM-compatible personal computers and UNIX for workstations. However, many of these desktop computers are now connected as networked or distributed systems. Computers in a networked system each have their operating system augmented with communication capabilities that enable users to remotely log into any system on the network and transfer information among machines that are connected to the network. The machines that make up a distributed system operate as a virtual single processor system from the user's point of view; a central operating system controls and makes transparent the location in the system of the particular processor or processors and file systems that are handling any given program.

EXERCISES

7–7 Make a table of computer generations with each entry containing the name of the generation, the dates of its existence, the component technology, and the type of operating system, if any, that was prevalent.

7–8 Who is generally credited with the development of the first electronic computer? What about the idea for the stored program computer?

7–9 What does a loader do and why is it needed?

---

6.   The Sun SPARCstation, the Digital DECstation, and the NeXT are examples of workstations that support time sharing and multiprogramming and are available for $6,000 or less.

7–10 Distinguish between a monoprogrammed and a multiprogrammed operating system.

7–11 What is the function of an operating system control language or shell?

7–12 Explain what is meant by "bootstrap loading."

7–13 What is a data channel and how does it work to enhance the performance of computing systems?

7–14 What is input/output buffering?

7–15 What advantage does the so-called disk operating system have over a tape operating system?

7–16 How does the restriction that user programs can utilize I/O devices only through system-provided routines protect a system's integrity?

7–17 How does the use of a spooler enhance system operating efficiency?

7–18 What is a CPU-bound job? an I/O-bound job?

7–19 Explain how an input spooler can be useful in the context of job scheduling, i.e., how does the presence of an input spooler help the job scheduler in the performance of its tasks?

7–20 What is the difference in function between the system scheduler and the system dispatcher?

COMPONENTS OF AN OPERATING SYSTEM

The historical survey of Section NO TAG provides a sense of perspective, from the user's point of view, of what an operating system does, along with a notion of how these various capabilities evolved to become components of the today's operating systems. The modern operating system is a complex program indeed. MINIX, a relatively simple UNIX lookalike for IBM PC and compatibles[5], contains some 12,000 lines of code; commercially available versions of UNIX for workstations contain substantially more. To design or even to understand such a system, it is essential to divide the system into manageable component parts. A modern operating system, exclusive of the networking and distributed computing facilities, may be divided into five components as shown in Figure 7–3:

The *processor management* component is responsible for allocation of the central processor among the currently active programs which are executing within the system. As such it includes the *dispatcher*, which is a low-level scheduler that allocates the CPU to a program already in the system, a facility for managing the interrelationships among the various programs and parts of programs, and routines for handling interrupts.

The *memory management* subsystem consists, as its title suggests, of the algorithms for the initial allocation of program space in the main memory, managing the flow of information between main memory and secondary memory to assure that the instructions to be executed are in main storage in time to be executed, keeping track of memory free space, and initiating memory exceptions in the event of a program's reference to storage locations outside of its allocated space.

The *input/output* component contains all of the detailed code necessary to facilitate the use of the various system peripheral devices. This includes the creation and maintenance of the various file and device descriptors, the interfaces for the language I/O procedures, the device drivers (one for each device type), and the buffering and spooling facilities.

The *file system* provides for longer term on-line storage and selected sharing of program and data information. This includes the capability for creating and removing files and reference to files by symbolic name; allocation and management of disk space for storage of the files in a way that the user does not need to know or care about its physical location; file directory management; facilitating the sharing of files among cooperating users but, at the same time, protecting files against unauthorized access; and providing a viable file backup system.

The *job scheduler and resource allocator* unit is responsible for determining which jobs should enter the system, making sure that resources needed for that job to successfully execute are available, ensuring that resource allocation does not lead to deadlock, and for collecting job accounting and resource information for system management and billing purposes.

Models for Operating System Design

It is clear that the design and implementation of an operating system is a major programming project. Our study of software design suggests that the proper approach is to look for an overall design and then successively divide the problem into subproblems until such decomposition yields easily programmable modules. Along the way, of course, it is important to consider the interconnection among these component parts. There are several approaches to this interconnection or system structure in use today.

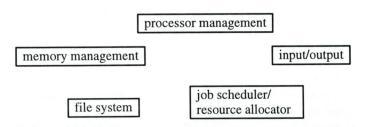

FIGURE 7–3 Components of an operating system.

Segmented Model In this scenario, the code for an operating system is segmented into a set of subroutines. These functions are independently compiled or assembled and linked together into one large load module. Each of these subroutines serves a particular function and may be called by any other procedure as needed. Such an organization has very little structure *per se*. The operating system is, to be sure, separated from the user programs by privileged instructions. To obtain some service, such as I/O, from the operating system, the user program issues a "supervisor call" (SVC) instruction which causes an interrupt. The interrupt handler moves the CPU from user program mode to supervisor mode, then interrogates the parameters of the SVC instruction to determine what service is being requested. Then, the interrupt handler (part of the kernel) transfers control to the request servicing subroutine. Following completion of the requested service, the CPU is returned to user mode, and control is restored to the requesting user program. Since any subroutine can call any other subroutine, the structure is manifest in the subroutine specifications and the parameters.

Layered Model An operating system design using the layered model is a very structured thing indeed. The idea is based on the notion that the computer hardware, because of the intricate detail required to understand the various instructions and operations, is, as a whole, not very useful to persons who use or design the operating system routines. Therefore, the operating system is recast as a series of layers, beginning with the hardware itself as the central layer. The next layer is built directly upon the hardware and provides a sort of virtual machine upon which to build the next layer, and so forth. Each layer provides system functions that use only the layers beneath it. Such an organization of the component parts of the system which were shown above in Figure 7–3 is portrayed as a layered model in Figure 7–4.

The layer just above the hardware, labeled processor management, is called the *kernel* because it provides the most basic interface between the machine itself and the rest of the operating system. The kernel is responsible for management of the central processor. The kernel includes the dispatcher to allocate the CPU among the various jobs in the system, an interrupt handler to determine the cause of an interrupt and initiate its processing, and some provision for communication among the various system and user tasks currently active in the system.

Above the kernel is the *memory management* layer. The memory management routines are responsible for the physical and logical organization of the hierarchical memory system, including the memory partitioning and movement of programs, or parts of programs (pages and/or segments), between main and secondary memory, effectively creating a virtual memory. In addition, memory management must provide for the relocation of programs and the protection of one program's memory space from another's.

Above memory management are the *Input/Output* routines. The I/O layer provides for transfer of data to and from a wide variety of physically unique devices via a general interface to the user. Thus, I/O routines take care of the initiation and organization of data transmission to and from devices, translation

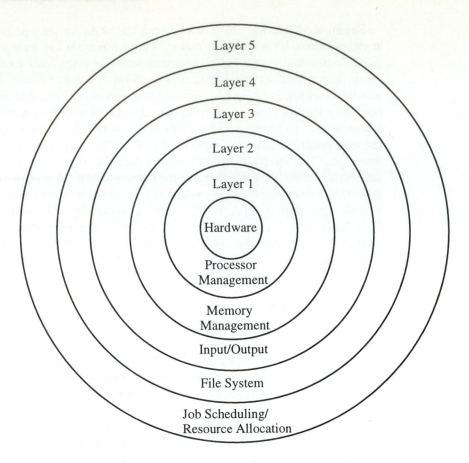

FIGURE 7–4 A layered operating system.

between unique device codes and the internal codes of the computer, maintenance of device request queues, buffering, and so forth.

The first four layers provide a fairly complete and usable system. Indeed, this is a reasonable portrayal of operating systems as they existed towards the end of the second generation. But as we saw in Section NO TAG, the third generation brought with it extensive multiprogramming and the appearance of time-sharing as a new delivery system for computing services. Since users were now running programs from remote terminals, it was unreasonable to expect them to continually retype programs and data each time they came to the terminal to work. For time-sharing to work effectively, it became necessary to provide for the long term storage of information on-line. Thus another layer, the *file system*, was added. In this organization, the file management routines depend only on the layers below. The resulting file system provides for secondary storage allocation and file directory management, sharing and protection of individual user's files, and for file system integrity by integrated backup systems.

The final operating system layer, the *job scheduling and resource allocation* layer, provides for admitting jobs into the system and managing the policies regarding system resource allocation in such a way that promotes system efficiency. This layer also detects and avoids system *deadlock*. Deadlock occurs whenever a number of active jobs within the system each hold resources that are simultaneously needed by another in such a way that the whole system comes to a complete halt. This layer also contains the data gathering routines necessary for analysis of system operation and billing.

The Client-Server Model   We saw in the layered model a very structured approach to operating systems organization manifest in the successive layers where each layer interfaced only with the layers above and below it and only the lowest layer interfaced directly with the computer hardware. The client-server model is similar in that most of the functions of the operating system are provided by subroutines which sit above a relatively small kernel, that is interfaced directly with the hardware, and provides just the most fundamental services.

In this model, only the small kernel runs in supervisor mode; the remaining system processes called *servers*, which do most of the system's work, run in user program mode. These servers provide systems services to user and other system programs called *clients*. The kernel here is mostly a communications processor which channels requests for services from clients to servers, and sends the results back from the servers to the clients. For example, a client program in need of a service, say to open a file, sends a message via the kernel to the file server process. The file server process, upon receipt of the message, provides the service—in this case, locating and making available the file—and informs the client by sending a return message.

You have probably already heard the terms "file server" and "printer server" used to refer to two of the more common server functions. However, the system also deals with some of the process management functions in a process server and memory management in a memory server, and so on. Such a structure has the advantages of the others in that the functions of the system are again divided into smaller and therefore more easily designed, written, and maintained parts. Since the servers run in user rather than privileged mode; and the kernel, which alone runs in privileged mode, is small; system bugs are more likely to result in the failure of an individual server process rather than causing the entire system to crash.

While the client-server approach is applicable and appropriate for use with a multiuser, stand-alone computer system, it also has the advantage of generalizing nicely for use in a networked or distributed complex of computers. In this case, the server processes may or may not be implemented on the same machine as the client process. When the kernel receives a message from a client requesting a service, it is essentially no different for the kernel to send the message to a server on another computer system than to one on its own machine, and the user (client) does not need to know or care.

This concept opens the possibility for greater resource sharing and more specialized use of resources, giving rise to a cooperative processing system where different parts of a given program can be processed by different, more special-ized machines. For example, with an application requiring intensive computa-tion applied to a large set of data, the kernel could request the input from a file server on a computer designed to handle large amounts of disk traffic, request the intensive computation from a compute server on another workstation or even minicomputer, and provide the output via a terminal server on the user's machine. Figure 7–5 shows a client-server model in a networked context.

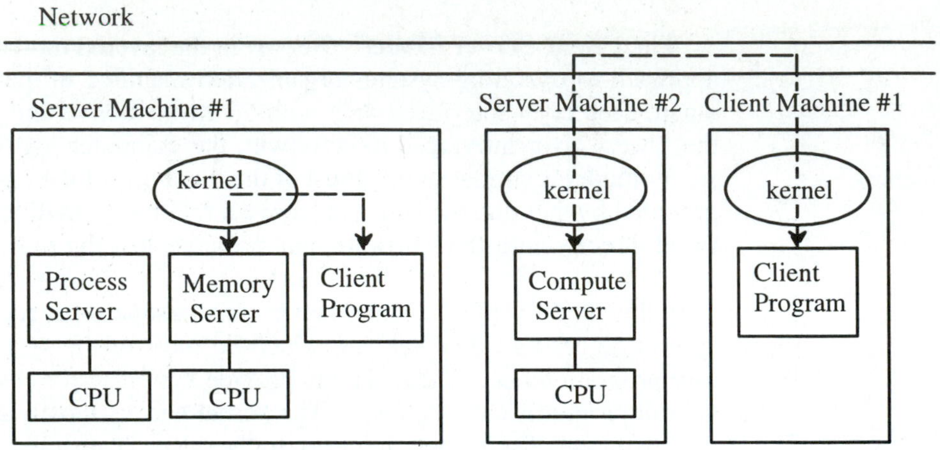

FIGURE 7–5 The client-server system design in a distributed context.

EXERCISES

7–21 List the five component parts of an operating system.

7–22 Give three functions of the processor management component of an op-erating system.

7–23 State four functions of the memory management component of an oper-ating system.

7–24 Design and coding of the input/output component of an operating sys-tem is a most difficult task, due to the variety of I/O devices which must be accommodated. Different devices have different codes for data rep-resentation (both printable and control), different data transfer rates, and operations which are device-dependent (for example, a tape can be re-wound, but it makes no sense to "rewind" a keyboard or screen). Sug-gest an overall design of an I/O component that addresses these issues and makes maximum reuse of code.

7–25 List three capabilities which a file maintenance system ought to provide for the system user.

7–26 Define system deadlock. What are the three conditions necessary for system deadlock to occur? You may need to find the answer in a text on operating systems.

7–27 Suggest a reasonable formula for billing jobs run in a multiprogrammed computer system. Would your formula provide reproducible bills. That is, if the same job were to be run twice, at different times, would the amount charged be exactly the same? Why or why not?

7–28 What is a privileged instruction?

7–29 Why do we require that programs use SVC to access system routines rather than the same "jump to subroutine" (JSR) instruction that is used in programming function calls?

7–30 Draw a characterization of a layered operating system. Why do you suppose that the Job Scheduling component is in the outer layer?

7–31 What are the advantages of the layered model over the segmented model? What is an advantage of the client-server model over the other two?

THE UNIX OPERATING SYSTEM: A CASE STUDY

Perhaps the most influential operating system in use today is UNIX. The origin of the UNIX system can be traced to Project MAC at MIT, where the MULTICS (**Mult**iplexed **I**nformation and **C**omputing **S**ystem) system was developed in the late 1960s. In 1969, after Bell Laboratories left the project, Ken Thompson, Dennis Ritchie, Rudd Canaday, and others from the MULTICS group used a PDP-7 computer as a platform for development of a small operating system and a control language interpreter. The control language interpreter was called "the shell" and the operating system UNICS, for *Un*iplexed *I*nformation and *C*omputing *S*ystem. The name was later changed to UNIX.

This original version of UNIX was written in assembly language. In 1970, Thompson and Ritchie adapted UNIX to run on a new and larger machine, the PDP-11/20. In 1972, much of the code was rewritten in a higher-level language called NB, which was based on BCPL. Subsequently, Ritchie designed and implemented a new programming language called C, which was also based on BCPL, but was designed specifically to obviate, in so far as possible, the systems programmer's need for writing assembly language code. UNIX was again rewritten in 1973, this time with the kernel and some of the input output coding written in C. This was followed by a fourth version whose code was mostly written in C.

By that time, UNIX included facilities for multiprogramming, pipes, and filters and was therefore much the same as it is today. The system began to be licensed to universities in 1974 and, in 1975, to commercial users. At about the same time, the University of California at Berkeley became a second locus for the development of UNIX. Thompson had gone there to teach an operating systems course and, with the help of some students, converted UNIX to run on a PDP-11/70. Subsequently, Bill Joy added virtual memory to this version. Thus, a Berkeley version of UNIX was born and, with the help of DARPA funding, was enhanced with a text editor known as *vi*, which replaced the original line editor, *ed*. The Berkeley Standard Distribution, version 3, BSD 3, was released and adopted by many universities. Subsequently BSD 4.1 (adding a C shell interface) was released in 1981, followed by BSD 4.2 (adding networking support) in 1983, and BSD 4.3 in 1986. Meanwhile, UNIX development continued at AT&T and resulted in the release of UNIX System V in 1983 and System V release 2 in 1984. Since then, although numerous other versions have been released, System V–Release 3.2 has become a quasi standard.

UNIX: A User Perspective

To the user, UNIX appears as a combination of commands, programming tools (such as editors, compilers, and debugging packages), utility programs (such as data transfer and directory management programs), application programs, and files. User interaction with a computer running under the UNIX system consists primarily of issuing commands to the so-called *shell* which, in turn, interprets the commands and schedules the program(s) needed to carry out the operations that are requested by the command. The UNIX shell, like any other operating system command interpreter, is designed to recognize and process a particular set of commands with their accompanying parameters.

This particular set of commands makes up what is sometimes called the system's *command language*. If you have been using an IBM PC or compatible for the design and running of your programs for this and previous courses, you have, most likely, been using the MS DOS command language which is similar in many respects to the UNIX command language. The command names are different (UNIX commands tend to be more terse), but otherwise the functions are often similar.

For example, in the MS DOS environment, one types `dir` (for directory) at the DOS prompt character, `C:`, to view a list of the files in the current directory. The analogous command in UNIX is `ls` (for "list"), which is typed at the UNIX prompt, `%`. To enter the Turbo Pascal environment in DOS, the command is `tp`, and from there one can enter a Pascal program and run it. To enter and run a C++ program in the UNIX system, one types the program using one of the UNIX editors, say `vi` or `emacs`. Thus, editing a program in UNIX requires issuing a separate command for the editor. Once the program text has been typed and saved as a file, the program is then compiled as a separate step via the command `g++`, and finally run using the command `a.out` (which is, in fact, the name of the executable object module).

Most interaction with UNIX involves files. UNIX files are one of three types: *plain*, *directory*, and *device*. Plain files, which are normally program and data files, are in directories as in DOS. Directory files contain lists of file names (along with other pertinent descriptive information such as file format and location). In the UNIX system, devices are represented as files, which means that writing data to, say, a printer is exactly the same as writing data to a file. This provides a uniform structure for all I/O in UNIX.

Files are organized into directories in a hierarchical structure as shown in Figure 7–6. All directories emanate from the root directory, which is indicated by the character /. In a conventional UNIX system, the children (one step down) of the root are: usr, which contains various user and locally installed files; bin, which contains the binary or object files for various system programs; dev, which contains the device files; etc, which contains files that just do not seem to fit into any of the other categories (e.g., the password file for user accounts); and tmp, for the various temporary files that are created during a UNIX session. Note that Figure 7–6 shows two directories named bin, one just below the root and the other a subdirectory of usr.

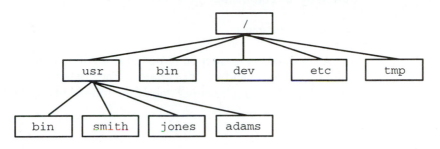

FIGURE 7–6 UNIX files and directories.

In such a hierarchical directory system, it is possible to have files and directories of the same name in different directories. In Figure 7–6, the directory smith is under usr and may be expected to contain John Smith's personal files. The files in the directory smith may be said to be at the end of a path beginning at the root directory and ending at the file in question. For example, if a file named prog1.cxx were in the directory smith, its complete name would include its path as a prefix, and hence would be written as:

/usr/smith/prog1.cxx

This is the file's *absolute name* and we note the two uses of the symbol /, the left-most occurrence designates the root directory; while subsequent appearances serve only to separate the directory names that comprise the path from the root to the file prog1.cxx.

The term *working directory* in UNIX refers to the directory containing the files the user is currently working with. For example, if the user were in the working directory smith, the same file could be referred to by the *relative file name*, prog1.cxx. When a user first logs into a UNIX system, the initial assigned directory is called the *home directory*. Users change directories in UNIX by issuing the command

cd directoryname

Here, `directoryname` may be a relative or absolute directory name representing the directory to be made the new working directory. By using `cd` with the argument `..` to move up one level, one can easily navigate around within the UNIX directory tree as needed. The command `cd` without an argument will return the user to the home directory. In case the identity of the current directory is forgotten, typing the command `pwd` (print the working directory) will display that directory name on the screen.

A new directory may be set up by the command:

```
mkdir arg
```

where `arg` is the pathname to the new directory. Similarly a directory can be removed by the command:

```
rmdir directoryname
```

However, a directory cannot be removed if it still contains files. Files can be deleted by the command `rm filename`. The contents of individual files may be printed to the screen by either one of the following commands:

```
cat filename
more filename
```

The former prints the entire file, while the latter displays the file one full screen at a time. A file may be copied by the command:

```
cp frompath topath
```

The move command `mv` is a little more complex, for it can do two things. First, `mv` can be used to *move* a file or directory to another directory. This is effected by either of the following:

```
mv [options] filename todirname
mv [options] dirname todirname
```

In addition, `mv` can be used to *rename* a file or directory as follows:

```
mv [options] oldfilename newfilename
mv [options] olddirname newdirname
```

The options field refers to a variety of optional "switches" which are permitted with many UNIX commands. For example, the switch `-i` when used with the `mv` command, means move interactively, that is if the particular move would overwrite another file, `-i` will cause the system to ask whether the move is really wanted. Similarly, `-f`, force, will cause `mv` to override any file permission restrictions for the owner of the files being rewritten.

UNIX provides file protection by means of access privileges. For this purpose, there are three classes of users: the *owner*, the owner's *group*, and all others. There are also three types of access for a file: *read*, *write*, and *execute*.

Thus, each file has a nine-bit field associated with it specifying read, write, and execute privileges for the owner, group, and others, respectively. For example, a directory such as /usr/smith might have the entries shown in Figure 7–7, which represents the display in response to the shell command ls -l (the operand -l means to display the "long" version of the directory listing). Here the directory entry prog1.cxx has read, write, and execute privileges for the owner; read and execute privileges for others in the same group; and only execute privileges for all others. The entry CS 101 is a directory name. (How would you interpret the privilege codes for this entry?) The permissions can be changed by the chmod command which has the form:

```
chmod mode filename
```

Here, mode is a three-digit octal value representing these protection bits. For each digit, 1 means execute only, 2 means write only, 3 means execute and write, 4 means read only, and so on up to 7 which means read, write, and execute.

```
-rwxr-x--x  1   smith      6251  Aug 11  10:48  prog1.cxx
drwxrwxr-x  4   smith       512  Aug 11  10:32  CS101
```

FIGURE 7–7 A UNIX directory listing.

UNIX: An Inside View

The kernel is at the heart of the UNIX system and serves as the resource manager. Resources managed by the kernel are:

- the CPU,
- the memory,
- the file system,
- the network interface,
- the process management code, and
- the device interfaces.

The various functions of the kernel are available to system and user programs through library procedures which effect system calls. The internal structure of the Sun Microsystems version of UNIX is shown in the block diagram of Figure 7–8. Details of what happens in some of these blocks will be discussed in the remainder of this chapter.

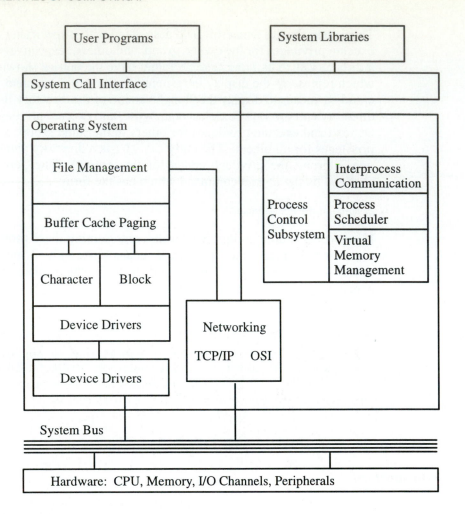

FIGURE 7–8 UNIX® internal structure on a Sun™ system.
(Modified and reprinted with the permission of Sun Microsystems, Inc.)

EXERCISES

7–32 In UNIX systems, most system documentation is available on-line through the man command. Use the man command to learn how to obtain a "long" version of a directory listing. Explain the meaning of as many of the fields in this long listing as you can.

7–33 How does one change the name of a file in a UNIX system?

7–34 List and differentiate the three types of UNIX files.

7–35 How is it possible to have two or more identical file or directory names in UNIX without ambiguity?

7–36 Distinguish between *home directory* and *working directory* in UNIX.

7–37 What is the effect of the command `cd` when used with no arguments?

7–38 Use the system `man` pages to determine the action of the `-r` switch when used with the `rm` command.

7–39 Decipher the privilege codes for the directory entry in Figure 7–7.

7–40 Suppose you are currently working in the directory

`/usr/student/yourname/CS2`

and you want to create the subdirectory `labs` under `CS2` for your lab exercises. What UNIX command(s) would you use to accomplish this?

TASKING AND PROCESSES

UNIX, as well as most other operating systems today, is a multiprogramming system. Systems such as these, where multiple independent programs are executing, must manage two difficult problems—concurrency and nondeterminacy. The concurrency problem arises from the coexistence of several active processes in the system during any given interval of time. Nondeterminacy arises from the fact that each process can be interrupted between any two of its steps. The unpredictability of these interruptions, coupled with the randomness that results from processes entering and leaving the system, make it impossible to predict the relative progress of interrelated processes through the system. A mechanism is needed to facilitate our thinking about, and ultimately dealing with, the problems associated with concurrency and nondeterminacy. An important part of that mechanism is the conceptual and operational isolation of the fundamental unit of computation that the operating system must manage. This unit is called the *task* or *process*.

> **Definition**   A *process* is a series of operations associated with the execution of a sequence of instructions which effect a particular system or user action.

Informally, a process or task is a program in execution.

A process, however, is not the same as a program — a program is a list of instructions representing an algorithm. Recall that an algorithm is a description of something that could be executed to perform some function. A process, on the other hand, is an active concept, embodying the idea of code being processed towards some specific end. A process is not the same as a function either. As in the case for a program, a function is not active *per se*. Moreover, a particular function may be a part of more than one process.

Take for example the method `insert` that adds an item to a `List`. This method can be used in any process that deals with list manipulation. Hence, knowing that `insert` is executing gives no insight into what user or system activity is being performed. A particular process may, in fact, require the execution of more than one method, as illustrated by executing some program made up of several routines. Further, the steps of a program or method are sequential in the sense that they are executed one after the other, and when a routine is called, the caller waits for it to complete before proceeding.

By contrast, processes execute concurrently, that is, when one process creates another, the two proceed without synchronization—the parent process does not wait for the child process to finish, but rather proceeds alongside it. For example, consider the two simple programs in Figures 7–9 and 7–11, each of which becomes a process when it begins to execute. In the program portrayed in Figure 7–9, the main program displays the digits 1 2 3, then calls a function that displays the digits 0 through 8, after which control returns to the main program to display the remaining digits from the first sequence, 4 through 9. The output is what we would expect, as shown in Figure 7–10.

```
//A Single Process

#include <iostream.h>

main()
//pre:  no input

{
     int i;
     for (i = 1; i <= 3; i++)
       cout << i;
     digits();
     for (i = 4; i <= 9; i++)
       cout << i;
//post:   output = 1 2 3 0 1 2 3 4 5 6 7 8 4 5 6 7 8 9}
}
digits()
{
// Displays the digits 0 through 8 in order.
//pre: no input and k is defined
     int k;
     for (k = 0; k <= 8; k++)
        cout << k;
//post:   output is display of sequence 0..8
}
```

FIGURE 7–9 Example of function call within a single process.

1 2 3 0 1 2 3 4 5 6 7 8 4 5 6 7 8 9

FIGURE 7–10 Output from the program of Figure 7–9.

In the second case, the program in Figure 7–11 begins with a main program that displays the first three digits as before, but then calls a function that creates[7] and initiates execution of a "child" process, `prdigits`, which executes the function `digits` that displays the integers 0 through 8. The output in this case is:

```
1 2 3 s1 s2 ... s15
```

where the `si` are digits representing output from the main program or the procedure `digits`, produced in order, but unpredictably intermingled with the output from the parent process. This program might, for example, produce the output shown in Figure 7–12.

```
// Two Processes

#include <iostream.h>

main()
//pre:  no input

{
    int i;
    for (i = 1; i <= 3; i++)
      cout << i;
    create ("prdigits", digits());
    for (i = 4; i <= 9; i++)
        cout << i;
//post:   output = 1 2 3 followed by the sequences {0..8} and {4..9}
//           randomly interspersed with one another.
}
digits()
{
// Displays the digits 0 through 8 in order.
//pre: no input and k is defined
    int k;
    for (k = 0; k <= 8: k++)
        cout << k;
//post:   output is display of sequence 0..8
}
```

FIGURE 7–11   Example of process creation within a process.

```
1 2 3 0 4 1 2 3 4 5 5 6 7 6 7 8 8 9
```

FIGURE 7–12   Possible output from the program in Figure 7–11.

---

7.   Assume, for the purpose of this example, that `create` is an operating system routine which has the general form: `create(processname, process_code_address)`. When called, it creates a process and gives it the name `processname` and initiates execution beginning with the instruction at process_code_address.

This occurs because the function call merely creates and initiates the child process and then returns to the calling program, whence the two active processes proceed concurrently. This explains the interaction between the two sequences in the output.

This concept of process allows us to get at the twin problems of concurrency and indeterminacy. Concurrency, as we have seen, occurs whenever there are two or more processes active within the system. Concurrency may be *real*, in the case where there is more than one processor and hence more than one process can execute simultaneously, or *apparent* whenever there are more processes than processors. In this latter case, it is necessary for the operating system to provide for the switching of processors from one process to another rapidly enough to present the illusion of concurrency to system users. But this is difficult, for whenever a processor is assigned to a new process (called *context switching*), it is necessary to recall where the first process was stopped in order to allow that process, when it gets the processor back, to continue where it left off.

The idea of context switching implies that a particular process can be interrupted. Indeed, a process may be interrupted, as necessary, between individual steps (machine instructions). Such interruptions occur most often when a particular process has used up its quota of processor time or when it has requested and must wait for completion of an I/O operation.

Nondeterminacy arises from the unpredictable order in which such interruptions can occur. Its effect is to make it impossible to judge the relative speed with which processes will proceed through the system, and hence the unpredictable order among the numbers displayed by the program in Figure 7–11. Evidently, then, if two processes are not independent (that is, one depends on the other for something, say I/O), then some mechanism for interprocess communication will have to be included in the system.

Process States

Since active processes in the system can be interrupted, each process can be in one of three states:

- *running*—the process is currently executing on a processor,

- *ready*—the process could use a processor if one were available, and

- *blocked*—the process is waiting for some event, such as I/O completion, to occur.

The relationship between these three states for a particular process is portrayed in Figure 7–13.

Here, we see that if a process is currently *running* and requests I/O, for example, it relinquishes its processor and goes to the *blocked* state. In order to maintain the illusion of concurrency, each process is assigned a fixed quantum of time, or *time slice*, which is the maximum time a running process can control

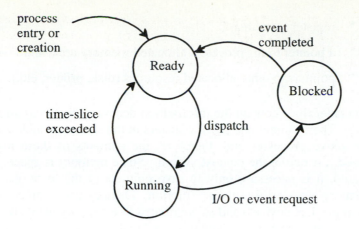

FIGURE 7–13 Process state transitions.

the processor. If a process is in the running state and does not complete or block before expiration of its time slice, that process is placed in the *ready* state and some other process is granted use of the processor for a quantum of time. A blocked process can move back to the ready state upon completion of the event which blocked it. A process in the ready state becomes running when it is assigned a processor by the system dispatcher.

All of these state changes are interrupt driven. A request for I/O is, as we have seen, effected by issuing a supervisor call via an I/O procedure which causes a system interrupt. I/O completion is signalled by an I/O interrupt from the data channel.[8] *Time-slice exceeded* results in a external interrupt from the system's interval timer. And, of course, movement from ready state to running results from the dispatcher giving control of the processor to the most eligible ready process. In each case, when a process gives up the processor, it is necessary to save the particulars of where the process was in its execution when it was interrupted so that it may properly resume later.

We now know enough to think about the representation of a process in the operating system.

The Process Control Block

Each process within the system will have an associated process control block (PCB). The PCB is a data structure containing the essential information about an active process including:

- process ID,

- current state of the process,

---

8. Recall that a data channel is the small special purpose computer which executes programs which actually do I/O concurrently with the main processor's program execution.

- register save area,

- a pointer to the process's allocated memory area, and

- pointers to other allocated resources (disk, printer, etc.).

The latter three contain the information necessary to restart an interrupted process. There is only one set of registers in the system, which is shared by all of the active processes and, therefore, the contents of these registers must be saved just before the context switch. Since memory is space, as well as time shared, it is necessary only to save pointers to the locations of the process' memory areas prior to its interruption. Devices vary; some are shareable (for example disk devices) and so are treated like memory, while others (such as the printer) are nonshareable and thus are "tied-up" by a process for as long as it is using them. In either case, it is necessary here to keep track only of the device ID and, perhaps, the current position in a file.

Now that we know what a process is, understand the meaning of the various states a process can be in, and can picture the representation of a process in the form of a process control block, we can begin to think about the flow of a given process into and through the computing system. The management of process flow into and through the system is, as we have seen in Figure 7–3, one of the key tasks of the operating system. Our next step, then, is to begin to think about the details of the implementation of the processor management component of an operating system. Actually, a true implementation of a processor manager is not possible here because we have neither a raw machine — that is, the hardware without an operating system — nor the intimate knowledge of the hardware which would be required to accomplish this task. But we can go part of the way by specifying a *model* of such hardware, designing a simple processor manager, and then using *simulation* to drive its operation for the implementation experience, analysis, and testing.

Process Management Simulation

In this section, we shall consider the data structures and some of the algorithms that can be used to simulate part of the process management facility of a simple operating system. Our goal is to be able to simulate the flow of user jobs into the computer system, and then through the processor for execution, and finally, when the job is complete, out of the system. The main procedure is basically a continuous loop that switches between a "Dispatcher" which allocates and deallocates the system processor among the various processes that are currently active within the system and an "Executor," which simulates execution of processes within the system.

The whole system is interrupt driven; that is, the currently executing process is eventually interrupted by either a system call (such as an I/O request) or time-slice exceeded. The dispatcher then assumes control and allocates the processor to the next best process in the ready queue. In our simple process manager, the ready queue is organized on a priority basis, and the dispatcher simply picks the top entry from the ready queue. Completion of I/O is, in reality, signalled by an interrupt from the data channel. This is simulated here by expiration of a quasi-random block time. In any case, completion of I/O causes a transfer of control to the dispatcher, which may return control to the just interrupted process or give the processor to what may now be a higher priority process in the ready queue. Note that, in an interactive environment, jobs enter the system randomly and are separated into processes and scheduled when the resources they need become available. Newly entering processes are placed in the ready queue according to their priority. The simulator also assumes that the processes have been priority-ordered in an input queue.

Actually, as indicated at the beginning of this chapter, we are interested in developing, as a case study, the implementation of a simulation model of several of the parts of a small operating system. That implementation will begin with the processor management component. We shall develop this software project using the MAPS methodology that was summarized earlier in the text.

Stage 1: The Dialogue   Before the process management facility can begin its job of managing the progress of a process through the system, one or more processes must enter the system. Since we are implementing a simulation model rather than an actual operating system, the system will deal with a *job specification* rather than an actual program to be executed. The input to the simulator will be a file of records as shown in Figure 7–14 describing the jobs to be processed by the system.

Stage 2: The Specifications   It is necessary to begin development of the simulation with some assumptions. The assumptions are designed to characterize both the simulated computer and the nature of the jobs it will process in order to facilitate modeling and to simplify the problem enough to make it more manageable and comprehensible. Specifically, we will assume:

- The input queue is the file of descriptors of the jobs to be run

- The scheduler takes programs from the input queue basically FIFO

- The dispatching algorithm will be round-robin with a 100 ms time slice

- Time is measured in units of 100 ms

- The clock will not run during scheduling or dispatching

Job Number	Execution Time (ms)	Memory Requirement (bytes)	I/O Block Rate

FIGURE 7–14 An input record for the simulation program.

- I/O blocks will occur at the rate given on the job's specification record. I/O block time will be randomly chosen to be between 100 ms and 50% of the job's execution time as indicated on its input specification.

Stage 3: The Breakdown The input record is represented as a `JobSpec` object in the program. The interface specification, from the header file, `jobspec.h`, is given in Figure 7–15.

```
// This is the header file for the JobSpec class
// that is a descendent of the Element class.  The
// class represents programs submitted to the computer
// for execution.#ifndef JOBSPEC_H

#define JOBSPEC_H
#include <iostream.h>
#include <iomanip.h>
#include "strg.h"
#include "elements.h"

class JobSpec:public Element
{
  protected:
      // DATA MEMBERS ...
      int jobnumber;
      int jobtime;
      long jobsize;
      float blockrate;

  public:
      // MEMBER FUNCTIONS ...
      // constructors - destructors
      JobSpec();
      JobSpec(int,int,long,float);
      JobSpec(int,ifstream&);
      virtual ~JobSpec();
      // display
      virtual void display();
      // access
      virtual int get_jobnumber();
      virtual int get_jobtime();
      virtual long get_jobsize();
      virtual float get_blockrate();
      // file in - file out
      virtual void file_in(ifstream&);
}; // end class JobSpec

      #endif
```

FIGURE 7–15 C++ header file for the `JobSpec` object.

Note the data members, `jobnumber`, `jobtime`, `jobsize`, and `blockrate` corresponding to the items in Figure 7–14. A Process Control Block (PCB) is needed for each job which enters the simulated system. A representation for the PCB is shown in Figure 7–16.

Job Number
Job Execute Time
Job Size
Job Elapsed Time
Block Rate
Block Time Remaining
State
Job Page
...

FIGURE 7–16 Process control block for the operating system simulator.

Once a job enters the system (here, its `JobSpec` is input to the simulator), then a process control block (PCB) is created. The PCB is represented as another object, which is a descendent of `JobSpec`. Note that in addition to the inherited instance variables of `jobnumber`, `jobtime`, etc., the PCB includes the process `state` and a number of other instance variables. The interface specification from the header file, `pcb.h`, is shown in Figure 7–17.

```
// This is the header file for the PCB(Process Control Block)
class
// that is a descendent of the JobSpec class.  This class repre-
sents
// a programming job in execution - a process.


#ifndef PCB_H
#define PCB_H


#include <iostream.h>
#include <iomanip.h>
#include <string.h>
#include "osconsts.h"
#include "strg.h"
#include "pagetab.h"
#include "random.h"
#include "jobspec.h"


class PCB:public JobSpec   // Process Control Block
{
   protected:
      // DATA MEMBERS ...
      int size_in_pages;
      string state;
      int current_vpage;
```

```
        int blocktime;
        PageTable* pcb_page_table;


    public:
        // MEMBER FUNCTIONS
        // constructors - destructors
        PCB(JobSpec*,int);
        virtual ~PCB();



        // display
        virtual void display();



        // access - modify
        void decr_jobtime(int);
        int get_size_in_pages();
        char* get_state();
        void set_state(string);
        int get_current_vpage();
        void set_current_vpage(int);
        int get_blocktime();
        void set_blocktime(int);
        void decr_blocktime(int);
        PageTable* return_page_table_ptr();
        boolean check_for_blocked_IO();
        boolean check_for_new_current_vpage();
        boolean test_if_page_in_MM();
        void select_new_current_vpage();
}; // end class PCB
```

FIGURE 7-17 C++ header file, pcb.h, for the PCB object.

The process ID is represented as jobnumber, inherited from JobSpec. The current state of the process is stored in state. The block time remaining for this process waiting for I/O is in blocktime. The size of the main memory area allocated to this process is stored in size_in_pages. In addition, the following parameters are needed:

Name	Meaning	Initial value
systemtime	System Time	0
blocktime	Job I/O block time	0

Stage 4: Defining abstractions The algorithm for the Job Scheduler is sketched in Figure 7-18. Here, the input queue is manifest as the object, Job-SpecQ, a descendent of the Queue class described in Chapter 4 and specified in an appendix to the corresponding chapter in the accompanying *Laboratory Manual*. In our implementation, the job scheduler is a method of the OSObj

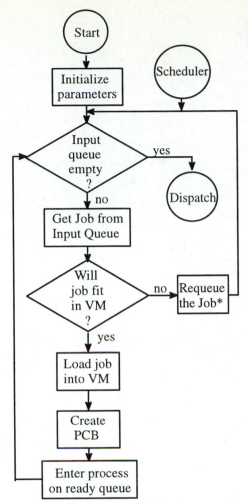

*or save it for next time. At any rate take care
not to loop on the same jobs which will not fit.

FIGURE 7–18 Job scheduler for the simulator.

object.[9] When the scheduler has loaded all the jobs from the input queue
that will fit, control is transferred to the dispatcher, a member function appropriately named dispatcher, of the OSObj object. After some system
housekeeping, dispatcher will assign the processor to the first job on the
Ready Queue, readyq, in the Simulator, as shown in Figure 7–19. Dispatching a job is simulated in our system by initializing or restoring the job's parameters (from its PCB) indicating where it is to begin or resume execution. For
the purposes of the simulation, we need only know the job's elapsed execution

---

9. Readers are encouraged to check out the hierarchical structure of the operating system simulator by
consulting the complete listing of the program code which appears in an appendix to this chapter.

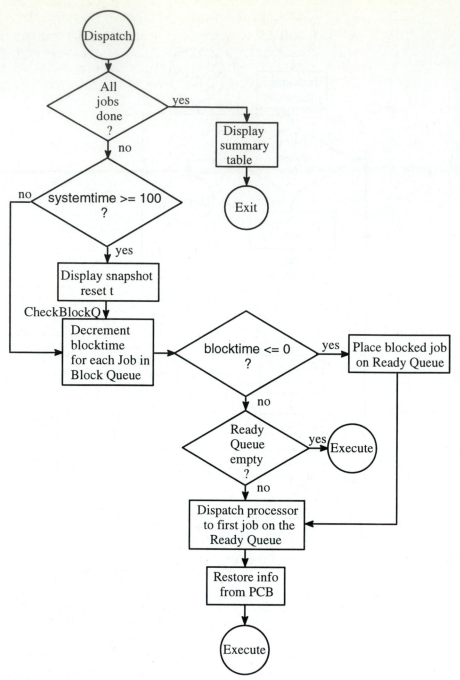

FIGURE 7–19 Dispatcher for the simulator.

time and which of its pages it was last executing from. If the job is just beginning execution, we assume it begins executing on its first page. We are now ready to begin a time slice of execution.

Execution in the simulator occurs by incrementing total system time, `systemtime`, and decrementing `jobtime`, the job's execution time, as shown in Figure 7–20. A pass through the execute component represents 1 time slice (100 ms). During a time slice, a process will execute until it completes, blocks for I/O, or exceeds its quota (the time slice time). If the job has completed, its

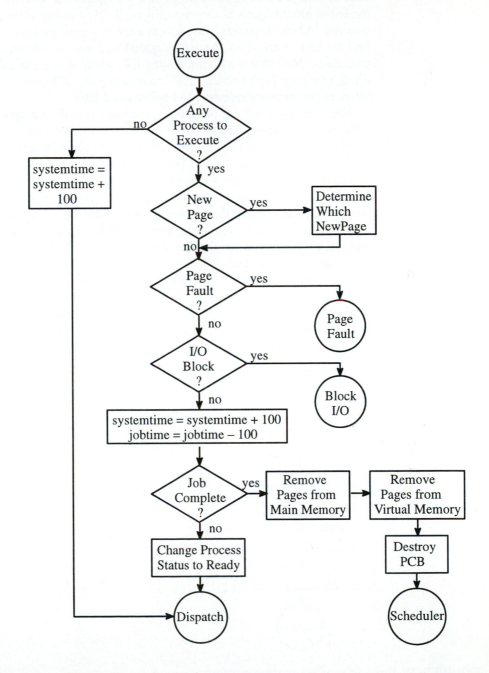

FIGURE 7–20 Execution of a time slice in the simulator.

system resources are returned and control goes back to the scheduler to see if additional jobs can be loaded into the system. I/O blocks occur at the rate, `blockrate`, given on the job's input record. This is handled in the simulation by calling a random number, using the random number generator specified in `random.h`, (between 0 and 1) and taking the I/O block if the random number exceeds the job's I/O `blockrate`. If a job blocks for I/O, the job is added to the list of blocked jobs as shown in Figure 7–21. Finally, if neither job completion nor I/O block occurs, the process executes until its time slice is exceeded and is then returned to the ready queue and control is transferred to `dispatcher`. Note that we do not distinguish when, if ever, in a time slice an I/O block or a page fault occurs. The remaining parts of Figure 7–20 refer to activities of the memory manager to be discussed later.

The remaining task for the process manager is to deal properly with the situation where an executing program requests I/O and becomes blocked waiting for the completion of the I/O data transfer. The algorithm is pictured in Figure 7–21. In the case of such an I/O block, the PCB for the currently executing job is located and the process's status is changed to `blocked`. The I/O Block component of the operating system, `blockio`, also a member function of the `OSObj` object, handles the change in the status of the current process from `running` to `blocked`, recording that status change in the corresponding PCB, and adding the process to the list of blocked jobs. In the simulation, the block time must also be calculated. The `block_time` for this job will be randomly chosen to be between 100 ms and 50% of the job's execute time, `jobtime`, as indicated on its input record as was specified in the assumptions above. The random number generator will be used to make the calculation. Once the job is blocked, control is returned to the `dispatcher` in order to find another job to execute.

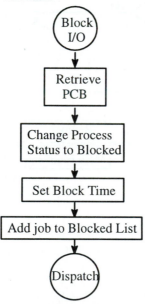

FIGURE 7–21 Block I/O routine for the simulator.

Stage 5: The code   The C++ program code for `scheduler`, a member function of the object, `OSObj`, appears in Figure 7–22.

```
// Function: OSObj::scheduler()
// Purpose:   To load programs into virtual memory.
//            To load jobs from the job input queue into virtual
//            memory as there is space available and the entire
//         job will fit.
// Pre:       The size of job_inputq = N, N>=0, and VM is not
//            full with M, M>=0 processes.
// Post:      The size of job_inputq = N - X, (N - X)>=0, and VM
//            now has N + X processes OR job_inputq is empty.
void OSObj::scheduler()
{
  JobSpec* current_job_ptr;
   scheduler_cnt++;
  boolean a_proc_will_fit = TRUE;
  boolean repeat_flag = FALSE;
  int repeat_jobnumber = -1;

  while(a_proc_will_fit){
    if(!job_inputq_ptr->is_empty()) // there are jobs
      current_job_ptr = (JobSpec*)job_inputq_ptr->front();
    else{
      //cout << "job_inputq empty" << endl;
      a_proc_will_fit = FALSE;
    }

    if(repeat_flag && (current_job_ptr->get_jobnumber()==
      repeat_jobnumber)){
      // The entire job_inputq has been examined.
      //cout << repeat_jobnumber;
     //cout << " did not fit and has been seen";
     //cout << " twice, stop" << endl;
      a_proc_will_fit = FALSE;
    }

    if(a_proc_will_fit){
      int proc_size_in_pages =
      calc_size_in_pages(current_job_ptr);
      if((virtual_memory_ptr->get_vm_free() -
      proc_size_in_pages)>=0){
    // the proc does fit
      cout << "Job: " << setw(3);
      cout << current_job_ptr->get_jobnumber();
      cout << " enters system at " << setw(8) << systemtime;
      cout << " ms." << endl;
    PCB* new_proc_ptr =
    new PCB(current_job_ptr,proc_size_in_pages);
    virtual_memory_ptr->load_proc_to_vm(new_proc_ptr);
    readyq_ptr->enter(new_proc_ptr);
    job_inputq_ptr->remove();
      }
      else{
    // proc did not fit in available VM
    if(!repeat_flag){
      // mark first job not to fit
```

```
                repeat_flag = TRUE;
                repeat_jobnumber = current_job_ptr->get_jobnumber();
                //cout << "first no fit, jobnumber: ";
                //cout << setw(8) << repeat_jobnumber << endl;
            }
                job_inputq_ptr->rotate();
            } // else
        } // if(a_proc_will_fit)
    } // while
    //cout << "call dispatcher from scheduler" << endl;
    taskflag = _dispatcher_;
} // end OSObj:::scheduler()
```

FIGURE 7–22 The C++ program code for the member function, `scheduler`, of the object, `OSObj`.

The entire simulation program begins at the "Start" oval of Figure 7–18. The parameter initialization is done in the main program `simdrv.cxx` by a message to the `OSObj` constructor. Again, the input queue is `JobSpecQ`; jobs will be extracted from `JobSpecQ` until either the input queue is completely empty, or it contains only jobs that by virtue of their `jobsize` are too big to fit into virtual memory (VM). After moving a job from the input queue to virtual memory (that is entering a job into the system), the job scheduler creates a PCB for that process with the statement:

```
PCB* new_proc_ptr = new PCB(current_job_ptr,proc_size_in_pages);
```

and enters the process on the ready queue with the following:

```
readyq_prt->enter(new_proc_ptr);
```

When the scheduler has "scheduled" as many jobs as it can, it transfers control to the dispatcher:

```
taskflag = _dispatcher_;
```

The variable, `taskflag`, is used as a switch in the case statement of the `execute` member function of the object, `OSObj`, to set control in the proper system routine. The details are provided by the code shown in Figure 7–22.

The `dispatcher`, like the `scheduler` above, is a method in the `OSObj` object. The C++ code for the method `dispatcher` appears in Figure 7–23.

```
// Function:  OSObj::dispatcher()
// Purpose:   To allocate the CPU to the first ready process.
//            To set the current process to the first available
//            one on the readyq. The function also checks the
//            blockq for  new ready processes and produces snap
//            shots of the system state.
// Pre:       readyq, blockq and current_proc_ptr are initialized

// Post:      Any process with blocktime <= 0 is placed on the
```

```
//              rear of the readyq by check_blockq. If readyq is
//              not empty then current_proc_ptr = readyq.front().
//              If SNAPINTV passes have occurred through the
//              dispatcher - display a map of MM and VM. If there
//              are still jobs taskflag =_timeslicer_ else
//              lastflag = TRUE and control returnsto the
//          dispatcher().
void OSObj::dispatcher()
{
   dispatcher_cnt++;
   if((!job_inputq_ptr->is_empty())||
      (!readyq_ptr->is_empty())||
      (!blockq_ptr->is_empty())){
     //cout << "There are still proc in the system." << endl;


     if(!blockq_ptr->is_empty())
        check_blockq();
     /*else
        cout << "blockq empty at dispatcher" << endl;*/
     eventflag = nada;


     if(dispatcher_cnt % SNAPINTV == 0){
        // time for a picture of the system
        cout << endl;
        cout << "Systemtime: " << setw(8) << systemtime << endl;
        virtual_memory_ptr->display();
        main_memory_ptr->display();
     }
     else
        main_memory_ptr->calc_mm_utilization();


     if(!readyq_ptr->is_empty()){
        //cout << "new running process" << endl;
        current_proc_ptr = (PCB*)readyq_ptr->front();
         current_proc_ptr->set_state("running");
        readyq_ptr->remove();
     }
     /*else
        cout << "readyq is empty at dispatcher" << endl;*/


     //cout << "Call timeslicer from dispatcher." << endl;
     taskflag = _timeslicer_;
   }
   else{
     //cout << "System is out of work." << endl;
     lastflag = TRUE;
   }
} // end OSObj::dispatcher()
```

FIGURE 7–23 C++ program code for the member function, dispatcher, from the object OSObj.

The `dispatcher` begins by checking to see that there are still processes in the system and then whether the appropriate interval for a snapshot picture of the system's status has passed. Next, the `dispatcher` looks at the queue of jobs blocked waiting for I/O completion. If the blocked queue is not empty, then the block time remaining for each of the jobs on the queue is decremented. This is accomplished by:

```
check_blockq();
```

The `dispatcher` begins its principal work by interrogating the status of the Ready Queue, `readyq`:

```
if(!readyq_ptr->is_empty())
```

If there are jobs on the ready queue, then the processor is dispatched to the first process on `readyq`:

```
current_proc_ptr = (PCB*)readyq_ptr->front();
current_proc_ptr->set_state("running");
readyq_ptr->remove();
```

The process's state in its PCB is marked `running` and that process is removed from the head of the ready queue. The `dispatcher` completes its work with a call to the executer, `timeslicer`.

The execution component of process management is simulated, like the `dispatcher` above, by a member function, `timeslicer`, of the `OSObj` object. The C++ code for the `timeslicer` appears in Figure 7–24. The process management parts of `timeslicer` are quite straightforward and follow the blocks of Figure 7–24 closely.

```
// Function: OSObj::timeslicer()
// Purpose:  To simulate the actions of the CPU cycle.
//           If there is a current process in the "running"
//           state, can it continue to execution? It may be
//           suspended if the current piece of code needed is
//           not in MM with a pagefault() or for input/output
//           with a call to blockio().  If yes, then decrement t
//           he process' runtime. If runtime is = 0, then
//           process has completed and it is removed from the
//           system else it is placed on the rear of the readyq.
// Pre:      systemtime = T ; current_proc-ptr, readyq and
//           blockq are initialized.
// Post:     If there is no current_proc with state = "running"
//           then systemtime = T + 100ms and call dispatcher()
//           else if the current vpage is not in memory
//               call pagefault()
//           else if process blocks for I/O
//               call blockio()
//           else if jobtime <= 0, proc finished
//               systemtime = T + 100
//               remove proc from system
//               call scheduler()
```

```
//            else jobtime > 0
//                jobtime -= 100ms
//                place current_proc on readyq.rear()
//                systemtime = T + 100ms
//                call dispatcher()
//
void OSObj::timeslicer()
{
  char ch;


  timeslicer_cnt++;
  if((current_proc_ptr == NULL) ||
     (readyq_ptr->is_empty() &&
     (strcmp(current_proc_ptr->get_state(),"running")!=0))){
    //cout << "In timeslicer with no processes to execute,";
    //cout << "call dispatcher." << endl;
    systemtime += 100;
    eventflag = idle; // No work for the CPU
    taskflag = _dispatcher_;
  }
  else{
    if(current_proc_ptr->get_current_vpage() == -1){
      //cout << "first time slice, install page 0" << endl;
      current_proc_ptr->set_current_vpage(0);
      taskflag = _pagefault_;
    }
    else{
      if(current_proc_ptr->check_for_new_current_vpage()){
      current_proc_ptr->select_new_current_vpage();
      if(!current_proc_ptr->test_if_page_in_MM()){
        //cout << "page fault in timeslicer, ";
        //cout << "new page not in MM" << endl;
        taskflag = _pagefault_;
          }
      /*else{
        cout << "new page in MM" << endl;
      }*/
      }
      else{
      //cout << "Remaining on the current page." << endl;
      if(!current_proc_ptr->test_if_page_in_MM()){
        //cout << "page fault in timeslicer, ":
        //cout << "current page not in MM" << endl;
        taskflag = _pagefault_;
      }
      /*else{
        cout << "current page in MM" << endl;
      }*/
      }// else remaining on current page
    }// else In timeslicer with a running process


    if(taskflag != _pagefault_){
      if(current_proc_ptr->check_for_blocked_IO()){
      //cout << "blockio called from timeslicer" << endl;
      taskflag = _blockio_;
```

```
          }
        else{
    //cout << "proc did not block in execution" << endl;
    systemtime += 100;
    current_proc_ptr->decr_jobtime(100);
    eventflag = exec;
    if(current_proc_ptr->get_jobtime() <= 0){
       cout << "Process ID: " << setw(8)
          << current_proc_ptr->get_jobnumber();
       cout << " completed execution at " << setw(8)
          << systemtime;
       cout << "ms" << endl;
       cout << "STRIKE RETURN" << endl;
       cin.get(ch);
       virtual_memory_ptr->remove_proc_from_vm(cur-
rent_proc_ptr);
       main_memory_ptr->release_memory(current_proc_ptr);
       delete current_proc_ptr;
        current_proc_ptr = NULL;
       //cout << "call scheduler from timeslicer" << endl;
       taskflag = _scheduler_;
       }
     else{
       //cout << "Current proc did not finish" << endl;
        current_proc_ptr->set_state("ready");
       readyq_ptr->enter(current_proc_ptr);
       //cout << "Call dispatcher from timeslicer" << endl;
       taskflag = _dispatcher_;
     }// else current proc did not finish
       }// else proc did not block
     }// if(taskflag! = _pagefault_)
   }// if in timeslicer without a running process
} // end OSObj::timeslicer()
```

FIGURE 7–24 C++ program code from OSObj for the operating system's execution component.

First, timeslicer checks to see whether, in fact, there is a process to execute:

```
if((current_proc_ptr == NULL) ||
    (readyq_ptr->is_empty() &&
    (strcmp(current_proc_ptr->get_state(),"running")!=0)))
```

An empty ready queue and no process running indicates the need to simulate the CPU in a wait state—there are still jobs in the system, in the block queue, but none currently able to execute. The timeslicer simulates wait state by incrementing the system time, systemtime, and then returning control to the dispatcher:

```
systemtime += 100;
eventflag = idle; // No work for the CPU
taskflag = _dispatcher_;
```

Assuming that there is a process to execute, the possibility then arises that the process requests I/O and blocks during this quantum:

```
if(current_proc_ptr->check_for_blocked_IO()){
    taskflag = _blockio_;
{
```

In this case, control is transferred to the Block I/O component of Figure 7–20.

If there is a process to execute, and that process does not block, we then execute for the period of the time slice. This is accomplished by incrementing the system time:

```
systemtime += 100;
```

and decrementing the job's total execute time:

```
current_proc_ptr->decr_jobtime(100);
```

Of course, the job's execution could become complete during this quantum:

```
if(current_proc_ptr->get_jobtime() <= 0)
```

in which case, it is necessary to remove the process code and data from virtual and main memory and then destroy the PCB for that job:

```
virtual_memory_ptr->remove_proc_from_vm(current_proc_ptr);
main_memory_ptr->release_memory(current_proc_ptr);
delete current_proc_ptr;
current_proc_ptr = NULL;
```

and return control to the job Scheduler. Otherwise, if the currently executing process did not complete during the quantum, it is returned to the ready queue and control goes to the dispatcher:

```
current_proc_ptr->set_state("ready");
readyq_ptr->enter(current_proc_ptr);
taskflag = _dispatcher_;
```

Whenever a block for I/O is encountered in timeslicer, control passes to blockio, another member function in the object OSObj. The C++ code for the member function, blockio, is shown in Figure 7–25. The block time is calculated by drawing a random number between 0 and 1 and scaling it to a range of 0 to 50% of the job execution time, i.e., .5*jobtime, and then adding 100 ms to provide a lower bound:

```
int block_time =(int)(random() * 0.5 *
        current_proc_ptr->get_jobtime()) + 100;
```

```
// Function: OSObj::blockio()
// Purpose:  To simulate the waiting for I/O — typically a disk
```

```
//              read or write. The function determines the amount
//              of time to assign to a proc's blocktime - how long
//              it must spend on the blockq and places it there.
// Pre:         current_proc_ptr->blocktime = 0, state = "running"
// Post:        blocktime = (0 to 0.5*jobtime)+100 ms, state =
//              "blocked", and call dispatcher().
void OSObj::blockio(){
  blockio_cnt++;
  int block_time =(int)(random() * 0.5 *
          current_proc_ptr->get_jobtime()) + 100;
  //cout << "Set blocktime to - " << block_time << " ms" ;
  //cout << endl;
  current_proc_ptr->set_blocktime(block_time);
  current_proc_ptr->set_state("blocked");
  blockq_ptr->enter(current_proc_ptr);
  //cout << "call to dispatcher from blockio" << endl;
  taskflag = _dispatcher_;
} // end OSObj::blockio()
```

FIGURE 7–25 C++ program code for the simulator's OSObj blockio member function.

The block time is recorded in the process' PCB:

```
current_proc_ptr->set_blocktime(block_time);
```

and the status is changed to blocked:

```
current_proc_ptr->set_state("blocked");
```

Finally, the blocked job is added to the block queue:

```
blockq_ptr->enter(current_proc_ptr);
```

and control is returned to the dispatcher.

Readers should study the C++ program code listing in the appendix until the various operations of process management are clear.

EXERCISES

7–41 What is the difference between a function and a process?

7–42 Explain how two processes can proceed "concurrently" on a single CPU. What is the difference between real and apparent concurrency?

7–43 List and describe the three possible states a process can be in. What are the two events that can cause a process to be removed from the "running" state?

7–44 Explain what is meant by the phrase "process state changes are interrupt driven."

7–45 What is a process control block? List and explain the need for the information in the PCB.

7–46 What is a context switch?

7–47 What is the difference between a shareable and a nonshareable device?

7–48 What changes are necessary in the process manager to facilitate a prioritized ready queue? A job's execution, or dispatching, priority could be externally specified—in the simulation as an additional entry in the input job specification. Can you think of a way to improve the overall operation of the operating system by dynamic priority adjustment, that is, changing a process's priority during its active life in the system? Suggest one such possibility.

MEMORY MANAGEMENT

A program's machine language code must be in the computer's main memory in order to execute. Assuring that at least the portion of code to be executed is in memory when a processor is assigned to a process is the job of the operating system *memory manager*. This task is complicated by two other aspects of modern computing systems.

The first is multiprogramming. From its definition, we know that multiprogramming means that several (at least two) processes can be active within the system during any particular time interval. But these multiple active processes result from various jobs entering and leaving the system in an unpredictable manner. Pieces, or blocks, of memory are allocated to these processes when they enter the system and are subsequently freed when the process leaves the system. Therefore, at any given moment, the computer's memory, viewed as a whole, consists of a pattern of blocks, some allocated to processes active at that moment, and others free and available to a new process which may, at any time, enter the system. This situation is portrayed in Figure 7–26.

The computer in Figure 7–26 has been running for some time, and consequently the memory allocation appears to be in a random pattern. Process A occupies the block of memory addresses 140K–340K, process G locations 475K–705K, and process X locations 875K–1M. The shaded areas are unused at the moment. A process about to enter the system could be placed in any of the remaining free areas, provided that a free block large enough to hold the new process exists. For example, suppose that the next program to enter requires a block of memory of 160K bytes. It could be placed in the second free area since this block, with addresses 705K through 875K, could accommodate a program of up to 170K bytes.

But there is another different, yet related, problem. Suppose that a new program, originally written in C++, were to be translated into a machine language program with actual storage addresses for a program designed to be placed in memory starting at, say, location 100. Such a program appears in Figure 7–27. The left-hand column of Figure 7–27 gives the storage locations (in decimal) of the instructions and data items found in column 2. Clearly, the program will

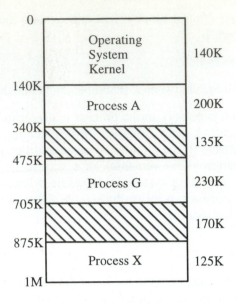

FIGURE 7–26 A snapshot of a computer's memory allocation.

not work correctly if placed in either of the available free areas of Figure 7–26 because the program code is set to execute from the actual storage addresses 100 to 114—a storage block not available in either of these two free areas. In fact, were the program to be loaded into one of the existing free areas, the only instruction in the program that would work correctly is the HALT instruction since it is the only instruction which does not make reference to any storage location.

```
Loc   Machine Code           Source              Comments

100   1011 000 00 1101111        LOAD N,R0     first number in loc N
101   1101 000 00 1110000        CMP  R0,N+1   second number in loc N=1
102   1110 010 00 1101000        BLT  L1
103   1110 000 00 1101001        BRA  L2
104   1011 000 00 1110000    L1  LOAD N+1,R0   larger of first 2 in R0
105   1101 000 00 1110001    L2  CMP  R0,N+2   third number in loc N+2
106   1110 010 00 1101100        BLT  L3
107   1110 000 00 1101101        BRA  L4
108   1011 000 00 1110001    L3  LOAD N+2,R0   largest of all in R0
109   1100 000 00 1110010    L4  STO  R0,MAX
110   1111 000 00 0000000        HALT              last instruction
111   0000000000001111      N   DC   15,2,673 data values
112   0000000000000010
113   0000000001000011
114   0000000000000000     MAX DS   1
                               END
```

FIGURE 7–27 An assembly language program with absolute addresses.

The initial LOAD instruction, for example, expects to load data from the storage location 111 into R0—something not possible if this program were in the block of storage with addresses 705K through 875K. Actually, the storage required for this program to execute correctly is currently occupied by the computer's operating system kernel. That is, the LOAD instruction's reference to location 111 would be an attempt to access the contents of a location in the kernel to load into R0. Worse yet, the store instruction at location 109 would attempt to write over a word which is, in fact, some part of the kernel. Such a store, by overwriting a part of the kernel would wreck the operating system if it were permitted to happen!

In general, then, programs designed to execute in this multiprogramming environment must be compiled so that they can execute from any block of storage available at the time of the program's execution. Such programs are called *relocatable* programs and the idea of placing them into any currently available block of storage is called *relocation*. Actually, the problem is even worse than we have portrayed it. For what would happen if the entering program were too large to fit into any of the available free blocks? For example, suppose that the entering program requires 300K bytes. The total amount of unused storage is certainly larger than 300K bytes, but no free area alone is sufficient in size. The new program could be accommodated if it would be possible to move one or more of the current processes so as to create a larger size free block, as shown in Figure 7–28.

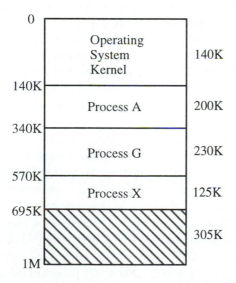

FIGURE 7–28 Memory after relocation.

Relocation of currently active programs is called *dynamic relocation*. If currently executing processes could be relocated, both the computer's response time and resource utilization could be improved.

Actual implementation of dynamic relocation is not trivial. The compiler can not possibly assign the correct addresses because a program must be compiled before it can be loaded and executed. Therefore, information about the number and sizes of the free blocks that will be available when the compiled program is to be executed (later) cannot be known (in advance) to the compiler. Thus, program relocation, especially dynamic relocation—the moving around of currently active processes—must be done by the operating system's *memory management facility.*

The second aspect of modern computing systems which bears upon memory management is the need to allow the programmer to use a range of program addresses which may be larger, perhaps significantly larger, than the range of memory locations actually available. That is, we want to provide the programmer with a *virtual memory*, that is a memory with characteristics (especially size) different from actual memory, and provide it in a way that is invisible to the programmer. This is accomplished by *extending* the actual memory with secondary memory such as disk. Providing an efficiently operating virtual memory is another task for the operating system memory management facility.

Relocation

Since dynamic relocation requires that a program be able to be moved at any time during its active life within the system, it follows that actual addresses cannot be formulated in advance. This means that the compiler cannot assign the actual storage locations. In fact, to enable dynamic relocation to take place, the actual storage locations cannot be assigned at all before the program begins to execute. Each storage reference, that is, each operand reference in an instruction, must have its address computed as a part of the memory reference. For example, the program of Figure 7–27 would be assembled with addresses as though it were to be loaded at address 0 (an impossibility since the operating system kernel occupies the lowest addresses of memory) as shown in Figure 7–29.

Then, if the program were actually loaded at, say, address 323654, the actual address of the first operand of the LOAD instruction will have to be computed as 323654+11, just before the actual reference is made. Since this kind of address computation must be done for *each* memory reference, hardware assistance is required in order to prevent an unacceptable slowdown of the program's execution. The simplest scheme is based on a hardware *relocation register*. In this case, whenever the dispatcher gives control of the processor to a particular process, the relocation register R is set to the beginning address of the process's assigned memory block. Then, all program addresses are interpreted as being *relative* to this relocation address. The hardware computes the actual address during the storage reference cycle as:

$$A(a) = C(R) + a$$ where $C(R)$ denotes the contents of the relocation register, a represents the program address, and $A(a)$ represents the memory address corresponding to a.

```
Loc  Machine Code           Source            Comments
000  1011 000 00 0001011        LOAD N,R0      first number in loc N
001  1101 000 00 0001100        CMP  R0,N+1    second number in loc N=1
002  1110 010 00 0000100        BLT  L1
003  1110 000 00 0000101        BRA  L2
004  1011 000 00 0001100   L1   LOAD N+1,R0    larger of first 2 in R0
005  1101 000 00 0001101   L2   CMP  R0,N+2    third number in loc N+2
006  1110 010 00 0001000        BLT  L3
007  1110 000 00 0001001        BRA  L4
008  1011 000 00 0001101   L3   LOAD N+2,R0    largest in R0
009  1100 000 00 0001110   L4   STO  R0,MAX
010  1111 000 00 0000000        HALT           last instruction
011  0000000000001111      N    DC   15,2,673  data values
012  0000000000000010
013  0000000001000011
014  0000000000000000      MAX DS  1
                               END
```

FIGURE 7–29 The program of Figure 7–27 assembled relative to address 0.

For example, if the program of Figure 7–29 were to be loaded beginning at storage location `323654`, then, when the dispatcher gives control of the processor to this program, the relocation register is set to `323654`, and during execution of the first LOAD instruction, the actual address of the first operand is computed to be `323654` + `11`, or `323665`, just exactly the correct location.

Given the needs for multiprogramming and virtual memory, and now having the mechanism of dynamic relocation, it is time to take a serious look at how one might design the actual memory manager.

Actual Memory Management

Creating and maintaining an environment which will sustain both multiprogramming and virtual memory consists basically of designing a memory management program which will facilitate the timely movement of blocks of program code into portions of main memory when they are about to be executed and out of main memory to secondary memory (disk) when they are no longer needed. There are basically three approaches to this problem. In the first approach, called *swapping*, all of the code for a particular process is transferred into main storage prior to dispatching the processor to the process. When the process becomes blocked or its time slice is used up, the entire block of code is again swapped out to secondary storage to be replaced by the block of code representing the next process to assume control of the processor, and so on. This approach, while reasonable when the size of main memory is limited, obviously causes a substantial execution delay overhead during the swapping itself. This overhead cost can sometimes be ameliorated by alternative approaches which move *parts* of the code for processes rather than code for entire processes.

The other two approaches are *segmentation* and *paging*. Both recognize the fact that only that portion of a process's code which is about to execute actually needs to be in main storage at a particular time. These approaches have two major advantages over swapping. First, if just a part of a currently executing process needs to be in main memory at a given time, then it follows that parts of more processes can be simultaneously in main store, and thus a greater degree of multiprogramming can be facilitated in the system. The term *degree of multiprogramming* refers to the number of processes currently active within the system.

The second advantage of segmentation or paging is that the capability to move just parts of programs allows part of a program to be loaded into memory and executed, and then be replaced by another part to be executed after the first, and so on, thus facilitating the execution of programs requiring a very large amount of memory, perhaps in total, more than the capacity of the computer's main store. But this would be, then, an implementation of virtual memory, as it has been described above.

These approaches would argue that perhaps swapping does too much. Both segmentation and paging move parts of programs back and forth between secondary storage and main memory as needed. Segmentation and paging differ from one another primarily in the way the code for a particular process is divided. In segmentation, a process's code is divided into a number of *variable sized blocks* corresponding to the logical blocks (such as functions, and data areas) of a process. Paging, on the other hand, divides the process's code into *fixed size blocks* called pages. It is evident that the more logical subdivision of segmentation makes program linking easier, while the fixed blocks of paging, being each interchangeable with the other, makes memory management easier. In either case, since portions of a program's code are being moved around during a program's execution, something like a hardware relocation register will be needed to compute actual addresses in order to avoid unacceptable slowdown in program execution times.

Paging   When paging is used as the basis for memory management, each process in the system is broken up into fixed length blocks called *pages*. Similarly, the main memory is conceptually divided into fixed length blocks called *page frames*. In this environment, each storage reference is represented by an ordered pair (p,d), where p represents a page name and d is the displacement of the referenced byte from the beginning of that page.

The implementation of a paging system requires that there be a *page table* for each active process and a hardware *page table register* which serves roughly the same purpose as the relocation register described above. The page table for a particular active process contains an entry for each page of that process as pictured in Figure 7–30. As shown, the entry for a particular page[10] contains a *presence indicator* field which records whether that particular page is currently in main storage or stored on the disk, and the *starting address* for that particular page.

---

10. In an actual implementation, there will be other fields in each entry in the page table which contain, for example, bits indicative of protection limitations on access to the page pointed to by that particular entry.

Page Table (one for each process)

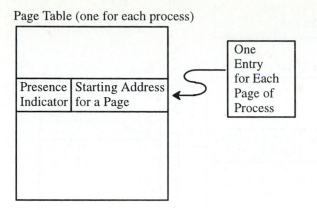

FIGURE 7–30 Page table for an active process.

The page table register is set to point to the page table of the currently dispatched process. As the process executes, reference is made to a particular byte
at (p,d). The storage access proceeds as follows:

- Reference is made to the page table through the page table register,

- The presence indicator field is checked; if the page is present, skip to the
  next step,
  if not, a *page fault* occurs, and the memory manager must:

  a. find the needed page on secondary storage;
  b. if no free page frames currently exist, then determine an expendable
      page to overlay;
  c. transfer the expendable page to secondary storage (if necessary)[11];
  d. copy the needed page from secondary to primary memory;
  e. update the page tables to indicate the "new page" is now resident in
      main memory and the "old" page is no longer resident;

- Calculate the actual address by addition of the displacement d from the
  reference address (p, d) to the the starting address of the page (from the
  page table).

This entire process is pictured in Figure 7–31.
However, this is not the whole story. It remains to consider how the original
set of pages gets into the page frames of memory and how the system decides
which page is expendable in case a page has to be removed during a page fault.

---

11. It is not necessary to recopy the page to be replaced back to secondary memory unless it has been
changed since it was last copied from secondary memory into main memory.

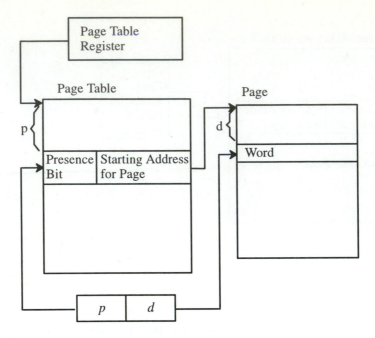

FIGURE 7–31 Operation of a paging system.

The first is fairly easy. There are two choices. We can attempt to anticipate needed pages and copy them from secondary to main memory in anticipation of a reference to instructions or data in them. This technique is called *prepaging*. As in all prognostication, prepaging is a pretty tricky business, and it is clear that there is a cost in terms of data transfer time to bring in what may, in fact, turn out to be an unneeded page. There is also a cost in the space that page occupies in the event that it is never used. Hence, it is more usual to follow an alternative system called *demand paging* in which pages are moved into main memory only when an execution reference requires it. This is a policy choice rather than a technical decision, and is known as the *system fetch policy*.

Determination of a *page replacement policy* is similar. We really want to minimize page traffic as it is basically system overhead. Therefore, in the case of a page fault, we want to remove the page least likely to be needed in the near future. A number of possibilities exist, including random replacement, first-in-first-out, and least-recently-used.

Random replacement, as the name suggests, consists of choosing, at random, some currently resident page to replace when the need arises. This policy, while easy to implement, has the disadvantage that the page which gets replaced may just be the one needed next in the execution of the current process or the next one to be dispatched. The first-in-first-out (FIFO) policy specifies that the page which has been resident in main memory for the longest time is the first to be replaced. FIFO, like random replacement, is easy to implement, but again, it is not necessarily so that the oldest page will not be needed again soon. The most frequently encountered page replacement policy is the *least-re-*

cently-used (LRU) policy. It is based on the assumption that if a particular page has not been used for a long time, it is unlikely to be used again in the near future and is, therefore, a good candidate for removal to secondary storage. The details of how and why LRU works as well as the alternatives are covered in most operating systems courses later in the curriculum.

Implementation of a Simple Memory Manager

We are now prepared to continue our discussion of the operating system simulator. First, note that the simulation does not specifically make use of the page table register and the page tables for the various jobs because the level of detail which these provide is only necessary when the jobs in the system are actually executing and therefore making specific storage references. Again, a true implementation of a memory management system is not possible here, but we can go part of the way by specifying a *model* of such hardware, designing a simple memory manager, and integrating it into the operating system *simulation* to drive its operation for the implementation.

The Model   The model represents a typical, though small, hierarchical memory system. Since this system is a dynamic memory manager based on paging, it will utilize a page table register, an actual main memory, and a virtual memory. These components are shown in Figure 7–32.

The page table register is part of the computer hardware, and the main memory represents the computer's physical central memory, that is, the 640K, or 1, 4, 8, 16, or 32 Megabyte memory in your PC, Macintosh, or workstation. The virtual memory represents the address space that is available to the programmers. It is generally much larger than the actual physical main memory. This virtual memory must be somewhere, and that somewhere is on one or more of the computer's disk drives (hard disk usually). We note that the model is kept purposely small to more easily demonstrate the principles involved. Thus, the main memory has space for only 12 page frames of 2K words each. The virtual memory, on the other hand, though still artificially small, is much larger than the main memory and can accommodate 48 pages.

The Memory Manager   All of the processes currently active in the system, including their data areas, are stored in the virtual memory. But, since instructions must be in main memory to be executed, the memory manager must move the page containing the needed instruction(s) into a page frame in main memory and ensure that memory references during a program's execution are to the right words in the right page frames. Moreover, it is responsible both for movement of information in pages between the virtual memory and main memory and back; and, just as important, keeping track of the current location of each page. In addition, the memory manager must ensure that a program's logical reference to a data item or instruction address is transformed into the

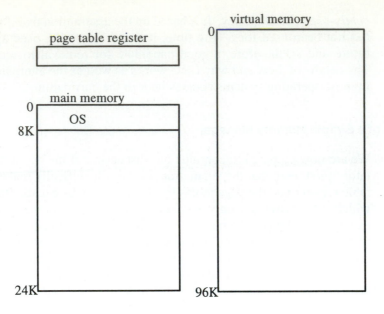

FIGURE 7–32 A memory system.

correct physical address in main memory of the particular data item or instruction needed. Since both main memory and virtual memory are divided into 2K word page frames, we number these as shown in Figure 7–33.

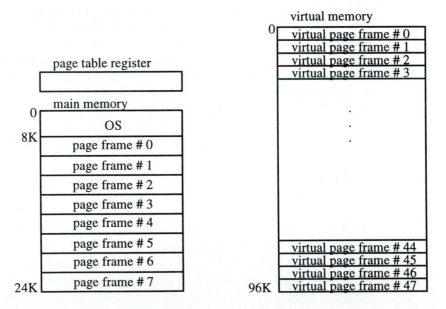

FIGURE 7–33 A memory system with main memory and virtual memory page frames.

If we assume that the system with the memory hierarchy portrayed in Figure 7–33 has been running for a while and that there are currently 4 active processes, the main and virtual memories might look like those shown in Figure 7–34. We note that when several pages from the same process are in main memory, they need not be stored contiguously. If process 2 is currently executing, at least the page with the current instruction must be in main memory. From Figure 7–34, we see that two of process 2's pages are already in main memory: page 0 at main memory page frame 0 and page 1 at page frame 4. Consider, for example, what happens when process 2 makes a storage reference to its logical location 2050 (decimal). This reference is to the second word of the second page of process 2. We also see that page 1 of process 2 is currently in main storage at page frame 4. Since this page frame begins at physical address 18,432, the memory manager must transform the logical reference to location 2050 to the physical address 18,434.

Thus, the purpose of this part of the project is to simulate the flow of user jobs into and through a computer system now including the flow of information into the virtual memory and from there to and from the modeled computer's main memory for simulated program execution. Again, we develop the case study using the MAPS methodology.

Stage 1: The dialogue   The problem is to simulate the operation of a simple memory management system. The details of the model of process management, the hierarchical memory and the simulation have been presented in the previous subsections. It remains to describe the input and output. The input to our simulation program has been previously described in Figure 7–14. The

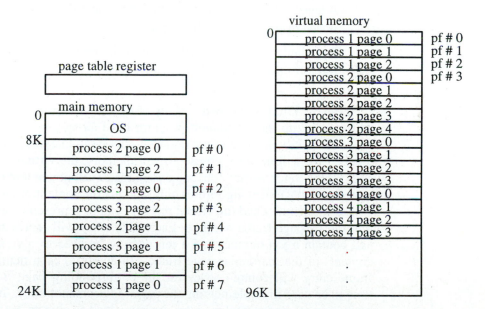

FIGURE 7–34 A snapshot of the computer memory hierarchy.

output from the program will consist of:

- Snapshots of main memory and virtual memory at given intervals of time, and

- A summary table giving statistics for each of the jobs "processed" by the system including:
  - *a.* times the jobs entered and left the system,
  - *b.* percentage I/O block time, number of pages used, number of page faults for each job, and
  - *c.* average CPU and memory utilization for the system as a whole over the simulated time period.

Stage 2:   The specifications   Since the program will be simulating the flow of the jobs through a computer rather than actually executing the jobs, it is necessary again to set out the assumptions:

- The size of the virtual memory is 96K,

- The size of the main memory is 24K,

- The operating system uses 8K of the main memory, which leaves 16K for user jobs,

- The page size will be 2K,

- All jobs begin execution in their first page,

- A snapshot of the contents of both main and virtual memory will be produced every 100 time slices, and

- Page faults for all jobs will occur at the rate of 1/2 of the percentage of the job's pages currently in main storage.

Stage 3:   The breakdown   Many of the data structures and the algorithms which make up the simulation program have already been described. It remains to specify how we might represent this small hierarchical memory in our model. We will need to represent main memory, the virtual memory, and the page table. Since we are concerned with the development and operation of the memory management algorithms only, and not the content of the various pages, both main memory and the virtual memory can be represented as simple tables, indexed by page frame number. Each table entry will represent a page frame and contain a job number and a job page to be used to represent the current contents of that particular page frame. In addition, each main memory page frame entry will contain space for the corresponding page frame's last load time to be used in implementing the page replacement policy. In the simulator, main memory and virtual memory are conceived as objects, MM and VM, respectively, which are both descendents of Element. The interface specifications for MM and VM from the header files, mm.h and vm.h respectively are shown in Figures 7–35 and 7–36.

Each process will require a page table. Page table entries will be indexed by virtual page number and will contain a presence bit and the physical page's location. Recall that our simulation model ignores, for the present, any read/write permission checks.

```cpp
// This is the header file for the MM(Main Memory) class
// that is a descendent of the Element class.  This class
// represents the physical memory of the system - your RAM.


#ifndef MM_H
#define MM_H


#include<iostream.h>
#include<iomanip.h>
#include "queue.h"
#include "standobj.h"
#include "osconsts.h"
#include "pagetab.h"
#include "pcb.h"
#include "elements.h"


class MM:public Element // Main Memory
{
 private:
  // DATA MEMBERS ...
  struct pageframe
  {
    int jobnumber;
    int jobpage;
    long loadtime;
  };



  pageframe* pageframe_array[MMTABLESIZE];

  Queue* mm_free_list_ptr;
  float mm_utilization;
  float mm_inst_utilization;

 public:
  // MEMBER FUNCTIONS ...
  // constructor - destructors
  MM::MM();
  MM::~MM();


  // display
  void display();
```

```
          // access - modify
          int get_jobnumber(int);
          void set_jobnumber(int,int);
          int get_jobpage(int);
          void set_jobpage(int,int);
          long get_loadtime(int);
          void set_loadtime(int,long);
          Queue* return_mm_free_list_ptr();
          int find_oldest_frame();
          void release_memory(PCB*);
          void calc_mm_utilization();
      }; // end class MM



      #endif
```

FIGURE 7–35 The C++header file for the object representing Main Memory, MM.

```
      // This is the header file for the VM(Virtual Memory) class
      // that is a descendent of the Element class.  This class
      // represents your disk or other mass storage device.


      #ifndef VM_H
      #define VM_H


      #include<iostream.h>
      #include<iomanip.h>
      #include "strg.h"
      #include "osconsts.h"
      #include "elements.h"
      #include "pagetab.h"
      #include "pcb.h"


      class VM:public Element // Virtual Memory
      {
       private:
         // DATA MEMBERS ...
         struct vpage
         {
           int jobnumber;
           int jobpage;
         };


         vpage* virtual_page_array[TABLESIZE];
         int vm_free;


       public:
         // MEMBER FUNCTIONS ...
```

```
    // constructor - destructor
    VM();
    ~VM();

    // display
    virtual void display();


    // access - modify
    int get_vm_free();
    void load_proc_to_vm(PCB*);
    void remove_proc_from_vm(PCB*);
}; // end VM class


#endif
```

FIGURE 7–36 The C++header file for the object representing virtual memory, VM.

A page table is represented in the simulation as the object, PageTable, also a descendent of Element. Its interface specification, pagetab.h, is shown in Figure 7–37.

```
// This is the header file for the PageTable class
// that is a descendent of the Element class.  The class
// supports the PCB class by mapping the use of main memory.


#ifndef PAGETAB_H
#define PAGETAB_H


#include <iostream.h>
#include <iomanip.h>
#include "osconsts.h"
#include "elements.h"


class PageTable:public Element
{
  private:
    // DATA MEMBERS
    struct page
    {
      int page_frame_num;
      boolean presence_bit;
      long loadtime;
    };


    page* page_table[TABLESIZE];
```

```
public:
    // MEMBER FUNCTIONS
    // constructors - destructors
    PageTable();
    virtual ~PageTable();

    //display
    void display();


    // access/modify
    int get_page_frame_num(int);
    void set_page_frame_num(int,int);
    boolean get_presence_bit(int);
    void set_presence_bit(int,boolean);
    long get_loadtime(int);
    void set_loadtime(int,long);
}; // end class PageTable


#endif
```

FIGURE 7–37 The C++ header file for the object representing page tables, `PageTable`.

The key parameters and variables are initialized in the header file, `os-consts.h`, as shown below:

Name	Meaning	Initial Value
VMSIZE	Size of virtual memory	64
MMSIZE	Size of main memory	32
PSIZE	Page size	2048

Stage 4: Defining Abstractions   The essential tasks of memory management, as we have seen, can be broken down into:

- loading and entering program into virtual memory,

- fetching pages from virtual memory to main memory as needed,

- calculating effective addresses for instruction and operand locations during program execution, and

- selecting and moving out of main memory and back to virtual memory those pages not immediately needed to make room for new pages essential for a process' continued execution.

The algorithm is shown in Figures 7–18, 7–19, and 7–20. This part of the simulator begins its work, after initializing the parameters, by scheduling as many jobs from the input queue (data input to the simulator) into the virtual memory as possible. A job cannot enter the system unless there are sufficient page frames available in virtual memory to hold all of the program's instruction and data pages. The details are shown in Figure 7–18.

Once a job's pages have been loaded into virtual memory and the job's PCB created, the job is ready to begin, or later, continue, execution when granted a processor by the `dispatcher`. To execute, the process must have pages in main memory, in particular, the page containing the code to be executed must be resident in main memory. Our earlier discussion indicated a preference for demand paging as a fetch policy. Hence, the memory manager's next task, fetching pages for execution, will take place in the execute phase of a program's processing. In our simulator, this occurs in the `OSObj` object's method `timeslicer`. The algorithm is sketched out in Figure 7–20.

A process which has been dispatched to the processor for a time slice is either a new process (with no pages) which will immediately cause a page fault, or it is a process continuing execution (after a block or time-slice exceeded) and thereby may or may not encounter a page fault during this time slice. In the latter case, we determine whether a page fault occurs in this time slice by applying the earlier algorithm:

1. Draw a random number;
2. Calculate the percentage of the process's virtual pages currently in store;
3. If the number exceeds that percentage, use the page fault algorithm.

But there is another possibility relevant to the process returning to continue its execution. During this time slice, the process's code to be executed may continue to come from the page used during the last execution cycle, or at some time during this quantum, the process may branch to code or refer to data in a different page. This is simulated by a two-step calculation. First, a random number between 0 and 1 is drawn (using `random` from the file `random.cxx`). If the random number is less than the reciprocal of the size of the process in pages plus 0.2, representing a somewhat greater than 20% likelihood of continuing to execute instructions from the same page, execution continues. If the random number is greater than or equal to the reciprocal of the size of the process in pages plus 0.2, we determine which new page is needed as follows:

1. Draw another random number;
2. Scale it to between 1 and the size of the current process, in pages;
3. If the resulting value (truncated) is not equal to the current page number, it becomes the number of the new page;
4. Otherwise, repeat steps 1–3.

Of course, if the needed new page is not resident in main memory, a page fault must be generated to get it. Note that this simple algorithm does give some recognition of programs' locality by assuming a significant chance of continuing execution from the same page. It is possible with this algorithm, as in real life, to have a program execute without using all of its pages.

Calculating effective addresses for instruction and operand references, an essential part of memory management, is not needed for the simulation model since no individual program instructions are to be executed.

A process may complete during a given time slice. In that case, the memory manager will need to remove that process's pages from main and virtual memory.

The last part of the memory manager is the page fault handler. Once the page fault has occurred (in `timeslicer`), it is necessary to locate the needed page in the virtual memory. Having found the desired page, we must determine whether there is space in main memory for it. If not (and this will normally be the case), we must determine which of the resident pages to remove. The simplest algorithm (though not the best) is FIFO, which entails removing the page which has been main memory resident for the longest time. Implementation of FIFO requires that the time each page is placed into main memory be maintained, thus explaining the need for the extra field, `loadtime`, in the main memory object for keeping the load time for all the resident pages. We assume that it will take 100 ms each to remove the oldest page and to move in the needed page. The details appear in Figure 7–38.

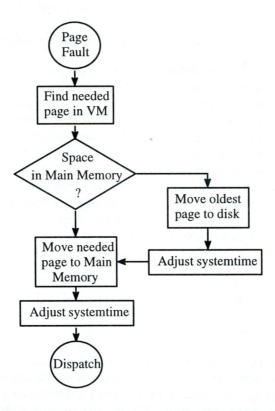

FIGURE 7–38 Page fault routine for the simulator.

Stage 5: The Code Loading entering programs into virtual memory is done by the object `OSObj` member function `scheduler`. The C++ program code for `scheduler` in Figure 7–22 is used again as a point of reference in the following discussion.

The `scheduler` loads jobs from the job input queue, `JobSpecQ`, into virtual memory until there are no jobs left which will fit, that is either `JobSpecQ` is empty or contains only jobs which need more pages than currently available in virtual memory:

```
while(a_proc_will_fit){
    if(!job_inputq_ptr->is_empty()) // there are jobs
      current_job_ptr = (JobSpec*)job_inputq_ptr->front();
    else{
        a_proc_will_fit = FALSE;
    }
```

It is careful not to continually attempt to load jobs which have already been found to be too big to fit:

```
if(repeat_flag && (current_job_ptr->get_jobnumber()==
        repeat_jobnumber)){
    // The entire job_inputq has been examined.
    a_proc_will_fit = FALSE;
    }
```

The actual calculations are done in the following statements (the processor management parts have already been discussed, and are omitted here):

```
if(a_proc_will_fit){
        int proc_size_in_pages =
        calc_size_in_pages(current_job_ptr);
        if((virtual_memory_ptr->get_vm_free() -
        proc_size_in_pages)>=0){
```

If the process will fit, it is loaded into virtual memory:

```
virtual_memory_ptr->load_proc_to_vm(new_proc_ptr);
```

and removed from the input queue:

```
job_inputq_ptr->remove();
```

Otherwise, the process will not fit and the flags `repeat_flag` and `repeat_jobnumber` are set. The remaining details are in Figure 7–22.

The memory management functions which take place during execution are performed by the member function `timeslicer` in the object `OSObj`, as shown in Figure 7–24. After determining that it is not in a wait state (see the previous discussion of the simulation of process management, Stage 5), the `timeslicer` determines whether the current process is new:

```
if(current_proc_ptr->get_current_vpage() == -1)
```

If so, it sets up the process's page 0 to begin execution:

```
current_proc_ptr->set_current_vpage(0);
```

and calls for a page fault to get it:

```
taskflag = _pagefault_;
```

If the process is continuing, we need to determine whether execution will continue from the page used in the last cycle, or some new page:

```
if(current_proc_ptr->check_for_new_current_vpage())
```

If execution continues from a new page:

```
current_proc_ptr->select_new_current_vpage();
```

it must be determined whether this new page is resident:

```
if(!current_proc_ptr->test_if_page_in_MM())
```

if not, set up for a page fault:

```
taskflag = _pagefault_;
```

It remains to determine whether the process completes during this time slice.

```
if(current_proc_ptr->get_jobtime() <= 0)
```

In the case of process completion, its pages must be returned to the free list. This is accomplished for the virtual memory:

```
virtual_memory_ptr->remove_proc_from_vm(current_proc_ptr);
```

and the main memory:

```
main_memory_ptr->release_memory(current_proc_ptr);
```

so that both will be available for loading and executing newly entering jobs.

The memory manager's page fault handler is called from timeslicer. The code is the method pagefault in the object OSObj, as shown in Figure 7–40.

```
// Function: OSObj::pagefault()
// Purpose:  A piece of needed code is copied into main memory.
//           To place a page for the current process in main
//           memory from virtual memory. If the number of free
//           page frames is > 0, the proc's current_vpage is
```

```
//              placed in MM, else a page replacement policy is
//              called. In this version that policy is FIFO: first
//              in - first out, to remove from memory a page of
//              some proc to make room. A single page move is
//           assumed to take 100ms.
// Pre:      MM has an initial set of pages in its pageframes
//              and current_proc_ptr->current_vpage = i.
//              free_frame_list is an initial list of unoccupied
//           pageframe numbers.
// Post:     If size of free_frame_list < 0 then
//              call page replacement policy and add a page to
//              mm_free.  In the first empty pageframe in
//              free_frame_list place i and change the
//              current_vpage's presence bit to reflect that it is //
//           now in MM.  systemtime += 100ms
//              Call dispatcher().
void OSObj::pagefault()
{
  pagefault_cnt++;
  eventflag = page_fault;

  if(main_memory_ptr->return_mm_free_list_ptr()->is_empty()){
    //cout << "There are no empty pageframes, ";
    //cout << "go to page replacement";
    //cout << endl;
    page_replacement_cnt++;
    fifo();
    eventflag = page_swap;
  }
  /*else
    cout << "There are unused frames in memory." << endl;*/


    // That is frames that have never been used or contain
    // pages for processes that have completed execution
    // or a page released by the page replacement policy.


    Queue* free_frame_list = main_memory_ptr->
      return_mm_free_list_ptr();
    int empty_frame = ((IntObj*)(free_frame_list->front()))->
      get_val();

    int newpage = current_proc_ptr->get_current_vpage();


    main_memory_ptr->set_jobnumber(empty_frame,
            current_proc_ptr->get_jobnumber());
    main_memory_ptr->set_jobpage(empty_frame,newpage);
    main_memory_ptr->set_loadtime(empty_frame,systemtime);


    PageTable* cp_table = current_proc_ptr->
      return_page_table_ptr();
    cp_table->set_page_frame_num(newpage,empty_frame);
    cp_table->set_presence_bit(newpage,TRUE);
    cp_table->set_loadtime(newpage,systemtime);
```

```
free_frame_list->remove();
systemtime += 100;


current_proc_ptr->set_state("ready");
readyq_ptr->enter(current_proc_ptr);
//cout << "call to dispatcher from pagefault" << endl;
taskflag = _dispatcher_;
} // end OSObj::pagefault()
```

FIGURE 7-39 The C++ program code for the member function `pagefault`.

Upon entering the page fault handler, it is first necessary to determine if there are any page frames free:

```
if(main_memory_ptr->return_mm_free_list_ptr()->is_empty())
```

If there is a free page frame, that is, a page frame that either is never used during the simulation run or currently contains a page from a process that has completed and left the system, then we find its page frame number:

```
Queue* free_frame_list = main_memory_ptr->
    return_mm_free_list_ptr();
  int empty_frame = ((IntObj*)(free_frame_list->front()))->
    get_val();
```

and then pick up the page to be moved from the virtual memory:

```
    int newpage = current_proc_ptr->get_current_vpage();
```

and put it in main memory, setting `loadtime` for the page replacement algorithm:

```
main_memory_ptr->set_jobnumber(empty_frame,
            current_proc_ptr->get_jobnumber());
  main_memory_ptr->set_jobpage(empty_frame,newpage);
  main_memory_ptr->set_loadtime(empty_frame,systemtime);
```

and then update the page tables:

```
PageTable* cp_table = current_proc_ptr->return_page_table_ptr();
  cp_table->set_page_frame_num(newpage,empty_frame);
  cp_table->set_presence_bit(newpage,TRUE);
  cp_table->set_loadtime(newpage,systemtime);
```

Alternatively, if we find the more likely possibility of a page fault with no empty page frames in main memory, the page replacement policy is invoked:

```
if(main_memory_ptr->return_mm_free_list_ptr()->is_empty()){
    page_replacement_cnt++;
    fifo();
```

In this case, we use the FIFO scheme. It is implemented in C++ code which may be found in Figure 7–40 as the `fifo` member function.

```cpp
// Function: OSObj::fifo()
// Purpose:  To implement the first in - first out (FIFO) page
//           replacement policy. The process with the pageframe
//           containing the oldest page in MM is freed and
//           placed on the mm_free_list. If fifo() is called you
//           are performing a page move, assumed to take 100ms.
//           That means a complete replacement with the page
//           the proc actually needs takes 200ms.
// Pre:      The size of mm_free_list = 0, MM is initialized and
//           the oldest pageframe M contains page I of proc N.
// Post:     The size of mm_free_list = 1, mm_free_list = (M)
//           and the presence_bit of page I for process N is
//           marked FALSE of process N. systemtime += 100 ms
void OSObj::fifo(){
  PCB* temp_ptr;


  int oldest_frame = main_memory_ptr->find_oldest_frame();
  int job_with_oldest_page = main_memory_ptr->
    get_jobnumber(oldest_frame);
  int oldest_page = main_memory_ptr->get_jobpage(oldest_frame);


  if(job_with_oldest_page == current_proc_ptr->get_jobnumber()){
    //cout << "oldest page belongs to current job" << endl;
    current_proc_ptr->return_page_table_ptr()->
    set_presence_bit(oldest_page,FALSE);
  }
  else{
    //cout << "oldest page belongs to non-current process";
    //cout << endl;
    // so search the blockq for the process
    boolean found = blockq_ptr->
    search_q(job_with_oldest_page,temp_ptr);

    if(!found){ // search the readyq for the process
      found = readyq_ptr->
       search_q(job_with_oldest_page,temp_ptr);
      if(!found){
    cout << "Program Error: Process in Main Memory cannot ";
    cout << "be found on the ready or block queues." << endl;
    cout << "ProcID: " << setw(8) << job_with_oldest_page ;
    cout << endl;
    cout << "If you get this message, ";
    cout << " you are in serious trouble.";
    exit(0);
      }
    }// if(!found)
    temp_ptr->return_page_table_ptr()->
    set_presence_bit(oldest_page,FALSE);
  }// else oldest page belongs to non-current process


  // add freed frame to mm_free_list
  IntObj* new_free_frame = new IntObj(oldest_frame);
```

```
        main_memory_ptr->return_mm_free_list_ptr()->
          enter(new_free_frame);
      systemtime += 100;
    } // end OSObj::fifo()
```

FIGURE 7–40 The C++ program code for the member function `fifo`.

First, the page which has been in main memory longest is found. This is accomplished by the member function, `find_oldest_frame` in the object MM:

```
// Function:  MM::find_oldest_frame()
// Purpose:   Return the the pageframe number with the oldest
//            loadtime
// Pre:       receiver is initialized
// Post:      find_oldest_frame() = i, where
//            pageframe_array[i].loadtime has the smallest value
//            of all pageframes
int MM::find_oldest_frame()
{
   int oldest_frame = 0;
   long min_time = pageframe_array[0]->loadtime;
   long tmp_time;
   for(int i = 1;i<MMTABLESIZE;i++)
   {
     tmp_time = pageframe_array[i]->loadtime;
     if(tmp_time < min_time)
     {
       min_time = tmp_time;
       oldest_frame = i;
     }
   }
   return oldest_frame;
} // end MM::find_oldest_frame()
```

Then, space is created on the free list for the `oldest_frame`:

```
IntObj* new_free_frame = new IntObj(oldest_frame);
```

and the page frame is added:

```
main_memory_ptr->return_mm_free_list_ptr()->en-
ter(new_free_frame);
```

the system timer is incremented to reflect the search time:

```
systemtime += 100;
```

and control is returned to `pagefault`. Much detail has been omitted here for clarity. The reader should study the code in Figures 7–39 and 7–40 for a fuller understanding of the complete `pagefault` algorithm.

EXERCISES

7–49 Explain how multiprogramming complicates the task of the memory manager.

7–50 Explain what is meant by program relocation. What is the difference between static and dynamic relocation?

7–51 What is virtual memory?

7–52 Consider the program of Figure 7–29. What is the actual address of the STOre instruction which has the label L4? What would its actual address be if the program were to be loaded at address 200,000? Use the single register relocation scheme to calculate your answers.

7–53 Distinguish between swapping and paging as techniques for memory management. List two advantages of paging over swapping.

7–54 Distinguish between segmentation and paging. List an advantage of each over the other.

7–55 Describe an entry in a process's page table.

7–56 Describe what happens when a page fault occurs.

7–57 Under what conditions does a page that is removed during a page fault, not need to be copied back to the secondary storage? How might the system track this condition?

7–58 Distinguish between demand paging and prepaging as a system fetch policy. Why is the latter rarely used?

7–59 Describe the data structures and an algorithm that could be used to implement a FIFO method for a page replacement policy.

7–60 Describe data structures and an algorithm which could be used to implement a LRU page replacement policy.

7–61 In the section on the implementation, a parenthetical phrase indicates that the FIFO page replacement scheme is not likely to be the best. Why is this so? Can you describe a better scheme? How about an optimal scheme? Why is this optimal scheme not used?

SUMMARY

This chapter has introduced the operating system as an example of a large software system. We see that the total amount of program code in an actual operating system is too immense to present or discuss in its entirety in such a small space as a chapter of a book. On the other hand, we have demonstrated once again, as in previous chapters, the value of simulation as a technique for modeling the behavior of certain "idealized" parts of an actual operating system—the memory management and process management functions.

The importance of object-oriented design, along with the particular classes developed here and in earlier chapters, is also emphasized. This design technique allows us to reuse software that had been developed under an entirely different application framework. Surely, stacks, queues, trees, and other fundamental classes have wide use across the computing discipline. Here they have been shown to be particularly valuable in the design of an operating system's software components.

The complete code for the simulator appears in the appendix to the corresponding chapter in the *Laboratory Manual*. Readers are encouraged to study the code and accompanying comments in detail and to follow up with the laboratory projects in the *Laboratory Manual*. Your study of these principles of operating systems and the transition from an understanding of principles to the design and implementation of the simulator positions you well not only for advanced study of operating systems but also for comfortably and confidently attacking a large software project. Both the process and the subject matter will be important in future study.

References

[1] Kernighan, Brian W. and Rob Pike, *The UNIX Programming Environment*, Prentice-Hall, Inc., Englewood Cliffs, NJ, 1984.

[2] Peterson, James L. and Abraham Silberschatz, *Operating System Concepts*, Second Edition, Addison-Wesley Publishing Company, Reading, MA, 1985.

[3] Sun Microsystems, STB Editor, "SunOS Subjects," *Sun Software Technical Bulletin*, Issue 1991-11 (November 1991), 15-21.

[4] Flynn, Ida M. and Ann McIver McHoes, *Understanding Operating Systems*, Brooks/Cole Publishing Company, Pacific Grove, CA, 1991.

[5] Tanenbaum, Andrew S., *Modern Operating Systems*, Prentice-Hall, Inc., Englewood Cliffs, NJ, 1992.

[6] Wilson, James, *Berkeley UNIX: A Simple and Comprehensive Guide*, John Wiley & Sons, Inc., New York, NY, 1991.

CHAPTER 8

SOFTWARE ENGINEERING: AN OVERVIEW

So far, we have considered the development, testing, measurement, and applications of several specific fundamental data structures in computing. The goal has been to lay groundwork that will enable us to understand the process of large software systems design. Because software has become a major industry in the world, a relatively new area of study, software engineering, has evolved in order to improve the overall quality and effectiveness of the process of developing software. This chapter explores the nature of software engineering as a field of study and a profession, so that readers will be prepared to study it in detail later in the curriculum.

THE CHALLENGE FOR MODERN SOFTWARE

The software industry has grown rapidly in many directions during the last three decades. It faces great challenges in order to enable modern computers to fulfill their inherent and evolving potential. The styles and techniques for developing quality software must change rapidly too, since recent methods have not effectively bridged the gap between promise and delivery.

The Changing Software Industry

The computer software industry has grown dramatically over the last several decades. In the 1960s, computer manufacturers provided most of the software to accompany their mainframes and minicomputers—compilers, operating systems, user interfaces, I/O and database systems, and so forth. Even software developed by users for their own applications was often remarketed by the manufacturers themselves. By 1970, the total U.S. expenditure for software was estimated at about $500 million annually [5].

By 1975, that number grew to an estimated $1 billion as mainframe manufacturers unbundled their software operations and independent software firms began to emerge in the information systems application area. By 1980, software sales approached $3 billion, and then the industry began an extremely rapid growth period which has not slowed down much since.

Current estimates (U.S. Department of Commerce, 1991) show that in 1990, software sales by American manufacturers alone totaled $35 billion, which accounts for more than 40 percent of the world's software market. This represents an approximate doubling of the market about every five years. Forecasts predict that the market will continue to grow at a rate exceeding 10 percent per year for the foreseeable future.

As the amount of software in use continues to grow, so does the enormity of the task of software maintenance; the process of keeping existing software systems operational and relatively bug-free. As we noted in Chapter 1, software maintenance consumes a majority of the total person power that is consumed by the software lifecycle.

The Software Crisis Persists

While the software market grows at a rapid rate, the ability of the software industry to provide timely products lags significantly behind the development of technology that might support these products. The inability, identified in Chapter 1, of the 1979 software industry to deliver effective software in a timely manner still persists in the 1990s. Here is an example.

A 1992 report entitled "Embedded Computer Systems: Significant Software Problems on C–17 Must Be Addressed" [8] typifies the severity of the current crisis. The U.S. Air Force has plans to buy 120 new C–17 transport aircraft, at an estimated cost of $36 billion. This aircraft has 19 different embedded computers incorporating over 80 microprocessors on board which utilize about 1.35 million lines of software code.

At present, this project has one developmental and 10 production aircraft currently under contract with McDonnell Douglas Corporation. At the outset, both the Air Force and the contractor agreed to use proven technology and existing software to reduce the complexity and technical risks associated with the C–17 software development effort. Later, however, it was discovered that the complexity and scope of this software project had been greatly underestimated. From 1985 to 1990, the number of specific software subsystems on the C–17 had grown from 4 to a total of 56.

As of March 1, 1992, the C–17 development effort had fallen two years behind schedule and had grown $1.5 billion over its projected cost. Software development has been a major factor in this delay. The report says that "the C–17 is a good example of how <u>not</u> to manage software development when procuring a major weapons system." Because the Air Force had originally assumed that software development would be a relatively low-risk aspect of this project, it did little to oversee or manage the contractor's work. The contractor, at the same time, took several short cuts that have substantially increased the risk of software failure as well as increased the eventual cost of software maintenance once the C–17 becomes operational.

In recognition of the extent of these problems, Congress has recently reduced funding for the program and required the Defense Department to assess the C–17's operational capability. GAO believes that more steps are needed in order to minimize future operational risks that may arise from faulty software.

EXERCISE

8–1 Go to the library and look for references (either oblique or direct) to the "software crisis" in the printed media over the past year. Possible sources are newspapers, magazines, and especially business publications (including the Wall Street Journal). List and briefly summarize the articles you found. On the basis of your investigation, write a short paper: "The Software Crisis: the Public Perception and its Implications."

METHODOLOGY TO MEET THE CHALLENGE: SOFTWARE ENGINEERING

Recall the nine qualities of "good" software that were portrayed in Figure 1-1, described in Chapter 1, and are reproduced in Figure 8–1. Different software methodologies have been proposed that are aimed at producing software that possesses these qualities. In general, these methodologies fall under the rubric of "software engineering." A definition was proposed at the first major software engineering conference in 1969 [3]:

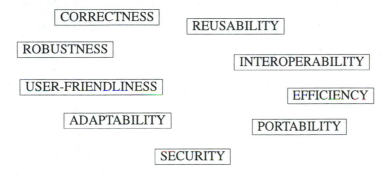

FIGURE 8–1   Nine qualities of a good software system.

Definition   *Software engineering* is the establishment and use of sound engineering principles in order to obtain economical software that is reliable and works efficiently on real machines.

Other definitions have been proposed, but all stress the importance of applying traditional engineering principles to the design, implementation, and maintenance of computer software. Software engineering can be viewed as a collection of tools and procedures that enable individuals, groups, and corporations to control the process of software development.

Software Models Revisited

To this end, various procedural methods have been proposed to address the problems of software development and maintenance. The two that have emerged most strongly over the last several years are the so-called "lifecycle model" and the "prototyping model."

The Lifecycle Model As outlined in Chapter 1, the lifecycle model divides software development and maintenance into six major steps, as pictured in Figure 8–2. For developing a single software project, these six downward-cascading steps often take place one time, in the order shown, and in relative isolation from the ultimate user who will be the beneficiary of the software.

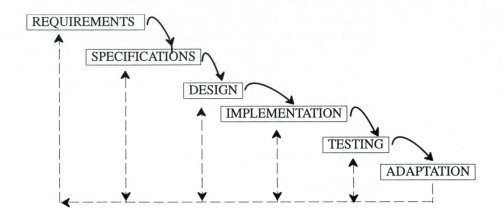

FIGURE 8–2 The software lifecycle (waterfall) model with feedback loops (dashed lines).

However, this need not be the case. Dashed lines in Figure 8–2 show different points at which the software can be respecified, redesigned, reimplemented (in part), and retested. In effect, at any stage of the cycle, a previous stage can be revisited. Moreover, if that loop includes input from the eventual users of the system, the outcome can ideally be quite well-suited to the user's expectations.

In spite of its potential and its widespread use in practice, the lifecycle model has been criticized in recent years. This criticism makes the following points:

- Real software projects often do not follow the sequence of steps proposed by the model.

- Rarely is the user in a position to predict all the system's requirements at the outset of the project.

- During the long time delay between the first and last stages of the project, the system's requirements themselves often change.

To help address these concerns, the alternative prototyping model has evolved in recent years.

The Prototyping Model   The prototyping model has as a guiding premise the idea that the user should be an active participant in the initial design of a system, and that design should be so simple that it can be developed rapidly (in the form of a "prototype" model of the final system). This process is pictured in Figure 8–3.

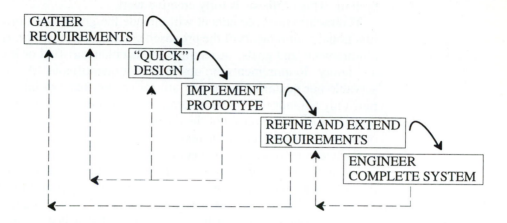

FIGURE 8–3   The prototyping model.

Here, we see a different configuration of the feedback loops. In particular, the steps of requirements gathering, initial design, and prototype implementation form a feedback loop that, with direct interaction from the user, enables a more informed design of the actual system to be eventually developed at the next step. This strategy is designed to ensure better success for the engineered product that will eventually come out of the fifth step.

Whether the traditional waterfall model or the prototyping model is used for software design, certain steps must inevitably take place. Moreover, either model allows the system to be designed in an object-oriented or a function-oriented style. The next few sections discuss these inevitable steps and alternatives in more detail. There, too, we introduce some of the tools that designers use during the process of software engineering.

REQUIREMENTS ANALYSIS

Requirements analysis is a process by which sponsors and developers reach agreements about the nature of a software system. In the traditional lifecycle model, the result of this negotiating process is a requirements document that becomes part of a contractual agreement between these two parties. The requirements document includes a complete specification of the behavior of the proposed system. Thus, the requirements document provides a basis for determining the correctness of the delivered product. The details of how this agreement is reached vary from system to system.

Requirements analysis is not straightforward. Sponsors and users may not have a clear picture of what they actually need, let alone the best technical solutions that meet this need. The developer may not have sufficient understanding of the domain of applications in which the user works. There may be conflicts among sponsors and/or users, as mentioned above. From all of this information, the systems analyst must infer and synthesize a broad outline for the new system. This synthesis is truly creative work.

The requirements document will include the goals, and functional and nonfunctional requirements of the proposed system. A distinction is made between requirements and goals. A requirement is either satisfied or it is not—without ambiguity. Requirements are observable or quantifiable. A goal is neither observable nor quantifiable. Goals are somewhat fuzzy or ambiguous, and thus play only a minor role in the requirements document. Usually, goals are stated in the introductory section of the document (in part, to inspire the development of forward-looking requirements).

Software requirements generally fall into two categories—*functional requirements* and *nonfunctional requirements*. A functional requirement is one that is *observable*, meaning that it relates to the input and output behavior of the system. Another way of stating this is that functional requirements relate to concrete services provided by the system (what it does). Nonfunctional requirements state constraints under which the proposed system will operate. Nonfunctional requirements must be stated in such a way that one can determine whether or not the requirement has been satisfied in the delivered system.

Typically, functional requirements consume more space in a requirements document than the nonfunctional requirements. The requirements are laid out in complete detail, with careful attention being paid to abnormal situations (to assure robustness). Very often, requirements specifications are written in English, using diagrams and formal notations that can be understood by both sponsors and developers. It is important that the sponsors understand the requirements document, or else they will not be willing to sign off on the document as a contractual agreement. For this reason, formal mathematical notations are not appropriate for specifying system behavior in a requirements document unless the sponsors themselves possess mathematical sophistication.

SOFTWARE SPECIFICATIONS

Software sponsors and users do not always possess the technical sophistication needed to understand the exact functional capabilities of the system. This fact makes it important for the designers to produce a second requirements document specifically for the system developers. This second document is normally called the *requirements specification* and it usually is more rigorous in its mathematical sophistication. The requirements specification often includes tentative design decisions, and often utilizes pre- and postconditions or some other formal language to specify the behavior of key system components. The requirements specification is used to guide the design process which follows. Figure 8–4 shows the outline of a typical requirements document.

I	INTRODUCTION
II	SYSTEM MODEL
III	FUNCTIONAL REQUIREMENTS
IV	NONFUNCTIONAL REQUIREMENTS
V	DATA DICTIONARY
VI	ANTICIPATED CHANGES
VII	GLOSSARY
VIII	INDEX

FIGURE 8–4   Outline of a typical requirements document.

The introduction of such a document explains the background of, and motivation for, the proposed system. This is where goals can be mentioned. The system model provides an overview of the functionality of the system, usually by means of diagrams. So-called *data flow diagrams*, which will be discussed below, are a popular method for presenting the system model. The functional requirements provide a detailed accounting of the services to be provided by the system. The nonfunctional requirements define the constraints under which the system will operate. The so-called *data dictionary* documents all data items mentioned in the system model, such as the data items and file formats that appear in data flow diagrams. *Anticipated changes* are documented in order to promote the graceful evolution of the system. The *glossary* includes both application-oriented terms (e.g., a definition for "backorder") and technical computer terms (e.g., random access file) for nontechnical users.

The nonfunctional requirements of a complex system can be quite extensive. Issues that may need to be addressed in this part of the requirements document include the following:

1. hardware issues
2. performance issues
3. human factors issues
4. security issues
5. interoperability issues

For example, the nonfunctional requirements describe the hardware that the system will require, constraints on the size and format of data files assumed by the system, necessary response times, the amount and nature of user documentation and training, constraints on the complexity of the user interface, constraints on the amount of time a typical user will need to learn to use the system, who will have access to the system, how often data files will need to be backed up, and other constraints that are related to interfacing the software with other systems.

Data Flow Diagrams   Data flow diagrams are often used to present the system model. They show the fundamental activities in the proposed system and the flow of data among those activities. Figure 8–5 shows one of the notational systems that are used for presenting data flow diagrams.

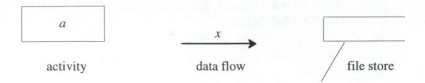

activity   data flow   file store

FIGURE 8–5   Symbols used in data flow diagrams.

Boxes represent activities, each of which normally has data flowing in and out. The flow of data is indicated by means of labeled arrows, and the labels name the data items that flow into and out of activities. Files (data stores) are distinguished by open-ended boxes. Figure 8–6 shows a data flow diagram for the fried chicken recipe shown below:

HOW TO PREPARE CHICKEN FOR FRYING

Cut in halves, quarters, or pieces.

Wash, dry well, and flour pieces by shaking several at a time in a paper bag containing . . .

> 1 cup GOLD MEDAL
> flour
> 2 tsp. salt
> 1/4 tsp. pepper
> 1/2 tsp. celery salt
> 1 tsp. paprika (if desired)

FRIED CHICKEN

Crisp and tender . . . according to the best Southern traditions.

Prepare *young, tender* Fryers as above. Place halves, or quarters (in heavy deep skillet) in 1/2" hot fat (part butter) skin side down. Brown on both sides and cover tightly. Cook over very low heat until tender (35 to 40 min.). To crisp the crust . . . remove the cover and cook 5 to 10 min. longer. Use the leftover flour plus extra, if needed, to make cream gravy (p. 356).

(Source: Betty Crocker's Picture Cook Book, General Mills, 1950, p. 283.)

Note in Figure 8–6 that a data flow diagram does not present an algorithm. It does not include control structures or any specification for the temporal order in which the activities are to occur. For example, Figure 8–6 does not specify whether we prepare the gravy before or after we brown the fryers.

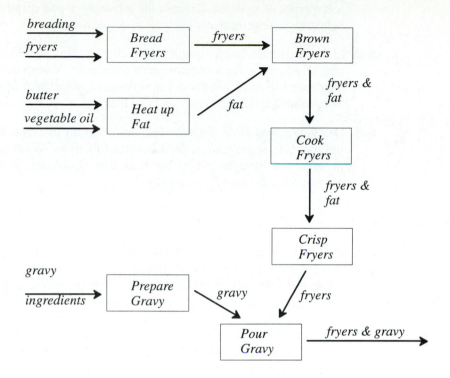

FIGURE 8–6   Data flow diagram for preparing fried chicken.

EXERCISES

8–2 Indicate whether each of the following statements represents a goal, a functional requirement or a nonfunctional requirement:

a. The system will provide a user-friendly interface for doing mathematics.

b. The user shall be able to utilize the full capabilities of the system after participating in a training course consisting of three training sessions of four hours each.

c. If the user chooses "integrate" from the compute subgenus, the system will compute the definite integral for the expression shown in the currently active expression window.

d. The system shall be able to display the derivative of any expression constructed by the user within 10 seconds.

e. The system requires 5 megabytes of RAM and 10 megabytes of disk space under the UNIX operating system.

8–3 Some software engineers recommend that the user's manual should be written before the system is designed and implemented. Some even suggest that the user's manual can serve as a requirements document for some types of systems. Discuss the advantages and disadvantages of this approach to requirements analysis and specification.

8–4 List and discuss briefly qualities which you think would constitute a notion of goodness for a requirements document. Compare your list to the characterization of goodness for software systems that appears in Figure 8–1. Which qualities appear in both lists?

8–5 Develop a data flow diagram for any program that you have written in the past. That program should contain functions. What features of your program are brought out by the data flow diagram? What features are obscured by the data flow diagram?

SOFTWARE DESIGN

During the design stage of the software lifecycle, developers produce a structural framework for the proposed system. This framework is presented as a *design document* that describes how the system is organized in terms of components, component behaviors, and component interactions. The design document is to a software project what a blueprint is to an architectural project. The design document must be checked against the requirements document for consistency. If the design document is consistent with the requirements document, the design is said to be *correct*.

Levels of Organization

Fundamentally, all design methodologies involve breaking up problems into subproblems. What distinguishes one methodology from another are the criteria that are used to perform this decomposition. The two dominant software design methodologies are *function-oriented design*, which views a system as a collection of interacting functions or routines, and *object-oriented design*, which views a system as a set of interacting objects. These design methodologies are introduced on pages 436 and 441.

In either case, design involves determining the basic building blocks, or components, for a software system. Usually, there are at least two levels of organization within a software system. These are the module level and the routine level. A *module* is a software component which can be separately compiled and provides services that can be utilized by other modules or systems. If Y utilizes the services of module X, then Y is said to be a *client* of X. Typical services that a module might provide for its clients are (1) declarations for special data types, variables and constants, and (2) definitions for one or more associated processes that the client will need to invoke.

Different languages have different names for software components at the module level, as shown in Table 8–1. We should note, for the sake of completeness, that the module level of organization available in the C language (program files with associated header files) is considered more primitive (and less effective, in some sense) than any of the other kinds of modules listed in Table 8–1. C++ was designed, in part, to provide a more powerful means of organizing C programs at the module level.

A *routine* is a software component that defines a particular activity that can be called by name. Such a process is usually parameterized. Routines have different names and take different forms in various languages. In C, routines are called functions. while in Pascal they are called functions and procedures.

TABLE 8–1   MODULE LEVEL COMPONENTS IN VARIOUS PROGRAMMING LANGUAGES

Language	Component Name(s)
C++	class
C	program file, header file
Turbo/THINK Pascal	class, unit
Modula-2	module
Ada	package

Properties of Good Modules

Earlier we discussed the ideal of "goodness" for software systems generally. Obviously, one of the goals of a design methodology is to produce good software components as opposed to bad software components. Table 8–2 lists desirable properties that contribute to this quality of goodness.

TABLE 8–2   DESIRABLE PROPERTIES FOR SOFTWARE COMPONENTS

Correspondence to syntactic units of the programming language
Intelligent coupling
Explicit interfaces
Information hiding
Cohesiveness
Clarity of coding and documentation
Clarity of pre- and postconditions

The first requirement is that software components should correspond to organizational components in the implementation language, such as C++ classes,

Ada packages, or Pascal units. This is as much a constraint on the implementation language as it is on the design. If a module does not correspond to a syntactic unit in the implementation language, it will be difficult to recognize as a fundamental module of the software system itself.

The second requirement is that software components should be intelligently coupled. That is, they should interact only if such interaction is explicit in the specifications, and in the way set forth in the specifications—no more and no less.

There are many kinds of couplings between components of a software system. Two routines can be coupled by sharing the same external file, by sharing a type declaration, by one routine assigning a value to a variable declared in another, by one routine calling another, by one routine being within the scope of another, by the passing of parameters and so forth. Poor couplings between routines can have one or more of the following undesirable effects:

1. They can make a program difficult to read and understand.
2. They can make a program difficult to debug and modify.
3. They can make it difficult to establish the correctness of a routine or program.
4. They encumber software reuse.

The software designer should make every effort to avoid interactions between software components that are not clearly reflected in the text of the program, such as the use of references to global variables. A routine's reference to a variable is *global* if no declaration for that variable occurs within that routine, either as a local variable or as a formal parameter. The presence of a global variable reference within a routine can have all four of the negative consequences listed above. For example, a global variable reference can make a routine difficult to understand, because one has to find the original declaration for the variable somewhere else. It mitigates against software reuse, because a routine with a global variable will not work properly when it is moved to an environment in which that global variable has not been declared.

The third requirement given in Table 8–2 is that software components must have explicit interfaces. By *interface*, we are referring to the parameter list of a routine, the header file that contains the declarations for a class, or the interface part of a module. (The interface part of a module declares the types, variables, constants and routines that the module provides as a service to its clients.) By *explicitness*, we mean that all possible interactions between software components should be apparent in the interface of that component. This is related to the intelligent coupling requirement given above. For example, a formal parameter list should include all data values that are passed to and from a routine.

The fourth requirement is that software components should hide implementation details from clients. This property is called *information hiding* and is one of the most important concepts in software design. Information hiding is related to the explicit interfaces requirement in that everything a client needs to know about a software component should be explicit in that component's interface. Beyond that, all implementation details should be hidden from the client. For example, suppose a client needs to have a list sorted and module X provides this service. The client should be able to use X's sorting service without having to know any of the internal details as to how X actually does the sorting. Ideally, module X will also use a standard, general list data type, so that the client need not know how lists themselves are to be represented internally. Information hiding is a fundamental aspect of data abstraction.

The fifth requirement is that software components should be highly cohesive. *Cohesiveness* is the conceptual glue that holds a component together. For example, at the routine level, the ideal is that each routine have a single purpose. A routine (e.g., a C++ function) should not be implemented as a grab bag of unrelated ideas. At the class or module level, the services that are collected together should represent a unified and coherent idea, and each routine within that module should have a single purpose. Implementing a module around the idea of an *abstract data type* is one example of cohesiveness. Another example would be to group together all types, variables, constants and routines that are needed for implementing a user interface if those entities are not portable from one graphics terminal to another. Packaging these hardware-dependent features as a single module makes it easier to port that software system to different graphics terminals, since the nonportable graphics features will be easy to locate.

The sixth requirement is that a software component should be clearly written and easy to understand with as little reference to external components as possible. For example, one should be able to understand a routine without having to refer to a lot of other routines.

The seventh requirement is that every software component should have clearly specified pre- and postconditions. This normally applies to routines. The pre- and postconditions for every software component must be included in the internal documentation for those components. These pre- and postconditions are also an intrinsic part of the design document itself.

EXERCISES

8–6 Compare the properties of good modules (Table 8–2) against the properties of a good requirements document which you prepared in doing Exercise 8–4. Is there any overlap? Do any of the properties of a good software module apply to a good requirements document? Discuss the relevance of modular design to the writing of a requirements document.

8–7 List as many kinds of couplings of C++ functions as you can. Are any of these intrinsically bad? Are any of these intrinsically unavoidable?

8–8 Explain information hiding relative to your use of the services provided by the C++ class `lists` which is documented in the laboratory manual. What does the client need to know about the class `lists` in order to use its services? What information is hidden from the client?

8–9 Analyze a program which you have written from the point of view of "cohesiveness." That is, check to see if the functions which you wrote satisfied the one routine – one purpose dictum. Would your program be better if you had strictly adhered to this dictum?

Using Abstract Data Types in Design

The idea of an abstract data type is a more limited one than that of a class, but it is useful for function-oriented programming as well as object-oriented programming. Abstract data types (ADTs) allow us to design and package collections of related routines that can be used in a wide range of application programs, but in a more limited way than classes. Thus, like a class, an ADT is designed to be used by many different and unrelated applications. Here is a definition of the general notion.

> **Definition** An *abstract data type* (often called an *ADT*), T, is a type t, along with a collection of associated routines r_1, r_2, ..., and r_n that can be applied to variables of that type.

The idea of an ADT is a forerunner of the object-oriented idea of a class, and it has no instance variables and no notion of hierarchy or inheritance. ADTs are used actively in function-oriented design as a vehicle to define, implement, and reuse various data structures that are fundamental to the disciplines of computer science and engineering.

For an example of an abstract data type, consider the idea of the C++ type int, along with its associated routines +, *, -, /, and %. This particular abstract data type is fully built into the language, since it is useful to a wide range of programming problems. Like classes, ADTs can be used to extend the C++ language through the use of separately compiled units. This alternative is often chosen within the framework of a function-oriented design paradigm, rather than an object-oriented one.

Design Methodology I: Function-Oriented Design

At the heart of a design methodology is the criteria for decomposing a problem into subproblems. Function-oriented design decomposes a problem into functions (or procedures). That is, function-oriented design has the central idea that a system consists of routines, and these routines receive inputs and produce outputs. There are two important elements in design specifications that are function-oriented:

1. A *structure chart* showing the decomposition of the problem into routines and the flow of information among those routines, and
2. A complete accounting of the *pre-* and *postconditions* for each routine. The routines identified in the structure chart are implemented as routines in the implementation language (e.g., as functions in C++).

Figure 8–7 introduces the basic symbols used in structure charts. Rectangles are used to denote routines, and an arrow going from rectangle P to rectangle Q means that routine P calls routine Q. An arrow with a darkened circle at its tail shows the flow of data into and out of a routine. Identifiers alongside these *data flow arrows* give the names of the data items flowing into and out of a process. In Figure 8–7, for example, we see that data x and y flow from routine P to routine Q at the time P calls Q, while data z flows from Q back to P at the time Q returns control to P.

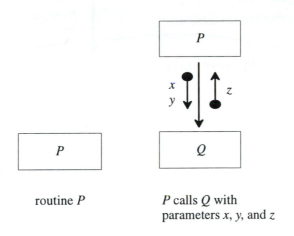

routine P

P calls Q with parameters x, y, and z

FIGURE 8–7   Symbols used in structure charts.

In function-oriented design, structure charts are often generated from the data flow diagrams which were presented in the system model section of the requirements document. Translating data flow diagrams into structure charts is somewhat of an art, since many alternative structure charts can be produced from a single data flow diagram. The following paragraphs offer some guidance concerning how this translation can be done effectively.

The first task is to decompose the data flow diagram into three parts, called the *afferent flow*, the *transform center*, and the *efferent flow*. The afferent and efferent flows are identified first, and whatever remains is the transform center. The afferent flow consists of all routines and data flow arrows that lead into the first routine that is a so-called "fundamental transformation" of the input data, including that routine itself. A routine constitutes a fundamental transformation if its inputs are not easily inferred from its outputs; fundamental transformations are irreversible. Similarly, the efferent flow consists of all routines and data flow arrows which lead out from the last routine that performs a fundamental transformation of the data, including that routine itself.

We can apply these ideas to the fried chicken data flow diagram from Figure 8–6, achieving the decomposition into afferent flow, efferent flow, and transform center shown in Figure 8–8.

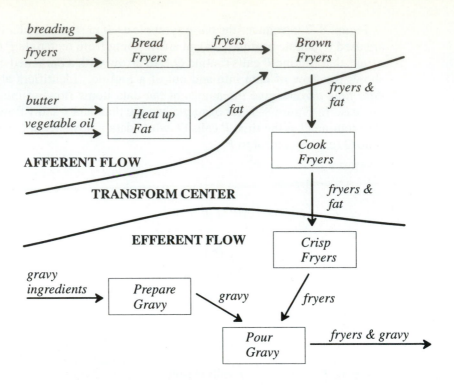

FIGURE 8–8   Afferent flow, efferent flow, and transform center for the fried chicken data flow diagram.

Once the afferent flow, efferent flow, and transform center have been identified, we can use the structure chart notations that are summarized in Figure 8–9. Here, we see a top level routine that calls three second level routines. These are an afferent routine (which corresponds to the afferent flow in the data flow diagram), a transform center routine (which corresponds to the transform center of the data flow diagram), and an efferent routine (which corresponds to the efferent flow in the data flow diagram). The top-level routine acts as the coordinator of these lower level routines.

In the fried chicken problem, we get the initial structure chart shown in Figure 8–10. The afferent flow is then captured as a new afferent routine, say *Bread N Brown*, which passes its output (fryers, which have been browned, along with the fat they are frying in) up to the first level. The first level acts as a coordinator, which then passes the fryers and fat to the transform center, *Cook Fryers*. This routine transforms the fryers by cooking them in fat until they are tender. The transform center returns the fryers (now brown and tender) and the used fat back to the top level coordinator, which then passes the fryers and the fat along to the efferent routine, say *Crisp N Pour*. This routine, in turn, is responsible for crisping the fryers, producing the gravy, and pouring the gravy over the fryers.

This method is recursively applied until the structure chart includes all the routines that were in the original data flow diagram. "Recursively" means here

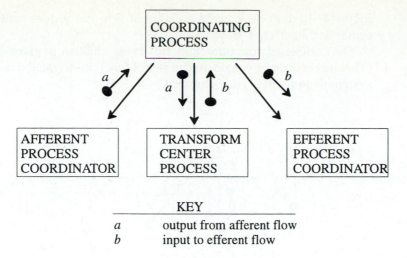

KEY

a	output from afferent flow
b	input to efferent flow

FIGURE 8–9   Structure chart notations for afferent flow, efferent flow, and transform center.

that whenever we identify an efferent flow (for example), that efferent flow is itself analyzed in terms of afferent flow, efferent flow and transform center, and so on until all the routines that were in the data flow diagram have been accounted for. For example, the efferent flow in Figure 8–10 has itself an afferent flow *Prepare Gravy*, an efferent flow *Pour Gravy*, and transform center *Crisp Fryers*. In this manner, we build the structure chart from the top down. As we develop a structure chart from a data flow diagram in this manner, some routines will be found that do not contain all three of the elements afferent flow, efferent flow, and transform center. For example, the afferent flow identified in

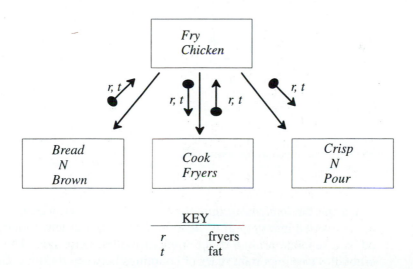

KEY

r	fryers
t	fat

FIGURE 8–10   Initial structure chart for frying chicken.

Figure 8–10 does not contain an afferent flow but it does contain a transform center and an efferent flow.

The completed structure chart for frying chicken is given in Figure 8–11. (This might even be considered an initial function-oriented design for a robotic system that produces fried chicken!)

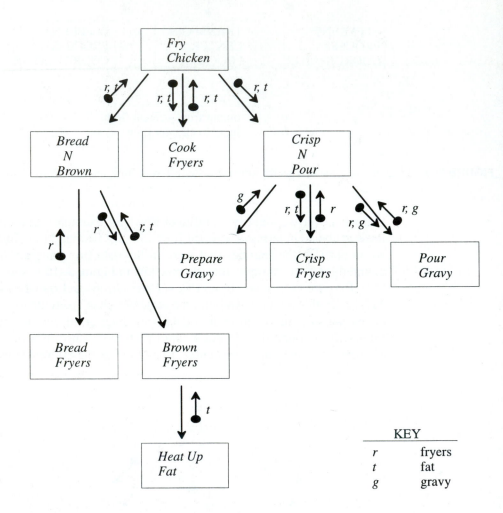

FIGURE 8–11   Completed structure chart for frying chicken.

During the *implementation phase* of a software project, the structure charts are converted into programs. Each routine in the structure chart is implemented as a separate routine in the implementation language. The structure chart embodies two important types of couplings between routines: namely the ways in which routines are coupled due to one routine calling another and the ways in which routines are coupled due to the passing of parameters.

The *design documentation* for a software system must include, for each routine, a description of the purpose of that routine, its input and output parameters, and its pre- and postconditions. For example, Figure 8–12 shows how the *Cook Fryers* process might be described in the design document.

ROUTINE NAME:	*Cook Fryers*
PURPOSE:	To cook fryers until they are tender
INPUT PARAMETERS:	fryers, fat
OUTPUT PARAMETERS:	fryers, fat
PRECONDITIONS:	Fryers are breaded $\wedge$ fat is hot
POSTCONDITIONS:	Fryers are breaded, brown, and tender $\wedge$ fat is hot

FIGURE 8–12   An example of the documentation for a process.

Note in this example that the preconditions and postconditions are declarative statements about the "state" of the parameters; as such, they can be written using symbols in the language of predicate logic.

Function-oriented design focuses on the module as a basic building block. Modules emerge by considering important abstractions that are often implicit in the functional decomposition. For example, suppose fried chicken preparation is just one aspect of a larger, computerized food-preparation system. Suppose in the larger system we often find ourselves preparing gravies of various types. This might lead us to develop a *Gravies* module which provides gravy production services for the rest of the system. This suggests how module-level components can emerge from a function-oriented design.

EXERCISES

8–10 Develop a second structure chart based upon an alternative analysis of the fried chicken data flow diagram (for instance, consider *Brown Fryers*, *Cook Fryers*, and *Crisp Fryers* as the transform center). Do you see any important difference between this alternate design and the one given in Figure 8–11?

8–11 Develop a structure chart for the data flow diagram you developed for Exercise 8–5. What aspects of your design become clearer in the structure chart than they were when you originally wrote the program?

Design Methodology II: Object-Oriented Design

If tomorrow you were to stumble into a research meeting of computer scientists and engineers, you would very likely hear people talking about object-oriented design, object-oriented programming, object-oriented languages, the object-oriented language paradigm, object-oriented user interfaces, object-oriented database systems, and so forth. In addition, you would probably hear terms that object-oriented people like to use in their conversations, such as "encapsulation," "inheritance," "class protocols," "polymorphism," "messages," "receivers," "constructors" and "destructors." By now, you should be fairly comfortable with most of these terms, having lived with them through most of the semester. Indeed, object orientation is rapidly emerging as a contemporary and promising alternative paradigm for designing large software systems.

In this section, we review and expand upon the ideas of object-oriented programming that were introduced throughout this text. Object-oriented design (OOD) is not the same as object-oriented programming (OOP), which is simply programming with an object-oriented language. While OOP occurs during the implementation stage of the software lifecycle, OOD occurs during the design stage. It thus provides an alternative way of thinking about and organizing the basic structure of the software system during its conception and before it is implemented. Object-oriented design will be described here in sufficient detail to distinguish it from function-oriented design. The methodology used here is consistent with that presented by Meyer [4] and others.

In object-oriented design, the focus is on identifying the basic *objects* that are part of an application rather than the basic routines. Routines are not ignored (of course), but they are organized as a concomitant part of the objects that comprise the system rather than vice versa. The design specification for an object-oriented design would contain four essential elements:

1. A listing of the *classes* (sometimes called *abstract data types*) for all objects that are a part of the solution.
2. A description of the *state variables* (local data) for each class.
3. A listing of all *methods* (member functions) that can act upon objects in each class.
4. For each method, a description of its purpose, its parameters, and its pre- and postconditions.

As a point of departure, we know that the idea of the class is a powerful generalization of the common idea of type in conventional programming languages.

Definition   A *class C* is a structure that defines both the nature of *objects* that belong to that class and the *methods (behaviors, member functions)* p_1, p_2, ..., and p_n that can act upon objects in that class. The nature of an object in a class is defined through a unified collection of *instance variables*. The collection of associated methods for a class is called the *class protocol*.

Several different objects can be declared as members of a class, in the same sense that several different variables in a program can be declared to have the same type.

An object-oriented design for the fried chicken system presented above would begin with an identification of its basic classes and objects. Most, if not all, of these objects are usually inherent in the problem statement itself—in this case, the fried chicken recipe. For instance, an important object is a batch of chicken parts (the "fryer" data item in the function-oriented design given earlier). Therefore, we need to declare a class `ChickenBatch`, so that objects in this class capture the essential features of a batch of chicken parts. Figure 8–13 shows the associated instance variables for any object in the `ChickenBatch` class. Note that each state variable itself is an object in some other class.

```
CLASS:  ChickenBatch

INSTANCE VARIABLE  CLASS

NumPieces           Integer
InitialWeight       Real
Breaded             Boolean
BrownFactor         0..10
TenderFactor        0..10
CrispFactor         0..10
GravyAmount         Real
```

FIGURE 8–13   State variables for objects in the class `ChickenBatch`.

Objects in class `ChickenBatch` capture the properties of a batch of chickens that are relevant to the application: the number of pieces in the batch, its initial weight (in ounces), whether the batch has been breaded or not, the brownness, tenderness, and crispness of the batch (on a scale of 0 – 10), and the amount of gravy (in liquid ounces) that has been poured onto the batch.

The methods associated with a class are those routines that are capable of acting upon objects in that class. When we want to apply a method to an object, we send that object a *message*. The message carries enough information to determine which routine to apply. The object that receives the message is the *receiver* of the message. The function-oriented analogy to a message is the function (and/or procedure, depending on the language) call.

Figure 8–14 shows the protocol for the class `ChickenBatch`. Class protocols include all the methods that can be applied to objects of the given class. Each method is defined using a comment explaining its purpose and a list of parameters (and their classes) in parentheses. Methods are grouped into five categories: *constructor/destructor* methods, *access* methods, *modify* methods, *display* methods, and *testing* methods. In this example, the constructor method causes the creation of a batch of chicken.

Figures 8–13 and 8–14 are intended to suggest the nature of an object-oriented design. Additional details are necessary to complete the design, and these would include state variables and class protocols for the classes `Scale`, `BreadStuff`, `CookingFat` and `Gravy`.

```
constructor method

CreateBatch
{creates a new batch of chicken parts for frying}

access methods

BreadFryers(breading: BreadStuff)
{covers the receiver batch with breading}

BrownFryers(fat: CookingFat)
{fries the receiver batch in fat until they are
 sufficiently brown}

CookFryers(fat: CookingFat)
{cooks the receiver batch in fat until they are
 sufficiently tender}

CoverWithGravy(creamGravy: Gravy)
{covers the receiver batch with gravy}

GravyAmount
{answers the amount of gravy which covers the
 receiver batch}

testing methods

IsBrown
{answers true if the receiver batch is sufficiently
 brown and false otherwise}

IsCrisp
{answers true if the receiver batch is sufficiently
 crisp and false otherwise}

IsTender
{answers true if the receiver batch is sufficiently
 tender and false otherwise}
```

FIGURE 8–14   Protocol for class `ChickenBatch`.

The documentation for an object-oriented design includes preconditions and postconditions for each method. Figure 8–15 illustrates this documentation style for the method `CookFryers`. This somewhat whimsical example has been designed to capture some of the flavor of an object-oriented design and to show how it contrasts fundamentally with more traditional function-oriented methodologies.

EXERCISE

8–12 Use the recipe for braised chicken given in Figure 8–16 to alter the design for objects in the class `ChickenBatch`, whose protocol is defined in Figure 8–14 and method `CookFryers` is defined in Figure 8–15.

```
METHOD:    CookFryers(fat: CookingFat)

{cooks the receiver batch in fat until they are
 sufficiently tender}

PARAMETERS: fat (belongs to class CookingFat)

{pre:    numPieces > 0
      ∧ initialWeight > 0
      ∧ breaded = true ∧ brownFactor > 8
      ∧ tenderFactor = 0 ∧ crispFactor = 0
      ∧ gravyAmount = 0}
{post: numPieces > 0 ∧ initialWeight > 0
      ∧ breaded = true ∧ brownFactor > 8
      ∧ tenderFactor > 8 ∧ crispFactor = 0
      ∧ gravyAmount = 0}
```

FIGURE 8–15   Preconditions and postconditions for the CookFryers method.

BRAISED CHICKEN*

The fried chicken of the Middle West.

Prepare as for Fried Chicken–*except* use a Larger Fryer and cut in serving pieces. After browning, add 3
tbsp. water. Cover; cook over low heat on top of stove,
or bake in a preheated oven . . . 325° (slow mod.) until
tender (45 to 60 min.). In either case, remove cover
the last 10 min. to crisp crust.

*Source: *Betty Crocker's Picture Cookbook*, General Mills.

FIGURE 8–16   Recipe for braised chicken.

IMPLEMENTATION ISSUES

The goal of the implementation stage of the software lifecycle is to produce a
correct, efficient and readable program based upon the design developed during the design stage. Implementation is the least time-consuming stage in a
software project. In general, four activities are involved in implementing a
software system:

1. Choice of a programming language.
2. Detailed design, in which data structures and algorithms are selected.

3. Coding, during which the actual program is written and documented.
4. Unit testing, during which software components are individually tested.

Note that "implementation" includes significant design and testing activities, in addition to program coding itself. The first two of these activities are discussed in this section. Testing methods are discussed beginning on page 448.

Choosing a Programming Language

The choice of a programming language may occur very early in a software project. For example, sponsors may require that a specific language be used to implement a system, so that this becomes part of the requirements document. Similarly, developers might be committed to a particular implementation language right from the start.

Table 8–3 lists factors that might influence the choice of an implementation language. A comparative study of programming languages is beyond the scope of this text; the emphasis here is on institutional and human factors.

TABLE 8–3   FACTORS THAT INFLUENCE THE CHOICE OF A PROGRAMMING LANGUAGE

1. Institutional inertia and commitment

2. Nature of the application

3. Availability and quality of languages and compilers

4. Quality of host operating systems and development tools

5. Objective language features

4. Quality of host operating systems and development tools

Institutional inertia and commitment are an important factor in the choice of a programming language. This factor operates on both the sponsor's and the developer's sides of the project. Sponsors may require that a system be coded in COBOL because their own in-house programming talent is in COBOL and because they have an enormous capital investment in existing COBOL applications. Developers may favor a particular language for similar reasons. The costs of hiring experts or retraining personnel in a new language may be prohibitive. A developer may also wish to take advantage of two important forms of reuse: reusing software components developed in earlier, similar projects; and reusing technical knowledge acquired during earlier projects.

The nature of the application can play a decisive role in the choice of a language. An increasingly large volume of systems software (compilers and operating systems) is being written in C and C++. Many database applications are developed either with special database languages or in COBOL, PL/I, or C enriched with database capabilities. Real-time systems (systems that must respond to environmental events as they occur, such as air traffic control systems or systems that monitor and control a nuclear reactor) are often written in C or Ada. Many expert systems are written in Prolog or some variation of Lisp.

A third factor that can influence the choice of a programming language is the reputation of that language, its compilers, the available operating systems, and development tools. (Development tools are programs that help developers to write, debug, test, and analyze programs.) The choice of the term "reputation" is deliberate. Computer professionals often discuss the virtues of different languages, compilers and operating systems. Word-of-mouth and the entire cultural ethos of the computing community play an important role in the perceived "goodness" of a particular language. This ethos includes personal and professional values, pride, and bias. Experienced computer professionals have a strong tendency to defend the language or system with which they are most familiar, since they have a large personal investment in learning and using that language. The personal cost of learning new languages and design techniques is significant.

Table 8–4 presents a short list of desirable properties for programming languages. Most of these properties are discussed in detail in more advanced courses on the principles of programming languages.

TABLE 8–4   DESIRABLE LANGUAGE PROPERTIES

1. Elegance, simplicity, and orthogonality

2. Defense in depth

3. Portability

4. Separate compilation (modularity)

5. Data abstraction

6. Genericity

7. Object-orientedness

What follows is a brief explanation for the other factors listed in Table 8–4. A language is orthogonal if its design is based on a few simple concepts and if these concepts are applied consistently throughout. "Defense in depth" refers to mechanisms for protecting programmers from certain types of errors. Strong typing, as in C++ and Pascal, is an example of this. Portability means that programs should be portable from one compiler to another, or from one hardware platform to another, for a given implementation language. Portability in this sense has much to do with language standards. Separate compilation is an absolute requirement for the construction of large systems. This implies the ability to compile chunks of program code separately, and later to combine those chunks into larger, executable chunks. For example, C++ classes or Pascal units provide this capability.

Choosing Data Structures and Algorithms

Much of this text has dealt with "detailed design" — the choice and design of concrete data structures and algorithms when we implemented the various classes. For the most part, a design specification developed using function-oriented or object-oriented design will leave unresolved the many issues concerning the choice of data structures and algorithms. For example, a function-oriented design may indicate that a list is passed among several routines, but it will say nothing about the concrete representation of that list in the implementation language. Will the list be represented using an array or will it use a dynamically linked structure? Will the list be implemented as an abstract data type? Choice of implementation strategies for different classes is so important that we have devoted an entire chapter and several laboratory manual exercises to it.

The aforementioned function-oriented design may indicate that one routine will sort a list in ascending order. The design documentation will present pre- and postconditions for the sorting routine, but it will not give the actual sorting algorithm itself. One aspect of detailed design is the decision to use one of the many alternative available sorting algorithms (such as selection sort, insertion sort heapsort, or quicksort) over all the others. This choice, for large lists, is governed by the computational complexity of the competing alternatives. Complexity issues play an important role in the choice of one algorithm over another, as we saw in Chapter 3.

TESTING, VALIDATION, AND VERIFICATION

The goal of software *testing* is to detect as many defects in a system as possible *before* it is delivered, installed, and made operational. Defects include bugs (the main focus of this section) as well as inefficiencies that might cause a system to not satisfy all of its requirements. The goal of software testing is not to *guarantee* that a system is completely bug-free; this is impossible in practice and even in principle. (Of course, we are assuming fairly large and complex systems. It might be possible to demonstrate that a trivial system is bug-free.)

Software testing is one aspect of two larger concerns, called *validation* and *verification*. Some computer scientists and engineers make a fine distinction between validation and verification. That is, *validation* refers to all of those activities in a systems development project that assure that a system is designed and implemented in conformity with the sponsor's needs. *Verification*, on the other hand, refers to all of those activities which, assuming conformity with sponsor needs, assure that a system is designed and implemented in conformity with the sponsor's requirements—that is, they are *correct* in some strong sense. For example, determining whether a sponsor wants a system to provide a specific service is a matter of validation. Determining the correctness of the data structures and algorithms which have been chosen to provide that service is a matter of verification.

Ideally, validation occurs during the requirements analysis phase in a software system's life cycle. However, in practice, issues may arise during system design and implementation that require further consultation with sponsors and users. Therefore, some verification activities occur during design and implementation. Checking whether a design conforms to a requirements specification and checking whether an implementation conforms to a design specification are examples of verification. Thus, the testing stage of the software life cycle actually embodies various kinds of verification activities.

Some testing activities require formal review meetings. For example, a requirements review is a formal meeting during which sponsors and developers review a requirements document. A *design review* is a formal meeting during which a design or part of a design is presented and critiqued. *Structured walkthroughs* are review meetings during which actual routines and modules are presented and critiqued. A formal meeting usually involves a presenter, a secretary, and a review committee, as well as the person or persons who will be responsible for implementing any changes that are recommended. The presenter presents the design or implementation and the secretary records any flaws that are found or any suggestions that are made by the review committee.

A more rigorous and thorough approach invokes formal proofs of program correctness, based upon axioms of program behavior and the formal application of rules of inference. That is, formal proofs show mathematically that a program or routine is correct. These proofs are sometimes categorized as *formal verification*, in order to distinguish them from various other verification and testing methods. Unlike testing, formal verification has as its goal to prove that a software module is *absolutely* correct for all possible inputs, rather than *relatively* correct for only a handful of test runs. However, formal proofs of correctness are not widely used in software systems development. They represent an attempt by computer scientists and engineers to discover and apply the logical foundations of computing. However, structured walkthroughs based upon less formal proofs of correctness are often utilized. Following this approach, in a review meeting, the presenter would argue, based upon mathematical reasoning, that a given implementation for a routine does indeed satisfy its pre- and postconditions. Loop invariants play an important role in this process. Our focus in the next two sections is on various testing methods and on formal verification methods.

Testing Methods

Testing is a process that involves either the actual execution of the software component being tested (called *dynamic testing*) or the execution of a static program analyzer against the software component being tested (called *static testing*). Static program analyzers detect possible errors or flaws by looking for suspicious patterns in the text of a program. Some compilers provide services of this nature. For example, some compilers detect situations in which a program declares a variable without ever assigning a value to it. Some static program analyzers can detect "dead code," or code that can never be reached. For example, if CAP is a C++ constant with the value of 100, then the first compound statement within the **if** statement below is dead code:

```
if (CAP < 50)
  {
      cout << "Enter an X value: " << endl;
      cin >> X;
  }
else
  {
      cout << "Enter a Y value: " << endl;
      cin >> Y;
  }
```

Dynamic testing techniques include the use of special programs, or so-called *profilers*, that analyze the performance of software components and systems. For example, a profiler would keep track of how much time it takes to execute a given routine, or how many times a given loop is repeated. This information may lead to the detection of an error, or it might suggest the need for a more efficient implementation of a particular routine.

An important part of dynamic testing techniques is the development of a *test suite* of data that sufficiently exercises the software module being tested. A test suite requires multiple executions, each execution using a different set of inputs from the test suite. The design of effective test suites requires considerable skill. We shall discuss strategies for designing test suites below.

However, before discussing dynamic testing, we need to make clear that the reason for doing it at all is not to prove that a software component is defect-free, but only to discover as many defects in a software component as is practically possible. For example, a test which fails to find a bug in a software component is not a successful test, since it does not guarantee the absence of bugs. A test that does discover a bug or other kind of defect is a successful test. Thus, the goal of the software tester is to become expert at the design of test suites that will have a high probability of finding software defects.

There are two fundamental reasons why we characterize the success of a software test in this negative manner. First, there are theoretical results which indicate that no algorithm can be written that can automatically establish the correctness of other algorithms. Second, it is not feasible and, in some cases, not possible to test a software component using all the different input values that it can possibly encounter.

Unit, Integration, and Acceptance Testing Dynamic testing techniques are used in three different situations, and these are called *unit testing*, *integration testing*, and *acceptance testing*, respectively.

Unit testing is testing of individual routines (e.g., C++ functions), either alone or in small groups. Unit testing is followed by integration testing, in which larger and larger subsystems of the final system are tested, ultimately resulting in a test of the entire system. Integration testing is followed by acceptance testing, whose two major parts are called *alpha testing* and *beta testing*. Alpha testing applies to systems that are custom-made for a particular sponsor. In alpha testing, the completed system is tested at the developer's site with the assistance of the sponsors. In contrast, beta testing applies to systems that are designed for a large number of customers. For example, a word processor is normally designed to be used by a large number of potential customers rather than a single sponsor. In beta testing, the proposed system is tested at a number of sites that are representative of the wide range of ultimate customer interests in and applications of the software.

Unit testing requires the development of special programs, called *drivers*, which supply data to the system components as they are individually exercised. There are two alternative forms of unit testing, called *black box testing* and *white box testing*. In black box testing, test suites are developed without knowing the actual algorithm a routine uses to solve a problem. The routine is treated like a black box, so that we know only the pre- and postconditions for the routine and design the test cases on this basis. White box testing is based upon knowledge of the algorithm that is embedded within the implementation of the routine. The goal of white box testing is to assure that each series of statements, or "code segment," within an algorithm is exercised at least once by the test suite.

Black box testing In black box testing, we know the input and output requirements of a routine (i.e., we know its pre- and postconditions), but we do not know the algorithm that is supposed to satisfy those pre- and postconditions. One important technique for black box testing is to identify "equivalence classes" among the legal input values for a routine. This technique is called "equivalence partitioning."

Definition A *partition* of a set S is the decomposition of that set into $N > 0$ mutually disjoint subsets $\{C_1 C_2 \ldots C_n\}$ of S which cover S. Two subsets C_j and C_k are mutually disjoint if $C_j \cap C_k = \emptyset$. These subsets C_i are called *equivalence classes*.

In equivalence partitioning, we design test cases by partitioning the set of possible input values into equivalence classes. Some of these equivalence classes emerge due to a statement of good and bad input values. Others emerge from a consideration of the outputs that are produced. For example, consider a C++ function ComputeLetterGrade which will convert an integer exam score in the range 0..100 into a letter grade. If the exam score is negative or greater than 100, this function will return the error code Z. Here is the function header for ComputeLetterGrade, including its pre- and postconditions:

```
char function ComputeLetterGrade(int NumericGrade);
{pre: NumericGrade is an integer}
{post: NumericGrade < 0 ∧ result = Z ∨
       0 ≤ NumericGrade < 60 ∧ result = F ∨
       60 ≤ NumericGrade < 70 ∧ result = D ∨
       70 ≤ NumericGrade < 80 ∧ result = C ∨
       80 ≤ NumericGrade < 90 ∧ result = B ∨
       90 ≤ NumericGrade ≤ 100 ∧ result = A ∨
       100 < NumericGrade ∧ result = Z}
```

The precondition for `ComputeLetterGrade` is simply that `NumericGrade` has an integer value. The postcondition requires that `result` be assigned a letter value in accordance with the range in which the value of NumericGrade falls.

An analysis of input values for this function yields the following three equivalence classes:

$$C_1 = \{\texttt{-INT\_MAX}, \ldots, -2, -1\}$$
$$C_2 = \{101, 102, \ldots, \texttt{INT\_MAX-1}\}$$
$$C_3 = \{0, 1, 2, \ldots, 100\}$$

Here, `INT_MAX` denotes the maximum value of an integer that can be represented by the computer and compiler in which we are testing this function. An analysis of the possible results shows that the class C_3 is best broken up into five distinct equivalence classes (corresponding to the letter grades A, B, C, D, and F), giving us seven equivalence classes altogether. We can therefore generate a test suite by randomly choosing a representative value from each of these equivalence classes and then hand-calculating the expected result for that value. The (perhaps dangerous) assumption behind equivalence partitioning is that the representative member chosen in each equivalence class fully represents that class in terms of the behavior of the function we are testing. This first version of our test suite is shown in Table 8–5.

TABLE 8–5 FIRST CUT AT A TEST SUITE FOR THE FUNCTION ComputeLetterGrade

Class	Description	Representative Member	Expected Result
C_1	$\{\texttt{-INT\_MAX}, \ldots, -2, -1\}$	-3	Z
C_2	$\{101, 102, \ldots, \texttt{INT\_MAX-1}\}$	110	Z
C_3	$\{0, 1, 2, \ldots, 59\}$	24	F
C_4	$\{60, 61, \ldots, 69\}$	65	D
C_5	$\{70, 71, \ldots, 79\}$	75	C
C_6	$\{80, 81, \ldots, 89\}$	85	B
C_7	$\{90, 91, \ldots, 100\}$	95	A

Experience tells us that boundary values are likely to be sources of error (for example, the program might mistakenly use a $\geq$ test instead of a $>$ test in comparing two values). Therefore, in testing, we need to pay special attention to input values near where a change in the value of the function will occur. With this in mind, Table 8–6 contains several representatives from each equivalence class, with boundary values taken into account in these selections.

TABLE 8–6   AN IMPROVED TEST SUITE FOR THE FUNCTION ComputeLetterGrade

Class	Description	Representative Members	Expected Result
C_1	{-INT_MAX, ..., -2, -1}	-3, -1	Z
C_2	{101, 102, ..., INT_MAX-1}	110, 101	Z
C_3	{0, 1, 2, ..., 59}	0, 24, 59	F
C_4	{60, 61, ..., 69}	60, 65, 69	D
C_5	{70, 71, ..., 79}	70, 75, 79	C
C_6	{80, 81, ..., 89}	80, 85, 89	B
C_7	{90, 91, ..., 100}	90, 95, 100	A

White box testing   White box testing complements black box testing. That is, both kinds of testing are recommended during the validation of a large software system. White box testing utilizes our complete knowledge of the code with each routine of the system. Its basic strategy is to assure that the test suite exercises every *code segment* within each routine at least once. A code segment is understood to be any contiguous sequence of statements that do not govern the flow of control. For instance, Figure 8–17 shows a schematic for a while loop that contains three code segments, which are enclosed in ovals and respectively labeled A, B, and C.

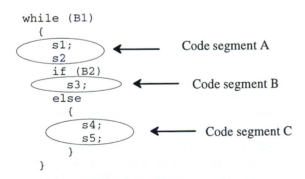

FIGURE 8–17   C++ code with three code segments A, B, and C.

Normally, the code segments are documented by means of a flow graph that shows the decisions (Boolean expressions) as nodes and the code segments as arcs. The arcs are labelled with the outcome of the previous decision (**true** or **false**) followed by the symbol for the relevant code segment (in this example

A, B, or C). Figure 8–18 presents the flow graph for the code given in Figure 8–17.

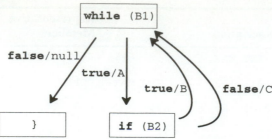

FIGURE 8–18   Flow graph for the C++ program code in Figure 8–17.

There are several alternative strategies for generating test cases from the flow graph. In one strategy, we design test cases that cover the entire flow graph. This strategy treats decisions in loops and conditionals in the same manner. A more demanding method requires that each loop be tested for 0 executions, 1 execution, and two or more executions. Table 8–7 shows the type of chart that could be used to help a tester develop test cases using this second strategy. Clearly, three well-designed test cases are sufficient to enable us to place checks in all five rows of the chart.

TABLE 8–7   RELATIONSHIP BETWEEN TEST CASES AND CONTROL STRUCTURES

| | | Test Cases | | |
Decision	Outcome	1	2	3
`while` (B1)	0 executions	X		
	1 execution		X	
	2 or more executions			X
`if` (B2)	true		X	
	false			X

Integration testing   To some extent, the white box and black box methods described above scale up to larger collections of system components. That is, while we have considered these methods for testing individual routines, the in-dividual routines that are tested in this manner do not need to be at the lowest level in the structure chart. Black box and white box methods can be applied in a bottom-up manner, starting at the lowest levels in the structure chart and progressing upwards so that larger and larger subsystems of the final system are being tested.

For example, consider Figure 8–19. This shows part of a structure chart for a system that includes the routine ComputeLetterGrade which calls four additional routines. This subsystem receives a string from the user (Get-NumericalGrade), converts that string into an integer (ConvertToNumber), checks to see if the resulting integer is between 0 and 100 (ValidateGrade), and converts the validated numerical grade to a letter grade (ConvertToLetter). Each of the routines called by ComputeLetterGrade can be tested using black box methods. Once this is done, ComputeLetterGrade can then be black box tested. In this sense, integration testing is a bottom-up process.

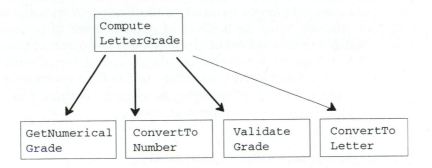

FIGURE 8–19   A subsystem that includes the routine ComputeLetterGrade.

Similarly, the individual routines and the coordinating routine ComputeLetterGrade in Figure 8–19 can be white box tested. In white box testing such a subsystem, it is important that each lower level routine be called at least once. In general, the strategy of testing a system by assuring that all possible routine calls occur at least once is called *structural testing*.

At the highest levels in the system, black box testing merges into *functional* testing. Functional testing involves the development of test suites based upon the functional requirements documented in the requirements document. All system services that were promised in the requirements document are systematically tested.

There are two additional types of tests that need to be mentioned for completeness. In *stress testing*, an integrated system is tested at the outer limits of its capabilities. (This is something like the final exam for a course). For example, if the nonfunctional requirements for an on-line banking system state that the system should be capable of processing ten thousand transactions in a single hour, a stress test would try running it with twelve or thirteen thousand transactions in an hour. The goal of stress testing would be to ensure that the system is able to handle stress "gracefully," or without crashing. *Performance tests* are done to check that the system meets additional temporal requirements, such as constraints on response times in a real-time system, and also to detect inefficiencies in the system's design or implementation.

Formal Verification Methods

There are many situations in software design where formal verification techniques can be used to provide assurance that the program absolutely satisfies its postconditions under all circumstances. In some of these situations, verification is in fact preferable to testing, since testing does not guarantee such satisfaction.

Formal verification is a process by which a routine or subsystem is analyzed statically, alongside its pre- and postconditions, by a someone who has the goal of mathematically proving that that routine or subsystem is correct. Persons who engage in formal verification of software systems utilize axioms and rules of inference about the behavior of different kinds of program constructs, as well as a healthy amount of experience in doing proofs of this sort.

It is, however, fair to state that the process of formal verification is not yet well enough developed to be widely used in the software industry at this time. Its methodology is still emerging in research problems, and may not become widely used for several years in the future.

SOFTWARE ENGINEERING AND THE USER INTERFACE

The design of effective software products in the 1990s must pay increasing attention to that element of the software that makes it readily usable; the so-called "user interface." Every software product has a user interface and, depending upon its nature and the nature of the hardware on which it runs, that user interface may have a number of different aspects and realizations.

> **Definition** A *user interface* is that part of the software system that is designed specifically and exclusively for the purpose of facilitating timely and accurate user interaction with the software on a regular basis. As such, it is composed of keyboard conventions, mouse clicks, screen menus and windows, and other information that facilitates this interaction.

The user interface always sits auspiciously at the junction between the software system, the hardware, and the user. In this position, it must merge the interests, strengths, and limitations of all three in providing maximum functionality and protection for the application program's effective utilization.

User Interface Devices Various hardware devices are designed to facilitate the design of effective user interfaces. Video display terminals and ASCII keyboards are the historical mainstay of the user interface, dating back to the early days of time sharing in the 1970s.

More recently, the advent of the microcomputer with its function keys (such as the IBM PC) and graphical user interface, or GUI (such as the Macintosh, Microsoft Windows, MIT's X-Windows, and Sun Microsystem's Open Look), have enabled software designers to radically alter the strategy of interaction that had dominated software use in the past. No longer is one constrained by the awkward keying conventions of the so-called "line editor" when altering a text with word processor, for instance. Instead, one uses a mouse as just one of the standard user interface devices, and edits a text by a series of highlightings, mouse clicks, and cut-and-paste operations.

For special graphical applications, users have access to sophisticated drafting tablets, color palettes, and drawing tools to assist with their work. More futuristic user interfaces will add to this repertoire the ability to converse with the machine orally and by way of abstract hand motions. Surely the potential for user interface design in the future is immense, due in part to the rapid development of alternative hardware and software devices for interaction beyond the keyboard and the video monitor.

User Interface Conventions and Toolkits for Software Designers   In the early years of software design, the user interface was designed from scratch for each new software product. More recently, libraries of routines and classes have evolved and circulated around the software industry, enabling many of the common interface conventions, such as the recording of a mouse click on a menu item, to be realized in a straightforward and reliable way. Needless to say, these libraries have greatly facilitated the process of software design, and have given many individuals access to the fast-growing and rapidly diversifying software industry.

Unfortunately, each operating system and hardware platform has its peculiarities with respect to the user interface, so that standardizing these libraries may be an impossible task. Contrast this situation, for instance, with the programming language C++ which is more or less standardized across a wide range of machine species. Where this standardization breaks down, however, is in the different libraries of classes and other functions for accomplishing routine tasks, like opening a window, recording a mouse click, and so on.

For example, UNIX users enjoy the programming conveniences that are afforded by the X-Windows user interface, whose operational features are significantly different from, say, the Macintosh user interface or the Microsoft Windows user interface for PC-type machines. Thus, when a software designer wants to develop a product that could be used across a wide range of different machines and operating systems, the user interface aspects of that product must be reprogrammed for each different system, even though the software might have been written in an otherwise-standardized language like C++. The C and C++ languages are somewhat more standardized than many others, including Pascal in this regard; however, machine-dependent differences still exist among different implementations of these languages.

EXERCISES

8–13 If you have access to both a PC with Microsoft Windows and a Macintosh, contrast the fundamental features of these two user interfaces. That is, explore how the hierarchy of data storage is realized using folders, files, and so on. What does it take to copy a file from a folder to a floppy disk. What are the dynamics of mouse-clicking, buttons, pull-down menus, windows, etc.?

8–14 For the particular version of C++ that you have been using in this course, explore its class library's features for user interface programming. What's involved in writing application program statements that will open a user window? How about recording a mouse click within a button on the user's screen?

SUMMARY

This chapter introduced the broader discipline of software engineering. You will encounter many of the concepts introduced here in later courses in the curriculum. While the concepts of software and module quality (reliability, robustness, interoperability, coupling, cohesion, information hiding, etc.) may seem to be somewhat abstract at this point, they do play a fundamental role in the development of reliable, efficient, and effective software products.

In addition to issues of quality, we have considered software models, contrasting the features of the software lifecycle model and the prototyping model. Requirements analysis, specifications, design, implementation, and testing were discussed in enough depth to give you a feel for the complexity of the issues involved. Function-oriented and object-oriented design were also introduced and contrasted. Methods for testing, verifying, and maintaining systems at various levels of integration were discussed . Special attention was given to black box and white box testing as alternatives to formal verification. Finally, we concluded the chapter with a brief discussion of the software user interface and user interface programming features.

References

[1]   Brooks, Frederick P., *The Mythical Man–Month: Essays on Software Engineering*, Addison–Wesley, Reading, MA, 1975.

[2]   Brooks, Frederick P., "No Silver Bullet: Essence and Accidents of Software Engineering", *IEEE Computer*, April 1987, pp. 10–19.

[3]   Jones, Gregory W., *Software Engineering*, Wiley, New York, NY, 1990.

[4]   Meyer, Bertrand, *Object-Oriented Software Construction*, Prentice-Hall, 1988.

[5]   Pressman, Roger S, *Software Engineering: A Practitioner's Approach*, 2nd ed., McGraw–Hill, New York, NY, 1987.

[6]   Schach, Stephen R., "Practical Software Engineering," Richard D. Irwin Associates, Homewood, IL (1992).

[7]   Schneiderman, B., *Designing the User Interface*, Addison–Wesley, Reading, MA (1986).

[8]   United States General Accounting Office, "Embedded Computer Systems: Significant Software Problems on C–17 Must Be Addressed," GAO/IMTEC–92–48, Washington, DC (May 1992).

CHAPTER 9

THE HUMAN DIMENSION
OF SOFTWARE SYSTEMS

In this chapter, we take an entirely different view of large software systems. This view takes into account the interests of organizations that *develop* and individuals who *use* computer software in their daily activities—these groups are part of the *social context* of the discipline of computing. This view reflects many of the design decisions that accompany the development and distribution of computer technology.

This discussion is framed in the context of two different points of view: that of the software user and that of the software designer. The duties of software designers and software users, together with the resulting benefits to each, lead to the following questions:

1. How can quality, reliability, and effectiveness be incorporated into the design and implementation of computer software so that the interests and goals of users and society at large are optimally served and their rights are simultaneously protected? In other words, what are the *duties of the software designer* that will ensure maximum *benefits to the user*?

2. Conversely, how can computers and software be protected against the various misuses that individuals can intentionally or unintentionally perpetrate against them? In other words, what are the *duties of the user* that will ensure protection *of the designer's rights*?

These two points of view are represented in Figure 9–1.

This chapter provides a careful look at three areas of major concern for the software industry in the 1990's. First, we introduce the dynamic idea of the "software team" as a vehicle through which effective software is developed and brought to market. Second, we review the question of software as intellectual property, taking into account recently published opinions of software developers regarding the so-called "look and feel" controversy, as well as recent court decisions which have developed out of that case. Third, we introduce the issue of software risks and liabilities—what are the possible damages when a software product fails, and who is responsible for such failures?

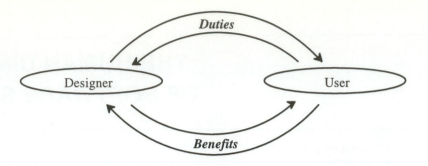

FIGURE 9–1   Duties and benefits: Incorporating the user's view.

There are a number of reasons for studying these issues here. First, the dramatic increase in software use throughout society requires that persons who are part of the "software industry" have a high level of understanding of the societal impact of their work. Many future software designers are now students in courses such as this. Second, most readers will sooner or later become computer and software users regardless of their choice of profession. Third, as computer technology and software continues to proliferate through modern society, so do the opportunities for its misuse. Computer crime is estimated by some to exceed the combined levels of all other kinds of crime in today's society. We should therefore understand the legal, ethical, and practical dimensions of software so that we become well-prepared to deal constructively with them as we confront them in the future.

SOFTWARE TEAMS

In January, 1988, Simpson Corporation added a new division which manufactured and sold health care products to hospitals, retail vendors, doctors, and physical therapists. The market's response to its products was immediate and positive. Health care products are often needed for emergencies, so Simpson needed to respond to telephone orders with same-day shipping. Also, prices for items and the decision as to whether or not to give credit required accurate information about a customer while that customer was on the phone. Thus Simpson needed a fast on-line database system to compete successfully.

Because Health Care was a new division for Simpson, it did not have its own software development staff. Thus, one needed to be formed to undertake a project of this size. A young programmer, employed by Simpson's central software development division, Rhonda Bailey, was transferred to the Health Care division and placed in charge of the new database project. She had never managed a team of programmers before; however, she was an outstanding programmer and had successfully solved several problems no else had been able to solve at the central division. She was given twelve months to finish the project. She was also told she could hire whatever staff she needed, and that after completion of the project they would become the permanent software staff for the Health Care division.

Bailey began by interviewing the supervisors of the Health Care staff who would be using the new database system. Based on these interviews, she did a preliminary design of the system and wrote specifications for each of the major components. She took this design back to the supervisors who approved it. While she was preparing the design, she hired four programmers and selected a software environment, a fourth generation language ("4GL" for short). During the time Bailey was finishing the software design, the new programmers familiarized themselves with the operating system and 4GL, and thus were ready to start as soon as she finished.

What Bailey most enjoyed about programming was being able to take a large problem, break it down into subproblems, design and code solutions for the subproblems, and then bring the whole problem to a working solution. She proceeded on the assumption that her programmers would like to operate the same way. Thus she assigned each of them the responsibility for a major component of the design while she kept one component and the main driver module for herself. The design, hiring, and software selection had taken three months; she gave each of her programmers eight months to finish their sections, and she allowed one month at the end for integration and testing.

Four months after completion of the design phase, she began to realize that the project had significant problems—morale on the programming team was very low—all four of the people she had hired were complaining about feeling overwhelmed by the task and they had produced little evidence of productive work. Furthermore, during a lunch time conversation, two of the programmers had discovered that they had each spent the last month writing a set of utility modules which were virtually identical in functionality, but which had different interfaces. Meanwhile, Rhonda, herself, felt completely bogged down in managerial details and was not progressing on her own components. Realizing that the project was only five months from its expected completion date, Bailey assessed as best she could the work each programmer had completed, subdivided each component and hired four more programmers. At the end of eleven months, her components were completed but they were the only ones done. She began at this point to read the specifications and code written by the other eight programmers and found a number of design and coding errors which she helped correct.

After sixteen months (and considerable overtime), most of the components were close enough to completion that she felt ready to assemble them into a complete system. Unfortunately, the interfaces between several modules were found to be inconsistent and some modules had unanticipated side effects. These problems required redesign and recoding of several modules. Integration was finally completed after 21 months. At that point, a suite of test data was designed. Testing uncovered an unfortunately large number of bugs, but the system was declared debugged after 25 months.

The software was finally delivered to the users, who immediately rebelled. They felt the interface was often confusing and was inconsistent across different subsystems. Also they were unhappy that it had been designed with their supervisor's input but without theirs. Occasional bugs still occurred often enough that it undermined the users' confidence. After six months of trying to use the new system, the supervisors reported to Bailey that they were discontinuing it. By this time four of Bailey's eight programmers had quit to take jobs in other firms. Bailey and the four remaining programmers decided to redesign the system to make it more useful. However, in the fall of 1991, the Simpson Board of Directors voted to discontinue the Health Care products line as it had shown a significant financial loss for twelve consecutive quarters and showed no evidence that it would become profitable in the near future. The four programmers Bailey had hired were released; she was offered a position as a programmer in central software development again; however, she chose to leave Simpson for another firm.

While the previous story is fictional, the details are based on real events. In an earlier chapter, we cited a study by the Comptroller General of the United States which found that among government software products studied, only 2% worked on delivery and 3% worked after minor corrections; 75% were never used. These failures are not necessarily due to incompetent programmers; like the Simpson Corporation example, they are frequently due to poor management.

Sometimes, though not often, the best programs are written by one or two individuals. For example, the Pascal language and its first compiler were written by Niklaus Wirth; the Unix operating system was created by Brian Kernighan and Dennis Ritchie; the original C language was designed and implemented by Dennis Ritchie; C++ was the work of Bjarne Stroustrup. However, large software projects can rarely be carried out by one person—e.g., consider a program which will take ten person-years to complete. One person could write the program in ten years or ten persons could write it in one year.[1] Because few organizations have the luxury of being able to wait ten years for completion of a software project, a software team is needed. Also, experience has shown that effective software teams produce higher quality software than the same individuals working alone. Thus it is critically important that computing students learn to work effectively in a team environment. In the remainder of this section, we shall discuss some principles of project planning and team organization that lead to effective software development teams.

Project Planning

The most commonly used method for planning large projects (superhighways, for example, as well as software projects) is called *PERT* (*P*rogram *E*valuation and *R*eview *T*echnique). It is popular because it uses an easily understood graphical tool called a PERT chart. For example, in Figure 9–2, we show a PERT chart one of the authors developed for construction of a basement recreation room; Figure 9–3 shows a PERT chart for a software project.

The development of a PERT chart is in itself a valuable activity. It forces one to define clearly and precisely exactly what steps need to be taken to com-

---

1. Assuming for the moment that projects are capable of being arbitrarily subdivided without loss of productivity; in fact this assumption is false. We shall say more about this below.

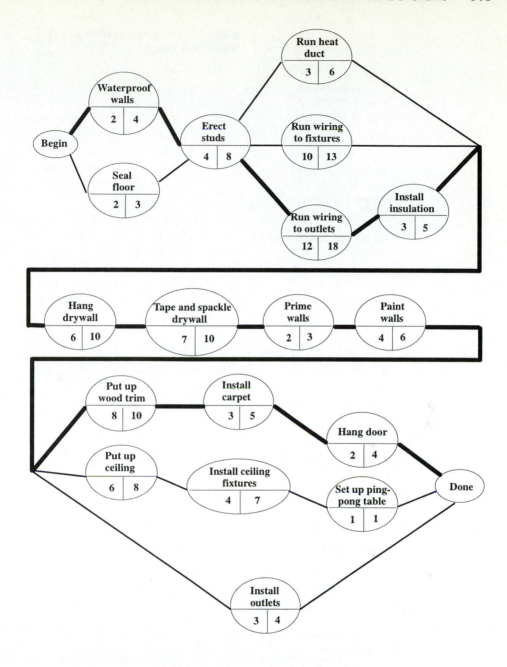

FIGURE 9–2 PERT chart for a project to construct a basement recreation room.

plete a project and to identify how they depend on each other. Also for each task, an expected completion time and a maximum completion time are estimated. (Note that we have indicated these on the chart for the recreation room project, but not the software project—since the latter is a generic chart, the

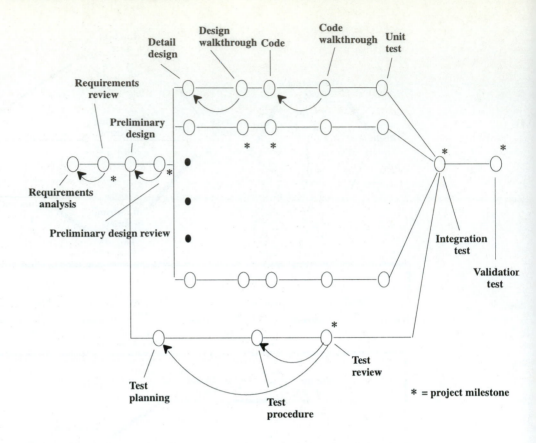

FIGURE 9–3   Pert chart for a software project.

times would have to be filled in for a specific project.) Use of PERT charts prevents many typical management problems, such as:

- having one group of workers complete a step in a project and being unable to continue on to the next step until someone else completes an overlooked piece of work

- not having resources on hand when workers are ready to begin a step

- having money tied up in resources which will not be used for months

- poor allocation of support; i.e., critical activities being undersupported while support is wasted somewhere else

- poor assignment of personnel

- poor estimates of job duration

- discouragement because a task is too big and perhaps cannot be done

Once a PERT chart has been constructed for a project, there is much valuable information that can be derived from it. Perhaps the most important is the identification of the "critical path."

Definition The *critical path* is the longest path from the initial node in the PERT chart to the terminating node.

The critical path in the PERT chart of Figure 9–2 is delineated by lines heavier than the other paths. It can be calculated using either the expected or the maximum completion times but it is usually calculated using the expected time. Thus, it calls a manager's attention to those steps which have the greatest potential for delaying completion of a project. Management which involves identifying these steps is called the *critical path method* (*CPM*). Often in large software projects, the programmers on the critical path are given the best workstations, first priority access to secretaries and technical support personnel, budget for overtime, and other perks—along with a lot of pressure. Programmers off the critical path can be more laid back, but often have to wait for programmers on the critical path when they share access to resources such as technical support personnel. Some other benefits of PERT charts are:

- The chart provides clear milestones so that managers and programmers can visualize their progress and feel a sense of accomplishment. This reduces the likelihood of discouragement.

- A completion date can be easily estimated.

- The chart can be dynamically modified as the project proceeds. Thus if one step takes more (or less) time than anticipated, the consequences of that delay (or gain) can be seen immediately. The critical path may need to be changed, resource allocations can be adjusted, and users can be informed early about possible delays.

- "Time windows" can be calculated for each step—i.e., the earliest time a manager can reasonably expect a step to begin and the latest time it can be completed without delaying the project. This is helpful in scheduling personnel assignments and resource allocations.

- The "float" can be computed for each step in the critical path—i.e., the amount of slippage that can be allowed before the entire project is delayed. This provides a measure of how close to critical certain steps are. Also it suggests where to look if personnel are temporarily needed somewhere else.

Team Organization

No team structure has been discovered which is clearly superior to all others. In this section, we will examine several structures which have been tried and discuss their pros and cons; we will closely parallel the work of Gregory Jones [7]. Later, we will look at some principles which underlie successful teams.

First, though, we must examine some of the roles that must be filled on a software team.

- **Analyst**   This is the individual who connects the software project with the outside world. He or she needs to be comfortable communicating both with users and with software designers and programmers. The analyst's chief responsibility in a project is to listen to users' requirements, help users to adjust them appropriately, and convert them into a set of formal specifications for the project.

- **Designer**   The designer takes the specifications formulated by the analyst, creates the software structure, and defines the interfaces between modules. In an object-oriented environment, this includes defining the appropriate objects and their methods.

- **Programmer**   This is the person who develops and debugs the code for the modules created by the designer.

- **Tester**   This person works in a formal adversarial role vis-a-vis the programmers and designers. The tester's responsibility is to create test data which will ferret out bugs in software. The tester is the person ultimately responsible for quality control.

- **Librarian**   The librarian makes sure that all versions of all modules, adequate documentation, and all test data and test results are saved in an organized fashion. Much of this role can be automated on contemporary systems.

- **Technical expert**   This person is the master of every idiosyncrasy of the operating system and whatever compiler the team is using.

There are several popular team structures in use. In the following paragraphs, we discuss the ideas behind natural teams, chief programmer teams, anarchistic teams, bureaucratic teams, democratic teams, and matrix-structured teams.

The natural organization   (See Figure 9–4.) This team really consists of two subgroups and a semi–independent analyst. The designer oversees the most purely technical personnel and is responsible for taking the project from specifications to functioning code. The manager oversees the less technical personnel and the tester, to protect the tester from conflict of interest. The manager is responsible for seeing that the final product is working correctly, is documented properly, and that the administrative support the designer's team needs is provided. He or she also handles the day-to-day administrative details of managing a project.

The chief programmer team   This is a variation of the natural structure, and is shown in Figure 9–5.

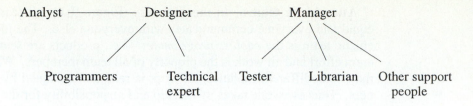

FIGURE 9–4   The "natural" team organization.

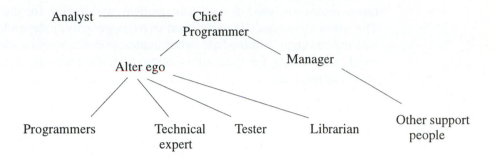

FIGURE 9–5   The chief programmer team organization.

In this structure, the chief programmer acts in a role analogous to that of a chief surgeon on a medical team. He or she does all of the design and, on small to medium size projects, all of the programming. In large projects, programmers may code modules designed by the chief programmer. Everyone else on the team exists primarily to free the chief programmer to do what he or she does best—design and write programs. The alter ego is expected to understand the design and code and interpret it to the technical expert, tester, librarian, and programmers. The alter ego is also a backup in case some disaster happens to the chief programmer.

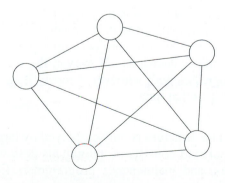

FIGURE 9–6   Anarchistic teams.

Anarchistic teams   In this structure (Figure 9–6), all team members are equal and everyone communicates with everyone else. The ideal in the anarchistic team is the *egoless programmer*—i.e., products are seen as the fruit of team effort and all work is the property of all team members. While individuals may code different modules, all work is read and critiqued by all team members. Thus everyone takes ownership and responsibility for the entire project.

The bureaucratic team   The team organization here is the typical bureaucratic tree structure (Figure 9–7). In this structure, the project manager at the top oversees analysis, design, management, and testing for the entire project. The software is typically partitioned into (supposedly) independent subsystems and the manager's immediate subordinates oversee analysis, design, management, and testing for their subsystem. Specific tasks are carried out at the leaves of the tree.

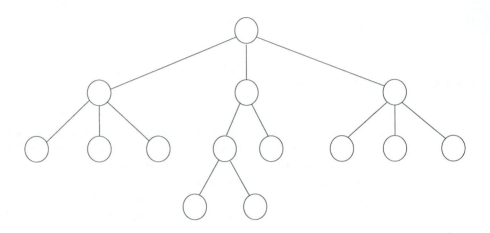

FIGURE 9–7   Bureaucratic team organization.

Democratic teams   This is a variation of the anarchistic team in which authority exists but much less formally than in the natural, chief programmer, or bureaucratic teams. At each stage of the project someone takes charge to provide direction and make minor decisions. However, the leader role typically rotates as the project progresses with whoever is most gifted at any particular phase taking the leadership at that time.

Matrix structures   This structure is only employed by large organizations. The software development staff consists of individuals designated as analysts, designers, coders, testers, and maintenance programmers (see Figure 9–8). The people in each section receive input from the previous section, do their part, then pass the project on. Thus, for instance, a proposal comes to an ana-

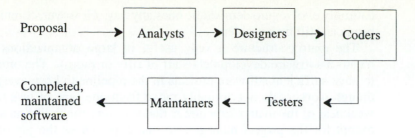

FIGURE 9–8   Matrix structured teams.

lyst who develops the specifications and turns them over to the designers, then moves on to another project. Projects are shepherded through the pipeline by a project manager who is the only individual who follows a project from inception to completion.

Each of these different team structures has its relative strengths and weaknesses. The natural structure fits the roles a software project entails well; however, its main disadvantage is that its most technically competent person—the designer—can easily get bogged down in the details of supervising a team of programmers and a technical expert.

The chief programmer concept attempts to correct this deficiency by providing an alter ego that handles the details and by creating a team climate in which the principal goal is to support the chief programmer. Its principal weakness is that there are very few people qualified to be a chief programmer. In actual practice, this structure is not used very widely; when the right person is placed in the chief programmer role, however, the structure can be quite successful. Chief programmer teams are very effective in small to moderate size projects, tend to be very productive, and the code produced shows a high degree of conceptual and stylistic unity. This makes it less error-prone and easier to maintain than other code.

Anarchistic teams also work well on small to medium sized projects if the team is a cohesive group of motivated programmers. Such teams tend to produce high-quality, relatively bug-free code. The weaknesses are that without formal leadership, anarchistic teams may lose their sense of direction; also they are only effective for relatively small projects. One explanation of this latter phenomenon is that the number of communication links on an anarchistic team is $\frac{n(n-1)}{2}$, or $O(n^2)$. (See Figure 9–6.) In a tree structured team like the natural, chief programmer, or bureaucratic structures, the number of links is $n-1$ $[O(n)]$. Thus for large projects, the communication overhead on an anarchistic team becomes so great that there is little time left to work effectively and the structure tends to break down.

The democratic team addresses the tendency of the anarchistic team to lose direction by providing informal leadership; in fact, anarchistic teams tend to naturally evolve into democratic ones anyway. However, communication overhead can still be a problem.

The matrix structure is only useful in large organizations (typically this means a software development staff of fifty or more). The organization needs to have sufficient software projects in the pipeline to keep everyone busy even though workers do not normally move from one type of task to another. The weakness of the matrix structure is that it is very much like an assembly line—except for the project manager, no one experiences the joy of working on a project from its beginning to its completion; thus the work tends to become routine, workers are less creative, and the code produced tends to include few innovations. Also there is a high potential for conflict between the project manager who sees a project through and the department supervisor who may have a different set of priorities.

Walkthroughs

Before we can discuss principles of effective team organization, we need to introduce one additional concept—walkthroughs. Walkthroughs originated with the concept of egoless programming as a means to give all team members input to the design and coding of all parts of the project. They proved so successful in improving program quality that they are now being used with many team structures; in fact, they have become an integral part of many contemporary programming teams.

In conducting a walkthrough, a programmer takes a completed design or piece of code and presents it to a small group of team members, usually in an informal setting. A team member's goal is to find errors in the design or code. While this might seem to create an adversarial relationship between a programmer and his or her colleagues, if done right, that need not happen; in fact, programmers who use the technique often find it quite helpful and enjoyable. Some guidelines for effective walkthroughs are:

- The author begins by presenting an overview of the work. At this point general questions or comments are allowed, but details are postponed. Following the overview, the author leads the team step by step through every detail. At this point, specific questions and test cases are permitted.

- Team members should point out errors, but not try to correct them; the author of a design or piece of code is responsible for correcting his or her own errors.

- Walkthroughs should be done as soon as a piece of work is finished and before the author has invested very much time in debugging it. In this way, the author has little ego involved in the work and is much less likely to be defensive when errors are found.

- The author is not allowed to explain how an error occurred—the error is simply mentioned, noted, and the walkthrough continues.

- Walkthroughs generally work best in an informal, relaxed atmosphere.

- It is often helpful to appoint a coordinator (frequently the chief designer if there is one on the team) who maintains order and resolves disagreements.

- Second walkthroughs are sometimes needed. At the end of a session, the team should decide if it needs to meet again.

- Create a team atmosphere in which it is clear that undetected bugs are everyone's responsibility equally—not just the author's. Having people sign off on a walkthrough report and then holding them responsible for any work they have signed off on often helps introduce a measure of accountability.

- Keep careful notes of all errors and suggestions which arise during the walkthrough.

Software reviews are an alternative technique similar to walkthroughs. They are generally more formal, occur less often, last longer, and typically include managers and customers. They are generally less effective than walkthroughs because they are infrequent, participants do not know each other very well, and their atmosphere tends to be more confrontational and defensive.

Principles of Effective Team Organization

As we have seen in the previous section, there is no single team structure which is ideal for all software development projects. The choice of structure depends on the size of the project, the skills and temperament of the personnel involved, and the culture of the organization in which the project is undertaken. However, whatever structure is chosen, there are some principles which, when followed, lead to greater productivity and higher-quality end results. Among these are:

- **Use a project planning tool.** A thorough, well-reviewed design and a PERT chart constructed by an experienced software engineer should enable the proper number of people to be assigned to a project before coding begins. Also such a tool allows a reasonable timeline to be established (and adjusted if necessary) and progress toward its attainment to be monitored carefully.

- **Establish measurable milestones**. Milestones are intermediate goals which can be clearly identified. They maintain a high level of motivation on a team—members can set attainable goals and feel a sense of accomplishment as they reach each one. The project doesn't become overwhelming. In *The Mythical Man–Month*, Frederick Brooks suggests that perhaps even milestones are too big and a project leader should think in terms of smaller "inch-pebbles" instead.

- **Do not assume that the person-years required to complete a project are linearly divisible**. Normally, fewer people and more time will yield a higher quality product than more people and less time. Thus, a balance needs to be struck between the demands of the project deadline and the need for a small cohesive team—often a team leader will need to negotiate a later deadline with customers or senior managers in order to ensure a quality product.

- **Assign clearly defined tasks organized by functional area**. This results in a product that has conceptual unity and does what was intended. It also makes for a more motivated programmer.

- **Use walkthroughs.** Some evidence at this point suggests that walkthroughs are the most effective method of software quality control—even better than formal verification! So walkthroughs are a critical component of any effective software team.

- **Do not add new programmers to an already late software project; this will only make it later**. This statement was first expressed in *The Mythical Man–Month* by Brooks and has since come to be known as Brooks' Law. It's not hard to see why this is true—when new people are added, they have to be trained. This takes substantial time away from people who are already working on the project. Also adding more people to a team significantly increases the possible lines of communication—this can reduce everyone's productivity.

- **Include representatives of all user groups on the development team.** Until the past few years, an analyst would interview users and that would end users' involvement until they tested the final product. This was often unsatisfactory as users frequently do not know what they want until they have tried the software. Recall that prototyping is a software development technique in which the user interface is designed first and iteratively refined by working with users even before a full-scale design is undertaken. Thus prototyping helps fulfill this guideline. Beyond prototyping, however, receiving user input throughout the development process ensures a higher level of user satisfaction with the final product.

- **Provide a supportive environment**. Adequate workstations, technical support, and secretarial help make a team far more productive.

At this point we can easily see why the project undertaken at Simpson Corporation, described in the introduction to this section, failed. First, planning was inadequate—a detailed design was not worked out before project components were assigned, no milestones were established, and libraries of shareable software were not defined. No tool for reviewing designs or code was utilized, team structure was only vaguely defined as the natural structure—but the tester, manager, and librarian roles were not explicitly assigned. New programmers were added in the middle of the project and users were not included on the development team. A complete set of test data was not designed until integration had been completed. In short, Bailey attempted to generalize from what worked for her as an individual programmer to a software team. But she did not take the operational dynamics of working together as a team into account.

An Example of a Successful Software Team

As we suggested earlier, there is no "right" structure for a software team. However, it is often helpful to examine successful teams which can serve as potential models for our own teams. We close this section by describing one such example. This particular project was carried out at the Summer Institute of Linguistics in Dallas, Texas. For more details, see the article by Marc Rettig [13] cited at the end of this chapter.

Before the project began, two team members, the project leader and the lead designer, spent nearly a person–year working together. In Rettig's words, "They accomplished three things:

- They sold upper management on the design concept and rallied user departments to participate in the development process.

- They agreed on the "guts" of the design, and wrote a set of design documents which described the components and their relation to each other.

- They laid out a plan for the first six months of development, including personnel requirements, time estimates, and complexity estimates."

At this point, the rest of the team was added—two programmer/analysts, an experienced manager with good technical knowledge, and part-time secretarial support. They set "team building" as their first task, and began this via a two day retreat which included spouses and child-care staff.

Besides team-building exercises and recreation, they all took a "social styles inventory" to understand potential communication problems, worked out a mission statement together, and worked out a team structure based on a concept by Larry Constantine [5] called "structured open teams." This structure is not a hierarchy like the natural, chief programmer, or bureaucratic structures, but it is not anarchical either. Rather it is a semidemocratic team in which certain roles are explicitly assigned. Thus one person is designated team leader and has veto power over decisions; otherwise decisions are made by consensus.

Other activities or needs that were identified were decision making, coordination, information management, critical feedback, application domain knowledge, and technical / analytic functions. These were allowed to rotate as the project progressed. In practice, the team found little difficulty reaching consensus, especially since there was a leader who could intervene in case of a stalemate. At the beginning there were many meetings to hash out structural details, but the necessity for these decreased with time.

The work was broken into small modules, each expected to take about two weeks for one person. There were group walkthroughs for both the design and coding phases for each module. Combined with weekly staff meetings, this required expenditure of time preparing for meetings or attending them. In order to keep meetings productive, the team agreed to a maximum of one meeting per day and scheduled all meetings at 4 PM. To reduce preparation time for the walkthroughs, one person was designated "principal reviewer" for each session. That person was expected to study the document carefully, prepare discussion topics, and give the author written comments before coming to the meeting.

Also each meeting had a scribe and a facilitator. Further roles (some of which were assigned for each meeting) included technical leader, process leader, librarian, technical and process critic, and domain expert. The scribe's job rotated, but because this team happened to have one individual who was a particularly effective facilitator, he was normally given this role. The critic or "devil's advocate" role was frequently rotated. A carefully designed document archive was developed and a curator assigned. The archive contained notes from all meetings, all versions of software and documentation, and any other documents the team produced. Development of the archive took some time, but once constructed, was easy to maintain and accessible to everyone.

The result of this was a harmonious team, a project that proceeded on schedule, and (in the judgement of the team) highly reliable software. Thus this is a good example of a successful software team organization.

EXERCISES

9–1 For your next programming project in this or another course, agree with one or two other students to conduct walkthroughs on each other's design and code. (Be sure your instructor knows you are doing this so that it is not regarded as plagiarism.)

9–2 For your next programming project in this or another course, create a PERT chart with time estimates in hours for each step.

9–3 For a team project in this course, organize yourselves according to one of the structures discussed in this section. Be sure that all of the relevant roles are explicitly assigned. Write an explanation of which structure you chose and also why you assigned the roles as you did before you start working. At the conclusion of the project, evaluate yourselves as a team and list possible improvements you could have made in your structure.

SOFTWARE AND INTELLECTUAL PROPERTY LAW

What do we mean when we use the term *intellectual property*? Intellectual property is not physical property, like a car or a house, but is instead an idea, an expression of an idea, or a representation of an idea in any of a variety of media. Formally, the definition can be given as follows:

Definition   *Intellectual property* is property that is not physical but nevertheless has rights that can be assigned, licensed, or used as collateral between its owner (vendor) and its users (clients).

This definition suggests that conventional means for protecting physical property rights apply also to intellectual property, and that is exactly the case. There are at least four different views of the notion of intellectual property which suggests four ways in which property rights can be identified, and hence protected: *copyright*, *patent*, *trademark*, and *trade secret*. These four means of protection for property rights are discussed in the following sections, paying special attention to their application to computer software as intellectual property.

As we know, *computer software* is a term that denotes any program that is designed and distributed to facilitate computer use by practitioners and students in some particular discipline, profession, or organization. For example, some computer software products facilitate the use of computers by banks and people who have bank accounts. Other products facilitate computing by publishers and people who use word processors to create manuscripts for publication. Still others are used by government agencies like the Internal Revenue Service and people who submit federal income tax statements.

We have had firsthand experience developing computer software throughout this text. If we view software as a commercial product, it has the basic characteristics of intellectual property. That is, as the authors of the software, we are its owners, in the same sense that we are the owners of our term papers, musical compositions, or creative works of art. As owners, we have explicit and exclusive property rights to our software creations.

For the purpose of the following discussion, suppose we define a *software product* as having three aspects (see Figure 9–9): a source program, an object

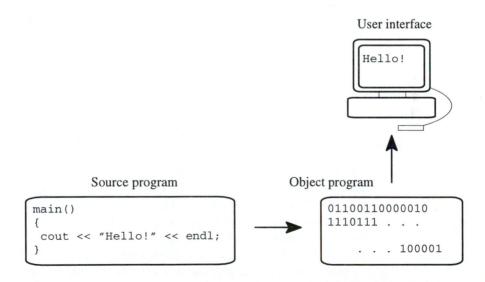

FIGURE 9–9   The three elements of a software product.

program, and a user interface. If we write a simple C++ program that displays the message "Hello!" on the screen, this software product has three basic elements, which are identified in Figure 9–9. These elements are intimately related. That is, the source program must be compiled into an equivalent object program in machine language, and that occurs before the program is run and produces a user interface. Thus, it is the object program whose steps are actually executed when the message "Hello!" appears on the screen at run time.

When a real software product, such as a word processor or a C++ compiler, is developed for commercial use, its source program is usually not distributed. Only its object program is distributed, along with some documentation and tutorial information. (A major exception to this pattern is in the world of education and research in computer science and engineering, where many software products are freely distributed in their source form.) The separation of source and object programs, nevertheless, is significant in situations where a software product is viewed as intellectual property.

Software user interfaces are many and varied. Their styles and capabilities depend on the nature of the application, the skills of the intended user, and on the particular computer for which the software is designed. In general, a software product's user interface includes the information presented on the screen by the software, the keyboard command sequences, the mouse-clicking activities, and all the other conventions for interaction that are required when users apply the software to their applications. For example, the user interface for a word processor (like WordPerfect) on a particular computer (like the IBM PC) includes all the text creation, insertion, saving, deletion, and other functions that users must assimilate when they type a manuscript using that word processor.

In the computer laboratory that accompanies this text, you have used the interface that comes with a particular C++ system. If you have been using Turbo C++ on an IBM PC, you are familiar with certain conventions for creating a C++ program text, saving the text, compiling the program, finding and correcting errors, running the program, and so on. If you have been using Symantec C++ on the Macintosh, you are familiar with a different suite of conventions for accomplishing these tasks. Those using a UNIX based system are familiar with yet another system of editing, compiling, and running programs. Each of these is an example of a user interface; as a C++ programmer, you are the user.

Software as Intellectual Property

When viewed as intellectual property, we can look at an item of software in two different ways. On the one hand, if we look at only the object program and the user interface, the software can be viewed as a *process or machine*. On the other hand, if we consider the source program and the object program together, the same software takes on the appearance of an *original work of authorship*. This duality of interpretation is illustrated in Figure 9–10.

When viewed as intellectual property, software is subject to intellectual property laws in a special way. Let's examine the details of those laws in this particular light.

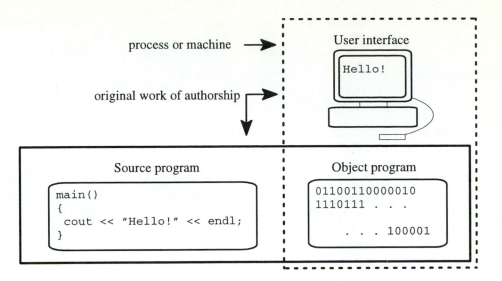

FIGURE 9–10   The dual interpretation of software.

Software Copyrights Because the source program and the user interface in a software product are original works of authorship, they are protected by copyright law. Copyright law protects all original works of authorship (historically, literary manuscripts, paintings, and musical compositions) against unauthorized copying. The law was amended in 1980 to explicitly cover computer programs, or software.

Note that in all these cases, the law *protects the expressions themselves* (that is, the verbatim text of the program) but not the ideas that underlie the expressions. For example, suppose we develop an original C++ program that computes grade point averages. Then the C++ text of this program is protected by copyright law, but the underlying idea (algorithm) that the text represents is not protected. Thus, someone else can independently arrive at the same algorithm, then express it in a different programming style. For example, another person's program might use different variable names, or use a do–while loop that has the same effect as our while loop. That person's program is therefore technically not in violation of our program's property rights. The second program would violate the first program's copyright protection only if the programmer derived it from the first by changing a few variable names or other program constructs.

A simpler example that illustrates different expressions of the same idea is shown in Figure 9–11. If any of the three programs in Figure 9–11 were independently created, it would not violate the others' copyright protection, since they represent different expressions of an idea. However, if either b or c were created as a derivative from program a, then a's copyright would be violated.

Any piece of academic work involving computer programs is governed by the same rules of plagiarism as a written term paper. *Plagiarism* can be defined

```
main()                  main()                        main()
{                       {                             {
  cout << "Hello!";      cout << "Hello!" << endl;     cout << "Hello!;
}                       }                              cout << endl;
                                                      }
```

        (a)   (b)   (c)

FIGURE 9–11   Three different expressions of the same idea.

as the failure to acknowledge another author's work when that work is included in one's own written work. Computer programs fall into the category of written work in this sense. Therefore, the use or adaptation of another's program without proper written acknowledgement generally constitutes plagiarism. College and university instructors, especially in computer science and engineering, usually make an explicit definition in their syllabi of what constitutes plagiarism for assignments that involve programming.

Copyright law applies to an original work of authorship immediately, from the day it is created until 50 years after the owner's death. It also applies *automatically*: the author or owner does not have to affix a copyright notice explicitly to the work. However, many copyright owners prefer to post explicit notice of copyright on all printed copies of the work (the C++ program listing, in our case), and that is suggested though not required by the law itself. Thus, all the programs written for this text are copyrighted immediately, and copyright protection will continue for 50 years after the authors die. It behooves us to affix the following kind of notice to all printed copies of this program if we intend to protect the property rights that apply to it:

Copyright 1991. Allen B. Tucker. All rights reserved.

Copyright protection means that the owner of the copyright has the exclusive right to make, use, and/or sell the original work.

Software Patents   Because the object program and user interface in a software product can also be interpreted as a "process or machine," software can also fall into the realm of patent protection. Patent law explicitly protects processes, machines, manufactured items, or compositions-of-matter inventions from unauthorized reproduction, use, or sale by anyone except the owner. The Supreme Court has ruled that software-related inventions can be judged for patentability in the same way as non-software-related inventions. Thus, patent law now can be fully applied to software.

Unlike a copyright, however, patent rights do not automatically apply to a piece of software at the time it is created. Instead, a software patent must be obtained by application to the U. S. Patent and Trademark Office, just as inventors apply to patent any other process, machine, or invention. Once obtained, a patent remains in force for a period of 17 years, after which the patented process or machine falls into the public domain. That is, it becomes freely available for use, adaptation, or sale by anyone.

The scope of a patent is wider than that of a copyright. Patent protection extends to the whole family of processes *that have the same effect as* the original patented product. Copyright protection, in contrast, applies only to one particular expression or realization of the process. Patent protection gives the owner of the patent the exclusive right to make, use, or sell the process.

Some algorithms can be patented. A famous one is Karmarkar's algorithm for solving certain types of problems which involve large numbers of simultaneous linear equalities and inequalities. In these problems, there are typically infinitely many "feasible" solutions—the problem is to find one that maximizes a given function of the variables. For many years these problems were solved with the "simplex algorithm" which used one variable at a time to step toward an optimal solution. Because of the number of equations and inequalities involved, this algorithm was often very slow. Karmarkar devised a much faster way to find the optimal solution, which involved changing several variables simultaneously. This was a truly unique and original algorithm, and the U.S. Patent and Trademark Office awarded a patent for it. The algorithms in this text, however, all use well-known techniques that are in the public domain and thus are not patentable. The main advantage to the patent holder is that now, if someone were to discover Karmarkar's algorithm independently, without knowing that it already exists, he or she could not use it without being in violation of the patent—no matter how the algorithm is expressed.

Software Trade Secrets A *trade secret* is generally any item of knowledge or characteristic of a product that makes it unique or valuable in comparison with the competition, but which is generally kept secret from the competition. In the special case of a software product, any feature that makes it especially efficient or unique in its capabilities, in comparison with its rivals in the marketplace, can be declared to be a trade secret. For example, a very fast spelling checker built into a word processor might be worth protecting as a trade secret if it makes that word processor unique in contrast with all others on the market.

A trade secret is easy to obtain, and no application procedure is required—in fact, that would be impossible, since the item is a secret! Trade secrets have unlimited life, but they are difficult to protect. Trade secrets often arise by contract, as through an employer-employee relationship. Many software developers require their employees to sign a "nondisclosure agreement" at the time they are hired. Under such an agreement, employees are bound not to reveal the software designs or implementations with which they come into contact. A nondisclosure agreement thereby protects against disclosure of a software trade secret. Given the high degree of software portability and employee mobility in the industry, this type of agreement is very difficult, if not impossible, to enforce—especially when an employee terminates employment with a company and begins working for a major competitor.

The "Look and Feel" of the Software User Interface

When discussing the intellectual property aspects of a software product's user interface, we must first try to define what it is that makes a user interface especially valuable or unique, in comparison with other user interfaces.

Consider the C++ compiler that you have been using. You have developed a certain level of skill in typing programs, running the compiler, finding and correcting syntax errors, and running programs. Much of that skill depends upon the effectiveness with which the software's user interface makes appropriate commands available to you as you need them. If you are running Turbo C++ on an IBM PC, for example, you use certain control key combinations to initiate these different kinds of operations. Moreover, the system keeps you informed about the status of your work by displaying certain messages on the screen as it completes the tasks you have designated. Similarly, if you are running Symantec C++ on a Macintosh, you perform operations through an entirely different kind of user interface—one that depends upon your skill at using a mouse, opening windows, making menu selections, and so on. Analogous remarks apply to a UNIX based user-interface. These alternative C++ systems present to the user a different "look and feel" when they are applied to the task of developing and running programs.

Some software manufacturers claim that the look and feel of a software user interface is protected under intellectual property laws. The term *look and feel* was actually coined in 1985 by two lawyers, Russo and Derwin, in an article [15] they published about aspects of user interfaces that might be protected under copyright law. They defined the "look" to mean the appearance of a user interface screen displays and the "feel" to denote how the software interacts with the user (i.e., the sequence of commands, keystrokes, mouse operations, and on-screen responses that occur when the software's various functions are performed by the user).

The validity of the look and feel argument for copyright protection has been tested in two recent court cases. Lotus Development Corporation sued Mosaic Software in 1987 for copyright infringement of the "Lotus 1-2-3" spreadsheet software product on the grounds that Mosaic copied the look and feel of that product's user interface. The second case involved a suit by Apple Computer Corporation against Microsoft Corporation in 1988 for copyright infringement of the graphical and visual elements of its Macintosh user interface. An example of the screen display in the Macintosh user interface appears in Figure 9–12.

Look and feel cases are difficult to prosecute, for several reasons. First, the originality of the user interface for which copyright protection may apply is difficult to determine. Recall that copyright protection applies only to an *original* work. In the case of Lotus 1-2-3's user interface, one can argue that it is a derivative of an older spreadsheet system called VisiCalc (circa 1982). It can similarly be shown that the basic elements of the MacIntosh user interface are derived from an earlier system developed by Xerox known as the "Star" system (circa 1980).

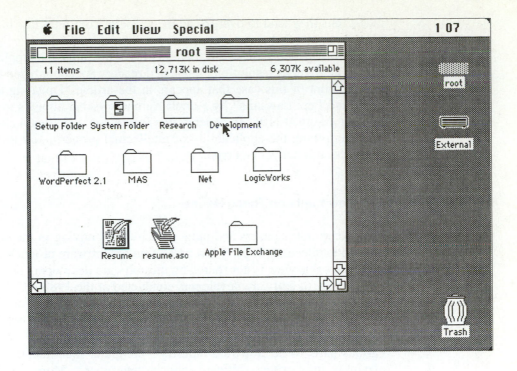

FIGURE 9–12   The Macintosh user interface.

The second problem that surrounds look and feel arguments is that the notion itself has (at best) an ambiguous standing in the law. Thus, some would argue that the alternative term *total concept and feel* may be applicable to copyright cases involving software user interfaces. Yet copyright law makes clear distinctions between the representation of a concept (which it does protect) and the concept itself (which it does not protect).

The third problem is that recent court cases reveal that judges are only lately beginning to understand the nature of user interfaces. It is not difficult to understand the artistry that is involved in creating a unique image on the screen, but nonprogrammers often do not understand the more complex ideas that encompass the interactive functionality of the software and how it uniquely allows the user to interact with the application.

The fourth problem is the confusion about boundaries between patent law and copyright law, as they apply to software in general and to user interfaces in particular. Some patent lawyers believe that the look and feel of a software user interface is patentable, and there are some precedents for this opinion. For example, IBM has a patent on a certain method of *highlighting* text on a word processor. Apple has a patent on the "pulldown menu" process, used with a mouse, which is a central aspect of its Macintosh user interface. Yet many judges are unaware that patents have been applicable to software user interfaces; thus they tend to overextend the scope of copyright law in cases that involve look and feel arguments.

While the Lotus case was resolved in favor of Lotus, the Apple case has had a more ambiguous resolution. Interested readers are encouraged to read the recent account of this case that appears in the article "Updating the Copyright Look and Feel Lawsuits" by Pamela Samuelson that appears in *Communications of the ACM* [19]. In general, it is fair to conclude that a clear legal basis for determining the applicability of intellectual property law to software user interfaces has not yet emerged.

Software Developers' Viewpoints on These Issues

While corporate lawyers and judges seem to be moving in the direction of increased intellectual property law protection for software products and their user interfaces, this view is not shared by the software developers themselves.

A survey of software developers conducted at the 1989 ACM SIGCCI conference on the question of copyright and patent protection for software in its various aspects was reported by Pamela Samuelson and Robert Glushko in *Communications of the ACM* [17]. That survey polled 667 developers from various parts of the software industry—computer manufacturers, R&D organizations, universities, software vendors, and others. More than 80 percent of the respondents opposed the extension of copyright protection for the look and feel of software user interfaces, although they strongly supported copyright protection for source and object programs. A more recent survey conducted in August 1991 at the ACM SIGGRAPH conference, and reported by Samuelson et al. in June of 1992 [18], reconfirmed these views.

The main reason for software developers' opposition to extending copyright law to user interface design is that copyright protection for look and feel would have a negative effect on the community, stifling creativity and adversely affecting the climate for open exchange and discussion of innovations that marks progress in the field. Yet 93 percent of the respondents in the first survey believed that source programs ought to fall under copyright or patent protection, and 85 percent thought that object programs ought to be so protected.

An important additional aspect of this survey is that it exposed the fact that a large number of software developers do not understand the legal issues surrounding the look and feel argument or the other aspects of intellectual property laws that apply to computer software.

No such survey data is available for the larger population of software users. However, there is anecdotal evidence which suggests that software users do not understand the legal and ethical dimensions of software any better than do the software developers themselves. For a variety of reasons, many individual users ignore the laws and copy whatever software they need in order to configure their computers to do useful work. Institutional users—corporations, colleges and universities, government agencies, and so on—tend to be more cautious than individuals in this regard, perhaps because managers fear the possibility of institutional exposure, embarrassment, and lawsuits.

Why do people illegally copy software? Several factors contribute to this activity, including cost, objection to the law, uncertainty about performance, convenience of copying, low level of use, and ignorance. Some have compared software copying in colleges and universities with plagiarism. Some users think that software product prices are unreasonably high and that vendors are gouging the public in the interest of making windfall profits. Others object to the fact that software is protected under the law in this way; they think that software is not "real" property, so the act of copying software is just copying and not stealing. Some people are uncertain whether a certain product is appropriate or effective for their needs, and they would prefer to have the software on a trial basis. However, vendors do not generally make their products available on this basis. Still other people justify illegal copying merely because it is convenient or because they expect to use the software only occasionally. And some people are simply ignorant of the intellectual property laws that protect software. In this sense, the software copying black market is similar to that which exists for video taped movies.

Nevertheless, unauthorized software copying is illegal and unethical, and it can be detrimental to future progress in computing technology. The U.S. patent law gives the inventor of a product the right to make a profit from his or her invention. Software developers need to recover the costs of inventing and distributing their products. If copying becomes widespread, it can deprive vendors of a fair return on investment. This, in turn, can discourage future investment in new software products by innovative firms. Furthermore, society needs a stronger vehicle for holding developers responsible for software errors (see the discussion in the next section), and software that does not enter into the normal stream of commerce cannot be so regulated.

EXERCISES

9–4 Identify the user interface for a program that you have recently written. Discuss the effects of making this program user-friendly upon its user interface: that is, how would these changes alter the look and feel of the user interface for the original program?

9–5 What is the difference between a software patent and a software copyright? Explain how any differences would affect a particular software product, such as one of your programs or a popular word processor with which you are familiar.

9–6 Read the article "Updating the Copyright Look and Feel Lawsuits" [19] that is cited at the end of this chapter. What is the notion of *summary judgment*? Explain the role of summary judgment in the Apple vs Microsoft case.

9–7 If you are a Macintosh user, describe the look and feel of the Macintosh user interface. How is that look and feel incorporated into the Symantec C++ software?

9–8 If you are a PC–Windows user, describe the look and feel of Microsoft Windows. How is that look and feel incorporated into the Turbo C++/Windows software? If, on the other hand, you are a PC user, describe the look and feel of your MS–DOS environment. How is that look and feel incorporated into or overridden by the Turbo C++ software?

9–9 If you are a UNIX system user, describe the look and feel of the UNIX or your UNIX-based user interface. How is that look and feel incorporated into or overridden by the C++ software?

RELIABILITY OF LARGE SOFTWARE SYSTEMS

Early in this text, software reliability was identified in terms of the correctness and robustness of a software product. The emphasis in this section is on the individual and social costs of software that is unreliable, that is, on software that fails. We should bear in mind that computer hardware can also fail. However, it does seem to be the case that developing reliable software is a much more difficult problem than developing reliable hardware.

In this section, we shall discuss the general nature of the software reliability problem and some of the proposed solutions to that problem. We shall give some dramatic examples of software that failed, and explore the ethical and professional issues inherent in this subject.

Software Is Pervasive

A fundamental fact of life as we approach the 21st century is that software is pervasive. It influences our lives in ever more complex and significant ways. We shall focus on two aspects of this pervasiveness: the multitudinous ways in which computer systems affect us as citizens, and the complex network of relationships which connects the computing professional with society at large.

Computer systems impact upon our lives in multitudinous ways. Not only are computer applications multiplying, they are becoming ever more critical to the physical and financial well-being of literally billions of people. Here is a list of some of the applications which now rely heavily upon computers:

- medicine
- nuclear power plants
- air traffic control
- communications
- financial systems
- financial markets (e.g., the stock market)

- civilian aircraft

- weapons systems

While there are many other applications for computer systems, these tend to carry a particularly high cost of failure. In fact, for each of these application areas we can cite at least one dramatic instance where a computer system failed with disastrous or potentially disastrous results. Forrester and Morrison [6] list dozens of examples of this nature. Many more are catalogued in each issue of the periodical *Software Engineering Notes*, a publication of the ACM's Special Interest Group on Software Engineering. Software systems that can have potentially devastating effects on human safety and health are known as "life-critical applications," while those that can have the same effects on financial institutions are called "finance-critical applications."

As suggested in the first section of this chapter, computing professionals sit in a complex web of relationships. It is important for them to be aware of those relationships in order to perform their own tasks in an effective and ethical manner. For example, imagine yourself just employed at a software firm that is developing an off-the-shelf income tax system for home use that will be used by millions of people. Your work places you in an enormous network of relationships which will slowly make its presence felt as you progress in your career. At first you may only be aware of your immediate co-workers and your supervisor, but as you progress you slowly realize the "big picture."

That big picture includes the larger picture at your company: the corporate battles and strategies, the conflicting personalities and interests. It includes the sort of raw human emotions that are not usually a part of your technical education. It includes your company's customers and their financial health. It includes your company's competitors and, if those competitors are overseas, global economic relationships and the possibility that your country will lose jobs to your competitor's country. It includes the broader social impact of the product which you are developing—upon tax accountants and lawyers, for example. Thus, working on a software project is not a small matter at all.

Imagine, now, the enormity of the "big picture" if you were working on software which will be used in a life-critical medical application (e.g., administering radiation dosages to cancer patients) or software that will be used to control the flight dynamics of an airplane. Now your network of relationships includes the lives of the potential patients and their families (in the case of the medical application) or the lives of the airplane crews and passengers (in the case of the flight control application). Computing professionals have enormous power and influence on the lives of others because the artifacts they create are so widely embedded in physical systems of all sorts. Computing professionals therefore need to understand, in the broadest sense, the network of relationships in which they work.

Dramatic Examples of Software Failure

When one reads a software disaster story, one cannot help but wonder about the environment in which the faulty software product was developed. Was an individual programmer ultimately responsible for the disaster? What was that programmer's attitude towards his or her work and what was that programmer's relationship to his or her colleagues? Did the corporate environment encourage sloppy work and/or cutting corners? What kind of software validation and verification procedures did the developers and testers use?

As Forrester and Morrison [6] point out, systems fail at many levels. In particular, a system can fail because it does not to meet the customer's requirements or it can fail because it is abandoned by the users or it can fail because of inordinate development or maintenance costs. In the extreme, a system may fail not only because it does not to meet the customer's requirements, but because it creates havoc and damage far beyond anything the customer could possibly have imagined.

One of the most horrible system failures on record was the USS Vincennes incident, which occurred in the late 1980s during the Iran-Iraq war [1]. The United States was not a combatant in that war, but American warships (including the USS Vincennes) were patrolling the Persian Gulf in order to assure the free flow of oil to Japan and Western Europe. The USS Vincennes was equipped with the Aegis anti-aircraft missile system. Aegis was designed to shoot down up to twenty aircraft simultaneously. At the heart of this system was sophisticated software to analyze radar data in order to identify aircraft over a large area. A synopsis of its analysis is shown visually on a computer screen. Unfortunately, the Aegis system mistook an Iranian civilian airliner for a fighter jet and the result was the loss of 290 civilian lives.

Some controversy surrounds the question of who is to blame for this tragic event. One school of thought is that the Aegis system's user interface contributed to the fatal missile firing. Others point out that the system was never tested in a realistic setting. Although its specifications include the ability to shoot down 20 targets simultaneously in a sea-air battle, the system was only tested in a New Jersey corn field. Others suggest that it is impossible to adequately test a weapons system such as this in a realistic setting, since one such test would cost many millions of dollars.

Here are some additional examples of software disasters. In the 1980s, a factory worker was killed by a robot in Japan. In various hospitals, patients have been killed by radiation overdoses due to faulty software. Fatal accidents have also been caused by pacemakers having either faulty hardware or faulty software. There have been numerous and costly errors involving financial systems. In November 1985, a system which handles electronic securities transactions failed and this resulted in a series of errors and desperate financial patches which eventually cost the Bank of New York five million dollars *in a single day*. During 1991 there were several incidents in which large metropolitan areas, including Pittsburgh, PA and Washington, DC had their telephone communications disrupted due to a bug in communications software.

A controversy in many cases is the question of whether to use computers to control the flight dynamics of an airplane, what is known as "fly-by-wire." This technology is already embedded in the European Airbus 320. Fly-by-wire involves, in part, replacing the metal cables which have historically connected the pilot to the plane's control surfaces (for example, the tail and wing flaps) with computer circuits. In the case of the European Airbus, computer software can control all aspects of flight dynamics without pilot intervention, including engine thrust. One pilot has testified that the Airbus can take off and land without a pilot at all. In one infamous incident, an Airbus crashed at the Paris Air Show killing one of its passengers. Initially the flight dynamics software was blamed for this accident. However, proponents of fly-by-wire claim, to the contrary, that the computer software actually prevented a more disastrous crash.

The causes of a more deadly crash, of a Midlands Boeing 737 in England in 1989, have been widely discussed in *Software Engineering Notes*. The 737 has two engines. In this crash, an engine malfunctioned but the pilot accidentally shut off the other engine, which had been working properly. Initially, it was thought that the cockpit user interface was at fault, but more recent speculation lays the blame on the software which interprets the information coming from sensors in the engine. This theory states that the software is designed to discount data which seems so unreasonable that it must be erroneous. According to this reconstruction of the Midlands disaster, the software incorrectly informed the pilot that the good engine was malfunctioning.

Perhaps the most dramatic incident of computer system failure involves nuclear weapons. In 1960, a computer system misinterpreted a moon rise as a Russian nuclear attack. On another occasion, the same system mistook a flock of geese as an incoming strike. During the 1980s, system failures caused NORAD to scramble B–52s on two occasions, out of the mistaken belief that a nuclear attack from the Soviet Union was under way.

During the 1980s the world entered into a particularly unsafe and unstable situation vis-a-vis nuclear weapons. At that time, both the United States and the Soviet Union had either implemented or were on the verge of implementing a "launch on warning" or "hair-trigger" nuclear defense. This meant that computers could launch missiles in retaliation for a presumed strike from the other side without human intervention. Perhaps humanity has never faced a greater threat to its survival than the prospect of a computer program, perhaps an unreliable program, bringing us to the edge of the nuclear abyss!

Why Is Designing Reliable Software So Difficult?

Earlier in this text, we mentioned the influential paper by Fred Brooks, "No Silver Bullet" [3]. This paper analyzes the prospects for a successful solution to the problem of producing reliable software. Brooks states that success is unlikely given the current technology because none of the proposed solutions to the problem addresses the essence of the problem. In Brooks' view, the essence of the problem is that software is inherently complex, changeable, subject to conformity to arbitrary standards, and nonvisualizable. To this list we might add the property that software is inherently unstable and unpredictable.

We have seen that software systems are being used in air traffic control, in nuclear power plants, in weapons systems, in medical applications, in communications, and in financial institutions. Both human life and world financial stability may be at risk if software systems fail. Yet, some of these software systems are so complex that it is beyond the ability of any single individual to understand them in their entirety. Imagine placing your life at the mercy of a program that no human being can possibly understand!

Complexity   A large software system consists of thousands, perhaps millions, of interacting elements (modules, routines, memory locations, data streams, and so forth). Even if an application is shown to be correct (a concept which itself is just an ideal), how does one prove that the compiler which is used to compile the program is correct, that the operating system that the compiler is built upon is correct, or that the hardware system in which the operating system and compiler reside is correct? It is safe to say that we cannot assume any of these to be correct, in the sense that they are fully reliable.

Furthermore, the interacting elements in a computer program are not standardized, but are unique for each application (for the most part). A sorting routine in an air traffic control application may be different from a sorting routine in process control software for a nuclear reactor. Even if these two sorting routines utilize the same algorithm, they may be written in different languages with different data types and structures. Software artifacts tend to have more uniqueness and variability than other engineering artifacts. The complexity of software makes it impossible to exhaustively test.

Beyond the purely technical issues, we cannot ignore the human and organizational implications of complexity, which were discussed briefly in an earlier section. Complex software is produced by teams of individuals. The more complex the software, the more complex the interactions among these individuals. In addition, there are interactions between the development team and the customers, the testers and the maintainers. This enormously complex web of interaction contains many difficulties and pitfalls in terms of assuring software reliability.

Changeability   Software evolves because requirements change and bugs are detected. Lehmann [8] presents some simple laws of software evolution, and one of those laws is that software becomes more complex as it evolves. Others have suggested that it may be better to work around a known bug in a large software system than to fix the bug, since fixing a known bug always contains the risk of introducing many new and potentially more devastating bugs.

Software also changes due to advances in hardware technology. A given software product may have to be revised repeatedly as it is ported from one host machine to another.

Conformity to Arbitrary Standards   Software must conform to standards that are not usually reflections of eternal or natural laws (as is the case for the laws of physics) but are rather the arbitrary output of various interest groups, each having its own agenda. "Arbitrary" does not imply that these standards are necessarily unreasonable (although this may be the case in some instances), but rather that the standards are not the consequences of orderly, natural principles. Thus, software developers cannot appeal to their intuition of natural order in order to solve a difficult problem. Instead, the software developer must surrender to the arbitrary order that is imposed by hardware designers, the design environment, and the users.

This is a profound but perhaps subtle point. Many of the great advances in mathematics, physics and other sciences came from an underlying faith in a natural order. One might say that this faith has served as an internal compass for many of the great scientists, such as Newton and Einstein. No comparable philosophical underpinning exists for software engineers. Their internal compasses must make frequent reference to arbitrary standards: hardware standards, operating system standards, language standards, design standards, coding standards, user interface standards—each developed by an interest group or committee with its own agenda and purposes.

The reality in the early 1990s is something like this. If you wish to develop a software application for a personal computer, you have to decide which computer and which operating system (especially the latter) you are going to use as your platform. That implies that you have to start to orient your creativity towards the standard hardware and operating systems currently available. If you choose the DOS operating system, you may be well-advised to conform to the *de facto* interface standard provided by Microsoft Windows. This is a standard. That standard provides the template, or context for your application. You must adjust your internal vision to conform to these existing standards. This is not good or bad. It is just a fact of life for software developers.

The Invisibility of Software   Brooks views the "invisibility" of software as a fundamental characteristic. This notion of invisibility refers to the fact that we have no means of representing complex software systems in a visual (or graphical) way. This is related to the complexity and conformity issues discussed earlier. If there were an effective way to visualize software, that visualization could provide a means for people to better understand how it works. Furthermore, effective software visualization would provide an intellectual tool that could lead to new fundamental discoveries and principles in software engineering.

As they engage the needs of the 1990s, software engineers have developed a variety of visual tools for representing systems (data flow diagrams, structure charts, entity–relationship diagrams, flow charts, Nassi–Schneiderman diagrams, etc.), but each of these captures only one tiny aspect of a system. There is no convenient notation for representing a complex software system all at once. This limitation has two implications. First, it mitigates against the use of visual tools to assist the process of discovery. Second, it makes unlikely the possibility that visual tools and visual languages will be useful to help solve the problem of software reliability.

The Instability and Unpredictability of Software Another factor that makes the development of reliable software difficult is the inherent instability and unpredictability of software. This has to do with the discrete nature of software systems. This is in contrast to many engineering artifacts which follow orderly laws based upon continuous functions.

For example, suppose the output from an engineering artifact is a continuous function of N inputs, as given by the equation:

```
output = f(input1, input2, .... , inputN)
```

The continuity of the function f assures that the output will depend upon the inputs in a predictable way. In particular, the system will be stable in the sense that small changes in one or more of the inputs will produce small changes in the output.

However, computer systems do not behave in this manner. Suppose we use a similar equation to describe the output from a computer system in terms of its N inputs:

```
output = f(input1, input2, .... , inputN)
```

If our computer system is a black box, it is generally impossible to establish whether or not the function f is stable (the discrete analogue of the notion of continuity). That is, we have no effective way to demonstrate that small changes in the inputs always produce small and predictable changes in the output. In fact, it is characteristic of computer systems that when they fail they fail spectacularly. In other words, a small change in an input can produce dramatic changes in output.

Even if our routine is treated as a white box and we are privy to its internal details, it may still be very difficult to establish that the function f is stable by running test cases which exercise all paths through the routine. It is for this reason that some software engineers are stressing the need to develop better formal verification techniques, such as those introduced earlier in this text, to help assure software reliability.

Possible Solutions

In its brief history, software engineering has tried to find a silver bullet that would permanently solve the problem of software unreliability. The following candidates are briefly discussed in the next few paragraphs.

- Object-oriented programming
- Formal program verification
- Automatic programming
- Visual languages and systems
- Software reuse technology

- Iterative design/prototyping

Brooks [3] asserts that, while object-oriented programming has some promise, it still does not attack the essential problems posed by the very nature of software—that it is complex, changeable, subject to arbitrary standards, nonvisualizable, and unstable.

While Mills and others advocate formal verification techniques, Brooks does not view this as a "silver bullet" for several reasons. First, formal proofs of correctness are themselves subject to errors. Second, formal proofs of correctness do not, in their current style, scale up well from the small routine level to the complex system level.

Automatic programming is the idea of using a formal specification language as a programming language. In other words, the formal specification would be given in a language that could be directly translated into a conventional programming language. Some software engineers view this as a potential silver bullet. For one thing, it is hoped that this technology would make it very simple to assure that a program satisfies its specifications because the program is developed automatically from its specifications by correctness-preserving transformations. Furthermore, this group can point to some success in the realm of database management systems where very high level application generators have been developed based upon the general idea of automatic programming.

Visual languages and systems are increasingly a part of modern CASE tools (tools for *C*omputer–*A*ided *S*oftware *E*ngineering). CASE tools rely heavily upon graphical representations of computer systems (such as data flow diagrams and structure charts) to aid the software design process. However, this approach is unlikely to provide the silver bullet unless Brooks [3] is wrong when he asserts that software is inherently unvisualizable.

Software reuse technology allows system developers to build new systems from existing reusable components. Reusable components which are known to be reliable can help build new systems that are, in turn, reliable. It will be some time before this technology comes to full fruition. Much research is needed in the areas of programming languages (new constructs to support reuse) and database systems (new database structures for storing and retrieving the reusable components). However, object-oriented techniques, such as those introduced in this text, seem to provide strong momentum in this direction.

Finally, new techniques for managing a software project may help to improve the situation. Iterative design and prototyping imply that users will have an opportunity to work extensively with a working model of a system before its requirements are finalized. This gives a greater likelihood that the product will be a success at least from the point of view of satisfying the users.

Ethical and Professional Issues

The current state of affairs, in which relatively unreliable software systems are being used in life-critical and finance-critical applications, raises many ethical and professional issues for the computing professional. Here are some of the ethical questions a computing professional might ask:

- What will be the impact of the product I am working on upon the quality of life, upon human safety and well-being, and upon the environment?

- What are the possible costs of failure of such a system, and have sufficient safeguards been implemented to prevent a catastrophic failure?

- Are the costs of failure so great that failure is unacceptable?

- Assuming that the system can be specified at all, can my organization really develop and deliver such a system?

- Has my organization communicated with the customer and users of the system the likelihood of failure and the costs of failure?

- Does my own experience qualify me to work on this sort of project?

- What is my role in the network of relationships surrounding this project?

- Am I approaching my work in an ethical and professional manner?

- Am I communicating my concerns to my co-workers and am I responsive to their concerns?

EXERCISES

9–10 The principle of the mythical man-month is that adding more people to a late software project makes the project later. Write down reasons why this may be so.

9–11 Why do you think a heterogeneous team (a team with a mixture of personality types) is generally more effective than a homogeneous team? (All members of a homogeneous team have the same personality type, be it task-oriented, self-oriented, or interaction-oriented.)

9–12 (Term Paper) Write a term paper concerning the reliability of large software systems. You may want to focus on software disasters in a particular applications domain. Some possible term paper topics might be:

    a. The fly-by-wire controversy
    b. Software and nuclear power
    c. Software in medicine
    d. Software and communications
    e. Software and the financial system
    f. Software and weapons systems

9–13 (Term Paper) One application that has been widely discussed in computer science journals is SDI or "Star Wars." In the mid-1980s President Reagan proposed Star Wars as a defense against nuclear attack. Star Wars poses many ethical and technical problems. These problems are discussed in detail in the book by Forrester and Morrison [6]. Forrester and Morrison also provide references to other discussions of this topic, including an influential paper by David Parnas [11]. Write a term paper about Star Wars software and its feasibility, along with the various ethical and professional issues that it raises.

References

[1]   Barry, John and Roger Charles, "Sea of Lies," *Newsweek* (July 13, 1992), 29-39.

[2]   Brooks, Frederick P., *The Mythical Man-Month: Essays on Software Engineering*, Addison–Wesley, Reading, MA, 1975.

[3]   Brooks, Frederick P., "No Silver Bullet: Essence and Accidents of Software Engineering," *IEEE Computer*, April 1987, 10-19.

[4]   Cobb, R. H. and H. D. Mills,. "Engineering Software Under Statistical Quality Control," *IEEE Software*, November 1990, 44-54.

[5]   Constantine, Larry, "Teamwork Paradigms and the Structured Open Team," *Proceedings of Software Development '90*, Miller Freeman Publications, 1990.

[6]   Forrester, T. and P. Morrison, *Computer Ethics: Cautionary Tales and Ethical Dilemnas in Computing*, MIT Press, Cambridge, MA (1990).

[7]   Jones, Gregory W., *Software Engineering*, Wiley, 1990.

[8]   Lehman, M. M., "Programs, Life Cycles and the Laws of Software Evolution," *Proceedings of the IEEE*, 15(3) (1980), 225-52.

[9]   National Research Council, *Intellectual Property Issues in Software*, National Academy Press, 1991.

[10] Nietzke, Frederic W., *A Software Law Primer*, Van Nostrand, 1984.

[11] Parnas, David L., "Software Aspects of Strategic Defence Systems," *Communications of the ACM* 28(12) (December 1985), 1326-35.

[12] Pressman, Roger S, *Software Engineering: A Practitioner's Approach*, 2nd ed., McGraw–Hill, New York, NY, 1987.

[13] Rettig, Marc, Software Teams, *Communications of the ACM* 33(10) (October, 1990), 23.

[14] Rubinstein and Hirsh, *The Human Factor*, Digital Press.

[15] Russo and Derwin, 1985 (source unknown).

[16] Samuelson, Pamela, "Why the Look and Feel of Software User Interfaces Should Not Be Protected by Copyright Law," *Communications of the ACM* 32(5) (May 1989).

[17] Samuelson, Pamela and Robert J. Glushko, "Survey on the Look and Feel Lawsuits," *Communications of the ACM* 33(5) (May 1990).

[18] Samuelson, Pamela, Michael Denber, and Robert J. Glushko, "Developments on the Intellectual Property Front, *Communications of the ACM* 35(6) (June 1992).

[19] Samuelson, Pamela, "Updating the Copyright Look and Feel Lawsuits," *Communications of the ACM* 35(9) (September 1992).

[20] Schneiderman, B., *Designing the User Interface*, Addison–Wesley, Reading, MA, 1986.

[21] *Wall Street Journal*, July 10, 1986 (author and title unknown).

[22] Yoches, E. Robert, "Legal Protection of Computer Software," *Communications of the ACM* 32(2) (February 1989).

[23] Yourdon, Edward, *Managing the System Life Cycle*, Prentice–Hall, Englewood Cliffs, NJ, 1988.

INDEX

A

Abstract class, 89

Abstract data type (ADT), 485

Abstractions, defining, 10

Ada, 483

Adaptability, 47

Adaptation, 51

Adjacency matrix, 338

ADT (Abstract Data Type), 486

Afferent flow, 487

Analyst, 516

Anarchistic team organization, 518

Ancestor, 295

Array addressing, in C++, 107

Array implementation for lists, 373

Assertion, 2, 16

Atanasoff, John, 405

B

Babbage, Charles, 405

Backus, John, 407

Base class, 95

Batch processing, 402, 407

Big-oh notation, 177

Binary search tree, 313

Binary tree
See also Classes
balanced, 307
complete, 302

Binary tree traversal
inorder, 311
postorder, 311
preorder, 311

Binary trees, implementation, 386

Boehm, Barry, 52

Booch, Grady, 54

Boot, 406

Breakdown, 10

Brooks, Fred, 45, 541

Buffered I/O, 408

Bureaucratic team organization, 518

C

C, 80

C++, 483, 496

Casting, type, 266

Changeability, 538

Channel program, 410

Chief programmer team organization, 516

Child, 295
left, 302
right, 302

Circular array, 354

Class, 54, 55, 343, 492

Class design, 56

Class hierarchy, 94, 134

Class protocol, 88

Classes
`BinaryTree`, 302, 307
`CharObj`, 87